Lecture Notes in Computer Science   8997

Commenced Publication in 1973
Founding and Former Series Editors:
Gerhard Goos, Juris Hartmanis, and Jan van Leeuwen

More information about this series at http://www.springer.com/series/7408

Ivan Lanese · Eric Madelaine (Eds.)

Formal Aspects
of Component Software

11th International Symposium, FACS 2014
Bertinoro, Italy, September 10–12, 2014
Revised Selected Papers

 Springer

Editors

Ivan Lanese
Department of Computer Science
  and Engineering
University of Bologna
Bologna
Italy

and

Inria Sophia Antipolis - Méditerranée
Sophia Antipolis
France

Eric Madelaine
Inria Sophia Antipolis - Méditerranée
Sophia Antipolis
France

ISSN 0302-9743   ISSN 1611-3349 (electronic)
Lecture Notes in Computer Science
ISBN 978-3-319-15316-2   ISBN 978-3-319-15317-9 (eBook)
DOI 10.1007/978-3-319-15317-9

Library of Congress Control Number: 2015930087

LNCS Sublibrary: SL2 – Programming and Software Engineering

Springer Cham Heidelberg New York Dordrecht London
© Springer International Publishing Switzerland 2015

Printed on acid-free paper

Springer International Publishing AG Switzerland is part of Springer Science+Business Media
(www.springer.com)

Preface

On behalf of the Program Committee, we are pleased to present the proceedings of the 11th International Symposium on Formal Aspects of Component Software (FACS 2014).

Component-based software development is a paradigm that has been proposing sound engineering principles and techniques for coping with the complexity of software-intensive systems. However, many challenging conceptual and technological issues remain that require further research. Moreover, the advent of service-oriented and cloud computing has brought to the fore new dimensions, such as quality of service and robustness to withstand inevitable faults, which require established concepts to be revisited and new ones to be developed in order to meet the opportunities offered by those architectures. As software applications become themselves components of wider sociotechnical systems, further challenges arise from the need to create and manage interactions, which can evolve in time and space, and rely on the use of resources that can change in noncomputable ways.

FACS 2014 was about how formal methods can be used to make component-based development fit for the new architectures of today and the systems that are now pervading the socioeconomic world. Formal methods have provided foundations for component-based software through research on mathematical models for components, composition, and adaptation, and rigorous approaches to verification, deployment, testing, and certification. While those avenues still needed to be further explored, the time was also ripe to bring new techniques to the fore, such as those based on stochastic models and simulation.

FACS 2014 was the 11th in a series of events initially created as international workshops by the United Nations University - International Institute for Software Technology (UNU-IIST), in 2003 in Pisa. In 2011, the FACS events were promoted to the status of International Symposium, with events located in Oslo (2011), Mountain View (2012), Nanchang (2013). For this 11th event FACS returned to Italy, hosted in the University Residential Center of Bertinoro, where it has been colocated with the 11th International Conference on Integrated Formal Methods (iFM 2014).

We received 44 submissions from 26 countries, out of which the Program Committee selected 20 papers, including 2 application and experience papers, 3 tool papers, and 15 research contributions. All submitted papers were reviewed by at least three referees. To minimize the preconference delays, the conference version of these papers was distributed in electronic form to the participants. Here, we have revised versions of these original contributions, taking into account also comments received during the symposium. The authors of a selected subset of accepted papers have also been invited to submit extended versions of their papers to appear in a special issue of Elsevier's Science of Computer Programming journal.

We are proud to have been endorsed by the European Association of Software Science and Technology (EASST) to deliver an EASST best paper award to the paper

"Compositional Analysis Using Component-Oriented Interpolation" by Viet Yen Nguyen, Benjamin Bittner, Joost-Pieter Katoen, and Thomas Noll.

We would like to express our gratitude to all the researchers who submitted their work to the symposium, to all colleagues who served on the Program Committee, as well as the external reviewers, who helped us to prepare a high-quality conference program. Particular thanks to the invited speakers, Helmut Veith from Technical University of Vienna, Rocco De Nicola from IMT Lucca, and Jean-Bernard Stefani from INRIA Grenoble, for the willingness to present their research and to share their perspective on formal methods for component software at the conference. Papers recalling the talks by Rocco De Nicola and Jean-Bernard Stefani are included in the proceedings, while a paper summarizing Helmut Veith's talk can be found in the proceedings of iFM 2014.

Without the support of the general chair and of the local organizers at Bertinoro and at University of Bologna, this conference could not have happened. In particular, we are deeply indebted to Gianluigi Zavattaro, Jacopo Mauro, and Monica Michelacci for their help in managing all practical aspects of preparation of this event. We also thank the Department of Computer Science and Engineering – DISI, of the University of Bologna, for its sponsorship.

December 2014   Ivan Lanese
                                                                       Eric Madelaine

Organization

Program Committee

Christian Attiogbé	University of Nantes, France
Luis Barbosa	Universidade do Minho, Portugal
Christiano Braga	Universidade Federal Fluminense, Brazil
Roberto Bruni	Università di Pisa, Italy
Carlos Canal	University of Málaga, Spain
Chunqing Chen	HP Labs Singapore, Singapore
Xin Chen	Nanjing University, China
Zhenbang Chen	National Laboratory for Parallel and Distributed Processing, China
José Luiz Fiadeiro	Royal Holloway, University of London, UK
Marcelo Frias	Buenos Aires Institute of Technology, Argentina
Lindsay Groves	Victoria University of Wellington, New Zealand
Rolf Hennicker	Ludwig-Maximilians-Universität München, Germany
Natallia Kokash	CWI, The Netherlands
Ivan Lanese	University of Bologna, Italy and Inria, France
Axel Legay	IRISA/Inria, France
Zhiming Liu	Birmingham City University, UK
Alberto Lluch Lafuente	Technical University of Denmark, Denmark
Antonia Lopes	University of Lisbon, Portugal
Markus Lumpe	Swinburne University of Technology, Australia
Eric Madelaine	Inria Sophia Antipolis - Méditerranée, France
Dominique Méry	Université de Lorraine, LORIA, France
Peter Olveczky	University of Oslo, Norway
Corina Pasareanu	CMU/NASA Ames Research Center, USA
Frantisek Plasil	Charles University in Prague, Czech Republic
Jose Proenca	Katholieke Universiteit Leuven, Belgium
Markus Roggenbach	Swansea University, UK
Gwen Salaün	Grenoble INP – Inria – LIG, France
Bernhard Schätz	TU München, Germany
Marjan Sirjani	Reykjavik University, Iceland
Meng Sun	Peking University, China
Neil Walkinshaw	University of Leicester, UK
Farn Wang	National Taiwan University, Taiwan
Naijun Zhan	Institute of Software, Chinese Academy of Sciences, China
Jianjun Zhao	Shanghai Jiao Tong University, China

Additional Reviewers

Abd Arrahman, Yehia
Abid, Rim
Afroozeh, Ali
Ahmad, Ehsan
Ait Ameur, Yamine
Ait Sadoune, Idir
Almeida Matos, Ana
Andre, Pascal
Boyer, Benoît
Carnevali, Laura
Chen, Yuting
Daniel, Jakub
Delahaye, Benoit

Farhadi, Alireza
Ferreira, Carla
Gerostathopoulos, Ilias
Hauzar, David
Jaber, Mohamad
Khamespanah, Ehsan
Kit, Michal
Lanoix, Arnaud
Li, Xiaoshan
Li, Yi
Milushev, Dimiter
Mohagheghi, Morteza
O'Reilly, Liam

Pastore, Fabrizio
Qamar, Nafees
Sabouri, Hamideh
Wang, Rui
Wang, Shuling
Xiao, Kejun
Yan, Rongjie
Ye, Lina
Yu, Hengbiao
Zhao, Liang
Zou, Liang
Zverlov, Sergey

Contents

Invited Speakers

Components as Location Graphs

Jean-Bernard Stefani[⊠]

INRIA, Saint-Ismier, France
jean-bernard.stefani@inria.fr

Abstract. This paper presents a process calculus framework for modeling ubiquitous computing systems and dynamic component-based structures as location graphs. A key aspect of the framework is its ability to model nested locations with sharing, while allowing the dynamic reconfiguration of the location graph, and the dynamic update of located processes.

1 Introduction

Motivations. Computing systems are increasingly built as distributed, dynamic assemblages of hardware and software components. Modelling these assemblages requires capturing different kinds of dependencies and containment relationships between components. The software engineering literature is rife with analyses of different forms of whole-part, aggregation or composition relationships, and of their attendants characteristics such as emergent property, overlapping lifetimes, and existential dependency [2]. These analyses explicitly consider the possibility for a component to be shared at once between different wholes, an important requirement in particular if one expects to deal with multiple architectural views of a system.

Consider, for instance, a software system featuring a database DB and a client of the database C. The database comprises the following (sub)components: a cache CC, a data store DS and a query engine QE. Both data store and query engine reside in the same virtual machine V_0, for performance reasons. Client and cache reside in another virtual machine V_1, also for performance reasons. We have here a description which combines two architectural views, in the sense of [17]: a *logical* view, that identifies two high-level components, the database DB and its client C, and the sub-components CC, QE and DS of the database, and a *process* view, that maps the above components on virtual machines V_0 and V_1. We also have two distinct containment or whole-part relationships: being placed in a virtual machine, and being part of the DB database. A virtual machine is clearly a container: it represents a set of resources dedicated to the execution of the components it contains, and it manifests a failure dependency for all the components it executes (should a virtual machine fail, the components it contains also fail). The database DB is clearly a composite: it represents the result of the composition of its parts (cache, query engine, and data store) together with their attendant connections and interaction protocols; it encapsulates the behavior of its subcomponents; and its lifetime constrains those of its parts (e.g. if the

© Springer International Publishing Switzerland 2015
I. Lanese and E. Madelaine (Eds.): FACS 2014, LNCS 8997, pp. 3–23, 2015.
DOI: 10.1007/978-3-319-15317-9_1

database is destroyed so are its subcomponents). The cache component CC in this example is thus part of two wholes, the database DB and the virtual machine V_1.

Surprisingly, most formal models of computation and software architecture do not provide support for a direct modelling of containment structures with sharing. On the one hand, one finds numerous formal models of computation and of component software with strictly hierarchic structures, such as Mobile Ambients and their different variants [6,7], the Kell calculus [25], BIP [4], Ptolemy [26], or, at more abstract level, Milner's bigraphs [20]. In bigraphs, for instance, it would be natural to model the containment relationships in our database example as instances of sub-node relationships in bigraphs, because nodes correspond to agents in a bigraph. Yet this is not possible because the sub-node relation in a bigraph is restricted to form a forest. To model the above example as a bigraph would require choosing which containment relation (placement in a virtual machine or being a subcomponent of the database) to represent by means of the sub-node relation, and to model the other relation by means of bigraph edges. This asymmetry in modelling is hard to justify for both containment relations are proper examples of whole-part relationships.

On the other hand, one finds formal component models such as Reo [1], π-ADL [22], Synchronized Hyperedge Replacement (SHR) systems [14], SRM-Light [15], that represent only interaction structures among components, and not containment relationships, and models that support the modeling of non-hierarchical containment structures, but with other limitations. Our own work on the Kell calculus with sharing [16] allows to model non-hierarchical containment structures but places constraints on the dependencies that can be modelled. For instance, the lifetime dependency constraints associated with the virtual machines and the database in our example above (if the aggregate or composite dies so do its sub-components) cannot be both easily modeled. The reason is that the calculus still enforces an ownership tree between components for the purpose of passivation: components can only passivate components lower down in the tree (i.e. suspend their execution and capture their state). The formal model which comes closer to supporting non strictly hierarchical containment structures is probably CommUnity [28], where component containment is modelled as a form of superposition, and can be organized as an arbitrary graph. However, in CommUnity, possible reconfigurations in a component assemblage are described as graph transformation rules that are separate from the behavior of components, making it difficult to model reconfigurations initiated by the component assemblage itself.

To sum up, we are missing a model of computation that allows us to directly model both different forms of interactions and different forms of containment relationships between components; that supports both planned (i.e. built in component behaviors) and unplanned (i.e. induced by the environment) dynamic changes to these relationships, as well as to component behaviors.

Contribution. In this paper, we introduce a model of computation, called *G-Kells*, which meets these requirements. We develop our model at a more concrete level than bigraph theory, but we abstract from linguistic details by developing a process calculus framework parameterized by a notion of process and certain semantical operations. Computation in our model is carried out by located processes, i.e. processes that execute at named *locations*. Locations can be nested inside one another, and a given location can be nested inside one or more locations at once. Locations constitute scopes for interactions: a set of processes can interact when situated in locations nested within the same location. Behaviors of located processes encompass interaction with other processes as well as reconfiguration actions which may change the structure of the location graph and update located processes. In addition, the G-Kells framework supports a notion of dynamic priority that few other component models support, apart from those targeting real-time and reactive systems such as BIP and Ptolemy.

Outline. The paper is organized as follows. The framework we introduce can be understood as an outgrowth of our prior work with C. Di Giusto [13], in which we proposed a process calculus interpretation of the BIP model. We recall briefly in Sect. 2 the main elements of this work, to help explain the extensions we introduce in our G-Kells framework. Section 3 presents the G-Kells framework and its formal operational semantics. Section 4 discusses the various features of the G-Kells framework, and related work. Section 5 concludes the paper.

2 CAB: A Process Calculus Interpretation of BIP

One way to understand the G-Kells model we introduce in the next section, is to see it as a higher-order, dynamic extension of the CAB model [13], a process calculus interpretation of the BIP model. We recall briefly in this section the main elements of CAB.

The CAB model captures the key features of the BIP model: (i) hierarchical components; (ii) composition of components via explicit "glues" enforcing multiway synchronization constraints between sub-components; (iii) priority constraints regulating interactions among components. Just as the BIP model, the CAB model is parameterized by a family $\mathcal{P}$ of primitive behaviors. A CAB component, named l, can be either a primitive component $C = l[P]$, where P is taken from $\mathcal{P}$, or a composite component $C = l[C_1, \ldots, C_n \star G]$, built by composing a set of CAB components $\{C_1, \ldots, C_n\}$ with a glue process G. When l is the name of a component C, we write $C.\mathrm{nm} = l$. We note $\mathcal{C}$ the set of CAB components, $\mathcal{N}_l$ the set of location names, and $\mathcal{N}_c$ the set of channel names. Behaviors in $\mathcal{P}$ are defined as labelled transition systems, with labels in $\mathcal{N}_c$.

In CAB, the language for glues G is a very simple language featuring:

- *Action prefix* $\xi.G$, where ξ is an action, and G a continuation glue (in contrast to BIP, glues in CAB can be stateful).
- *Parallel composition* $G_1 \mid G_2$, where G_1 and G_2 are glues. This operator can be interpreted as an *or* operator, that gives the choice of meeting the priority and synchronization constraints of G_1 or of G_2.
- *Recursion* $\mu X. G$, where X is a process variable, and G a glue.

Actions embody synchronization and priority constraints that apply to subcomponents in a composition. An action ξ consists of a triplet $\langle \pi \cdot a \cdot \sigma \rangle$, where π is a priority constraint, σ is a synchronization constraint, and a is a channel name, signalling a possibility of synchronization on channel a. Priority and synchronization constraints take the same form: $\{l_i : a_i \mid i \in I\}$, where l_i are location names, and a_i are channel names. A synchronization constraint $\sigma = \{l_i : a_i \mid i \in I\}$ requires each sub-component l_i to be ready to synchronize on channel a_i. Note that in a synchronization constraint $\sigma = \{l_i : a_i \mid i \in I\}$ we expect each l_i to appear only once, i.e. for all $i, j \in I$, if $i \neq j$ then $l_i \neq l_j$. A priority constraint $\pi = \{l_i : a_i \mid i \in I\}$ ensures each subcomponent named l_i is *not* ready to synchronize on channel a_i.

Example 1. A glue G of the form $\langle \{l : a\}; c; \{l_1 : a_1, l_2 : a_2\} \rangle.G'$ specifies a synchronization between two subcomponents named l_1 and l_2: if l_1 offers a synchronization on channel a_1, and l_2 offers a synchronization on a_2, then their composition with glue G offers a synchronization on c, provided that the subcomponent named l does not offer a synchronization on a. When the synchronization on a takes place, implying l_1 and l_2 have synchronized with composite on a_1 and a_2, respectively, a new glue G' is put in place to control the behavior of the composite.

Note that the same component l can appear in both the priority and the synchronization constraint of the same action ξ.

Example 2. An action of the form $\langle \{l : a\} \cdot c \cdot \{l : b, l' : b\} \rangle$ specifies that a synchronization on c is possible provided both subcomponents l and l' offer a synchronization on b, and component l does not offer a synchronization on a.

The operational semantics of the CAB model is defined as the labeled transition system whose transition relation, $\rightarrow \subseteq \mathcal{C} \times (\mathcal{N}_l \times \mathcal{N}_c) \times \mathcal{C}$, is defined by the inference rules in Fig. 2, where we use the following notations:

- $\mathbf{C}$ denotes a finite (possibly empty) set of components
- $\mathbf{C}_\sigma$ denotes the set $\{C_i \mid i \in I\}$, i.e. the set of subcomponents involved in the multiway synchronization directed by the synchronization constraint σ in rule COMP. Likewise, $\mathbf{C}'_\sigma$ denotes the set $\{C'_i \mid i \in I\}$.
- $\mathbf{C} \models_p \{l_i : a_i \mid i \in I\}$ denotes the fact that $\mathbf{C}$ meets the priority constraint $\pi = \{l_i : a_i \mid i \in I\}$, i.e. for all $i \in I$, there exists $C_i \in \mathbf{C}$ such that $C_i.\mathrm{nm} = l_i$ and $\neg(C_i \xrightarrow{l_i:a_i})$, meaning there are no C' such that $C_i \xrightarrow{l_i:a_i} C'$.

The COMP rule in Fig. 2 relies on the transition relation between glues defined as the least relation verifying the rules in Fig. 1.

The transition relation is well defined despite the presence of negative premises, for the set of rules in Fig. 2 is stratified by the height of components, given by the function `height`, defined inductively as follows:

$$\mathtt{height}(l[P]) = 0 \qquad \mathtt{height}(l[\mathbf{C} \star G]) = 1 + \max\{\mathtt{height}(C) \mid C \in \mathbf{C}\}$$

$$\text{Act } \xi.G \xrightarrow{\xi} G \qquad\qquad \text{Rec } \frac{G\{^{\mu X.G}/x\} \xrightarrow{\xi} G'}{\mu X.G \xrightarrow{\xi} G'}$$

$$\text{Parl } \frac{G \xrightarrow{\xi} G'}{G \mid G_2 \xrightarrow{\xi} G' \mid G_2} \qquad\qquad \text{Parr } \frac{G \xrightarrow{\xi} G'}{G_2 \mid G \xrightarrow{\xi} G_2 \mid G'}$$

Fig. 1. LTS semantics for CAB glues

$$\text{Prim } \frac{P \xrightarrow{\alpha} P'}{l[P] \xrightarrow{l:\alpha} l[P']}$$

$$\text{Comp } \frac{G \xrightarrow{\langle \pi \cdot a \cdot \sigma \rangle} G' \qquad \sigma = \{l_i : a_i \mid i \in I\} \qquad \forall i \in I, C_i \xrightarrow{l_i : a_i} C_i' \qquad \mathbf{C} \models_p \pi}{l[\mathbf{C} \star G] \xrightarrow{l:a} l[(\mathbf{C} \setminus \mathbf{C}_\sigma) \cup \mathbf{C}'_\sigma \star G']}$$

Fig. 2. LTS semantics for CAB($\mathcal{P}$)

Indeed, in rule COMP, if $\texttt{height}(l[\mathbf{C} \star G]) = n$, then the components in $\mathbf{C}$ that appear in the premises of the rule have a maximum height of $n - 1$. The transitions relation $\rightarrow$ is thus the transition relation associated with the rules in Fig. 2 according to Definition 3.14 in [5], which is guaranteed to be a minimal and supported model of the rules in Fig. 2 by Theorem 3.16 in [5].

We now give some intuition on the operational semantics of CAB. The evolution of a primitive component $C = l[P]$, is entirely determined by its primitive behavior P, following rule PRIM. The evolution of a composite component $C = l[\mathbf{C} \star G]$ is directed by that of its glue G, which is given by rules ACT, PARL, PARR and REC. Note that the rules for glues do not encompass any synchronization between branches G_1 and G_2 of a parallel composition $G_1 \mid G_2$. Rule COMP specifies how glues direct the behavior of a composite (a form of superposition): if the glue G of the composite $l[\mathbf{C} \star G]$ offers action $\langle \pi \cdot a \cdot \sigma \rangle$, then the composite offers action $l : a$ if both the priority ($\mathbf{C} \models_p \pi$) and synchronization constraints are met. For the synchronization constraint $\sigma = \{l_i : a_i \mid i \in I\}$ to be met, there must exist subcomponents $\{C_i \mid i \in I\}$ ready to synchronize on channel a_i, i.e. such that we have, for each i, $C_i \xrightarrow{l_i : a_i} C_i'$, for some C_i'. The composite can then evolve by letting each each C_i perform its transition on channel a_i, and by letting untouched the components in $\mathbf{C}$ not involved in the synchronization (in the rule COMP, the components C_i in $\mathbf{C}$ are simply replaced by their continuation C_i' on the right hand side of the conclusion).

The CAB model is simple but already quite powerful. For instance, it was shown in [13] that CAB($\emptyset$), i.e. the instance of the CAB model with no primitive components, is Turing complete[1]. Priorities are indispensable to the result, though: as shown in [13], CAB($\emptyset$) without priorities, i.e. where glue actions have empty priority constraints, can be encoded in Petri nets. We now turn to the G-Kells model itself.

3   G-Kells: A Framework for Location Graphs

3.1   Syntax

The G-Kells process calculus framework preserves some basic features of the CAB model (named locations, actions with priority and synchronization constraints, multiway synchronization within a location) and extends it in several directions at once:

- First, we abstract away from the details of a glue language. We only require that a notion of process be defined by means of a particular kind of labelled transition system. The G-Kells framework will then be defined by a set of transition rules (the equivalent of Fig. 2 for CAB) that takes as a parameter the transition relation for processes.
- We do away with the tree structure imposed by CAB for components. Instead, components will now form directed graphs between named locations, possibly representing different containment relationships among components.
- In addition, our location graphs are entirely dynamic, in the sense that they can evolve as side effects of process transitions taking place in nodes of the graphs, i.e. locations.
- CAB was essentially a pure synchronization calculus, with no values exchanged between components during synchronization. The G-Kells framework allows higher-order value passing between locations: values exchanged during synchronization can be arbitrary, including names and processes.

The syntax of G-Kells components is quite terse, and is given in Fig. 3. The set of G-Kells components is called $\mathcal{K}$. Let us explain the different constructs:

- 0 stands for the null component, which does nothing.
- $l[P]$ is a *location* named l, which hosts a *process* P. As we will see below, a process P can engage in interactions with other processes hosted at other locations, but also modify the graph of locations in various ways.
- $l.r \rightarrow h$ denotes an *edge* in the location graph. An edge $l.r \rightarrow h$ connects the *role* r of a location l to another location h.
- $C_1 \parallel C_2$ stands for the parallel composition of components C_1 and C_2, which allows for the independent, as well as synchronized, evolution of C_1 and C_2.

A role is just a point of attachment to nest a location inside another. A role r of a location l can be *bound*, meaning there exists an edge $l.r \rightarrow h$ attaching a

---

[1] The CAB model is defined in [13] with an additional rule of evolution featuring silent actions. For simplicity, we have not included such a rule in our presentation here, but the stated results still stand for the CAB model presented in this paper.

$$C ::= \; \mathbf{0} \;\; | \;\; l[P] \;\; | \;\; l.r \rightarrowtail h \;\; | \;\; C \parallel C$$

$$l, h \in \mathcal{N}_l \quad r \in \mathcal{N}_r$$

Fig. 3. Syntax of G-Kells components

location h to r, or unbound, meaning that there is no such edge. We say likewise that location h is bound to location l, or to a role in location l, if there exists an edge $l.r \rightarrowtail h$. Roles can be dynamically attached to a location, whether by the location itself or by another location. One way to understand roles is by considering a location $l[P]$ with unbound roles $r_1, \ldots, r_n$ as a frame for a composite component. To obtain the composite, one must complete the frame by binding all the unbound roles $r_1, \ldots, r_n$ to locations $l_1, \ldots, l_n$, which can be seen as subcomponents. Note that several roles of a given location can be bound to the same location, and that a location can execute with unbound roles.

Locations serve as scopes for interactions: as in CAB, interactions can only take place between a location and all the locations bound to its roles, and a location offers possible interactions as a result. Unlike bigraphs, all interactions are thus local to a given location. One can understand a location in two ways: either as a composite glue superposing, as in CAB, priority and synchronization constraints on the evolution of its subcomponents, i.e. the locations bound to it, or as a connector, providing an interaction conduit to the components it binds, i.e. the locations bound to it. More generally, one can understand intuitively a whole location graph as a component C, with unbound locations acting as external interfaces for accessing the services provided by C, locations bound to these interfaces corresponding to subcomponents of C, and unbound roles in the graph to possible places of attachment of missing subcomponents.

We do not have direct edges of the form $l \rightarrowtail h$ between locations to allow for processes hosted in a location, say l, to operate without knowledge of the names of locations bound to l through edges. This can be leveraged to ensure a process is kept isolated from its environment, as we discuss in Sect. 4. We maintain two invariants in G-Kells components: at any one point in time, for any location name l, there can be at most one location named l, and for any role r and location l, there can be at most one edge of the form $l.r \rightarrowtail k$.

Example 3. Let us consider how the example we discussed in the introduction can be modeled using G-Kells. Each of the different elements appearing in the configuration described (database DB, data store DS, query engine QE, cache CC, client C, virtual machines V_0 and V_1) can be modeled as locations, named accordingly. The database location has three roles s, q, c, and we have three edges $DB.s \rightarrowtail DS, DB.q \rightarrowtail QE, DB.c \rightarrowtail CC$, binding its three subcomponents DS, QE and CC. The virtual machines locations have two roles each, 0 and 1, and we have four edges $V_1.0 \rightarrowtail C, V_1.1 \rightarrowtail CC, V_0.0 \rightarrowtail DS, V_0.1 \rightarrowtail QE$, manifesting the placement of components C, CC, DS, QE in virtual machines.

Now, the database location hosts a process supporting the semantics of composition between its three subcomponents, e.g. the cache management protocol directing the interactions between the cache and the other two database subcomponents[2]. The virtual machine locations host processes supporting the failure semantics of a virtual machine, e.g. a crash failure semantics specifying that, should a virtual machine crash, the components it hosts (bound through roles 0 and 1) should crash similarly. We will see in Sect. 4 how this failure semantics can be captured.

3.2   Operational Semantics

We now formally define the G-Kells process calculus framework operational semantics by means of a labelled transition system.

Names, Values and Environments

Notations. We use boldface to denote a finite set of elements of a given set. Thus if S is a set, and s a typical element of S, we write $\mathbf{s}$ to denote a finite set of elements of S, $\mathbf{s} \subseteq S$. We use ϵ to denote an empty set of elements. We write $\wp_f(S)$ for the set of finite subsets of a set S. If S_1, S_2, S are sets, we write $S_1 \uplus S_2 = S$ to mean $S_1 \cup S_2 = S$ and S_1, S_2 are disjoint, i.e. S_1 and S_2 form a partition of S. We sometimes write $s, \mathbf{s}$ to denote $\{s\} \cup \mathbf{s}$. If C is a G-Kell component, $\Gamma(C)$ represents the set of edges of C. Formally, $\Gamma(C)$ is defined by induction as follows: $\Gamma(0) = \emptyset$, $\Gamma(l[P]) = \emptyset$, $\Gamma(l.r \rightarrowtail h) = \{l.r \rightarrowtail h\}$, $\Gamma(C_1 \parallel C_2) = \Gamma(C_1) \cup \Gamma(C_2)$.

Names and Values. We use three disjoint, infinite, denumerable sets of names, namely the set $\mathcal{N}_c$ of channel names, the set $\mathcal{N}_l$ of location names, and the set $\mathcal{N}_r$ of role names. We set $\mathcal{N} = \mathcal{N}_c \cup \mathcal{N}_l \cup \mathcal{N}_r$. We note $\mathcal{P}$ the set of processes. We note $\mathcal{V}$ the set of values. We posit the existence of three functions $\mathtt{fcn} : \mathcal{V} \rightarrow \mathcal{N}_c$, $\mathtt{fln} : \mathcal{V} \rightarrow \mathcal{N}_l \mathtt{frn} : \mathcal{V} \rightarrow \mathcal{N}_r$ that return, respectively, the set of free channel names, free location names, and free role names occurring in a given value. The restriction of $\mathtt{fcn}$ (resp. $\mathtt{fln}, \mathtt{frn}$) to $\mathcal{N}_c$ (resp. $\mathcal{N}_l, \mathcal{N}_r$) is defined to be the identity on $\mathcal{N}_c$ (resp. $\mathcal{N}_l, \mathcal{N}_r$). The function $\mathtt{fn} : \mathcal{V} \rightarrow \mathcal{N}$, that returns the set of free names of a given value, is defined by $\mathtt{fn}(V) = \mathtt{fcn}(V) \cup \mathtt{fln}(V) \cup \mathtt{frn}(V)$. The sets $\mathcal{N}$, $\mathcal{P}$ and $\mathcal{V}$, together with the functions $\mathtt{fcn}$, $\mathtt{fln}$, and $\mathtt{frn}$, are parameters of the G-Kells framework. We denote by $\mathcal{E}$ the set of edges, i.e. the set of triples $l.r \rightarrowtail h$ of $\mathcal{N}_l \times \mathcal{N}_r \times \mathcal{N}_l$. We stipulate that names, processes, edges and finite sets of edges are values: $\mathcal{N} \cup \mathcal{P} \cup \mathcal{E} \cup \wp_f(\mathcal{E}) \subseteq \mathcal{V}$. We require the existence of a relation $\mathtt{match} \subseteq \mathcal{V}^2$, used in ascertaining possible synchronization.

---

[2] Notice that the database location does not run inside any virtual machine. This means that, at this level of abstraction, our *process* architectural view of the database composite is similar to a network connecting the components placed in the two virtual machines.

Environments. Our operational semantics uses a notion of *environment*. An environment Γ is just a subset of $\mathcal{N} \cup \mathcal{E}$, i.e. a set of names and a set of edges. The set of names in an environment represents the set of *already used* names in a given context. The set of edges in an environment represents the set of edges of a location graph. the set of environments is noted $\mathcal{G}$.

Processes

Process transitions. We require the set of processes to be equipped with a transition system semantics given by a labelled transition system where transitions are of the following form:

$$P \xrightarrow{\langle \pi \cdot \alpha \cdot \sigma \cdot \omega \rangle} P'$$

The label $\langle \pi \cdot \alpha \cdot \sigma \cdot \omega \rangle$ comprises four elements: a priority constraint π (an element of Pr), an offered interaction α, a synchronization constraint σ (an element of S), and an effect ω (an element of A). The first three are similar in purpose to those in CAB glues. The last one, ω, embodies queries and modifications of the surrounding location graph.

An offered interaction α takes the form $\{a_i \langle V_i \rangle \mid i \in I\}$, where I is a finite index set, a_i are channel names, and V_i are values.

Evaluation functions. We require the existence of evaluation functions on priority constraints ($\mathtt{eval}_\pi$), and on synchronization constraints ($\mathtt{eval}_\sigma$) of the following types $\mathtt{eval}_\pi : \mathcal{G} \times \mathcal{N}_l \times \mathsf{Pr} \to \wp_f(\mathcal{N}_l \times \mathcal{N}_r \times \mathcal{N}_c)$, and $\mathtt{eval}_\sigma : \mathcal{G} \times \mathcal{N}_l \times \mathsf{S} \to \wp_f(\mathcal{N}_l \times \mathcal{N}_r \times \mathcal{N}_c \times \mathcal{V})$. The results of the above evaluation functions are called *concrete (priority or synchronization) constraints*. The presence of evaluation functions allows us to abstract away from the actual labels used in the semantics of processes, and to allow labels used in the operational semantics of location graphs, described below, to depend on the environment and the surrounding location graph.

Example 4. One can, for instance, imagine a kind of broadcast synchronization constraint of the form $* : a\langle V \rangle$, which, in the context of an environment Γ and a location l, evaluates to a constraint requiring all the roles bound to a locations in Γ to offer an interaction on channel a, i.e.: $\mathtt{eval}_\sigma(\Gamma, l, * : a\langle V \rangle) = \{l.r : a\langle V \rangle \mid \exists h, l.r \twoheadrightarrow h \in \Gamma\}$.

We require the existence of an evaluation function on effects ($\mathtt{eval}_\omega$) with the type $\mathtt{eval}_\omega : \mathcal{G} \times \mathcal{N}_l \times \mathsf{A} \to \wp_f(\mathsf{E})$, where E is the set of *concrete effects*. A concrete effect can take any of the following forms, where l is a location name:

- $l : \mathtt{newl}(h, P), l : \mathtt{newch}(c), l : \mathtt{newr}(r)$, respectively to create a new location named h with initial process P, to create a new channel named c, and to create a new role named r.
- $l : \mathtt{add}(h, r, k), l : \mathtt{rmv}(h, r, k)$, respectively to add and remove a graph edge $h.r \twoheadrightarrow k$ to and from the surrounding location graph.

- l : gquery(Γ), to discover a subgraph Γ of the surrounding location graph.
- l : swap(h, P, Q), to swap the process P running at location h for process Q.
- l : kill(h), to remove location h from the surrounding location graph.

Concrete effects embody the reconfiguration capabilities of the G-Kells framework. Effects reconfiguring the graph itself come in pairs manifesting introduction and elimination effects: thus, adding and removing a node (location) from the graph (newl, kill), and adding and removing an edge from the graph (add, rmv). Role creation (newr) is introduced to allow the creation of new edges. Channel creation (newch) allows the same flexibility provided by name creation in the π-calculus. The swap effect (swap) is introduced to allow the atomic update of a located process. The graph query effect (gquery) is perhaps a bit more unorthodox: it allows a form of reflection whereby a location can discover part of its surrounding location graph. It is best understood as an abstraction of graph navigation and query capabilities which have been found useful for programming reconfigurations in component-based systems [11].

Operational Semantics of Location Graphs

Transitions. The operational semantics of location graphs is defined by means of a transition system, whose transition relation $\rightarrow$ is defined, by means of the inference rules presented below, as a subset of $\mathcal{G} \times \mathcal{K} \times \mathcal{L} \times \mathcal{K}$. Labels take the form $\langle \pi \cdot \sigma \cdot \omega \rangle$, where π and σ are *located priority and synchronization constraints*, respectively, and ω is a finite set of *located effects* (for simplicity, we reuse the same symbols than for constraints and effects). The set of labels is noted $\mathcal{L}$.

A located priority constraint π is just a concrete priority constraint, and takes the form $\{l_i.r_i : a_i \mid i \in I\}$, where I is a finite index set, with l_i, r_i, a_i in location, role and channel names, respectively. A located synchronization constraint takes the form $\{u_j : a_j \langle V_j \rangle\}$, where a_j are channel names, u_j are either location names l_j or pairs of location names and roles, noted $l_j.r_j$, and V_j are values. Located effects can take the following forms: l : rmv$(h, r, k), l$: swap$(h, P, Q), l$: kill$(h), h : \overline{\text{rmv}}(h, r, k), h : \overline{\text{swap}}(h, P, Q), and h : \overline{\text{kill}}(h)$, where l, h, k are location names, r is a role name, P, Q are processes. The predicate located on E identifies located effects. In particular, for a set $\omega \subset$ E, we have located(ω) if and only if all elements of ω are located.

A transition $\langle \Gamma, C, \langle \pi \cdot \sigma \cdot \omega \rangle, C' \rangle \in \rightarrow$ is noted $\Gamma \rhd C \xrightarrow{\langle \pi \cdot \sigma \cdot \omega \rangle} C'$ and must obey the following constraint:

- If $\Gamma = \mathbf{u} \cup \Delta$, where $\mathbf{u}$ is a set of names, and Δ is a set of edges, then $\text{fn}(\Delta) \subseteq \mathbf{u}$ and $\text{fn}(\Gamma) = \mathbf{u}$.
- $\text{fn}(C) \subseteq \text{fn}(\Gamma)$, i.e. the free names occurring in C must appear in the already used names of Γ.
- If $l.r \twoheadrightarrow h$ and $l.r \twoheadrightarrow k$ are in $\Gamma \cup \Gamma(C)$, then $h = k$, i.e. we only have a single edge binding a role r of a given location l to another location h.

Auxiliary relation $\rightarrow_\bullet$. The definition of $\rightarrow$ makes use of an auxiliary relation $\rightarrow_\bullet \subseteq \mathcal{G} \times \mathcal{K} \times \mathcal{L}_\bullet \times \mathcal{K}$, where $\mathcal{L}_\bullet$ is a set of elements of the form $\langle \pi \cdot \sigma \cdot \omega \rangle$ where π and σ are located priority and synchronizaton constraints, and where ω is a finite set of concrete effects. Relation $\rightarrow_\bullet$ is defined as the least relation satisfying the rules in Fig. 4, where we use the following notation: if $\alpha = \{a_i \langle V_i \rangle \mid i \in I\}$, then $l : \alpha = \{l : a_i \langle V_i \rangle \mid i \in I\}$, and if $\alpha = \epsilon$, then $l : \alpha = \epsilon$.

Rule ACT simply expresses how process transitions are translated into location graph transitions, and process level constraints and effects are translated into located constraints and concrete effects, via the evaluation functions introduced above. Rule NEWL specifies the effect of an effect $l : \texttt{newl}(h, Q)$, which creates a new location $h[Q]$. Notice how effect $l : \texttt{newl}(h, Q)$ is removed from the set of effects in the transition label in the conclusion of the rule: auxiliary relation $\rightarrow_\bullet$ is in fact used to guarantee that a whole set of concrete effects are handled atomically. All the rules in Fig. 4 except ACT, which just prepares for the evaluation of effects, follow the same pattern. Rules NEWC and NEWR specify the creation of a new channel name and of a new role name, respectively. The rules just introduce the constraint that the new name must not be an already used name in the environment Γ. Our transitions being in the early style, the use of the new name is already taken into account in the continuation location graph C (in fact in the continuation process P' appearing on the left hand side of the instance of rule ACT that must have led to the building of C). This handling of new names is a bit unorthodox but it squares nicely with the explicitly indexed labelled transition semantics of the π-calculus given by Cattani and Sewell in [8]. Rule ADDE specifies the effect of adding a new edge to the location graph. Rule GQUERY allows the discovery by processes of a subgraph of the location graph. In the rule premise, we use the notation Γ_l to denote the set of edges reachable from location l, formally: $\Gamma_L = \{h.r \twoheadrightarrow k \in \Gamma \mid l \rightarrow_\Gamma^+ h\}$, where $l \rightarrow_\Gamma^+ h$ means that there exists a non-empty chain $l.r \twoheadrightarrow l_1, l_1.r_1 \twoheadrightarrow l_2, \ldots, l_{n-1}.r_{n-1} \twoheadrightarrow l_n, l_n.r_n \twoheadrightarrow h$, with $n \geq 1$, linking l to h in the location graph Γ. As in the case of name creation rules, the exact effect on processes is left unspecified, the only constraint being that the discovered graph be indeed a subgraph of the location graph in the environment.

Transition relation $\rightarrow$. The transition relation $\rightarrow$ is defined by the rules in Fig. 5. We use the following notations and definitions in Fig. 5:

– Function $\texttt{seval}$ is defined by induction as follows (for any $l, r, h, V, \sigma, \sigma'$):

$$\texttt{seval}(\Gamma, \sigma) = \texttt{seval}(\Gamma, \sigma') \qquad if\ \sigma = \{l.r : a\langle V \rangle, h : a\langle W \rangle\} \cup \sigma'$$
$$\wedge\, l.r \twoheadrightarrow h \in \Gamma \wedge \texttt{match}(V, W)$$
$$\texttt{seval}(\Gamma, \sigma) = \sigma \qquad\qquad otherwise$$

$$\text{ACT}_{\bullet} \quad \frac{\pi_{\bullet} = \text{eval}_{\pi}(\Gamma, l, \pi) \qquad P \xrightarrow{\langle \pi \cdot \alpha \cdot \sigma \cdot \omega \rangle} P' \qquad \sigma_{\bullet} = \text{eval}_{\sigma}(\Gamma, l, \sigma) \qquad \omega_{\bullet} = \text{eval}_{\omega}(\Gamma, l, \omega)}{\Gamma \triangleright l[P] \xrightarrow{\langle \pi_{\bullet} \cdot l : \alpha \cup \sigma_{\bullet} \cdot \omega_{\bullet} \rangle}_{\bullet} l[P']}$$

$$\text{NewL} \quad \frac{\Gamma \triangleright l[P] \xrightarrow{\langle \pi \cdot \sigma \cdot l : \text{newl}(h, Q), \omega \rangle}_{\bullet} C \qquad h \notin \Gamma}{\Gamma \triangleright l[P] \xrightarrow{\langle \pi \cdot \sigma \cdot \omega \rangle}_{\bullet} C \parallel h[Q]}$$

$$\text{NewC} \quad \frac{\Gamma \triangleright l[P] \xrightarrow{\langle \pi \cdot \sigma \cdot l : \text{newch}(c), \omega \rangle}_{\bullet} C \qquad c \notin \Gamma}{\Gamma \triangleright l[P] \xrightarrow{\langle \pi \cdot \sigma \cdot \omega \rangle}_{\bullet} C}$$

$$\text{NewR} \quad \frac{\Gamma \triangleright l[P] \xrightarrow{\langle \pi \cdot \sigma \cdot l : \text{newr}(r), \omega \rangle}_{\bullet} C \qquad r \notin \Gamma}{\Gamma \triangleright l[P] \xrightarrow{\langle \pi \cdot \sigma \cdot \omega \rangle}_{\bullet} C}$$

$$\text{AddE} \quad \frac{\Gamma \triangleright l[P] \xrightarrow{\langle \pi \cdot \sigma \cdot l : \text{add}(h, r, k), \omega \rangle}_{\bullet} C \qquad \neg(\exists k, h.r \rightarrow k \in \Gamma)}{\Gamma \triangleright l[P] \xrightarrow{\langle \pi \cdot \sigma \cdot \omega \rangle}_{\bullet} C \parallel h.r \rightarrow k}$$

$$\text{GQuery} \quad \frac{\Gamma \triangleright l[P] \xrightarrow{\langle \pi \cdot \sigma \cdot l : \text{gquery}(\Delta), \omega \rangle}_{\bullet} C \qquad \Delta \subseteq \Gamma_l}{\Gamma \triangleright l[P] \xrightarrow{\langle \pi \cdot \sigma \cdot \omega \rangle}_{\bullet} C}$$

Fig. 4. Rules for auxiliary relation $\rightarrow_{\bullet}$

$$\text{SWAP} \quad \Gamma \triangleright l[P] \xrightarrow{\langle \epsilon \cdot \epsilon \cdot \overline{\text{swap}}(l, P, Q) \rangle} l[Q] \qquad\qquad \text{KILL} \quad \Gamma \triangleright l[P] \xrightarrow{\langle \epsilon \cdot \epsilon \cdot \overline{\text{kill}}(l) \rangle} 0$$

$$\text{RMV} \quad \Gamma \triangleright h.r \rightarrow k \xrightarrow{\langle \epsilon \cdot \epsilon \cdot \overline{\text{rmv}}(h, r, k) \rangle} 0$$

$$\text{ACT} \quad \frac{\Gamma \triangleright l[P] \xrightarrow{\langle \pi \cdot \sigma \cdot \omega \rangle}_{\bullet} C \qquad \text{located}(\omega)}{\Gamma \triangleright l[P] \xrightarrow{\langle \pi \cdot \sigma \cdot \omega \rangle} C}$$

$$\text{COMP} \quad \frac{\begin{array}{c} \Gamma' = \Gamma \cup \Gamma(C_1) \cup \Gamma(C_2) \qquad \pi = \pi_1 \cup \pi_2 \qquad \mathbf{fn}(\Gamma') \uplus \Delta_1 \uplus \Delta_2 = \mathcal{N} \\ \Gamma' \triangleright (\!|C_1 \parallel C_2|\!)_{\pi} \models \pi \qquad \sigma = \text{seval}(\Gamma', \sigma_1 \cup \sigma_2) \qquad \omega = \text{aeval}(\Gamma', \omega_1 \cup \omega_2) \\ \Gamma' \cup \Delta_1 \triangleright C_1 \xrightarrow{\langle \pi_1 \cdot \sigma_1 \cdot \omega_1 \rangle} C_1' \qquad \Gamma' \cup \Delta_2 \triangleright C_2 \xrightarrow{\langle \pi_2 \cdot \sigma_2 \cdot \omega_2 \rangle} C_2' \end{array}}{\Gamma \triangleright C_1 \parallel C_2 \xrightarrow{\langle \pi \cdot \sigma \cdot \omega \rangle} C_1' \parallel C_2'}$$

Fig. 5. Rules for transition relation $\rightarrow$

– Function `aeval` is defined by induction as follows (for any $l, r, h, k, P, Q, \sigma, \sigma'$):

$$\text{aeval}(\Gamma, \sigma) = \text{aeval}(\Gamma, \sigma') \quad if \quad \sigma = \{l : \text{swap}(h, P, Q), \overline{\text{swap}}(h, P, Q)\} \cup \sigma'$$

$$\text{aeval}(\Gamma, \sigma) = \text{aeval}(\Gamma, \sigma') \quad if \quad \sigma = \{l : \text{rmv}(h, r, k), \overline{\text{rmv}}(h, r, k)\} \cup \sigma'$$

$$\text{aeval}(\Gamma, \sigma) = \text{aeval}(\Gamma, \sigma') \quad if \quad \sigma = \{l : \text{kill}(h), \overline{\text{kill}}(h)\} \cup \sigma'$$

$$\text{aeval}(\Gamma, \sigma) = \sigma \qquad\qquad otherwise$$

– Assume $\pi = \{l_i.r_i : a_i \mid i \in I\}$, then $(\!|C|\!)_\pi$ is obtained by replacing in C all the locations $\{l_i[P_i] \mid i \in I\}$ with locations $\{l_i[(\!|P_i|\!)] \mid i \in I\}$, where $(\!|P|\!)$ is defined by the LTS obtained from that of P by the following rule:

$$\text{TRIM} \quad \dfrac{P \xrightarrow{\langle \pi \cdot \alpha \cdot \sigma \cdot \omega \rangle} P'}{(\!|P|\!) \xrightarrow{\langle \epsilon \cdot \alpha \cdot \sigma \cdot \omega \rangle} P'}$$

In other terms, $(\!|C|\!)_\pi$ is obtained by disregarding the priority constraints that are generated by locations l_i mentioned in the priority constraint π.

– $\Gamma \triangleright C \models \{l_i.r_i : a_i \mid i \in I\}$ means that, for all $i \in I$, $\Gamma \triangleright C \models l_i.r_i : a_i$. We write $\Gamma \triangleright C \models l.r : a$ to mean that

$$\neg(\exists h, \pi, \sigma, \omega, V, C', l.r \twoheadrightarrow h \wedge \Gamma \triangleright C \xrightarrow{\langle \pi \cdot l:a\langle V \rangle, \sigma \cdot \omega \rangle} C')$$

Rule SWAP specifies that at any point in time a location can see its process swapped for another. Likewise, rules KILL and RMV specify that at any point in time a location or an edge, respectively, can be removed from a location graph. Rule ACT specifies the termination of the atomic execution of a set of concrete effects. All the effects remaining must be located effects, which expect some counterpart (provided by the rules SWAP, KILL, and RMV, when invoking rule COMP) to proceed.

Rule COMP is the workhorse of our operational semantics of location graphs. It specifies how to determine the transitions of a parallel composition $C_1 \parallel C_2$, by combining the priority constraints, synchronization constraints and effects obtained from the determination of contributing transitions from C_1 and C_2. The latter takes place in extended environment Γ', that contains the original environment Γ, but also the edges present in C_1 and C_2, defined as $\Gamma(C_1)$ and $\Gamma(C_2)$, respectively. To ensure the names created as side effects of C_1 and C_2 transitions are indeed unique, the determination of the contributing transition of C_1 takes place in an environment where the already used names include those in Γ as well as those in Δ_1, which gathers names that may be created as a side effect of the contributing transition of C_2. Likewise for determining the contributing transition of C_2. The constraint $\text{fn}(\Gamma') \uplus \Delta_1 \uplus \Delta_2 = \mathcal{N}$ ensures that names in Δ_1 and Δ_2 are disjoint, as well as disjoint from the already used names of $\text{fn}(\Gamma')$.

The original aspect of rule COMP lies with the computation of located synchronization constraints and effects resulting from the parallel composition of G-Kells components: we allow it to be dependent on the global environment Γ' with the clauses $\sigma = \text{seval}(\Gamma', \sigma_1 \cup \sigma_2)$ and $\omega = \text{aeval}(\Gamma', \omega_1 \cup \omega_2)$, which, in turn, allows to enforce constraints dependent on the location graph as in the definition of function `seval`. In fact, as we discuss in Sect. 4 below, we can envisage instances of the framework where different types of location-graph-dependent constraints apply.

The use of environments in rule COMP to obtain a quasi-compositional rule of evolution is reminiscent of the use of environment and process *frames* in the parallel rule of the ψ-calculus framework [3]. We say our rule COMP is *quasi-compositional* for the handling of priority is not compositional: it relies on the global condition $\Gamma' \triangleright (\!|C_1 \parallel C_2|\!)_\pi$, which requires computing with (an altered view of) the whole composition. The use of the $(\!|\cdot|\!)_-$ operator in rule COMP is reminiscent of the handling of priorities in other works [9]. An easy way to turn rule COMP into a completely compositional rule would be to adopt a more "syntactic" approach, defining $(\!|C|\!)_\pi$ to be obtained by replacing *all* locations $l[P]$ in C by their trimmed version $l[(\!|P|\!)]$, and defining environments to include information on possible actions by trimmed locations. On the other hand, we can also adopt a purely "semantic" (albeit non-compositional) variant by defining $(\!|C|\!)_\pi$ to be just C. However, in this case, we don't know whether the completeness result in Theorem 1 below still stands.

Example 5. To illustrate how the rules work, consider the following process transitions:

$$P \xrightarrow{\langle \epsilon \cdot \epsilon \cdot *:a\langle V\rangle \cdot \mathtt{newl}(h,P)\rangle} P' \qquad P_1 \xrightarrow{\langle \epsilon \cdot a\langle V_1\rangle \cdot \epsilon \cdot \{\mathtt{newl}(h_1,P_1)\}\rangle} P_1' \qquad P_2 \xrightarrow{\langle \epsilon \cdot a\langle V_2\rangle \cdot \epsilon \cdot \epsilon\rangle} P_2'$$

Let $\Gamma = \{l, l_1, l_2\} \cup \{l.r_1 \twoheadrightarrow l_1, l.r_2 \twoheadrightarrow l_2\}$, and let Δ, Δ' be such that $\Delta \uplus \Delta' = \mathcal{N} \setminus \{l, l_1, l_2, h, h_1\}$. We assume further that $\mathtt{match}(V, V_1)$ and $\mathtt{match}(V, V_2)$, that all names l, l_1, l_2, h, h_1 are distinct, and that

$$\mathtt{eval}_\sigma(\Gamma, l, * : a\langle V\rangle) = \{l.r_1 : a\langle V\rangle, l.r_2 : a\langle V\rangle\}$$
$$\mathtt{eval}_\omega(\Gamma, l, \{\mathtt{newl}(h, P)\}) = \{l : \mathtt{newl}(h, P)\}$$
$$\mathtt{eval}_\omega(\Gamma, l_1, \{\mathtt{newl}(h_1, P_1)\}) = \{l_1 : \mathtt{newl}(h_1, P_1)\}$$
$$\mathtt{eval}_\omega(\Gamma, l_2, \epsilon) = \epsilon \quad \mathtt{eval}_\pi(\Gamma, l, \epsilon) = \epsilon \quad \mathtt{eval}_\pi(\Gamma, l_1, \epsilon) = \epsilon \quad \mathtt{eval}_\pi(\Gamma, l_2, \epsilon) = \epsilon$$

Applying rule ACT$_\bullet$, we get

$$\Gamma \cup \{h_1\}, \Delta \triangleright l[P] \xrightarrow{\langle \epsilon \cdot \{l.r_1:a\langle V\rangle, l.r_2:a\langle V\rangle\} \cdot \{l:\mathtt{newl}(h,P)\}\rangle}_\bullet l[P']$$
$$\Gamma \cup \{h\}, \Delta' \triangleright l_1[P_1] \xrightarrow{\langle \epsilon \cdot l_1:a\langle V_1\rangle \cdot \{l_1:\mathtt{newl}(h_1,P_1)\}\rangle}_\bullet l_1[P_1']$$
$$\Gamma \cup \{h\}, \Delta' \triangleright l_2[P_2] \xrightarrow{\langle \epsilon \cdot l_2:a\langle V_2\rangle \cdot \epsilon\rangle}_\bullet l_2[P_2']$$

Applying rule NEWL, we get

$$\Gamma \cup \{h_1\}, \Delta \triangleright l[P] \xrightarrow{\langle \epsilon \cdot \{l.r_1:a\langle V\rangle, l.r_2:a\langle V\rangle\} \cdot \epsilon\rangle}_\bullet l[P'] \parallel h[P]$$
$$\Gamma \cup \{h\}, \Delta' \triangleright l_1[P_1] \xrightarrow{\langle \epsilon \cdot \{h_1:a\langle V_1\rangle\} \cdot \epsilon\rangle}_\bullet l_1[P_1'] \parallel h_1[P_1]$$

Applying rule ACT we get

$$\Gamma \cup \{h_1\}, \Delta \rhd l[P] \xrightarrow{\langle \epsilon \cdot \{l.r_1:a\langle V \rangle, l.r_2:a\langle V \rangle\} \cdot \epsilon \rangle} l[P'] \parallel h[P]$$

$$\Gamma \cup \{h\}, \Delta' \rhd l_1[P_1] \xrightarrow{\langle \epsilon \cdot \{l_1:a\langle V_1 \rangle\} \cdot \epsilon \rangle} l_1[P_1'] \parallel h_1[P_1]$$

$$\Gamma \cup \{h\}, \Delta' \rhd l_2[P_2] \xrightarrow{\langle \epsilon \cdot \{l_2:a\langle V_2 \rangle\} \cdot \epsilon \rangle} l_2[P_2']$$

Finally, applying rule COMP we get

$$\Gamma \cup \{h\}, \Delta' \rhd l_1[P_1] \parallel l_2[P_2] \xrightarrow{\langle \epsilon \cdot \{l_1:a\langle V_1 \rangle, l_2:a\langle V_2 \rangle\} \cdot \epsilon \rangle} l_1[P_1'] \parallel h_1[P_1] \parallel l_2[P_2']$$

$$\Gamma \rhd l[P] \parallel l_1[P_1] \parallel l_2[P_2] \xrightarrow{\langle \epsilon \cdot \epsilon \cdot \epsilon \rangle} l[P'] \parallel h[P] \parallel l_1[P_1'] \parallel h_1[P_1] \parallel l_2[P_2']$$

Transition relation $\rightarrow$ *as a fixpoint.* Because of the format of rule COMP, which does not *prima facie* obey known SOS rule formats [21], or conform to the standard notion of transition system specification [5], the question remains of which relation the rules in Figs. 4 and 5 define. Instead of trying to turn our rules into equivalent rules in an appropriate format, we answer this question directly, by providing a fixpoint definition for $\rightarrow$. We use the fixpoint construction introduced by Przymusinski for the three-valued semantics of logic programs [23].

Let $\sqsubseteq$ be the ordering on pairs of relations in $\mathcal{T} = \mathcal{G} \times \mathcal{K} \times \mathcal{L} \times \mathcal{K}$ defined as:

$$\langle R_1, R_2 \rangle \sqsubseteq \langle T_1, T_2 \rangle \iff R_1 \subseteq T_1 \wedge T_2 \subseteq R_2$$

As products of complete lattices, $(\mathcal{T}, \subseteq)$ and $(\mathcal{T}^2, \sqsubseteq)$ are complete lattices [10]. One can read the COMP rule in Fig. 5 as the definition of an operator $\mathcal{F} : \mathcal{T}^2 \to \mathcal{T}^2$ which operates on pairs of sub and over-approximations of $\rightarrow$. Let $\rightarrow_0$ be the relation in $\mathcal{T}^2$ obtained as the least relation satisfying the rules in Figs. 4 and 5, with rule COMP omitted. Operator $\mathcal{F}$ is then defined as follows:

$$\mathcal{F}(R_1, R_2) = (\rightarrow_0 \cup R_1 \cup r(\rightarrow_0 \cup R_1, R_2), R_2 \sqcap r(R_2, \rightarrow_0 \cup R_1))$$
$$r(R_1, R_2) = \{t \in \mathcal{T} \mid t = (\Gamma, C_1 \parallel C_2, \langle \pi \cdot \sigma \cdot \omega \rangle, C_1' \parallel C_2')$$
$$\wedge \; \mathrm{comp}(\Gamma, C_1, C_2, \pi, \sigma, \omega, C_1', C_2', R_1, R_2)\}$$

where the predicate `comp` is defined as follows:

$$\mathrm{comp}(\Gamma, C_1, C_2, \pi, \sigma, \omega, C_1', C_2', R_1, R_2) \iff$$
$$\exists \pi_1, \pi_2, \sigma_1, \sigma_2, \omega_1, \omega_2, \Delta_1, \Delta_2, \Gamma',$$
$$\Gamma' = \Gamma \cup \Gamma(C_1) \cup \Gamma(C_2)$$
$$\wedge \; \pi = \pi_1 \cup \pi_2$$
$$\wedge \; \mathbf{fn}(\Gamma') \uplus \Delta_1 \uplus \Delta_2 = \mathcal{N}$$
$$\wedge \; \sigma = \mathbf{seval}(\Gamma', \sigma_1 \cup \sigma_2)$$
$$\wedge \; \omega = \mathbf{aeval}(\Gamma', \omega_1 \cup \omega_2)$$
$$\wedge \; (\Gamma' \cup \Delta_1, C_1, \langle \pi_1 \cdot \sigma_1 \cdot \omega_1 \rangle, C_1') \in R_1$$
$$\wedge \; (\Gamma' \cup \Delta_2, C_2, \langle \pi_2 \cdot \sigma_2 \cdot \omega_2 \rangle, C_2') \in R_1$$
$$\wedge \; \Gamma' \rhd (\!| C_1 \parallel C_2 |\!)_\pi \models_{R_2} \pi$$

where $\Gamma \triangleright C \models_R \{l_i : a_i \mid i \in I\}$ means that, for all $i \in I$, $\Gamma \triangleright C \models_R l_i : a_i$, and where $\Gamma \triangleright C \models_R l : a$ stands for:

$$\neg(\exists \pi, \sigma, \omega, V, C', (\Gamma, C, \langle \pi \cdot \{l : a\langle V\rangle\} \cup \sigma \cdot \omega\rangle, C') \in R)$$

The definition of the predicate comp mimics the definition of rule COMP, with all the conditions in the premises appearing as clauses in comp, but where the positive transition conditions in the premises are replaced by transitions in the sub-approximation R_1, and negative transition conditions (appearing in the $\Gamma' \triangleright (C_1 \parallel C_2)_\pi \models \pi$ condition) are replaced by equivalent conditions with transitions not belonging to the over-approximation R_2. With the definitions above, if R_1 is a sub-approximation of $\rightarrow$, and R_2 is an over-approximation of $\rightarrow$, then we have $R_1 \subseteq \pi_1(\mathcal{F}(R_1, R_2))$ and $\pi_2(\mathcal{F}(R_1, R_2)) \subseteq R_2$, where π_1, π_2 are the first and second projections. In other terms, given a pair of sub and over approximations of $\rightarrow$, $\mathcal{F}$ computes a pair of better approximations.

From this definition, if it is easy to show that $\mathcal{F}$ is order-preserving:

Lemma 1. *For all $R_1, T_1, R_2, T_2 \in \mathcal{T}^2$, if $(R_1, R_2) \sqsubseteq (T_1, T_2)$, then $\mathcal{F}(R_1, R_2) \sqsubseteq \mathcal{F}(T_1, T_2)$.*

Since $\mathcal{F}$ is order-preserving, it has a least fixpoint, $\mathcal{F}_* = (D, U)$, by the Knaster-Tarski theorem. We can then define $\rightarrow$ to be the first projection of $\mathcal{F}_*$, namely D. With the definition of $(C)_\pi$ we have adopted, and noting that it provides a form of stratification with the number of locations in a location graph with non-empty priority constraints, it is also possible to show that $\rightarrow = U$, meaning that $\rightarrow$ as just defined is *complete*, using the terminology in [27]. In fact, using the terminology in [27], we can prove the theorem below, whose proof we omit for lack of space:

Theorem 1. *The relation $\rightarrow$ as defined above is the least well-supported model of the rules in Figs. 4 and 5. Moreover $\rightarrow$ is complete.*

4 Discussion

We discuss in this section the various features of the G-Kells framework and relevant related work.

Introductory example. Let's first revisit Example 3 to see how we can further model the behavior of its different components. We can add, for instance, a crash action to the virtual machine locations, which can be triggered by a process transition at a virtual machine location of the form $P \xrightarrow{\langle \epsilon \cdot \epsilon \cdot \epsilon \cdot \text{kill}(*) \rangle} 0$ with the following evaluation function:

$$\text{eval}_\omega(\Gamma, l, \text{kill}(*)) = \{\text{kill}(h) \mid \exists r, l.r \twoheadrightarrow h \in \Gamma\}$$

yielding, for instance, the following transition (where **u** includes all free names in $V_0[P] \parallel C[P_C] \parallel CC[P_{CC}]$):

$$\mathbf{u}, \{V_0.0 \twoheadrightarrow C, V_0.1 \twoheadrightarrow CC\} \triangleright V_0[P] \parallel C[P_C] \parallel CC[P_{CC}] \xrightarrow{\langle \epsilon \cdot \epsilon \cdot \epsilon \rangle} V_0[0] \parallel 0 \parallel 0$$

This crash behavior can be extended to an arbitrary location graph residing in a virtual machine, by first discovering the location graph inside a virtual machine via the gquery primitive, and then killing all locations in the graph as illustrated above.

Early style. Our operational semantics for location graphs is specified in an early style [24], with values in labels manifesting the results of successful communication. This allows us to remain oblivious to the actual forms of synchronization used. For instance, one could envisage pattern matching as in the ψ-calculus [3], or even bi-directional pattern matching: for instance we could have a process synchronization constraint $r : a\langle x, V \rangle$ matching an offered interaction $h : a\langle W, y \rangle$, which translate into matching located synchronization constraints $l.r : a\langle W, V \rangle$ and $h : a\langle W, V \rangle$.

Mobility vs higher-order. Our operational semantics comprises both mobility features with location binding, and higher-order features with swapping and higher-order interactions. One could wonder whether these features are all needed as primitives. For instance, one could argue that mobility features are enough to model higher-order phenomena as in the π-calculus [24]. Lacking at this point a behavioral theory for the G-Kells framework, we cannot answer the question definitely here. But we doubt that mobility via location binding is sufficient to faithfully encode higher-order communication. In particular, note that we have contexts (location graphs) that can distinguish the two cases via the ability to kill locations selectively.

Directed graphs vs acyclic directed graphs. Location graphs form directed graphs. One could wonder whether to impose the additional constraints that such graphs be acyclic. While most meaningful examples of ubiquitous systems and software structures can be modeled with acyclic directed graphs, our rules for location graphs function readily with arbitrary graphs. Enforcing the constraint that all evolutions of a location graph keep it acyclic does not seem necessary.

Relationship with CAB. The G-Kells model constitutes a conservative extension of CAB. A straightforwward encoding of CAB in the G-Kells framework can be defined as in Fig. 6, with translated glues $[\![G]\!]$ defined with the same LTS, mutatis mutandis, as CAB glues. The following proposition is then an easy consequence of our definitions:

Proposition 1. *Let C be a CAB component. We have $C \xrightarrow{l:a} C'$ if and only if* $[\![C]\!] \xrightarrow{\langle \epsilon \cdot \{l:a\} \cdot \epsilon \rangle} [\![C']\!]$.

Graph constraints in rules. For simplicity, the evaluation functions seval and aeval have been defined above with only a simple graph constraint in the first clause of the seval definition. One can parameterize these definitions with additional graph constraints to enforce different policies. For instance, one could

$$\llbracket l[P] \rrbracket = l[P]$$

$$\llbracket l[C_1, \ldots, C_n \star G] \rrbracket = l_1[C_1] \parallel l.1 \twoheadrightarrow l_1 \parallel \ldots \parallel l_n[C_n] \parallel l.n \twoheadrightarrow l_n \parallel l[\llbracket G \rrbracket]$$

$$\llbracket 0 \rrbracket = 0$$

$$\llbracket \langle \pi \cdot l : a \cdot \sigma \rangle.G \rrbracket = \langle \llbracket \pi \rrbracket \cdot \{l : a\} \cdot \llbracket \sigma \rrbracket \rangle.\llbracket G \rrbracket$$

$$\llbracket G_1 \mid G_2 \rrbracket = \llbracket G_1 \rrbracket \mid \llbracket G_2 \rrbracket$$

$$\llbracket \mu X. G \rrbracket = \mu X. \llbracket G \rrbracket$$

$$\llbracket \{l_i : a_i \mid i \in I\} \rrbracket = \{i : a_i \mid i \in I\}$$

$$\mathtt{eval}_\pi(\Gamma, l, i : a_i) = l.i : a_i \qquad \mathtt{eval}_\sigma(\Gamma, l, i : a_i) = l.i : a_i$$

Fig. 6. Encoding CAB in the G-Kells framework

constrain the use of the swap, kill and edge removal operations to locations dominating the target location by adding a constraint of the form $l \twoheadrightarrow^* h$ to each of the clauses in the definition of $\mathtt{aeval}$, where $l \twoheadrightarrow_\Gamma^* h$ means that there exists a (possibly empty) chain $l.r \twoheadrightarrow l_1, l_1.r_1 \twoheadrightarrow l_2, \ldots, l_{n-1}.r_{n-1} \twoheadrightarrow l_n, l_n.r_n \twoheadrightarrow h$ linking l to h in the location graph Γ. Similar constraints could be added to rule ADDE. Further constraints could be added to rule GQUERY to further restrict the discovery of subgraphs, for instance, preventing nodes other than immediate children to be discovered.

Types and capabilities. The framework presented in this paper is an untyped one. However, introducing types similar to i/o types capabilities in the π-calculus [24] would be highly useful. For instance, edges of a location graph can be typed, perhaps with as simple a scheme as different colors to reflect different containment and visibility semantics, which can be exploited in the definition of evaluation functions to constrain effects and synchronization. In addition, location, role and channel names can be typed with capabilities constraining the transfer of rights from one location to another. For instance, transferring a location name l can come with the right to swap the behavior at l, but not with the right to kill l, or with the right to bind roles of l to locations, but not with the ability to swap the behavior at l. We believe these capabilities could be useful in enforcing encapsulation and access control policies.

Relation with the ψ-calculus framework and SCEL. We already remarked that our use of environments is reminiscent of the use of frames in the ψ-calculus framework [3]. An important difference with the ψ-calculus framework is the fact that we allow interactions to depend on constraints involving the global environment, in our case the structure of the location graph. Whether one can faithfully encode the G-Kells framework (with mild linguistic assumptions on processes) with the ψ-calculus framework remains to be seen.

On the other hand, it would seem worthwhile to pursue the extension of the framework presented here with ψ-calculus-like assertions. We wonder in particular what relation the resulting framework would have with the SCEL language for autonomous and adaptive systems [12]. The notion of *ensemble*, being assertion-based, is more fluid than our notion of location graph, but it does not have the ability to superimpose on ensembles the kind of control actions, such as swapping and killing, that the G-Kells framework allows.

Relation with SHR. The graph manipulation capabilities embedded in the G-Kells framework are reminiscent of synchronized hyperdege replacement (SHR) systems [18]. In SHR, multiple hyperedge replacements can be synchronized to yield an atomic transformation of the underlying hypergraph in conjunction with information exchange. Intuitively, it seems one can achieve much the same effects with G-Kells: located effects can atomically build a new subgraph and modify the existing one, and they can be synchronized across multiple locations thanks to synchronization constraints. In contrast, SHR systems lack priorities and the internalization of hyperedge replacement rules (the equivalent of our processes) in graph nodes to account for inherent dynamic reconfiguration capabilities. We conjecture that SHR systems can be faithfully encoded in the G-Kells framework.

5   Conclusion

We have introduced the G-Kells framework to lift limitations in existing computational models for ubiquitous and reconfigurable software systems, in particular the ability to describe dynamic structures with sharing, where different aggregates or composites can share components. Much work remains to be done, however. We first intend to develop the behavioral theory of our framework. Indeed we hope to develop a first-order bisimulation theory for the G-Kells framework, avoiding the difficulties inherent in mixing higher-order features with passivation described in [19]. We also need to formally compare G-Kells with several other formalisms, including SHR systems and the ψ-calculus framework. And we definitely need to develop a typed variant of the framework to exploit the rich set of capabilities that can be attached to location names.

Ackowledgements. Damien Pous suggested the move to an early style semantics. The paper was much improved thanks to comments by Ivan Lanese on earlier versions.

References

1. Baier, C., Sirjani, M., Arbab, F., Rutten, J.J.M.M.: Modeling component connectors in reo by constraint automata. Sci. Comput. Program. **61**(2), 75–113 (2006)
2. Barbier, F., Henderson-Sellers, B., Le Parc, A., Bruel, J.M.: Formalization of the whole-part relationship in the unified modeling language. IEEE Trans. Softw. Eng. **29**(5), 459–470 (2003)
3. Bengtson, J., Johansson, M., Parrow, J., Victor, B.: Psi-calculi: a framework for mobile processes with nominal data and logic. Logical Meth. Comput. Sci. **7**(1) (2011)
4. Bliudze, S., Sifakis, J.: A notion of glue expressiveness for component-based systems. In: van Breugel, F., Chechik, M. (eds.) CONCUR 2008. LNCS, vol. 5201, pp. 508–522. Springer, Heidelberg (2008)

5. Bol, R.N., Groote, J.F.: The meaning of negative premises in transition system specifications. J. ACM **43**(5), 863–914 (1996)
6. Bugliesi, M., Castagna, G., Crafa, S.: Access control for mobile agents: the calculus of boxed ambients. ACM Trans. Prog. Lang. Syst. **26**(1), 57–124 (2004)
7. Cardelli, L., Gordon, A.: Mobile ambients. Theor. Comput. Sci. **240**(1), 177–213 (2000)
8. Cattani, G.L., Sewell, P.: Models for name-passing processes: interleaving and causal. Inf. Comput. **190**(2), 136–178 (2004)
9. Cleaveland, R., Lüttgen, G., Natarajan, V.: Priority in process algebra. In: Handbook of Process Algebra. Elsevier (2001)
10. Davey, B.A., Priestley, H.A.: Introduction to Lattices and Order, 2nd edn. Cambridge University Press, New York (2002)
11. David, P.C., Ledoux, T., Léger, M., Coupaye, T.: Fpath and fscript: language support for navigation and reliable reconfiguration of fractal architectures. Ann. Telecommun. **64**(1–2), 45–63 (2009)
12. De Nicola, R., Loreti, M., Pugliese, R., Tiezzi, F.: A formal approach to autonomic systems programming: the SCEL language. ACM Trans. Auton. Adapt. Syst. **9**(2), 7:1–7:29 (2014)
13. Di Giusto, C., Stefani, J.-B.: Revisiting glue expressiveness in component-based systems. In: De Meuter, W., Roman, G.-C. (eds.) COORDINATION 2011. LNCS, vol. 6721, pp. 16–30. Springer, Heidelberg (2011)
14. Ferrari, G.-L., Hirsch, D., Lanese, I., Montanari, U., Tuosto, E.: Synchronised hyperedge replacement as a model for service oriented computing. In: de Boer, F.S., Bonsangue, M.M., Graf, S., de Roever, W.-P. (eds.) FMCO 2005. LNCS, vol. 4111, pp. 22–43. Springer, Heidelberg (2006)
15. Fiadeiro, J.L., Lopes, A.: A model for dynamic reconfiguration in service-oriented architectures. Softw. Syst. Model. **12**(2), 349–367 (2013)
16. Hirschkoff, D., Hirschowitz, T., Pous, D., Schmitt, A., Stefani, J.-B.: Component-oriented programming with sharing: containment is not ownership. In: Glück, R., Lowry, M. (eds.) GPCE 2005. LNCS, vol. 3676, pp. 389–404. Springer, Heidelberg (2005)
17. Kruchten, P.: Architectural blueprints - the 4+1 view model of software architecture. IEEE Softw. **12**(6), 42–50 (1995)
18. Lanese, I., Montanari, U.: Mapping fusion and synchronized hyperedge replacement into logic programming. Theory Pract. Logic Program. **7**(1–2), 123–151 (2007)
19. Lenglet, S., Schmitt, A., Stefani, J.B.: Characterizing contextual equivalence in calculi with passivation. Inf. Comput. **209**(11), 1390–1433 (2011)
20. Milner, R.: The Space and Motion of Communicating Agents. Cambridge University Press, New York (2009)
21. Mousavi, M.R., Reniers, M.A., Groote, J.F.: SOS formats and meta-theory: 20 years after. Theor. Comput. Sci. **373**(3), 238–272 (2007)
22. Oquendo, F.: π-ADL: an architecture description language based on the higher-order π-calculus for specifying dynamic and mobile software architectures. ACM Softw. Eng. Notes **29**(4), 1–14 (2004)
23. Przymusinski, T.C.: The well-founded semantics coincides with the three-valued stable semantics. Fundamenta Informaticae **13**, 445–464 (1990)
24. Sangiorgi, D., Walker, D.: The π-calculus: A Theory of Mobile Processes. Cambridge University Press, New York (2001)
25. Schmitt, A., Stefani, J.-B.: The kell calculus: a family of higher-order distributed process calculi. In: Priami, C., Quaglia, P. (eds.) GC 2004. LNCS, vol. 3267, pp. 146–178. Springer, Heidelberg (2005)

26. Tripakis, S., Stergiou, C., Shaver, C., Lee, E.A.: A modular formal semantics for ptolemy. Math. Struct. Comput. Sci. **23**(4), 834–881 (2013)
27. van Glabbeek, R.J.: The meaning of negative premises in transition system specifications II. J. Log. Algebr. Program. **60–61**, 229–258 (2004)
28. Wermelinger, M., Fiadeiro, J.L.: A graph transformation approach to software architecture reconfiguration. Sci. Comput. Program. **44**(2), 133–155 (2002)

A Formal Approach to Autonomic Systems Programming: The SCEL Language

(Long Abstract)

Rocco De Nicola[✉]

IMT – Institute for Advanced Studies, Lucca, Italy
rocco.denicola@imtlucca.it

Abstract. Software-intensive cyber-physical systems have to deal with massive numbers of components, featuring complex interactions among components and with humans and other systems. Often, they are designed to operate in open and non-deterministic environments, and to dynamically adapt to new requirements, technologies and external conditions. This class of systems has been named ensembles and new engineering techniques are needed to address the challenges of developing, integrating, and deploying them. In the paper, we briefly introduce SCEL (Software Component Ensemble Language), a kernel language that takes a holistic approach to programming autonomic computing systems and aims at providing programmers with a complete set of linguistic abstractions for programming the behavior of autonomic components and the formation of autonomic components ensembles, and for controlling the interaction among different components.

Software-intensive cyber-physical systems have to deal with massive numbers of components, featuring complex interactions among components and with humans and other systems. Often, they are designed to operate in open and non-deterministic environments, and to dynamically adapt to new requirements, technologies and external conditions. This class of systems has been named *ensembles*. Sometimes, ensembles are assembled from systems that are independently controlled and managed, while their interaction "mood" might be cooperative or competitive; then one has to deal with systems coalitions or so-called *systems of systems*. Due to their inherent complexity, today's engineering methods and tools do not scale well with such systems. Therefore, new engineering techniques are needed to address the challenges of developing, integrating, and deploying them.

A possible answer to the problems posed by such complex systems is to make them able to self-manage by continuously monitoring their behavior and their working environment and by selecting the actions to perform to best deal with the current status of affairs. Self-management could be exploited also to face situations in which humans intervention is limited or even absent and components have to collaborate to achieve specific goals. This requires increasing systems' self-management capabilities and guaranteeing what now are known as

© Springer International Publishing Switzerland 2015
I. Lanese and E. Madelaine (Eds.): FACS 2014, LNCS 8997, pp. 24–28, 2015.
DOI: 10.1007/978-3-319-15317-9_2

self- * properties (self-configuration, self-healing, self-optimization, self-protection) of *autonomic computing*.

The main challenges posed to language designers by these classes of systems are:

- to devise appropriate abstractions and linguistic primitives to deal with the large dimension of systems,
- to guarantee systems adaptation to (possibly unpredicted) changes of the working environment,
- to take into account evolving requirements,
- to control the emergent behaviors resulting from complex interactions.

During the invited talk, we proposed facing these challenges by taking as starting point the notions of *autonomic components* and *autonomic components ensembles* and defining programming abstractions to model their evolutions and their interactions. These notions are the means we propose to use to structure systems into well-understood, independent and distributed building blocks that interact and adapt in different ways.

Autonomic components are entities with dedicated knowledge units and resources; awareness is guaranteed by providing them with information about their state and behavior via their knowledge repositories. These repositories can be also used to store and retrieve information about the working environment of components, and can thus be used to adapt components' behavior to the perceived changes. Each component is equipped with an *interface*, consisting of a collection of *attributes*, describing different component's features such as its identity, functionalities, spatial coordinates, group memberships, trust level, response time.

Attributes play a crucial rôle, they are used by components to dynamically organize themselves into ensembles. Indeed, one of the main novelties of our approach is the way sets of partners are selected for interaction and thus how ensembles are formed. Communication partners of a specific component can be not only selected by using their identities, but also by exploiting the attributes in their interfaces. Predicates over such attributes are used to specify the targets of communication actions, to guarantee a sort of *attribute-based* communication. In this way, the formation rule of ensembles is endogenous to components: members of an ensemble are connected by the interdependency relations defined through predicates. An *autonomic-component ensembles* is therefore not a rigid fixed network but rather a highly flexible structure where components' linkages are dynamically established.

In the talk, we presented SCEL (Software Component Ensemble Language), a kernel language that takes a holistic approach to programming autonomic computing systems and aims at providing programmers with a complete set of linguistic abstractions for programming the behavior of autonomic components and the formation of autonomic components ensembles, and for controlling the interaction among different components. These abstractions permit describing autonomic systems in terms of *Behaviors*, *Knowledge* and *Aggregations*, according to specific *Policies* depicted in Fig. 1 and described below.

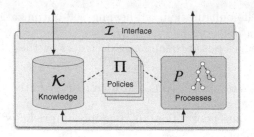

Fig. 1. SCEL component

- *Behaviors* describe how computations progress; they are modeled as processes executing actions, in the style of process calculi.
- *Knowledge* repositories provide the high-level primitives to manage pieces of information coming from different sources. Each knowledge repository is equipped with operations for *adding, retrieving,* and *withdrawing* knowledge items.
- *Aggregations* describe how different elements are brought together to form components and to construct the software architecture of components ensembles. Composition and interaction are implemented by exploiting the attributes exposed in components interfaces.
- *Policies* control and adapt the actions of the different components for guaranteeing accomplishment of specific tasks or satisfaction of specific properties.

Components, by accessing and manipulating their own knowledge repository or the repositories of other components, acquire information about their status (*self-awareness*) and their environment (*context-awareness*) and can perform *self-adaptation*, initiate *self-healing* actions to deal with system malfunctions, or install *self-optimizing* behaviors. All these *self-** properties, as well as *self-configuration*, can be naturally expressed by exploiting SCEL's higher-order features, namely the capability to store/retrieve (the code of) processes in/from the knowledge repositories and to dynamically trigger execution of new processes. Moreover, by implementing appropriate security policies, e.g. limiting information flow or external actions, components can set up *self-protection* mechanisms.

To show expressiveness and effectiveness of SCEL's design, we briefly introduced a Java implementation of the proposed abstractions and showed how it had been exploited for programming the robotics scenario that was used as a running example for describing achievements and potentials of the proposed approach.

The results presented in the talk have been developed within the EU-FET project ASCENS [2] and most of them are presented in [9]. Other important features have been described in various other papers to which the reader is referred to for details about specific results and for references to related work. In particular:

- jRESP, the Java Run-time Environment for SCEL Programs that provides an API for using SCEL's linguistic constructs in JAVA programs is described in [11]. There, it is also discussed how jRESP can be exploited to perform statistical model checking of SCEL programs.
- Policies and their integration with the run time environment are studied in [12,13]. A full instantiation of the SCEL language, called PSCEL (Policed SCEL) that relies on modeling knowledge by means of distributed tuple spaces (à la Klaim [7]) and on FACPL for specifying policies is introduced in [13]. In [12], jRESP is extended to encompass PSCEL and thus to deal also with policies.
- Knowledge handling mechanisms alternative to distributed *tuple spaces* that are instead based on *constraints* are studied in [15]. It is discussed how soft constraints can be exploited to deal with partial knowledge and guarantee multi-criteria optimization.
- Quantitative variants are considered in [10]. There, a stochastic version of SCEL is introduced that enriches terms with information about actions duration, and can be used to support quantitative analysis of autonomic systems. Investigation of these issues will continue in QUANTICOL [16] another EU-FET project.
- Adaptation patterns and the possibility of modeling them via the SCEL abstractions are considered in [6]. Modelling of self-expression in SCEL is instead considered in [5].
- The extension of SCEL with reasoning capabilities that are guaranteed by external reasoners is presented in [3]. There, the solid semantics foundations of SCEL is also exploited to develop MISSCEL, an implementation of SCEL's operational semantics in MAUDE to pave the way towards using the rich verification tool set of this framework.
- In [8] it is instead shown how the SPIN model checker can be used to prove properties of SCEL programs by translating them into Promela, the input language of SPIN.
- Specific case studies taken from the automotive and cloud computing scenarios are considered in [4,14].
- A core calculus with attribute-based communication obtained by distilling the key concepts of SCEL is presented [1] with the aim of initiating fundamental studies to understand the full impact of this novel communication paradigm.

Acknowledgement. As evident from the list of the papers mentioned in the bibliography below, design, implementation and exploitation of SCEL has been a collective effort. I would like to thank all involved colleagues for their fundamental contributions. I take the occasion to thank also Ivan Lanese and Eric Madelaine for giving me the possibility of presenting our work at the FACS conference and in the proceedings.

References

1. Abd Alrahman, Y., De Nicola, R., Loreti, M., Tiezzi, F., Vigo, R.: A calculus for attribute-based communication. In: Proceedings of SAC 2015 (2015, to appear)
2. ASCENS. Autonomic service-components ensemble, a FET-EU project. http://www.ascens-ist.eu/ (2014). Accessed 28 Nov 2014
3. Belzner, L., De Nicola, R., Vandin, A., Wirsing, M.: Reasoning (on) service component ensembles in rewriting logic. In: Iida, S., Meseguer, J., Ogata, K. (eds.) Specification, Algebra, and Software. LNCS, vol. 8373, pp. 188–211. Springer, Heidelberg (2014)
4. Bures, T., De Nicola, R., Gerostathopoulos, I., Hoch, N., Kit, M., Koch, N., Valentina Monreale, G., Montanari, U., Pugliese, R., Serbedzija, N. B., Wirsing, M., Zambonelli, F.: A life cycle for the development of autonomic systems: the e-mobility showcase. In: Proceedings of SASOW, pp. 71–76. IEEE (2013)
5. Cabri, G., Capodieci, N., Cesari, L., De Nicola, R., Pugliese, R., Tiezzi, F., Zambonelli, F.: Self-expression and dynamic attribute-based ensembles in SCEL. In: Margaria, T., Steffen, B. (eds.) ISoLA 2014, Part I. LNCS, vol. 8802, pp. 147–163. Springer, Heidelberg (2014)
6. Cesari, L., De Nicola, R., Pugliese, R., Puviani, M., Tiezzi, F., Zambonelli, F.: Formalising adaptation patterns for autonomic ensembles. In: Fiadeiro, J.L., Liu, Z., Xue, J. (eds.) FACS 2013. LNCS, vol. 8348, pp. 100–118. Springer, Heidelberg (2014)
7. De Nicola, R., Ferrari, G.L., Pugliese, R.: Klaim: a kernel language for agents interaction and mobility. IEEE Trans. Softw. Eng. $\mathbf{24}(5)$, 315–330 (1998)
8. De Nicola, R., Lluch Lafuente, A., Loreti, M., Morichetta, A., Pugliese, R., Senni, V., Tiezzi, F.: Programming and verifying component ensembles. In: Bensalem, S., Lakhneck, Y., Legay, A. (eds.) From Programs to Systems. LNCS, vol. 8415, pp. 69–83. Springer, Heidelberg (2014)
9. De Nicola, R., Loreti, M., Pugliese, R., Tiezzi, F.: A formal approach to autonomic systems programming: the SCEL language. TAAS $\mathbf{9}(2)$, 7 (2014)
10. Latella, D., Loreti, M., Massink, M., Senni, V.: Stochastically timed predicate-based communication primitives for autonomic computing. In: Bertrand, N., Bortolussi, L. (eds.) Proceedings of QAPL 2014, Electronic Proceedings in Theoretical Computer Science, EPTCS, 2014, pp. 1–16. ISSN: 2075–2180, doi:10.4204/EPTCS.154.1
11. Loreti, M.: jRESP: a run-time environment for SCEL programs. Technical report, Sept 2014. http://rap.dsi.unifi.it/scel/ and http://code.google.com/p/jresp/
12. Loreti, M., Margheri, A., Pugliese, R., Tiezzi, F.: On programming and policing autonomic computing systems. In: Margaria, T., Steffen, B. (eds.) ISoLA. LNCS, vol. 8802, pp. 164–183. Springer, Heidelberg (2014)
13. Margheri, A., Pugliese, R., Tiezzi, F.: Linguistic abstractions for programming and policing autonomic computing systems. In: UIC/ATC, pp. 404–409. IEEE (2013)
14. Mayer, P., Klarl, A., Hennicker, R., Puviani, M., Tiezzi, F., Pugliese, R., Keznikl, J., Bures, T.: The autonomic cloud: a vision of voluntary, peer-2-peer cloud computing. In: Proceedings of SASOW, pp. 89–94. IEEE (2013)
15. Montanar, U., Pugliese, R., Tiezzi, F.: Programming autonomic systems with multiple constraint stores. In: De Nicola, R., Hennicker, R. (eds.) Software, Services and Systems. LNCS. Springer, Heidelberg (2015)
16. QUANTICOL. A quantitative approach to management and design of collective and adaptive behaviours, a FET-EU project. http://blog.inf.ed.ac.uk/quanticol/. Accessed 28 Nov 2014

Compositional Approaches

Verified Service Compositions
by Template-Based Construction

Sven Walther[✉] and Heike Wehrheim

Department of Computer Science,
University of Paderborn, Paderborn, Germany
{swalther,wehrheim}@mail.upb.de

Abstract. Today, service compositions often need to be assembled or changed on-the-fly, which leaves only little time for quality assurance. Moreover, quality assurance is complicated by service providers only giving information on their services in terms of *domain specific* concepts with only limited semantic meaning.

In this paper, we propose a method to construct service compositions based on *pre-verified templates*. Templates, given as workflow descriptions, are typed over a (domain-independent) template ontology defining concepts and predicates. Templates are proven correct using an *abstract semantics*, leaving the specific meaning of ontology concepts open, however, only up to given *ontology rules*. Construction of service compositions amounts to instantiation of templates with domain-specific services. Correctness of an instantiation can then simply be checked by verifying that the domain ontology (a) adheres to the rules of the template ontology, and (b) fulfills the constraints of the employed template.

1 Introduction

Concepts like component-based software engineering (CBSE) or service-oriented architectures (SOA) ease the construction of software by combining off-the-shelf components or services to compositions. Today, such compositions often need to be assembled or changed *on-the-fly*, thereby imposing strong timing constraints on quality assurance. "Quality" of service compositions might refer to either non-functional properties (like performance [7]), or functional requirements like adherence to protocols (e.g., [8]), to given pre- and postconditions [21], or to properties specified with temporal logic [25]. Quality assurance methods typically translate the composition (e.g., an architecture model, or a workflow description) into an analysis model, which captures the semantics of the composition and allows – at the best – for a fully automatic quality analysis. Both the transformation into the analysis model and the analysis itself are time-costly and thus difficult to apply in an on-the-fly composition scenario.

In this paper, we propose a technique for service composition and analysis based on *templates*. Templates can capture known compositional patterns,

This work was partially supported by the German Research Foundation (DFG) within the Collaborative Research Centre "On-The-Fly Computing" (SFB 901).

© Springer International Publishing Switzerland 2015
I. Lanese and E. Madelaine (Eds.): FACS 2014, LNCS 8997, pp. 31–48, 2015.
DOI: 10.1007/978-3-319-15317-9_3

and thus allow for the generally proven principle of pattern usage in software engineering [12]. In this paper, templates are workflow descriptions with *service placeholders*, which are replaced with concrete services by instantiations. Our templates are already *verified*, i.e., all template instances will be *correct by construction*. Every template specification contains pre- and postconditions (with associated meaning "if precondition fulfilled then postcondition guaranteed"), and a correct template provably adheres to this specification. This poses a non-trivial task on verification: Since templates should be usable in a wide range of contexts and the instantiations of service placeholders are unknown at template design time, we cannot give a fixed semantics to templates. Rather, the template semantics needs to be *parameterized* in usage context and service instantiation. A template is only correct if it is correct for all (allowed) usage contexts.

Technically, we capture the usage contexts by *ontologies*, and the interpretation of concepts and predicates occurring therein by *logical structures*. A *template ontology* fixes the concepts and predicates of a template. Furthermore, a template specification contains *constraints* fixing additional conditions on instantiations. These constraints allow us to verify the correctness of the template despite unknown usage and unknown fixed semantics. A template instantiation replaces the template ontology with a homomorphous *domain ontology*, and the service placeholders with concrete services of this domain. Verification of the instantiation then amounts to checking whether the (instantiated) template constraints are valid within the domain ontology, and thus can be carried out on-the-fly.

Section 2 describes ontologies and logical structures. Section 3 continues with the syntax of templates, and Sect. 4 proceeds with their semantics and correctness. Section 5 explains instantiation and presents the central result of our approach: instantiation of correct templates yields correct service compositions, if constraints are respected. Section 6 discusses related work, and Sect. 7 concludes.

2   Foundations

We assume service compositions to be assembled of services which are specified by a signature and pre- and postconditions. Languages to describe signatures with pre- and postconditions are already in use (e.g., OWL-S [21]). Such service descriptions rely on domain specific concepts. *Ontologies* formally specify a conceptualization of domain knowledge [13]; the semantics can be defined, e.g., by *description logics* [5]. For this paper, we retain a high-level view of ontologies, and focus on *concepts*, *roles* (relating concepts), and *rules* (formalizing additional knowledge).

Definition 1. *Let C be a finite set of* concept *symbols, and P a finite set of* role *(or* predicate*) symbols, where every $p \in P$ denotes a unary or higher order relation on concepts. Let R be a set of rules of the form $b_0 \wedge \cdots \wedge b_n \rightarrow h_0 \wedge \cdots \wedge h_m$, where b_i, h_i are negated or non-negated predicates denoting concepts of C, or roles from P. Then $K = (C, P, R)$ denotes a* rule-enhanced ontology.

We assume every variable in the rules to be implicitly all-quantified, and rules to be *consistent*, i.e., not to contain contradictions. For details about ontologies and rules, we refer to [11,14]. In classical ontologies, predicates are always binary; however, roles (predicates) relating to boolean types can be expressed unary, and n-ary predicates with $n > 2$ can be translated to binary predicates by introducing supplementary concepts. To avoid technicalities, we allow for a more general notion of predicates here.

Example 1 introduces a template ontology. It will be used later in a "filter" template, which extracts "good" elements from a set using a filter predicate.

Example 1. The template ontology $K_T = (C_T, P_T, R_T)$ has two concepts, two predicates, and no rules:

$$C_T = \{Elem, Value\}, P_T = \{fp : Value \to \textbf{bool}, g : Elem \to \textbf{bool}\}, R_T = \{\} .$$

Signatures and pre- and postconditions are specified using concepts and roles, viz. predicates, of ontologies. To allow standard types like integers, we inductively define the set $\mathcal{T}_K$ of *types over an ontology* $K = (C_K, P_K, R_K)$ by these three rules: (i) $c \in C_K \to c \in \mathcal{T}_K$, (ii) $\textbf{int} \in \mathcal{T}_K$, $\textbf{bool} \in \mathcal{T}_K$, and (iii) $T \in \mathcal{T}_K \to$ $\textbf{set } T \in \mathcal{T}_K$. We furthermore assume that all predicate symbols of ontologies are typed as well[1], thus, e.g., a binary predicate p relating concepts T_1 and T_2 has type $T_1 \times T_2 \to \textbf{bool}$. We therefore implicitly extend purely domain specific ontologies by standard types.

Types are used to fix the types of inputs and outputs of services; the predicates can occur in pre- and postconditions. We assume that we have – in addition to the predicates of an ontology K – standard predicate symbols, operations and constants on integers, booleans and sets available, e.g., $true, <, >, \leq, =, \in$, $\cup, \cap, \emptyset, \ldots$ These make up a set $\mathcal{P}_K$ (for predicate symbols) and a set $\mathcal{F}_K$ (for function symbols). We assume that $P_K \subset \mathcal{P}_K$. Note that the ontology itself does not define any function symbols. From $\mathcal{P}_K$ and $\mathcal{F}_K$, we construct first-order logic formulae in the usual way. To only get type-correct formulae, we assume a set of typed variables *Var*, i.e., given an ontology K we assume a typing function $type : Var \to \mathcal{T}_K$.

We assume typed *terms* based on function symbols $\mathcal{F}_K$ and typed variables to be defined in the usual way. Note that the set of terms over different ontologies might only use different variables, but always use the same (standard) function symbols; also constants like *true* or 1 are nullary function symbols. Using typed terms, we define the set of first-order logic formulae over K.

Definition 2. *Let K be an ontology with types $\mathcal{T}_K$, predicate symbols $\mathcal{P}_K$, and function symbols $\mathcal{F}_K$. The set of first order formulae over K, Φ_K, is inductively defined as follows:*

– *if $p \in \mathcal{P}_K$ is a predicate symbol of arity k and type $T_1 \times \ldots \times T_k \to \textbf{bool}$ and $e_1, \ldots e_k$ are terms of type $T_1, \ldots, T_k$, respectively, then $p(e_1, \ldots, e_k) \in \Phi_K$,*

---

[1] In expressive ontology languages and description logics, it is possible to express notions similar to sub-classing; as we restrict ourselves to a simple version of ontologies, we can assume our roles to be typed even with this simple type system.

– if $\varphi_1, \varphi_2 \in \Phi_K$ then $\neg\varphi_1 \in \Phi_K$ and $\varphi_1 \vee \varphi_2 \in \Phi_K$,
– if $\varphi \in \Phi_K$ then $\forall x : \varphi \in \Phi_K$ and $\exists x : \varphi \in \Phi_K$.

As usual, we write $free(F)$ to denote the free and $bound(F)$ for the bound variables of a formula F.

The meaning of first-order logic is usually defined with respect to a *logical structure*. A logical structure fixes the universe out of which elements of the types are taken as well as an interpretation of the predicate and function symbols.

Definition 3. *Let K be an ontology with types $\mathcal{T}_K$, predicate symbols $\mathcal{P}_K$, and function symbols $\mathcal{F}_K$. A logical structure over K, $\mathcal{S}_K = (\mathcal{U}, \mathcal{I})$, consists of*

– $\mathcal{U} = \bigcup_{T \in \mathcal{T}_K} \mathcal{U}_T$ *the universe of values split up for the different types, and*
– $\mathcal{I}$ *an interpretation of the predicate and function symbols, i.e., for every $p \in \mathcal{P}_K$ of type $T_1 \times \ldots \times T_K \rightarrow \boldsymbol{bool}$ and every $f \in \mathcal{F}_K$ of type $T_1 \times \ldots \times T_K \rightarrow T$ we have a predicate $\mathcal{I}(p) : \mathcal{U}_{T_1} \times \ldots \times \mathcal{U}_{T_k} \rightarrow \mathcal{U}_{\boldsymbol{bool}}$ and a function $\mathcal{I}(f) : \mathcal{U}_{T_1} \times \ldots \times \mathcal{U}_{T_k} \rightarrow \mathcal{U}_T$, respectively.*

We assume standard domains and interpretations for integers, sets, and boolean, e.g., $\mathcal{U}_{\boldsymbol{bool}} = \{true, false\}$. Therefore all logical structures of an ontology agree on standard types and their operations, but may differ on domain specific parts.

To define a semantics for formulae with free variables, we need a valuation of variables. We let $\sigma : V \rightarrow \mathcal{U}$ be a valuation of $V \subseteq Var$ with (type-correct) values from $\mathcal{U}$. We write $\sigma \models_\mathcal{S} F$ for a structure $\mathcal{S}$ and a formula F if $\mathcal{S}$ together with σ is a model for F (viz. F holds true in $\mathcal{S}$ and σ); refer to, e.g., [1] for a formal definition. If the formula contains no free variables, we can elide σ and just write $\models_\mathcal{S} F$, or $\mathcal{S} \models F$. Note that an ontology usually does not fix a structure because it neither gives a universe nor an interpretation for its predicates. It does, however, define constraints on valid interpretations by the rules R.

Definition 4. *A structure $\mathcal{S}$ over an ontology $K = (C, P, R)$ satisfies the rules R of the ontology, $\mathcal{S} \models R$, if it satisfies every rule in R, i.e., $\forall r \in R : \mathcal{S} \models r$.*

Note that rules do not contain free variables, and therefore no σ is needed here.

3 Services and Templates

The ontology and logical formulae over the ontology are basic building blocks for services and compositions. A *service* in our notation is an entity which generates outputs for given inputs. The signature fixes the types of inputs and outputs.

Definition 5. *A service signature over an ontology K specifies the name of the service as well as the type, order, and number of inputs $T_1 \times \cdots \times T_j$ and the type, order, and number of outputs $T_{j+1} \times \cdots \times T_k$, where each $T_i \in \mathcal{T}_K$.*

Additionally, a service is specified by its *pre-* and *postcondition* (also: effect). Both of these are given as first-order formulae. They are formulated over a set of input and output variables.[2]

---

[2] In combination also known as IOPE (Input/Output/Precondition/Effect) in SOA.

Definition 6. *A service description of a service Svc over an ontology K consists of service signature, lists of input variables I and output variables O, a precondition pre_{Svc} and a postcondition $post_{Svc}$, both elements of Φ_K. Variables are typed according to the signature of Svc, that is, for $Svc : T_1 \times \cdots \times T_j \rightarrow T_{j+1} \times \cdots \times T_k$:*

– $I = (i_1, \ldots, i_j)$ with $type(i_l) = T_l$ for all $0 < l \le j$, and
– $O = (i_{j+1}, \ldots, i_k)$ with $type(i_l) = T_l$ for all $j < l \le k$.

The precondition describes only inputs, the postcondition inputs and outputs: $free(pre_{Svc}) \subseteq I$ and $free(post_{Svc}) \subseteq I \cup O$.

The set of service descriptions over an ontology K is denoted $\mathcal{SVC}_K$. Services are composed using a *workflow* describing the order of execution of the services. Workflows comprise control flow (using control structures) and data flow (using variables) between services. While different notations are in practical use (e.g., WS-BPEL [23]), we use a simple programming language style notation here.

Definition 7. *Let K be an ontology. The syntax of a workflow W over K can be described by the following rules:*

$$W ::= \text{skip} \mid u := t \mid W_1; W_2 \mid (u_{j+1}, \ldots, u_k) := Svc(i_1, \ldots, i_j)$$
$$\mid \text{if } B \text{ then } W_1 \text{ else } W_2 \text{ fi} \mid \text{while } B \text{ do } W \text{ od}$$
$$\mid \text{foreach } a \in A \text{ do } W \text{ od}$$

*with variables u, a, A; expression t of type $type(u)$; A of type **set** T; a of type $T \in \mathcal{T}_K$; $B \in \Phi_K$; and Svc a service call with service description Svc, with inputs $i_1, \ldots, i_j$, and outputs $u_{j+1}, \ldots, u_k$, with type and order fixed by the signature.*

Here, we augment usual imperative programming elements with an iteration construct for set types and with service calls. Workflows are build over arbitrary sets of services, defined on the same ontology. For template workflows, we do not use concrete services but service *placeholders*. Formally, a service placeholder has a signature like a service, but instead of formulae for pre- and postconditions we just write pre_{Svc}^{sp} and $post_{Svc}^{sp}$. We write $\mathcal{SP}_K$ to denote the set of service placeholders over K.

Example 2. The template in Fig. 1 accepts one input and produces one output, both of a set type with element type *Elem*. It uses one service placeholder, V, and the predicates fp and g from Example 1. Its workflow initializes the output variable A', and then iterates over the input set A. Every element is given to the service placeholder V, and then filtered by applying fp to the result of the service call. If filtering succeeds, the element is put in the output set A'.

Like services, templates have pre- and postconditions: they define the correctness properties which we intend to achieve with the template, and allow us to treat instantiated templates as any other services. The last part we find in a template are *constraints*. They define conditions on instantiations: if a template instantiation cannot guarantee these constraints, the postcondition of the template might not be achieved, i.e., the template concretion might not be correct. We will make this more precise in Sect. 5.

Name	: FILTER
Inputs	: A with $type(A) = \textbf{set } Elem$
Outputs	: A' with $type(A') = \textbf{set } Elem$
Services	: $V : Elem \rightarrow Value$
Precondition	: $\{\forall a \in A : pre_V^{sp}(a)\}$
Postcondition	: $\{A' = \{a \in A \mid g(a)\}\}$
Constraints	: $\{\forall x, y : post_V^{sp}(x, y) \wedge fp(y) \Rightarrow g(x),$
	$\quad \forall x, y : post_V^{sp}(x, y) \wedge \neg fp(y) \Rightarrow \neg g(x)\}$

```
1  A' := ∅ ;
2  foreach a ∈ A do
3  │    (y) := V(a) ;
4  │    if fp(y) then  A' := A' ∪ {a} fi ;
5  od
```

Fig. 1. Template to filter a list, using a filter fp and a validation service V

Definition 8. *A* workflow template *WT over an ontology K consists of*

- *a name N,*
- *a list of typed input variables I and typed output variables O,*
- *a set of services placeholders $\mathcal{SP}_K$,*
- *a precondition $pre \in \Phi_K$ and a postcondition $post \in \Phi_K$,*
- *a set of constraint rules C as in Definition 1, and*
- *a workflow description W.*

In short: $WT = (N, I, O, \mathcal{SP}_K, pre, post, C, W)$.

Later, we see how templates get instantiated. To this end, we need concrete, existing services described by a *domain ontology*, to replace the service placeholders. However, our ultimate aim is to show correctness on the level of templates, and inherit their correctness onto instantiations. Thus, we will now define the semantics of templates and, with this help, their correctness.

4   Semantics of Templates

The key principle of our approach is to take correct templates, instantiate them, and afterwards be able to check correctness of instances by checking simple side-conditions. We start with the meaning of "correctness of templates". Figure 1 shows a template with pre- and postconditions and constraints. Basically, these state the property which the template should guarantee: if the precondition holds and the constraints are fulfilled, then the postcondition is achieved. All these parts contain undefined symbols: neither do we know the pre- and post-conditions of the employed services (they are placeholders), nor the meaning of the predicates of the template ontology. The definition of a semantics of templates and their correctness therefore necessarily has to be *abstract*, i.e., defined modulo a concrete meaning. This meaning can only be fixed once we have a logical structure. This is, however, not given by an ontology; thus the logical structure is a parameter for our semantics. The second parameter to the semantics is the concretion of service placeholders with actual services, given by a mapping $\pi : \mathcal{SP}_K \rightarrow \mathcal{SVC}_K$.

Definition 9. *Let K be an ontology, $\mathcal{SP}_K$ a set of service placeholders over K, and $\mathcal{SVC}_K$ be a set of service descriptions over K. Then $\pi : \mathcal{SP}_K \rightarrow \mathcal{SVC}_K$ is a concretion of service placeholders, if it respects signatures, i.e.*

$$\text{if } \pi(sp) = svc \text{ and } sp : T_1 \times \cdots \times T_k \rightarrow T_{k+1} \times \cdots \times T_N \text{ ,}$$
$$\text{then } svc : T_1 \times \cdots \times T_k \rightarrow T_{k+1} \times \cdots \times T_N \text{ .}$$

We lift the definition of π to replace pre- and postconditions of service placeholders with their counterparts of the corresponding service, such that $\pi(pre^{sp}) \in \Phi_K$ with $free(\pi(pre^{sp})) = I_{svc}$, and $\pi(post^{sp}) \in \Phi_K$ with $free(\pi(post^{sp})) = I_{svc} \cup O_{svc}$. We use π to replace placeholders in any formula.

We define an operational semantics for workflows, much alike [1], however, always parameterized with a structure $\mathcal{S}$ and a concretion π. The semantics is defined by a transition relation between *configurations*. A configuration consists of a workflow to be executed and a state. We introduce a failure state `fail` which is entered once a service is called outside its preconditions. The workflow stops in `fail`, thus we define a *blocking semantics* for service calls here.

Definition 10. *Let $\mathcal{S} = (\mathcal{U}, \mathcal{I})$ be a structure of an ontology K, and Var a set of variables. A state σ over $\mathcal{S}$ is a type-correct mapping from Var to $\mathcal{U}$. The set of all states over $\mathcal{S}$ is denoted $\Sigma_{\mathcal{S}}$. We let $\Sigma_{\mathcal{S}}^{fail} = \Sigma_{\mathcal{S}} \cup \{fail\}$.*

For a formula $F \in \Phi_K$ we define the set of states satisfying F with respect to a structure $\mathcal{S}$ as $[\![F]\!]_{\mathcal{S}} = \{\sigma \in \Sigma_{\mathcal{S}} \mid \sigma \models_{\mathcal{S}} F\}$.

A configuration $\langle W, \tau \rangle$ has a workflow W over K and a state $\tau \in \Sigma_{\mathcal{S}}^{fail}$.

We use E to stand for the empty workflow. Later, the semantics of workflows $[\![\cdot]\!]$ will map initial to final configurations. For this, we first define transitions between configurations by means of the set of axioms and rules given in Fig. 2. The main deviation from the standard semantics given in [1] is that we take two parameters into account: evaluation of conditions is parameterized in the interpretation of predicates as given in the structure $\mathcal{S}$, and influenced by the concretion of placeholders, π. We also add rules for the **foreach** statement and for service calls. Note that both introduce nondeterminism into the transition system: **foreach** iterates over the set of elements in an arbitrary order, and service calls can have more than one successor state.

Consider, e.g., rules (a) and (b) in Fig. 2: if a conditional statement is to be executed in state σ, then W_1 is selected as the next statement if and only if the condition B is true in the given structure $\mathcal{S}$ (with placeholders replaced); otherwise, W_2 is the next statement. In both cases, the state remains the same, as these rules only deal with the selection of the next workflow statement. Note that the states σ in the rules exclude the failure state, i.e., configurations $\langle W, \texttt{fail} \rangle$ have no outgoing transitions.

$$\langle skip, \sigma \rangle \rightarrow_S^\pi \langle E, \sigma \rangle$$

$$\langle u := t, \sigma \rangle \rightarrow_S^\pi \langle E, \sigma[u := \sigma(t)] \rangle$$

$$\frac{\langle W_1, \sigma \rangle \rightarrow_S^\pi \langle W_2, \tau \rangle}{\langle W_1; W, \sigma \rangle \rightarrow_S^\pi \langle W_2; W, \tau \rangle}$$

$$\langle \text{if } B \text{ then } W_1 \text{ else } W_2 \text{ fi}, \sigma \rangle \rightarrow_S^\pi \langle W_1, \sigma \rangle \qquad \text{if } \sigma \models_S \pi(B) \qquad (a)$$

$$\langle \text{if } B \text{ then } W_1 \text{ else } W_2 \text{ fi}, \sigma \rangle \rightarrow_S^\pi \langle W_2, \sigma \rangle \qquad \text{if } \sigma \models_S \neg\pi(B) \qquad (b)$$

$$\langle \text{while } B \text{ do } W \text{ od}, \sigma \rangle \rightarrow_S^\pi \langle W; \text{while } B \text{ do } W \text{ od}, \sigma \rangle$$

$$\text{if } \sigma \models \pi(B)$$

$$\langle \text{while } B \text{ do } W \text{ od}, \sigma \rangle \rightarrow_S^\pi \langle E, \sigma \rangle \qquad \text{if } \sigma \models \neg\pi(B)$$

$$\langle \text{foreach } a \in A \text{ do } W \text{ od}, \sigma \rangle \rightarrow_S^\pi \langle E, \sigma \rangle \qquad \text{if } \sigma(A) = \emptyset$$

$$\langle \text{foreach } a \in A \text{ do } W \text{ od}, \sigma \rangle \rightarrow_S^\pi \langle W; \text{foreach } a \in A \text{ do } W \text{ od}, \sigma' \rangle$$

$$\text{if } \sigma(A) \neq \emptyset \wedge \sigma'(a) = v \wedge$$

$$v \in \sigma(A) \wedge \sigma'(A) = \sigma(A) \setminus \{v\}$$

$$\langle (u_{j+1}, \ldots, u_k) := Svc(i_1, \ldots, i_j), \sigma \rangle \rightarrow_S^\pi$$

$$\{\langle E, \sigma[u_{j+1} := v_{j+1}, \ldots, u_k := v_k] \rangle \mid \pi(post_{Svc}^{sp}(\sigma(i_1), \ldots, \sigma(i_j), v_{j+1} \ldots, v_k))\}$$

$$\text{if } \sigma \models_S \pi(pre_{Svc}^{sp}(\sigma(i_1), \ldots, \sigma(i_j)))$$

$$\langle (u_{j+1}, \ldots, u_k) := Svc(i_1, \ldots, i_j), \sigma \rangle \rightarrow_S^\pi \langle (u_{j+1}, \ldots, u_k) := Svc(i_1, \ldots, i_j), \text{fail} \rangle$$

$$\text{if } \sigma \models_S \neg\pi(pre_{Svc}^{sp}(\sigma(i_1), \ldots, \sigma(i_j)))$$

Fig. 2. Transition axioms and rules based on [1], with additional rules for service calls and **foreach** constructs

The transition rules are used to derive the semantics of workflows. In this paper, we only define a partial correctness semantics, i.e., we do not specifically care about termination. Transitions lead to *transition sequences*, where a non-extensible transition sequence of a workflow W starting in σ is a *computation* of W. If it is finite and ends in $\langle E, \tau \rangle$ or $\langle W', \text{fail} \rangle$, then it *terminates*. We use the transitive, reflexive closure $\rightarrow^*$ of $\rightarrow$ to describe the effect of finite transition sequences. The semantics of partial correctness is again parameterized with a logical structure and a concretion mapping for service placeholders.

Definition 11. *Let S be a logical structure and π a concretion mapping. The partial correctness semantics of a workflow W with respect to S and π maps an initial state to a set of possible final states*

$$[\![W]\!]_S^\pi : \Sigma_S \rightarrow 2^{\Sigma_S \cup \{\text{fail}\}}, \text{ with } [\![W]\!]_S^\pi(\sigma) = \{\tau \mid \langle W, \sigma \rangle \rightarrow_S^{\pi*} \langle W', \tau \rangle\}$$

where $W' = E$ or $\tau = \text{fail}$.

We define a workflow template to be *correct*, if all computations starting in a state which satisfies the precondition, end in a state which fulfills the postcondition. Since services are only placeholders, correctness can only be stated when the template works correctly for arbitrary concretions, as long as they obey the concretized constraints of the template. So far, we only operate on the template ontology, and thus arbitrary concretion means inserting arbitrary formulae for pre- and postconditions of placeholders. Therefore, our concretion mapping $\pi : \mathcal{SP}_K \to \mathcal{SVC}_K$ maps placeholders to arbitrary service descriptions over K.

Definition 12. *Let* $WT = (N, I, O, \mathcal{SP}_K, pre, post, C, W)$ *be a workflow template, and* $K = (C_K, P_K, R_K)$ *the corresponding ontology. We say* WT *is* correct *if the following holds:*

$$\forall \text{ logical structures } \mathcal{S} \text{ over } K, \forall \text{ concretions } \pi : \mathcal{SP}_K \to \mathcal{SVC}_K \text{ s.t.}$$
$$\mathcal{S} \models R_K \wedge \mathcal{S} \models \pi(C) : [\![\, W \,]\!]_{\mathcal{S}}^{\pi}([\![\, \pi(pre) \,]\!]_{\mathcal{S}}) \subseteq [\![\, \pi(post) \,]\!]_{\mathcal{S}} \; .$$

There are different ways of proving template correctness. The verification approach introduced in [27] encodes correctness as satisfiability problem. For brevity, we provide a correctness proof for Example 2 in terms of Hoare-style verification. Since our semantics is almost the same as that in [1], we can readily use their proof calculus (augmenting it with rules for **foreach** and service calls; rules omitted here). The proof outline in Fig. 3 shows that, starting from the precondition, the postcondition is reached by the workflow; to do this, we rewrite the **if** without **else** into an **if-then-else** with an empty **else** (skip) construct.

5   Template Instantiation

Templates are used to describe generic forms of service compositions, independent of concrete domains and thus concrete services. To describe templates we employ template ontologies which fix the concepts usable in a template. For instantiation, we replace service placeholders with concrete services, which are typed over concrete domain ontologies. To this end, we define a *mapping* between a template ontology and a domain ontology. While general ontology mapping has to deal with different *ontology conflicts* [19,22], we assume a perfect mapping without conflicts.

Definition 13. *Let* $K_T = (C_T, P_T, R_T)$ *be a template ontology and* $K_D = (C_D, P_D, R_D)$ *be a domain ontology. Then* $K_T \triangleright_f K_D$ *is an homomorphous ontology mapping from* K_T *to* K_D *by* f, *if* f *is a pair of mappings* $f = (f_C : C_T \to C_D, f_P : P_T \to P_D)$ *such that*

- f_P *preserves signatures with respect to* f_C, *that is* $\forall p \in P_T$ *with* $p : T_1 \times \cdots \times T_n \to$ **bool** *we have* $f_P(p) : f_C(T_1) \times \cdots \times f_C(T_n) \to$ **bool**;
- f *preserves the rules* R_T, *that is* $\forall r \in R_T$ *with* $r = b_1 \wedge \cdots \wedge b_n \to h_1 \wedge \cdots \wedge h_m$, *there is* $r' \in R_D$ *with* $r' = f(b_1) \wedge \cdots \wedge f(b_n) \to f(h_1) \wedge \cdots \wedge f(h_m)$.

We assume the mapping pair f to map standard types to themselves, e.g., $f(\textbf{bool}) = \textbf{bool}$, $f(\textbf{set } T) = \textbf{set } (f(T))$. For brevity, we use f as a shorthand notation for the application of the correct mappings f_C, f_P, or rule preservation.

To replace service placeholders (typed over a template ontology K_T) with service descriptions (typed over a domain ontology K_D), we define an concretion π_f for two ontologies with $K_T \triangleright_f K_D$.

```
1   {∀a ∈ A : pre_V^sp(a) ∧ A_0 = A}
2   A' := ∅
3   {inv: A' = {a' ∈ A_0 \ A | g(a')}}
4   foreach a ∈ A do
5   │   {A' = {a' ∈ A_0 \ (A ∪ {a}) | g(a')}}
6   │   (y) := V(a)
7   │   {post_V^sp(a, y) ∧ A' = {a' ∈ A_0 \ (A ∪ {a}) | g(a')}} // service call
8   │   if fp(y) then
9   │   │   {fp(y) ∧ post_V^sp(a, y) ∧ A' = {a' ∈ A_0 \ (A ∪ {a}) | g(a')}}
10  │   │   A' := A' ∪ {a}
11  │   │   {g(a) ∧ A' = {a' ∈ A_0 \ (A ∪ {a}) | g(a')} ∪ {a}} // constr./set union
12  │   │   {inv}
13  │   else
14  │   │   {¬fp(y) ∧ post_V^sp(a, y) ∧ A' = {a' ∈ A_0 \ (A ∪ {a}) | g(a')}}
15  │   │   skip
16  │   │   {¬g(a) ∧ A' = {a' ∈ A_0 \ (A ∪ {a}) | g(a')}} // constraint
17  │   │   {inv}
18  │   fi
19  │   {inv}
20  od
21  {inv ∧ A = ∅} // foreach
22  {A' = {a' ∈ A_0 | g(a')}}
```

Fig. 3. Proof outline for correctness of the filter template; comments refer to the semantics definition

Definition 14. *Let K_T and K_D be ontologies with $K_T \triangleright_f K_D$, let SP_T be the set of service placeholders over K_T, and SVC_D be the set of service descriptions over K_D. Then $\pi_f : SP_T \to SVC_D$ is a concretion of service placeholders from K_T to K_D, if it respects signatures with respect to f, that is,*

$$\text{if } \pi_f(sp) = svc \text{ and } sp : T_1 \times \cdots \times T_k \to T_{k+1} \times \cdots \times T_N ,$$
$$\text{then } svc : f(T_1) \times \cdots \times f(T_k) \to f(T_{k+1}) \times \cdots \times f(T_N) .$$

We lift π_f to pre- and postconditions of placeholders, such that $\pi_f(pre^{sp}) \in \Phi_D$ and $free(\pi_f(pre^{sp})) = I_{svc}$, as well as $\pi_f(post^{sp}) \in \Phi_D$ and $free(\pi_f(post^{sp})) = I_{svc} \cup O_{svc}$. In short, π_f maps placeholders to services, using the ontology mapping f of $K_T \triangleright_f K_D$ to translate types from the template to the domain ontology.

As the semantics of workflows rely on logical structures, we need to clarify the relation of structures over K_T to structures over K_D: if a structure satisfies the rules of K_D, then there exists a corresponding one satisfying the rules of K_T.

Proposition 1. *Let $K_T = (C_T, P_T, R_T)$ and $K_D = (C_D, P_D, R_D)$ be ontologies and $S = (\mathcal{U}, \mathcal{I})$ a logical structure over K_D. If $K_T \triangleright_f K_D$, and $S \models R_D$, then we can construct a corresponding logical structure $S^{\triangleright_f}$, where*

$$\mathcal{S}^{\triangleright_f} = (\mathcal{U}^{\triangleright_f}, \mathcal{I}^{\triangleright_f}), \quad \text{with} \quad \mathcal{U}_T^{\triangleright_f} = \mathcal{U}_{f(T)} \text{ and}$$
$$\mathcal{I}^{\triangleright_f}(p) = \mathcal{I}(f(p)) \text{ for } p \in \mathcal{P}_T$$

such that $\mathcal{S}^{\triangleright_f} \models R_T$.

Later, we will reason about formulae containing placeholders, which are satisfied by a logical structure, and which follow from the rules of an ontology. Therefore, in addition to the construction of a corresponding logical structure, we construct a corresponding mapping from placeholders to service descriptions as well.

Proposition 2. *Let* $K_T = (C_T, P_T, R_T)$ *and* $K_D = (C_D, P_D, R_D)$ *be ontologies with* $K_T \triangleright_f K_D$, *and* $\mathcal{S} = (\mathcal{U}, \mathcal{I})$ *a logical structure over* K_D. *Let* $\pi_f : \mathcal{SP}_T \to \mathcal{SVC}_D$ *be a concretion, and* $\Psi \in \Phi_T$ *be a formula containing placeholders from* $\mathcal{SP}_T$. *If* $\mathcal{S}$ *satisfies the rules of* K_D *and the concretized formula* $\pi_f(\Psi)$, *then we can construct a corresponding concretion* $\pi_f^{\triangleright_f} : \mathcal{SP}_T \to \mathcal{SVC}_T$ *within the template ontology; let signature names be* $sp \in \mathcal{SP}_T$, $svc \in \mathcal{SVC}_D$, $svc' \in \mathcal{SVC}_T$ *and* $\pi_f(sp) = svc$, $\pi_f^{\triangleright_f}(sp) = svc'$, *and* svc *and* svc' *refer to the same name; if* $\pi_f^{\triangleright_f}$ *is signature preserving (Definition 14), and*

$$\pi_f^{\triangleright_f}(sp) = svc' \text{ with } svc' : T_1 \times \cdots \times T_j \to T_{j+1} \times \cdots \times T_N ,$$

then we also know, that

$$\pi_f(sp) = svc \text{ with } svc : f(T_1) \times \cdots \times f(T_j) \to f(T_{j+1}) \times \cdots \times f(T_N)$$
$$pre_{svc'} \in \Phi_T \text{ such that } f(pre_{svc'}) = pre_{svc}$$
$$post_{svc'} \in \Phi_T \text{ such that } f(post_{svc'}) = post_{svc} ;$$

and we can conclude $\mathcal{S}^{\triangleright_f} \models \pi_f^{\triangleright_f}(\Psi)$.

Proof: Consider some state $\sigma \models_{\mathcal{S}} \pi_f(\Psi)$ with $\Psi \in \Phi_T$. Then, the interpretations $\mathcal{I}_D$ are fix for every predicate. We can construct $\mathcal{S}^{\triangleright_f}$ by Proposition 1, where the interpretations of template predicates are by construction the same as the interpretations of the corresponding (by f) domain predicates. The only predicates without interpretations are the pre- and postconditions of placeholders. We can construct $\pi_f^{\triangleright_f}$ such that $f(\pi_f^{\triangleright_f}(pre_{svc}^{sp})) = \pi_f(pre_{svc}^{sp})$ (same for postcondition). By definition, the interpretations are then mapped to the corresponding predicates, and $\sigma \models_{\mathcal{S}} \pi_f(\Psi) \Rightarrow \sigma \models_{\mathcal{S}^{\triangleright_f}} \pi_f^{\triangleright_f}(\Psi)$.

The same is true for $\sigma \not\models_{\mathcal{S}} \pi_f(\Psi)$, therefore $\sigma \models_{\mathcal{S}} \pi_f(\Psi) \Leftrightarrow \sigma \models_{\mathcal{S}^{\triangleright_f}} \pi_f^{\triangleright_f}(\Psi)$. $\square$

We can conclude that the set of states satisfying a formula with instantiated placeholders under a structure $\mathcal{S}$, is the same as for the corresponding $\mathcal{S}^{\triangleright_f}$:

Lemma 1. *Let* $K_T = (C_T, P_T, R_T)$ *a template ontology and* $K_D = (C_D, P_D, R_D)$ *a domain ontology with* $K_T \triangleright_f K_D$, *a concretion* π_f, *a formula* $F \in \Phi_T$ *containing placeholders from* $\mathcal{SP}_T$, *and a structure* $\mathcal{S} \models \pi_f(F)$, *then*

$$[\![\pi_f(F)]\!]_{\mathcal{S}} = [\![\pi_f^{\triangleright_f}(F)]\!]_{\mathcal{S}^{\triangleright_f}} .$$

Note that we do not need to give an interpretation for the standard function and predicate symbols since their interpretation is always the same.

We continue our example with a domain ontology and a service description.

Example 3. Let K_D be an ontology of the (simplified) domain of restaurants with concepts $C_D = \{Restaurant, Rating\}$, predicates $P_D = \{isMinRating : Rating \rightarrow \textbf{bool}, goodRestaurant : Restaurant \rightarrow \textbf{bool}, fastFood : Restaurant \rightarrow \textbf{bool}, cheap : Restaurant \rightarrow \textbf{bool}, hasRating : Restaurant \times Rating \rightarrow \textbf{bool}\}$ and rules[3]

$$fastFood(res) \Rightarrow cheap(res)$$
$$hasRating(res, rat) \wedge isMinRating(rat) \Rightarrow goodRestaurant(res)$$
$$hasRating(res, rat) \wedge \neg isMinRating(rat) \Rightarrow \neg goodRestaurant(res)$$

We define a mapping $f = (f_C, f_P)$ from K_T of Example 1 with $K_T \rhd_f K_D$ as:

$$f_C : Elem \mapsto Restaurant, Value \mapsto Rating$$
$$f_P : fp \mapsto isMinRating, g \mapsto goodRestaurant .$$

Since the template ontology has no rules, f trivially preserves them. For our restaurant ontology, we assume a service *Vld* to provide a lookup service for ratings of restaurants. It consists of the signature $Restaurant \rightarrow Rating$, an input *res*, an output *rat*, precondition $pre_{Vld} = true$ (it provides ratings for all restaurants), and postcondition $post_{Vld} = hasRating(res, rat)$ (the returned rating belongs to the input restaurant).

Such services can replace service placeholders in the template. In addition, instantiation requires replacing boolean conditions in the template workflow (because they use template predicates) with their counterparts in the domain ontology. To this end, we apply the ontology mapping f to the boolean conditions.

Definition 15. *Let* $WT = (N, I, O, \mathcal{SP}_T, pre, post, C, W)$ *be a workflow template over a template ontology* K_T, *let* K_D *be a domain ontology with set of services* $\mathcal{SVC}_D$ *and* $K_T \rhd_f K_D$ *with* $f = (f_C, f_P)$. *Let* $\pi_f : \mathcal{SP}_T \rightarrow \mathcal{SVC}_D$ *be a concretion of the service placeholders in* WT *to services of the domain ontology. The* instantiation *of the workflow* W *with respect to* π *and* f, $\pi_f(W)$, *is inductively defined as follows:*

---

[3] Ontology languages provide dedicated constructs to specify different properties of predicates, e.g., transitivity or cardinality ("every restaurant has exactly one rating"). These constructs can be expressed using rules, but for simplicity, we omitted them in this example.

$$\pi_f(\text{skip}) := \text{skip} \qquad \pi_f(u := t) := u := t$$
$$\pi_f((u_{j+1}, \ldots, u_k) := Svc(i_1, \ldots, i_j)) := (u_{j+1}, \ldots, u_k) := \pi_f(Svc)(i_1, \ldots, i_j)$$
$$\pi_f(W_1; W_2) := \pi_f(W_1); \pi_f(W_2)$$
$$\pi_f(\textbf{if } B \textbf{ then } W_1 \textbf{ else } W_2 \textbf{ fi}) := \textbf{if } f(B) \textbf{ then } \pi_f(W_1) \textbf{ else } \pi_f(W_2) \textbf{ fi}$$
$$\pi_f(\textbf{while } B \textbf{ do } W \textbf{ od}) := \textbf{while } f(B) \textbf{ do } \pi_f(W) \textbf{ od}$$
$$\pi_f(\textbf{foreach } a \in A \textbf{ do } W \textbf{ od}) := \textbf{foreach } a \in A \textbf{ do } \pi_f(W) \textbf{ od} \ .$$

Note that terms t do not need to be mapped by f since they only contain function symbols over standard types.

Name   : RESTAURANTFILTER
Inputs   : A with $type(A) = \textbf{set } Restaurant$
Outputs   : A' with $type(A') = \textbf{set } Restaurant$
Services   : $Vld : Restaurant \to Rating$
Precondition : $\{\forall a \in A : pre_{Vld}(a)\}$
Postcondition : $\{A' = \{a \in A \mid g(a)\}\}$
Constraints   : $\{\forall x, y : post_{Vld}(x, y) \wedge isMinRating(y) \Rightarrow goodRestaurant(x),$
$\forall x, y : post_{Vld}(x, y) \wedge \neg isMinRating(y) \Rightarrow \neg goodRestaurant(x)\}$

```
1  A' := ∅ ;
2  foreach a ∈ A do
3  |    (y) := Vld(a);
4  |    if isMinRating(y) then  A' := A' ∪ {a} fi ;
5  od
```

Fig. 4. Instantiation of the Filter template with a restaurant ontology and a rating acquisition service

When templates are instantiated, we get *service compositions*. A service composition is a workflow (over a domain ontology) without service placeholders. Figure 4 shows an instantiation of the filter template from Fig. 1, using the ontology mapping of Example 3 and $\pi_f(V) = Vld$.

For the semantics of service compositions, we re-use the semantics definition of templates. This time, however, we can omit the parameter π_f, since all services are concrete. Therefore, the only parameter left for the semantics is the logical structure: the interpretation of domain ontology predicates is still not fixed. The correctness condition can thus directly be re-used, except that service compositions do not come with fixed pre- and postconditions (unlike templates).

Definition 16. *A service composition W over a domain ontology K is correct with respect to some precondition $pre \in \Phi_K$ and some postcondition $post \in \Phi_K$ if the following holds:*

$$\forall \text{ logical structures } \mathcal{S} \text{ s.t. } \mathcal{S} \models R_K : [\![W]\!]_{\mathcal{S}}([\![pre]\!]_{\mathcal{S}}) \subseteq [\![post]\!]_{\mathcal{S}} \ .$$

We have defined correctness of templates and service compositions as well as semantics for both. If a template and a composition are typed over the same ontology, we can conclude from the definitions that they have the same semantics.

Lemma 2. *Let WT be a template with workflow W, and $\pi : \mathcal{SP}_K \to \mathcal{SVC}_K$ be an instantiation with services over ontology K. Then the following holds:*

$$\forall \text{ logical structures } \mathcal{S}: \quad [\![W]\!]_{\mathcal{S}}^{\pi} = [\![\pi(W)]\!]_{\mathcal{S}} \ .$$

From the semantics and correctness definitions above, and assuming that the template is already proven correct, we state the following: To prove correctness of a service composition, it is sufficient to show that the instantiated constraints of the template can be derived from the rules of the domain ontology.

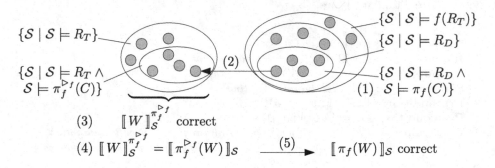

Fig. 5. Overview of the proof of Theorem 1, with main steps (1) to (5)

Theorem 1. *Let $WT = (N, I, O, \mathcal{SP}_T, pre, post, C, W)$ be a correct workflow template over a template ontology K_T, K_D a domain ontology such that $K_T \rhd_f K_D$ with a mapping $f = (f_C, f_P)$, and let $\pi_f : \mathcal{SP}_T \to \mathcal{SVC}_D$ be a concretion of service placeholders in the template with services of the domain ontology.*

If $R_D \models \pi_f(C)$ then $\pi_f(W)$ is correct with respect to $\pi_f(pre)$ and $\pi_f(post)$.

Figure 5 gives an overview of the proof. First, we select a structure which satisfies the concretized constraints of the template (1). Then, we construct the corresponding structure which satisfies the original constraints (2). By definition, we know the semantics of the template (3) and can conclude that its instantiation has the same semantics (4). As the template is correct, the instantiation is also correct (5). We will now give the formal proof.

Proof: Let $WT = (N, I, O, \mathcal{SP}_T, pre, post, C, W)$ be a correct workflow template over a template ontology K_T, and $\pi_f(W)$ be a service composition over a domain ontology K_D with $K_T \rhd_f K_D$. We have to show that, for any concretion π_f where the domain ontology satisfies the concretized template constraints, $\pi_f(W)$ is indeed a correct instantiation of template WT, that is, it is correct with respect to the concretized precondition and postcondition of WT. Formally: for all structures $\mathcal{S}_D$ and instantiations π_f the following has to hold:

$$\mathcal{S}_D \models R_D \wedge R_D \models \pi_f(C) : [\![\pi_f(W)]\!]_{\mathcal{S}_D}([\![\pi_f(pre)]\!]_{\mathcal{S}_D}) \subseteq [\![\pi_f(post)]\!]_{\mathcal{S}_D} \ .$$

To start, fix $\mathcal{S}_D$ and π_f such that

$$\mathcal{S}_D \models R_D \wedge R_D \models \pi_f(C) \ .$$

If $\mathcal{S}_D$ satisfies its rules, then it satisfies the subset of rules that is the range of the homomorphous mapping:

$$\mathcal{S}_D \models R_D \Rightarrow \mathcal{S}_D \models f(R_T) \text{ because } f(R_T) \subseteq R_D \text{ (by Definition 13).}$$

Also, if both $R_D \models \pi_f(C)$ and $\mathcal{S}_D \models R_D$, then $\mathcal{S}_D \models \pi_f(C)$. Therefore

$$\mathcal{S}_D \models f(R_T) \wedge \mathcal{S}_D \models \pi_f(C)$$

of course also holds. Now we "switch" to the template ontology; by $K_T \rhd_f K_D$, we can construct a corresponding structure over the template ontology (Proposition 1) along with a mapping $\pi_f^{\rhd_f} : \mathcal{SP}_T \rightarrow \mathcal{SVC}_T$ (Proposition 2):

$$\exists \mathcal{S}^{\rhd_f}, \exists \pi_f^{\rhd_f} : \mathcal{S}^{\rhd_f} \models R_T \wedge \mathcal{S}^{\rhd_f} \models \pi_f^{\rhd_f}(C) .$$

By Definition 12, and because WT is correct, we know

$$\exists \mathcal{S}^{\rhd_f}, \exists \pi_f^{\rhd_f} :$$

$$\mathcal{S}^{\rhd_f} \models R_T \wedge \mathcal{S}^{\rhd_f} \models \pi_f^{\rhd_f}(C) : [\![W]\!]_{\mathcal{S}^{\rhd_f}}^{\pi_f^{\rhd_f}} ([\![\pi_f^{\rhd_f}(pre)]\!]_{\mathcal{S}^{\rhd_f}}) \subseteq [\![\pi_f^{\rhd_f}(post)]\!]_{\mathcal{S}^{\rhd_f}} .$$

As we are currently solely in the template ontology, by Lemma 2 we know that a template and an instantiation have the same semantics, and therefore

$$\exists \mathcal{S}^{\rhd_f}, \pi_f^{\rhd_f} :$$

$$\mathcal{S}^{\rhd_f} \models R_T \wedge \mathcal{S}^{\rhd_f} \models \pi_f^{\rhd_f}(C) : [\![\pi_f^{\rhd_f}(W)]\!]_{\mathcal{S}^{\rhd_f}} ([\![\pi_f^{\rhd_f}(pre)]\!]_{\mathcal{S}^{\rhd_f}}) \subseteq [\![\pi_f^{\rhd_f}(post)]\!]_{\mathcal{S}^{\rhd_f}} .$$

If we "switch back" to the domain ontology, by Lemma 1, we can use our original $\mathcal{S}_D$ again:

$$\mathcal{S}_D \models R_D \wedge \mathcal{S}_D \models \pi_f(C) : [\![\pi_f(W)]\!]_{\mathcal{S}_D} ([\![\pi_f(pre)]\!]_{\mathcal{S}_D}) \subseteq [\![\pi_f(post)]\!]_{\mathcal{S}_D} .$$

It is therefore sufficient to show that $R_D \models \pi_f(C)$, if the template is already proven to be correct, and $K_T \rhd_f K_D$ holds. $\square$

For our example template, we look at the instantiation $\pi_f(V) = Vld$ from Fig. 4. It can easily be shown that the concretized constraints follow from the rules R_D of the restaurant domain. Thus the service composition as given by the instantiated template is correct with respect to the mapped pre- and postconditions of the template which are $\forall a \in A : true$ (precondition) and $A' = \{a \in A \mid goodRestaurant(a)\}$.

6   Discussion

Our approach contains the following aspects: (1) we have correct templates with a formal, parameterized semantics, (2) instantiate them with services of a concrete domain, and (3) show correctness of the instantiation by correctness of simple side-conditions. As instantiated templates come along with a full-fledged service description, they can be treated as services themselves, and therefore be re-used as services in other template instantiations.

On a basic level, verification of service compositions is not fundamentally different from verification of programs. However, especially the context of on-the-fly composition and verification comes with timing constraints; we therefore believe that it is not feasible to prove correctness of service compositions individually. Domain-independent templates can, on the other hand, be verified without timing constraints (e.g., by dedicated specialists). Then, instantiations can be created on-the-fly, without the necessity of a complete verification: checking the validity of the instantiated constraints is sufficient.

Working with templates in general is common in modular software design methods, component-based software development, and service-oriented architectures, either by dedicated modeling constructs, or by best-practices. However, templates are not necessarily verified.

An early approach of formally specifying a service composition as a parameterized template, and to get provably correct instantiations, is the CARE approach [16,20]. In CARE so-called *fragments* are used for modeling: *primitives*, which come with a black-box description and are proven to be correct externally; and *composites*, which are used to model complex algorithms. The Z modeling language [28] is used as a concise formal notation. For a composition's specification, a *proof obligation* is derived automatically and can be proven by an automated (and/or interactive) theorem prover to show that the instantiation is correct wrt. the requirements. In contrast to CARE, we define correctness for an *incomplete* template, and show that it is sufficient to proof that an instantiation adheres to come constraints, instead of proving correctness for the complete instantiation. Also, we integrate formalized domain knowledge into our approach. [15] also uses the CARE method, but focuses on matching and adaptation.

Based on the development of adaptation techniques, [9] advocates the need for verification at runtime, to verify compositions which changed while already deployed. SimuLizar [6] extends the Palladio Component Model (PCM, [7]) with fuzzy requirements for adaptation using the temporal-logic-based RELAX language, targeting scalability analysis. While both focus on non-functional properties, it would be promising to apply our template- and constraint-based verification to similar runtime contexts.

There is also more research to define formal semantics for existing industrial workflow languages. While [26] defines an event algebra for general workflows, [10] defines a semantic for WS-BPEL [23] based on abstract machines, and [24] based on Petri nets. [18] derives a data flow network from BPEL and translate it to a Promela [17] model.

Also based on generalized data flow networks, the REO approach [3] focuses on communication between entities (e.g., services), by using channel-based communication models, and defining a semantics based on times data streams [2].

While we use a simple imperative programming style language to present our approach, we believe it is possible to apply our results to existing workflow or software architecture languages. To do this, the target language needs a notion of placeholders, and a proper mapping between the languages has to be defined. Our own ongoing experiments are based on an extension of PCM (esp. with pre-/postconditions, [4]), where we also work on SAT-based verification of the instantiation process.

7 Conclusion

In this paper, we presented an approach to create service compositions for different domains by instantiation of domain-independent templates. Moreover, if these templates are provably correct, we have shown that verification of service compositions can be reduced to verification of side-conditions of the instantiation: the instantiated template constraints have to hold in the target domain.

To prove this, we defined an abstract semantics for workflow templates containing service placeholders, which is parameterized with concretions (of placeholders), and logical structures (which fix the concrete meaning). We defined correctness with respect to pre- and postconditions based on this parameterized semantics. If templates formalize instantiation constraints in the form of rules, we have shown that all possible template instantiations are correct, if the (corresponding) instantiation of these constraints are correct.

Therefore, using this approach to create service compositions, their verification can be reduced to verification of side-conditions.

We would like to thank our colleague Felix Mohr for several discussions about the use of templates in service compositions, as well as the anonymous reviewers for their feedback.

References

1. Apt, K., de Boer, F., Olderog, E.R.: Verification of Sequential and Concurrent Programs. Springer, London (2009)
2. Arbab, F., Rutten, J.J.M.M.: A coinductive calculus of component connectors. In: Wirsing, M., Pattinson, D., Hennicker, R. (eds.) WADT 2003. LNCS, vol. 2755, pp. 34–55. Springer, Heidelberg (2003)
3. Arbad, F.: Reo: a channel-based coordination model for component composition. Math. Struct. Comput. Sci. **14**, 329–366 (2004)
4. Arifulina, S., Becker, M., Platenius, M.C., Walther, S.: SeSAME: modeling and analyzing high-quality service compositions. In: Proceedings of the 29th IEEE/ACM International Conference on Automated Software Engineering (ASE 2014), Tool Demonstrations. ACM, 15–19 September 2014, to appear
5. Baader, F., Horrocks, I., Sattler, U.: Description logics. In: Frank van Harmelen, V.L., Porter, B. (eds.) Foundations of Artificial Intelligence, vol. 3, pp. 135–179. Elsevier (2008)
6. Becker, M., Luckey, M., Becker, S.: Performance analysis of self-adaptive systems for requirements validation at design-time. In: QoSA, pp. 43–52. ACM (2013)
7. Becker, S., Koziolek, H., Reussner, R.: The palladio component model for model-driven performance prediction. J. Syst. Softw. **82**(1), 3–22 (2009). Special Issue: Software Performance - Modeling and Analysis

8. Bures, T., Hnetynka, P., Plasil, F.: SOFA 2.0: balancing advanced features in a hierarchical component model. In: SERA, pp. 40–48 (2006)
9. Calinescu, R., Ghezzi, C., Kwiatkowska, M., Mirandola, R.: Self-adaptive software needs quantitative verification at runtime. Commun. ACM **55**(9), 69–77 (2012)
10. Farahbod, R., Glässer, U., Vajihollahi, M.: Abstract operational semantics of the business process execution language for web services. Technical report (2005)
11. Franconi, E., Tessaris, S.: Rules and queries with ontologies: a unified logical framework. In: Ohlbach, H.J., Schaffert, S. (eds.) PPSWR 2004. LNCS, vol. 3208, pp. 50–60. Springer, Heidelberg (2004)
12. Gamma, E., Helm, R., Johnson, R., Vlissides, J.: Design Patterns: Elements of Reusable Object-Oriented Software. Addison-Wesley, Boston (1995)
13. Gruber, T.R.: A translation approach to portable ontology specifications. Knowl. Acquisition **5**(2), 199–220 (1993)
14. Guarino, N., Oberle, D., Staab, S.: What is an ontology? In: Staab, S., Studer, R. (eds.) Handbook on Ontologies: International Handbooks on Information Systems, pp. 1–17. Springer, Heidelberg (2009)
15. Hemer, D.: Semi-automated component-based development of formally verified software. In: Proceedings of the 11th Refinement Workshop (REFINE 2006), Electronic Notes in Theoretical Computer Science, vol. 187, pp. 173–188 (2007)
16. Hemer, D., Lindsay, P.: Reuse of verified design templates through extended pattern matching. In: Fitzgerald, J.S., Jones, C.B., Lucas, P. (eds.) FME 1997. LNCS, vol. 1313, pp. 495–514. Springer, Heidelberg (1997)
17. Holzmann, G.J.: The model checker SPIN. IEEE Trans. Softw. Eng. **23**(5), 279–295 (1997)
18. Kovács, M., Gönczy, L.: Simulation and formal analysis of workflow models. Electron. Notes Theor. Comput. Sci. **211**, 221–230 (2008)
19. Kumar, S.K., Harding, J.A.: Ontology mapping using description logic and bridging axioms. Comput. Ind. **64**(1), 19–28 (2013)
20. Lindsay, P.A., Hemer, D.: An industrial-strength method for the construction of formally verified software. In: Australian Software Engineering Conference, p. 27 (1996)
21. Martin, D., Paolucci, M., McIlraith, S.A., Burstein, M., McDermott, D., McGuinness, D.L., Parsia, B., Payne, T.R., Sabou, M., Solanki, M., Srinivasan, N., Sycara, K.: Bringing semantics to web services: the OWL-S approach. In: Cardoso, J., Sheth, A.P. (eds.) SWSWPC 2004. LNCS, vol. 3387, pp. 26–42. Springer, Heidelberg (2005)
22. Noy, N.F.: Ontology mapping. In: Staab, S., Studer, R. (eds.) Handbook on Ontologies: International Handbooks on Information Systems, pp. 573–590. Springer, Heidelberg (2009)
23. OASIS: Web services business process execution language v2.0. http://docs.oasis-open.org/wsbpel/2.0/OS/wsbpel-v2.0-OS.pdf
24. Ouyang, C., Verbeek, E., van der Aalst, W.M.P., Breutel, S., Dumas, M., ter Hofstede, A.H.M.: Formal semantics and analysis of control flow in WS-BPEL. Sci. Comput. Program. **67**(2–3), 162–198 (2007)
25. Pnueli, A.: The temporal logic of programs. In: FOCS, pp. 46–57 (1977)
26. Singh, M.P.: Formal aspects of workflow management - part 1: semantics (1997)
27. Walther, S., Wehrheim, H.: Knowledge-based verification of service compositions - an SMT approach. In: ICECCS, pp. 24–32 (2013)
28. Woodcock, J., Davies, J.: Using Z: Specification, Refinement, and Proof. Prentice Hall, Upper Saddle River (1996)

Compositional Verification of Asynchronously Communicating Systems

Jan Martijn E.M. van der Werf[✉]

Department of Information and Computing Science, Utrecht University,
P.O. Box 80.089, 3508 TB Utrecht, The Netherlands
j.m.e.m.vanderwerf@uu.nl

Abstract. Within a network of asynchronously communicating systems,
the complete network is often not known, or even available at run-time.
Consequently, verifying whether the network of communicating systems
behaves correctly, i.e., the network does not contain any deadlock or livelock, is impracticable. As such systems are highly concurrent by nature,
Petri nets form a natural choice to model these systems and their communication.

This paper presents a formal framework based on a generic communication condition to verify correctness of the system by pairwise checking
whether these systems communicate correctly and fulfill some condition,
then the whole network is guaranteed to behave correctly. As an example,
this paper presents the elastic communication condition.

1 Introduction

Dividing the functionality of a system into subsystems such that each subsystem
implements its own specific functionality is not new. Already in the sixties of the
last century, McIlroy [17] suggested to use components to design and implement
software systems. A component implements a specific part of the specification,
masking its internal design [22].

A component offers some functionality, and, in order to deliver this, it uses
functionality of other components. This way, a component has two roles: it is a
provider and a *consumer*. From a business oriented view, a component *sells* functionality, and to meet its commitments, it *buys* functionality of other components
[4,12].

With the advent of paradigms like Service Oriented Architectures [3,18], systems become more and more distributed. Some of the components of the system
may be offered by third parties. As these third parties do not expose which components their systems use, the individual systems form a, possibly unknown,
large scale ecosystem: a *dynamic network* of communicating components. These
systems communicate via *messages*: a component *requests functionality* from
another component, which in turn *eventually sends its answer*. Hence, communication between the components is *asynchronous* by nature. Verification of
asynchronously communicating systems is known to be a hard problem.

The nature of this class of communicating systems is asymmetric. A provider
commits itself to deliver some functionality. It does not matter what other

© Springer International Publishing Switzerland 2015
I. Lanese and E. Madelaine (Eds.): FACS 2014, LNCS 8997, pp. 49–67, 2015.
DOI: 10.1007/978-3-319-15317-9_4

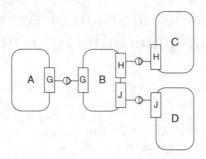

Fig. 1. Example of a component tree of four components A, B, C and D.

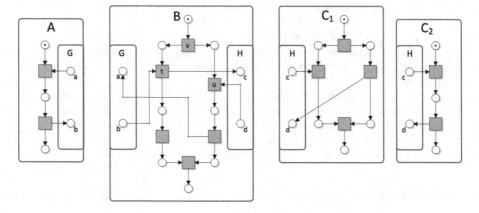

Fig. 2. Four components A, B, C_1 and C_2, such that $A \oplus_G B \oplus_H C_1$ is sound, but $A \oplus_G B \oplus_H C_2$ is not.

components that provider needs, as long as it keeps delivering the requested functionality. Therefore, the connections between components have a direction: they are initiated by some client, and accepted by a provider. Consider the component architecture depicted in Fig. 1. There are four components, A, B and C, which are connected via ports G, H and J. The $\oslash$ operator indicates the direction of the communication. In this example, component B delivers a service to component A over port G, and to do so, it uses the functionality of its children C and D.

At run-time, components use other components to deliver their functionality. In this way, the components form a *component tree*. The dynamic binding of components causes the component tree to be unknown at design time. This makes verification of behavioral correctness very hard. Thus, if we want to ensure behavioral correctness, we need a verification method that only considers pairwise compositions of components: if each component is sound, and all pairwise connected components satisfy some condition, the whole tree should be sound.

Current compositional verification techniques start with the verification of a pair of components, compose these into a larger component, and then use this larger composition for the next pairwise composition. However, this way of verification does not take the dynamic nature of service oriented approaches into account: if one of the components changes, the whole network needs to be checked again. Consider for example the components A, B, C_1 and C_2 depicted in Fig. 2. In this example, the composition of A, B and C_1 is sound. However, if B decides to use C_2 instead of C_1, the communication with A is hampered. Current compositional verification techniques have to re-verify the whole network for soundness again.

In [16], the authors prove that in general verification of such a dynamic, distributed setting is undecidable. Current research results (cf. [15,20,25,26]) are based on a message bound.

In this paper, we present a framework based on communication conditions to verify a subclass of asynchronously communicating systems compositionally [24]. The formal foundation of the framework is *Petri nets*, in which communication is asynchronous by nature. *Petri nets* can be used both for modeling the *internal activities* of a component, as well as for the interaction between components. We focus on *soundness* of systems: a system should always have a possibility to terminate.

This paper is structured as follows. Section 2 presents the basic notions used throughout the paper. Next, Sect. 3 introduces the notion of components and their composition. In Sect. 4, we present a general framework to verify correctness of component trees compositionally. Next, Sect. 5 shows a subclass of communicating systems based on this general framework. Section 6 concludes the paper.

2 Preliminaries

Let S be a set. The powerset of S is denoted by $\mathcal{P}(S) = \{S' \mid S' \subseteq S\}$. We use $|S|$ for the number of elements in S. Two sets U and V are *disjoint* if $U \cap V = \emptyset$. A *bag* m over S is a function $m : S \to I\!N$, where $I\!N = \{0, 1, 2, \ldots\}$ denotes the natural numbers. We denote e.g. the bag m with an element a occurring once, b occurring three times and c occurring twice by $m = [a, b^3, c^2]$. The set of all bags over S is denoted by $I\!N^S$. Sets can be seen as a special kind of bag were all elements occur only once. We use $+$ and $-$ for the sum and difference of two bags, and $=, <, >, \leq, \geq$ for the comparison of two bags, which are defined in a standard way. The projection of a bag $m \in I\!N^S$ on elements of a set $U \subseteq S$, is denoted by $m_{|U}$, and is defined by $m_{|U}(u) = m(u)$ for all $u \in U$ and $m_{|U}(u) = 0$ for all $u \in S \setminus U$. Furthermore, if for some $n \in I\!N$, disjoint sets $U_i \subseteq S$ with $1 \leq i \leq n$ exist such that $S = \bigcup_{i=1}^{n} U_i$, then $m = \sum_{i=1}^{n} m_{|U_i}$.

A *sequence* over S of length $n \in I\!N$ is a function $\sigma : \{1, \ldots, n\} \to S$. If $n > 0$ and $\sigma(i) = a_i$ for $i \in \{1, \ldots, n\}$, we write $\sigma = \langle a_1, \ldots, a_n \rangle$. The length of a sequence is denoted by $|\sigma|$. The sequence of length 0 is called the *empty sequence*, and is denoted by ϵ. The set of all finite sequences over S is denoted by S^*. We write $a \in \sigma$ if a $1 \leq i \leq |\sigma|$ exists such that $\sigma(i) = a$. *Concatenation* of two sequences $\nu, \gamma \in S^*$, denoted by $\sigma = \nu; \gamma$, is a sequence defined by

$\sigma : \{1, \ldots, |\nu| + |\gamma|\} \to S$, such that $\sigma(i) = \nu(i)$ for $1 \leq i \leq |\nu|$, and $\sigma(i) = \gamma(i - |\nu|)$ for $|\nu| + 1 \leq i \leq |\nu| + |\gamma|$.

A projection of a sequence $\sigma \in S^*$ on elements of a set $U \subseteq S$ (i.e. eliminating the elements from $S \setminus U$) is denoted as $\sigma_{|U}$. The bag denoted the elements of a sequence σ and their occurrences is called the *Parikh vector* and is denoted by $\overrightarrow{\sigma}$.

Labeled transition systems. To model the behavior of a system, we use a *labeled transition system*. A *labeled transition system* (LTS) is a 5-tuple $(S, \mathcal{A}, \to, s_0, \Omega)$ where S is a set of *states*; $\mathcal{A}$ is a set of *actions*; $\to \subseteq (S \times (\mathcal{A} \cup \{\tau\}) \times S)$ is a *transition relation*, where $\tau \notin \mathcal{A}$ is the silent action. $(S, \to, \emptyset)$ is a labeled directed graph, called the *reachability graph*; $s_0 \in S$ is the *initial state*; and $\Omega \subseteq S$ is the set of *accepting states*.

Let $L = (S, \mathcal{A}, \to, s_i, \Omega)$ be an LTS. For $s, s' \in S$ and $a \in \mathcal{A} \cup \{\tau\}$, we write $(L : s \xrightarrow{a} s')$ if and only if $(s, a, s') \in \to$. An action $a \in \mathcal{A} \cup \{\tau\}$ is called *enabled* in a state $s \in S$, denoted by $(L : s \xrightarrow{a})$ if a state s' exists such that $(L : s \xrightarrow{a} s')$. If $(L : s \xrightarrow{a} s')$, we say that state s' is *reachable* from s by an action labeled a. A state $s \in S$ is called a *deadlock* if no action $a \in \mathcal{A} \cup \{\tau\}$ exists such that $(L : s \xrightarrow{a})$. We define $\implies$ as the smallest relation such that $(L : s \implies s')$ if $s = s'$ or $\exists s'' \in S : (L : s \implies s'' \xrightarrow{\tau} s')$. As a notational convention, we may write $\xrightarrow{\tau}$ for $\implies$. For $a \in \mathcal{A}$, we define $\xRightarrow{a}$ as the smallest relation such that $(L : s \xRightarrow{a} s')$ if $\exists s_1, s_2 \in S : (L : s \implies s_1 \xrightarrow{a} s_2 \implies s')$.

We lift the notation of actions to sequences. For the empty sequence ϵ, we have $(L : s \xrightarrow{\epsilon} s')$ if and only if $(L : s \implies s')$. Let $\sigma \in \mathcal{A}^*$ be a sequence of length $n > 0$, and let $s_0, s_n \in S$. Sequence σ is a *firing sequence*, denoted by $(L : s_0 \xrightarrow{\sigma} s_n)$, if states $s_{i-1}, s_i \in S$ exist such that $(L : s_{i-1} \xRightarrow{\sigma(i)} s_i)$ for all $1 \leq i \leq n$. We write $(L : s \xrightarrow{*} s')$ if a sequence $\sigma \in \mathcal{A}^*$ exists such that $(L : s \xrightarrow{\sigma} s')$, and say that s' is *reachable* from s. The set of reachable states from some state $s \in S$ is defined as $\mathcal{R}(L, s) = \{s' \mid (L : s \xrightarrow{*} s')\}$. We lift the notation of reachable states to sets by $\mathcal{R}(L, M) = \bigcup_{s \in M} \mathcal{R}(L, s)$ for $M \subseteq S$. A set of states $M \subseteq S$ is called a *livelock* if $M \subseteq \mathcal{R}(L, M)$. An LTS $L = (S, \mathcal{A}, \to, s_0, \Omega)$ is called *weakly terminating* if $\Omega \subseteq \mathcal{R}(L, s_0)$.

Petri nets. A *Petri net* [19] is a 3-tuple $N = (P, T, F)$ where (1) P and T are two disjoint sets of *places* and *transitions* respectively; (2) $F \subseteq (P \times T) \cup (T \times P)$ is a *flow relation*. The elements from the set $P \cup T$ are called the *nodes* of N. Elements of F are called *arcs*. Places are depicted as circles, transitions as squares. For each element $(n_1, n_2) \in F$, an arc is drawn from n_1 to n_2. Two Petri nets $N = (P, T, F)$ and $N' = (P', T', F')$ are *disjoint* if and only if $(P \cup T) \cap (P' \cup T') = \emptyset$. Let $N = (P, T, F)$ be a Petri net. Given a node $n \in (P \cup T)$, we define its *preset* ${}^{\bullet}_N n = \{n' \mid (n', n) \in F\}$, and its *postset* $n^{\bullet}_N = \{n' \mid (n, n') \in F\}$. We lift the notation of preset and postset to sets. Given a set $U \subseteq (P \cup T)$, ${}^{\bullet}_N U = \bigcup_{n \in U} {}^{\bullet}_N n$ and $U^{\bullet}_N = \bigcup_{n \in U} n^{\bullet}_N$. If the context is clear, we omit the N in the superscript.

A *marking* of N is a bag $m \in \mathbb{N}^P$, where $m(p)$ denotes the number of *tokens* in place $p \in P$. If $m(p) > 0$, place p is called *marked* in marking m. A Petri net

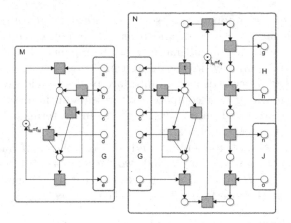

Fig. 3. Two components N and M with three ports G, H and J, where components N and M share port G.

N with corresponding marking m is written as (N, m) and is called a *marked Petri net*.

A *system* is a 3-tuple $S = (N, m_0, \Omega)$ where (N, m_0) is a marked Petri net with $N = (P, T, F)$ and $\Omega \subseteq \mathbb{N}^P$ is the set of *final markings*. Its semantics is defined by an LTS $\mathcal{N}(S) = (\mathbb{N}^P, T, \rightarrow, m_0, \Omega)$ such that $(m, t, m') \in \rightarrow$ iff ${}^\bullet t \leq m$ and $m' + {}^\bullet t = m + t^\bullet$ for $m, m' \in \mathbb{N}^P$ and $t \in T$. We write $(N : m \xrightarrow{t} m')$, $\mathcal{R}(N, m_0)$, $\mathcal{L}(N, m_0)$, and $\mathcal{T}(N, m_0)$ as a shorthand notation for $(\mathcal{N}(N, m_0) : m \xrightarrow{t} m')$, $\mathcal{R}(\mathcal{N}(N, m_0))$, $\mathcal{L}(\mathcal{N}(N, m_0))$, and $\mathcal{T}(\mathcal{N}(N, m_0))$, respectively. A marking $m \in \mathcal{R}(N, m_0)$ is a home marking if $m \in \mathcal{R}(N, m')$ for all $m' \in \mathcal{R}(N, m_0)$.

3   Asynchronously Communicating Systems

In a network of asynchronously communicating systems, systems communicate via message passing. We call these systems *components* of the network. Two components are connected via some interface that defines which messages are exchanged between the systems. As communication is asynchronous, Petri nets [19] form a natural choice to model the communication between these components. We model the different messages that can be sent and received via special places, called *interface places*. A component either receives messages from an interface place, which is then called an *input place*, or it sends messages to an interface place, which we then call an *output place*.

As components communicate with multiple components, we partition the interface places of a system into *ports*. A transition can send or receive messages via a port. For this, we introduce the notion of a transition sign. A transition sends messages to a port (sign !), receives messages from a port (sign ?) or does not communicate at all with a port (sign τ).

The marking of a component represents the internal state of the component, together with messages it has sent and received. As initially no messages have been sent or received, the initial marking of a component has no messages in its interface places. Similarly, in the desired final marking of a component, all messages have been processed, i.e., all interface places should be empty. Often, the desired final marking of a component represents an idle state, from which the component can respond on new messages again. In terms of Petri nets, the final marking is often a home marking.

Figure 3 depicts two components N and M. Component M has a single port G with three input places a, c and d, and two output ports b and e. Component N has three ports, G, H and J. The internal structure of a component, i.e., the component without the interface places, is called the *skeleton*.

Definition 1 (Component, skeleton, sign). *A Component is defined as an 8-tuple* $(P, I, O, T, F, \mathcal{G}, i, f)$ *where* $((P \cup I \cup O), T, F)$ *is a Petri net; P is a set of* internal *places; I is the set of* input *places, O is the set of* output *places such that P, I and O are pairwise disjoint and* $^\bullet I = O^\bullet = \emptyset$; $\mathcal{G} \subseteq \mathcal{P}(I \cup O)$ *is a partitioning of the interface places, an element of $\mathcal{G}$ is called a* port; *a transition either sends or receives messages, i.e.,* $^\bullet G \cap G^\bullet = \emptyset$ *for all $G \in \mathcal{G}$. $i \in \mathbb{N}^P$ is the initial marking, and $f \in \mathbb{N}^P$ is the final marking.*

Two components N and M are called disjoint *if* $(P_N \cup I_N \cup O_N \cup T_N) \cap (P_M \cup I_M \cup O_M \cup T_M) = \emptyset$. *A component N is called* closed *if $I_N = O_N = \emptyset$. The set of all components is denoted by $\mathfrak{N}$. As a shorthand notation, we write $\mathcal{R}(N, m)$ for $\mathcal{R}((P_N \cup I_N \cup O_N, T_N, F_N), m)$ for $m \in \mathbb{N}^{P_N \cup I_N \cup O_N}$.*

The skeleton *of N is defined as the Petri net $\mathcal{S}(N) = (P_N, T_N, F)$ with $F = F_N \cap ((P_N \times T_N) \cup (T_N \times P_N))$. The* skeleton system *of N is defined as the system $\overline{\mathcal{S}}(N) = (\mathcal{S}(N), i_N, \{f_N\})$.*

The sign *of a transition with respect to a port $G \in \mathcal{G}$ is a function $\lambda_G : T \to \{!, ?, \tau\}$ defined by $\lambda_G(t) = !$ if $t^\bullet \cap G \neq \emptyset$, $\lambda_G(t) = ?$ if $^\bullet t \cap G \neq \emptyset$, and $\lambda_G(t) = \tau$ otherwise, for all $t \in T$.*

It is desired that from every reachable marking of a component, the component should be able to reach its desired final marking. This property is expressed in the notion of weak termination. Another basic sanity check for components is to check whether it internally behaves correctly, i.e., ignoring the interface places, the component should be able to always reach its final marking. As this property is closely related to soundness of workflow nets [1], We call this property *soundness*.

Definition 2 (Weak termination and soundness). *Let N be a component. It is* weakly terminating, *if for each marking $m \in \mathcal{R}(N, i_N)$, we have $f_N \in \mathcal{R}(N, m)$. It is* sound, *if the system defined by its skeleton is weakly terminating.*

Notice that this definition does not require the final marking of a component to be a deadlock. Instead, the final marking can be seen as a home marking, in which the component is in rest.

Components communicate via their ports. To be able to compose two components so that they are able to communicate, the components should have inverted ports: input places of the one should be output places of the other, and vice versa.

Definition 3 (Composition of components). *Two components A and B are composable with respect to port $G \in \mathcal{G}_A \cap \mathcal{G}_B$, denoted by $A \oplus_G B$, if and only if $(P_A \cup I_A \cup O_A \cup T_A) \cap (P_B \cup I_B \cup O_B \cup T_B) = (I_A \cap O_B) \cup (O_A \cap I_B) = G$.*

If A and B are composable with respect to port G, their composition *results in a component $A \oplus_G B = (P, I, O, T, F, \mathcal{G}, i, f)$ where $P = P_A \cup P_B \cup H$; $I = (I_A \cup I_B) \backslash H$; $O = (O_A \cup O_B) \backslash H$; $T = T_A \cup T_B$; $F = F_A \cup F_B$; $\mathcal{G} = (\mathcal{G}_A \cup \mathcal{G}_B) \backslash \mathcal{H}$; $i = i_A + i_B$; and $f = f_A + f_B$. If a port $G \in \mathcal{G}_A \cap \mathcal{G}_B$ exists such that $A \oplus_G B$, we write $A \oplus B$.*

Consider again the components N and M of Fig. 3. Both components share port G, where the input places a, c and d of M are output places of N, and the output places b and d are input places of N. Their composition results in a component $N \oplus M$, where the places a, b, c, d and e become internal places of the composition.

The composition operator is commutative and associative, provided that the components are composable.

Corollary 4 (Composition is commutative and associative). *Let A, B and C be three components, such that $A \cap C = \emptyset$, and let $G \in \mathcal{G}_A \cap \mathcal{G}_B$ and $H \in \mathcal{G}_B \cap \mathcal{G}_C$. If A and B are composable w.r.t some port $G \in \mathcal{G}_A \cap \mathcal{G}_B$, then $A \oplus_G B = B \oplus_G A$; Also, $(A \oplus_G B) \oplus_H C$ exists iff $A \oplus_G (B \oplus_H C)$ exists. If the compositions exist, they are identical.*

In the remainder of this section, we discuss some properties of the composition operator. Composition only restricts behavior, i.e., the composition of two components A and B does not introduce any new behavior. In [24], it is shown that the projection of a composition to either one of its constituents is a simulation relation [10]. As a consequence, a firing sequence in the composition of two components is a firing sequence of its constituents, after hiding the transitions of the other component, and any reachable marking in the composition results in a reachable marking of that constituent.

Corollary 5. *Let A and B be two composable components with respect to some port $G \in \mathcal{G}_A \cap \mathcal{G}_B$. Define $N = A \oplus_G B$. Let $m, m' \in \mathcal{R}(\overline{\mathcal{S}}(N))$ and $\sigma \in T_N^*$ such that $(\mathcal{S}(N) : m \xrightarrow{\sigma} m')$. Then $m_{|P_A} \in \mathcal{R}(\overline{\mathcal{S}}(A))$ and $m_{|P_B} \in \mathcal{R}(\overline{\mathcal{S}}(B))$, $(\mathcal{S}(A) : m_{|P_A} \xrightarrow{\sigma_{|T_A}} m'_{|P_A})$, and $(\mathcal{S}(B) : m_{|P_B} \xrightarrow{\sigma_{|T_B}} m'_{|P_B})$.*

4   A General Verification Framework

In this section we present a formal framework for compositional verification of soundness on component trees. Proving the soundness of a component tree is

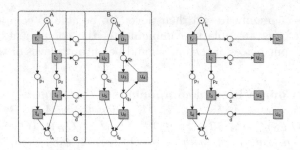

Fig. 4. Composition $A \oplus_G B$ and its subnet $N_1 = \mathcal{C}_B(A)$

done in two steps. First of all, each component should be sound itself. Next, each connection is checked against some communication condition, from which soundness of the composition, and of the whole tree can be concluded. Such a condition should satisfy some criteria. A component may not notice the difference whether it is communicating with a single component or with a component tree. We therefore search for a *sequence relation* $\varphi : T_N^* \times T_N^* \to \mathbb{B}$, which is a predicate on the firing sequences of component N, such that this property is guaranteed.

As shown in [4], soundness is not a sufficient condition. Consider for example the composition in Fig. 2. In this example, it is easy to verify that both compositions $A \oplus_G B$ and $B \oplus_H C_2$ are sound. However, in the composition $A \oplus_G B \oplus_H C_2$, transition t is only enabled once it received a message from component A, which in turn requires a message from component C_2. Consequently, the composition of the tree is not sound.

As soundness is not a sufficient condition, we need to strengthen the soundness property by stating that for all reachable markings in the composition of B and C and firing sequence σ in B, a firing sequence $\tilde{\sigma}$ should exist in the composition such that σ and $\tilde{\sigma}$ satisfy the predicate φ.

Definition 6 (Communication condition). *Let B and C be two components such that $B \oplus_H C$ for some $H \in \mathcal{G}_B \cap \mathcal{G}_C$. Define $N = B \oplus_H C$ and let $\varphi :$ $T_B^* \times T_N^* \to \mathbb{B}$ be a sequence relation. The* communication condition $\mathrm{com}_\varphi(B, C)$ *holds if and only if:*

$$\forall m \in \mathcal{R}(\mathcal{S}(N), i_N), \sigma \in T_B^* :$$

$$(\mathcal{S}(B) : m_{|P_B} \xrightarrow{\sigma} f_B) \implies (\exists \tilde{\sigma} \in T_N^* : (\mathcal{S}(N) : m \xrightarrow{\tilde{\sigma}} f_N) \wedge \varphi(\sigma, \tilde{\sigma}))$$

In fact, the communication condition states that $B \oplus C$ is able to follow B. For any φ, this condition implies soundness, which directly follows from Corollary 5.

Lemma 7 (φ-communication condition implies soundness). *Let B and C be two components that are composable with respect to port $G \in \mathcal{G}_B \setminus \mathcal{G}_C$. Let φ be a sequence relation. If B is sound and $\mathrm{com}_\varphi(B, C)$ holds for some sequence relation φ, then $B \oplus_H C$ is sound.*

Condition com_φ is sufficient for deciding the soundness of two components. Let A, B and C be three components such that A communicates with B, B communicates with C, but A and C do not communicate, i.e., A and C are disjoint. We prove that if the composition $A \oplus B$ is sound, and components B and C satisfy $com_\varphi(B, C)$, then the composition of A, B and C is sound. In order to provide a sufficient condition for concluding soundness of a tree of three components, such a sequence relation needs to satisfy several criteria. These criteria follow directly from the proof.

To prove soundness of the component tree, we need to show that given a reachable marking of the component tree, the final marking should be reachable. As the composition of A and B is sound, we have a firing sequence in $A \oplus B$ from this marking leading to the final marking of $A \oplus B$. Condition $com_\varphi(B, C)$ should guarantee that this firing sequence projected on B is still possible in the component tree. The condition ensures the existence of a firing sequence in $B \oplus C$ such that it satisfies the sequence relation φ.

Hence, we have a firing sequence in $A \oplus B$ and a firing sequence in $B \oplus C$ satisfying the sequence relation φ. We should be able to interweave these firing sequences, so that the resulting sequence is a firing sequence in the component tree. Therefore, we divide the composition of $A \oplus B$ into two subnets, N_1 and N_2. The first subnet, N_1, covers component A and the transitions of B that communicate with A. Figure 4 depicts the division of the composition $A \oplus B$ into N_1. Net N_2 is the skeleton of component B. Note that the union of nets N_1 and N_2 is the skeleton of the composition. The transitions of B that communicate with A are common for the two subnets, the places of N_1 and N_2 are disjoint.

Definition 8. *Let A and B be two components such that A and B are composable with respect to some port $G \in \mathcal{G}_A \cap \mathcal{G}_B$. Define $N = A \oplus_G B$. The Petri net $\mathcal{C}_B(A)$ is defined as $\mathcal{C}_B(A) = (P, T, F)$ where $P = P_A \cup G$, $T = T_A \cup {}_N^\bullet G \cup G_N^\bullet$ and $F = F_N \cap ((P \times T) \cup (T \times P))$.*

Every firing sequence in $A \oplus B$ can be turned into a firing sequence of $\mathcal{C}_B(A)$ by leaving out all transitions of T_B, except the transitions of B that communicate with A. The proof follows directly from Corollary 5.

Corollary 9. *Let A and B be two OPNs that are composable with respect to some port $G \in \mathcal{G}_A \cap \mathcal{G}_B$. Define $N = A \oplus B$ and $L = \mathcal{C}_B(A)$. Then for all $\sigma \in T_N^*$ and $m, m' \in \mathbb{N}^{P_N}$ such that $(\mathcal{S}(N) : m \xrightarrow{\sigma} m')$ holds $(L : m_{|P_L} \xrightarrow{\sigma_{|T_L}} m'_{|P_L})$.*

In the soundness proof, the firing sequence in $A \oplus B$ is projected on $\mathcal{C}_B(A)$, and it will be interweaved with the resulting firing sequence of the communication condition. The interweaving property will guarantee that this interweaving is possible.

Property 10 (Interweaving firing sequences). Let A and B be two components that are composable with respect to some port $G \in \mathcal{G}_A \cap \mathcal{G}_B$. Let φ be a sequence relation as defined in Definition 6. Let $N_1 = \mathcal{C}_B(A)$ and $N_2 = \mathcal{S}(B)$. Let $\mu \in T_{N_1}^*$ and $m, m' \in \mathbb{N}^{P_{N_1}}$ such that $(N_1 : m \xrightarrow{\mu} m')$. Let $\nu \in T_{N_2}^*$ and $\overline{m}, \overline{m}' \in \mathbb{N}^{P_{N_2}}$

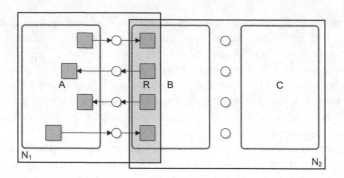

Fig. 5. The composition $A \oplus B \oplus C$ is split into $N_1 = \mathcal{C}_B(A)$ and $N_2 = \mathcal{S}(B \oplus C)$

such that $(N_2 : \overline{m} \xrightarrow{\nu} \overline{m}')$ and $\varphi(\mu, \nu)$. Then a $\sigma \in T_N^*$ exists such that $(\mathcal{S}(N) : m + \overline{m} \xrightarrow{\sigma} m' + \overline{m}')$, $\varphi(\mu, \sigma)$ and $\varphi(\nu, \sigma)$.

The interweaving property expresses that two sequences can be combined into a single firing sequence that is executable and satisfies the sequence relation. Also, the sequence relation should hold for a firing sequence, and its firing sequence in which all transitions are hidden except for the transitions that communicate. Rephrased, the sequence relation φ should not consider all transitions in B, but only the transitions of B that communicate with A. This is expressed in the next property.

Property 11. Let B and C be two components that are composable, and let $G \in \mathcal{G}_B \setminus \mathcal{G}_C$. Define $N = B \oplus C$ and $R = {}_N^\bullet G \cup G_N^\bullet$. Let φ be a sequence relation as defined in Definition 6. Let $\sigma \in T_B^*$ and $\tilde{\sigma} \in T_N^*$. If $\varphi(\sigma, \tilde{\sigma})$, then $\varphi(\sigma_{|R}, \tilde{\sigma})$ and $\varphi(\sigma, \tilde{\sigma}_{|R})$.

This leads to the main theorem, that the communication condition com_φ is a sufficient condition for soundness. Note that to prove the main theorem for a specific sequence relation, we need to show that both properties hold for the sequence relation.

Theorem 12 (Communication condition sufficient for soundness). *Let A, B and C be three components such that A and B are composable with respect to port $G \in \mathcal{G}_A \cap \mathcal{G}_B$, B and C are composable, A and C are disjoint and $A \oplus_G B$ is sound. Let φ be a sequence relation as defined in Definition 6.*
If $\mathrm{com}_\varphi(B, C)$ holds, then $A \oplus_G B \oplus_H C$ is sound.

Proof. Define $N = A \oplus_G B \oplus_H C$, $M = A \oplus_G B$, $N_2 = \mathcal{S}(B \oplus_H C)$ and $N_1 = \mathcal{C}_B(A)$. Let $m \in \mathcal{R}(\overline{\mathcal{S}}(N))$. Since M is sound, a $\sigma \in T_M^*$ exists such that $(\mathcal{S}(M) : m_{|P_M} \xrightarrow{\sigma} f_M)$. By Corollary 5, the firing sequence $\sigma_{|T_B}$ is also a firing sequence in $\mathcal{S}(B)$, i.e. $(\mathcal{S}(B) : m_{|P_B} \xrightarrow{\sigma_{|T_B}} f_B)$. By Corollary 5, $m_{|P_{N_2}} \in \mathcal{R}(N_2, i_M)$. Hence, we can apply the communication condition $\mathrm{com}_\varphi(B, C)$ on $m_{|P_{N_2}}$ and $\sigma_{|T_B}$, which results in a firing sequence $\tilde{\sigma} \in T_{N_2}^*$ such that $(N_2 : m_{|P_{N_2}} \xrightarrow{\tilde{\sigma}} f_{N_2})$ and

$\varphi(\sigma_{|T_B}, \tilde{\sigma})$. Hence, we have a firing sequence σ in M and a firing sequence $\tilde{\sigma}$ in N_2, which we need to interweave.

We split the composition N in N_1 and N_2, as shown in Fig. 5. By Corollary 9, $(N_1 : m_{|P_{N_1}} \xrightarrow{\sigma_{|T_{N_1}}} f_A)$. By Property 11, the sequence relation also holds for the projected firing sequence, i.e. $\varphi(\sigma_{|T_{N_1}}, \tilde{\sigma})$ holds. Then the Interweaving Property (10) applied on $(N_1, m_{|P_{N_1}})$ with firing sequence $\sigma_{|T_{N_1}}$ and $(N_2, m_{|P_{N_2}})$ with firing sequence $\tilde{\sigma}$ results in a firing sequence $\overline{\sigma} \in T_N^*$ such that $(\mathcal{S}(N) : m \xrightarrow{\overline{\sigma}} f_A + f_{N_2} = f_N)$. Hence, N is sound. $\square$

From Theorem 12, it follows that com_φ is a sufficient condition to conclude soundness of a component tree consisting of three components if Properties 10 and 11 hold for the sequence relation. Hence, if two connected components satisfy com_φ, the composition is guaranteed to be sound, and it can be used for compositional verification. In fact, $\text{com}_\varphi(A, B)$ implies a direction in the component tree: component A *uses* component B to provide its service on port G, or, rephrased, B *provides a service* to A.

Definition 13 (Component uses another component). *Let A and B be two composable components with respect to port $G \in \mathcal{G}_A \cap \mathcal{G}_B$, and let φ be a sequence relation as defined in Definition 6.*

We say A uses B, denoted by $A \oslash_\varphi B$, if $A \oplus_G B$ and $\text{com}_\varphi(A, B)$.

In this way, we can construct a *component tree* of components that uses other components to deliver their service. A component tree is a tree of components connected to each other such that components can only "subcontract" work to other components. The structure of the tree is defined by the tree function c. Each node A is a component that delivers a service to its parent $c(A)$ using the services of its children $c^{-1}(A)$. Each component only communicates with its parent and its children, communication with other components is not allowed. Note that the communication implied by this function is asymmetric: the parent uses its children to deliver the service requested. By requiring that the transitive closure of c is irreflexive, we ensure the component tree to be a tree.

Definition 14 (component tree). *A component tree is a pair $(\mathcal{O}, c)$ where $\mathcal{O}$ is a set of components, and $c : \mathcal{O} \rightharpoonup \mathcal{O}$ is a partial function called the parent function such that the transitive closure c^* of c is irreflexive, for all $A, B \in \mathcal{O}$:*

– $c(B) = A \implies |\mathcal{G}_A \cap \mathcal{G}_B| = 1 \wedge A \oslash_\varphi B$; and
– $A \cap B \neq \emptyset \implies c(A) = B \vee c(B) = A$.

and for all $A \in \mathcal{O}$ a $B \in \mathcal{O}$ exists such that $(A, B) \in c^*$ or $(B, A) \in c^*$.

An example is shown in Fig. 1, where component A uses component B, which in turns uses components C and D.

In a component tree, each parent should use the services of its children. Hence, if the root is sound, and each parent uses its children, the component tree should be sound. This is expressed in the next theorem. The proof uses the associativity and commutativity of the composition operator and Theorem 12.

Theorem 15 (Soundness of component trees). *Let* $(\mathcal{O}, c)$ *be a component tree. If all components of* $\mathcal{O}$ *are sound, then* $\bigoplus_{X \in \mathcal{O}} X$ *is sound.*

Proof. Assume all components in $\mathcal{O}$ are sound. As $(\mathcal{O}, c)$ is a tree, a topological sort $\sqsubseteq$ exists on the nodes $\mathcal{O}$. Let $\mathcal{O} = \{O_1, \ldots, O_n\}$ such that $O_i \sqsubseteq O_{i+1}$ for $1 \leq i < n$. We prove the lemma by induction on i. For $i = 1$, the statement holds trivially.

Now assume $1 < i < n$ and $\bigoplus_{X \in \mathcal{O}'} X$ is sound where $\mathcal{O}' = \{O_1, \ldots, O_i\}$. Let $B = O_{i+1}$. Since $\sqsubseteq$ is a topological sort, there exists a unique $A \in \mathcal{O}'$ such that $A \oslash_\varphi B$, and B is disjoint with all OPNs in $\mathcal{O}' \setminus \{A\}$.

By associativity and commutativity, we have $\bigoplus_{X \in \mathcal{O}'} X = (\bigoplus_{X \in \mathcal{O}' \setminus \{A\}} X) \oplus A$, and $\bigoplus_{X \in \mathcal{O}' \setminus \{A\}} X$ is disjoint with B. As $A \oslash_\varphi B$, we have $\mathrm{com}_\varphi(A, B)$, and thus by Theorem 12, $(\bigoplus_{X \in \mathcal{O}' \setminus \{A\}} X) \oplus A \oplus_G B$ is sound. Again by associativity and commutativity, $(\bigoplus_{X \in \mathcal{O}' \setminus \{A\}} X) \oplus A \oplus_G B = \bigoplus_{X \in \mathcal{O}' \cup \{B\}} X$. Hence, the statement holds. $\square$

5   Elastic Communication

In this section, we present a communication condition that satisfies both Properties 10 and 11. Let A, B and C be three components such that A and B, and B and C are both composable, and A and C are disjoint. In [4], it is shown that checking whether the composition $B \oplus C$ behaves as component B on the interface with A, i.e., identical communication, is sufficient to prove soundness of a component tree. In fact, it is easy to show that this condition satisfies Properties 10 and 11 [24]. However, this identical communication condition is very restrictive. One way to weaken the condition of [4] is by allowing to permute port transitions within a communication block, i.e., a block of only sending or receiving transitions, possibly interweaved with silent transitions. Although this already weakens the condition, it remains very restrictive [24]. Consider for example the composition of Fig. 6. It is clear that the composition $A \oplus_G B$ is sound. Now, take the sequence $\sigma = \langle t_1, t_2, t_3, t_4, t_5 \rangle$. Although it is easy to verify that the composition $A \oplus B \oplus C$ is sound, no firing sequence can be found that behaves as σ, even when swaps within the same communication block is allowed. The main problem of the net is that the b message is sent too early for some of the sequences. This example shows that messages may be sent earlier without violating the soundness property. Soundness only requires that messages should be on time, i.e., components may send messages earlier, as long as they can both terminate properly. We reflect this in the *elastic communication condition*.

The condition allows sending transitions to be shuffled, as long as for each receiving transition at least the same sending transitions occur, or rephrased, sending transitions may occur at any position within its communication block, or it can be moved forward in the firing sequence. Although transitions sending messages may be moved forward in the firing sequence, the condition ensures that from every marking reachable, the final marking is reachable.

Consider the composition $A \oplus_G B$ of two components A and B. In the proof of Theorem 12, the composition is split into two nets, $N_1 = \mathcal{C}_B(A)$ and $N_2 = \mathcal{S}(B)$,

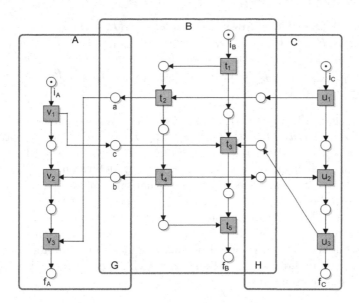

Fig. 6. Although net $A \oplus_G B \oplus_H C$ is sound, identical communication does not hold

and a firing sequence in N_1 is interweaved with a firing sequence in N_2. Let μ be a firing sequence in N_1 and ν a firing sequence in N_2. To be able to interweave the two firing sequences, ν has to produce the tokens it sends in time, and μ has to ensure that ν has sufficient tokens to be able to produce these tokens. In net N_1, all transitions of B either have an empty preset, or an empty postset. The set of transitions of B with an empty preset is labeled R_{out}, the set of transitions of B with an empty postset is labeled R_{in}. If in μ a transition of R_{out} fires, it means that a message from B is needed for A to continue. On the other hand, firing a transition of R_{in} in ν indicates that B needs a message from A.

To interweave sequences μ and ν into a firing sequence σ in the composition, if a transition in R_{in} is the next transition of ν to be added to σ, then the transition should already have fired in μ, since otherwise the transition cannot be enabled in the composition. Likewise, if a transition in R_{out} is the next transition of μ to be added to σ, then the transition should already have fired in ν, since otherwise the transition cannot be enabled in σ. If both conditions do not hold, we cannot create a firing sequence in the composition. Hence, the following formula has to hold:

$$\neg \exists\, 0 \le k < |\mu|, 0 \le l < |\nu| :$$
$$(\overrightarrow{\mu_{[1..k+1]}}_{|R_{out}} > \overrightarrow{\nu_{[1..l]}}_{|R_{out}}) \wedge (\overrightarrow{\nu_{[1..l+1]}}_{|R_{in}} > \overrightarrow{\mu_{[1..k]}}_{|R_{in}})$$

If such a pair k, l would exist, we cannot interweave the firing sequences: we cannot add the next transition of μ, since it needs tokens of ν that are not yet generated, and we cannot add the next transition of ν, since that transition needs tokens of μ that are not yet generated. If such a pair does not exist, we say the sequences are *elastic* to each other.

Definition 16 (Elastic sequences). *Let $N = (P, T, F)$ be a Petri net and $G \subseteq P$. Define $R_{in} = \{t \in T \mid \lambda_G(t) =?\}$ and $R_{out} = \{t \in T \mid \lambda_G(t) =!\}$. Let $\mu, \nu \in T_N^*$. Sequence μ is elastic to sequence ν, denoted by $\mu \rightarrowtail_G \nu$ if and only if: $(\overrightarrow{\mu_{[1..k+1]}}_{|R_{out}} \leq \overrightarrow{\nu_{[1..l]}}_{|R_{out}}) \vee (\overrightarrow{\nu_{[1..l+1]}}_{|R_{in}} \leq \overrightarrow{\mu_{[1..k]}}_{|R_{in}})$ for all $0 \leq k < |\mu|$ and $0 \leq l < |\nu|$.*

Consider again Fig. 6. As an example, take the firing sequences $\sigma = \langle t_1, t_2, t_3, t_4, t_5 \rangle$ and $\tilde{\sigma} = \langle t_1, u_1, t_2, t_4, u_2, u_3, t_3, t_5 \rangle$. In $\tilde{\sigma}$, the firing of transition t_3 is moved forward with respect to σ, i.e., sending message b is "delayed" in σ. Since $\sigma_{[1..0]} = \epsilon$ for each firing sequence σ, we have by definition $\sigma_{[1..0]} \rightarrowtail_G \tilde{\sigma}_{[1..0]}$. The index of $\tilde{\sigma}$ may be increased up to the situation that $\sigma_{[1..0]} \rightarrowtail_G \tilde{\sigma}_{[1..6]}$, since then t_3 needs to be fired in $\sigma_{[1..0]} = \epsilon$, which is obviously not the case. Hence, we need to increase the index of σ, which is allowed up to $\sigma_{[1..5]} \rightarrowtail_G \tilde{\sigma}_{[1..6]}$. Then, it is allowed to increase the index of $\tilde{\sigma}$ up to $\sigma_{[1..5]} \rightarrowtail_G \tilde{\sigma}_{[1..8]}$. Hence, σ is elastic to $\tilde{\sigma}$. The sequences not only should be elastic, but also the number of messages sent and received by both sequences should match. These two requirements form the elastic sequence relation.

Definition 17 (Elastic communication condition). *Let B and C be two components that are composable with respect to port $G \in \mathcal{G}_B \setminus \mathcal{G}_C$. Let $\mu \in T_B^*$ and $\nu \in T_{B \oplus_H C}^*$. We define the elastic sequence relation $\psi_G : T_B^* \times T_{B \oplus_H C}^* \rightarrow \mathbb{B}$ by $\psi_G(\mu, \nu)$ if and only if $\overrightarrow{\mu}_{|R} = \overrightarrow{\nu}_{|R}$ and $\mu_{|R} \rightarrowtail_G \nu$, where $R = \{t \in T_B \mid \lambda_G(t) \neq \tau\}$. The elastic communication condition is defined as $\text{com}_{\psi_G}(B, C)$.*

In order to show that the elastic communication condition com_ψ is a sufficient condition, we need to show that Properties 10 and 11 hold for the elastic sequence relation. The latter follows directly from the definition of the elastic sequence relation.

Corollary 18. *Let A and B be two components that are composable with respect to port $G \in \mathcal{G}_B \setminus \mathcal{G}_C$. Define $N = A \oplus B$. Let $\mu \in T_B^*$ and $\nu \in T_N^*$ such that $\psi_G(\mu, \nu)$. Define $R = {}_N^\bullet G \cup G_N^\bullet$. Then $\psi_G(\mu_{|R}, \nu)$ and $\psi_G(\mu, \nu_{|R})$.*

To combine a firing sequence μ with a firing sequence ν it is elastic to, we need to consider the elasticity, i.e., the structure of the sequences. Hence, to prove Property 10 for ψ, we need to show that we can interweave firing sequences μ and ν. If $\overrightarrow{\mu_{[1..k+1]}}_{|R_{out}} \leq \overrightarrow{\nu_{[1..l]}}_{|R_{out}}$, we concatenate σ and $\langle \mu(k+1) \rangle$ if $\mu(k+1)$ is not in R_{in} or R_{out}, and if $\overrightarrow{\nu_{[1..l+1]}}_{|R_{in}} \leq \overrightarrow{\mu_{[1..k]}}_{|R_{in}}$, we concatenate σ and $\langle \nu(l+1) \rangle$. Since μ is elastic to ν, always at least one of the two cases holds for each $k < |\mu|$ and $l < |\nu|$. This operation results in the algorithm IsElasticTo. In the algorithm, the If-□-Fi construction indicates that if multiple guards are true, non-deterministically one of the guards evaluating true is chosen.

In this algorithm, if both conditions of the if clauses fail, sequence μ cannot be elastic to sequence ν, and hence, the algorithm fails. Otherwise, an interweaved firing sequence σ is returned, such that both $\mu \rightarrowtail_G \sigma$ and $\nu \rightarrowtail_G \sigma$.

Procedure IsElasticTo(μ,ν)

$(k, l, \sigma) := (0, 0, \epsilon)$;

{**Inv**: $\mu_{[1..k]} \rightarrowtail_G \nu_{[1..l]} \wedge \mu_{[1..k]} \rightarrowtail_G \sigma \wedge \nu_{[1..l]} \rightarrowtail_G \sigma$ }

while $(k < |\mu| \vee l < |\nu|)$ **do**

   if $k < |\mu| \wedge \overrightarrow{\mu_{[1..k+1]}}_{|R_{out}} \leq \overrightarrow{\nu_{[1..l]}}_{|R_{out}}$ **then**

      if $\mu(k+1) \notin (R_{in} \cup R_{out})$ **then**

       | $\sigma := \sigma; \langle \mu(k+1) \rangle$;

      fi

      $k := k+1$;

   □ $l < |\nu| \wedge \overrightarrow{\nu_{[1..l+1]}}_{|R_{in}} \leq \overrightarrow{\mu_{[1..k]}}_{|R_{in}}$ **then**

    | $(\sigma, l) := (\sigma; \langle \nu(l+1) \rangle, l+1)$;

   else

   | **return** ϵ;

   fi

od

return σ

Corollary 19. *Let N be a component and let $G \in \mathcal{G}_N$. Let $\mu, \nu \in T_N^*$. Then an invariant for procedure isElasticTo(μ,ν) is*

$$\mu_{[1..k]} \rightarrowtail_G \nu_{[1..l]} \wedge \mu_{[1..k]} \rightarrowtail_G \sigma \wedge \nu_{[1..l]} \rightarrowtail_G \sigma$$

Next, we need to show that the firing sequence constructed via IsElasticTo is executable. Given two OPNs A and B that are composable with respect to port G, we split the composition into $N_1 = \mathcal{C}_B(A)$ and $N_2 = \mathcal{S}(B)$. Every marking in the composition can be split into a marking in $\mathcal{S}(A)$, $\mathcal{S}(B)$ and some tokens in the interface places G. The marking in the interface G can again be split into places that are input for B, which we name x, and places that are output for B, which we name y. As shown in the next lemma, the elastic communication condition ensures that at each point in time, there are sufficient tokens in the interface places to continue.

Lemma 20. *Let A and B be two components such that they are composable with respect to some port $G \in \mathcal{G}_A \cap \mathcal{G}_B$. Define $G_I = G \cap I_B$, $G_O = G \cap O_B$, $N_1 = \mathcal{C}_B(A)$, $N_2 = \mathcal{S}(B)$ and $N = N_1 \cup N_2$. Let $m_0 \in \mathbb{N}^{P_{N_1}}$ be a marking, and let $\mu \in T_{N_1}^*$ be a firing sequence of length k such that for all $1 \leq i \leq |\mu|$, markings $m_{i-1}, m_i \in \mathbb{N}^{P_{N_1}}$ exist with $(N_1 : m_{i-1} \xrightarrow{\mu(i)} m_i)$. Let $\overline{m}_0 \in \mathbb{N}^{P_B}$ be a marking, and let $\nu \in T_B^*$ be a firing sequence of length l such that $\mu \rightarrowtail_G \nu$ and for all $1 \leq i \leq |\nu|$, markings $\overline{m}_{i-1}, \overline{m}_i \in \mathbb{N}^{P_{N_2}}$ exist with $(N_2 : \overline{m}_{i-1} \xrightarrow{\nu(i)} \overline{m}_i)$. Then, a firing sequence $\sigma \in T_N^*$ and a marking $m \in \mathbb{N}^{P_N}$ exist such that: (1) $\sigma = \text{IsElasticTo}(\mu,\nu)$; (2) $\sigma_{|T_A} = \mu_{|T_A}$ and $\sigma_{|T_B} = \nu_{|T_B}$; (3) $(N : m_0 + \overline{m}_0 \xrightarrow{\sigma} m)$; and (4) $m_{k|P_A} \leq m$, and $\overline{m}_l \leq m$.*

Proof. Define $R_{in} = \{t \in T_B \mid \lambda_G(t) = ?\}$, $R_{out} = \{t \in T_B \mid \lambda_G(t) = !\}$ and $R = R_{in} \cup R_{out}$. Note that $R = T_{N_1} \setminus T_{N_2}$.

We prove the lemma by induction on the structure of $\mu \rightarrowtail_G \nu$. The statement holds trivially for $\sigma = \epsilon$ and $m = m_0 + \overline{m}_0$.

Suppose the statement holds for some $\mu' \leq \mu$ and $\nu' \leq \nu$ such that $\mu' \rightarrowtail_G \nu'$, i.e. let $k = |\mu'|$ and $l = |\nu'|$, then for μ' and ν' a firing sequence $\sigma' \in T_N^*$ and marking $m' \in I\!N^{P_N}$ exist such that $\sigma' = \text{IsElasticTo}(\mu', \nu')$, $\sigma'_{|T_A} = \mu'_{|T_A}$ and $\sigma'_{|T_B} = \nu'_{|T_B}$ $(N : m_0 + \overline{m}_0 \xrightarrow{\sigma'} m')$ and $m_k \leq m'$, and $\overline{m}_l \leq m'$.

By the structure of $\rightarrowtail_G$, two cases need to be considered: $k < |\mu|$ and $\overrightarrow{\mu_{[1..k+1]}}_{|R_{out}} \leq \overrightarrow{\nu_{[1..l]}}_{|R_{out}}$ or (2) $l < |\nu|$ and $\overrightarrow{\nu_{[1..l+1]}}_{|R_{in}} \leq \overrightarrow{\mu_{[1..k]}}_{|R_{in}}$.

First suppose $k < |\mu|$ and $\overrightarrow{\mu_{[1..k+1]}}_{|R_{out}} \leq \overrightarrow{\nu_{[1..l]}}_{|R_{out}}$. Let $t = \mu(k+1)$. If $t \in R$, then $t \in T_B$. Hence, firing transition t does not change the internal marking of A, i.e. $m_{k|P_A} = m_{k+1|P_A}$. Choose $\sigma = \sigma'$ and $m = m'$. Then clearly the statement holds.

Otherwise, $t \notin R$. There are two cases to consider: either (a) ${}_N^\bullet t \cap G = \emptyset$ or (b) ${}_N^\bullet t \cap G \neq \emptyset$. If (a) ${}_N^\bullet t \cap G = \emptyset$, then ${}_N^\bullet t \leq m_{k|P_A} \leq m'$. Let $\sigma = \sigma'; \langle t \rangle$ and $m \in I\!N^{P_N}$ such that $(N : m' \xrightarrow{t} m)$. Hence, σ and m have the desired property. Next, suppose (b) ${}_N^\bullet t \cap G \neq \emptyset$. Then, transition t needs input from some places in the interface G. Since $t \notin R$, we have $\overrightarrow{\mu_{[1..k]}}_{|R_{out}} = \overrightarrow{\mu_{[1..k+1]}}_{|R_{out}} \leq \overrightarrow{\nu_{[1..l]}}_{|R_{out}} = \overrightarrow{\sigma'}_{|R_{out}}$. Let $p \in {}_N^\bullet t \cap G$ be an interface place in the preset of transition t. Since transition t is enabled in (N, m_k), we have $m_k(p) > 0$. By the marking equation, $m_k(p) = m_0(p) + \sum_{u \in {}^\bullet p} \overrightarrow{\mu_{[1..k]}}(u) - \sum_{u \in p^\bullet} \overrightarrow{\mu_{[1..k]}}(u)$. As place p is an interface place, $m_k(p) \leq m'(p)$. Thus, transition t is enabled in (N, m'). Let $\sigma = \sigma'; \langle t \rangle$ and $m \in I\!N^{P_N}$ such that $(N : m' \xrightarrow{t} m)$.

Suppose (2) $l < |\nu|$ and $\overrightarrow{\nu_{[1..l+1]}}_{|R_{in}} \leq \overrightarrow{\mu_{[1..k]}}_{|R_{in}}$. Let $t = \nu(l + 1)$. If ${}_N^\bullet t \cap G = \emptyset$, then ${}_N^\bullet t \leq m_l$. Hence, the statement holds for $\sigma = \sigma'; \langle t \rangle$ and $m \in I\!N^{P_N}$ such that $(N : m' \xrightarrow{t} m)$.

Otherwise, ${}_N^\bullet t \cap G \neq \emptyset$. Then $\lambda_G(t) =?$ and transition t needs input from A in order to be enabled in N. Hence, $t \in R_{in}$ and $\nu_{[1..l]|R_{in}}(t) < \mu_{[1..k]|R_{in}}(t)$. Let $p \in {}_N^\bullet t \cap G$ be an interface place in the preset of t. Consequently, $m_k(p) < m'(p)$, and transition t is enabled in (N, m'). Let $\sigma = \sigma'; \langle t \rangle$ and $m \in I\!N^{P_N}$ such that $(N : m' \xrightarrow{t} m)$. $\qquad \square$

Lemma 20 shows that a firing sequence and a firing sequence it is elastic to may be interweaved into a new firing sequence that is elastic to both sequences. As in elastic communication the number of occurrences of each communicating transition should be equal, we may directly conclude that Property 10 holds for the elastic sequence relation ψ.

Corollary 21 (Harlem shuffle). *Let A and B be two OPNs that are composable with respect to port $G \in \mathcal{G}_A \cap \mathcal{G}_B$. Let $N_1 = \mathcal{C}_B(A)$ and $N_2 = \mathcal{S}(B)$. Let $\mu \in T_{N_1}^*$ and $m, m' \in I\!N^{P_{N_1}}$ such that $(N_1 : m \xrightarrow{\mu} m')$. Let $\nu \in T_{N_2}^*$ and $\overline{m}, \overline{m}' \in I\!N^{P_{N_2}}$ such that $(N_2 : \overline{m} \xrightarrow{\nu} \overline{m}')$ and $\psi_G(\mu, \nu)$. Then, there exists $\sigma \in T_N^*$ such that $(\mathcal{S}(N) : m + \overline{m} \xrightarrow{\sigma} m' + \overline{m}')$, $\psi_G(\mu, \sigma)$ and $\psi_G(\nu, \sigma)$.*

From Corollaries 18 and 21 we can directly conclude that Condition com_ψ is a sufficient condition for compositional verification.

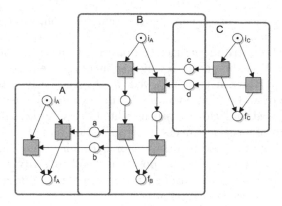

Fig. 7. Although net $A \oplus_G B \oplus_H C$ is sound, condition $\Psi_G(B, C)$ does not hold.

Theorem 22 (Elastic communication condition sufficient for soundness). *Let A, B and C be three OPNs such that A and B are composable with respect to $G \in \mathcal{G}_A \cap \mathcal{G}_B$, B and C are composable, A and C are disjoint and $A \oplus_G B$ is sound. If $\mathrm{com}_{\psi_G}(B, C)$ holds, then $A \oplus_G B \oplus_H C$ is sound.*

The framework does not provide a necessary condition. As shown in Fig. 7, also the elastic communication condition is not necessary. In this example, component A either receives an a or a b from component B. In the composition $B \oplus_H C$, component C decides which message will be sent by component B. Consider the marking $[i_B, d, f_C]$ of the composition $B \oplus C$. In this marking, the composition can only decide to send message b, whereas if we project this marking on B, i.e. we consider only the marking $[i_B]$, also message a could be sent. Hence, the condition does not hold for the example.

6   Conclusions

In this paper, we considered a sub class of dynamic networks of asynchronously comunicating systems. We presented a framework for compositional verification of such systems based on communication conditions.

The elastic communication condition is an example of using this framework. Given two sequences, the elastic communication condition allows transitions that send messages to occur earlier in the firing sequence, as long as it is produced before the token needs to be consumed. A simple algorithm exists to decide whether a firing sequence is elastic to another firing sequence, and if so, the algorithm returns an interweaved firing sequence of the two.

Related Work. In [7] the authors give a constructive method preserving the inheritance of behavior. As shown in [2] this can be used to guarantee the correctness of interorganizational processes. Other formalisms, like I/O automata [14] or interface automata [6] use synchronous communication, whereas we focus on asynchronous communication.

In [23], the author introduces place composition to model asynchronous communication focusing on the question which subnets can be exchanged such that the behavior of the whole net is preserved. In [13] the authors focus on deciding *controllability* of an OPN and computing its *operating guidelines*. Operating guidelines can be used to decide substitutability of services [21], or to prove that an implementation of a service meets its specification [5].

In [8], the authors propose to model choreographies using Interaction Petri nets. Similarly the authors of [11] propose a method to verify whether services agree to a choreography specification. However, in these approaches the whole network should be known at design-time.

In [9], the authors introduce an abstract component and interface algebra based on logic, where consistency is based on the composition of, possibly infinite, sets of traces of both the connections and the services. Although closely related, the approach presented in this paper focuses more on the process aspects of component-based design.

Future Work. Although we have shown that the elastic communication condition is sufficient, decidability of the condition remains future work. The proposed framework shows that post-design verification is a challenging task. As, in limitations one first shows oneself the master, we search for similar approaches as presented in [12] that guarantees the presented conditions during the construction of a network of asynchronously communication systems.

References

1. van der Aalst, W.M.P.: Verification of workflow nets. In: Azéma, P., Balbo, G. (eds.) ICATPN 1997. LNCS, vol. 1248, pp. 407–426. Springer, Heidelberg (1997)
2. van der Aalst, W.M.P.: Inheritance of interorganizational workflows: how to agree to disagree without loosing control? Inf. Technol. Manage. J. 4(4), 345–389 (2003)
3. van der Aalst, W.M.P., Beisiegel, M., van Hee, K.M., König, D., Stahl, C.: An SOA-based architecture framework. Int. J. Bus. process Integr. Manage. 2(2), 91–101 (2007)
4. van der Aalst, W.M.P., van Hee, K.M., Massuthe, P., Sidorova, N., van der Werf, J.M.: Compositional service trees. In: Franceschinis, G., Wolf, K. (eds.) PETRI NETS 2009. LNCS, vol. 5606, pp. 283–302. Springer, Heidelberg (2009)
5. van der Aalst, W.M.P., Lohmann, N., Massuthe, P., Stahl, C., Wolf, K.: Multiparty contracts: agreeing and implementing interorganizational processes. Comput. J. 53(1), 90–106 (2010)
6. de Alfaro, L., Henzinger, T.A.: Interface automata. SIGSOFT Softw. Eng. Notes 26(5), 109–120 (2001)
7. Basten, T., van der Aalst, W.M.P.: Inheritance of behavior. J. Logic Algebraic Program. 47(2), 47–145 (2001)
8. Decker, G., Weske, M.: Local enforceability in interaction petri nets. In: Alonso, G., Dadam, P., Rosemann, M. (eds.) BPM 2007. LNCS, vol. 4714, pp. 305–319. Springer, Heidelberg (2007)

9. Fiadeiro, J.L., Lopes, A.: An interface theory for service-oriented design. Theor. Comput. Sci. **503**, 1–30 (2013)
10. van Glabbeek, R.J.: The linear time - branching time spectrum II. In: Best, E. (ed.) CONCUR 1993. LNCS, vol. 715, pp. 66–81. Springer, Heidelberg (1993)
11. Gössler, G., Salaün, G.: Realizability of choreographies for services interacting asynchronously. In: Arbab, F., Ölveczky, P.C. (eds.) FACS 2011. LNCS, vol. 7253, pp. 151–167. Springer, Heidelberg (2012)
12. van Hee, K.M., Sidorova, N., van der Werf, J.M.: Construction of asynchronous communicating systems: weak termination guaranteed!. In: Baudry, B., Wohlstadter, E. (eds.) SC 2010. LNCS, vol. 6144, pp. 106–121. Springer, Heidelberg (2010)
13. Lohmann, N., Massuthe, P., Wolf, K.: Operating guidelines for finite-state services. In: Kleijn, J., Yakovlev, A. (eds.) ICATPN 2007. LNCS, vol. 4546, pp. 321–341. Springer, Heidelberg (2007)
14. Lynch, N.A., Tuttle, M.: Hierarchical correctness proofs for distributed algorithms. In: 6th Annual ACM Symposium on Principles of Distributed Computing (1987)
15. Massuthe, P.: Operating guidelines for services. Ph.D. thesis, Technische Universiteit Eindhoven (2009)
16. Massuthe, P., Serebrenik, A., Sidorova, N., Wolf, K.: Can I find a partner? Undecidability of partner existence for open nets. Inf. Process. Lett. **108**(6), 374–378 (2008)
17. McIlroy, M.D.: Mass produced software components. In: Naur, P., Randell, B. (eds.) Proceedings of NATA Software Engineering Conference, Garmisch Germany, vol. 1, pp. 138–150 (1968)
18. Papazoglou, M.P.: Web Services: Principles and Technology. Pearson/Prentice Hall, Tappan (2007)
19. Reisig, W.: Petri Nets: An Introduction. Monographs in Theoretical Computer Science: An EATCS Series, vol. 4. Springer, Berlin (1985)
20. Stahl, C.: Service substitution. Ph.D. thesis, Technische Universiteit Eindhoven (2009)
21. Stahl, C., Massuthe, P., Bretschneider, J.: Deciding substitutability of services with operating guidelines. In: Jensen, K., van der Aalst, W.M.P. (eds.) Transactions on Petri Nets and Other Models of Concurrency II. LNCS, vol. 5460, pp. 172–191. Springer, Heidelberg (2009)
22. Szyperski, C.: Component Software - Beyond Object-Oriented Programming. Addison-Wesley/ACM Press, New York (1998)
23. Vogler, W.: Asynchronous communication of petri nets and the refinement of transitions. In: Kuich, W. (ed.) Automata, Languages and Programming. LNCS, vol. 623, pp. 605–616. Springer, Heidelberg (1992)
24. van der Werf, J.M.E.M.: Compositional design and verification of component-based information systems. Ph.D. thesis, Technische Universiteit Eindhoven (2011)
25. Wolf, K.: Does my service have partners? In: Jensen, K., van der Aalst, W.M.P. (eds.) Transactions on Petri Nets and Other Models of Concurrency II. LNCS, vol. 5460, pp. 152–171. Springer, Heidelberg (2009)
26. Wolf, K., Stahl, C., Weinberg, D., Ott, J., Danitz, R.: Guaranteeing weak termination in service discovery. Fundam. Inf. **108**(1–2), 151–180 (2011)

Compositional Analysis Using Component-Oriented Interpolation

Viet Yen Nguyen[1,2]([✉]), Benjamin Bittner[3,4], Joost-Pieter Katoen[2], and Thomas Noll[2]

[1] Fraunhofer IESE, Kaiserslautern, Germany
`vietyen.nguyen@iese.fraunhofer.de`
[2] Software Modeling and Verification Group, RWTH Aachen University, Aachen, Germany
[3] Embedded Systems Group, Fondazione Bruno Kessler, Trento, Italy
[4] ICT School, University of Trento, Trento, Italy

Abstract. We present a novel abstraction technique that exploits the compositionality of a concurrent system consisting of interacting components. It uses, given an invariant and a component of interest, bounded model checking (BMC) to quickly interpolate an abstraction of that component's environment. The abstraction may be refined by increasing the BMC bound. Furthermore, it is only defined over variables shared between the component and its environment, resulting in an aggressive abstraction with several applications. We demonstrate its use in a verification setting, as we report on our open source implementation in the NuSMV model checker which was used to perform a practical assessment with industrially-sized models from satellite case studies of ongoing missions. These models are expressed in a formalized dialect of the component-oriented and industrially standardized Architecture Analysis and Design Language (AADL).

1 Introduction

An earlier work [11] reports on the application of a wide range of model checking techniques for validating a satellite platform of an ongoing mission. This industrially-sized model was expressed in a formalized dialect [2] of the Architecture Analysis and Design Language [12]. This AADL dialect is a component-oriented formalism in which components interact through data and event ports (i.e. shared variables). The sheer size of models was particularly visible once failures were injected. The nominal state space of roughly 48 million states exploded by a factor 213563 due to the activation of failure modes and the fault management functionality for handling it. The model checkers used in literature had a hard time on this model. Various techniques have been proposed in literature to cope with similar instances of the infamous state space explosion problem. In the context of this paper, compositional reasoning and interpolation are particularly relevant.

© Springer International Publishing Switzerland 2015
I. Lanese and E. Madelaine (Eds.): FACS 2014, LNCS 8997, pp. 68–85, 2015.
DOI: 10.1007/978-3-319-15317-9_5

The compositional reasoning technique by [8] was our starting point. It generates a so-called split invariant defined over the system's global variables for each parallel process. The split invariants are then checked against the property instead of the full composition of processes. It was shown later [15,18] that this technique, along with Cartesian abstract interpretation [18] and thread-modular verification [13], is conceptually the same as the classical Owicki-Gries paradigm, but differs in the details. They generally work well for parallel systems where processes communicate over a *small* set of *global variables*, i.e. variables that are visible to *all* processes. In the satellite models, components are highly cohesive through *shared variables*, as variables of one component are only visible to a handful of other components. The techniques from the Owicki-Gries paradigm are ineffective here as naively all shared variables would have to be interpreted as global variables, which would make it a near-monolithic model checking problem again. Another branch of compositional reasoning is the rely/assume guarantee/provide techniques. There is a huge body of work behind this. The most related ones are the automated methods that use learning techniques to generate assumptions [5]. Our work is a twist on this, because instead of learning we use *interpolation* to generate an environment. That environment can be then viewed as an assumption for which the property of interest may hold. The use of interpolation techniques [9] in model checking was pioneered by McMillan [19]. Also this led to a substantial body of work. To our knowledge, it however has not been cast into a compositional reasoning scheme as we describe in this paper.

Contributions: The contributions of this paper are as follows.

- A theory inspired by Craig interpolation that results in an aggressive abstraction of the environment of a component of interest, resulting into a component-oriented interpolant.
- A rudimentary (re)verification algorithm that exploits this theory.
- An open source implementation of the algorithm in NuSMV 2.5.4 [4].
- An evaluation of the theory and implementation using industrially-sized models from satellite platform case studies of ongoing missions.

Organization: Section 2 explains applicable background information and introduces the majority of the formal notation used in this paper. Section 3 describes the theoretical contribution of this paper, the component-oriented interpolant. We implemented it into an algorithm and evaluated it using satellite platform case studies on which we report in Sect. 4. Related work and the conclusions are discussed respectively in Sects. 5 and 6.

2 Preliminaries

Our work builds upon existing works in satisfiability (SAT) solving, bounded model checking and Craig interpolation. These are discussed in the following.

SAT Solving: Propositional formulae consist of literals, which are Boolean variables (e.g. x_1) that can be negated (e.g. $\neg x_1$), and are combined by AND (i.e. $\wedge$) and OR (i.e. $\vee$) operators. They are typically processed from their conjunctive normal form (CNF) where the formula consists of conjuncted clauses (e.g. $(\neg x_1) \wedge (x_1 \vee \neg x_2)$) and each clause is a disjunction of literals (e.g. $(x_1 \vee \neg x_2)$). As we can view CNF formulae as a set of clauses, we use the set membership notation to check whether a clause is part of a CNF formulae, e.g. $(x_1 \vee \neg x_2) \in A$ with A being a CNF formula. A classical decision problem is whether, given a propositional formula, there exists a satisfying assignment, i.e. a vector of values holding either true (i.e. $\top$) or false (i.e. $\bot$) for each variable. This is the NP-complete SAT problem. Yearly competitions have highly stimulated research in this area, progressing modern SAT-solvers to handle formulae with thousands of variables in mere seconds. They typically generate the satisfying assignment, denoted as σ, as a proof of satisfiability. In case of unsatisfiability, some SAT-solvers provide a resolution refutation graph as a proof [19]. An example of a resolution refutation graph is shown in Fig. 2. It is a directed acyclic graph $G = (V, E)$, where V is a set of clauses (not necessarily a subset of the original formula). If a vertex $v \in V$ is a root (there are usually multiple), then it is a clause in the original formula. Otherwise the vertex has exactly two predecessors, v_1 and v_2 of the form $v_1 = x \vee D$ and $v_2 = \neg x \vee D'$. The clause v is the simplification of $D \vee D'$ and x is its *pivot variable*. There is only one leaf which is the empty clause $\bot$. The resolution graph reasons how clauses, starting from the root clauses, have pivot variables that can be eliminated, as they contribute to the inconsistency. Once all variables are eliminated, the empty clause $\bot$ is reached, indicating unsatisfiability.

Bounded Model Checking: Propositional formulae can be used to verify a property (e.g. ϕ) of a model $M = (I, T)$. The initial condition $I(\bar{s})$ is a Boolean formula over a finite set of variables, e.g. $\bar{s} = s_1, \ldots, s_n$. The set of occurring variables is denoted by the predicate *var*, e.g. $var(I) = \{s_1, \ldots, s_n\}$. Whenever a particular valuation σ of $\bar{s}$ satisfies I, i.e. $\sigma(I) = \top$, then σ is an initial state. Multiple distinct initial states may satisfy I. The transition function, denoted as $T(\bar{s} \times \bar{s}')$, is a propositional function with $\bar{s} = s_1, \ldots, s_n$ and $\bar{s}' = s_1', \ldots, s_n'$. Note that the cardinalities of $\bar{s}$ and $\bar{s}'$ are equal. If for a pair of valuations σ and σ' the transition function holds, i.e. $\sigma\sigma'(T) = \top$, then σ' is a valid successor state to state σ. The initial condition and the transition function are used to compute the reachable states up to a natural bound k using the formula $I[\bar{s}/\bar{r}_0] \wedge \bigwedge_{i=1}^{k} T[\bar{s}/\bar{r}_{i-1}, \bar{s}'/\bar{r}_i]$. It uses the substitution operator $T[x/y]$ to denote that all occurrences of x in T are substituted by y. We refer to $I_0 \wedge T_1 \wedge \cdots \wedge T_k$ as its simplified notation. An invariant ϕ can be verified by conjuncting its negated unrolling, $\bigvee_{i=0}^{k} \neg\phi[\bar{s}/\bar{r}_i]$, to it. To ease notation, we simply refer to this formula as $\neg\phi$. The resulting formula, $I_0 \wedge \bigwedge_{i=1}^{k} T_i \wedge \neg\phi$, can be checked for satisfiability. If it is satisfiable, the satisfying assignment is a counterexample to the invariant. If it is unsatisfiable, then the invariant holds up to bound k, which is denoted by $M \models_k \phi$. An outcome w.r.t. the full state space is however inconclusive [1].

Example 1 (Two-Bit Counter). Part of our running example is a simple two-bit counter that is initialized to 0. It is incremented by 1 with each transition until it hits the value 3. The Boolean encodings of its initial condition and transition functions look as follows:

$$I = \neg\alpha \wedge \neg\beta$$
$$T = (\neg\alpha \vee \alpha') \wedge (\neg\alpha \vee \beta') \wedge (\alpha \vee \neg\alpha' \vee \beta) \wedge (\alpha \vee \neg\beta \vee \neg\beta') \wedge (\alpha' \vee \beta')$$

Its one-step unrolling looks as follows:

$$I_0 \wedge T_1 = (\neg\alpha_0 \wedge \neg\beta_0) \wedge (\neg\alpha_0 \vee \alpha_1) \wedge (\neg\alpha_0 \vee \beta_1)$$
$$\wedge (\alpha_0 \vee \neg\alpha_1 \vee \beta_0) \wedge (\alpha_0 \vee \neg\beta_0 \vee \neg\beta_1) \wedge (\alpha_1 \vee \beta_1)$$

(end of example)

Interpolation: Our work is heavily inspired by Craig's seminal result [9].

Theorem 1 (Craig's Interpolation Theorem). *Let A and B be formulae of first-order logic. If $A \implies B$ holds, then there exists an interpolant C expressed using the common variables of A and B, i.e. $var(C) \subseteq var(A) \cap var(B)$, such that $A \implies C$ and $C \implies B$ holds.*

A proof of this theorem restricted to propositional logic can be found in [3]. The beauty of this theorem is that the interpolant C is expressed using a subset of the variables in A. This powerful notion inspired us for developing our compositional reasoning technique.

Note that Craig's theorem only postulates the existence of an interpolant when $A \implies B$. This can be verified with a SAT-solver. Observe that $A \implies B$ is equivalent to $\neg(A \wedge \neg B)$. This means its tautology infers the contradiction of $A \wedge \neg B$. By Craig's interpolation theorem it follows that if $A \wedge \neg B$ is unsatisfiable, there exists an interpolant C such that $A \implies C$ holds and $C \wedge \neg B$ is unsatisfiable. Thus in this shape, the unsatisfiability of a formula indicates the existence of an interpolant. It is shown in [20] how an interpolant C is generated from the resolution refutation proof resulting from the unsatisfiability of $A \wedge \neg B$. We use a similar approach to abstract a component's environment as a transition function.

3   Component-Oriented Interpolation

Our setting is a concurrent system composed of processes (also referred to as components with behavior) using a parallel composition operator. We leverage this composition to reason over its behaviour in a compositional manner. In the upcoming, we will describe our approach in the synchronous case only, i.e. all components transit per global transition. It can however be extended to the asynchronous case (i.e. interleaving transitions) by complementing the asynchronous model with an interleaving scheduler component that regulates which component progresses upon a transition.

Consider a synchronous composition of n processes $M^1, \ldots, M^n$, with their associated transition relations T^i and initial conditions I^i such that $T = \bigwedge_{i=1}^{n} T^i$ and $I = \bigwedge_{i=1}^{n} I^i$. When this is applied to the bounded model checking formula, the result is $\bigwedge_{i=1}^{n} I_0^i \wedge \bigwedge_{i=1}^{n} T_1^i \wedge \ldots \wedge \bigwedge_{i=1}^{n} T_k^i \wedge \neg\phi$. We can now isolate any process M^p such that the remainder processes, i.e. process p's environment, shall be abstracted through interpolation. It then becomes more apparent how A and $\neg B$ from Theorem 1 are to be determined:

$$\underbrace{I_0^p \wedge T_1^p \wedge \ldots \wedge T_k^p \wedge \neg\phi}_{\neg B} \wedge \underbrace{I_0^{\neq p} \wedge T_1^{\neq p} \wedge \ldots \wedge T_k^{\neq p}}_{A} \tag{1}$$

In the above, $I_0^{\neq p} = \bigwedge_{q \in \{1,\ldots,n\} \setminus \{p\}} I_0^q$, and similarly for $T_i^{\neq p}$.

Example 2 (Counter Monitor). Let us refer to the counter example of Example 1 as M^1. We now add a monitoring process, M^2, that among its functions, raises a flag when the counter exceeds 2. The Boolean encoding of M^2, where both δ and γ are flags and the latter being the flag of interest, looks as follows:

$$I^2 = \neg\gamma \wedge \delta$$
$$T^2 = (\neg\alpha \vee \neg\beta \vee \neg\delta') \wedge (\neg\alpha \vee \gamma') \wedge (\alpha \vee \neg\gamma) \wedge (\alpha \vee \neg\gamma') \wedge (\beta \vee \neg\gamma) \wedge (\delta' \vee \gamma)$$

From this point on we shall use the synchronous composition $M^1 \wedge M^2$ as our ongoing running example. Let us say we are interested to see whether the flag γ always stays unraised, i.e. the invariant $\neg\gamma$. And let us isolate process M^1, i.e. $p = 1$, from the synchronous composition. This isolation on a two-step BMC unrolling would look as follows:

$$\underbrace{I_0^1 \wedge T_1^1 \wedge \wedge T_2^1 \wedge (\gamma_0 \vee \gamma_1 \vee \gamma_2)}_{\neg B} \wedge \underbrace{I_0^2 \wedge T_1^2 \wedge \wedge T_2^2}_{A} \tag{2}$$

(end of example)

From Theorem 1, it follows that whenever the invariant holds within bound k, there exists an interpolant C, such that it is implied by A. Intuitively, the interpolant C can be perceived as an abstraction of the k-fold unrolled environment of process p. It is significantly smaller than the original formula representing the k-bounded environment, since it is only defined over the variables used for interacting with process p over bound k. That is, $var(C) \subseteq var(I_0^{\neq p}, T_1^{\neq p}, \ldots, T_k^{\neq p}) \cap var(I_0^p, T_1^p, \ldots, T_k^p, \phi)$, where $var(S_1, \ldots, S_n)$ is a shorthand for $var(S_1) \cup \ldots \cup var(S_n)$. Observe that C is not a formula over current/next states, because it is interpolated from the unrolling of $T^{\neq p}$ instead of $T^{\neq p}$ itself. In that form, the interpolant C is only useful for k-bounded reverification of component p. It would only conclude whether the invariant still holds for a partial state space, namely up to a depth k. We strive for a different kind of interpolant that can conclude whether the invariant still holds for the full state space. We call it the *component-oriented interpolant*.

To this end, let us have a closer look at the sharing of variables in the component-oriented interpolation setting, as it is slightly different from Craig interpolation. In the latter, there are two sets of variables that can be partitioned into three disjoint sets of variables, namely $var(A) \setminus var(B)$, $var(B) \setminus var(A)$ and $var(A) \cap var(B)$. This is shown in Fig. 1a where the sets are respectively denoted

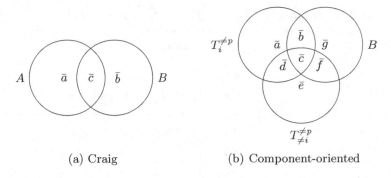

(a) Craig   (b) Component-oriented

Fig. 1. Relation of variables in both interpolation settings.

as $\bar{a}$, $\bar{b}$, $\bar{c}$. In our component-oriented setting, there are three sets of variables which can be partitioned into seven disjoint sets. See Fig. 1b. Consider any step i by component p's environment, i.e. $T_i^{\neq p}(\bar{a}, \bar{b}, \bar{c}, \bar{d})$. The remainder environment transition steps are $T_{\neq i}^{\neq p}(\bar{e}, \bar{d}, \bar{c}, \bar{f})$ and the transition steps by component p and the property ϕ are $B(\bar{g}, \bar{f}, \bar{c}, \bar{b})$. The variables of $I_0^{\neq p}$ are omitted here for clarity and are covered w.l.o.g. by the variables of $T_1^{\neq p}$.

Example 3 (Variable Sharing in Counter Monitor). Reconsider Eq. (2), the two-step BMC unrolling of the counter monitor (cf. Example 2). The variable partitioning of that unrolling in the Craig interpolation case is: $\bar{a} = \{\alpha_2, \beta_2\}$, $\bar{b} = \{\alpha_0, \alpha_1, \beta_0, \beta_1, \gamma_0, \gamma_1, \gamma_2\}$ and $\bar{c} = \{\delta_0, \delta_1, \delta_2\}$.

The partitions are more fine-grained in the component-oriented interpolation case. If we would take $p = 1$ and $i = 1$ on our running example, we would get the following arrangement out of Eq. (2):

$$\underbrace{I_0^1 \wedge T_1^1 \wedge \wedge T_2^1 \wedge (\gamma_0 \vee \gamma_1 \vee \gamma_2)}_{\neg B} \wedge \underbrace{I_0^2 \wedge T_1^2}_{T_1^{\neq 1}} \wedge \underbrace{\wedge T_2^2}_{T_{\neq 1}^{\neq 1}}$$

The partitioning of Fig. 1b then applies, resulting in the following partitioning:

$\bar{a} = \{\delta_0, \delta_1\}$	$\bar{d} = \{\}$	$\bar{g} = \{\alpha_2, \beta_2\}$
$\bar{b} = \{\alpha_0, \beta_0, \gamma_0\}$	$\bar{e} = \{\delta_2\}$	
$\bar{c} = \{\gamma_1\}$	$\bar{f} = \{\alpha_1, \beta_1, \gamma_2\}$	

(end of example)

We use the finer grained notion of variable sharing in Fig. 1b to construct component-oriented interpolants by traversing the resolution refutation graph of Eq. (1) for each step i of component p's environment:

Definition 1 (Component-Oriented Interpolant Construction). *Let us consider step $i \leq k$ of a component p's environment. Furthermore, let $G = (V, E)$ be the resolution refutation graph of Eq. (1) and partition the occurring variables* *into disjoint sets according to Fig. 1b. For each non-root vertex $v \in V$, let v_1 and v_2 be its predecessors and x its pivot variable. Then, with each $v \in V$ we associate a Boolean formula C_v^i given as follows*

$$C_v^i = \begin{cases} \bot & \text{if } v \in T_i^{\neq p} \text{ and } v \text{ is root} \\ \top & \text{if } v \in T_{\neq i}^{\neq p} \cup I^{\neq p} \cup B \text{ and } v \text{ is root} \\ (\neg x \wedge C_{v_1}^i) \vee (x \wedge C_{v_2}^i) & \text{if } x \in \bar{b} \cup \bar{c}, x \in v_1, \neg x \in v_2, \text{ and } v \text{ is non-root} \\ C_{v_1}^i \vee C_{v_2}^i & \text{if } x \in \bar{a} \cup \bar{d} \text{ and } v \text{ is non-root} \\ C_{v_1}^i \wedge C_{v_2}^i & \text{if } x \in \bar{g} \cup \bar{f} \cup \bar{e} \text{ and } v \text{ is non-root} \end{cases}$$

We refer to the formula C_v^i for the leaf vertex $v = \bot$ as the full interpolant *of step i. All other interpolants are referred to as* partial interpolants.

If Definition 1 is applied starting from the leaf $\bot$, one gets a component-oriented interpolant for $T_i^{\neq p}$.

Example 4 (Component-Oriented Interpolation on Counter Monitor). Consider Fig. 2. As it is an unrolling for two steps, there are partial interpolants for the first and second step, i.e. respectively C_v^1 and a C_v^2. Take for example the upper-left three-node subtree. That is $v = \neg\gamma_1$ and its two predecessors as $v_1 = \alpha_0 \vee \neg\gamma_1$ and $v_2 = \neg\alpha_0$. The pivot is therefore α_0. As we determined earlier in Example 3 that α_0 is in $\bar{b}$, the partial interpolant of v for transition step 1 becomes $(\neg\alpha_0 \wedge C_{v_1}^1) \vee (\alpha_0 \wedge C_{v_2}^1)$. Since $C_{v_1}^1 = \bot$ and $C_{v_2}^1 = \top$, this is simplified to $C_v^1 = \alpha_0$.
(end of example)

This interpolant is weak enough to preserve the over-approximation from Craig interpolation, i.e. $T_i^{\neq p} \implies C_\bot^i$. This is captured by the following lemma:

Lemma 1 (Over-Approximation by Component-Oriented Interpolant).
Let σ be a valuation such that $\sigma(v) = \bot$ for any $v \in V$ in Definition 1. For any $1 \leq i \leq k$, the following holds:

$$\sigma(C_v^i) = \bot \implies \exists a \in T_i^{\neq p} :: \sigma(a) = \bot \tag{3}$$

Intuitively, this means that whenever the partial interpolant C_v^i evaluates to false for a particular valuation, a clause of $T_i^{\neq p}$ evaluates to false as well for the same valuation, causing the whole formula (see Eq. (1)) to evaluate to false.

Proof. Due to paper size constraints, we only provide a proof sketch. The full proof is by induction on the structure of C_v^i and follows the reasoning in [21]. The base case is trivial to show. For the inductive step, there are three cases, namely that the pivot variable x of vertex v is either in $\bar{b} \cup \bar{c}$ or in $\bar{a} \cup \bar{d}$ or in $\bar{g} \cup \bar{f} \cup \bar{e}$. See Fig. 1.

By the definition of the resolution refutation graph, each non-root vertex has two predecessors v_1 and v_2. It can be shown that regardless of each of the three cases, whenever $\sigma(C_v^i) = \bot$ either predecessor branch evaluates to false for both the intermediate component-oriented interpolant and the predecessor vertex, e.g. $\sigma(v_1) = \bot$ and $\sigma(C_{v_1}^i) = \bot$. Then by induction, Eq. (3) can be concluded. $\square$

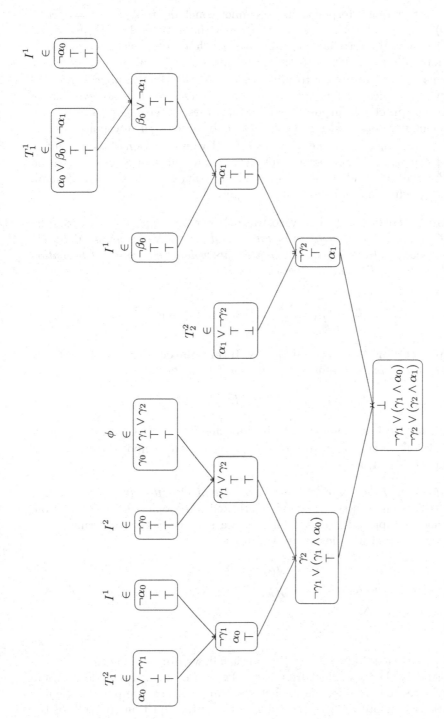

Fig. 2. An annotated resolution refutation graph from our two-step BMC unrolling of Eq. (2). Each node contains three lines. The first line identifies the vertex $v \in V$. The second and third lines are respectively C_v^1 and C_v^2 obtained through the application of Definition 1. The root nodes are annotated with $\in$, meaning that the clause identifying the vertex is part of the formula, e.g. $\neg\alpha_0 \in I^1$.

Contrary to Craig interpolation, we cannot conclude $\sigma(C_v^i) = \top \implies \exists b \in$ $B :: \sigma(b) = \bot$ and thus preserve the unsatisfiability of Eq. (1) using the component-oriented interpolant. It could also be that whenever the component-oriented interpolant evaluates to true, a clause in $T_{\neq i}^{\neq p}$ evaluates to false. Or that a clause in $I^{\neq p}$ evaluates to false. In that sense, the component-oriented interpolant is significantly weaker than a Craig interpolant. It is however strong enough for our practical purposes, as is demonstrated later in Sect. 4.

The component-oriented interpolant $C_\bot^i$ only derives an interpolated environment for transition step i, i.e. $T_i^{\neq p} \implies C_\bot^i$. By substitution of the occurring variables to current and successor-state variables, it can be used as a transition function for the unbounded case. This holds for each $1 \le i \le k$. So in general, the following definition and theorem are applicable:

Definition 2 (Interpolated Environment). *Let the component-oriented interpolants $C_\bot^1, \ldots, C_\bot^k$ be derived from the resolution refutation graph of Eq. (1) using Definition 1. The component-oriented interpolated environment transition function, defined as E^p, can be derived as such:*

$$E^p = \bigwedge_{i=1}^{k} C_\bot^i (\bar{r}_{i-1}, \bar{r}_i)[\bar{r}_{i-1}/\bar{s}, \bar{r}_i/\bar{s}']$$

Theorem 2 (Over-Approximation by Interpolated Environment). *Let E^p be given according to Definition 2. It then follows that*

$$T^{\neq p} \implies E^p \tag{4}$$

Proof. This follows from Lemma 1 which shows that $T_i^{\neq p} \implies C_\bot^i$. As $var(C_\bot^i) \subseteq var(T_i^{\neq p})$, it follows that $T^{\neq p} \implies C_\bot^i[\bar{r}_{i-1}/\bar{s}, \bar{r}_i/\bar{s}']$. By composition of implications of each i, Eq. (4) follows.   □

Example 5 (Transition Function from Component-Oriented Interpolants). Let us apply Definition 2 on the component-oriented interpolants $C_\bot^1$ and $C_\bot^2$ from our running example (cf. Fig. 2). That is, we substitute the occurring timed variables into current and next-state variables:

$$\begin{aligned} E^p &= C_\bot^1[\alpha_0/\alpha, \gamma_1/\gamma'] \wedge C_\bot^2[\alpha_1/\alpha, \gamma_2/\gamma'] \\ &= (\neg\gamma_1 \vee (\gamma_1 \wedge \alpha_0))[\alpha_0/\alpha, \gamma_1/\gamma'] \wedge (\neg\gamma_2 \vee (\gamma_2 \wedge \alpha_1))[\alpha_1/\alpha, \gamma_2/\gamma'] \\ &= \neg\gamma' \vee (\gamma' \wedge \alpha) \\ &= \alpha \vee \neg\gamma' \end{aligned}$$

Since we partitioned $T^{\neq p} = T^2$ in Eq. (2), it follows from Eq. (4) that $T^2 \implies \alpha \vee \neg\gamma'$. This is clearly evident from the definition of T^2 in Example 2, where the interpolated environment is in fact the third clause. Component-oriented interpolation therefore reduces the original transition function to $1/6^{\text{th}}$ of the amount of clauses.   *(end of example)*

Applications: Theorem 2 can be applied in several ways. We elaborate on a few possible applications in the following.

Manual inspection for example becomes more feasible. Models as large and complex as the one mentioned in Sect. 1 are labor-intensive to analyze manually, yet this is often the pragmatical approach by industry for verifying/validating involved requirements. The interpolated environment of Theorem 2 can support this. Assume one is intimate with a particular (set of) component(s), e.g. the power system. The remainder components can be viewed as a rather unfamiliar environment that can be abstracted in terms of variables shared with the power system. Such an abstraction is significantly smaller and thus eases manual inspection. The abstraction is cheap to compute, as it can be obtained for a bound as small as $k = 1$, although a larger k is preferable since this possibly strengthens the accuracy of the environment.

It can also be used as an abstraction method in model checking. Consider the invariant checking case and assume a tractable bound k for $M \models_k \phi$. Yet it is unclear whether it holds beyond the tractable bound k. One can pick a component p and use Theorem 2 to over-approximate the remainder to E^p. Heuristically it is wise to include at least the component directly referred to by ϕ as p, as they directly affect the property of interest. Then the smaller model $(I^p, T^p \wedge E^p)$ can be subjected to unbounded model checking to verify $M \models \phi$. An example of such an algorithm is discussed later in Sect. 4. Note that the transition function $T^p \wedge E^p$ could be too weak. Thus, if a counterexample is found during unbounded model checking, one has to distinguish whether it is a false-negative due to over-approximation of E^p, or whether it is a counterexample that also occurs in the original model. Techniques from CEGAR (counterexample guided abstraction refinement) [7,10] can be utilized for this. Theorem 2 can also supplement existing CEGAR techniques, as it can generate computationally cheap abstractions.

Partial model reverification is also a suitable application. In monolithic model checking, refinements or changes of the model require a full reverification round. Theorem 2 can speed this up. Assume only a part of the model is changed, for example component p. The unchanged environment can be interpolated from previous verifications. The resulting interpolated environment is smaller in size. Instead of reverifying the full model, the modified component p and the interpolant of the unchanged environment E^p can be used. Since reverification with the smaller model $(I^p, T^p \wedge E^p)$ is likely to be faster, as less variables are present, it can be used less reluctantly upon changes to component p, thus providing more direct and continuous feedback during the construction of the model. Note that here over-approximation might cause false counterexamples as well and therefore warrant the use of CEGAR techniques.

4   Evaluation on Satellite Case Studies

We developed a prototype implementation utilizing Theorem 2 in NuSMV 2.5.4 and applied it to industrially-sized models of satellite case studies reported in [11]. The resulting data provides an indication of the quality of the abstraction, as well as its effectiveness when used for manual inspection or (re)verification.

Tool Implementation: The prototype implementation is an extension of NuSMV 2.5.4 [4]. We reused NuSMV's data structures and functionality for representing and handling propositional formulae. The SAT-solving was performed by MiniSAT 1.14p. We deliberately chose version 1.14p over newer versions, as it is – at the moment – the only publicly available version that can generate resolution refutation graphs upon unsatisfiability. Additionally, NuSMV has a preexisting integration with MiniSAT which we extended for handling those graphs. The models are expressed in SLIM, a formalized dialect of AADL. We used the SLIM-to-SMV translator built in the COMPASS toolset for obtaining their SMV representations [2].

Case Description: We ran our evaluation with two large industrially-sized models. They are system-software models based on design data of Earth-orbiting satellites in development.

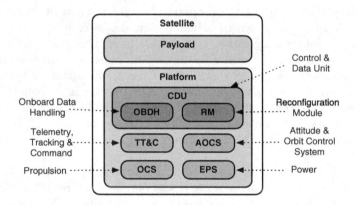

Fig. 3. Decomposition of the PDR satellite model.

The first model is from the case study reported in [11]. We call it the PDR satellite platform model. It was constructed from the design data available during the satellite's preliminary design review (PDR). Its global decomposition into subsystems is shown in Fig. 3. The OCS consists of a series of controllable thrusters for orbital corrections. The AOCS is a control system consisting of several kinds of sensors for acquiring and maintaining a correct attitude and orbit. The CDU is the main computer. The EPS consists of solar arrays and batteries for powering the satellite and the TT&C is the radio communication interface for ground control on Earth. The focus of the PDR model is the relation of the system's nominal behavior, its erroneous behavior (e.g. faults) and the subsequent behaviors resulting from the fault tolerance strategies by the fault management design. Its nominal state space is roughly 48 million states.

This number multiplies rapidly when failures are injected, thus activating failure modes and the associated fault management strategies. The case is modeled in our AADL dialect and comprises 3,831 lines of code, not counting comments.

The second model is a refinement of the PDR model. We call it the CDR model. It was crafted from the design data available during the critical design review (CDR) of the same satellite mission. During the CDR, more design details have been decided upon. It is estimated that the amount of design data increased twofold. The CDR model's nominal behavior state space nevertheless counts 2,341 states thanks to the effective modeling lessons learned from the PDR case study. The CDR model is however more detailed, more complex and more difficult to analyze. Akin to the PDR model, its state space multiplies once failures are injected. It is composed of 6,357 lines of AADL code, not counting comments. A more detailed report of this model is currently being prepared for publication.

We considered several configurations of the PDR and the CDR models. The final configurations outlined below are known to require a bound $k > 1$ for proving or disproving the invariant property of interest [11]. The first two configurations are from the PDR model, whereas the remaining three are from the CDR model. Note that the models are based on proprietary designs. Their details are therefore not publicly available.

Model	Fault injections	Property
PDR-1	Earth sensor failure	Fail-operational flag is set
PDR-2	Propulsion failure	AOCS status flags are consistent
CDR-3	Various platform failures	Not in safe mode
CDR-4	(none, i.e. nominal behaviour)	Solar voltage level is consistent
CDR-5	(none, i.e. nominal behaviour)	Not in safe mode

Comparison Factors: All experiments were run on a Linux 64-bits machine equipped with a 2.33 GHz multi-core CPU and 32 GB RAM. We set the maximum computation time to 900 s. Our implementation is however single-threaded. The exploitation of the multiple cores in a multi-threaded fashion is future work.

We intended to use NuSMV's BDD-based verification as the baseline. We however quickly learned that the BDDs were ineffective on both the PDR and CDR model. BDD-based verification was a magnitude slower on PDR configurations than the other techniques we considered (see Table 1). On CDR configurations, the time for constructing the transition functions exceeded the 900 s by far, thus leaving no time for the verification. We therefore omit BDD-verification data and decided upon another technique as the baseline.

We used McMillan's interpolation-based unbounded model checking technique for invariants [20] instead. It starts by k-bounded model checking the property. Then it (Craig) interpolates the first transition step $C \implies I \wedge T_1$. This interpolant is a weakened characterization of one-step successor states $\bar{s}_1$.

These states are added to I by variable substitution, i.e. $I \leftarrow I \vee C[\bar{s}_1/\bar{s}_0]$. The new I is a characterization of the original initial states and the one-step successor states. It is then used to bounded model check the property up to bound k, thus reaching a search depth of $k+1$. This is repeated until a fixpoint is reached. A sketch of the algorithm can be found in [20]. It is furthermore also part of Algorithm 1 from lines 5 to 8, which we shall explain shortly after. We implemented the algorithm in NuSMV as there was no pre-existing implementation. The interpolation scheme we implemented is by McMillan as well [19] and it has been studied thoroughly for use in this setting [10].

The component-oriented interpolation technique has been casted into a verification scheme. We heuristically chose the components p by selecting those directly referred in the property. Given this, the remaining procedure is shown in Algorithm 1. Intuitively, it obtains an interpolated environment (line 3), which is then used in an inner reachability analysis (lines 5–8) until a fixpoint is encountered (line 8), meaning that the property holds. Otherwise, the bound is increased in the hope for a stronger interpolated environment (line 9). The overall algorithm can terminate in two ways: either a concrete (and real) counterexample is eventually found at depth k while executing line 2, or reachability analysis on the over-approximated model reaches a fixpoint without violation of the property (line 8). Note that even though any inner reachability algorithm could be used, we employed McMillan's interpolant-based invariant checking algorithm here. This is mainly for efficiency reasons of staying in a SAT-based context. If for example BDD-based reachability techniques were used, we would have to convert E^p, I^p and T^p to BDDs, resulting in additional overhead.

Algorithm 1. Component-Oriented Interpolation-based Invariant Checking.

1: $k \leftarrow 1$
2: **while** $\neg\phi \wedge I_0^p \wedge T_1^p \wedge \cdots \wedge T_k^p \wedge I_0^{\neq p} \wedge T_1^{\neq p} \wedge \cdots \wedge T_k^{\neq p}$ is unsatisfiable **do**
3:    $E^p \leftarrow$ component-oriented interpolant of $I_0^{\neq p} \wedge T_1^{\neq p} \wedge \cdots \wedge T_k^{\neq p}$
4:    $R \leftarrow I^p$
5:    **while** $R \wedge T_1^p \wedge E_1^p \wedge \cdots \wedge T_k^p \wedge E_k^p \neg\phi$ is unsatisfiable **do**
6:       $C \leftarrow$ Craig interpolant of $R \wedge T_1^p \wedge E_1^p$
7:       **if** $C \wedge \neg R$ is satisfiable **then** $R \leftarrow R \vee C$
8:       **else**[no new states explored] **return** ϕ holds
9:    $k \leftarrow k + 1$
10: **return** counterexample extracted from the satisfying assignment

---

Experiment Data and Discussion: A summary of the experiment data is presented in Table 1. We kept track of the depth needed to determine whether the property holds or whether there exists a counterexample. This depth k is the column "Bound" in Table 1. A smaller bound indicates a faster convergence of the abstraction.

The results indicate that the CDR model has a higher complexity than the PDR model. This was expected due to the doubling of design details in the CDR design data. The results furthermore indicate that the verification by

Table 1. Summary of verification outcome, needed bound k, verification time and peak memory consumption for McMillan's interpolation-based invariant checking (MCM) and the component-oriented interpolation-based invariant checking (COMP).

Case	Technique	Outcome	Bound	Time (sec)	Mem (Mb)
PDR-1	MCM	Counterexample	3	2.42	95.9
	COMP	Counterexample	3	3.52	111.9
PDR-2	MCM	Counterexample	2	1.77	92.0
	COMP	Counterexample	2	2.28	100.4
CDR-3	MCM	Counterexample	11	486.06	651.0
	COMP	Counterexample	11	338.56	865.5
CDR-4	MCM	Holds	4	7.10	125.7
	COMP	Holds	3	7.00	138.0
CDR-5	MCM	Holds	7	69.20	171.5
	COMP	Holds	3	8.10	137.0

the component-oriented interpolation method is competitive. This is in particular visible for CDR-3 and CDR-5, where the computation time is significantly better. The reason for this is the needed bound k. A small k appears to suffice for a quality abstraction. Note that these measures cannot be trivially generalized. Timings depend heavily on the used SAT-solver, in particular on the heuristics it employs, the possibly imposed randomness influenced by the order of clauses, or by the choice of the target system. These factors are inherent to the nature of current-day SAT-solvers. The numbers should therefore be interpreted as indications.

While the experiment data indicate a positive influence of component-oriented interpolation, we suspect that the way it is used in this evaluation suffers from double abstraction. Observe that in Algorithm 1 two abstraction techniques are jointly used. The first comes from component-oriented interpolation which is a possible source of false counterexamples. The second comes from inner reachability analysis (line 6 of Algorithm 1), which may add further false counterexamples. Each abstract counterexample of the inner reachability analysis turns the while condition in line 5 of Algorithm 1 to false, leading to an unnecessary increase of k. An exact, rather than an approximative, inner reachability would resolve this. We are however not aware of any exact unbounded SAT-based reachability techniques. BDD-based techniques might work, but we suspect that the repeated conversion from SAT-based data structures to BDDs would add too much overhead to be competitive. Hence, we leave further optimization in this area as future work.

As elaborated in Sect. 3, there are other applications for the component-oriented interpolated environment, like manual inspection or partial model reverification. Their algorithms look slightly different from Algorithm 1, but the essential computational steps are there. For manual inspection, the emphasis is

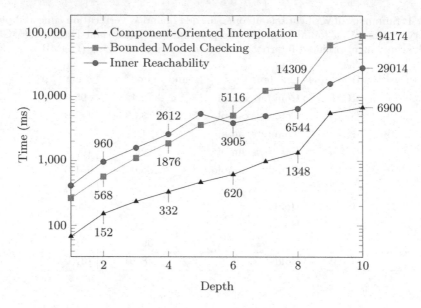

Fig. 4. Plots of time spent in milliseconds at each depth k for bounded model checking, component-oriented interpolation and inner reachability (respectively lines 2, 3 and 5–8 of Algorithm 1) on experiment configuration CDR-3 (checking avoidance of safe mode in the presence of various platform failures).

on the bounded model checking step (line 2) and component-oriented interpolation (line 3). For reverification on the other hand, the emphasis lies on inner reachability (lines 5–10). To extrapolate the effectiveness of component-oriented interpolation for those two applications, we logged the time spent on parts of Algorithm 1 at each step k. A summary is shown in Fig. 4 for experiment configuration CDR-3, which is representative for the other experiment configurations. Note that the y-axis has a logarithmic scale. The bottom line is that the step for constructing the interpolated environment has little impact on the overall running time, as it only takes a fraction of the time spent on bounded model checking and inner reachability. Note that the (most time-costly) bounded model checking step is avoided for partial model reverification, whereas inner reachability is omitted for manual inspection. This is where time is saved for the overall analysis.

5   Related Work

There is a huge body of work on compositional analysis in literature. In the introduction, Sect. 1, we have briefly explained the main differences between our work and what has been reported in literature. We continue this discussion in this section.

Contrary to many works from the Owicki-Gries paradigm, which often make distinctions between global and local variables, our work fits the *shared variables* paradigm. Global variables are typical to parallel systems, where multiple (identical) concurrent processes are active at the same time and interact with each others through a small set of global variables. The technique by [7] essentially abstracts and redefines the concurrent processes in terms of those global variables and calls this notion the split invariant. The technique by [13] is similar to that, as well as the technique by [18]. Our work expresses environments in terms of those variables that are *shared* with other components, thus not requiring a model structure in which global variables are explicitly defined by the user. The shared variable paradigm is therefore a generalization of the global/local variables paradigm.

In this work, we show, so far, how the environments are interpolated using the unsatisfiability proof from bounded model checking of an invariant. This can be extended to a larger class of properties. Akin to [8], where the notion of a process environment is described, the interpolated environments, as it currently is formalized, can also be used to verify safety and liveness properties. In fact, our notion of the interpolated environment was inspired by that. We however foresee that the interpolated environment is not strong enough for verifying liveness properties and that techniques from CEGAR are a necessity here. Particular techniques in this setting are by [8,17]. As these works were carried out for the global/local variables paradigm, it requires further investigation how these techniques are extendable to the shared variables paradigm. For the moment, Algorithm 1 naively increases the bound k as a refinement step without checking whether an abstract counterexample is a false-positive or not.

With regard to rely/assume guarantee/provide reasoning, we remarked in the introduction that the automated approaches are closely related to ours. In [14], a technique based on automata determinization is described to generate weakest assumptions. In subsequent work [5], assumptions are learned using an automaton learning algorithm, like L*. Our work is a twist on this, as we describe a method using Craig interpolation.

Rely/assume guarantee/provide reasoning has also been applied to AADL models, like for example [6]. The scope and semantic base of [6] differs from ours. Our satellite models for example are expressed in a formalized dialect of AADL by [2]. It is designed to provide a rigorous and coherent semantics for a system's nominal, erroneous and degraded behavior. The work by [6] appears to focus only on the nominal behavior. Furthermore, their approach does not generate assumptions nor guarantuees as we do, but rather provides a tool-supported reasoning framework over them once provided by the user.

Interpolation in model checking has become an active field since the pioneering work by [19]. It has been further studied since, covering applications such as a monolithic abstraction of the transition relation [16], or more theoretical investigations studying the differences in strength of interpolants as a consequence of a chosen interpolation generation scheme [10]. We were inspired by [20] and devised a modified interpolation scheme that is suitable for compositional reasoning that is reported in this paper.

6   Conclusions

We have described and experimentally evaluated a technique for deriving an abstract environment transition condition from a component-oriented model using a Craig interpolation-inspired method. We call it the component-oriented interpolant. It particularly fits models where highly cohesive components communicate through shared variables, which is a generalization over the global/local variables setting. To our knowledge it is the first application of interpolation-like techniques to exploit a model's composition of components.

Through our work, we identified several open points for future work. In particular a study of the component-oriented interpolant's strength would be interesting. We know from Lemma 1 that the component-oriented interpolant over-approximates, but we do not know how strong it is such that the property still holds up to bound k. This is in contrast to classical Craig interpolation, where its interpolant does have this property. It requires further study to understand how and whether the component-oriented interpolant can be strengthened. Inspiration can be drawn from the strengthening techniques for classical interpolation, where the reordering of vertices in the resolution refutation proof and asymmetric interpolation schemes have been studied for this purpose [10].

Studying the strength of the component-oriented interpolant also benefits its suitability for verifying more expressive properties, like safety and liveness properties. We estimate that the component-oriented interpolation scheme of Definition 2 overapproximates too much for that purpose and thus the straight-forward usage of the interpolated environment to safety/liveness properties would yield too many false-positive counterexamples.

Furthermore, Algorithm 1 in Sect. 4 is open for further investigation. It suffers from double abstraction, because it does not perform an exact inner reachability analysis using the interpolated environment. Exact methods would alleviate that. Especially ones that work in a SAT-based context are preferable, because that would avoid the overhead of converting the used data-structures.

We have made our implementation available on http://www-i2.informatik.rwth-aachen.de/~nguyen/coi/ under the LGPL open source license.

Acknowledgements. This work was partially supported by ESA/ESTEC (contract no. 4000100798), Thales Alenia Space (contract no. 1520014509/01) and EU FP7-ICT D-MILS (reference 318772).

References

1. Biere, A., Cimatti, A., Clarke, E., Zhu, Y.: Symbolic model checking without BDDs. In: Cleaveland, W.R. (ed.) TACAS 1999. LNCS, vol. 1579, pp. 193–207. Springer, Heidelberg (1999)
2. Bozzano, M., Cimatti, A., Katoen, J.-P., Nguyen, V.Y., Noll, T., Roveri, M.: Safety, dependability and performance analysis of extended AADL models. Comput. J. **54**(5), 754–775 (2011)
3. Buss, S.R.: Propositional proof complexity. In: Berger, U., Schwichtenberg, H. (eds.) Computational Logic. Springer, Heidelberg (1997)

4. Cimatti, A., Clarke, E., Giunchiglia, E., Giunchiglia, F., Pistore, M., Roveri, M., Sebastiani, R., Tacchella, A.: NuSMV 2: an opensource tool for symbolic model checking. In: Brinksma, E., Larsen, K.G. (eds.) CAV 2002. LNCS, vol. 2404, pp. 359–364. Springer, Heidelberg (2002)
5. Cobleigh, J.M., Giannakopoulou, D., Păsăreanu, C.S.: Learning assumptions for compositional verification. In: Garavel, H., Hatcliff, J. (eds.) TACAS 2003. LNCS, vol. 2619, pp. 331–346. Springer, Heidelberg (2003)
6. Cofer, D., Gacek, A., Miller, S., Whalen, M.W., LaValley, B., Sha, L.: Compositional verification of architectural models. In: Goodloe, A.E., Person, S. (eds.) NFM 2012. LNCS, vol. 7226, pp. 126–140. Springer, Heidelberg (2012)
7. Cohen, A., Namjoshi, K.S.: Local proofs for global safety properties. Formal Methods Syst. Des. **34**(2), 104–125 (2009)
8. Cohen, A., Namjoshi, K.S.: Local proofs for linear-time properties of concurrent programs. In: Gupta, A., Malik, S. (eds.) CAV 2008. LNCS, vol. 5123, pp. 149–161. Springer, Heidelberg (2008)
9. Craig, W.: Three uses of the Herbrand-Gentzen theorem in relating model theory and proof theory. J. Symb. Log. **22**(3), 269–285 (1957)
10. D'Silva, V., Kroening, D., Purandare, M., Weissenbacher, G.: Interpolant strength. In: Barthe, G., Hermenegildo, M. (eds.) VMCAI 2010. LNCS, vol. 5944, pp. 129–145. Springer, Heidelberg (2010)
11. Esteve, M.-A., Katoen, J.-P., Nguyen, V.Y., Postma, B., Yushtein, Y.: Formal correctness, safety, dependability and performance analysis of a satellite. In: Proceedings of 34th Software Engineering (ICSE), pp. 1022–1031. IEEE (2012)
12. Feiler, P.H., Gluch, D.P.: Model-Based Engineering with AADL: An Introduction to the SAE Architecture Analysis & Design Language. Addison-Wesley, Upper Saddle River (2012)
13. Flanagan, C., Qadeer, S.: Thread-modular model checking. In: Ball, T., Rajamani, S.K. (eds.) SPIN 2003. LNCS, vol. 2648, pp. 213–224. Springer, Heidelberg (2003)
14. Giannakopoulou, D., Pasareanu, C.S., Barringer, H.: Assumption generation for software component verification. In: Proceedings of 17th Automated Software Engineering (ASE), pp. 3–12. IEEE (2002)
15. Gupta, A., Popeea, C., Rybalchenko, A.: Threader: a constraint-based verifier for multi-threaded programs. In: Gopalakrishnan, G., Qadeer, S. (eds.) CAV 2011. LNCS, vol. 6806, pp. 412–417. Springer, Heidelberg (2011)
16. Jhala, R., McMillan, K.L.: Interpolant-based transition relation approximation. In: Etessami, K., Rajamani, S.K. (eds.) CAV 2005. LNCS, vol. 3576, pp. 39–51. Springer, Heidelberg (2005)
17. Malkis, A., Podelski, A., Rybalchenko, A.: Thread-modular counterexample-guided abstraction refinement. In: Cousot, R., Martel, M. (eds.) SAS 2010. LNCS, vol. 6337, pp. 356–372. Springer, Heidelberg (2010)
18. Malkis, A., Podelski, A., Rybalchenko, A.: Thread-modular verification is Cartesian abstract interpretation. In: Barkaoui, K., Cavalcanti, A., Cerone, A. (eds.) ICTAC 2006. LNCS, vol. 4281, pp. 183–197. Springer, Heidelberg (2006)
19. McMillan, K.L.: Interpolation and SAT-based model checking. In: Hunt Jr., W.A., Somenzi, F. (eds.) CAV 2003. LNCS, vol. 2725, pp. 1–13. Springer, Heidelberg (2003)
20. McMillan, K.L.: Applications of Craig interpolants in model checking. In: Halbwachs, N., Zuck, L.D. (eds.) TACAS 2005. LNCS, vol. 3440, pp. 1–12. Springer, Heidelberg (2005)
21. Nguyen, V.Y.: Trustworthy spacecraft design using formal methods. Ph.D. thesis, RWTH Aachen University, Germany (2012)

Adaptation and Evolution

Impact Models for Architecture-Based Self-adaptive Systems

Javier Cámara Moreno[1]([⊠]), Antónia Lopes[2],
David Garlan[1], and Bradley Schmerl[1]

[1] Institute for Software Research, Carnegie Mellon University,
Pittsburgh, PA 15213, USA
{jcmoreno,garlan,schmerl}@cs.cmu.edu
[2] Department of Informatics, Faculty of Sciences,
University of Lisbon, Lisbon, Portugal
mal@di.fc.ul.pt

Abstract. Self-adaptive systems have the ability to adapt their behavior to dynamic operation conditions. In reaction to changes in the environment, these systems determine the appropriate corrective actions based in part on information about which action will have the best impact on the system. Existing models used to describe the impact of adaptations are either unable to capture the underlying uncertainty and variability of such dynamic environments, or are not compositional and described at a level of abstraction too low to scale in terms of specification effort required for non-trivial systems. In this paper, we address these shortcomings by describing an approach to the specification of impact models based on architectural system descriptions, which at the same time allows us to represent both variability and uncertainty in the outcome of adaptations, hence improving the selection of the best corrective action. The core of our approach is an impact model language equipped with a formal semantics defined in terms of Discrete Time Markov Chains. To validate our approach, we show how employing our language can improve the accuracy of predictions used for decision-making in the Rainbow framework for architecture-based self-adaptation.

1 Introduction

Self-adaptive systems have the ability to autonomously change their behavior in response to changes in their operating conditions, thus preserving the capability of meeting certain requirements. For instance, to provide timely response to service requests, a news website with self-adaptive capabilities can react to high

This work is supported in part by award N000141310401 from the Office of Naval Research, by the Foundation for Science and Technology via project CMU-PT/ELE/0030/2009, and is based upon work funded and supported by the Department of Defense under Contract No. FA8721-05-C-0003 with Carnegie Mellon University for the operation of the Software Engineering Institute, a federally funded research and development center. This material has been approved for public release and unlimited distribution. (DM-0001079).

I. Lanese and E. Madelaine (Eds.): FACS 2014, LNCS 8997, pp. 89–107, 2015.
DOI: 10.1007/978-3-319-15317-9_6

response latencies by activating more servers, or reducing the fidelity of contents being served [6,12].

Deciding which adaptations should be carried out in response to changes in the execution environment requires that systems embody knowledge about themselves. Knowledge about the impact of adaptation choices on system's properties is particularly important when the decision process involves comparing alternative adaptations at runtime, as is often the case [5,11,14,17].

The effectiveness of the enacted changes, which affects the system's ability to meet its requirements, strongly depends on the accuracy of the analytical models that are used for decision making. Exact models, if attainable at all, tend to be quite complex and costly to obtain. As argued in [8], an alternative is to attend to the uncertainty underlying the knowledge models in the decision process.

However, existing models used to describe the impact of adaptations are either unable to capture the underlying uncertainty and variability of such dynamic execution environments, or are not compositional and described at a level of abstraction too low to scale in terms of specification effort required for non-trivial systems.

In this paper, we address the specification of probabilistic impact models for architecture-based self-adaptive systems that support the representation of: (i) uncertainty in the outcome of adaptation actions (e.g., the activation of a server can fail with some given probability), and (ii) context variability (e.g., the impact on response time of activating a single server will progressively reduce with a growing number of active servers). The core of our approach is a declarative specification language for expressing complex probabilistic constraints over state transitions that is equipped with a formal semantics defined in terms of Discrete Time Markov Chains (DTMC). This language provides the means for expressing impact models in a flexible and compact way.

We illustrate how the proposed impact models can be used in the context of the Rainbow framework [11] for architecture-based self-adaptation, and quantify the benefits of using probabilistic impact models instead of constant impact vectors [5].

The rest of the paper is organized as follows. Section 2 describes related work. Section 3 provides a formal account of the concepts required to define impact models. Section 4 presents the syntax and semantics of a new specification language of probabilistic impact models and Sect. 5 shows how our impact models can be used in the context of Rainbow for adaptation strategy selection. Next, experimental results that quantify the benefits of using probabilistic impact models instead of impact vectors are presented in Sect. 6. Finally, Sect. 7 presents some conclusions and future work.

2 Related Work

Environment domain models are a key element used by adaptive systems to determine their behavior [1,18]. These models capture the knowledge that the system has about itself and its environment by describing how system and environment respond to adaptation actions. Approaches to self-adaptation can be divided into two categories, depending on the way in which environment domain models are built.

A first category takes a systematic approach to modeling the impact of individual adaptation actions, which can be composed to reason about system behavior under adaptation. An example is the approach presented in [5], developed around Stitch, a language that enables the specification of adaptation strategies composed of individual adaptation actions. The impact of these action is specified in terms of constant impact vectors which describe how the execution of adaptation actions affects system quality attributes. The same type of impact models is used in several approaches to optimization of service compositions, such as the approach presented in [14]. Adaptation actions in this approach target service composition instances and the optimal criteria relies on impact models that are defined per adaptation action and system property as constant functions. Slightly more expressive impact models are considered in the approach presented [17], which targets component-based systems where impact models are defined per adaptation action and key performance indicators (KPIs), as functions over a given set of KPIs. These approaches address the specification of environment domain models in a compositional way and at a very high level of abstraction, thus facilitating specification and promoting reuse. However, they severely limit the ability to represent environment domain knowledge in a realistic way, since they are unable to model uncertainty and provide limited support to capture variability.

The second category consists of approaches that consider the behavior of the system and its environment modeled in a monolithic way in terms of more powerful models defined at a lower level of abstraction [1,2,9]. For example, in the approach presented in [2], DTMCs are used to model, for each system configuration, the future state of a system and its environment if that configuration is used. These models are expressive enough to model variability and the uncertainty underlying adaptation outcomes. The main drawback here is that these models being defined at the level of system configurations are system specific. For instance, in the case of a news website that can react to high response latencies by activating more servers, a DTMC that models the effect of activating one server in a system that can use up to 4 servers is completely different from another that models the same on a system that can use up to 10 servers, although the effect of activating one server does not depend on the maximum number of servers. Moreover, these models are both difficult and cumbersome to write. The specification of a DTMC tends to be a non-trivial task, even using description languages such as the one built into the probabilistic model checker PRISM [13].

The approach described in this paper aims at striking a balance between the ease of specification and reusability found in compositional approaches, and the expressive power of monolithic approaches that use probabilistic models. We present a language for the specification of impact models, which is: (i) more intuitive than describing DTMCs in other probabilistic approaches, since it is based on architectural descriptions and therefore raises the level of abstraction, (ii) able to capture both variability and probabilistic outcomes of adaptation actions, and (iii) scalable in terms of specification effort, since developers can focus on smaller units of conceptualization (i.e., architectural properties) and reason about them individually.

3   Modeling Adaptation

We address the modeling of impact in the context of architecture-based approaches to self-adaptation, that take the architectural style of the managed system as a basis for the system adaptation. The aim is to support the specification of impact models for families of systems that share the same architectural style. The semantics of such specifications assigns, for each system in the family, an impact model (a DTMC).

In this section, we provide a formal account of the concepts required to define impact models, namely architectural style and system state. We start by introducing the running example used in the rest of the paper.

3.1   Running Example

Znn.com [3] is a case study portraying a representative scenario for the application of self-adaptation in software systems which has been extensively used to assess different research in self-adaptive systems. Znn.com is able to reproduce the typical infrastructure for a news website, and has a three-tier architecture consisting of a set of servers that provide contents from backend databases to clients via front-end presentation logic (Fig. 1). The system uses a load balancer to balance requests across a pool of replicated servers, the size of which can be adjusted according to service demand. A set of clients makes stateless requests, and the servers deliver the requested contents.

The main objective for Znn.com is to provide content to customers within a reasonable response time, while keeping the cost of the server pool within a certain operating budget. It is considered that from time to time, due to highly popular events, Znn.com experiences spikes in requests that it cannot serve adequately, even at maximum pool size. To prevent loss of customers, the system can provide minimal textual content during

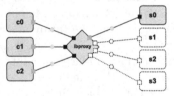

Fig. 1. Znn.com architecture

such peak times, to avoid not providing service to some of its customers. Concretely, there are two main quality objectives for the self-adaptation of the system: (i) performance, which depends on request response time, server load, and network bandwidth, and (ii) cost, which is associated with the number of active servers.

3.2   Architectural Style

As discussed in [4], when the architectural style of the managed system is taken as a basis for the system adaptation, it has to define not only the class of models to which the managed system architecture belongs but also to determine the operators representing available configuration changes on systems in that style and prescribes what aspects of a system and its execution context need to be monitored.

An architectural style defines a vocabulary of component and connector types that can be used in instances of that style and the properties of each of these types. In the context of self-adaptive systems, it is essential to distinguish between managed and monitored properties. *Managed properties* correspond to properties that are uniquely under system control. Their values can be defined at startup and changed subsequently by the control layer to regulate the system. *Monitored properties* correspond to properties of the managed system or its execution context that need to be monitored and made available to the control layer. While the properties of the execution context are not under the system control (e.g., available bandwidth), monitored properties also include those that the system aims to control (e.g., response time).

As an example, we consider the architectural style of Znn.com. It has one connector type — HttpConnT, and three component types — ClientT, ServerT and ProxyT. For instance, ServerT has two managed properties — isTextualMode:bool and cost:int. The former defines whether web pages are served by a given server in textual or multimedia mode and the latter reflects the cost of an active server per unit time. Since these properties are defined as uniquely under the system's control, the cost of each server included in the system must be defined at deployment time, and whether it will start serving pages in textual or multimedia mode. Additionally, ServerT has two monitored properties — load:double and isActive:bool. The latter property is defined as monitored, since even if its activation can be controlled, a server may crash anytime.

Formally, architectural signatures are defined as follows.

Definition 1 (Architectural Signature). *An architectural signature Σ consists of a tuple of the form $\langle CompT, ConnT, \Pi^o, \Pi^m \rangle$, where CompT and ConnT are two disjoint sets (the sets of, respectively, component and connector types) and, Π^o and Π^m are functions that assign, to architectural types $\kappa \in CompT \cup ConnT$, mutually disjoint sets whose elements are typed by datatypes in a fixed set $\mathcal{D}$ ($\Pi^o(\kappa)$ and $\Pi^m(\kappa)$ represent, respectively, the managed and monitored properties of the type κ). We abbreviate $\Pi^o(\kappa) \cup \Pi^m(\kappa)$ by $\Pi(\kappa)$ and, for $p \in \Pi(\kappa)$, will use dtype($\kappa.p$) to denote its datatype.*

The architectural configurations of systems with architectural signature Σ, hereafter called Σ-system states, are captured in terms of graphs of components and connectors with state. State of architectural elements consist of the values taken by their monitored and managed properties.

We formally define Σ-system states assuming there is a fixed universe $\mathcal{A}_\Sigma$ of architectural elements (components and connectors) for Σ, i.e., a countable set whose elements are typed by elements in $CompT \cup ConnT$. We use $type(c)$ to denote c's type.

Definition 2 (Σ-System State). *A Σ-system state s consists of (i) a simple graph $\mathcal{G}$, (ii) a function type that assigns an architectural type to every node of $\mathcal{G}$, (iii) an injective function I^s from the set of nodes of $\mathcal{G}$ to $\mathcal{A}_\Sigma$ such that $type(I^s(c)) = type(c)$ and (iv) a function that assigns a value $[\![c.p]\!]^s$ in the domain of dtype($\kappa.p$), to every pair $c.p$ such that c is a node of $\mathcal{G}$, $\kappa = type(c)$ and $p \in \Pi(\kappa)$. We denote by $\mathcal{S}_\Sigma$ (or simply $\mathcal{S}$ when Σ is clear from the context) the set of all Σ-system states.*

An architectural style also defines the ways one can change systems with that style. For instance, the Znn architectural style defines that property isTextualMode of servers can be modified through setLowFidelity and setHighFidelity operators, that set isTextualMode to, true and false, respectively.

Generically, these operators can range from primitive operations, such as changing the value of a property of a given connector type or replacing an implementation of a component type with another, to higher-level operations that exploit restrictions of that style. However, in practice, most approaches to self-adaptation consider only primitive operations. Hence, we focus on architectural styles that define the set of operators provided by the target system for (i) changing the values of the managed properties of its components and connectors and (ii) replacing a component or connector of a given type by another of the same type. Notice that, in these architectural styles, only the last two components of a system state —I^s and $[\![\ ]\!]^s$— can change at runtime. The structure of the system, defined by the graph and *type* function, does not change.

3.3 Adaptation Actions

The adaptation of the managed system is achieved through the execution of adaptation actions defined at design-time. Adaptation actions define actions packaged as applications of one or more operators, with a condition of applicability. In the Znn example we could, for instance, define an adaptation action switchToTextualMode applicable only if there is at least one active service not serving pages in textual mode, prescribing the application of operator setLowFidelity to all servers in these conditions. A different adaptation action for Znn is enlistServer that is applicable when there is at least one inactive server, and prescribes the application of startServer to one inactive server.

Applicability conditions of adaptation actions are formulas of a constraint language that are evaluated over system states. For illustration purposes, we consider a constraint language inspired by that of Acme [10][1] in which, for instance, (exists s:ServerT | exists k:HttpConnT | attached(k,s) and s.isActive) holds in a system state iff the state includes at least one active server attached to one http connector.

4   Modeling Impact

Deciding how to best adapt the system when a certain anomaly is detected involves analyzing models describing the effects, in terms of costs and benefits, of the available adaptation actions defined for the system. These models capture the causal relationship between an adaptation action's execution and its impact on the different system properties. Because 100 % accurate models are in general not attainable, it is important to have means to address the underlying uncertainty.

In this section, we describe an expressive language to model adaptation action execution, which is able to capture: (i) the context that might influence the

---

[1] Acme is in turn derived from OCL [16], with the addition of functions that relate to architectural structure.

outcome of an adaptation action's execution, and (ii) the intrinsic uncertainty that pervades self-adaptive systems. Specifically, this language enables the description of models of the expected impact of each adaptation action on the different system properties. These models are based on DTMCs [15], and enable us to express alternative possible outcomes of the execution of the same adaptation action with some given probability.

4.1   Impact Model Language

The impact model of adaptation actions is defined in terms of probabilistic expressions in a language that allows one to express probabilistic constraints over state transitions (regarded as pairs of before and after system states), incorporating some elements of the PRISM language [13].

The language targets systems whose structure does not change at runtime. For this reason, it is built over a language $\mathcal{E}$ for specifying sets of components and connectors in a system state. For illustration purposes, we use a language in line with the one that we use to express constraints, in which, for instance, (s: ServerT | s.isActive) describes the set of active servers in a system state. To handle data, we assume that the fixed set of datatypes $\mathcal{D}$ is equipped with the relevant operations. We denote by $\mathcal{T}$ the term language used to describe data values and by $\mathcal{T}_d(\Sigma, X)$ the set of terms built over variables in X denoting values of datatype d. Similarly, we use $\mathcal{E}_\kappa(\Sigma, X)$ to denote the set of expressions defined over the variables in X denoting sets of architectural elements of type κ.

Definition 3 (Probabilistic Expressions). *Let X be a set of variables typed by architectural types in an architectural signature Σ. The set $\mathcal{P}(\Sigma, X)$, of probabilistic expressions over variables in X, is defined by the following grammar:*

$$\alpha ::= x.p' = t \qquad \text{with } x \in X, \ p \in \Pi(\kappa), \ t \in \mathcal{T}_d(\Sigma, x_\Pi),$$
$$\text{where } \kappa = type(x) \ and \ d = dtype(p)$$

$$| \ \textbf{forall } x : \epsilon \ | \ \alpha_1$$
$$| \ \textbf{foreach } x : \epsilon \ | \ \alpha_1$$
$$| \ \textbf{foreach } x : \epsilon \ \textbf{minus } D \ | \ \alpha_1 \qquad \text{with } x \notin X, \ \epsilon \in \mathcal{E}_\kappa(\Sigma, X),$$
$$\alpha_1 \in \mathcal{P}(\Sigma, X \cup \{x : \kappa\}) \ and \ D \subseteq X_\kappa$$

$$| \ \{\alpha_1 \& \dots \& \alpha_n\}$$
$$| \ \{[p_1]\alpha_1 + [p_2]\alpha_2 + \cdots + [p_n]\alpha_n\} \qquad \text{with, for } 1 \leq i \leq n, \ \alpha_i \in \mathcal{P}(\Sigma, X),$$
$$0 \leq p_i \leq 1 \ and \ \Sigma_{i=1}^n p_i = 1$$

where $x_\Pi = \{x.p : d \mid p \in \Pi(type(x)), d = dtype(p)\}$ and $X_\kappa = \{x \in X : type(x) = \kappa\}$. $\mathcal{P}(\Sigma)$ is the set of probabilistic expressions without free variables, i.e., $\mathcal{P}(\Sigma, \emptyset)$.

The atomic expression $x.p' = t$ defines the value of the property p in the next state (after the execution of the adaptation action), for every component or connector denoted by x. This value can be defined in terms of the values of the properties of the same element as well as other architectural elements in the system, but the free variables of t are limited to variables representing properties of x. For instance, assuming that s is a variable of type ServerT, we can write s.isActive' = !s.isActive to express that every server denoted by s has its isActive property toggled.

The operator **forall** is used to impose the same constraints over a set of architectural elements of the same type, denoted by a given expression in $\mathcal{E}$. The operator **foreach** is used to define a number of alternative outcomes, all with the same probability. For instance, **foreach** x:ServerT | x.isActive' = true states that all servers have the same probability of having their isActive property set to true. Adding **minus** D to the expression reduces the target to elements not included in the denotation of variables in D.

For instance, **foreach** x:E | **foreach** y:E **minus** x | {x.isActive'=true &y.isActive'= true} where E is (s:ServerT|!s.isActive), expresses that exactly two servers are activated and that all pairs of distinct inactive servers have the same probability of being activated.

A fixed number of constraints over the next state are expressed through conjunction (&). Probabilities that sum to one are assigned to a fixed number of expressions defining constraints over alternative outcomes of the adaptation action execution. Assigning a probability to an expression with $[p]\alpha$ has the effect of world closure: all properties of components and connectors not constrained by α are considered to keep the same value in the next state.

To capture that an adaptation action may have different impacts under different conditions, impact models are defined as sets of guarded probabilistic expressions with mutually exclusive guards (i.e., at most one guard holds in any system state). As before, we abstract from the language used for expressing the guard conditions and assume a fixed language $\mathcal{C}$ of constraints over system states.

Definition 4 (Impact Model). *An impact model $\mathcal{I}$ of an adaptation action is a finite set of pairs $\langle \phi, \alpha \rangle$ where ϕ is a constraint in $\mathcal{C}(\Sigma)$ and α is a probabilistic expression in $\mathcal{P}(\Sigma)$ such that all ϕ are mutually exclusive.*

An example of a simple impact model is presented below for the adaptation action switchToTextualMode. For the sake of clarity, we present all examples making use of a concrete syntax that supports the definition of abbreviations and in which guarded expressions are represented as $\phi \rightarrow \alpha$.

```
1    define S=(s:ServerT | !s.isTextualMode and s.isActive) and define k=size(S)
2    define f(x)=x*(1−k/(2*(k+1))) and define g(x)=x*(1−k/(k+1))
3    impactmodel switchToTextualMode
4       k>0 → { [0.8] { forall s:S | s.isTextualMode'=true & forall c:ClientT | c.expRspTime'=f(c.expRspTime) }
5             + [0.2] { forall s:S | s.isTextualMode'=true & forall c:ClientT | c.expRspTime'=g(c.expRspTime) }}
```

Listing 1.1. Impact model for adaptation action switchToTextualMode.

This model expresses the impact of the adaptation action over manipulated properties, where the fact that operator setLowFidelity sets the property isTextualMode to true is represented by s.isTextualMode'=true. Moreover, the model foresees that switchToTextualMode can impact the response time of *all clients* in two ways, both decreasing its value, considering the number of servers that were changed to low fidelity. The more severe reduction of the response time is defined to be the least likely, with probability 0.2. According to this (simplistic) model, the execution of this adaptation action is not expected to affect the remaining properties of servers, clients, or http connectors.

Alternatively, we could specify that switchToTextualMode can impact the response time of *each client* in two ways as follows:

```
1  impactmodel switchToTextualMode
2    k>0 → forall c:ClientT | { [0.8] { forall s:S | s.isTextualMode'=true & c.expRspTime'=f(c.expRspTime) }
3                              + [0.2] { forall s:S | s.isTextualMode'=true & c.expRspTime'=g(c.expRspTime) }}
```

Listing 1.2. Alternative impact model for switchToTextualMode.

While we have considered that the property isTextualMode of servers is subject only to system control, isActive was defined as a monitored property and it was considered that the activation of a server, through the execution of operator startServer, may fail. An impact model for enlistServer that captures this aspect is presented below.

```
1  define m=size(s:ServerT | s.isActive) and define S= (s:ServerT | !s.isActive)
2  define f(x)=x∗(1−((1/log(100∗m,2))∗(m/(2∗m+1)))) and define g(x)=x∗(1−1/log(100∗m,2))
3  impactmodel enlistServer
4    m>0 → { [0.95] { foreach s:S | s.isActive'=true &
5                      { [0.7] forall c:ClientT | c.expRspTime'=f(c.expRspTime)
6                      + [0.3] forall c:ClientT | c.expRspTime'=g(c.expRspTime) }}
7          + [0.05] { forall s:ServerT | s.isActive'=s.isActive & forall c:ClientT | c.expRspTime'=c.expRspTime }}
```

Listing 1.3. Impact model for adaptation action enlistServer.

This impact model implicitly states that the starting of the server is expected to fail with probability 0.05 and foresees that the adaptation action may impact client response time in two ways, both considering the number of servers that were already active.

Moreover, isActive is also defined as a monitored property, since a server could become spontaneously inactive (e.g., due to a server crash). The impact model above does not define any impact of the adaptation action over the property isActive of already active servers, hence the probability of an active server crashing while executing enlistServer is considered to be so small that it can be neglected. Alternatively, we can define the probability of each relevant crash scenario (e.g., for one server, two servers, etc.). For instance, the impact model presented below defines that the probability of exactly one active server crashing while executing enlistServer is 0.001.

```
1  define T=(s:ServerT | s.isActive)
2  impactmodel enlistServer
3    m>0 → { [0.999] { foreach s:S | s.isActive'=true &
4                       { [0.7] forall c:ClientT | c.expRspTime'=f(c.expRspTime) +
5                       [0.3] forall c:ClientT | c.expRspTime'=g(c.expRspTime) } }
6          + [0.001] { foreach s:S | s.isActive'=true & foreach t:T | t.isActive'=false &
7                       forall c:ClientT | c.expRspTime'=c.expRspTime } }
```

Listing 1.4. Alternative impact model for adaptation action enlistServer.

4.2   Impact Model Semantics

The semantics of impact models is formally defined in terms of DTMCs. Since a DTMC has a discrete state space, we have to limit properties of components and connectors to take values in discrete sets and perform quantization.

Quantization. For each property p that takes values in a datatype $d \in \mathcal{D}$ that has a non-countable domain $\mathcal{I}_d$, it is necessary that a countable set $[\mathcal{I}_d]_p$ and a quantization function $Q_p : \mathcal{I}_d \to [\mathcal{I}_d]_p$ be defined. For each property $p : d$ such that $\mathcal{I}_d$ is countable we take $[\mathcal{I}_d]_p = \mathcal{I}_d$ and Q_p as the identity function.

The quantization of the properties of component and connector types can be propagated to the level of system states, defining a discrete set of states $[\mathcal{S}] = \{[s] : s \in \mathcal{S}\}$. In $[s]$, the value of a property p of a component or connector c is obtained by applying the corresponding quantization function to the value it has in s, i.e., $[\![c.p]\!]^{[s]} = Q_p([\![c.p]\!]^s)$.

The semantics of adaptation action impact models is defined in terms of DTMCs over $[\mathcal{S}]$. We start by providing the semantics of the probabilistic expressions used to assemble such models.

The interpretation of a probabilistic expression α over a set of variables X is defined in the context of a system state s and an *interpretation* ρ of X assigning to each variable $x{:}\kappa$, a set of elements in s of type κ. This interpretation, denoted by $[\![\alpha]\!]^s_\rho$, consists of a set Y of properties of component and connectors in s — those which are constrained by α — and a function P defining the probability of a transition between any pair of Y-states. As an example, consider $[\![\text{x.isActive'=true}]\!]^s_\rho$ where $x : \mathsf{ServerT}$, s is a state with servers $z_1, \ldots, z_n$ and $\rho : x \mapsto \{z_1\}$. The expression constrains only the property *isActive* of z_1, i.e., $Y = \{z_1.isActive\}$ and, hence, in this case, a Y-state is just a truth value for $z_1.isActive$. Its interpretation is that the probability of a transition from any Y-state to $\{z_1.isActive \mapsto true\}$ is 1 and to $\{z_1.isActive \mapsto false\}$ is 0.

Formally, given a set Y of properties, a Y-state s is a function defining the value of each property in $y \in Y$, subject to the corresponding quantization functions. As for system states, we simply write $[\![y]\!]^s$ and use $[\mathcal{S}_Y]$ for referring to the set of all Y-states.

An important operation over probabilistic expressions is world closure through assignment of a probability. As mentioned before, when we write $[p]\alpha$, all properties of components and connectors not constrained by α are considered to keep the same value in the next state. World closure can be captured by the following notion of closure over transition probability matrices:

Definition 5 (Closure). *Let* $Y {\subseteq} Y'$ *be two sets of properties. Given a function* $P{:}[\mathcal{S}_Y] \times [\mathcal{S}_Y] \to [0,1]$, *the closure of* P *to* Y' *is the function* $P^{Y'}{:}[\mathcal{S}_{Y'}] \times [\mathcal{S}_{Y'}] \to [0,1]$ *s.t.*

$$P^{Y'}(s_1, s_2) = \begin{cases} P(s_{1|Y}, s_{2|Y}) & \text{if } \forall y \in Y' \setminus Y, \; [\![y]\!]^{s_2} = [\![y]\!]^{s_1} \\ 0 & \text{otherwise} \end{cases}$$

where $s_{|Y}$ *is the* Y-state *obtained through the restriction of* s *to the properties in* Y.

The closure of P corresponds to extending the probabilities given by P to states with more properties, considering that their values do not change.

Definition 6 (Interpretation of Probabilistic Expressions). *The interpretation* $[\![\alpha]\!]^s_\rho$ *of* $\alpha \in \mathcal{P}(\Sigma, X)$ *in a system state* s *and an interpretation* ρ *of* X *is a pair of the form* $\langle Y, P{:}[\mathcal{S}_Y] \times [\mathcal{S}_Y] \to [0,1] \rangle$ *defined inductively in the structure of* α *as follows:*

- $[\![x.p' = t]\!]_\rho^s = \langle Y, P \rangle$

$$Y = \{c.p : c \in \rho(x)\} \text{ and } P(s_1, s_2) = \begin{cases} 1 & \text{if } \forall c \in \rho(x), [\![c.p]\!]^{s_2} = [\![t]\!]_{\rho_c}^{s_1} \\ 0 & \text{otherwise} \end{cases}$$

with $\rho_c = \{x.q \mapsto [\![c.q]\!]^{s_1} : q \in \Pi(type(x))\}$

- $[\![\textbf{forall } x : \epsilon \mid \alpha]\!]_\rho^s = [\![\alpha]\!]_{\rho'}^s$, with $\rho' = \rho \oplus x \mapsto [\![\epsilon]\!]^s$

- $[\![\textbf{foreach } x : \epsilon \mid \alpha]\!]_\rho^s = \langle Y, P \rangle$

Let $C = [\![\epsilon]\!]^s$. If $|C| = 0$, then $Y = \emptyset$ and P is the empty function to $[0, 1]$. Otherwise, let $\rho_c = \rho \oplus x \mapsto \{c\}$, for every $c \in C$, and $[\![\alpha]\!]_{\rho_c}^s = \langle Y_c, P_c \rangle$.

$$Y = \bigcup_{c \in C} Y_c \text{ and } P(s_1, s_2) = \sum_{c \in C} \frac{1}{|C|} \cdot P_c^Y(s_{1|Y_c}, s_{2|Y_c})$$

- $[\![\textbf{foreach } x : \epsilon \textbf{ minus } D \mid \alpha]\!]_\rho^s = \langle Y, P \rangle$

Let $C = [\![\epsilon]\!]^s \setminus \rho(D)$. If $|C| = 0$, then $Y = \emptyset$ and P is the empty function to $[0, 1]$. Otherwise, let $\rho_c = \rho \oplus x \mapsto \{c\}$, for every $c \in C$, and $[\![\alpha]\!]_{\rho_c}^s = \langle Y_c, P_c \rangle$.

$$Y = \bigcup_{c \in C} Y_c \text{ and } P(s_1, s_2) = \sum_{c \in C} \frac{1}{|C|} \cdot P_c^Y(s_{1|Y_c}, s_{2|Y_c})$$

- $[\![\{\alpha_1 \& \cdots \& \alpha_n\}]\!]_\rho^s = \langle Y, P \rangle$

Let $[\![\alpha_i]\!]_\rho^s = \langle Y_i, P_i \rangle$, for $i = 1, .., n$. If the sets $Y_1, \cdots, Y_n$ are not mutually disjoint, then $Y = \emptyset$ and P is the empty function to $[0, 1]$. Otherwise,

$$Y = \bigcup_{i=1,..,n} Y_i \text{ and } P(s_1, s_2) = \prod_{i=1}^{n} P_i(s_{1|Y_i}, s_{2|Y_i})$$

- $[\![\{[p_1]\alpha_1 + \cdots + [p_n]\alpha_n\}]\!]_\rho^s = \langle Y, P \rangle$

Let $[\![\alpha_i]\!]_\rho^s = \langle Y_i, P_i \rangle$, for $i = 1, .., n$.

$$Y = \bigcup_{i=1,..,n} Y_i \text{ and } P(s_1, s_2) = \sum_{i=1}^{n} p_i \cdot P_i^Y(s_{1|Y_i}, s_{2|Y_i})$$

Notice that there are some state-dependent semantic restrictions over probabilistic expressions. If, in a given state s, an expression α does not meet these conditions, then α does not impose any restriction in the evolution of the system state (i.e., $Y = \emptyset$).

Proposition 1. If $[\![\alpha]\!]_\rho^s = \langle Y, P : [S_Y] \times [S_Y] \to [0, 1] \rangle$, then P is a transition probabilistic matrix, i.e., $\sum_{s_2 \in [S_Y]} P(s_1, s_2) = 1$, for every $s_1 \in [S_Y]$.

The quantization of component and connector properties may invalidate an impact model, by making pairs of constraints that were mutually exclusive, non mutually exclusive anymore. Invalid adaptation action models are inconsistent (i.e., they do not admit any interpretation) and, hence, we limit our attention to valid impact models.

Definition 7 (Semantics of Impact Models). *An impact model $\mathcal{I}$ is valid if for every $s \in \mathcal{S}$, there exists at most one element $\langle \phi, \alpha \rangle \in \mathcal{I}$ such that $[s] \models \phi$.*

The semantics of a valid impact model $\mathcal{I}$ is the DTMC $\langle [\mathcal{S}], P : [\mathcal{S}] \times [\mathcal{S}] \to [0,1] \rangle$ where P is defined as follows:

If the graph of s_1 and s_2 is not the same then $P(s_1, s_2) = 0$,

else if exists $\langle \phi, \alpha \rangle \in \mathcal{I}$ s.t. $s_1 \models \phi$ then $P(s_1, s_2) = P_\alpha^{Y_{s_1}}(s_{1|Y_\alpha}, s_{2|Y_\alpha})$

else if $s_1 \neq s_2$ then $P(s_1, s_2) = 0$ else $P(s_1, s_2) = 1$

where Y_s denotes the set of all properties of components and connectors in a system state s, i.e., $Y_s = \{c.p : d \mid c$ is a node in $s, p \in \Pi(type(c)), d = dtype(p)\}$.

As an example, consider an impact model defined by $\langle size(E)>0, \alpha \rangle$ with $\alpha =$ (**foreach** x:E | x.isActive' = true) and E=(s:ServerT||!s.isActive). Let s, s_1, s_2 be three system states with servers z_1, z_2, z_3 that only differ in the number of active servers: (i) in s only z_3 is active, (ii) in s_1 only z_2 is inactive and (iii) in s_2 only z_1 is inactive. According to definition above, we have for instance that $P(s, s_1) = P(s, s_2) = \frac{1}{2}$ and $P(s, s') = 0$, for every other system state s' different from s_1 and s_2.

5   Predicting Adaptation Strategy Impact

In this section we show how the proposed impact models can be used when the adaptation of the managed system is achieved through the execution of an adaptation strategy selected from a portfolio of strategies specified in Stitch [5].

5.1   Adaptation Strategies

Strategies are built from tactics, which are Stitch's adaptation actions. Strategies have an applicability condition and a body. The body of a strategy σ is a tree T_σ whose edges $n \to m$ are labelled by a guard condition, a tactic and a success condition. Once at node n, if the guard condition is true, it means that the edge can be taken. When a edge is taken, the corresponding tactic is executed. Upon its termination the success condition is evaluated to determine if the tactic achieved what was expected and node m is reached. Guards include a special symbol *success* capturing whether the last tactic had succeeded or not.

An example of a strategy for Znn is simpleReduceResponseTime presented in Fig. 2. hiLoad, hiLatency and hiRspTime are formulas expressing respectively that the system load, latency and response time is high. hiRspTime, for instance, is defined in terms of the average response time of the clients by:

(sum(c.expRspTime|c: ClientT)/count(c: ClientT) > MAX_RSPTIME)

The body of the strategy defines that initially there are three alternatives, depending on the load and latency of the system. If the latency is high, then a possibility defined by the strategy is to just apply the tactic switchToTextualMode. The success condition in this case is hiRspTime that expresses that the average response time is below a given threshold. If the load is high, then a possibility is to apply the tactic enlistServer and, depending on the success of the application of this tactic, either terminate with skip or still try the application of the tactic switchToTextualMode. If neither the latency nor the load is high, the strategy does not offer any remedy.

Table 1. Utility functions and preferences for Znn

$U_R(w_{U_R} = 0.6)$				$U_C(w_{U_C} = 0.4)$		
0 : 1.00	200 : 0.99	1000 : 0.70	2000 : 0.25	0 : 1.00	2 : 0.90	4 : 0.00
100 : 1.00	500 : 0.90	1500 : 0.50	4000 : 0.00	1 : 1.00	3 : 0.30	

5.2 Strategy Selection

A particular situation that requires adaptation can typically be addressed in different ways by executing alternative adaptation strategies, many of which may be applicable under the same run time conditions. Different strategies impact quality attributes in different ways; thus there is a need to choose a strategy that will result in the best outcome with respect to achieving the system's desired quality objectives. To enable decision-making for selecting strategies Stitch uses utility functions and preferences, which are sensitive to the context of use and able to consider trade-offs among multiple potentially conflicting objectives. Specifically, the process

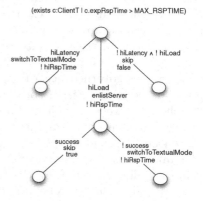

Fig. 2. A strategy for Znn.

consists in selecting the strategy that maximizes its expected utility, which entails: (i) defining quality objectives, relating them to specific run-time conditions, and (ii) assessing the expected aggregate utility of every applicable strategy, based on the impact model of its tactics on the system's quality objectives (using utility functions and preferences).

Defining Quality Objectives. Defining quality objectives requires identifying the concerns for the different stakeholders. In Znn, users are concerned with experiencing service without any disruptions, which can be mapped to specific run-time conditions such as response time. In contrast, the organization is interested in minimizing the cost of operating the infrastructure, which can be mapped to the cost of specific resources used at run-time (e.g., active servers). In short, we identify two quality objectives: maintaining low client response time (R), and cost (C). Table 1 summarizes the utility functions for Znn defined by an explicit set of value pairs (where intermediate points are linearly interpolated). Function U_R maps low response times (up to 100 ms) with maximum utility, whereas values above 2000 ms are highly penalized (utility below 0.25), and response times above 4000 ms provide no utility. Function U_C maps a increasing cost (derived from the number of active servers) to lower utility values. Utility preferences capture business preferences over the quality dimensions, assigning a specific weight (w_{U_R}, w_{U_C}) to each one of them. In Znn, preference is given to performance over cost.

To compute the utility of a given system state s (denoted as $Util(s)$), we first need to map the values of the different qualities [2] to their corresponding utility values. In a system state with 1250 ms of response time and a cost of 2 usd/hour, based on the utility functions defined in Table 1, we have $[U_R(1250), U_C(2)] = [0.625, 0.9]$. Finally, all utilities are combined into a single value, using utility preferences: $0.625*0.6+0.9*0.4=0.735$.

Assessing the Aggregate Utility of Strategies. The expected utility of a strategy σ in a given system state s can be formulated in terms of a tree like that presented in Fig. 3, i.e., a labelled tree with two types of nodes — normal and chance nodes, that alternate in consecutive depth levels of the tree. As with decision trees, chance nodes represent situations in which the choice between the different alternatives is external (i.e., not under the system's control), and is governed according to a given probability distribution function. Normal nodes, as decision nodes of decision trees, represent situations in which the choice between the different alternatives is internal. These nodes reflect situations of non-determinism during the execution of the strategy (that arise when more than one edge can be executed) that we assume are solved by a fair scheduler and, hence, all alternatives have the same probability of being taken. In this way, all edges $\langle n, m \rangle$ of the tree are labelled with a probability p; if n is a normal node then the edge is additionally labelled by a tactic t. For short we write, respectively, $n \xrightarrow{p} m$ and $n \xrightarrow{p}_{t} m$. Chance nodes are not labelled whereas every normal node n is labelled by a system state.

Formally, this type of labelled trees can be represented as a tuple $\langle N, st, E, l \rangle$ with $N = H \cup A$, where H and A are the sets of, respectively, chance and normal nodes, st is a function that labels nodes in H with system states, E is the set of edges and l labels edges with a probability and, optionally, a tactic. The tree defined by a strategy σ in a given system state s, which we denote by $T_{\mathcal{I}}(\sigma, s)$, is defined as follows.

Definition 8 ($T_{\mathcal{I}}(\sigma, s)$). *Let σ be a strategy and s a system state. Given an impact model $\mathcal{I}_t$ for every tactic t used in σ, $T_{\mathcal{I}}(\sigma, s)$ is the labelled tree obtained as follows:*

1. *Start with an empty set of chance nodes and edges and with a single normal node $root(T_\sigma)$ labelled by $[s]$.*
2. *While there exists a normal node n that has not been considered before:*
   (a) Find the edges of T_σ that start in n and can be executed in state $st(n)$:
   $$E_n = \{n \xrightarrow{\langle \phi, t, \psi \rangle} m \text{ in } T_\sigma : st^*(n) \vDash \phi\}$$
   where, supposing that k is the parent node of n and ψ' is the success condition of the edge that leads to n in T_σ, $st^*(n)$ is the extension of $st(n)$ with the interpretation of success with true if ψ' holds in $st(k)$ and false, otherwise.

---

[2] For utility calculation, we assume a representation of system state in terms of qualities. In Znn, we take the average of response time in all clients and the sum of the costs of active servers.

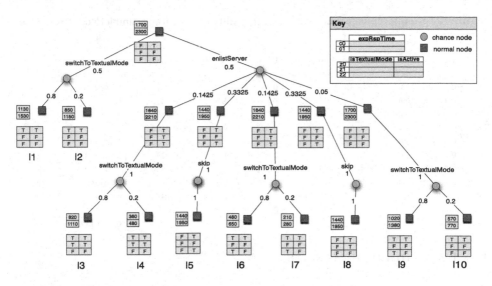

Fig. 3. Tree for simpleReduceResponseTime and a system state with 2000 ms of response time, and a cost of 2 usd/h.

(b) For every $n \xrightarrow{\langle \phi, t, \psi \rangle} m \in E_n$:

    i. add m to the set of chance nodes and $n \xrightarrow{1/|E|}_t m$ to the set of edges.

    ii. for every state s' such that $p = P_{\llbracket \mathcal{I}_t \rrbracket}(st(n), s') > 0$, add the node $m^{s'}$ labelled by s' to the set of normal nodes and $m \xrightarrow{p} m^{s'}$ to the set of edges.

Figure 3 presents the tree $T_{\mathcal{I}}(\mathsf{simpleReduceResponseTime}, s)$ where s is system state with two clients (c_0, c_1) and three servers (z_0, z_1, z_2). Only server z_0 is active in s and is not working in textual mode. The cost assigned to all servers is 1 and the load assigned to z_0, z_1, z_2 is, respectively, 2, 0 and 0. The response time for c_0 is 1700 and for c_1 is 2300. The considered impact models for tactics switchToTextualMode and enlistServer were those presented, respectively, in Listings 1.1 and 1.3. For readability reasons we represented in the figure only the part of the system state that is directly manipulated or affected by the two tactics. Then, using the utility profile, we can calculate the utility of the state associated with each leaf node. The expected utility of the strategy is given by the sum of these utilities weighted by the probability of the path that leads to that node.

Definition 9 (Expected Utility of a Strategy). *Given a set of impact models $\mathcal{I}$, the expected utility of a strategy σ in a system state s is given by*

$$\sum_{n \in leaves(T_{\mathcal{I}}(\sigma, s))} p_n \cdot Util(st(n))$$

where p_n is the product of the probabilities in the path leading from the root to n.

Table 2 illustrates the utility calculation for strategy simpleReduceResponseTime that corresponds to the tree shown in Fig. 3. Note that nodes l1 and l2 contribute half of the utility, and that the sum of all p_n assigned to leaf nodes adds to one.

Table 2. Sample calculation of aggregate utility for strategy simpleReduceResponse Time

n	p_n	avg. expRspTime (ms)	cost (usd/hour)	$U_R(st(n))$	$U_C(st(n))$	$Util(st(n))$	$p_n \cdot Util(st(n))$
l1	0.4	1330	1	0.585	1	0.751	0.3004
l2	0.1	1000	1	0.75	1	0.85	0.085
l3	0.057	965	2	0.7605	0.9	0.8163	0.046529
l4	0.01425	410	2	0.927	0.9	0.9162	0.013056
l5	0.16625	1695	2	0.4025	0.9	0.6105	0.1014496
l6	0.057	565	1	0.8805	1	0.9283	0.052913
l7	0.01425	245	2	0.9765	1	0.9859	0.014049
l8	0.16625	1695	2	0.4025	0.9	0.6105	0.101496
l9	0.02	1200	1	0.65	1	0.79	0.0158
l10	0.005	670	1	0.849	1	0.9094	0.004245
total	1	-	-	-	-	-	**0.734937**

6   Experimental Results

To quantify the benefits of using probabilistic impact models in Rainbow, we considered two alternative models of Znn, one using impact vectors[3] and the other using the proposed impact models. We manually encoded the two models in the language of PRISM [13] and assessed the quality of the models that we are able to specify in each case by quantifying: (i) impact of tactics on the state of the target system, and (ii) impact of strategies on system utility. In addition, both models incorporate an M/M/c queuing model [7], which is able to compute the response time of the system based on the rate of request arrivals to the system, number of active servers, and the service rate (i.e., the time that it takes to service a request, which in this case is directly proportional to the fidelity level). In our experiments, we assume that the response time computed with the queuing model is considered as the actual response time of the system, against which we compare the predictions made using either vectors or probabilistic models.

Using each of the alternative models, we explored a state space $[S] = [1, 9] \times [1, 3]$, which includes the request arrival rate in the interval $[1, 9]$ requests/s, and the number of active servers in the interval $[1, 3]$ (i.e., a valid system configuration can have up to a maximum of 4 active servers). For the sake of clarity, we fixed in our experiments the values of other variables which could have been considered as additional dimensions in our state space (network latency is 0 ms, whereas service rate is fixed at 1 ms).

6.1   Impact of Tactics on System State

To quantify the improvement obtained using vectors with the results of employing probabilistic models, we focused on the enlistServer tactic, for which we encoded two alternative impact descriptions:

---

[3] The impact of individual adaptation actions is specified in terms of constant impact vectors (called cost/benefit attribute vectors) which describe how the execution of adaptation actions affects system quality attributes [5].

Cost-benefit Attribute Vectors. For the vector-based version of the model, we computed the average impact in response time of adding a server in all points of the explored region of the state space, making use of the M/M/c queuing model, which is the best approximation that can be obtained, given by $(\sum_{s \in [S]} MMc(ar_s, as_s + 1) - MMc(ar_s, as_s))/|[S]|$, where $MMc(a, b)$ returns the response time for request arrival rate a and number of active servers b. Moreover, ar_s and as_s designate the request arrival rate, and number of active servers in state s, respectively.

For our state space, this calculation yielded a reduction of response time of 714 ms. Since the cost is increased in 1 unit, and fidelity is not changed by enlistServer, the vector used in our experiments for the tactic is $[-714, +1, 0]$.

Probabilistic Impact Models. The probabilistic version of the model employed for the experiments is analogous to the one described in Listing 1.3.

Figure 4 shows the deviation from actual response time impact values (computed using the M/M/c model) for tactic enlistServer. The values computed using the probabilistic impact model (right) are much more accurate, since their deviation is far less prominent than the one presented when computing impact with vectors (average deviation Δ_{rt} in values computed using vectors is $\simeq 315\%$ wrt the values obtained using impact models). Moreover, while the values computed using vectors are not sensitive to context, presenting reduced deviations wrt actual response times only in states that are close to the average (e.g., 1 server, 3–5 requests/s), values obtained with the probabilistic model better approximate actual impact, reflecting the fact that a higher number of active servers noticeably reduces the impact of the tactic on response time.

6.2 Impact of Strategies on System Utility

The use of different models to express the impact of tactics on system state also affects the predictions that concern the expected utility of the system after the execution of adaptation strategies. To assess how utility prediction is affected by the constructs available to express tactic impact, we included in our PRISM

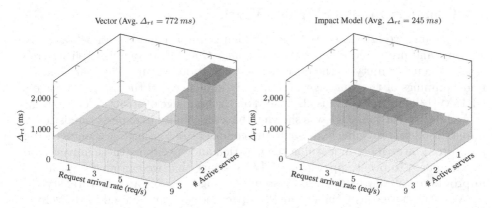

Fig. 4. Deviation in response time impact prediction for tactic enlistServer: cost/benefit vector (left) and probabilistic impact model (right).

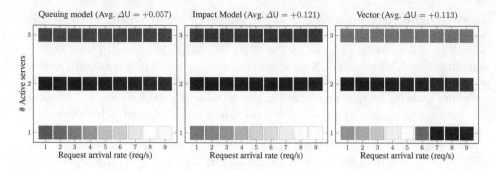

Fig. 5. Utility prediction for the execution of strategy reduceResponseTime based on: queuing model, impact model, and impact vector. Lighter colors represent higher utility improvements.

model an encoding of the strategy simpleReduceResponseTime shown in Fig. 2, and computed the expected utility after its execution for each of the states included in $[S]$ for each of the alternatives.

Figure 5 shows how the utility values predicted using probabilistic impact models (center) exhibit a similar pattern to the one obtained using the queuing model (left). In contrast, vectors (right) show an entirely different pattern, which only coincides with the one resulting from the queuing model in the area in which the impact of tactics is close to their average impact (i.e., when there are two active servers).

It is worth noticing that the overall average difference in utility ΔU across the state space does not constitute a representative indicator of the accuracy of utility predictions, since positive and negative utility deltas in different states can cancel each other (i.e., the average ΔU yielded by vectors is +0.113, which is closer to the one obtained with the queuing model of +0.057, even if the absolute value of the deviation in individual states in vectors is greater than in the case of impact models).

7   Conclusions and Future Work

In this paper we addressed the specification of impact models for self-adaptive systems and presented a declarative language that allows one to explicitly represent the uncertainty in the outcome of adaptation actions. The mathematical underpinnings of the language were heavily influenced by the input language of PRISM [13], but its syntax is also based on the language of structural constraints of Acme [10]. The language was shown to have the ability to express sophisticated impact models, providing expressive and compact descriptions. Although there is an upfront investment in learning the notation and specifying these impact models compared to other approaches [5,17], the fact that we can model variability improves reusability (e.g., across systems sharing the same architectural style).

We also showed how the proposed impact models can be used in the context of Rainbow with adaptation strategies defined in the language Stitch [5], and proposed a new method for calculating the utility of a strategy. The benefits of the proposed impact models can be extended to other architecture-based approaches to self-adaptation that rely on impact models for adaptation decision-making such as [17] and [14].

Regarding future work, we plan on extending our declarative language to cater to architectural styles that support structural changes. Moreover, we plan on leveraging and furthering formal analysis of adaptation behavior by encoding impact models described in our language into existing tools. A third research direction aims at further refining our approach to consider time as a first-class entity in impact models.

References

1. Calinescu, R., Ghezzi, C., Kwiatkowska, M., Mirandola, R.: Self-adaptive software needs quantitative verification at runtime. Commun. ACM **55**(9), 69–77 (2012)
2. Calinescu, R., Kwiatkowska, M.Z.: Using quantitative analysis to implement autonomic IT systems. In: ICSE (2009)
3. Cheng, S., et al.: Evaluating the effectiveness of the rainbow self-adaptive system. In: SEAMS. IEEE (2009)
4. Cheng, S.-W., et al.: Using architectural style as a basis for system self-repair. In: WICSA. Kluwer, B.V. (2002)
5. Cheng, S.-W., Garlan, D.: Stitch: a language for architecture-based self-adaptation. J. Syst. Softw. **85**(12), 2860–2875 (2012)
6. Cheng, S.-W., Garlan, D., Schmerl, B.R.: Raide for engineering architecture-based self-adaptive systems. In: ICSE Companion. IEEE (2009)
7. Chiulli, R.: Quantitative Analysis: An Introduction. Automation and Production Systems. Taylor & Francis, London (1999)
8. Esfahani, N., Malek, S.: Uncertainty in self-adaptive software systems. In: de Lemos, R., Giese, H., Müller, H.A., Shaw, M. (eds.) Software Engineering for Self-Adaptive Systems. LNCS, vol. 7475, pp. 214–238. Springer, Heidelberg (2013)
9. Filieri, A., Ghezzi, C., Leva, A., Maggio, M.: Self-adaptive software meets control theory: a preliminary approach supporting reliability requirements. In: ASE (2011)
10. Garlan, D., et al.: Acme: an architecture description interchange language. In: CASCON (1997)
11. Garlan, D., et al.: Rainbow: architecture-based self-adaptation with reusable infrastructure. IEEE Comput. **37**(10), 46–54 (2004)
12. Klein, C., et al.: Brownout: building more robust cloud applications. In: ICSE. ACM (2014)
13. Kwiatkowska, M., Norman, G., Parker, D.: PRISM 4.0: verification of probabilistic real-time systems. In: Gopalakrishnan, G., Qadeer, S. (eds.) CAV 2011. LNCS, vol. 6806, pp. 585–591. Springer, Heidelberg (2011)
14. Leitner, P., Hummer, W., Dustdar, S.: Cost-based optimization of service compositions. IEEE Trans. Serv. Comput. **6**(2), 239–251 (2013)
15. Norris, J.R.: Markov Chains. Cambridge Series in Statistical and Probabilistic Mathematics. Cambridge University Press, Cambridge (1998)
16. OMG. Object Constraint Language V2.4 (2014). http://www.omg.org/spec/OCL/2.4
17. Rosa, L., Rodrigues, L., Lopes, A., Hiltunen, M.A., Schlichting, R.D.: Self-management of adaptable component-based applications. IEEE Trans. Software Eng. **39**(3), 403–421 (2013)
18. Sykes, D., et al.: Learning revised models for planning in adaptive systems. In: ICSE (2013)

Decentralised Evaluation of Temporal Patterns over Component-Based Systems at Runtime

Olga Kouchnarenko[1,2] and Jean-François Weber[1(✉)]

[1] FEMTO-ST CNRS, University of Franche-Comté, Besançon, France
{okouchnarenko,jfweber}@femto-st.fr
[2] Inria/Nancy-Grand Est, Villers-lès-Nancy, France

Abstract. Self-adaptation allows systems to modify their structure and/
or their behaviour depending on the environment and the system itself.
Since reconfigurations must not happen at any but in suitable circumstances, guiding and controlling dynamic reconfigurations at runtime is
an important issue. This paper contributes to two essential topics of the
self-adaptation—a runtime temporal properties evaluation, and a decentralization of control loops. It extends the work on the adaptation of
component-based systems at runtime via policies with temporal patterns
by providings (a) specific *progressive semantics* of temporal patterns and
(b) a *decentralised* method which is suitable to deal with temporal patterns of component-based systems at runtime. The implementation with
the *GROOVE* tool constitutes a practical contribution.

1 Introduction

Self-adaptation—the ability of systems to modify their structure and/or their
behaviour in response to their interaction with the environment and the system
itself, and their goals—is an important and active research field with applications
in various domains [1]. Since dynamic reconfigurations that modify the architecture of component-based systems without incurring any system downtime must
not happen at any but in suitable circumstances, adaptation policies are used to
guide and control reconfigurations at runtime. For triggering adaptation policies
and specifying behaviours of component-based systems, a linear temporal logic
based on Dwyer's work on patterns and scopes [2], called FTPL, has been used
in [3]. In this adaptation context, choosing a suitable adaptation policy in a
current component-based system configuration depends on a *runtime temporal
patterns evaluation* which is one of the essential topics of the self-adaptation [1].

We consider *open* component-based systems interacting with their environment, therefore, their behaviour depends on both external and internal events.
Since our component-based systems are modelled by infinite state transition

---

This work has been partially funded by the Labex ACTION, ANR-11-LABX-0001-01.

I. Lanese and E. Madelaine (Eds.): FACS 2014, LNCS 8997, pp. 108–126, 2015.
DOI: 10.1007/978-3-319-15317-9_7

systems, for our pattern-based verification to remain tractable, we consider a non-blocking environment with incomplete information about the component-based system that enables all the external events.

In this setting, providing values for temporal patterns is a difficult task. In [3], a centralised evaluation of temporal patterns at runtime has been proposed. In order to contribute to *decentralization of control loops*—another self-adaptation topic, this paper addresses the FTPL *decentralised* evaluation problem on a reconfiguration path, and presents a method that is suitable to deal with temporal patterns of component-based systems. Indeed, as these patterns contain conjunctions or disjunctions of properties over components' parameters and relations, the evaluation of temporal patterns in a decentralised manner makes sense, and the sooner the better.

Inspired by the LTL decentralised evaluation [4] for closed systems, this paper provides a progressive FTPL semantics allowing a decentralised evaluation of FTPL formulae over open component-based systems – the first contribution. The second contribution consists of an algorithm to answer the temporal pattern decentralised evaluation problem in $\mathbb{B}_4$ and of the correctness and uniqueness results saying that whenever an FTPL property is evaluated in the decentralised manner, it matches the FTPL evaluation using the basic semantics in [3]. The implementation with the *GROOVE* tool [5] constitutes a practical contribution.

Related work. When checking properties of open systems, the idea is to satisfy a property no matter how the environment behaves. For non-universal temporal logics, this problem, called *module-checking*, is in general much harder than model-checking of closed systems in finite as well as in infinite settings [6,7], and it becomes undecidable with imperfect information about the control states [8]. Fortunately, for universal temporal logics as LTL, the module checking problem with both complete or incomplete information remains decidable in finite setting [6]; in particular, it is PSPACE-complete for LTL.

As temporal properties often cannot be evaluated to true or false during the system execution, in addition to *true* and *false* values, *potential true* and *potential false* values are used whenever an observed behaviour has not yet led to an acceptance or a violation of the property under consideration, forming the $\mathbb{B}_4$ domain like in RV-LTL [9]. Like in [10], in our framework external events can be seen as invocations of methods performed by (external) sensors when a change is detected in their environment.

Let us remark that this work is motivated by applications in numerous frameworks that support the development of components together with their monitors/controllers, as, e.g., Fractal [11], CSP‖B [12], FraSCAti [13], etc.

More generally, this paper aims to contribute to the development of new verification approaches for complex systems that integrate ideas of distributed algorithms [14].

Layout of the paper. After a short overview of a component-based model and of a linear temporal patterns logic in Sects. 2, 3 presents a specific progressive semantics of temporal patterns. Afterwards, Sect. 4 addresses the temporal pattern decentralised evaluation problem on a reconfiguration path by providing an algorithm for such an evaluation in $\mathbb{B}_4$. Section 5 describes the implementation with the *GROOVE* tool and details an example of a location composite component. Finally, Sect. 6 presents our conclusion.

2   Background: Reconfiguration Model and Temporal Patterns

The reconfigurations we consider here make the component-based architecture evolve dynamically. They are combinations of basic reconfiguration operations such as instantiation/destruction of components; addition/removal of components; binding/unbinding of component interfaces; starting/stopping components; setting parameter values of components. In the remainder of the paper, we focus on reconfigurations that are combinations of basic operations.

In general, a system configuration is the specific definition of the elements that define or prescribe what a system is composed of. As in [15], we define a configuration to be a set of architectural elements (components, required or provided interfaces, and parameters) together with relations (binding, delegation, etc.) to structure and to link them, as depicted in Fig. 1.

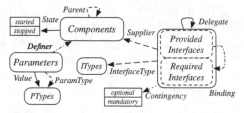

Fig. 1. Configurations = architectural elements and relations

Given a set of configurations $\mathcal{C} = \{c, c_1, c_2, \ldots\}$, let CP be a set of configuration properties on the architectural elements and the relations between them specified using first-order logic formulae. The interpretation of functions, relations, and predicates is done according to basic definitions in [16] and in [15]. A configuration *interpretation* function $l : \mathcal{C} \rightarrow CP$ gives the largest conjunction of $cp \in CP$ evaluated to true on $c \in \mathcal{C}^1$.

Among all the configuration properties, the architectural *consistency constraints CC* express requirements on component assembly common to all the component architectures. These constraints introduced in [17] allow the definition of *consistent configurations* regarding, in particular, the following rules:

- a component *supplies* one provided interface, at least;
- the composite components have no parameter;
- a sub-component must not include its own parent component;
- two bound interfaces must have the same interface type and their containers are sub-components of the same composite;
- when binding two interfaces, there is a need to ensure that they have not been involved in a delegation yet; similarly, when establishing a delegation link between two interfaces, the specifier must ensure that they have not yet been involved in a binding;

---

[1] By definition in [16], this conjunction is in CP.

- a provided (resp. required) interface of a sub-component is delegated to at most one provided (resp. required) interface of its parent component; the interfaces involved in the delegation must have the same interface type;
- a component is *started* only if its mandatory required interfaces are bound or delegated.

Definition 1 (Consistent configuration). *Let* $c = \langle Elem, Rel \rangle$ *be a configuration and* CC *the architectural consistency constraints. The configuration* c *is* consistent, *written* **consistent**(c), *if* $l(c) \Rightarrow CC$.

Let $\mathcal{R}$ be a finite set of reconfiguration operations, and run a generic running operation. The possible evolutions of the component architecture via the reconfiguration operations are defined as a transition system over $\mathcal{R}_{run} = \mathcal{R} \cup \{run\}$.

Definition 2 (Reconfiguration model). *The operational semantics of component systems with reconfigurations is defined by the labelled transition system* $S = \langle \mathcal{C}, \mathcal{C}^0, \mathcal{R}_{run}, \rightarrow, l \rangle$ *where* $\mathcal{C} = \{c, c_1, c_2, \ldots\}$ *is a set of consistent configurations,* $\mathcal{C}^0 \subseteq \mathcal{C}$ *is a set of initial configurations,* $\mathcal{R}$ *is a finite set of reconfigurations,* $\rightarrow \subseteq \mathcal{C} \times \mathcal{R}_{run} \times \mathcal{C}$ *is the reconfiguration relation.*

Let us write $c \xrightarrow{ope} c'$ when c' is reached from c by $ope \in \mathcal{R}_{run}$. An evolution path σ (or a path for short) in S is a (possibly infinite) sequence of configurations $c_0, c_1, c_2, \ldots$ such that $\forall i \geq 0$. $(\exists\, ope_i \in \mathcal{R}_{run}.(c_i \xrightarrow{ope_i} c_{i+1}))$. Let $\sigma(i)$ denote the i-th configuration of a path σ, σ_i a suffix path starting with $\sigma(i)$, and Σ the set of paths. An execution is a path σ in Σ such that $\sigma(0) \in \mathcal{C}^0$.

In this section, we also briefly recall the FTPL[2] logic patterns introduced in [18]. In addition to configuration properties (cp) in CP mentioned above, the proposed logic contains external events (ext), as well as events from reconfiguration operations, temporal properties (tpp) together with trace properties (trp) embedded into temporal properties. Let $Prop_{FTPL}$ denote the set of the FTPL formulae obeying the FTPL grammar below. The FTPL semantics from [3] is summarized in the long version of this paper [19].

```
<FTPL>   ::= <tpp> | <events> | cp
<tpp>    ::= after <events> <tpp> | before <events> <trp> | <trp> until <events> | <trp>
<trp>    ::= always cp | eventually cp | <trp> ∧ <trp> | <trp> ∨ <trp>
<events> ::= <event>,<events> | <event>
<event>  ::= ope normal | ope exceptional | ope terminates | ext
```

In the rest of the paper, let AE be the set of atomic events composed of atomic propositions from CP and of basic FTPL events. An *event* θ is an element of $\Theta = 2^{AE}$. Let us suppose that each component C_i of the component-based system has a local monitor M_i attached to it, from the set $\mathcal{M} = \{M_0, \ldots, M_{n-1}\}$ of monitors[3]. Let us introduce the projection function Π_i to restrict events to

---

[2] FTPL stands for TPL (Temporal Pattern Language) prefixed by 'F' to denote its relation to Fractal-like components and to first-order integrity constraints over them.
[3] Implemented as controllers in CSP‖B, Fractal, FraSCAti, etc.

the local view of the monitor M_i. For atomic events, $\Pi_i : 2^{AE} \to 2^{AE}$, and we write $AE_i = \Pi_i(AE)$. We assume $\forall i, j \leq n.i \neq j \Rightarrow AE_i \cap AE_j = \varnothing^4$. Similarly, for events, we define $\Pi_i : 2^\Theta \to 2^\Theta$, with $\Theta_i = \Pi_i(\Theta)$, and we assume $\forall i, j \leq n.i \neq j \Rightarrow \Theta_i \cap \Theta_j = \varnothing$.

Let $ev : \mathcal{C} \to \Theta$ be a function to associate events with configurations. Given a configuration $\sigma(j)$ of a path σ with $j \geq 0$, the corresponding event is $\theta(j) = ev(\sigma(j))$. In this setting, an individual *behaviour* of a component C_i can be defined as a (finite or infinite) sequence of events $\theta_i = \theta_i(0) \cdot \theta_i(1) \cdots \theta_i(j) \cdots$ s.t. $\forall j \geq 0.\theta_i(j) = \Pi_i(ev(\sigma(j))) \in \Theta_i$, also called a *trace*. Finite (resp. infinite) traces over Θ are elements of Θ^* (resp. Θ^ω); the set of all traces is $\Theta^\infty = \Theta^* \cup \Theta^\omega$.

3   FTPL Progression and Urgency

This section provides the underpinnings to allow a decentralised evaluation of FTPL formulae. Inspired by definitions in [4], our notions of progression and urgency are adapted to the FTPL semantics: they take into account external and internal events as well as scopes of linear temporal patterns.

For decentralised evaluation of the FTPL formulae, instead of the set $\mathbb{B}_4$ as in [3], let us consider the set $\mathbb{B}_5 = \{\bot, \bot^p, \#, \top^p, \top\}$, where $\bot, \top$ stand resp. for *false* and *true* values, $\bot^p, \top^p$ for *potential false* and *potential true* values, and $\#$ for *unknown* value. We consider $\mathbb{B}_5$ together with the truth non-strict ordering relation $\sqsubseteq_5$ satisfying $\bot \sqsubseteq_5 \bot^p \sqsubseteq_5 \top^p \sqsubseteq_5 \top \sqsubseteq_5 \#$. On $\mathbb{B}_5$ we define two binary symmetric operations $\sqcap_5, \sqcup_5$ resp. as the minimum and maximum interpreted wrt. $\sqsubseteq_5$. Thus, $(\mathbb{B}_5, \sqsubseteq_5)$ is a finite lattice but not a Boolean nor a de Morgan lattice. Let $\forall \varphi \in Prop_{FTPL}.\varphi \sqcap_5 \# = \varphi$. We write $\sqcup$ and $\sqcap$ instead of $\sqcup_5$ and $\sqcap_5$ when it is clear from the context. For any formula $\varphi \in Prop_{FTPL}$, let $\hat{\varphi}$ denote the value of φ in $\mathbb{B}_5$.

In the context of a decentralised evaluation, each monitor may not be aware of information related to a given property and may be not able to evaluate it. This property is then written as a formula in terms of the current configuration. However, after the transition to the next configuration, such a formula may be not relevant. To compensate for this, we define the progression function to rewrite FTPL formulae in a way relevant to the next configuration of a path. Intuitively, given an FTPL formula and a set of atomic events, the progression function provides either the value of the property, if available, or the rewritten formula otherwise.

Definition 3 (Progression Function for *Events*). *Let* $\varepsilon, \varepsilon_1, \varepsilon_2 \in AE$, $e = e_1, e_2 \ldots e_m$, *a list of FTPL events from* AE, *and* $\theta(i)$ *an event. The progression function* $P : Prop_{FTPL} \times \Theta \to Prop_{FTPL}$ *is inductively defined by:*

---

[4] For relations involving two components (like *Delegate* or *Parent*) we consider that only the parent component is *aware* of the relation. For the *Binding* relation, only the component owning the *required* (or *client*) interface is *aware* of the binding.

$$P(\varepsilon, \theta(i)) \quad\quad = \top \; if \; \varepsilon \in \theta(i), \bot \; otherwise \;;$$
$$P(\varepsilon_1 \vee \varepsilon_2, \theta(i)) = P(\varepsilon_1, \theta(i)) \vee P(\varepsilon_2, \theta(i)) \quad\quad ;$$
$$P(\neg\varepsilon, \theta(i)) \quad\quad = \neg P(\varepsilon, \theta(i)) \quad\quad\quad\quad\quad\quad ;$$
$$P(e, \theta(i)) \quad\quad\quad = \bigvee_{1 \leq j \leq m} P(e_j, \theta(i)) \quad\quad\quad ;$$

$$P(\bot, \theta(i)) \quad = \quad \bot$$
$$P(\bot^p, \theta(i)) = \quad \bot^p$$
$$P(\top^p, \theta(i)) = \quad \top^p$$
$$P(\top, \theta(i)) \quad = \quad \top$$

Let us now introduce, in order to establish progression formulae, the $\overline{\mathbf{X}}$-operator that precedes an FTPL property to denote its evaluation at the configuration preceding the current one, i.e., $P(\overline{\mathbf{X}}\xi, \theta(i)) = P(\xi, \theta(i-1))$. We write $\overline{\mathbf{X}}^m \xi$ to denote $\overline{\overline{\mathbf{X}\mathbf{X}} \ldots \overline{\mathbf{x}}}^{m}\varepsilon$. Also, when $m = 0$, $\overline{\mathbf{X}}^m \xi = \xi$.

Because of lack of room, the progression function is not given for every type of FTPL property. Instead, we provide a definition for the **always** trace property (Definition 4), lists of events (Definition 5), and the **before** temporal property (Definition 6). The reader can extrapolate these definitions for the remaining FTPL properties, using the FTPL progressive semantics introduced in [3].

Definition 4 (Progression of the *always* FTPL trace property's evaluation formulae on a (suffix) path). *Let cp be a configuration property and ϕ a trace property of the form $\phi = $ **always** cp. The progression function P for the **always** property on a (suffix) path is defined by:*

$$P(\phi_{\sigma_k}, \theta(i)) = \begin{cases} P(cp, \theta(i)) \sqcap \top^p & for \; i = k \\ P(cp, \theta(i)) \sqcap P(\overline{\mathbf{X}}\phi_{\sigma_k}, \theta(i)) & for \; i > k \end{cases} \tag{1}$$

Definition 5 (Progression of FTPL list of events properties' evaluation formulae on a (suffix) path). *Let e be a list of FTPL events, the progression function P for FTPL lists of events on a (suffix) path is defined by:*

$$P(e_{\sigma_k}, \theta(i)) = \begin{cases} P(e, \theta(i)) & for \; i = k \\ P(e, \theta(i)) \sqcup (\top^p \sqcap P(\overline{\mathbf{X}}e_{\sigma_k}, \theta(i))) & for \; i > k \end{cases} \tag{2}$$

Definition 6 (Progression of the *before* FTPL temporal property's evaluation formulae on a (suffix) path). *Let e be a list of FTPL events, trp a trace property, and β a temporal property of the form $\beta = $ **before** e trp. The progression function P for the **before** property on a (suffix) path is defined by:*

$$P(\beta_{\sigma_k}, \theta(i)) = \begin{cases} \top^p & for \; i = k \\ F_{\mathcal{B}}(P(e_{\sigma_k}, \theta(i)), P(\overline{\mathbf{X}}trp'_{\sigma_k}, \theta(i)), P(\overline{\mathbf{X}}\beta_{\sigma_k}, \theta(i))) & for \; i > k \end{cases} \tag{3}$$

where $F_{\mathcal{B}}$ is based on the FTPL progressive semantics and defined as follows:

$$F_{\mathcal{B}}(\varepsilon, trp, tpp) = \begin{cases} \top^p & if \; \varepsilon = \bot \\ \bot & if \; \varepsilon = \top \wedge trp \in \{\bot, \bot^p\} \\ tpp & otherwise \end{cases} \tag{4}$$

Example 1. Let be $\varphi = $ **before** $e\ trp$ where e is an FTPL list of events and trp a trace property. To evaluate φ at the configuration of index $i > 0$ on the suffix path σ_0, let us set $P(e_{\sigma_0}, \theta(i)) = e_{\sigma_0}(i) = \top$ and $P(trp_{\sigma_0}, \theta(i-1)) = trp_{\sigma_0}(i-1) = \perp^p$. Then by Equalities (3) and (4) we have:

$$
\begin{aligned}
P(\varphi_{\sigma_0}, \theta(i)) &= F_{\mathcal{B}}(P(e_{\sigma_0}, \theta(i)), P(\overline{\mathbf{X}}trp_{\sigma_0}, \theta(i)), P(\overline{\mathbf{X}}\varphi_{\sigma_0}, \theta(i))) \\
&= F_{\mathcal{B}}(P(e_{\sigma_0}, \theta(i)), P(trp_{\sigma_0}, \theta(i-1)), P(\varphi_{\sigma_0}, \theta(i-1))) \\
&= F_{\mathcal{B}}(\top, \perp^p, P(\varphi_{\sigma_0}, \theta(i-1))) \\
&= \perp
\end{aligned}
$$

In order to perform evaluation in a decentralised manner, we define below the *Normalised Progression Form* (NPF) to describe the point up to which a formula should be developed, using the progression function.

Definition 7 (NPF). *Let φ be an FTPL property and θ an event. A formula $P(\varphi, \theta)$ is in NPF if the $\overline{\mathbf{X}}$-operator only precedes atomic events.*

Theorem 1 (Existence of NPF). *Let φ be an FTPL property and θ an event. Every $P(\varphi, \theta)$ can be rewritten into an equivalent[5] formula in NPF.*

Proof. The proof is by induction on the indexes of the events (i.e., on the trace) using Definitons 4 to 6 (and definitions for the remaining FTPL properties).

Example 2. Let be $\varphi = $ **before** $e\ trp$, $e = a, b$, and $trp = $ **always** cp, where a and b are FTPL events s.t. a, b, and $cp \in CP$ are atomic events. The resulting formula in NPF is obtained using Eq. 3.

$P(\varphi_{\sigma_0}, \theta(0)) = \top^p$

$P(\varphi_{\sigma_0}, \theta(1)) = F_{\mathcal{B}}(P(e_{\sigma_0}, \theta(1)), P(\overline{\mathbf{X}}trp_{\sigma_0}, \theta(1)), P(\overline{\mathbf{X}}\varphi_{\sigma_0}, \theta(1)))$

$\qquad = F_{\mathcal{B}}(P(e, \theta(1)) \sqcup (\top^p \sqcap P(\overline{\mathbf{X}}e_{\sigma_0}, \theta(1))), P(trp_{\sigma_0}, \theta(0)), P(\varphi_{\sigma_0}, \theta(0)))$

$\qquad = F_{\mathcal{B}}(P(a, \theta(1)) \sqcup P(b, \theta(1)) \sqcup (\top^p \sqcap P(e_{\sigma_0}, \theta(0))), P(cp, \theta(0)) \sqcap \top^p, \top^p)$

$\qquad = F_{\mathcal{B}}(P(a, \theta(1)) \sqcup P(b, \theta(1)) \sqcup (\top^p \sqcap P(e, \theta(0))), P(cp, \theta(0)) \sqcap \top^p, \top^p)$

$\qquad = F_{\mathcal{B}}(P(a, \theta(1)) \sqcup P(b, \theta(1)) \sqcup (\top^p \sqcap (P(a, \theta(0)) \sqcup P(b, \theta(0)))), P(cp, \theta(0)) \sqcap \top^p, \top^p)$

$\qquad = F_{\mathcal{B}}(P(a, \theta(1)) \sqcup P(b, \theta(1)) \sqcup (\top^p \sqcap (P(\overline{\mathbf{X}}a, \theta(1)) \sqcup P(\overline{\mathbf{X}}b, \theta(1)))), P(\overline{\mathbf{X}}cp, \theta(1)) \sqcap \top^p, \top^p)$

As in [4] for LTL, a monitor M_j for the component C_j accepts as input an event $\theta(i)$ and FTPL properties. Applying Definition 3 to atomic events could lead to wrong results in a decentralised context. For example, if $\varepsilon \notin \theta(i)$ holds locally for the monitor M_j it could be due to the fact that $\varepsilon \notin AE_j$. The decentralised progression rule should be adapted by taking into account a local set of atomic events. Hence, the progression rule for atomic events preceded by the $\overline{\mathbf{X}}$-operator is given below.

$$
P(\overline{\mathbf{X}}^m \varsigma, \theta(i), AE_j) = \begin{cases} \top & \text{if } \varsigma = \varsigma' \text{ for some } \varsigma' \in AE_j \cap \Pi_j(\theta(i-m)), \\ \perp & \text{if } \varsigma = \varsigma' \text{ for some } \varsigma' \in AE_j \setminus \Pi_j(\theta(i-m)), \\ \overline{\mathbf{X}}^{m+1} \varsigma & \text{otherwise.} \end{cases}
$$

$$(5)$$

---

[5] wrt. the semantics.

We complete the specification of the progression function with the special symbol $\# \notin AE$ for which the progression is defined by $\forall j.P(\#, \theta, AE_j) = \#$. Finally, among different formulae to be evaluated, the notion of urgency allows determining a set of urgent formulae. In a nutshell, the urgency of a formula in NPF is 0 if the formula does not contain any $\overline{\mathbf{X}}$-operator or the value of the greatest exponent of the $\overline{\mathbf{X}}$-operator. Using formulae in NPF, any sub-formula ς following an $\overline{\mathbf{X}}$-operator is atomic ($\exists j.\varsigma \in AE_j$) and can only be evaluated by a single monitor M_j. A formal definition of urgency can be found in [19].

4   Decentralised Evaluation Problem

As FTPL patterns contain conjunctions or disjunctions of properties over components' parameters and relations, the evaluation of temporal patterns in a decentralised manner makes sense. Section 4.1 addresses the temporal pattern decentralised evaluation problem on a reconfiguration path by providing an algorithm for such an evaluation in $\mathbb{B}_4$. Its properties are studied in Sect. 4.2.

4.1   Problem Statement and Local Monitor Algorithm

Let $\hat{\varphi}_{\sigma_k}(s)$ denote the value of φ at configuration of index s on the suffix path σ_k. While considering components with their monitors, because of a decentralised fashion, the evaluation of $\varphi_{\sigma_k}(s)$ by a monitor M_i may be delayed to configuration $\sigma(t)$ with $t > s$, and the progression comes into play. In this case, let $_i\varphi^s_{\sigma_k}(t)$ denote the decentralised formula as progressed to the configuration $\sigma(t)$ by M_i, for the evaluation of φ started at configuration $\sigma(s)$. Therefore, we consider the following decision problem.

Temporal Pattern Decentralised Evaluation on a Path (TPDEP)
Input: an FTPL temporal property φ, a suffix path σ_k with $k \geq 0$, a configuration $\sigma(s)$ with $s \geq k$, and a number $n = |\mathcal{M}|$ of monitors.

Output: $i, j < n$, and $_i\hat{\varphi}^s_{\sigma_k}(s + j) \in \mathbb{B}_4$, the value of φ at $\sigma(s + j)$ by M_i.

We consider as the basic TPDEP case the situation when only *run* operations occur after the TPDEP problem input, and until an output is returned, communications between monitors being covered by *run* operations.

The idea of a decentralised evaluation is as follows. Similarly to [4], at the configuration $\sigma(t)$, if $_i\varphi^s(t)$ cannot be evaluated in $\mathbb{B}_4$, a monitor M_i progresses its current formula $_i\varphi^s(t)$ to $_i\varphi^s(t+1) = P(_i\varphi^s(t), \theta(t), AE_i)$ and sends it to a monitor that can evaluate its most urgent sub-formula. After $_i\varphi^s(t+1)$ is sent, M_i sets $_i\varphi^s(t+1) = \#$. When M_i receives one or more formulae from others monitors, each of them is added to the current formula using the $\sqcap$ operator.

Unlike [4], where LTL decentralised monitoring determines the *steady* value of a property in $\mathbb{B}_2$, our decentralised method allows values of FTPL properties in $\mathbb{B}_4$ to vary at different configurations, depending notably on the property scopes and on external events. To this end, a result in $\mathbb{B}_4$ obtained by a monitor is broadcast to other monitors, allowing them to maintain a complete but

```
1  (*LDMon*)                                      14 |  |   IF (Prop(φ)∩AE_i ≠ ∅ ∧ _iφ^s_{σ_k}(t) ≠ #) DO
2  Input                                          15 |  |  |  send(_iφ^s_{σ_k}(t))
3     i       (*current monitor index*)           16 |  |  |  _iφ^s_{σ_k}(t) = #
4     AE_i    (*current monitor atomic events*)   17 |  |   FI
5     s       (*input configuration index*)       18 |  |   receive({_jφ^s_{σ_k}(t)}_{j≠i})
6     φ       (*FTPL property to evaluate*)        19 |  |   _iφ^s_{σ_k}(t) := _iφ^s_{σ_k}(t) ⊓ ⊓_{j≠i} _jφ^s_{σ_k}(t)
7     σ_k     (*suffix path*)                      20 |  ENDWHILE
8  Variables                                       21 |  IF (∀j ≠ i._jφ̂^s_{σ_k}(t) ∉ B_4) DO
9     t := s : integer                             22 |  |  broadcast(_iφ̂^s_{σ_k}(t))
10 Begin                                           23 |  FI
11 |  WHILE (_iφ̂^s_{σ_k}(t) ∉ B_4) DO              24 |  RETURN _iφ̂^s_{σ_k}(t)
12 |  |  _iφ̂^s_{σ_k}(t+1) := P(_iφ̂^s_{σ_k}(t), θ_i(t), AE_i)   25 End
13 |  |  t := t+1
```

Fig. 2. Algorithm LDMon

bounded history that can be used to invoke the TPDEP problem at the following configurations.

To answer the TPDEP problem, we propose the LDMon algorithm displayed in Fig. 2. It takes as input the index i of the current monitor, its set AE_i of atomic events, the index s of the current configuration, an FTPL temporal property φ to be evaluated, and the index k of the suffix path on which φ is supposed to be evaluated. An integer variable t indicates the index of the current configuration as it evolves. The algorithm broadcasts to all monitors, as soon as it is determined, the result of the evaluation of φ in $\mathbb{B}_4$. We chose this method to transmit the results because we prefer to focus on the feasibility of a decentralised evaluation of temporal patterns and we consider that the transmission of result is a related issue outside of the scope of this paper.

Three functions are used in this algorithm: (a) $\mathtt{send}(\varphi)$, sends φ (as well as its sub-formulae evaluated at the current configuration) to monitor M_j (different from the current monitor) where ψ is the most urgent sub-formula[6] such that $Prop(\psi) \subseteq AE_j$ holds, with $Prop : Prop_{FTPL} \rightarrow 2^{AE}$ yielding the set of events of an FTPL formula; (b) $\mathtt{receive}(\{\varphi, \dots\})$, receives formulae sent (and broadcast) by other monitors; and (c) $\mathtt{broadcast}(\varphi)$, broadcasts φ to all other monitors.

As long as an evaluation of φ in $\mathbb{B}_4$ is not obtained (line 11), the LDMon algorithm loops in the following way: the evaluation formula is progressed to the next configuration (line 12) and the current configuration index t is incremented (line 13). If at least one event of the current formula belongs to the set of atomic events AE_i ($Prop(\varphi) \cap AE_i \neq \varnothing$) and if no progressed formula was sent (or if such a formula was sent and at least one from another monitor was received) at the previous configuration ($_i\varphi^s_{\sigma_k}(t) \neq \#$), the progressed formula is sent to the monitor that can solve its most urgent sub-formula (line 15) and is set to $\#$ (line 16). Progressed formulae (and broadcast results) from other monitors are received (line 18) and are combined to the local formula using the $\sqcap$-operator

---

[6] In the case where there are two or more equally urgent formulae, φ is sent to a monitor determined by an arbitrary order with the function $Mon : \mathcal{M} \times 2^{AE} \rightarrow \mathcal{M}$. $Mon(M_i, AE') = M_{j_{min}}$ s.t $j_{min} = min(j \in [1,n]\backslash\{i\}|AE' \cap AE_j \neq \varnothing)$.

(line 19). If the result is not in $\mathbb{B}_4$, the loop continues, otherwise if the result of the formula has not already been provided by another monitor (line 21), the result is broadcast (line 22) and returned (line 24).

4.2 Correctness, Uniqueness, and Termination

In this section several properties of the LDMon algorithm are studied. Proposition 1, below, guarantees that the LDMon algorithm provides an output within a finite number of configurations, communications being covered by *run* operations.

Proposition 1 (Existence). *Let* $\varphi \in Prop_{FTPL}$, σ_k *a suffix path*, $k \geq 0$. *For a given configuration* $\sigma(s)$ *with* $s \geq k$, *when using a number* $n = |\mathcal{M}|$ *of monitors, the* LDMon *algorithm provides an output such that* $\exists i, j. i, j < n \wedge {}_i\hat{\varphi}^s_{\sigma_k}(s+j) \in \mathbb{B}_4$.

Proof. (*Sketch.*) Let $M_0, M_1, \ldots, M_{n-1}$ be n monitors. At a given configuration of index s, if one of the monitors $M_i \in \mathcal{M}$ is able to evaluate its formula in $\mathbb{B}_4$, the proposition holds with $j = 0$. Otherwise, each monitor M_i ($0 \leq i < n$) progresses its formula ${}_i\varphi^s_{\sigma_k}(s)$ into ${}_i\varphi^s_{\sigma_k}(s+1)$ and sends it to another monitor, according to *Mon*, able to answer its most urgent sub-formula.

We assume that ${}_{i_1}\varphi^s_{\sigma_k}(s+1)$ is sent to the monitor $M_{i_2 \neq i_1}$. At the next configuration of index $s + 1$, the monitor M_{i_2} receives ${}_{i_1}\varphi^s_{\sigma_k}(s+1)$ and combines it with ${}_{i_2}\varphi^s_{\sigma_k}(s+1)$ as well as other formulae (if any) received from other monitors using the $\sqcap$-operator. If one of these formulae (or a sufficient number of sub-formulae) can be evaluated in $\mathbb{B}_4$, the proposition holds with $j = 1$ and ${}_i\hat{\varphi}^s_{\sigma_k}(s+1)$. Otherwise, each monitor M_i progresses the formula ${}_i\varphi^s_{\sigma_k}(s+1)$ into ${}_i\varphi^s_{\sigma_k}(s+2)$ and sends it to another monitor according to *Mon* which is able to answer its most urgent sub-formula.

We assume that ${}_{i_2}\varphi^s_{\sigma_k}(s+2)$ is sent to the monitor M_{i_3} with $i_3 \neq i_2$. Also $i_3 \neq i_1$ because previously, all sub-formulae of ${}_{i_1}\varphi^s_{\sigma_k}(s+1)$ that could be solved using the set of atomic events AE_{i_1} were already solved. This way, the problem is reduced from n to $n-1$ monitors. Since for a single monitor the output of the algorithm is $\hat{\varphi}_{\sigma_k}(s)$ with $j = 0$, we can infer that for n monitors, there is at least one monitor M_{i_0} such that ${}_{i_0}\hat{\varphi}^s_{\sigma_k}(s+j) \in \mathbb{B}_4$ with $j < n$. □

As explained before, when evaluating $\varphi_{\sigma_k}(s)$, the formula ${}_i\varphi^s_{\sigma_k}(t)$ at configuration of index t by M_i either has a result ${}_i\hat{\varphi}^s_{\sigma_k}(t) \in \mathbb{B}_4$ or progresses to $\#$. The latter is written ${}_i\hat{\varphi}^s_{\sigma_k}(t) = \#$. Thus ${}_i\hat{\varphi}^s_{\sigma_k}(t) \in \mathbb{B}_5$.

Theorem 2 (Semantic Correctness). ${}_i\hat{\varphi}^s_{\sigma_k}(t) \neq \# \Leftrightarrow {}_i\hat{\varphi}^s_{\sigma_k}(t) = \hat{\varphi}_{\sigma_k}(s)$.

Proof. (*Sketch.*)

$\Rightarrow$ If ${}_i\hat{\varphi}^s_{\sigma_k}(t) \neq \#$, a result has been obtained in $\mathbb{B}_4$, otherwise ${}_i\hat{\varphi}^s_{\sigma_k}(t)$ would equal $\#$. Therefore, we only have to verify that the progression function of Definitions 3 to 6 (and definitions for the remaining FTPL properties) matches the FTPL semantics in $\mathbb{B}_4$ as defined in [3]. It is done by induction on the path length.

$\Leftarrow$ ${}_i\hat{\varphi}^s_{\sigma_k}(t) = \hat{\varphi}_{\sigma_k}(s) \Rightarrow {}_i\hat{\varphi}^s_{\sigma_k}(t) \in \mathbb{B}_4 \Rightarrow {}_i\hat{\varphi}^s_{\sigma_k}(t) \neq \#$.

Corollary 1 (Uniqueness). *If $_i\hat{\varphi}^s_{\sigma_k}(t) \neq \#$ and $_j\hat{\varphi}^s_{\sigma_k}(t) \neq \#$ for $i \neq j$, then $_i\hat{\varphi}^s_{\sigma_k}(t) = {_j}\hat{\varphi}^s_{\sigma_k}(t)$.*

Corollary 2 (Generalised Uniqueness). *Let be $_S\hat{\varphi}^s_{\sigma_k}(t) = \underset{i \in S}{\sqcap} {_i}\varphi^s_{\sigma_k}(t)$ for $S \subseteq [1, n]$. If $_S\hat{\varphi}^s_{\sigma_k}(t) \neq \#$ then for all $j \in S$, $_j\hat{\varphi}^s_{\sigma_k}(t) \neq \#$ implies $_j\hat{\varphi}^s_{\sigma_k}(t) = {_S}\hat{\varphi}^s_{\sigma_k}(t)$.*

Corollary 2 allows a monitor to simplify the combination of formulae with the operator $\sqcap$. For a given property, a conjunction in $\mathbb{B}_4$ of formulae received from other monitors with the formula of the current monitor can be replaced by any of these formulae provided that its value is different from $\#$.

Example 3. Let us consider again $\varphi = $ **before** $e\ trp$. Let A, B, and C be the components with their respective monitors M_A, M_B, and M_C such that $_i\varphi^s(t) = F_\mathcal{B}(_ie^s(t), {_i}trp^{s-1}(t), {_i}\varphi^{s-1}(t))$ for $i \in \{A, B, C\}$ (Definition 6). Let us assume $\varphi(s) = F_\mathcal{B}(e(s), trp(s-1), \varphi(s-1))$, with $\varphi(s), e(s), trp(s-1)$, and $\varphi(s-1)$ being evaluated in $\mathbb{B}_4$. By Corollary 2, $e(s) = {_A}e^s(t) \sqcap {_B}e^s(t) \sqcap {_C}e^s(t)$ (resp. $trp(s-1) = {_A}trp^{s-1}(t) \sqcap {_B}trp^{s-1}(t) \sqcap {_C}trp^{s-1}(t)$, $\varphi(s-1) = {_A}\varphi^{s-1}(t) \sqcap {_B}\varphi^{s-1}(t) \sqcap {_C}\varphi^{s-1}(t))$ if it exists at least one i such that the value of $_ie^t(s)$ (resp. $_itrp^{s-1}(t)$, $_i\varphi^{s-1}(t)$) is in $\mathbb{B}_4$; in this case, $_ie^s(t) = e(s)$ (resp. $_itrp^{s-1}(t) = trp(s-1)$, $_i\varphi^{s-1}(t) = \varphi(s-1))$.

For example, if $_A\varphi^s(t) = F_\mathcal{B}(\top, \phi, {_A}\varphi^{s-1}(t))$, $_B\varphi^s(t) = F_\mathcal{B}(\varepsilon, \top^p, {_B}\varphi^{s-1}(t))$, and $_C\varphi^s(t) = F_\mathcal{B}(\epsilon, \psi, \top^p)$, with ϕ, $_A\varphi^{s-1}(t)$, ε, $_B\varphi^{s-1}(t)$, ϵ, and ψ not being evaluated in $\mathbb{B}_4$. It implies $_Ae^s(t) = e(s) = \top$ (resp. $_Btrp^{s-1}(t) = trp(s-1) = \top^p$, $_C\varphi^{s-1}(t) = \varphi(s-1) = \top^p$) and $\varphi(s) = F_\mathcal{B}(\top, \top^p, \top^p) = \top^p$.

Proposition 2 (Correctness and Uniqueness). *The output provided by the* LDMon *algorithm answers the TPDEP problem. For a given configuration $\sigma(s)$, this answer is unique.*

Proof. (Sketch.) By Proposition 1 LDMon provides an output $_i\hat{\varphi}^s_{\sigma_k}(s+j)$ for at least one monitor M_i, within a finite number j of configurations. By Theorem 2 this output answers the TPDEP problem. Furthermore Corollary 1 establishes that for any i_0, if $_{i_0}\hat{\varphi}^s_{\sigma_k}(s+j)$ is the output of the LDMon algorithm for the monitor M_{i_0} then $_{i_0}\hat{\varphi}^s_{\sigma_k}(s+j) = {_i}\hat{\varphi}^s_{\sigma_k}(s+j)$. □

Proposition 3 (Termination). *The* LDMon *algorithm always terminates, either at the configuration when an output is provided or at the next one. Furthermore, the number of configurations needed to reach a result is at most $|\mathcal{M}|$.*

Proof. (sketch) Propositions 1 and 2 establish that the LDMon algorithm terminates and answers the TPDEP problem for at least one monitor M_i after a finite number of reconfigurations $j < |\mathcal{M}|$. Such monitor M_i broadcasts the result to all other monitors before finishing (line 22 of the LDMon algorithm, Fig. 2). This enables any monitor for which the LDMon algorithm did not finish at configuration

$s + j$ to receive the result of the broadcast and to finish its instance of the LDMon algorithm at configuration $s + j + 1 \leq s + |\mathcal{M}|$.   □

In general, decentralised algorithms tend to be very hard for creating a consensus and moreover they require significant communication overhead. Let us emphasize the fact that Proposition 2 guarantees the correctness and uniqueness of a result, which implies such a consensus. As a consequence of Propositions 2 and 3 adaptation policies relying on the decentralised evaluation of FTPL temporal properties can be applied to component-based systems for their dynamic reconfiguration at runtime.

Let us now discuss communication overhead. We consider a component-based system of N components reporting their status in $\mathbb{B}_4$ to a central controller at each configuration as described for in [3]. In the centralised context, thanks to the progressive semantics, the evaluation of a given FTPL property φ would mean that N messages should be sent to conclude in $\mathbb{B}_4$. With the decentralised approach, assuming that atomic events of φ would be distributed among n components ($n \leq N$), we would need, at most, $n^2 - 1$ messages to evaluate φ.

This means that to evaluate a formula involving $n = 10$ components of a component-based system of $N = 100$ components, in the worst case the decentralised fashion would need 99 messages versus 100 for the centralised approach to evaluate φ which is a ratio of 99 %. If, however, the total number N of components of the system is much greater than the number n of components involved in the evaluation of φ, the communication overhead ratio can be even lower (e.g., 9.9 % for $N = 1000$). Reciprocally, if a great proportion of the system is involved in the property to evaluate, the centralised method would lead to better results. Let q be such a proportion, i.e., $n = qN$, the communication overhead ratio is $Nq^2 - 1/N$.

This is different from the result in [4] where the decentralised algorithm outperforms its centralised counterpart by a proportion of 1 to 4 in terms of communication overhead, to conclude in $\mathbb{B}_2$. Such a difference is due to the fact that in our case, as soon as a property is evaluated in $\mathbb{B}_4$ for a given configuration of the path, another evaluation is initiated for another configuration. Nevertheless, we have better results while monitoring only components concerned with the temporal property, that can be determined syntactically. To sum up, our approach is suitable for systems with a large number of components when the FTPL property to evaluate involves a small proportion of them.

5   Implementation and Experiment

This section describes how the LDMon algorithm has been implemented within the *GROOVE* graph transformation tool [5]. This implementation is then used to experiment with a case study.

5.1   Implementing with *GROOVE*

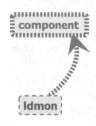

Fig. 3. Rule `remove OrphanMon` (Color figure online)

GROOVE uses simple graphs for modelling the structure of object-oriented systems at design-time, compile-time, and runtime. Graphs are made of nodes and edges that can be labelled. Graph transformations provide a basis for model transformation or for operational semantics of systems. Graphs are transformed by rules consisting of (a) patterns that must be present (resp. absent) for the rule to apply, (b) elements (nodes and edges) to be added (resp.deleted) from the graph, and (c) pairs of nodes to be merged. Colour and shape coding allow these rules to be easily represented. For example, our implementation uses the graph rule `removeOrphanMon` represented Fig. 3 that can be interpreted as follows: (a) The red (dashed fat) "embargo" elements, representing a node of type *component* and an edge defining a monitoring relation between monitors, of type *ldmon*, and *components*, must be absent, (b) the blue (dashed thin) "eraser" element, representing a node of type *ldmon*, must be present, and (c) if both conditions are satisfied, the blue (dashed thin) element is deleted. This means that if a monitor of type *ldmon* is not monitoring a *component*, the monitor node, *ldmon*, must be deleted. The reader interested in *GROOVE* is referred to [5].

Our implementation uses the *GROOVE* typed mode to guarantee that all graphs are well-typed. It consists of generic types and graph rules that can manage assigned priorities in such a way that a rule is applied only if no rule of higher priority matches the current graph. The input is a graph containing an FTPL formula and a component-based system, both represented using the model presented in Sect. 2. Figure 4 shows a screenshot of *GROOVE* displaying, in the main panel, a graph modelling the *location* component-based system used in the case study below. *Components* are represented in blue, *Required* (resp. *Provided) Interfaces* in magenta (resp. red), *Parameters* in black, and both *ITypes* and *PTypes* in grey. The top left panel shows graph rules ordered by priority, whereas the bottom left panel contains *GROOVE* types.

5.2   Case Study

In this section we illustrate the `LDMon` algorithm with an example of a location composite component, and afterwards we provide several details on its implementation in *GROOVE*. The location system is made up of different positioning systems, like GPS or Wi-Fi, a merger and a controller. Thanks to adaptation policies with temporal patterns, the location composite component can be modified to use either GPS or Wi-Fi positioning systems, depending on some properties, such as available energy, occurrences of indoor/outdoor positioning external events, etc. For example, when the level of energy is low, if the vehicle is in a tunnel where there is no GPS signal, it would be useful to remove the GPS

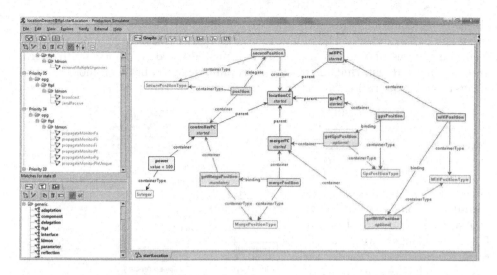

Fig. 4. Model of the location component-based system displayed with *GROOVE*

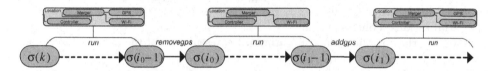

Fig. 5. Representation of the suffix configuration path σ_k

component (cf. Fig. 5). To save energy, this component may not be added back before the level of energy reaches an acceptable value.

This example has been fully implemented with *GROOVE* together with adaptation policies. Let G be the *GROOVE* graph representing this example. Let us consider the FTPL temporal property $\varphi =$ **after removegps normal (eventually** ($power \geq 33$) **before addgps normal**), which can be written as $\varphi =$ **after** e_0 ϕ, with $e_0 =$ **removegps normal**, $\phi = trp$ **before** e_1, $trp =$ **eventually** cp, $e_1 =$ **addgps normal**, and $cp = (power \geq 33)$. Intuitively, φ represents the requirement "After the GPS component has been removed, the level of energy has to be greater than 33 % before this component is added back". Figure 6 shows how φ is represented in our implementation.

Let M_c, M_m, M_g, and M_w be four monitors pertaining respectively to the controller, merger, GPS, and Wi-Fi components. Monitor Mc has access to the value of the configuration property **power_ge_33** ($\top$ if $power \geq 33$, or $\bot$ otherwise) while M_m is aware of the values of **addgps_normal** (resp. **removegps_normal**) which are $\top$ at the configuration following the addition (resp. removal) of the GPS component, or $\bot$ otherwise. Since monitors, M_g and M_w do not have access to any atomic event having an influence on the evaluation of φ (i.e., $Prop(\varphi) \cap AE_g = Prop(\varphi) \cap AE_w = \varnothing$), M_g and M_w do not send messages, which has a beneficial effect on the communication overhead. In our implementation, each monitor is a subgraph of G containing the monitored component via an edge named *monitor*. Communications between monitors are represented by edges named *sentreceived* and *broadcast*. Recall that in the model, communications between monitors are covered by *run* operations as they do not directly affect the system's architecture.

Let us consider a reconfiguration path σ representing the sequences of configurations of the location composite component where the transitions between configurations are reconfiguration operations. In the suffix path σ_k displayed in Fig. 5, we suppose that all the reconfiguration operations are *run*, except between $\sigma(i_0 - 1)$ and $\sigma(i_0)$ (resp. $\sigma(i_1 - 1)$ and $\sigma(i_1)$), where it is **removegps** (resp. **addgps**). During runtime, an adaptation controller—in charge of the application of adaptation policies—needs to

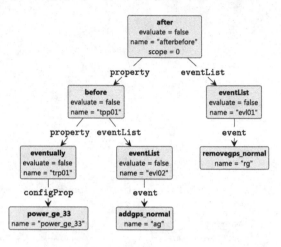

Fig. 6. Representation of the φ FTPL property

evaluate FTPL properties. To do so, the adaptation controller uses the LDMon algorithm to evaluate φ. When a result is returned by a monitor, the most suitable adaptation policy is applied, and the algorithm is used again to evaluate φ at the following configuration, where it may vary because of the scope, for example. In the following, we describe how, at each configuration of index s ($k \leq s \leq i_1$) the adaptation controller requests the evaluation of φ to the monitors using the LDMon algorithm, and receives the answer at the same configuration $\sigma(s)$. In Fig. 7 green (dashed) arrows represent broadcast communications, blue (plain) arrows represent formulae being sent, and red (dotted) arrows indicate that (a) the destination component is able to solve the most urgent sub-formula of the source component and (b) no communication is made between these components. Because neither M_g nor M_w has access to atomic events impacting their formulae, they do not send any message during the run described below.

   At configuration $\sigma(k)$, since M_m can evaluate $e_0 = \bot$, by definition of the **after** FTPL property, $_m\hat{\varphi}_{\sigma_k}^k(k) = \top^p$ is established and broadcast. Other monitors progress their formulae and determine that the most urgent sub-formula can be solved by M_m (Fig. 7a); consequently, M_c sends its formulae[7] to M_m.

---

[7] The formula to evaluate as well as its sub-formulae evaluated at the current state.

At every configuration $\sigma(s)$ for $k + 1 \leq s \leq i_0 - 1$, since e_0 does not occur, the decentralised evaluation consists in evaluating φ by M_m that returns and broadcasts the result. Other monitors receive the result from the previous configuration broadcast by M_m[8]. They also progress their current formulae, which cause M_c to send its formulae to M_m. This is diplayed in Fig. 7b, where $F_{\mathcal{A}}$ represents the FTPL temporal property **after** *in the same way $F_{\mathcal{B}}$ does for the* **before** *property in Definition 6. At configuration $\sigma(i_0)$, the event $e_0 =$* **removegps normal**, *signifying the GPS normal removal, occurs. The M_m monitor, being aware of this occurrence, evaluates φ:* $_m\hat{\varphi}_{\sigma_k}^{i_0}(i_0) =$ $_m\hat{\phi}_{\sigma_{i_0}}^{i_0}(i_0) = \mathsf{T}^p$ *because the* **"before"** *FTPL pattern is defined to be T^p at the first configuration of its scope. The result is then retuned and*

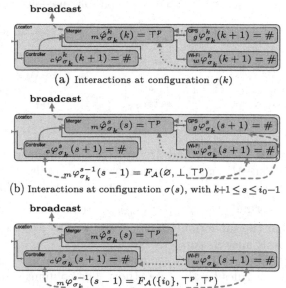

broadcast

(a) Interactions at configuration $\sigma(k)$

broadcast

(b) Interactions at configuration $\sigma(s)$, with $k{+}1 \leq s \leq i_0{-}1$

broadcast

(c) Interactions at configuration $\sigma(s)$, with $i_0{+}1 \leq s \leq i_1{-}1$

broadcast

(d) Interactions at configuration $\sigma(i_1)$

Fig. 7. Interactions between monitors (Color figure online)

broadcast. In the meantime, M_c and M_w receive the result broadcast at the previous configuration and M_c sends its formulae to M_m.

At configuration $\sigma(s)$ for $i_0 + 1 \leq s \leq i_1 - 1$, because e_0 occurred once, M_m computes $_m\hat{\varphi}_{\sigma_k}^s(s) = _m\hat{\phi}_{\sigma_{i_0}}^s(s) = \mathsf{T}^p$, since $\phi = trp$ **before** e_1 and e_1 has not yet occurred; the result is then returned and broadcast. M_c and M_w receive the result broadcast at the previous configuration which contains, as a subformula, the information that e_0 occurred at configuration $\sigma(i_0)$. The formula progressed by M_c contains $_c\phi_{\sigma_{i_0}}^s(s + 1) = F_{\mathcal{B}}(\overline{\mathbf{X}}e_1, t\hat{r}p_{\sigma_{i_0}}^{s-1}(s), \mathsf{T}^p)$. We suppose that there is a configuration $\sigma(s')$ s.t. $s' > i_0$, where the power rises over 33%, i.e., $cp = (power \geq 33) = \mathsf{T}$ and then $t\hat{r}p_{\sigma_{i_0}}^s(s) = cp \sqcup t\hat{r}p_{\sigma_{i_0}}^{s-1}(s) = \mathsf{T}$ for $s \geq s'$. In this case, the set of formulae M_c sends to M_m (Fig. 7c) contains $F_{\mathcal{B}}(\overline{\mathbf{X}}e_1, \mathsf{T}, \mathsf{T}^p)$ and $trp_{\sigma_{i_0}}^s(s)$.

At configuration $\sigma(i_1)$, $e_1 =$ **addgps terminates** *just occurred.* We assume that the reconfiguration terminated normally and that the GPS component was

---

[8] This allows all monitors to keep a history of $|\mathcal{M}| + 1$ configurations.

Table 1. Graph rules used at configuration $\sigma(s)$

Index s of configuration	Number of graph rules	Reconfiguration	Part of formula to be evaluated
$s = k$	85		after removegps normal...
$k + 1 \leq s \leq i_0 - 1$	111 − 162		after removegps normal...
$s = i_0$	237	removegps	...before addgps normal
$i_0 + 1 \leq s \leq i_1 - 1$	149		...before addgps normal
$s = i_1$	253	addgps	...eventually ($power \geq 33$)...

added. M_c, M_g, and M_w receive the result broadcast at the previous configuration. M_c and M_w behave in a way similar than above at configuration $\sigma(s)$ with $i_0 + 1 \leq s \leq i_1 - 1$, whereas M_g behaves like M_w. Finally, M_m evaluates its formula to $_m\hat{\varphi}^{i_1}_{\sigma_k}(i_1) = {}_m\hat{\phi}^{i_1}_{\sigma_{i_0}}(i_1) = F_{\mathcal{B}}(\top, \overline{\mathbf{X}}trp_{\sigma_{i_0}}, \top^p) = \top^p$ using the fact that the sub-formula $\overline{\mathbf{X}}trp_{\sigma_{i_0}}$ was sent by M_c at the previous configuration. This result answers correctly the TPDEP.

Back to the implementation, Table 1 gives information on the *GROOVE* graph rules for the case study. The columns show, from left to right, the possible values of the index of the considered configurations, the number of graph rules used, the reconfiguration occurring (if any), and the part of the FTPL formula that must be evaluated to obtain a result in $\mathbb{B}_4$. At configuration $\sigma(k)$ 85 rules are used, rules concerning the evaluation of FTPL events are the ones used the most; as long as the event removegps normal has not occurred yet, only the evaluation of the part "**after** removegps **normal**..." of the formula is needed to obtain a result. At configuration $\sigma(s)$, with $k + 1 \leq s \leq i_0 - 1$, from 111 to 162 graph rules are used, depending of the length of the history being built at the beginning of the run; once the length of history has reach its maximum, i.e., $|\mathcal{M}| + 1$, the most used graph rules are the ones designed to clear outdated history. At configuration $\sigma(i_0)$, the reconfiguration removegps occurs, then as long as the event addgps normal has not occurred yet, only the evaluation of the part "...**before** addgps **normal**" of the formula is needed to obtain a result; 237 graph rules are used, most of them doing a cleaning of the elements of the subgraph representing the monitor of the GPS component being removed. At configuration $\sigma(s)$, with $k + 1 \leq s \leq i_0 - 1$, 149 graph rules are used, mainly to clear outdated history. At configuration $\sigma(i_1)$, the reconfiguration addgps occurs, then only the evaluation, at the previous configuration, of the part "...**eventually** ($power \geq 33$)..." of the formula is needed to obtain a result; 253 graph rules are used, mainly to clear outdated history and to update the scope of the property.

6   Conclusion

This paper has addressed the decentralised evaluation problem for linear temporal patterns on reconfiguration paths of component-based systems. To this end, we have proposed a specific progressive semantics of temporal patterns, and an algorithm for their decentralised evaluation using monitors associated with components. We have shown that when reached, the decentralised evaluation results coincide with the results obtained by the centralised evaluation of temporal patterns at runtime. We have described the implementation with *GROOVE* and its application to a location composite component.

In this paper, for the sake of readability, monitors only deal with a single FTPL property. To evaluate several FTPL formulae, we can either use a single monitor (per component) dealing with all the formulae, as herein described, or a monitor per formula of interest. Depending on the context, each method can have its own advantages and drawbacks.

In the case of the removal of a component, the corresponding monitor terminates and is removed. Thanks to the adaptation policies' controller, this should not influence any ongoing temporal pattern evaluation. When a component is added, its monitor starts with a blank history. Furthermore, when a monitored primitive component is replaced with a composite component whose sub-components contain (among other) the same parameters as the original component, the monitor shall keep working seamlessly. Since no additional monitor is added, this mechanism allows us to mitigate the communication overhead that could be incurred by the increase of the number of components.

As a future work, we intend to extend the analysis of the TPDEP problem to the case when several reconfiguration operations occur. It would be possible when reconfigurations lead to configurations whose atomic events do not interfere with the evaluation of the temporal property of interest (the TPDEP input). In this case the adaptation controller can authorize reconfigurations of independent parts of the component-based system. On the implementation side, we plan to exploit the decentralised evaluation method for the implementation handling the adaptation policies. The overall goal is to exploit its results to apply adaptation policies to the component-based system under scrutiny at runtime. So far we have considered the components having monitors to be all on the same architectural level, i.e., they all are siblings. As a future work, we plan to *delegate* part of the monitoring of composite components to their subcomponents.

References

1. de Lemos, R., et al.: Software engineering for self-adaptive systems: a second research roadmap. In: de Lemos, R., Giese, H., Müller, H.A., Shaw, M. (eds.) Software Engineering for Self-Adaptive Systems. LNCS, vol. 7475, pp. 1–32. Springer, Heidelberg (2013)
2. Dwyer, M.B., Avrunin, G.S., Corbett, J.C.: Patterns in property specifications for finite-state verification. In: Software Engineering, pp. 411–420 (1999)
3. Kouchnarenko, O., Weber, J.-F.: Adapting component-based systems at runtime via policies with temporal patterns. In: Fiadeiro, J.L., Liu, Z., Xue, J. (eds.) FACS 2013. LNCS, vol. 8348, pp. 234–253. Springer, Heidelberg (2014)
4. Bauer, A., Falcone, Y.: Decentralised LTL monitoring. In: Giannakopoulou, D., Méry, D. (eds.) FM 2012. LNCS, vol. 7436, pp. 85–100. Springer, Heidelberg (2012)
5. Ghamarian, A.H., de Mol, M., Rensink, A., Zambon, E., Zimakova, M.: Modelling and analysis using GROOVE. Int. J. Softw. Tools Technol. Trans. **14**, 15–40 (2012)

6. Kupferman, O., Vardi, M.Y., Wolper, P.: Module checking. Inf. Comput. **164**, 322–344 (2001)
7. Bozzelli, L., Murano, A., Peron, A.: Pushdown module checking. In: Sutcliffe, G., Voronkov, A. (eds.) LPAR 2005. LNCS (LNAI), vol. 3835, pp. 504–518. Springer, Heidelberg (2005)
8. Aminof, B., Legay, A., Murano, A., Serre, O., Vardi, M.Y.: Pushdown module checking with imperfect information. Inf. Comput. **223**, 1–17 (2013)
9. Bauer, A., Leucker, M., Schallhart, C.: Comparing LTL semantics for runtime verification. Int. J. Logic Comput. **20**, 651–674 (2010)
10. Kim, M., Lee, I., Shin, J., Sokolsky, O., et al.: Monitoring, checking, and steering of real-time systems. ENTCS **70**, 95–111 (2002)
11. Bruneton, E., Coupaye, T., Leclercq, M., Quéma, V., Stefani, J.B.: The fractal component model and its support in java. Softw. Pract. Exper. **36**, 1257–1284 (2006)
12. Schneider, S., Treharne, H.: CSP theorems for communicating B machines. Formal Asp. Comput. **17**, 390–422 (2005)
13. Seinturier, L., Merle, P., Rouvoy, R., Romero, D., Schiavoni, V., Stefani, J.B.: A component-based middleware platform for reconfigurable service-oriented architectures. Softw. Practice Experience **42**, 559–583 (2012)
14. Garavel, H., Mateescu, R., Serwe, W.: Large-scale distributed verification using cadp: Beyond clusters to grids. Electr. Notes Theor. Comput. Sci. **296**, 145–161 (2013)
15. Dormoy, J., Kouchnarenko, O., Lanoix, A.: Runtime verification of temporal patterns for dynamic reconfigurations of components. In: Arbab, F., Ölveczky, P.C. (eds.) FACS 2011. LNCS, vol. 7253, pp. 115–132. Springer, Heidelberg (2012)
16. Hamilton, A.G.: Logic for Mathematicians. Cambridge University Press, Cambridge (1978)
17. Dormoy, J., Kouchnarenko, O., Lanoix, A.: When structural refinement of components keeps temporal properties over reconfigurations. In: Giannakopoulou, D., Méry, D. (eds.) FM 2012. LNCS, vol. 7436, pp. 171–186. Springer, Heidelberg (2012)
18. Dormoy, J., Kouchnarenko, O., Lanoix, A.: Using temporal logic for dynamic reconfigurations of components. In: Barbosa, L.S., Lumpe, M. (eds.) FACS 2010. LNCS, vol. 6921, pp. 200–217. Springer, Heidelberg (2012)
19. Kouchnarenko, O., Weber, J.F.: Decentralised Evaluation of Temporal Patterns over Component-based Systems at Runtime (2014). Long version of the present paper available at: http://hal.archives-ouvertes.fr/hal-01044639

Formal Rules for Reliable Component-Based Architecture Evolution

Abderrahman Mokni[1]([✉]), Marianne Huchard[2], Christelle Urtado[1],
Sylvain Vauttier[1], and Huaxi (Yulin) Zhang[3]

[1] LGI2P, Ecole Nationale Supérieure des Mines Alès, Nîmes, France
{Abderrahman.Mokni,Christelle.Urtado,Sylvain.Vauttier}@mines-ales.fr
[2] LIRMM, CNRS and Université de Montpellier 2, Montpellier, France
huchard@lirmm.fr
[3] Laboratoire MIS, Université de Picardie Jules Verne, Amiens, France
yulin.zhang@u-picardie.fr

Abstract. Software architectures are the blueprint of software systems construction and evolution. During the overall software lifecycle, several changes of its architecture may be considered (*e.g.* including new software requirements, correcting bugs, enhancing software performance). To ensure a valid and reliable evolution, software architecture changes must be captured, verified and validated at an early stage of the software evolution process. In this paper, we address this issue by proposing a set of evolution rules for software architectures in a manner that preserves consistency and coherence between abstraction levels. The rules are specified in the B formal language and applied to a three-level ADL that covers the three steps of software development: specification, implementation and deployment. To validate our rules, the approach is tested on a running example of Home Automation Software.

Keywords: Software architecture evolution · Component reuse · Consistency checking · Coherence checking · Evolution rules · Formal models · Abstraction level · B formal language

1 Introduction

The great importance of evolution and maintenance in software systems engineering has been noticed over more than two decades ago. According to a highly cited survey conducted by Lientz and Swanson in the late 1970s [1], it has been proven that software maintenance represents the main part of a software lifecycle in terms of cost and time. In particular, this high fraction relates to component-based software engineering that tackles the development of complex software architectures (thanks to modularity, abstraction and reuse). Indeed, an ill mastered software system maintenance or a misconception during its evolving process may lead to serious architectural mismatches and inconsistencies. A famous problem that software architecture evolution is subject to is erosion. Introduced by Perry and Wolf [2] in 1992 and studied over many years [3], erosion can be

© Springer International Publishing Switzerland 2015
I. Lanese and E. Madelaine (Eds.): FACS 2014, LNCS 8997, pp. 127–142, 2015.
DOI: 10.1007/978-3-319-15317-9_8

defined as the deterioration or violation of architectural design decisions by the software implementation. It is usually due to software aging and an undisciplined evolution of its architecture. While a lot of work was dedicated to architectural modeling and evolution, there is still a lack of means and techniques to tackle architectural inconsistencies, and erosion in particular. Indeed, almost existing ADLs hardly support the whole life-cycle of a component-based software and it often creates a gap between design and implementation, requirements and design or even both. These gaps make evolution harder and increase the risk of non-conformance between requirements, design and implementation hence leading to erosion.

In previous work [4,5], we proposed Dedal, an ADL that supports the full lifecycle process of component-based software systems. Dedal proposes to model architectures at three abstraction levels that correspond to the three steps of software development: specification, implementation and deployment. However, at this stage the ADL handles evolution in an *adhoc* manner and lacks rigorous support for reliable and automatic software evolution. In this paper, we propose a set of evolution rules specified using the B formal language [6] to automatically handle forward and reverse evolution among Dedal levels in a reliable way. We also show how evolution can be simulated at an early stage using the proposed rules, anticipating and preventing inconsistencies.

The remainder of this paper is outlined as follows: Sect. 2 discusses related work. Section 3 gives a brief overview of Dedal architecture levels and their formalization. Section 4 presents the three-level evolution approach, illustrated by some evolution rules. Section 5 gives the simulation of an evolution scenario example using the proposed rules. Finally, Sect. 6 concludes the paper and discusses future work.

2   Related Work

Over the two past decades, a wide area of related work has addressed the problem of software evolution. Indeed, many ADLs have been proposed [7]. Examples include C2SADL [8], Wright [9], Rapide [10], ACME [11], Darwin [12] and π-ADL [13]. While "box-and-line" seems to be the easiest way to represent architectures for practitioners [14], this notation is informal and leads to ambiguity and imprecision. For this reason, the use of a formalism and its integration into an ADL is crucial. To cope with software evolution and particularly dynamic change, existing ADLs use several kinds of formal ground depending on their application domain. For instance, C2SADL uses event-based processes to model concurrent systems while Dynamic-Wright lies on CSP [15], a process algebra formalism to support the specification and analysis of interactions between components. ACME, which was basically designed to define a common interchange language for architecture design tools, is based on first-order logic. The ADL was extended with Plastik [16] to support dynamic reconfiguration of architectures. π-ADL was designed for concurrent and mobile systems. It lies on π-calculus [17], a higher-order logic formalism to model and evolve the behavior of the architectures. C2SADL, Pi-ADL, ACME and Dynamic-Wright support dynamic reconfiguration of architectures. However, they lack analysis support for the evolution activity and hardly cover the whole lifecycle of component-based software.

In our work, we propose a solution for the simulation and verification of software architecture evolution using B [6] formal models. The choice of B is motivated by its rigorism (first-order logic) and its expressiveness that enables modeling concepts in a reasonable easy way. The B formal models correspond to the definitions of our three-level Dedal ADL that covers the whole lifecycle of a software system (*i.e.* specification, implementation and deployment). Hence, we address both static and dynamic evolution by proposing change rules at each of the three abstraction levels of our ADL.

3 Overview of Dedal

3.1 Dedal Abstraction Levels

Dedal is a novel ADL that covers the whole life-cycle of a component-based software. It proposes a three-step approach for specifying, implementing and deploying software architectures as a reuse-based process(*cf.* Fig. 1).

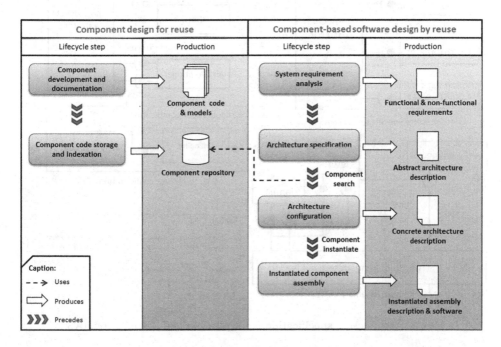

Fig. 1. Dedal overall process [5]

To illustrate the concepts of Dedal, we propose to model a home automation software (HAS) that manages comfort scenarios. Here, it automatically controls the building's lighting and heating in function of the time and ambient temperature. For this purpose, we propose an architecture with an orchestrator component that interacts with the appropriate devices to implement the desired scenario.

The abstract architecture specification is the first level of software architecture descriptions. It represents the architecture as imagined by the architect to meet the requirements of the future software. In Dedal, the architecture specification is composed of component roles, their connections and the expected global behavior. Component roles are abstract and partial component type specifications. They are identified by the architect in order to search for and select corresponding concrete components in the next step. Figure 2a shows a possible architecture specification for the HAS. In this specification, five component roles are identified. A component playing the *Orchestrator* role controls four components playing the *Light*, *Time*, *Thermometer* and *CoolerHeater* roles.

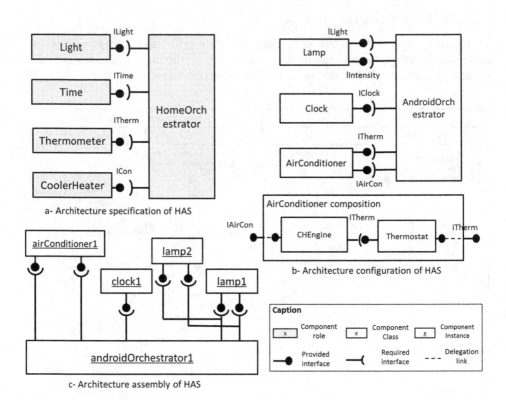

Fig. 2. Architecture specification, configuration and assembly of HAS

The concrete architecture configuration is an implementation view of software architectures. It results from the selection of existing component classes in component repositories. Thus, an architecture configuration lists the concrete component classes that compose a specific version of the software system.

In Dedal, component classes can be either primitive or composite. *A primitive component class* encapsulates executable code. *A composite component class* encapsulates an inner architecture configuration (*i.e.* a set of connected component classes which may, in turn, be primitive or composite). A composite component class exposes a set of interfaces corresponding to unconnected interfaces of its inner components.

Figure 2b shows a possible architecture configuration for the HAS example as well as an example of an *AirConditioner* composite component and its inner configuration. As illustrated in this example, a single component class may realize several roles in the architecture specification as with the *AirConditioner* component class, which realizes both *Thermometer* and *CoolerHeater* roles. Conversely, a component class may provide more services than those listed in the architecture specification as with the *Lamp* component class which, provides an extra service to control the intensity of light.

The instantiated architecture assembly describes software at runtime and gathers information about its internal state. The architecture assembly results from the instantiation of an architecture configuration. It lists the instances of the component and connector classes that compose the deployed architecture at runtime and their assembly constraints (such as maximum numbers of allowed instances).

Component instances document how component classes in an architecture configuration are instantiated in the deployed software. Each component instance has an initial and current state defined by a list of valued attributes. Figure 2c shows an instantiated architecture assembly for the HAS example.

3.2   Dedal Formal Model

Dedal is enhanced by a formal model using the B specification language. The proposed model covers all Dedal concepts and includes rules for substitutability and compatibility among each level as well as the rules that govern interrelations between the different levels (*cf.* Fig. 3). These rules, which were discussed in previous work [18], are the basis for controlling the evolution process. Indeed, evolution needs a subtyping mechanism to manage change locally (at the same abstraction level) and then, inter-level rules to propagate change to the other levels.

For the sake of simplicity, we present in Table 1 a generic formal model covering the underlying concepts of Dedal.

For instance, the concept of *component* is specialized into *compRole* at the specification level and the concept of *architecture* is specialized into *configuration* at the configuration level.

This model is used to set generic evolution rules which are specialized for each of the three abstraction levels of Dedal. An evolution scenario is presented in Sect. 5 as an illustration.

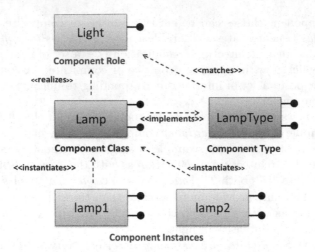

Fig. 3. Component interrelations in Dedal

Table 1. Formal specification of underlying concepts

MACHINE *Arch_concepts*
INCLUDES *Basic_concepts*
SETS
ARCHS; *COMPS*; *COMP_NAMES*
VARIABLES
architecture, arch_components, arch_connections, component,
comp_name, connection, comp_interfaces, client, server
arch_clients, arch_servers
INVARIANT
/* **A component has a name and a set of interfaces** */
    $component \subseteq COMPS \land$
    $comp\_name \in component \rightarrow COMP\_NAMES \land$
    $comp\_interfaces \in component \rightarrowtail \mathcal{P}(interface) \land$
/* **A client (resp. server)is a couple of a component and an interface** */
    $client \in component \leftrightarrow interface \land$
    $server \in component \leftrightarrow interface \land$
/* **A connection is a relation between a client and a server** */
    $connection \in client \leftrightarrow server \land$
/* **An architecture has a set of components and connections** */
    $architecture \subseteq ARCHS \land$
    $arch\_components \in architecture \rightarrow \mathcal{P}(component) \land$
    $arch\_connections \in architecture \rightarrow \mathcal{P}(connection)$
/* **Arch_clients (resp. arch_servers) lists the connected clients(reps. servers)**
within an architecture */
    $arch\_clients \in architecture \rightarrow \mathcal{P}(client) \land$
    $arch\_servers \in architecture \rightarrow \mathcal{P}(server)$
Specific B notations:
    $\leftrightarrow$: relation $\rightarrowtail$: injection $\mathcal{P}(\text{<set>})$: powerset of <set>

4   The Formal Evolution Approach

In this section, we present our approach to handle multi-level software evolution
as a reuse-based process. The objective of this approach is twofold: (1) capture software change and control its impact on architecture consistency and,

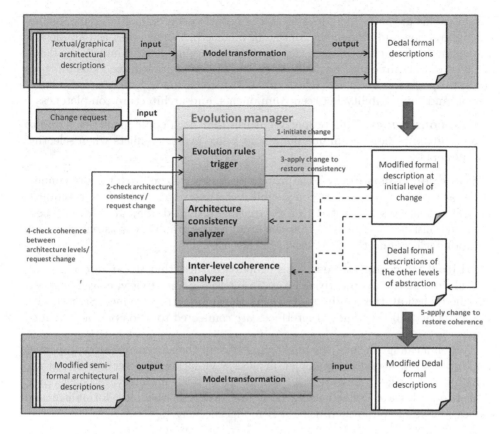

Fig. 4. The formal evolution process

(2) propagate change between multiple architecture levels to preserve global coherence. The approach is formal model-based since it relies on the formal models of our three-level ADL and uses consistency and coherence properties and a set of evolution rules (*cf.* Fig. 4). The approach is also dynamic in the sense that it performs analysis and simulates change on executable models. The formal models may be generated through a MDE (Model Driven Engineering) process where the source models are textual or graphical (UML profile) descriptions of Dedal. Since the transformation is not tooled yet, this issue is out of the scope of the present paper.

The evolution management is composed of three main activities: consistency analysis, inter-level coherence analysis and evolution rules triggering. In the remainder, we present the foundations and the mechanisms of each of these three activities.

4.1 Architecture Consistency Analysis

Taylor *et al.* [19] define consistency as an internal property intended to ensure that different elements of an architectural model do not contradict one another.

Usually, this property includes five sorts of consistency: name, interface, behavior, interaction and refinement consistency. Some properties such as parameters, names and interfaces are taken into account by adding constraints in the definition of our architectural formal model [18]. In our approach, we focus on three main properties: name consistency, connection consistency, which includes interaction and compatibility between components, and architecture completeness.

Name consistency. This property ensures that each component belonging to the architecture holds a unique name and hence avoids conflicts when selecting components.

Connection consistency. This property ensures that all architecture connections are correct and satisfy compatibility between both sides (*i.e.* a required interface is always connected to a compatible provided one). In addition, connection consistency stipulates that the architecture graph is consistent (*i.e.* each component is connected to at least another one).

Architecture completeness. This property ensures that the architecture realizes all its functional objectives. From an internal point of view, completeness is satisfied when all the required services in the architecture are met. Structurally, it means that all the required interfaces are connected to a compatible provided one.

When a change occurs, the analyzer checks all the aforementioned properties and notify the evolution manager in case a violation is detected. Then, the adequate evolution rules are triggered to reestablish architecture consistency. The properties are defined using B, a first order set-theoretic formalism and hence analysis is performed using a B model checker.

4.2   Inter-level Coherence Properties

Coherence analysis is managed using inter-level rules (*cf.* Fig. 5). These rules are defined to check whether a configuration conforms to its specification or a software instantiation is coherent with its configuration.

Coherence between specification and configuration. A specification is a formal description of software requirements that is used to guide the search for suitable concrete component classes to implement the software. An architecture definition is coherent when all component roles are realized by component classes in the configuration. This results in a many-to many relation. Indeed, several component roles may be realized by a single component class while, conversely, a composition of component classes may be needed to realize a single role. Formally:

$$
\begin{aligned}
&implements \in configuration \leftrightarrow specification \wedge \\
&\forall\,(Conf,\,Spec).(Conf \in configuration \wedge Spec \in specification \\
&\quad \Rightarrow \\
&\qquad (Conf,\,Spec) \in implements \\
&\qquad \Leftrightarrow \\
&\quad \forall\,CR.(CR \in compRole \wedge CR \in spec\_components(Spec) \Rightarrow \\
&\qquad \exists\,CL.(CL \in compClass \wedge CL \in config\_components(Conf) \wedge \\
&\qquad\quad (CL, CR) \in realizes)))
\end{aligned}
$$

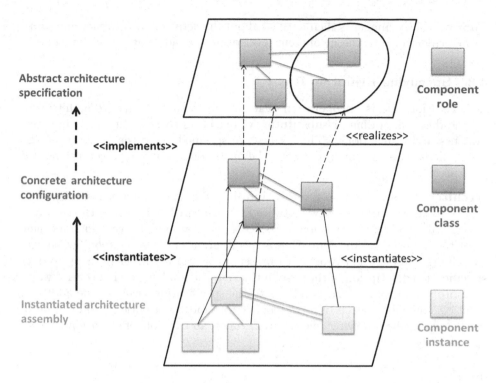

Fig. 5. Coherence between architecture levels

Coherence between configuration and assembly. Coherence between configuration and assembly levels is satisfied when all the classes of the configuration are instantiated at least once in the architecture assembly and, conversely, all instances of the assembly are instances of the component classes of the configuration. Formally:

$$
\begin{aligned}
&instantiates \in assembly \to configuration \land \\
&\forall (Asm, Conf).(Asm \in assembly \land Conf \in configuration \\
&\Rightarrow \\
&((Asm, Conf) \in instantiates \\
&\quad \Leftrightarrow \\
&\forall CL.(CL \in compClass \land CL \in config\_components(Conf) \\
&\quad \Rightarrow \\
&\quad\ \exists CI.(CI \in compInstance \land CI \in assm\_components(Asm) \land \\
&(CI, CL) \in comp\_instantiates)) \land \\
&\forall CI.(CI \in compInstance \land CI \in assm\_components(Asm) \\
&\quad \Rightarrow \\
&\quad\ \exists CL.(CL \in compClass \land CL \in config\_components(Conf) \land \\
&(CI, CL) \in comp\_instantiates))))
\end{aligned}
$$

Coherence analysis comes after consistency checking returns a positive result. Indeed, it is necessary that software system descriptions are consistent at all abstraction levels before checking coherence between them. When a change occurs at any level, this may result in erosion or drift (for instance, some higher level decisions are violated or not taken into account by the lower level).

The evolution manager is then notified about the detected incoherence and propagates the change to the incoherent levels using the adequate evolution rules.

4.3   Specifying Evolution Rules

An evolution rule is an operation that changes a target software architecture by the deleting, adding or substituting of one of its constituent elements (components and connections). These rules are specified using the B notation and each rule is composed of three parts: the operation signature, preconditions and actions.

Architecture specification evolution. Evolving an architecture specification is usually a response to a new software requirement. For instance, the architect may need to add new functionalities to the system and hence add some new roles to the specification. Moreover, a specification may also be modified during the change propagation process to preserve coherence and keep an up-to-date specification description of the system that may be implemented in several ways. The proposed evolution rules related to the specification level are the addition, deletion and substitution of a component role and the addition and deletion of connections. The following role addition rule is an example of evolution rules at specification level:

```
addRole(spec, newRole) =
PRE
spec ∈ arch_spec ∧ newRole ∈ compRole ∧ newRole ∉ spec_components(spec) ∧
/* spec does not contain a role with the same name*/
∀ cr.(cr ∈ compRole ∧ cr ∈ spec_components(spec)
     ⇒ comp_name(cr) ¬ comp_name(newRole))
THEN
        spec_servers(spec) := spec_servers(spec) ∪ servers(newRole) ||
        spec_clients(spec) := spec_clients(spec) ∪ clients(newRole) ||
        spec_components(spec) := spec_components(spec) ∪ {newRole}
END;
```

Architecture configuration evolution. Change can be initiated at configuration level whenever new versions of software component classes are released. Otherwise, an implementation may also be impacted by change propagation either from the specification level, in response to new requirements, or from the assembly level, in response to a dynamic change of the system. Indeed, a configuration may be instantiated several times and deployed in multiple contexts. At configuration level, there is a need for two more evolution rules: the connection and the disconnection of the exposed services. Indeed, a component class used in a configuration may hold more provided interfaces than the component role that it implements. These extra interfaces may be left unconnected. On the contrary, a specification sets by definition the requirements, and hence the provided interfaces of all roles must be connected to keep the architecture consistent. As an example of evolution rule at configuration level, we list the following component class substitution rule:

```
replaceClass(config, oldClass, newClass) =
   PRE
        oldClass ∈ compClass ∧ newClass ∈ compClass ∧ config ∈ configuration ∧
oldClass ∈ config_components(config) ∧
/* The old component class can be substituted for the new one
      (verified by the component substitution rule)*/
        newClass ∉ config_components(config) ∧ (oldClass, newClass) ∈ class_substitution
      THEN
        config_components(config) := (config_components(config) - {oldClass}) ∪ {newClass} ||
        config_clients(config) := (config_clients(config) - clients(oldClass)) ∪ clients(newClass)
   END
```

Architecture assembly evolution. Since the architecture assembly represents the software at runtime, evolving software at assembly level is a dynamic evolution issue. Several kinds of change may occur at runtime. For instance, dynamic software change may be needed due to a change in the execution context (*e.g.* lack of memory, CPU). Unanticipated changes are one of the most important issues in software evolution. Indeed, some software systems have to be self-adaptive to keep providing their functions despite environmental changes. This issues are handled by the evolution manager which monitors the execution state of the software through its corresponding formal model. It then triggers the assembly evolution rules to restore consistency when it is violated. These rules include component instance deployment, component instance removal, component instance substitution, component instance connection/disconnection and service connection/disconnection. As an example of dynamic evolution rule, we state the following component instance addition rule:

```
deployInstance(asm, inst, class, state) =
      PRE
         asm ∈ assembly ∧ class ∈ compClass ∧
/* The instance is a valid instantiation of an existing component class*/
         inst ∈ compInstance ∧ class = comp_instantiates(inst) ∧ inst ∉ assm_components(asm) ∧
/* The state given to the instance is a valid value assignment to the attributes
      of the instantiated component class*/
         state ∈ 𝒫 (attribute_value) ∧ card(state) = card(class_attributes(class)) ∧
/* The maximum number of allowed instances of the given component class
      is not already reached*/
         nb_instances(class) < max_instances(class)
      THEN
/*initial and current state initialization*/
         initiation_state(inst) := state ||
         current_state(inst) := state ||
/*updating the number of instances and the assembly architecture*/
         nb_instances(class) := nb_instances(class) + 1 ||
         assm_components(asm) := assm_components(asm) ∪ {inst} ||
         assm_servers(asm) := assm_servers(asm) ∪ servers(inst) ||
         assm_clients(asm) := assm_clients(asm) ∪ clients(inst)
   END;
```

5   Implementing an Evolution Scenario

To illustrate the use of evolution rules, we propose to evolve the HAS architecture by adding of a new device that manages the building's shutters. The evolution simulation is performed using ProB [20], an animator and model checker of B models. Once the formal models corresponding to the three architecture descriptions are successfully checked, we use the ProB solver to trigger change as a goal to reach. In the remainder, we give some details about the example instances and the different steps of the evolution process.

5.1   Intra-level Change

Figure 6 illustrates the old architecture specification and the evolved one.

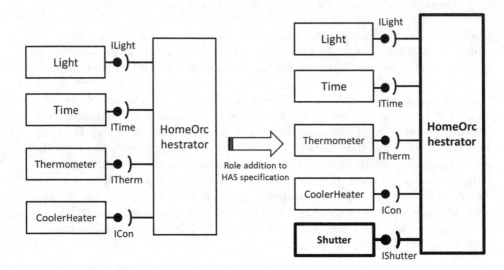

Older version of HAS specification   Evolved version of HAS specification

Fig. 6. Evolving the HAS specification by role addition

Initially, the instantiation of the formal HAS specification is as follows:

compRole := $\{cr1, cr1a, cr2, cr3, cr4, cr4a, cr5, cr6\}$||
comp_name := $\{cr1 \mapsto Light, cr1a \mapsto ELight, cr2 \mapsto Time,$
    $cr3 \mapsto Thermometer, cr4 \mapsto HomeOrchestrator,$
    $cr4a \mapsto HomeOrchestrator, cr5 \mapsto CoolerHeater,$
    $cr6 \mapsto Shutter\}$||
arch_spec := $\{HAS\_spec\}$||
spec_components := $\{HAS\_spec \mapsto \{cr1, cr2, cr3, cr4, cr5\}\}$||
spec_connections := $\{HAS\_spec \mapsto \{$
    $((cr4, rintILight) \mapsto (cr1, pintILight)),$
    $((cr4, rintITime) \mapsto (cr2, pintITime)),$
    $((cr4, rintITherm2) \mapsto (cr3, pintITherm1)),$
    $((cr4, rintICon) \mapsto (cr5, pintICon))\}\}$||
spec_clients := $\{(HAS\_spec \mapsto \{(cr4, rintILight), (cr4, rintITime),$
    $(cr4, rintITherm2), (cr4, rintICon)\}\}$||
spec_servers := $\{(HAS\_spec \mapsto \{(cr1, pintILight), (cr2, pintITime),$
    $(cr3, pintITherm1), (cr5, pintICon)\})\}$

The change is requested by the execution of the role addition operation that takes as arguments the HAS_spec HAS architecture specification and the *Shutter* ($cr6$) component role.

addRole($HAS\_spec, cr6$)

The change process is initiated by setting a goal. When the goal cannot be reached, the change process rolls back to the initial state of the architecture. In this case, the goal is to add a *Shutter* to the HAS specification while maintaining architecture consistency (as defined in Sect. 4):

$GOAL == changeOperation = ADDITION \land selectedRole = cr6 \land$
$\quad selectedSpec = HAS\_spec \land specification\_consistency$

The change entails the disconnection of all servers, the deletion of the old orchestrator (cr4), the addition of the new orchestrator (cr4a) and finally the connection of all servers. These operations are automatically generated by the ProB solver:

$disconnect(HAS\_spec, (cr4, rintILight), (cr1, pintILight))$
$disconnect(HAS\_spec, (cr4, rintITime), (cr2, pintITime))$
$disconnect(HAS\_spec, (cr4, rintITherm1), (cr3, pintITherm))$
$disconnect(HAS\_spec, (cr4, rintICon), (cr5, pintICon))$
$deleteRole(HAS\_spec, cr4)$
$generateAddRole(HAS\_spec, cr4a)$
$connect(HAS\_spec, (cr4a, rintILight), (cr1, pintILight))$
$connect(HAS\_spec, (cr4a, rintITime), (cr2, pintITime))$
$connect(HAS\_spec, (cr4a, rintITherm1), (cr3, pintITherm))$
$connect(HAS\_spec, (cr4a, rintICon), (cr5, pintICon))$
$connect(HAS\_spec, (cr4a, rintIShutter), (cr6, pintIShutter))$

5.2 Propagating Change to Other Levels

Once the change is successfully achieved at the specification level, the propagation rules are triggered in the other levels to attempt to restore coherence with the new specification architecture.

Propagating change to the HAS configuration. To restore conformity with the new HAS specification, the new configuration must realize the added *Shutter* role and its connection to the orchestrator device to perform the new required behavior. In the given example, the solution is to search for a concrete component class that realizes the *Shutter* role and can be connected to a compatible *orchestrator* class. Initially, the HAS configuration (illustrated by Fig. 7) is formally instantiated as follows:

compClass := $\{cl1, cl2, cl3, cl4, cl3a, cl3b, cl4a, cl6\}||$
comp_name := $\{cl1 \mapsto Lamp, cl2 \mapsto Clock, cl3 \mapsto AirConditioner,$
$\quad cl3a \mapsto CHEngine, cl3b \mapsto Thermostat,$
$\quad cl4 \mapsto AndroidOrchestrator, cl4a \mapsto AndroidOrchestrator,$
$\quad cl6 \mapsto AndroidShutter\}||$
configuration := $\{HAS\_config, AirConConfig\}||$
compositeComp := $\{cl3\}$
composite_uses := $\{cl3 \mapsto AirConConfig\}$
config_components := $\{HAS\_config \mapsto \{cl1, cl2, cl3, cl4\},$
$\quad AirConConfig \mapsto \{cl3a, cl3b\}||$
spec_connections := $\{HAS\_config \mapsto \{$
$\quad ((cl4, rintIPower) \mapsto (cl1, pintIPower)),$
$\quad ((cl4, rintIIntensity) \mapsto (cl1, pintIIntensity)),$
$\quad ((cl4, rintIClock) \mapsto (cl2, pintIClock)),$
$\quad ((cl4, rintITherm2) \mapsto (cl3, pintITherm2)),$
$\quad ((cl4, rintICon) \mapsto (cl3, pintICon))\},$
$\quad AirConConfig \mapsto \{((cl3a, rintITherm1) \mapsto (cl3b, pintITherm1)),$
$\quad ((cl4, rintITime) \mapsto (cl2, pintILamp))\}||$
config_clients := $\{(HAS\_config \mapsto \{(cl4, rintILamp), (cl4, rintIIntensity),$
$\quad (cl4, rintIClock), (cl4, rintITherm2), (cl4, rintICon))\}\}||$
config_servers := $\{(HAS\_config \mapsto \{(cl1, pintILamp), (cl1, pintIIntensity),$
$\quad (cl2, pintITime), (cl3, pintITherm2), (cl3, pintICon)\})\}$

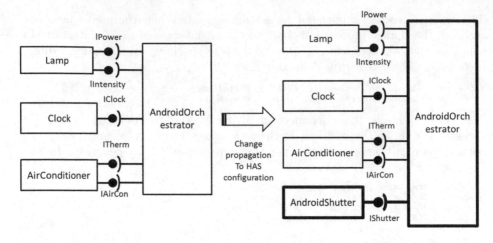

Fig. 7. Change propagation to HAS configuration

Again, we use the ProB solver giving it the following goal to restore coherence property with the new HAS specification:

$GOAL == selectedConfig = HAS\_config \land configuration\_consistency \land specConfigCoherence$

We note that *specConfigCoherence* is the conformity rule defined in Sect. 4 to check conformity between a specification and a configuration.

A potential solution generated by the solver is:

$disconnect(HAS\_config, (cl4, rintILamp), (cl1, pintILamp))$
$disconnect(HAS\_config, (cl4, rintIIntensity), (cl1, pintIItensity))$
$disconnect(HAS\_config, (cl4, rintIClock), (cl2, pintIClock))$
$disconnect(HAS\_config, (cl4, rintITherm2), (cl3, pintITherm2))$
$disconnect(HAS\_config, (cl4, rintICon), (cl3, pintICon2))$
$deleteClass(HAS\_config, cl4)$
$addClass(HAS\_config, cl4a)$
$connect(HAS\_config, (cl4a, rintILamp2), (cl1, pintILamp))$
$connect(HAS\_config, (cl4a, rintIIntensity2), (cl1, pintIItensity))$
$connect(HAS\_config, (cl4a, rintIClock), (cl2, pintIClock))$
$connect(HAS\_config, (cl4a, rintITherm3), (cl3, pintITherm2))$
$connect(HAS\_config, (cl4a, rintICon2), (cl3, pintICon2))$
$connect(HAS\_config, (cl4a, rintIShutter), (cl6, pintIShutter))$

Propagating change to the HAS assembly. In the same way, change is propagated to assembly level by disconnecting and deleting the instance of the old *AndroidOrchestrator* and by creating, deploying and connecting an instance of the new added *Shutter* device.

The solver is given the following goal:

$GOAL == selectedAssembly = HAS\_assembly \land assembly\_consistency\land$
$\quad assemblyConfigCoherence$

The *assemblyConfigCoherence* is the defined property to check coherence between an assembly and a configuration (*cf.* Sect. 4).

The solution generated by the solver is as follows:

```
unbind(HAS_assembly, (ci4, rintILampInst), (ci11, pintILampInst1))
unbind(HAS_assembly, (ci4, rintIIntensityInst), (ci11, pintIItensity1Inst))
unbind(HAS_assembly, (ci4, rintILampInst), (ci12, pintILampInst2))
unbind(HAS_assembly, (ci4, rintIIntensityInst), (ci12, pintIItensityInst2))
unbind(HAS_assembly, (ci4, rintIClockInst), (ci2, pintIClockInst))
unbind(HAS_assembly, (ci4, rintITherm2Inst), (ci3, pintITherm2Inst))
unbind(HAS_assembly, (ci4, rintIConInst), (ci3, pintICon2Inst))
removeInstance(HAS_assembly, ci4)
deployInstance(HAS_assembly, ci4a, cl4a, {})
bind(HAS_assembly, (ci4a, rintILamp2Inst), (ci11, pintILampInst1))
bind(HAS_assembly, (ci4a, rintIIntensity2Inst), (ci11, pintIItensityInst1))
bind(HAS_assembly, (ci4a, rintIClockInst), (ci2, pintIClockInst))
bind(HAS_assembly, (ci4a, rintILamp2Inst), (ci12, pintILampInst2))
bind(HAS_assembly, (ci4a, rintITherm3Inst), (ci3, pintITherm2Inst))
bind(HAS_assembly, (ci4a, rintICon2Inst), (ci3, pintICon2Inst))
bind(HAS_assembly, (ci4a, rintIIntensity2Inst), (ci12, pintIItensityInst2))
bind(HAS_assembly, (ci4a, rintIShutterInst), (ci6, pintIShutterInst))
```

At this stage, change is simulated and verified semi-automatically since the models are instantiated manually. Moreover, a manual checking is needed to validate the proposed evolution rules. A perspective is to fully automate the evolution management process and to study the scalability of the solver to timely handle complex goals.

6 Conclusion and Future Work

In this paper, we proposed a set of rules to evolve software architectures. These rules defined as a B formal model of our three-level Dedal ADL that covers the whole lifecycle of software systems. Our approach enables simulation and early validation of software evolution at design time (specification and implementation) as well as runtime (deployment). At this stage, the proposed consistency properties and evolution rules are checked and validated using a B animator and model checker. As a future work, we aim to extend the use of the proposed evolution rules in order to consider the semantics of changes. Another perspective is to generate multiple candidate evolution paths that can be evaluated using some criteria (*e.g.* quality of service, cost, change priority) as proposed by Barnes *et al.* [21].

We are also considering several MDE techniques to develop an eclipse-based environment for Dedal that automatically manages software architecture evolution.

References

1. Lientz, B.P., Swanson, E.B., Tompkins, G.E.: Characteristics of application software maintenance. Commun. ACM **21**(6), 466–471 (1978)
2. Perry, D.E., Wolf, A.L.: Foundations for the study of software architecture. SIGSOFT Softw. Eng. Notes **17**(4), 40–52 (1992)

3. de Silva, L., Balasubramaniam, D.: Controlling software architecture erosion: a survey. J. Syst. Softw. **85**(1), 132–151 (2012)
4. Zhang, H.Y., Urtado, C., Vauttier, S.: Architecture-centric component-based development needs a three-level ADL. In: Babar, M.A., Gorton, I. (eds.) ECSA 2010. LNCS, vol. 6285, pp. 295–310. Springer, Heidelberg (2010)
5. Zhang, H.Y., Zhang, L., Urtado, C., Vauttier, S., Huchard, M.: A three-level component model in component-based software development. In: Proceedings of the 11th GPCE, pp. 70–79. ACM, Dresden, September 2012
6. Abrial, J.R.: The B-book: Assigning Programs to Meanings. Cambridge University Press, New York (1996)
7. Medvidovic, N., Taylor, R.N.: A classification and comparison framework for software architecture description languages. IEEE TSE **26**(1), 70–93 (2000)
8. Medvidovic, N.: ADLs and dynamic architecture changes. In: Joint Proceedings of the Second International Software Architecture Workshop and International Workshop on Multiple Perspectives in Software Development on SIGSOFT 1996 Workshops, pp. 24–27. ACM, New York (1996)
9. Allen, R., Garlan, D.: A formal basis for architectural connection. ACM TOSEM **6**(3), 213–249 (1997)
10. Luckham, D.C., Kenney, J.J., Augustin, L.M., Vera, J., Bryan, D., Mann, W.: Specification and analysis of system architecture using rapide. IEEE TSE **21**, 336–355 (1995)
11. Garlan, D., Monroe, R., Wile, D.: ACME: an architecture description interchange language. In: Proceedings of CASCON. IBM Press (1997)
12. Magee, J., Kramer, J.: Dynamic structure in software architectures. ACM SIGSOFT Softw. Eng. Notes **21**(6), 3–14 (1996)
13. Oquendo, F.: Pi-ADL: an architecture description language based on the higher-order typed pi-calculus for specifying dynamic and mobile software architectures. SIGSOFT Softw. Eng. Notes **29**(3), 1–14 (2004)
14. Shaw, M., Garlan, D.: Formulations and formalisms in software architecture. In: van Leeuwen, J. (ed.) Computer Science Today. LNCS, vol. 1000, pp. 307–323. Springer, Heidelberg (1995)
15. Hoare, C.A.R.: Communicating sequential processes. Commun. ACM **21**(8), 666–677 (1978)
16. Joolia, A., Batista, T., Coulson, G., Gomes, A.T.A.: Mapping ADL specifications to an efficient and reconfigurable runtime component platform. In: Proceedings of the 5th WICSA, pp. 131–140. IEEE, Washington (2005)
17. Milner, R., Parrow, J., Walker, D.: A calculus of mobile processes. I. Inf. Comput. **100**(1), 1–40 (1992)
18. Mokni, A., Huchard, M., Urtado, C., Vauttier, S., Zhang, H.Y.: Towards automating the coherence verification of multi-level architecture descriptions. In: Proceedings of the 9th ICSEA, Nice, October 2014
19. Taylor, R., Medvidovic, N., Dashofy, E.: Software Architecture: Foundations, Theory, and Practice. Wiley, Chichester (2009)
20. Leuschel, M., Butler, M.: ProB: an automated analysis toolset for the B method. Int. J. Softw. Tools Technol. Transfer **10**(2), 185–203 (2008)
21. Barnes, J., Garlan, D., Schmerl, B.: Evolution styles: foundations and models for software architecture evolution. Softw. Syst. Model. **13**(2), 649–678 (2014)

Application and Experience

Solving Parity Games in Scala

Antonio Di Stasio, Aniello Murano$^{(\boxtimes)}$, Vincenzo Prignano,
and Loredana Sorrentino

Università degli Studi di Napoli Federico II, Napoli, Italy
murano@na.infn.it, vincenzo.prignano@gmail.com

Abstract. *Parity games* are two-player games, played on directed
graphs, whose nodes are labeled with priorities. Along a play, the maximal priority occurring infinitely often determines the winner. In the
last two decades, a variety of algorithms and successive optimizations
have been proposed. The majority of them have been implemented in
PGSolver, written in OCaml, which has been elected by the community
as the de facto platform to solve efficiently parity games as well as evaluate their performance in several specific cases.

PGSolver includes the *Zielonka Recursive Algorithm* that has been
shown to perform better than the others in randomly generated games.
However, even for arenas with a few thousand of nodes (especially over
dense graphs), it requires minutes to solve the corresponding game.

In this paper, we deeply revisit the implementation of the recursive
algorithm introducing several improvements and making use of *Scala
Programming Language*. These choices have been proved to be very successful, gaining up to two orders of magnitude in running time.

1   Introduction

Parity games [13,35] are abstract infinite-duration games that represents a powerful mathematical framework to address fundamental questions in computer
science and mathematics. They are strict connected with other games of infinite duration, such as *mean* and *discounted* payoff, *stochastic*, and *multi-agent*
games [7–10].

In formal system design and verification [12,25], parity games arise as a natural evaluation machinery to automatically and exhaustively check for reliability
of distributed and reactive systems [1,3,26]. More specifically, in formal verification, *model-checking* techniques [11,31] allow to verify whether a system is
correct with respect to a desired behavior by checking whether a mathematical model of the system meets a formal specification of the expected execution.
In case the latter is given by means of a μ-calculus formula [24], the model
checking problem can be translated, in linear-time, into a parity game [13].
Hence, every parity game solver can be used in practice as a model checker for a
μ-calculus specification (and vice-versa). Using this approach, *liveness* and *safety*

Aniello Murano—Partially supported by the FP7 European Union project 600958-
SHERPA and OR.C.HE.S.T.R.A. MIUR PON project.

I. Lanese and E. Madelaine (Eds.): FACS 2014, LNCS 8997, pp. 145–161, 2015.
DOI: 10.1007/978-3-319-15317-9_9

properties can be addressed in a very elegant and easy way [28]. Also, this offers a very powerful machinery to check for component software reliability [1,3].

In the basic settings, parity games are two-player turn-based games, played on directed graphs, whose nodes are labeled with *priorities* (i.e., natural numbers). The players, named *player* 0 and *player* 1, move in turn a token along graph's edges. Thus, a play induces an infinite path and player 0 wins the play if the greatest priority visited infinitely often is even; otherwise, player 1 wins the play.

The problem of finding a winning strategy in parity games is known to be in UPTime ∩ CoUPTime [21] and deciding whether a polynomial time solution exists or not is a long-standing open question. Aimed to find the right complexity of parity games, as well as come out with solutions working efficiently in practice, several algorithms have been proposed in the last two decades. In Table 1, we report the most common ones along with their known computational complexities, where parameters n, e, and d denote the number of nodes, edges, and priorities in the game, respectively (for more details, see [15,16]).

Table 1. Parity algorithms along with their computational complexities.

Condition	Complexity
Recursive [35]	$O(e \cdot n^d)$
Small Progress Measures [22]	$O(d \cdot e \cdot (\frac{n}{d})^{\frac{d}{2}})$
Strategy Improvement [34]	$O(2^e \cdot n \cdot e)$
Dominion Decomposition [23]	$O(n^{\sqrt{n}})$
Big Step [32]	$O(e \cdot n^{\frac{1}{3}d})$

All above mentioned algorithms have been implemented in *PGSolver*, written in *OCaml* by Oliver Friedman and Martin Lange [15,16], a collection of tools to solve, benchmark and generate parity games. Noteworthy, PGSolver has allowed to declare the Zielonka Recursive Algorithm as the best performing to solve parity games in practice, as well as explore some optimizations such as decomposition into strong connect components, removal of self-cycles on nodes, and priority compression [2,22].

Despite the enormous interest in finding efficient algorithms for solving parity games, less emphasis has been put on the choice of the programming language. Mainly, the scientific community relies on OCaml as the best performing programming language to be used in this setting and PGSolver as an optimal and *the de facto* platform to solve parity games. However, starting from graphs with a few thousand of nodes, even using the Zielonka algorithm, PGSolver would require minutes to decide the given game, especially on dense graphs. Therefore a natural question that arises is whether there exists a way to improve the running time of PGSolver. We identify three research directions to work on, which specifically involve: the algorithm itself, the way it is implemented, and the chosen programming language. As a result we introduce, in this paper, a slightly improved version of the Classic Zielonka Algorithm along with a heavily optimized implementation in *Scala Programming Language* [29,30]. Scala is a high-level language, proven to be well performing [20], with object and functional oriented features, that recently has come to the fore with useful applications in several fields of computer science including *formal verification* [4]. Our experiments show that, by using all Scala features extensively, we are able of gaining two order of magnitude in running time with respect to the implementation of the Zielonka algorithm in PGSolver.

In details, the main goal of this work is the design and development of a new tool for solving parity games, based on an improved version of the Zielonka Recursive Algorithm, with performance in mind. Classical Zielonka algorithm requires to decompose the graph game into multiple smaller arenas, which is done by computing, in every recursive call, the *difference* between the current graph and a given set of nodes. This operation (Fig. 1, lines 10 and 15) turns out to be quite expensive as it requires to generate a new graph at each iteration. Somehow such a difference operation has the flavor of the complicancy of complementing automata in formal verification [33]. Remarkably, our improved version guarantees that the original arena remains immutable by tracking the removed nodes in every subsequent call and checking, in constant time, whether a node needs to be excluded or not. Casting this idea in the above automata reasoning, it is like enriching the state space with two flags (*removed*, $\neg$*removed*), instead of performing a complementation.

In this paper we consider and compare four implementations. The Classic (C) and Improved (I) Recursive (R) algorithms implemented in Scala (S) and OCaml (O). Using random generated games, we show that IRO gains an order of magnitude against CRO, *as well as* CRS against CRO. Remarkably, we show that these improvements are cumulative by proving that IRS gains two order of magnitude against CRO.

We have been able to achieve this kind of performance optimization by deeply studying the way the classic Recursive algorithm has been implemented in PGSolver and concentrating on the following tasks of the algorithm, which we have deeply improved: finding the maximal priority, finding all nodes with a given priority, and removing a node (including related edges) from the graph. Parsing the graph in Scala, we allocate an *Array*, whose size is fixed to the number of nodes of the graph. In addition we populate at the same time the adjacency list and incidence list for each node, which avoids to build a transposed graph. We make also use of an open source Java library called *Trove* that provides a fast and lightweight implementation of the *java.util* Collection API.

Finally, we want to remark that, among all programming languages, we have chosen to investigate Scala as it shares several modern and useful programming language aspects. Among the others, Scala carries functional and object-oriented features, compiles its programs for the JVM, is interoperable with Java and an high-level language with a concise and clear syntax. The results we obtain strongly support our choice and allow to declare Scala as a clear winner over OCaml, in terms of performance.

Outline. The sequel of the paper is structured as follows. In Sect. 2, we give some preliminary concepts about parity games. In Sect. 3, we describe the Classic Recursive Zielonka Algorithm. In Sect. 4, we introduce our improved algorithm based on the Zielonka algorithm that we implement in Sect. 5 using Scala programming language. In Sect. 6 we study, analyze, and benchmark the Classic and Improved Algorithms in OCaml (PGSolver) and Scala.

Finally we report that the tool is available as an open source project at https://github.com/vinceprignano/SPGSolver.

2   Parity Games

In this section we report some basic concepts about parity games including the Zielonka Recursive Algorithm. For more details we refer to [14,35].

A *parity game* is a tuple $G = (V, V_0, V_1, E, \Omega)$ where (V, E) forms a directed graph whose set of nodes is partitioned into $V = V_0 \cup V_1$, with $V_0 \cap V_1 = \emptyset$, and $\Omega : V \to N$ is the *priority function* that assigns to each node a natural number called the *priority* of the node. We assume E to be *total*, i.e. for every node $v \in V$, there is a node $w \in V$ such that $(v, w) \in E$. In the following we also write vEw in place of $(v, w) \in E$ and use $vE := \{w \,|\, vEw\}$.

Parity games are played between two players called *player 0* and *player 1*. Starting in a node $v \in V$, both players construct an infinite path (the *play*) through the graph as follows. If the construction reaches, at a certain point, a finite sequence $v_0...v_n$ and $v_n \in V$ then player i selects a node $w \in v_n E$ and the play continues with the sequence $v_0...v_n w$. Every play has a unique winner, defined by the priority that occurs infinitely often. Precisely, the *winner* of the play $v_0 v_1 v_2...$ is player i iff $max\{p \,|\, \forall j . \exists k \geq j \,:\, \Omega(v_k) = p\} \, mod\, 2 = i$. A *strategy* for player i is a partial function $\sigma : V^*V \to V$, such that, for all sequences $v_0...v_n$ with $v_{j+1} \in v_j E$, with $j = 0, ..., n-1$, and $v_n \in V_i$ we have that $\sigma(v_0...v_n) \in v_n E$. A play $v_0 v_1...$ *conforms* to a strategy σ for player i if, for all j we have that, if $v_j \in V_i$ then $v_{j+1} = \sigma(v_0...v_j)$. A strategy σ for player i (σ_i) is a winning strategy in node v if player i wins every play starting in v that conforms to the strategy σ. In that case, we say that player i *wins* the game G starting in v. A strategy σ for player i is called *memoryless* if, for all $v_0...v_n \in V^*V_i$ and for $w_0...w_m \in V^*V_i$, we have that if $v_n = w_m$ then $\sigma(v_0...v_n) = \sigma(w_0...w_m)$. That is, the value of the strategy on a path only depends on the last node on that path. Starting from G we construct two sets $W_0, W_1 \subseteq V$ such that W_i is the set of all nodes v such that player i wins the game G starting in v. Parity games enjoy *determinacy* meaning that for every node v either $v \in W_0$ or $v \in W_1$ [13].

The problem of solving a given parity game is to compute the sets W_0 and W_1, as well as the corresponding *memoryless* winning strategies, σ_0 for player *0* and σ_1 for player *1*, on their respective winning regions. The construction procedure of winning regions makes use of the notion of *attractor*. Formally, let $U \subseteq V$ and $i \in \{0, 1\}$. The i-attractor of U is the least set W s.t. $U \subseteq W$ and whenever $v \in V_i$ and $vE \cap W \neq \emptyset$, or $v \in V_{1-i}$ and $vE \subseteq W$ then $v \in W$. Hence, the i-attractor of U contains all nodes from which player i can move "towards" U and player $1 - i$ *must* move "towards" U. The i-attractor of U is denoted by $Attr_i(G, U)$. Let A be an arbitrary attractor set. The game $G \setminus A$ is the game restricted to the nodes $V \setminus A$, i.e. $G \setminus A = (V \setminus A, V_0 \setminus A, V_1 \setminus A, E \setminus (A \times V \cup V \times A), \Omega_{|V \setminus A})$. It is worth observing that the totality of $G \setminus A$ is ensured from A being an attractor.

Formally, for all $k \in \mathbb{N}$, the i-attractor is defined as follows:

$$Attr_i^0(U) = U \; ;$$
$$Attr_i^{k+1}(U) = Attr_i^k(U) \cup \{v \in V_i \,|\, \exists w \in Attr_i^k(U) \; s.t. \; vEw\}$$
$$\cup \{v \in V_{1-i} \,|\, \forall w : vEw \implies w \in Attr_i^k(U)\} \; ;$$
$$Attr_i(U) = \bigcup_{k \in \mathbb{N}} Attr_i^k(U).$$

3   The Zielonka Recursive Algorithm

In this section, we describe the Zielonka Recursive Algorithm using the basic concepts introduced in the previous sections and some observations regarding its implementation in PGSolver.

The algorithm to solve parity games introduced by Zielonka comes from a work of McNaughton [27]. The Zielonka Recursive Algorithm, as reported in Fig. 1, uses a divide and conquer technique. It constructs the winning sets for both players using the solution of subgames. It removes the nodes with the highest priority from the game, together with all nodes (and edges) attracted to this set. The algorithm $win(G)$ takes as input a graph G and, after a number of recursive calls over ad hoc built subgames, returns the winning sets (W_0, W_1) for player 0 and player 1, respectively. The running time complexity of the Zielonka Recursive Algorithm is reported in Table 1.

```
function win (G):
    if V == ∅:
        (W₀, W₁) = (∅, ∅)
    else:
        d = maximal priority in G
        U = { v ∈ V | priority(v) = d }
        p = d % 2
        j = 1 - p
        A = Attrₚ(U)
        (W₀', W₁') = win (G \ A)
        if Wⱼ' == ∅:
            Wₚ = Wₚ' ∪ A
            Wⱼ = ∅
        else:
            B = Attrⱼ(W₁ʲ)
            (W₀', W₁') = win (G \ B)
            Wₚ = Wₚ'
            Wⱼ = Wⱼ' ∪ B
    return (W₀, W₁)
```

Fig. 1. Zielonka Recursive Algorithm

3.1   The Implementation of the Zielonka Algorithm in PGSolver

PGSolver turns out to be of a very limited application in several real scenarios. In more details, even using the Zielonka Recursive Algorithm (that has been shown to be the best performing in practice), PGSolver would require minutes to decide games with few thousands of nodes, especially on dense graphs. In this work we deeply study all main aspects that cause such a bad performance.

Specifically, our investigation beginnings with the way the (Classic) Recursive Algorithm has been implemented in PGSolver by means of the OCaml programming language. We start observing that the graph data structure in this framework is represented as a fixed length *Array* of tuples. Every tuple has all information that a node needs, such as the player, the assigned priority and the adjacency list. Before every recursive call is performed, the program computes the difference between the graph and the attractor, as well as it builds the transposed graph. In addition the attractor function makes use of a *TreeSet* data structure that is not available in the OCaml's standard library, but it is imported from *TCSlib*, a multi-purpose library for OCaml written by Oliver Friedmann and Martin Lange. Such library implements this data structure using *AVL-Trees* that guarantees logarithmic search, insert, and removal. Also, the same function calculates the number of successors for the opponent player in *every* iteration when looping through every node in the attractor.

4   The Improved Algorithm

```
function win (G):
   T = G.transpose()
   Removed = {}
   return winI (G, T, Removed)

function winI (G, T, Removed):
   if |V| == |Removed|:
      return (∅, ∅)
   W = (∅, ∅)
   d = maximal priority in G
   U = { v ∈ V | priority(v) = d }
   p = d % 2
   j = 1 - p
   W' = (∅, ∅)
   A = Attr (G, T, Removed, U, p)
   (W'_0, W'_1) = winI (G, T, Removed ∪ A)
   if W'_j == ∅:
      W_p = W'_p ∪ A
      W_j = ∅
   else:
      B = Attr (G, T, Removed, W'_j, j)
      (W'_0, W'_1) = winI (G, T, Removed ∪ B)
      W_p = W'_p
      W_j = W'_j ∪ B
   return (W_0, W_1)
```

Fig. 2. Improved Recursive Algorithm

```
function Attr (G, T, Removed, A, i):
   tmpMap = []
   for x = 0 to |V|:
      if x ∈ A tmpMap = 0
      else tmpMap = -1
   index = 0
   while index < |A|:
      for v_0 ∈ adj(T, A[index]):
         if v_0 ∉ Removed:
            if tmpMap[v_0] == -1:
               if player(v_0) == i:
                  A = A ∪ v_0
                  tmpMap[v_0] = 0
               else:
                  adj_counter = -1
                  for x ∈ adj(G, v_0):
                     if (x ∉ Removed):
                        adj_counter += 1
                  tmpMap[v_0] = adj_counter
                  if adj_counter == 0:
                     A = A ∪ v_0
            else if (player(v_0) == j
                  and tmpMap[v_0] > 0):
               tmpMap[v_0] -= 1
               if tmpMap[v_0] == 0:
                  A = A ∪ v_0
   return A
```

Fig. 3. Improved Recursive Attractor

In this section we introduce an improved version based on the Classic Recursive Algorithm by Zielonka. The new algorithm is depicted in Fig. 2. In Fig. 3 we also report an improved version of the attractor function that the new algorithm makes use of.

Let G be a graph. Removing a node from G and building the transposed graph takes time $\Theta(|V| + |E|)$. Thus dealing with dense graph such operation takes $\Theta(|V|^2)$. In order to reduce the running time complexity caused by these graph operations, we introduce an immutability requirement to the graph G ensuring that every recursive call uses G without applying any modification to the state space of the graph. Therefore, to construct the subgames, in the recursive calls, we keep track of each node that is going to be removed from the graph, adding all of them to a set called *Removed*.

The improved algorithm is capable of checking if a given node is excluded or not in constant time as well as it completely removes the need for a new graph in every recursive call. At first glance this may seem a small improvement with respect to the Classic Recursive Algorithm. However, it turns out to be very successful in practice as proved in the following benchmark section. Further evidences that boost the importance of such improvement can be related to the fact that the difference operation has somehow the same complicance of complementing automata [33]. Using our approach is like avoiding such complementation by adding constant information to the states, i.e. a flag (*removed*, ¬*removed*).

Last but not least, about the actual implementation, it is also worth mentioning that general-purpose *memory allocators* are very expensive as the per-operation cost floats around one hundred processor cycles [18]. Through these years many efforts have been made to improve memory allocation writing custom allocators from scratch, a process known to be difficult and error prone [5,6].

4.1 Implementation in OCaml for PGSolver

Our implementation of the Improved Recursive Algorithm, listed in Fig. 4, does not directly modify the graph data structure (that is represented in PGSolver as an array of tuples), but rather it uses a set to keep track of removed nodes.

The Improved Recursive Algorithm, named *solver*, takes three parameters: the Graph, its transposed one, and a set of excluded nodes. Our Improved Attractor function, uses a *HashMap*, called *tempMap* to keep track of the number of successors for the opponent player's nodes. In addition, we use a *Queue*, from OCaml's standard library, to loop over the nodes in the attractor. Aiming at performance optimizations, the attractor function, implemented in PGSolver also returns the set of excluded nodes that *solver* passes to the next recursive call.

```
let rec win game tgraph exc =
  let w = Array.make 2 InteSet.empty in
  if(not ((Array.length game) =
    (InteSet.cardinal exc))) then (
    let (d,u) = (max_prio_and_set game exc) in
    let p = d mod 2 in
    let j = 1 - p in
    let w1 = Array.make 2 InteSet.empty in
    let (attr,excl) = attr_fun game
                               exc tgraph u p in
    let (sol0,sol1) = win game
                           tgraph excl in
    w1.(0) <- sol0;
    w1.(1) <- sol1;
    if (InteSet.is_empty w1.(j)) then (
      w.(p) <- (InteSet.union w1.(p) attr);
      w.(j) <- InteSet.empty;
    ) else (
      let (attr_B,exc2) =
        attr_fun game exc tgraph w1.(j) j in
      let (sol_0,sol_1) = win game
                               tgraph exc2 in
      w1.(0) <- sol_0;
      w1.(1) <- sol_1;
      w.(p) <- w1.(p);
      w.(j) <- (InteSet.union w1.(j) attr_B);
    )
  );
  (w.(0),w.(1))
;;
```

Fig. 4. Improved Recursive in OCaml

5   Scala

Scala [29,30] is the programming language designed by Martin Odersky, the codesigner of Java Generics and main author of *javac* compiler. Scala defines itself as a *scalable* language, statically typed, a fusion of an object-oriented language and a functional one. It runs on the *Java Virtual Machine* (JVM) and supports every existing Java library. Scala is a purely object-oriented language in which, like Java and Smalltalk, every value is an object and every operation is a method call. In addition Scala is a functional language where every function is a first class object, also is equipped with efficient immutable and mutable data structures, with a strong selling point given by Java interoperability. However, it is not a purely functional language as objects may change their states and functions may have side effects. The functional aspects are perfectly integrated with the object-oriented features. The combination of both styles makes possible to express new kinds of patterns and abstractions. All these features make Scala programming language as a clever choice to solve these tasks, in a strict comparison with other programming languages available such as C, C++ or Java. Historically, the first generation of the JVM was entirely an interpreter; nowadays the JVM uses a Just-In-Time (*JIT*) compiler, a complex process aimed to improve performance at runtime. This process can be described in three steps: (1) source files are compiled by the Scala Compiler into Java Bytecode, that will be feed to a JVM; (2) the JVM will load the compiled classes at runtime and execute proper computation using an interpreter; (3) the JVM will analyze the application method calls and compile the bytecode into native machine code. This step is done in a lazy manner: the JIT compiles a code path when it knows that is about to be executed. JIT removed the overhead of interpretation and allows programs to start up quickly, in addition this kind of compilation has to be fast to prevent influencing the actual performance of the program. Another interesting aspect of the JVM is that it verifies every class file after loading them. This makes sure that the execution step does not violate some defined safety properties.

The checks are performed by the verifier that includes a complete type checking of the entire program. The JVM is also available on all major platforms and compiled Java executables can run on all of them with no need for recompilation. The Scala compiler *scalac* compiles a Scala program into Java class files. The compiler is organized in a sequence of successive steps. The first one is called *the front-end step* and performs an analysis of the input file, makes sure that is a valid Scala program and produces an attributed abstract syntax tree (*AST*); the

```scala
def win(G: GraphWithSets)
: (ArrayBuffer[Int],
   ArrayBuffer[Int]) = {
 val W =
   Array(ArrayBuffer.empty[Int],
   ArrayBuffer.empty[Int])
 val d = G.max_priority()
 if (d > -1) {
   val U = G.priorityMap.get(d)
     .filter(p => !G.exclude(p))
   val p = d % 2
   val j = 1 - p
   val W1 =
     Array(ArrayBuffer.empty[Int],
     ArrayBuffer.empty[Int])
   val A = Attr(G, U, p)
   val res = win(G -- A)
   W1(0) = res._1
   W1(1) = res._2
   if (W(j).size == 0) {
     W(p) = W1(p) ++= A
     W(j) = ArrayBuffer.empty[Int]
   } else {
     val B = Attr(G, W1(j), j)
     val res2 = win(G -- B)
     W1(0) = res2._1
     W1(1) = res2._2
     W(p) = W1(p)
     W(j) = W1(j) ++= B
   }
 }
 (W(0), W(1))
}
```

Fig. 5. Improved Algorithm in Scala

back-end step simplifies the AST and proceeds to the generation phase where it produces the actual class files, which constitute the final output. Targeting the JVM, the Scala Compiler checks that the produced code is type-correct in order to be accepted by the JVM bytecode verifier.

In [20], published by *Google*, Scala even being an high level language, performs just 2.5x slower than C++ machine optimized code. In particular it has been proved to be even faster than Java. As the paper notes: "*While the benchmark itself is simple and compact, it employs many language features, in particular high level data structures, a few algorithms, iterations over collection types, some object oriented features and interesting memory allocation patterns*".

5.1   Improved Algorithm in Scala

In this section we introduce our implementation of the Improved Recursive Algorithm in Scala, listed as Figs. 5 and 6.

Aiming at performance optimizations we use a *priority HashMap* where every *key* is a certain priority and a *value* is a set of each node v where $priority(v) = key$. As fast and JVM-Optimized *HashMaps* and *ArrayLists* we use the ones included in the open source library *Trove*. In addition, using the well known *strategy pattern* [17] we open the framework for further extensions and improvements. The intended purpose of our algorithm is to assert that the performance of existing tools for solving parity games can be improved using the improved algorithm and choosing Scala as the programming language. We rely on Scala's internal

```
def Attr(G: GraphWithSets,
    A: ArrayBuffer[Int], i: Int)
    : ArrayBuffer[Int] = {
  val tmpMap = Array
    .fill[Int](G.nodes.size)(-1)
  var index = 0
  A.foreach(tmpMap(_) = 0)
  while (index < A.size) {
    G.nodes(A(index))
      .< .foreach(v0 => {
        if (!G.exclude(v0)) {
          val flag = G.nodes(v0).player == i
          if (tmpMap(v0) == -1) {
            if (flag) {
              A += v0
              tmpMap(v0) = 0
            } else {
              val tmp = G.nodes(v0)
                .~>
                .count(x => !G.exclude(x)) - 1
              tmpMap(v0) = tmp
              if (tmp == 0) A += v0
            }
          } else if (!flag && tmpMap(v0) > 0){
            tmpMap(v0) -= 1
            if (tmpMap(v0) == 0) A += v0
          }
        }
      })
    index += 1
  }
  A
}
```

Fig. 6. Improved Attractor in Scala

features and standard library making heavy use of the dynamic *ArrayBuffer* data structure. In order to store the arena we use an array of *Node* objects. The Node class contains: a list of adjacent nodes, a list of incident nodes, its priority and the player; the data structure also implements a factory method called "$--(set : ArrayBuffer[Int])$" that takes an ArrayBuffer of integers as input, flags all the nodes in the array as excluded, and returns the reference to the new graph. In addition, there is also a method called $max\_priority()$ that will return the maximal priority in the graph and the set of nodes with that priority.

The Attractor function makes deeply use of an array of integers named $tmpMap$ that is preallocated using the number of nodes in the graph with a negative integer as default value; we use $tmpMap$ when looping through every node in the set A given as parameter, to keep track of the number of successors for the opponent player. We add a node $v \in V$ to the attractor set when its counter (stored in $tmpMap[v]$) reaches 0 ($adj(v) \subseteq A$ and $v \in V_{opponent}$) or if $v \in V_{player}$; using an array of integers, or an HashMap, to serve this purpose, guarantees a constant time check if a node was already visited and ensures that the count for the opponent's node adjacency list takes place one time only. These functions are inside a singleton object called $ImprovedRecursiveSolver$ that extends the $Solver$ interface.

6   Benchmarks

In this section we study, analyze and evaluate the running time of our four implementations: $Classic\ Recursive\ in\ OCaml\ (CRO)$, $Classic\ Recursive\ in\ Scala$ (CRS), $Improved\ Recursive\ in\ OCaml\ (IRO)$ and $Improved\ Recursive\ in\ Scala$ (IRS). We have run our experiments on multiple instances of random parity games. We want to note that IRS does not apply any preprocessing steps to the arena before solving. All tests have been run on an Intel(R) Xeon(R) CPU E5620 @ 2.40 GHz, with 16 GB of Ram (with no Swap available) running Ubuntu 14.04. Precisely, we have used 100 random arenas generated using PGSolver of each of the following types, given $N = i \times 1000$ with i integer and $1 \le i \le 10$ and a timeout set at 600 s. In the following, we report six tables in which we show the running time of all experiments under fixed parameters. Throughout

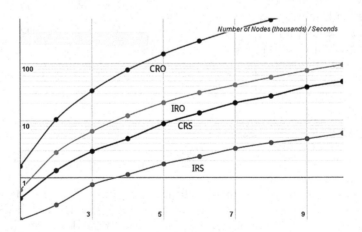

Fig. 7. Random Games Chart in Logarithmic Scale

this section we define abo_T when the program has been aborted due to excessive time and abo_M when the program has been killed by the Operating System due to memory consumption. In Fig. 7 we also report the trends of the four implementations using a logarithmic scale with respect to *seconds*. This figure is based on the averages of all results reported in the tables below.

N nodes, N colors, $adj(\frac{N}{2}, N)$

N	IRS	CRO	CRS	IRO
1×10^3	**0.204**	1.99	0.505	0.752
2×10^3	**0.456**	13.208	1.918	3.664
3×10^3	**1.031**	41.493	2.656	6.147
4×10^3	**1.879**	96.847	6.728	15.966
5×10^3	**2.977**	183.589	12.616	27.272
6×10^3	**3.993**	306.104	19.032	41.051
7×10^3	**4.989**	486.368	27.05	50.367
8×10^3	**6.103**	abo_T	36.597	70.972
9×10^3	**7.287**	abo_T	55.171	97.216
10×10^3	**8.468**	abo_T	68.303	113.36

N nodes, N colors, $adj(1, N)$

N	IRS	CRO	CRS	IRO
1×10^3	**0.179**	1.21	0.454	0.583
2×10^3	**0.389**	8.075	1.173	2.366
3×10^3	**0.868**	25.097	2.656	6.147
4×10^3	**1.279**	57.186	4.23	10.452
5×10^3	**2.273**	108.983	9.206	20.377
6×10^3	**2.772**	183.884	12.562	27.489
7×10^3	**3.748**	291.077	17.942	37.521
8×10^3	**3.942**	418.377	22.105	47.502
9×10^3	**4.989**	593.721	23.93	61.593
10×10^3	**6.413**	abo_T	42.408	80.508

N nodes, 2 colors, $adj(\frac{N}{2}, N)$

N	IRS	CRO	CRS	IRO
1×10^3	**0.189**	1.98	0.481	0.702
2×10^3	**0.469**	12.941	1.55	3.17
3×10^3	**1.046**	41.584	3.995	7.428
4×10^3	**1.712**	96.545	5.378	13.823
5×10^3	**2.414**	181.225	11.273	22.575
6×10^3	**3.458**	307.233	16.472	35.269
7×10^3	**4.612**	484.159	26.448	49.311
8×10^3	**6.003**	abo_T	28.968	65.674
9×10^3	**7.03**	abo_T	43.666	85.909
10×10^3	**8.938**	abo_T	57.18	110.814

N nodes, 2 colors, $adj(1, N)$

N	IRS	CRO	CRS	IRO
1×10^3	**0.159**	1.226	0.385	0.468
2×10^3	**0.341**	7.965	1.004	2.162
3×10^3	**0.797**	25.114	2.305	6.014
4×10^3	**1.123**	56.422	3.699	9.421
5×10^3	**1.704**	108.584	6.12	14.971
6×10^3	**2.243**	182.935	10.099	22.621
7×10^3	**3.324**	286.503	13.898	32.335
8×10^3	**3.95**	430.265	19.743	44.281
9×10^3	**4.597**	abo_T	28.742	56.81
10×10^3	**5.651**	abo_T	33.639	71.434

N nodes, $\sqrt{N}$ colors, $adj(\frac{N}{2}, N)$

N	IRS	CRO	CRS	IRO
1×10^3	**0.204**	1.978	0.468	0.71
2×10^3	**0.456**	13.114	1.575	3.203
3×10^3	**1.031**	41.493	3.868	7.492
4×10^3	**1.621**	96.55	5.744	13.97
5×10^3	**2.439**	183.589	10.72	22.98
6×10^3	**3.372**	307.426	15.978	34.78
7×10^3	**4.662**	485.826	26.432	48.875
8×10^3	**6.499**	abo_T	34.741	66.423
9×10^3	**7.147**	abo_T	48.915	86.645
10×10^3	**8.988**	abo_T	56.656	111.492

N nodes, $\sqrt{N}$ colors, $adj(1, N)$

N	IRS	CRO	CRS	IRO
1×10^3	**0.162**	1.218	0.384	0.475
2×10^3	**0.344**	7.947	1.034	2.195
3×10^3	**0.788**	25.029	2.406	5.944
4×10^3	**1.105**	57.307	3.835	9.608
5×10^3	**1.678**	108.623	6.34	15.165
6×10^3	**2.281**	182.154	9.871	22.859
7×10^3	**3.193**	285.28	14.338	32.536
8×10^3	**4.185**	422.74	20.362	44.515
9×10^3	**5.009**	599.071	24.347	57.022
10×10^3	**5.76**	abo_T	35.024	72.291

6.1   Trends Analysis for Random Arenas

The speedup obtained by our implementation of the Improved Recursive Algorithm is in most cases quite noticeable. Figure 8 shows the running time trend for Improved and Classic Algorithm on each platform. The seconds are limited to [0, 100]. As a result we show that even with all preprocessing steps enabled in PGSolver, *IRS* is capable of gaining two orders of magnitude in running time.

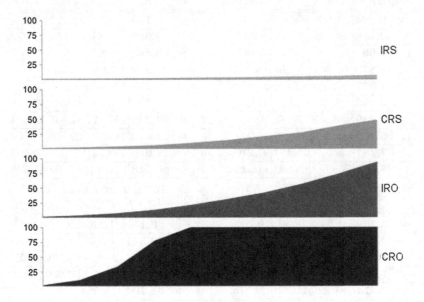

Fig. 8. Trends Chart

6.2   Trends Analysis for Special Games

Focusing on Classic Recursive in PGSolver and our Improved Recursive in Scala, here we show the running times for non-random games generated by PGSolver. In particular we use four types of non-random games, these experiments have been run against PGSolver using the Classic Recursive Algorithm with all optimizations disabled and all solutions were matched to ensure correctness.

Clique[n] games are fully connected games without self-loops, where n is the number of nodes. The set of nodes is partitioned into V_0 and V_1 having the same size. For all $v \in V_p$, $priority(v) \% 2 = p$. For our experiments we set $n = 2^k$ where $8 \leq k \leq 14$. Table below reports the running time for our experiments and these results are drawn in Fig. 9.

n	2^8	2^9	2^{10}	2^{11}	2^{12}	2^{13}	2^{14}
IRS	0.05	0.07	0.12	0.46	1.18	4.87	17.39
CRO	0.09	0.61	4.37	29.58	229.78	abo_T	abo_M

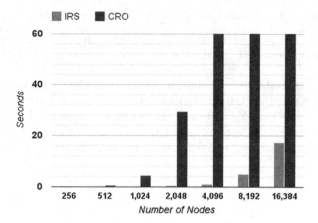

Fig. 9. Clique Trends

In *Ladder[n]* game, every node in V_0 has priority 2 and every node in V_1 has priority 1. In addition, each node $v \in V$ has two successors: one in V_0 and one in V_1, which form a node pair. Every pair is connected to the next pair forming a *ladder* of pairs. Finally, the last pair is connected to the top. The parameter n specifies the number of node pairs. For our tests, we set $n = 2^k$ where $7 \le k \le 19$ and report our experiments in the table below whose trend is drawn in Fig. 10. Figure 10 shows better performance for *CRO* than *IRS* using low-scaled values as input parameter. This behaviour is not surprising as there is a *warming-up* time required by the Java Virtual Machine.

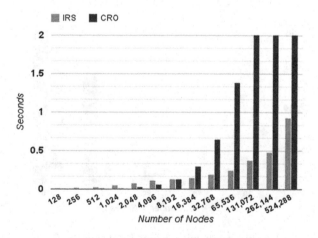

Fig. 10. Ladder Trends

n	2^7	2^8	2^9	2^{10}	2^{11}	2^{12}	2^{13}	2^{14}	2^{15}	2^{16}	2^{17}	2^{18}	2^{19}
IRS	0.01	0.02	0.03	0.05	0.08	0.11	0.13	0.15	0.19	0.25	0.38	0.48	0.93
CRO	0.00	0.00	0.01	0.01	0.03	0.06	0.13	0.3	0.65	1.39	2.93	6.21	11.71

Model Checker Ladder[n] consists of overlapping blocks of four nodes, where the parameter n specifies the number of desidered blocks. Every node is owned by player 1, $V_1 = V$ and $V_0 = \emptyset$, and the nodes are connected such that every cycle passes through a single point of colour 0. For our experiments we set $n = 2^k$ where $7 \leq k \leq 19$, report our experiments in the table below and draw the trends in Fig. 11.

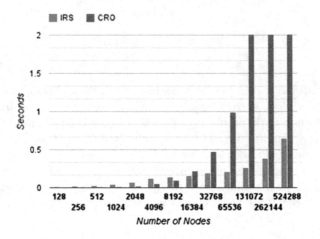

Fig. 11. Model Checker Ladder Trends

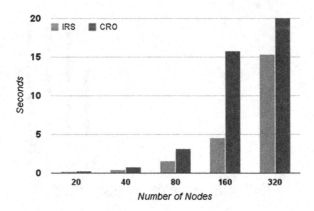

Fig. 12. Jurdiznski Trends with a Fixed Parameter of $n = 10$ Layers

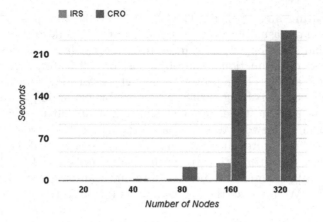

Fig. 13. Jurdiznski Trends with a Fixed Parameter of $m = 10$ Blocks

n	2^7	2^8	2^9	2^{10}	2^{11}	2^{12}	2^{13}	2^{14}	2^{15}	2^{16}	2^{17}	2^{18}	2^{19}
IRS	0.01	0.02	0.03	0.04	0.07	0.12	0.14	0.16	0.19	0.21	0.26	0.39	0.65
CRO	0.00	0.00	0.01	0.01	0.02	0.05	0.10	0.22	0.47	0.99	2.12	4.16	8.31

Jurdzinski[n, m] games are designed to generate the worst-case behaviour for the Small Progress Measure Solver [22]. The parameter n is the number of layers, where each layer has m repeating blocks that are inter-connected as described in [22]. As this game takes two parameters, in our test we ran two experiments: one where n is fixed to 10 and $m = 10 \times 2^k$, for $k = 1, 2, 3, 4, 5$ and one where m is fixed to 10 and $n = 10 \times 2^k$, for $k = 1, 2, 3, 4, 5$. The results of our experiments are reported in the tables below. The trends are drawn in Figs. 12 and 13.

m	10×2^1	10×2^2	10×2^3	10×2^4	10×2^5	n	10×2^1	10×2^2	10×2^3	10×2^4	10×2^5
IRS	0.21	0.48	1.54	4.55	15.31	*IRS*	0.28	0.77	3.02	30.02	232.24
CRO	0.23	0.79	3.14	15.77	65.85	*CRO*	0.42	2.94	22.69	184.12	abo_T

7   Conclusions

PGSolver is a well-stablished framework that collects multiple algorithms to decide parity games. For several years now this platform has been the only one available to solve and benchmark in practice. Given PGSolver's limitations addressing huge graphs, several attempts of improvement have been carried out recently. Some of them have been implemented as preprocessing steps in the tool itself (such as priority compression or SCC decomposition and the like), while others chose parallelism techniques, such as Cuda [19], applied to the algorithms. However these improvements often do not show the desired performance.

In this paper we started from scratch by revisiting the Zielonka Recursive Algorithm, implemented an improved and the classic versions in Scala and

OCaml, comparing among them. The choice of Scala as a programming language has been not casual, but rather it comes out from a deep study focused on performance and simplicity. Scala is interoperable with Java libraries, has a concise and clear syntax, functional and object oriented features, runs on the Java Virtual Machine and has been proven to be high performing. Our main result is a new and fast tool for solving parity games capable of gaining up to two orders of magnitude in running time. In conclusion we state that there is place for a faster and better framework to solve parity games and this work is a starting point raising several interesting questions. For example, what if one implements the other known algorithms to solve parity games in Scala? PGSolver showed that Zielonka's algorithm is the best performing. Can one reproduce the same results in Scala? We leave all these questions as future work.

References

1. Aminof, B., Mogavero, F., Murano, A.: Synthesis of hierarchical systems. Sci. Comp. Program. **83**, 56–79 (2013)
2. Antonik, A., Charlton, N., Huth, M.: Polynomial-time under-approximation of winning regions in parity games. ENTCS **225**, 115–139 (2009)
3. Aminof, B., Kupferman, O., Murano, A.: Improved model checking of hierarchical systems. Inf. Comput. **210**, 68–86 (2012)
4. Barringer, H., Havelund, K.: TRACECONTRACT: a scala DSL for trace analysis. In: Butler, M., Schulte, W. (eds.) FM 2011. LNCS, vol. 6664, pp. 57–72. Springer, Heidelberg (2011)
5. Berger, E.D., Zorn, B.G., McKinley, K.S.: Composing high-performance memory allocators. ACM SIGPLAN Not. **36**, 114–124 (2001)
6. Berger, E.D., Zorn, B.G., McKinley, K.S.: OOPSLA 2002: reconsidering custom memory allocation. ACM SIGPLAN Not. **48**(4), 46–57 (2013)
7. Berwanger, D.: Admissibility in infinite games. In: Thomas, W., Weil, P. (eds.) STACS 2007. LNCS, vol. 4393, pp. 188–199. Springer, Heidelberg (2007)
8. Chatterjee, K., Doyen, L., Henzinger, T.A., Raskin, J.-F.: Generalized mean-payoff and energy games. In: FSTTCS'10, LIPIcs 8, pp. 505–516 (2010)
9. Chatterjee, K., Henzinger, T.A., Jurdzinski, M.: Mean-payoff parity games. In: LICS'05, pp. 178–187 (2005)
10. Chatterjee, K., Jurdzinski, M., Henzinger, T.A.: Quantitative stochastic parity games. In: SODA'04, pp. 121–130 (2004)
11. Clarke, E.M., Emerson, E.A.: Design and synthesis of synchronization skeletons using branching time temporal logic. In: Kozen, D. (ed.) Logic of Programs 1981. LNCS, vol. 131, pp. 52–71. Springer, Heidelberg (1982)
12. Clarke, E., Grumberg, O., Peled, D.: Model Checking. MIT Press, Cambridge (2002)
13. Emerson, E., Jutla, C.: Tree automata, μ-calculus and determinacy. In: FOCS'91, pp. 368–377 (1991)
14. Friedmann, O.: Recursive algorithm for parity games requires exponential time. RAIRO-Theor. Inform. Appl. **45**(04), 449–457 (2011)
15. Friedmann, O., Lange, M.: The pgsolver collection of parity game solvers. University of Munich (2009)
16. Friedmann, O., Lange, M.: Solving parity games in practice. In: Liu, Z., Ravn, A.P. (eds.) ATVA 2009. LNCS, vol. 5799, pp. 182–196. Springer, Heidelberg (2009)

17. Gamma, E., Helm, R., Johnson, R., Vlissides, J.: Design Patterns: Elements of Reusable Object-Oriented Software. Pearson Education, New Jersey (1994)
18. Gay, D., Aiken, A.: Memory management with explicit regions. ACM Sigplan Not. **33**, 313–323 (1998)
19. Hoffmann, P., Luttenberger, M.: Solving parity games on the GPU. In: Van Hung, D., Ogawa, M. (eds.) ATVA 2013. LNCS, vol. 8172, pp. 455–459. Springer, Heidelberg (2013)
20. Hundt, R.: Loop recognition in c++/java/go/scala. In: 2011 Proceedings of Scala Days (2011)
21. Jurdzinski, M.: Deciding the winner in parity games is in up ∩ co-up. Inf. Process. Lett. **68**(3), 119–124 (1998)
22. Jurdziński, M.: Small progress measures for solving parity games. In: Reichel, H., Tison, S. (eds.) STACS 2000. LNCS, vol. 1770, pp. 290–301. Springer, Heidelberg (2000)
23. Jurdzinski, M., Paterson, M., Zwick, U.: A deterministic subexponential algorithm for solving parity games. SIAM J. Comput. **38**(4), 1519–1532 (2008)
24. Kozen, D.: Results on the propositional mu-calculus. TCS **27**(3), 333–354 (1983)
25. Kupferman, O., Vardi, M., Wolper, P.: An automata theoretic approach to branching-time model checking. JACM **47**(2), 312–360 (2000)
26. Kupferman, O., Vardi, M., Wolper, P.: Module checking. IC **164**(2), 322–344 (2001)
27. McNaughton, R.: Infinite games played on finite graphs. Ann. Pure Appl. Log. **65**(2), 149–184 (1993)
28. Mogavero, F., Murano, A., Sorrentino, L.: On promptness in parity games. In: McMillan, K., Middeldorp, A., Voronkov, A. (eds.) LPAR-19 2013. LNCS, vol. 8312, pp. 601–618. Springer, Heidelberg (2013)
29. Odersky, M., Altherr, P., Cremet, V., Emir, B., Maneth, S., Micheloud, S., Mihaylov, N., Schinz, M., Stenman, E., Zenger, M.: An overview of the scala programming language (2004)
30. Odersky, M., Spoon, L., Venners, B.: Programming in Scala. Artima Inc, Sunnyvale (2008)
31. Queille, J., Sifakis, J.: Specification and verification of concurrent programs in CESAR. In: Dezani-Ciancaglini, M., Montanari, U. (eds.) International Symposium on Programming. LNCS, vol. 137, pp. 337–351. Springer, Heidelberg (1982)
32. Schewe, S.: Solving parity games in big steps. In: Arvind, V., Prasad, S. (eds.) FSTTCS 2007. LNCS, vol. 4855, pp. 449–460. Springer, Heidelberg (2007)
33. Thomas, W.: Automata on infinite objects. In: van Leeuwen, J. (ed.) Handbook of Theoretical Computer Science, vol. B, pp. 133–191. MIT Press, Cambridge (1990)
34. Vöge, J., Jurdzinski, M.: A discrete strategy improvement algorithm for solving parity games. In: Emerson, E.A., Sistla, A.P. (eds.) CAV 2000. LNCS, vol. 1855, pp. 202–215. Springer, Heidelberg (2000)
35. Zielonka, W.: Infinite games on finitely coloured graphs with applications to automata on infinite trees. Theor. Comput. Sci. **200**(1–2), 135–183 (1998)

Synthesis of a Reconfiguration Service
for Mixed-Criticality Multi-Core Systems:
An Experience Report

Md Tawhid Bin Waez[1]([⊠]), Andrzej Wąsowski[2], Juergen Dingel[1],
and Karen Rudie[1]

[1] Queen's University, Kingston, Canada
{waez,dingel}@cs.queensu.ca, karen.rudie@queensu.ca
[2] IT University of Copenhagen, Copenhagen, Denmark
wasowski@itu.dk

Abstract. Task-level reconfiguration techniques in automotive applications aim to reallocate tasks to computation cores during failures to
guarantee that the desired functionality is still delivered. We consider
a class of mixed-criticality asymmetric multi-core systems inspired by
our collaboration with a leading automotive manufacturing company,
for which we automatically synthesize task-level reconfiguration services
to reduce the number of processing cores and decrease the cost without weakening fault-tolerance. We admit the following types of faults:
safety violations by tasks, permanent core failures, and temporary core
failures. We use timed games to synthesize the controllers. The services
suspend and reinstate the periodic executions of the non-critical tasks
to ensure enough processing capacity for the critical tasks by maintaining lookup tables, which keep track of processing capacity. We present a
methodology to synthesize the services and use a case study to show that
suitable abstractions can dramatically improve the scalability of timed
games-based tools for solving industrial problems.

1 Introduction

We synthesize task-level reconfiguration services to ensure fault-tolerance of a
mixed-criticality automotive system that consists of an asymmetric multi-core
processor (AMP). The system has a fault-intolerant AMP scheduler. We augment
the existing scheduler with supplementary reconfiguration services, which we
synthesize. The services assure the periodic executions of all the critical tasks in
the presence of faults from a fault model.

We use timed games at synthesis-time and lookup tables at runtime to
provide task-level reconfiguration, a cost-effective fault-tolerance technique, for
mixed-criticality multi-core systems. System-level requirements for embedded,
real-time software in many domains (such as automotive) have enough flexibility
to reallocate tasks from one processing core to another. A task-level reconfiguration technique reduces the number of redundant cores those are used only
to provide fault-tolerance by reallocating the loads of the failed cores to the

© Springer International Publishing Switzerland 2015
I. Lanese and E. Madelaine (Eds.): FACS 2014, LNCS 8997, pp. 162–180, 2015.
DOI: 10.1007/978-3-319-15317-9_10

non-redundant operational cores. Reduction in the amount of expensive hardware makes task-level reconfiguration a promising fault-tolerance technique in the automotive industry, where cost-efficiency and fault-tolerance are both crucial issues. Since this economical technique can handle tasks with different levels of criticality, one of its prospective application sectors is next-generation automotive systems, most of which are expected to be mixed-criticality multi-core systems.

Formal methods have been used for the development of fault-tolerant real-time systems. However, in industry, fault-tolerance problems are typically designed, analyzed, and solved using classical control theory [1,2]. Timed game theory [3–5], a dense-time automata-based game theory, is almost unexplored in industrial applications. The use of timed game theory to solve industrial problems is attractive because of automated controller synthesis, visual modeling, and dense-time formal analysis. Nevertheless, applying timed game theory to solve industrial problems is challenging because of its high computational complexity.

We use timed games to synthesize the embedded controllers of the reconfiguration services. Our approach guarantees fault-tolerance up to a certain maximal number of concurrent faults after inserting the services into the system. Such reliable and accurate information is helpful to build mixed-criticality systems cost effectively. Intellectual property regulations do not allow us to present the case study on the systems of our industrial partner. Instead we demonstrate the approach using a small system, which is complex enough to show the essence of the problem and our approach, yet simple enough to allow a compact presentation.

Structure of Paper. In Sect. 3 we propose a service-based task-level reconfiguration technique to guarantee fault-tolerance of mixed-criticality multi-core systems. Timed games are used to synthesize controllers that select safe operational cores to reallocate the periodic executions of critical tasks from failed cores. Lookup tables are used at runtime to suspend and reinstate the periodic executions of non-critical tasks to ensure that operational cores have enough free processing capacity for the executions of the newly reallocated critical tasks. We synthesize the reconfiguration services in six steps:

Section 4. Identification of modeling abstractions and required system parameters to construct a scalable model.
Sections 4.1–4.3. Construction of a timed game model where unsafe locations are reachable if and only if a core exceeds its load capacity.
Section 5.1. Analysis of the model for the existence of a central controller that ensures no unsafe location is reachable; binary search for the maximal value of the concurrent-failures–limit for which such a controller exists; and automated synthesis of the controller of the maximal concurrent-failures–limit.
Section 5.2. Synthesis of the services by distributing the synthesized central controller and combining the abstracted elements of Sect. 4.
Section 5.3. Leverage scalability of the whole process for industrial systems using aggressive abstractions.

Section 5.4. Generalization of the synthesis process to apply to other multi-core systems, such as for symmetric multi-core processing (SMP) systems.

We use Uppaal Tiga [6]—a solver for timed games—to model, analyze, and synthesize. The methodology, however, can be applied using any solver for timed games, such as Synthia [7]. The paper concludes in Sect. 6.

2   Related Work

A real-time control problem can be viewed as a two-player timed game [3–5] between the controller and the environment, where the controller aims to find a strategy to guarantee that the system will satisfy a given property, no matter what the environment does [8]. An example of such reformulation is to find a strategy for the controller (or a reconfiguration service) to prevent the system from becoming unstable in the presence of the faults of the fault model.

We use a dense-time model-based approach to synthesize the services because dense-time models also can capture uncontrollable behaviors which may occur other than at discrete time units. Timed automata (TA) [9,10]—finite automata with dense-time clocks, clock constraints, and clock resets—are a prominent class of formal models to analyze safety and reachability properties of real-time systems. Clocks, clock constraints, and clock resets are used to express timing behaviors in TA. Timed automata have been used for many purposes [10] including fault diagnosis [11–13], analyzing multi-core systems [14,15], task models [16], and analyzing mixed-criticality systems [17].

A timed I/O automaton (TIOA) [18,19] is a timed automaton which has an input alphabet and a set of uncontrollable transitions along with a regular (output) alphabet and a set of regular (controllable) transitions. The controller plays controllable transitions and the environment plays uncontrollable transitions; thus TIOA are a natural model for real-time games. Uppaal Tiga [6] is a well-known timed games-based tool that uses TIOA for modeling.

3   Task-Level Reconfiguration Technique

We introduce a service-based task-level reconfiguration technique to assure fault-tolerance of mixed-criticality multi-core systems.

3.1   Systems

We consider a class of multi-core systems having asymmetric processing cores. Different asymmetric cores may exhibit different performance for the same task. The systems under consideration are mixed-criticality systems, because they execute both critical tasks and non-critical tasks with two different priorities.

Definition 1. *A mixed-criticality system consists of*

- *N asymmetric processing cores:* $core_1$, $core_2$, $\cdots$, $core_N$.
- *M tasks:* $task_1$, $task_2$, $\cdots$, $task_M$.
- *P critical tasks, where $P < M$.*
- *Predicate* `criticality(`$task_i$`)` *holds only for critical tasks.*
- *A fault-intolerant criticality-unaware asymmetric multi-core processor (AMP) scheduler with a static allocation of tasks.*
- *Function* `primary(`$task_i$`)` *maps* $task_i$ *to the core on which the task runs in the initial system-state.*
- `load(`$task_i$`, `$core_j$`)` *is a function mapping each task-core pair to the worst-case load that the task generates on the core, represented as a number $\{0, 1, \cdots, 100\}$ $\cup \{+\infty\}$, where $+\infty$ represents incompatibility between the core and the task.*
- *Each task is executed periodically. Tasks always terminate within the pre-scribed periods. Each task is described as a timed I/O automaton. These automata do not communicate[1]. Every task can be killed (and resumed) in any of its states by a reconfiguration technique.*
- *Fault Model: The system is fault-free in its initial system-state. In the other system-states, the system might suffer three types of faults: safety violations by tasks, permanent core failures, and temporary core failures. Critical tasks are assumed not to breach any safety constraints[2]. Non-critical tasks may violate safety constraints. Every core of the system may fail. However, all cores of a system concurrently cannot be in their failed states. The maximal number of cores that can fail concurrently is restricted by the concurrent-failures–limit (CFL). No limit is imposed on the total number of fault occurrences in a run.*

Given a mixed-criticality system of Definition 1, we want to obtain a task allocation policy that is able to cope with the failures admitted by the fault model. We will synthesize distributed reconfiguration services that assure uninterrupted execution of all the critical tasks. Section 3.2 explains how the reconfiguration technique is expected to work using an example.

3.2 Task-Level Reconfiguration Service

We propose a service-based reconfiguration technique for the fault-tolerance of mixed-criticality systems, where the system has a task-level reconfiguration service each per core. The services manage critical tasks differently than non-critical tasks. Consider, for instance, a simple mixed-criticality AMP system $system_1$, one of the systems that are described in Sect. 3.1. System $system_1$ executes six periodic tasks S, W, D, N_1, N_2, and N_3. Only three tasks S, W, and D are the critical

---

[1] More generally, the communication can be abstracted by suitable understanding of worst and best case execution times, and terminations are independent of communication.

[2] Critical tasks are developed using formal methods and control theory; therefore we assume that they do not violate safety constraints. However, the main principle of the presented synthesis process works even after removing this assumption.

tasks, where in an execution S records exactly one update of a speedometer, and W (respectively, D) records at most one update of a wiper (resp., door). The system has three cores $core_1$, $core_2$, and $core_3$, which are asymmetric but each core is able to execute all six tasks.

Figure 1 presents a trace of a desirable behavior of $system_1$ in the presence of different faults after inserting the reconfiguration services; the figure omits suspended non-critical tasks to avoid clutter. At any given time, the periodic execution of a task can be assigned to at most one operational core. A task is assigned to its primary core in the initial system-state, where a core is responsible for executing only its primary tasks. For instance, $core_1$ is the primary core of task S, and S is a primary task of $core_1$ in Fig. 1. We call a non-primary core a backup core of a critical task when that core can execute that task; similarly, a task is a backup task of its backup core. Whenever a core fails, the services assign the critical tasks that were previously assigned to that failed core to the operational cores. The services may kill and suspend temporarily one or more non-critical tasks on the operational cores during a reallocation process to ensure enough processing capacity for the reallocated critical tasks. In Fig. 1, core $core_2$ fails in system-state s_2; in the next system-state, the periodic execution of critical task W is assigned to a backup core $core_3$ and the periodic execution of non-critical task N_3 is suspended temporarily on $core_3$ to have enough processing capacity for W. A critical task is allowed to execute further on a backup core only if the primary core is in a failed state. The services kill a critical task on a backup core (if that task is initialized or released) and cancel the assignment of that task to that backup core, whenever the primary core recovers from a temporary failure. As an example, core $core_2$ recovers from a temporary failure in system-state s_6, and after that only $core_2$ is again assigned to perform critical task W. The services reinstate a suspended non-critical task as soon as enough processing capacity for that task is regained due to the recovery of a core from a temporary failure; for example, the periodic execution of non-critical task N_3 is reinstated in system-state s_7. The services permanently suspend a non-critical

	$core_1$: operational S: primary N_1: safe	$core_2$: operational W: primary N_2: safe	$core_3$: operational D: primary N_3: safe
s_1			
s_2	$core_1$: operational S: primary N_1: safe	$core_2$: failed W: primary N_2: safe	$core_3$: operational D: primary N_3: safe
s_3	$core_1$: operational S: primary N_1: safe	$core_2$: failed	$core_3$: operational D: primary W: backup
s_4	$core_1$: operational S: primary N_1: unsafe	$core_2$: failed	$core_3$: operational D: primary W: backup
s_5	$core_1$: operational S: primary	$core_2$: failed	$core_3$: operational D: primary W: backup
s_6	$core_1$: operational S: primary	$core_2$: operational	$core_3$: operational D: primary W: backup
s_7	$core_1$: operational S: primary	$core_2$: operational W: primary N_2: safe	$core_3$: operational D: primary N_3: safe

Fig. 1. Sample trace of $system_1$ with reconfiguration

task when it performs some harmful activities, such as illegal memory access. For instance, non-critical task N_1 performs some harmful activities in system-state s_4, and the task is permanently suspended in system-state s_5.

Problem Statement. Given a mixed-criticality system as specified in Definition 1, the problem is to synthesize a reconfiguration service $service_i$ for each core $core_i$ such that $service_i$ reacts whenever any other core fails or a core recovers (including $core_i$), or a non-critical task violates a safety constraint on $core_i$ at that time $service_i$ may kill, resume, and suspend any task running on $core_i$ and as long as $core_i$ is in a failure state, none of its tasks or $service_i$ executes. All reconfiguration services of a system together satisfy a property that at all times critical tasks are allocated to operating cores as long as the CFL limit is observed, and any non-critical task that has violated a safety constraint is suspended from execution indefinitely.

4   Modeling

We construct a timed game model of the system in a way that an unsafe location becomes reachable when a core exceeds its processing capacity. The model explicitly or implicitly captures the behaviors of the scheduler, the reconfiguration services, the cores, and the tasks.

To obtain a scalable model: (i) we model only a single (central) reconfiguration service for the whole system, instead of one service per core; (ii) we assume that every non-idle state of a task requires the worst-case core load of the task on the current core; and (iii) we abstract away the non-critical tasks. These three assumptions do not prevent synthesis of a distributed reconfiguration service per core, which will be shown in Sect. 5. Our model depends on four system parameters: (i) the release period of each task (constants pS, pW, pD); (ii) the worst-case load of each task on each core, in percent of the processing capacity of that core (constants 1S1, 1W1, 1D1, 1S2, 1W2, 1D2, 1S3, 1W3, 1D3); (iii) the worst-case execution time (WCET) of each task on all cores (constants wS, wW, wD); and (iv) the best-case execution time (BCET) of each task on all cores (constants bS, bW, bD).

Now we illustrate the design process by constructing a concrete model of mixed-criticality system $system_1$. The main design principle behind this model is to describe each component of the system in detail as a timed I/O automaton to obtain an intuitive model by composing all the components using parallel composition [19]. The concrete model has 13 TIOA, which follow five different templates. In general, the concrete model has at most $(N \times K) + N + 1$ TIOA and $K + 2$ templates, where N is the number of total cores, K is the number of total critical tasks: $N \times K$ TIOA represent execution of K critical tasks on N cores, N TIOA represent the cores, one automaton represent the service, K templates for the tasks, one template for the cores, and one template for the service.

Each automaton of the concrete model represents exactly one rectangle of Fig. 2. The automata synchronize using both actions and global variables.

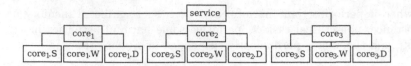

Fig. 2. Architecture of system$_1$ after adapting abstractions of Sect. 4

The model does not have any local variables and constants. A task automaton models initialization, killing, resumption, termination, and state information of a task on a specific core; for example, task automaton core$_1$.S at the bottom of Fig. 3 represents the activities of task S on core$_1$. A core may fail only if the fault model allows it to fail. A core automaton models initializations and terminations of tasks on a core along with failures of the core and safety violations; for instance, core automaton core$_1$ in the middle of Fig. 3 represents the activities of core core$_1$. The service automaton on top of Fig. 3 models reallocations of the critical tasks when a core fails or recovers. In the model a failed core may recover at any time. All automata of the model are presented in a technical report [20].

The models are built in Uppaal Tiga [6], which displays controllable transitions as solid arrows (edges 1–4), and uncontrollable transitions as dashed arrows (edges 5–8). The core automata follow the same template. For instance, automaton core$_1$ uses action kS1 to model the killing of task S on core$_1$ (edge 16 in Fig. 3), kW1 to model the killing of task W on core$_1$ (edge 17), kD1 to model the killing of task D on core$_1$ (edge 18), and global variable L1 to record the current worst-case load on core$_1$ (edges 9–14,16–18); similarly, automaton core$_2$ uses action kS2 to model the killing of S on core$_2$ and global variable L2 to record the current worst-case load on core$_2$. The automata modeling the same task—but on different cores—follow the same template.

4.1 Task Automata

A task automaton represents two types of activities of a task on a core:

Task Life-Cycle Activities (edges 1–5). Every task can be initialized, killed, and resumed by performing controllable actions. Task terminations are modeled using uncontrollable actions because neither the scheduler nor the reconfiguration services can control the exact termination period of a task. The duration between an initialization and the immediate termination of a task represents one complete execution of that task. A task can be killed and then resumed arbitrarily many times in a single execution. Initialization, killing, resumption, and termination of task S on core$_1$ are modeled by performing actions iS1 (edge 1), kS1 (edges 3–4), rS1 (edge 2), and tS1 (edge 5), respectively. Every task automaton has at least two locations: Idle and Active. The task is either killed or yet to be initialized in location Idle. Every non-idle location has an invariant to force the task to terminate within the WCET; for instance, an automaton modeling task S has invariant $x \leq wS$ to force termination, where global clock x records the amount of time passed since the last initialization of S and global constant wS

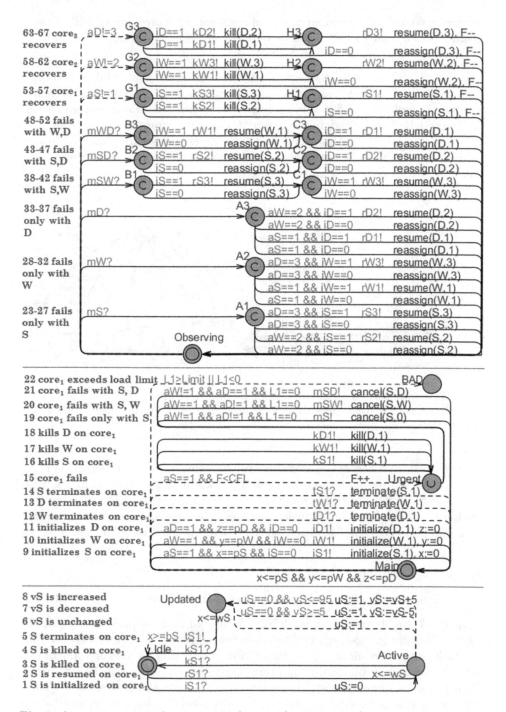

Fig. 3. Automata core₁.S (in the bottom), core₁ (in the middle), service (in the top) of the concrete model (and comments are on the left)

stores the WCET of S. Similarly, global constant bS stores the BCET of task S. Hence, clock guard $x \geq bS$ prevents task S from terminating before the BCET (edge 5).

Task Specific Activities (edges 6–8). Task S records exactly one update of a digital speedometer (modeled as global variable vS) in an execution: vS represents the speed in multiples of five varying from zero to hundred. Boolean variable uS is 1 if and only if the speedometer is updated in the current execution of S.

Task automata core_1.W and core_1.D in the concrete model are presented in the technical report [20]. The automata model the task life-cycle activities and task specific activities of tasks W and D.

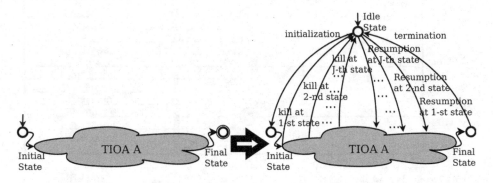

Fig. 4. Transformation of a timed I/O automaton representing a task (in Definition 1) to a task automaton: from single to periodic executions with kill and resumption at all internal states

In general, a timed I/O automaton representing a task (in Definition 1) is transformed (see Fig. 4) to a corresponding task automaton by adding controllable transitions to capture periodic (or cyclic) initialization of the task (by the scheduler), killing by reconfiguration services at all internal states (of interest), and resumption by reconfiguration services at all internal states (of interest).

4.2   Core Automata

A core automaton in the concrete model can carry out two types of activities:

Operation-Time Activities (edges 9–14). A core automaton periodically initializes a task at its release period if the corresponding core is assigned to execute that task. A task terminates voluntarily after completing its assigned functions. A task between its initialization and termination uses a portion of the resources. When a task terminates (resp., is initialized) on a core, the corresponding core automaton decreases (resp., increases) a variable modeling the current worst-case load. In location Main, task S is initialized by performing action iS1 (edge 9) if S is assigned to core_1 (aS==1), and S is not initialized yet (iS==0), and clock x hits the value of the release period of S (x==pS). Automaton $core_1$ (edge 14) receives action tS1 from task automaton $core_1$.S (edge 5) whenever S terminates its execution on this core. Function terminate(S,1) decreases (resp., initialize(S,1) increases) variable L1, modeling the worst-case load on $core_1$, by constant 1S1, the worst-case load of task S on core $core_1$, and resets Boolean variable iS to 0 (resp., 1), which means task S terminates (resp., is initialized).

Failure-Time Activities (edges 15–22). Core automaton $core_1$ models failures of the core by traversing an uncontrollable edge. In order to respect the concurrent failure limit, this edge is only admitted if the number of currently failed cores (F) is less than CFL (CFL). Location Urgent is reached from Main whenever $core_1$ fails. Urgent is one of the urgent locations, denoted as Ⓤ in Uppaal Tiga syntax, which means the automaton cannot spend time in this location (edges 15–21). When the core fails, the automaton instantaneously kills all tasks currently released on it—to simulate that no task can continue to run on a failed core (edges 16–18). Then the automaton instantaneously performs specific actions to communicate the information which tasks are currently assigned to the failed core; i.e., action mS is performed if S is the only assigned task, action mSW is performed if S and W are the only assigned tasks, and action mSD is performed if S and D are the only assigned tasks (edges 19–21). Note that tasks W and task D cannot be assigned to core $core_1$ without task S because a task (S) must be assigned to its operational primary core ($core_1$). At runtime, the reconfiguration services use a distributed monitoring system to identify these (task) assignments because no failed core can broadcast a message. An unsafe location BAD becomes reachable when the current worst-case load on $core_1$ exceeds the load limit of $core_1$ because of the failure of some other core(s) (edge 22). This prevents the synthesis algorithm from producing a strategy that would require illegal loads.

A core automaton in Fig. 5 is constructed for a core, which is compatible with K number of critical tasks of the system. The automaton has three locations: Main, Urgent, and BAD. The initial location Main has K controllable (resp., K uncontrollable) self-loops to simulate initializations (resp., terminations) of K critical tasks on the core. Location Urgent is reached from Main when the core fails. At Urgent all the active tasks are killed instantaneously by traversing maximum K self-loops. After that, Main is reached instantaneously by broadcasting the assigned critical tasks to the core. There are 2^{K-J} edges to broadcast all

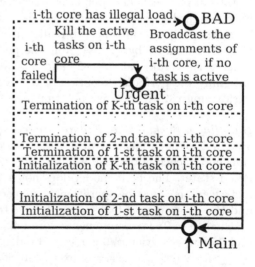

Fig. 5. A core automaton in general

combinations of assigned tasks to the core, where J is the number of primary critical tasks of the core. However, the number of compatible cores for a task (resp., K) in an AMP system is typically low. The environment may take the game to location BAD when the respective core has more load than its load limit.

4.3   Service Automaton

A service automaton spends most of its time in observing states waiting for a fault to occur (or for a core recovery from a temporary failure). The automaton reallocates a task in two steps: (i) assigns the periodic execution of the task to a suitable operational core, and (ii) resumes the task on the assigned core if the task was initialized before the reallocation. Other than Observing, all locations are committed, denoted as ⓒ in Uppaal Tiga syntax. They model states in which reconfiguration decisions are taken, which are expected to be instantaneous and get precedence even over the urgent transitions of the other automata. Activities of the automaton can be divided into three groups described in the following.

Handling a Primary Core Failure (edges 23–37). Recall the invariant that an operating core is always assigned to execute its primary tasks, so in $system_1$ when a core (say $core_1$) is assigned to execute only one task then it must be a primary task (S). In the model a failure message is broadcast using an action (e.g., mS) linked to the currently assigned tasks of the failed core, instead of the name of the core. Therefore, whenever a core failing with only assignment of the periodic execution of task S (or action mS is performed) then $core_1$, the primary core of S, must be that failed core. At that point, task S is reallocated to either $core_2$ or $core_3$. For example, location A1 is reached from location Observing when $core_1$ fails (edges 23–27); in A1 the focus is reallocating S, the primary task of $core_1$, to core $core_2$ (bottom two outgoing edges) or to core $core_3$ (top two outgoing edges). Details of reallocation depend on whether the task was initialized (and needs to be reassigned and then resumed) or is yet to be initialized (and just needs to be reassigned). For instance, to reallocate task S to $core_2$, location Observing is reentered from A1 by: (i) assigning the periodic execution of S to $core_2$ (aS:=2) if $core_2$ is operational (aW==2) and S was yet to be initialized (iS==0), or (ii) assigning the periodic execution of S to $core_2$ and resuming S on the core (by performing rS2) if $core_2$ is operational and S was initialized (iS==1).

Handling a Backup Core Failure (edges 38–52). In our example, when a core is assigned to execute two critical tasks then one of them must be a backup task of that core; hence, after such a failure at least two cores concurrently are in their failed states. The fault model does not allow all cores to fail concurrently. For instance, $core_1$ must be operational when $core_2$ and $core_3$ are in their failed states; and the executions of tasks W and D have to be assigned to $core_1$. Location B1 is reached from Observing when a core fails that is responsible to execute both W and D or when action mWD is received (edges 48–52). Location C1 is reached from B1 by assigning the periodic execution of W to the only operational core $core_1$ and resuming W, if necessary (iW==1). Then Observing is reached by assigning the periodic execution of D to $core_1$ and resuming D, if necessary (iD==1).

Handling a Primary Core Recovery (edges 53–67). The periodic execution of a task must be assigned to its primary core when it is operational. Therefore, a task must be reallocated from a backup core to the primary core whenever it recovers from a temporary failure. The periodic execution of task S can be assigned to a backup core (aS!=1) only if its primary core $core_1$ is in a failed state. Location G1 is reached from location Observing when $core_1$ recovers from a failure (edges 53–57). In G1 the controller has two main choices depending on the initialization condition of the task: S is yet to be initialized and needs to be only reassigned to its primary core (the bottom outgoing edge); and S is initialized on a backup core and needs to be killed (the top two outgoing edges) and then resumed on the primary core (the outgoing edge from location H1).

In general, the service automaton of Fig. 6 remains in observing states unless a core fails or recovers. Reconfiguration services need at least one operational core to run tasks. In the worst case when a failure occurs, CFL-1 cores are in their failed states (because if CFL cores had already failed, then no further failure can happen before some of the cores recover).

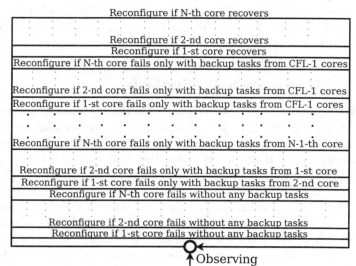

Reconfigure if N-th core recovers

Reconfigure if 2-nd core recovers

Reconfigure if 1-st core recovers

Reconfigure if N-th core fails only with backup tasks from CFL-1 cores

Reconfigure if 2-nd core fails only with backup tasks from CFL-1 cores

Reconfigure if 1-st core fails only with backup tasks from CFL-1 cores

Reconfigure if N-th core fails only with backup tasks from N-1-th core

Reconfigure if 2-nd core fails only with backup tasks from 1-st core

Reconfigure if 1-st core fails only with backup tasks from 2-nd core

Reconfigure if N-th core fails without any backup tasks

Reconfigure if 2-nd core fails without any backup tasks

Reconfigure if 1-st core fails without any backup tasks

Observing

Fig. 6. A service automaton in general

When a task is failing as the last failure admitted by the fault model, there are 2^{CFL-1} possible subsets of cores from which its currently running task might have been migrated (so they are backup tasks). Therefore in total $N \times 2^{CFL-1}$ edges are used to match these situations, where the total number of cores is N. The construction is exponential in CFL, however usually CFL is much smaller than N. Similarly, the internal edges of core recoveries depend on CFL and task-core compatibility ($load(task_i, core_j)$) relationships.

5   Synthesis

A reconfiguration service runs on a core, which can fail. Hence, fault tolerance cannot be achieved using only one central reconfiguration service. We propose that each core executes its own reconfiguration service consisting of three components: a distributed controller to reallocate critical tasks, a monitoring system

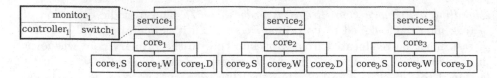

Fig. 7. Architecture of system$_1$ at runtime

to observe the system's conditions, and a switch to cancel and reinstate the periodic execution of non-critical tasks. All the distributed controllers of a system differ from each other—but complement each other in a way that they all together work similarly with a central controller, which is synthesized by analyzing the model of Sect. 4. Figure 7 presents the architecture of system$_1$ with the reconfiguration services.

5.1   Central Controller Synthesis

We perform a controller synthesis for the monolithic model of Sect. 4 against a safety objective "A[] not (core$_1$.BAD or core$_2$.BAD or core$_3$.Bad)", meaning that there is a strategy to always avoid locations core$_1$.BAD, core$_2$.BAD, and core$_3$.BAD. If the property holds, the strategy—which is our central controller—is automatically synthesized by a timed game solver.

In order to obtain the most fault-tolerant controller possible, we synthesize it for the maximal concurrent-failures–limit (MCFL), the maximal value of CFL for which such a controller still exists. We use binary search to find MCFL. If MCFL is zero, then no safe controller exists. The higher MCFL is the better the fault-tolerance offered by the reconfiguration services. The value of MCFL is strictly bounded by the total number of processing cores. Consider, for instance, configuration C1 in Table 1 where the release period, the WCET, the BCET of every task is 10, 5, and 4 time units, respectively; the worst-case load of tasks S, W, and D on core$_1$ (resp., core$_2$, core$_3$) are 60 % (10 %, 10 %), 45 % (80 %, 5 %), and 5 % (5 %, 85 %), respectively. Configuration C1 does not have a controller for CFL 2. However, there is a controller for CFL 1. Hence, the MCFL for system$_1$ in configuration C1 is 1.

5.2   Service Synthesis

We synthesize the distributed reconfiguration service of a core by combining its distributed controller with an embedded monitor and an embedded switch.

Distributed Controller. The functions of the central controller are completely and exclusively distributed into separate controllers for each core. A distributed controller is responsible for killing, reassignment, and resumption of critical tasks only on its core. A timed game represents all the possible transitions of the controller. As a result, a timed game may have non-deterministic choices for the controller. For example, in Fig. 1 the controller has non-deterministic choices at system-state s_4 when only $core_2$ fails and the other two cores are operational (edges 28–32). A strategy removes non-determinism for the controller. By directing the controller to take the correct paths, the strategy plays a crucial role when in the model some paths guarantee satisfaction of a property (say reallocating task W to $core_3$ at system-state s_5 in Fig. 1) and some paths do not (say reallocating W to $core_1$). For example, when $core_2$ fails (edges 28–32) a strategy (or the central controller) may say, "if the system-state fulfills condition X then reallocate task W to $core_3$, otherwise to $core_1$"; then the distributed controller of this portion (edges 28–32) for $core_3$ is "if the system-state fulfills condition X then reallocate task W to $core_3$"; and the distributed controller of this portion (edges 28–32) for $core_1$ is "if the system-state does not fulfill condition X then reallocate task W to $core_1$". Thus, deriving the distributed controllers from the central controller is a mechanical process and cannot fail.

Monitor. The monitor of a reconfiguration service periodically broadcasts health messages of the corresponding core. A health message has three parts: (a) name of its core, (b) currently assigned critical tasks to its core, and (c) currently initialized critical tasks on its core. A monitor periodically also receives health messages—from the other reconfiguration services—and manipulates received messages. It marks a core as a failed core if two consecutive health messages of that core are not received. The monitor concludes core recovery when it receives a message from a previously failed core. In the same way, the monitor detects when the scheduler releases a task and when a task terminates on a core.

Switch. A reconfiguration service has a static lookup table and a dynamic lookup table. The static lookup table lists the worst-case core load of every critical task (of the system) on this core and of every non-critical task assigned to this core. The dynamic lookup table keeps a list of the assigned tasks, temporarily suspended non-critical tasks, and permanently suspended non-critical tasks. The controllers reallocate critical tasks from a failed or to a recovered core without considering the existence of non-critical tasks. The switch of a reconfiguration service (of the targeted core) suspends a set of non-critical tasks on its core using the lookup tables when the residual capacity on the core is insufficient to run the newly reallocated task safely. The distributed controllers first take necessary steps related to primary tasks of the recovered core whenever a core recovers. After that the switches reinstate the periodic executions of a set of suspended non-critical tasks on each source core where free processing capacity is revived due to the recovery. The switch permanently suspends a non-critical task when it violates safety constraints.

5.3   Scalability

The scalability of our service synthesis process mostly depends on the central controller synthesis as the remaining steps are mechanical and cannot fail.

The concrete model has a very large state space. For example, configuration C1 in Table 1 generates a strategy of size 290,663 KB in 94.20 s for this model when CFL is 1. Moreover, for many configurations (C3–C6 in Table 1) the solver runs out of memory during analysis. Detailed and monolithic models like the concrete model are easy to construct, understand, and present. However, large state spaces make them a poor choice for analysis.

The main purpose of the strategy is to resolve non-determinism among enabled controllable transitions in a way that guarantees satisfaction of the desired property. Hence, one can abstract away every detail from a timed game model that does not contribute to the non-determinism (or to the property). For instance, task specific activities and their non-deterministic updates of the tasks, which do not have any impact on our property, can be removed from a timed game model of system$_1$. Using such aggressive abstractions we construct the abstract model of system$_1$. Presented in Fig. 8, the model has only one automaton.

The abstract model uses all the modeling abstractions and system parameters of Sect. 4. It models only task initializations (edges 68–70), task terminations (edges 71–76), core failures (edges 77–79), core recovery (edges 80–94), and safety violations (edge 95) explicitly. Like task killings and resumptions, task initializations and terminations change the load on a core; thus they play an important role in the required property (or the safety checking). The invariant is used to release or initialize the tasks periodically. While a task termination within the WCET is forced by allowing an additional controllable transition (edges 74–76). Reallocation is a function which combines task killings,

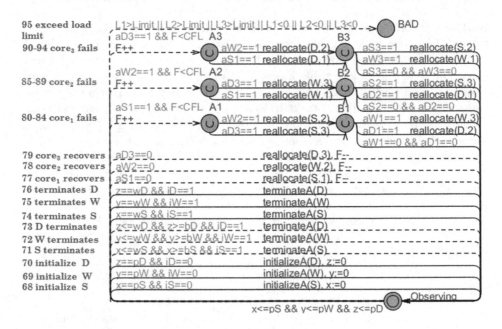

Fig. 8. The abstract model (with comments on the left)

reassignments, and resumptions (edges 77–94). The model uses nine Boolean variables aS1, aW1, aD1, aS2, aW2, aD2, aS3, aW3, and aD3 to keep track of the currently assigned tasks to cores: the value of aS1 (resp., aW1, aD1) is 1 when the periodic execution of task S (resp., W, D) is assigned to core $core_1$, otherwise the value is 0; similarly, aS2 (resp., aW2, aD2) is 1 if and only if the periodic execution of task S (resp., W, D) is assigned to core $core_2$. If both the concrete model and the abstract model use a variable or constant then it is used for the same purpose; for example, variable iS in both the models is used to identify when task S is initialized.

In general, the abstract model (in Fig. 9) combines all automata of the concrete model into a single automaton. In both models, one clock per task is used for the execution times, and the worst-case loads have been used. A task can be killed and resumed in any internal state, and the internal control behaviors of a task cannot be effected by other tasks (see Definition 1). Therefore, internal executions of the tasks can be abstracted away by only tracking task assignments along with task initializations—which is actually done in the abstract model. The abstract model hides communication among automata of the concrete model but keeps its effects. For example, in a core automaton (in Fig. 3 or in Fig. 5) when the core fails, all the initialized tasks on the core are instantaneously killed by sending kill messages to the corresponding task automata and instantaneously broadcast the assignments to the service automaton; the abstract model sim-

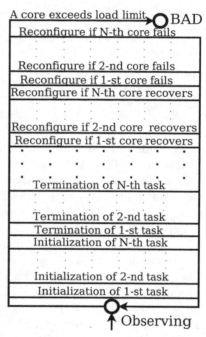

Fig. 9. The abstract model in general

ulates core failures and hides the following two communication steps (but performs necessary changes in the variables). Similarly, communication in the concrete model between the service automaton and a task automaton related to task killing and resumption is abstracted away in the abstract model. The abstract model also hides obvious details of the concrete model. For example, in the service automaton (in Fig. 3) to reallocate, an initialized task is (reassigned and then) resumed and an uninitialized task is only reassigned; the abstract model (in Fig. 8) models only task reallocations (and hides the other details of resumptions and reassignments). Therefore, a strategy extracted from the abstract model can be used for the concrete model by augmenting these communications and obvious details.

Experimental Results. We analyze the two models with different configurations. All the analyses and controller syntheses were performed by Uppaal Tiga-0.17

Table 1. Comparisons of the two models with respect to their controller synthesis time (in s) and the strategy size (in KB), for different configurations (release period, WCET, and BCET have abstract time units; and loads are in % of the respective core)

	Period of task			WCET of task			BCET of task			Load on core$_1$ of task			Load on core$_2$ of task			Load on core$_3$ of task			CFL	Comparison concrete model		abstract model	
	S	W	D	S	W	D	S	W	D	S	W	D	S	W	D	S	W	D		time	size	time	size
C1	10	10	10	5	5	5	4	4	4	60	45	5	10	80	5	10	5	85	2	No controller exists			
																			1	94.20	290663	0.08	73
C2	10	10	10	5	5	5	0	0	0	60	45	5	10	80	5	10	5	85	2	No controller exists			
																			1	115.71	296524	0.11	107
C3	10	15	20	5	5	5	0	0	0	60	45	5	10	80	5	10	5	85	2	No controller exists			
																			1	Out of memory		0.14	242
C4	10	15	20	5	5	5	0	0	0	60	35	5	10	80	5	10	5	85	2	Out of memory		0.25	712
																			1			0.14	266
C5	10	15	20	5	5	5	0	0	0	43	37	7	11	67	19	23	13	59	2	Out of memory		0.25	712
																			1			0.14	266
C6	10	15	20	5	5	5	0	0	0	43	37	59	11	67	39	23	13	59	2	No controller exists			
																			1				

on a PC with an Intel Core i3 CPU at 2.4 GHz, 4 GB of RAM, and running 64-bit Windows 7. Table 1 shows that the abstract model improves the scalability dramatically. Other than aggressive abstraction, it encodes the whole model into a single automaton to avoid parallel composition, because parallel composition typically increases the size of the state space very rapidly. The larger the difference between WCET and BECT the longer the analysis time, and the sparser the strategy (configuration C1 vs. configuration C2). The smaller the least common denominator of the clock ranges (or the execution times and release periods) the smaller the state space, the shorter the analysis time, and the more compact the strategy (C2 vs. C3). However, variations in the least common denominator of other variables, such as different loads, do not have any significant impact on the analysis (C4 vs. C5). Uppaal Tiga takes less time and generates asmaller strategy for a higher value for CFL (C4, C5). The MCFL of system system$_1$ depends on its configuration: the MCFL is 1 for the first three configurations (C1–C3); 2 for the next two configurations (C4, C5); and 0 for the last configuration (C6).

5.4   Discussion

We briefly discuss the handling of systems with slightly different properties. For systems with asymmetric cores, which are unable to execute some tasks on some of the other cores, we do not model the initialization, termination, killing, reassignment, and resumption for the illegal combinations of tasks and cores. For symmetric multi-core processing (SMP) one simply has to set the same load parameters on all the cores for each task. The synthesized reconfiguration services are oblivious to the tasks having substructure (sub-tasks), if they can be consistently abstracted by a single set of parameters (WCET, BCET and load).

  We have assumed that an initialized task reallocated from a failed core should resume in the same state. If this is not required, i.e., a task can start from the initial state on the new core at its next release period, then the model can be simplified, by removing the edges modeling resumption. We have not investigated the synthesis process for a scheduler with dynamic allocation yet. In another paper, we presented a theoretical framework for hierarchical dynamic open systems (such as system $system_1$) having any number of control hierarchies [21]. The framework supports an automated state-space reduction technique to allow timed games-based analysis for industrial hierarchical dynamic open systems.

6   Conclusion

We have presented the synthesis process using a mixed-criticality AMP system having a fault-intolerant criticality-unaware scheduler with fixed allocation. This includes two different design principles to model the problem using timed games, based on a selection of simplifications and abstractions. We compared the models for scalability, showing that solving the problem using strategy synthesis for timed games is feasible. We have observed that reducing action based synchronization, the state space, and especially shared states, improves efficiency of algorithms. Our reconfiguration services are distributed, and the synthesis process applies to mixed-criticality systems, both in symmetric and asymmetric scenarios. We demonstrated this on a case study from the automotive domain. To the best of our knowledge, this is the first case study applying timed games to the synthesis reconfiguration services for fault-tolerance.

Acknowledgements. We would like to express our gratitude to the engineers and scientists of our industrial partner who contributed in this project. We also thank Alexandre David for his help with Uppaal Tiga.

References

1. Zhang, Y., Jiang, J.: Bibliographical review on reconfigurable fault-tolerant control systems. ARC **32**(2), 229–252 (2008)
2. Hwang, I., Kim, S., Kim, Y., Seah, C.E.: A survey of fault detection, isolation, and reconfiguration methods. IEEE Trans. Control Syst. Technol. **18**(3), 636–653 (2010)
3. Maler, O., Pnueli, A., Sifakis, J.: On the synthesis of discrete controllers for timed systems. In: Mayr, E.W., Puech, C. (eds.) STACS 1995. LNCS, vol. 900, pp. 229–242. Springer, Heidelberg (1995)
4. Asarin, E., Maler, O., Pnueli, A., Sifakis, J.: Controller synthesis for timed automata. In: SSC (1998)
5. de Alfaro, L., Faella, M., Henzinger, T.A., Majumdar, R., Stoelinga, M.: The element of surprise in timed games. In: Amadio, R.M., Lugiez, D. (eds.) CONCUR 2003. LNCS, vol. 2761, pp. 144–158. Springer, Heidelberg (2003)
6. Behrmann, G., Cougnard, A., David, A., Fleury, E., Larsen, K.G., Lime, D.: UPPAAL-Tiga: time for playing games!. In: Damm, W., Hermanns, H. (eds.) CAV 2007. LNCS, vol. 4590, pp. 121–125. Springer, Heidelberg (2007)

7. Peter, H.-J., Ehlers, R., Mattmüller, R.: Synthia: verification and synthesis for timed automata. In: Gopalakrishnan, G., Qadeer, S. (eds.) CAV 2011. LNCS, vol. 6806, pp. 649–655. Springer, Heidelberg (2011)
8. David, A., Grunnet, J.D., Jessen, J.J., Larsen, K.G., Rasmussen, J.I.: Application of model-checking technology to controller synthesis. In: Aichernig, B.K., de Boer, F.S., Bonsangue, M.M. (eds.) FMCO 2010. LNCS, vol. 6957, pp. 336–351. Springer, Heidelberg (2011)
9. Alur, R., Dill, D.L.: A theory of timed automata. TCS **126**, 183–235 (1994)
10. Waez, M.T.B., Dingel, J., Rudie, K.: A survey of timed automata for the development of real-time systems. CSR **9**, 1–26 (2013)
11. Tripakis, S.: Fault diagnosis for timed automata. In: Damm, W., Olderog, E.-R. (eds.) FTRTFT 2002. LNCS, vol. 2469, pp. 205–221. Springer, Heidelberg (2002)
12. Bouyer, P., Chevalier, F., D'Souza, D.: Fault diagnosis using timed automata. In: Sassone, V. (ed.) FOSSACS 2005. LNCS, vol. 3441, pp. 219–233. Springer, Heidelberg (2005)
13. Waszniowski, L., Krákora, J., Hanzálek, Z.: Case study on distributed and fault tolerant system modeling based on timed automata. J. Syst. Softw. **82**, 1678–1694 (2009)
14. Lv, M., Yi, W., Guan, N., Yu, G.: Combining abstract interpretation with model checking for timing analysis of multicore software. In: RTSS (2010)
15. Dalsgaard, A.E., Laarman, A., Larsen, K.G., Olesen, M.C., van de Pol, J.: Multicore reachability for timed automata. In: Jurdziński, M., Ničković, D. (eds.) FORMATS 2012. LNCS, vol. 7595, pp. 91–106. Springer, Heidelberg (2012)
16. Fersman, E., Krčál, P., Pettersson, P., Yi, W.: Task automata: schedulability, decidability and undecidability. Inf. Comput. **205**, 1149–1172 (2007)
17. Socci, D., Poplavko, P., Bensalem, S., Bozga, M.: Modeling mixed-critical systems in real-time BIP. In: ReTiMiCS (2013)
18. Kaynar, D.K., Lynch, N.A., Segala, R., Vaandrager, F.W.: The theory of timed I/O automata. In: SLCS (2006)
19. David, A., Larsen, K.G., Legay, A., Nyman, U., Wąsowski, A.: Timed I/O automata: a complete specification theory for real-time systems. In: HSCC (2010)
20. Waez, M.T.B., Wąsowski, A., Dingel, J., Rudie, K.: Synthesis of a reconfiguration service for mixed-criticality multi-core systems. Technical Report 2014–619, Queen's University, ON (2014). http://research.cs.queensu.ca/TechReports/Reports/2014-619.pdf
21. Waez, M.T.B., Wąsowski, A., Dingel, J., Rudie, K.: A model for industrial real-time systems. In: D'Souza, D., Lal, A., Larsen, K.G. (eds.) VMCAI 2015. LNCS, vol. 8931, pp. 153–171. Springer, Heidelberg (2015)

Tools

From HELENA Ensemble Specifications to Executable Code

Annabelle Klarl$^{(\boxtimes)}$, Lucia Cichella, and Rolf Hennicker

Ludwig-Maximilians-Universität München, Munich, Germany
klarl@pst.ifi.lmu.de

Abstract. The HELENA approach [5] provides a modeling technique for distributed systems where components dynamically collaborate in ensembles. Models of such systems are formalized with ensemble specifications. They can be implemented using the jHELENA framework [6]. In this paper, we present a domain-specific language for ensemble specifications and provide an Eclipse plug-in featuring an editor and an automatic code generator for translating ensemble specifications into executable code.

1 Motivation

Exploiting global interconnectedness in distributed systems, autonomic components can dynamically form ensembles to collaborate for some global goal. The EU project ASCENS [1,9] develops foundations, techniques and tools to support the whole life cycle for the construction of Autonomic Service Component ENSembles. In this context, several approaches to formalize and implement ensemble-based systems have been developed. SCEL [3,4] provides a kernel language for abstract programming of autonomic systems, whose components rely on knowledge repositories, and models interaction by knowledge exchange. In SCEL (and its implementation jRESP) ensembles are understood as group communications. DEECo [2] introduces an explicit specification artifact for ensembles dynamically formed according to a given membership predicate. Interaction is realized by implicit knowledge exchange managed by DEECo's runtime infrastructure. Related approaches have been developed in the context of multi-agent systems and multi-party session types, for instance in the Scribble framework [10]. Recently, we proposed the HELENA approach [5] which is centered around the notion of *roles*. Roles can be adopted by components to collaborate in ensembles. The introduction of roles helps (1) to focus on the particular tasks which components fulfill in specific collaborations and (2) to structure the implementation of ensemble-based systems. In the jHELENA framework [6], roles are implemented as Java threads on top of a component. Role objects are bound to specific ensembles while components can adopt many roles in different, concurrently running ensembles. So far, there is no tool support for writing ensemble specifications and their implementation in jHELENA must be derived by hand. In this paper, we present HELENATEXT, a domain-specific language for

This work has been partially sponsored by the EU project ASCENS, 257414.

I. Lanese and E. Madelaine (Eds.): FACS 2014, LNCS 8997, pp. 183–190, 2015.
DOI: 10.1007/978-3-319-15317-9_11

ensemble specifications, and provide an Eclipse plug-in for writing specifications and generating code following the strategy proposed in [6].

2   HELENA in a Nutshell

HELENA is based on a rigorous typing discipline, distinguishing between types and instances. Component instances classified by *component types* are considered as carriers of basic information relevant across many ensembles. Whenever a component instance joins an ensemble, the component adopts a role by creating a new role instance and assigning it to itself. The kind of roles a component is allowed to adopt is determined by role types. Given a set CT of component types, a *role type rt* over CT is a tuple $rt = (nm, compTypes, roleattrs, rolemsgs)$ such that nm is the name of the role type, $compTypes \subseteq CT$ is a finite, non-empty subset of component types (whose instances can adopt the role), *roleattrs* is a set of role specific attribute types for role-specific information, and *rolemsgs* is a set of message types capturing incoming, outgoing, and internal messages supported by the role type rt. We want to illustrate the use of HELENA at a peer-2-peer network supporting the distributed storage of files which can be retrieved upon request. Several peers work together to request and transfer a file: One peer plays the role of the `Requester` of the file, other peers act as `Routers` and the peer storing the requested file adopts the role of the `Provider`. All these roles can be adopted by components of the type `Peer`. Figure 1a shows the role type `Router` in graphical representation similar to a UML class. The notation `Router:{Peer}` indicates that any component instance of type `Peer` can adopt the role `Router`. The `Router` has no role-specific attributes and supports one incoming and two outgoing messages types. The full specification and implementation of the example can be found in [5,6].

A HELENA *ensemble specification EnsSpec = (Σ, RoleBeh)* consists of two parts, an *ensemble structure Σ* and a family *RoleBeh* of *role behavior specifications RoleBeh$_{rt}$* (one for each role type rt occurring in Σ). The ensemble structure $\Sigma = (roleTypes, rconnTypes)$ specifies a set *roleTypes* of pairs, consisting of a role type and an associated multiplicity. Each multiplicity (like 0..1, 1, *, 1..* etc.) determines how many instances of that role type may contribute to the ensemble. The set *rconnTypes* of *role connector types* specifies which types of messages can be exchanged between role instances. Each role connector type must be equipped with a source and a target role type which must be declared in *roleTypes*. Figure 1b shows a graphical representation of the ensemble structure for the p2p example. It consists of three role types (`Requester`, `Router`, `Provider`) with associated multiplicities and five role connector types. For instance, the connector type `ReqAddrConn` consists of the single message type `reqAddr(Requester req)(String fn)` with source type `Requester` and with target type `Router`. It will be used for requesting the address of a provider for file `fn` such that the file can be directly downloaded afterwards using the connectors between `Requester` and `Provider`.

A *role behavior specification RoleBeh$_{rt}$* for a role type rt specifies the life cycle of each instance of rt. We represent role behaviors by labeled transition systems derived from process expressions [8]. The labels denote actions which must fit to the declared ensemble structure. There are actions for creating role instances, sending (!) or receiving (?) messages, and performing internal computations. For instance, Fig. 1c shows the behavior specification of a `Router`. Initially, a router is able to receive a request for an address either via the role connector `ReqAddrConn` (from the requester) or via `FwdReqAddrConn` (from another router). Depending on whether the router knows the peer storing `fn` or not, it either creates a provider role instance `prov` and sends it back to the requester (right branch) or it forwards the request to another router (left branch). The formal ensemble specification serves as an analysis model, e.g. to eliminate collaboration mismatches between different roles at early stages, and as a design model for implementation.

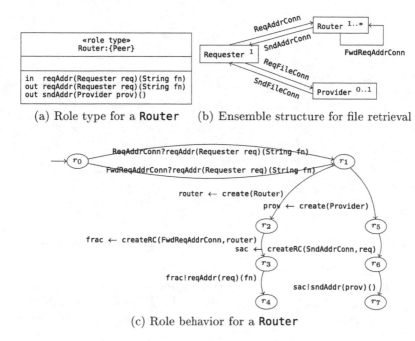

(a) Role type for a **Router**   (b) Ensemble structure for file retrieval

(c) Role behavior for a **Router**

Fig. 1. Ensemble specification in graphical notation (excerpt)

For the implementation and execution of ensembles, we provide the Java framework jHELENA [6]. The framework contains two layers and a system manager; cf. upper part of Fig. 2. The `metadata` layer implements the types used in ensemble structures, i.e. component types, role types, etc. All types and ensemble structures themselves are represented by objects of the `metadata` classes which are linked according to the formal definitions. While the `metadata` layer is related to the type level, the `developer interface` is related to the instance level. It contains abstract base classes which must be extended to implement subclasses for particular components, roles etc. The `SysManager` class provides basic functionality for the administration of ensembles. Its abstract operations must be implemented by a concrete system manager for configuring particular ensemble

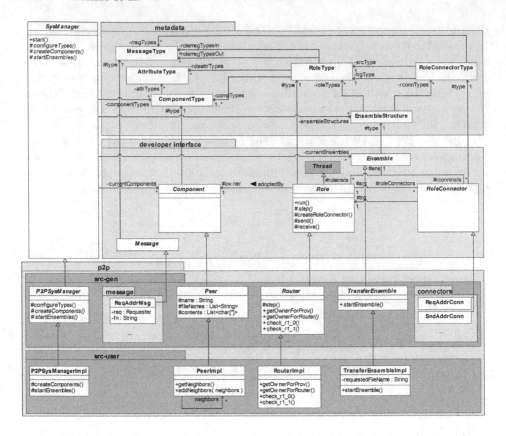

Fig. 2. jHELENA framework and generated p2p ensemble application (excerpts)

structures and the necessary types, creating the underlying component instances and instantiating and starting an ensemble. The framework controls that the created ensembles are built in accordance with previously configured ensemble structures.

3   HELENATEXT and Code Generation

When modeling and implementing an ensemble-based system according to HELENA, the developer may experience two pitfalls. Without any editor support, the developer has to ensure herself that her specifications conform to HELENA and respect all constraints formulated in the formal definitions. To implement an ensemble, she has to translate an ensemble specification to jHELENA code by hand and has no guarantee that the implementation indeed respects the formal specification. We therefore define HELENATEXT, a domain-specific language (DSL) which provides a concrete syntax for ensemble specifications supporting roles and ensemble structures as first-class citizens. We also provide Eclipse integration which features a full HELENATEXT editor including syntax highlighting, content assist, and validation. Moreover, we define a set of rules for the automatic generation of jHELENA code from HELENATEXT.

HELENATEXT. For defining the syntax of HELENATEXT we use XTEXT (www. eclipse.org/Xtext/), a framework for the development of DSLs fully integrated into Eclipse. We define a grammar in a BNF-like notation following the formal definitions of types, ensemble structures and role behaviors. Constraints which cannot be included into the DSL grammar are formulated as validation rules written with XTEND. For instance, Listing 1.1 shows the grammar for the declaration of ensemble structures which must start with the key word **ensembleStructure** followed by its name. In curly braces the two parts (*roleTypes, rconnTypes*) of an ensemble structure Σ (cf. Sect. 2) are specified: **roleTypes** is a list of role types with multiplicity, **rconnTypes** is a list of role connector types (their specifications including source and target types are not shown). However, in the DSL grammar we cannot express the constraint that each role connector type must be equipped with a source and a target role type defined in *roleTypes*. For that, a validation rule in XTEND is added (cf. Listing 1.2) which iterates over all role connector types in the ensemble structure and reports an error if the context condition is not satisfied. The concrete syntax for the declaration of the ensemble structure of Fig. 1b is shown in Listing 1.3. The concrete syntax for role behaviors is a textual representation of labeled transition systems not shown here. The rules for all syntactic constructs of HELENATEXT can be found at [7].

```
1  EnsembleStructure:
2    'ensembleStructure' name=ValidID '{'
3      'roleTypes' '=' '{'
4        roleTypes+=RoleTypeWithMultiplicity (','roleTypes+=RoleTypeWithMultiplicity)*'}'';'
5      'rconnTypes' '=' '{'
6        rconnTypes+=[RoleConnectorType] (','rconnTypes+=[RoleConnectorType])*'}'';'
7    '}';
```
Listing 1.1: HELENATEXT grammar rule for ensemble structures

```
1  @Check
2  def check_es_rtsContainRcSrcAndTrgRoles(EnsembleStructure es) {
3    var rts = es.roleTypes.getRoleTypeList;
4    for (RoleConnectorType rct : es.rconnTypes) {
5      if (!(rts.contains(rct.srcType) && rts.contains(rct.trgType))) {
6        error('srcType and trgType of roleConnectorType not listed in roleTypes',...)
7  }}}
```
Listing 1.2: Validation rule for ensemble structures

```
1  ensembleStructure TransferEnsemble {
2    roleTypes = {<Requester,1>,<Router,1..*>,<Provider,0..1>};
3    rconnTypes = {ReqAddrConn,SndAddrConn,FwdReqAddrConn,ReqFileConn,SndFileConn};
4  }
```
Listing 1.3: Ensemble structure for file retrieval in HELENATEXT

Code generation. The code generator takes a HELENATEXT file containing a particular ensemble specification and generates a package for the ensemble application which is split into two parts, the (sub)packages **src-gen** and **src-user**;

see Fig. 2. The package `src-gen` is already complete and must not be touched by the user. It contains a subclass (here `P2PSysManager`) of the `SysManager` class which implements the method `configureTypes()`. The method body creates objects for the metadata classes to represent types and the ensemble structure in accordance with the specification. Moreover, `src-gen` contains subclasses for the abstract base classes of the developer interface. These subclasses, like `Peer`, `Router`, correspond to the types of the given ensemble structure.

To define templates for the code generation, we use template expression in XTEND. Listing 1.4 shows an excerpt of such an XTEND rule. The operation `body` is called for any role type given in a HELENATEXT specification and generates the corresponding class declaration in jHELENA. Basically anything in the operation `body` is written to the generated class file except text enclosed in tag brackets «» which must be evaluated first. For example, in line 3 the class-header is built. The name of the class is dynamically evaluated from the expression «`classname`». This is a function of `RoleType` which is called for the first parameter `it` of the operation (see line 1) and retrieves the name of the role type `it` (the resulting class-header for the role type `Router` is shown in line 1 of Listing 1.5). Afterwards, in line 4-6 of the XTEND rule all attributes of the role type are generated (which are none for the role type `Router`). Lines 8–18 declare additional attributes for any created instances or parameters of incoming messages in the role behavior of the role type such that their values can be accessed throughout the execution of the role behavior. For example, for the role behavior of the `Router` in Fig. 1c we need attributes to store the values of the two created role instances `router` and `prov`, of the role connector instances `frac` and `sac` as well as of the parameters `req` and `fn` of the incoming message `reqAddr`. For the role behavior itself the method `step` is generated from the textual labeled transition system representation in HELENATEXT (see line 22, template not shown here). Basically, a simple

```
1  def body(RoleType it, ImportManager im)
2  '''
3  public abstract class «it.classname» extends Role {
4     «FOR a:it.roleattrs»
5        «attrTypeGenerator.compile(a,im)»
6     «ENDFOR»
7
8     «IF it.roleBehavior != null»
9        «var instsAndParams = it.roleBehavior.getInstancesAndBindingParams(null, null)»
10       «FOR instOrParam : instsAndParams»
11          «IF(instOrParam instanceof AbstractInstance)»
12             «var inst = instOrParam as AbstractInstance»
13             «attrVisibility» «inst.type.name» «inst.name» = null;
14          «ELSEIF (instOrParam instanceof AbstractParam)»
15             ...
16          «ENDIF»
17       «ENDFOR»
18    «ENDIF»
19
20    public «it.classname»(Ensemble ens){ ... }
21
22    protected synchronized void step() throws ... { ... }
23 }'''
```

Listing 1.4: Generation rule for role types (excerpt)

```
 1  public abstract class Router extends Role {
 2      protected Router router = null;
 3      protected FwdReqAddrConn frac = null;
 4      protected Provider prov = null;
 5      protected SndAddrConn sac = null;
 6      protected Requester req = null;
 7      protected String fn = null;
 8
 9      public Router(Ensemble ens) { ... }
10
11      protected synchronized void step() throws ... {
12          if (this.currentState == RouterState.r0) {
13              ReqAddrMessage reqAddr = (ReqAddrMessage) this.receive(
14                  new ExpectedMsgTypes(ReqAddrConn.class, ReqAddrMessage.class),
15                  new ExpectedMsgTypes(FwdReqAddrConn.class, ReqAddrMessage.class));
16              this.currentState = RouterState.r1;
17          }
18          else if (this.currentState == RouterState.r1) {
19              if (check_r1_0()) {
20                  this.router = this.ens.createRole(RouterImpl.class, this.getOwnerForRouter());
21                  this.currentState = RouterState.r2;
22              }
23              else if (check_r1_1()) {
24                  this.prov = this.ens.createRole(ProviderImpl.class, this.getOwnerForProv());
25                  this.currentState = RouterState.r5;
26  ...
```

Listing 1.5: Generated jHELENA code for a **Router** (excerpt)

state machine is implemented which will be called repeatedly by the run method implemented in the base class Role of the developer interface in jHELENA.

Lines 11–26 in Listing 1.5 show an excerpt of the step method generated from the behavior specification of Router shown graphically in Fig. 1c. The code generator creates a sequence of case distinctions to determine the next action depending on the current state. If there is only one transition starting from the current state, the action can directly be translated from HELENATEXT to code. If there are several alternatives for one state, like for r0 or r1 in Fig. 1c, the nondeterminism between those branches has to be resolved. In HELENA there are no mixed states in a role behavior meaning that whenever an incoming message is an alternative in a certain state then the other alternatives must also be incoming messages. Nondeterminism for incoming messages can be resolved easily by waiting for several messages in parallel; cf. line 13–15 in Listing 1.5. For all other actions, the code generator cannot decide which transition to take. Therefore, for each such branch an abstract boolean method is called, cf. line 19 and 23, which must be implemented by the user to decide which branch should be taken. This mechanism is also used for the creation of new role instances. In fact, the user has to decide on which component the role instance should be deployed; cf. call to the abstract method getOwnerForRouter() in line 20. To implement user decisions, the code generator constructs the package src-user which includes implementation classes for all abstract classes in src-gen. The package src-user also contains a concrete manager class (here P2pSysManagerImpl). The user has to implement the methods createComponents() and startEnsembles() for creating components and for creating and starting ensembles, which can run concurrently. We have only described here the basic ideas behind the code generation. Formally it is based on a set of generation rules written in XTEND which define, for each model element in HELENATEXT, how it is translated to jHELENA code. The rules for all syntactic constructs of HELENATEXT can be found at [7].

Next steps. In the near future we intend to provide a graphical DSL in addition to HELENATEXT which implements our UML-like notation used throughout the paper. Moreover, we want to investigate collaboration requirements and integrate tools for the analysis of ensemble specifications to check the absence of collaboration errors.

References

1. The ASCENS Project (2014). http://www.ascens-ist.eu
2. Bures, T., Gerostathopoulos, I., Hnetynka, P., Keznikl, J., Kit, M., Plasil, F.: DEECo: an ensemble-based component system. In: Proceedings of 16th International Symposium on Component-Based Software Engineering, pp. 81–90. ACM (2013)
3. De Nicola, R., Ferrari, G., Loreti, M., Pugliese, R.: A language-based approach to autonomic computing. In: Beckert, B., Damiani, F., de Boer, F.S., Bonsangue, M.M. (eds.) FMCO 2011. LNCS, vol. 7542, pp. 25–48. Springer, Heidelberg (2012)
4. De Nicola, R., Loreti, M., Pugliese, R., Tiezzi, F.: SCEL: a language for autonomic computing. Technical report, IMT, Institute for Advanced Studies Lucca, Italy (2013)
5. Hennicker, R., Klarl, A.: Foundations for ensemble modeling – the HELENA approach. In: Iida, S., Meseguer, J., Ogata, K. (eds.) Specification, Algebra, and Software. LNCS, vol. 8373, pp. 359–381. Springer, Heidelberg (2014)
6. Klarl, A., Hennicker, R.: Design and implementation of dynamically evolving ensembles with the HELENA framework. In: Proceedings of the 23rd Australasian Software Engineering Conference, pp. 15–24. IEEE (2014)
7. Klarl, A., Hennicker, R.: The Helena Framework (2014). http://www.pst.ifi.lmu.de/Personen/team/klarl/helena
8. Klarl, A., Mayer, P., Hennicker, R.: HELENA@Work: modeling the science cloud platform. In: Margaria, T., Steffen, B. (eds.) ISoLA 2014, Part I. LNCS, vol. 8802, pp. 99–116. Springer, Heidelberg (2014)
9. Wirsing, M., Hölzl, M., Tribastone, M., Zambonelli, F.: ASCENS: engineering autonomic service-component ensembles. In: Beckert, B., Damiani, F., de Boer, F.S., Bonsangue, M.M. (eds.) FMCO 2011. LNCS, vol. 7542, pp. 1–24. Springer, Heidelberg (2012)
10. Yoshida, N., Hu, R., Neykova, R., Ng, N.: The scribble protocol language. In: Abadi, M., Lluch Lafuente, A. (eds.) TGC 2013. LNCS, vol. 8358, pp. 22–41. Springer, Heidelberg (2014)

MAccS: A Tool for Reachability by Design

Guillaume Verdier$^{(\boxtimes)}$ and Jean-Baptiste Raclet

IRIT/CNRS, 118 Route de Narbonne, 31062 Toulouse Cedex 9, France
{verdier,raclet}@irit.fr

Abstract. MAccS is a tool for the modular design of complex IT systems. Component specifications are given in the form of marked acceptance specifications which are acceptance specifications, an extension of modal specifications, enriched with reachability constraints on states. The tool supports the crucial operators for a complete specification theory: satisfaction checking, consistency, refinement, product, quotient and conjunction. These operators can be used to build larger systems by composing or decomposing component specifications while ensuring some reachability properties.

1 Introduction

The basic idea underlying modular design is to break down complex systems into individual components that can be implemented concurrently or possibly taken off-the-shelf, and later composed to obtain the targeted system. This approach can be supported by a specification theory in which a formalism is defined for the component specifications together with dedicated operators allowing to perform different steps of a system design flow.

The tool MAccS implements a specification theory based on *marked acceptance specifications* (MAS) [1]. As an example of MAS, consider the specification *Server* shown in Fig. 1. It consists of a finite deterministic transition system with, associated to any state q, a set Acc(q) of sets of actions that may be enabled in a model of the specification. In general terms, a MAS characterizes a (possibly infinite) set of finite transition systems called its *models*. Now Fig. 2 depicts two models of *Server* (for a formal definition of satisfaction, see [1]). In each state of the model, the set of outgoing transitions must be an element of the acceptance set of the specification. For example, the state 2 of the MAS *Server* allows either to do only one transition labeled *response* or two transitions labeled *response* and *ban*. In the model on the right of Fig. 2, the state 2 chose this last option (both *response* and *ban*) while the state 4 only realizes the transition *response*.

Observe that *logout* and *ban* are optional respectively in state 1 and in state 2 of *Server* as these actions are not present in all sets in Acc(1) and Acc(2) and thus may not be present in some models of the specification. Moreover, state 3 of *Server* is marked to encode the constraint that it must be reached in any

---

Source code of MAccS, screenshots and more examples are available at http://irit.fr/Guillaume.Verdier.

© Springer International Publishing Switzerland 2015
I. Lanese and E. Madelaine (Eds.): FACS 2014, LNCS 8997, pp. 191–197, 2015.
DOI: 10.1007/978-3-319-15317-9_12

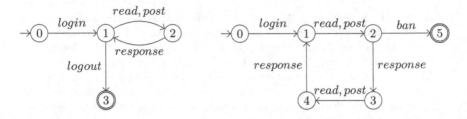

$$Acc(0) = \{\{login\}\}$$
$$Acc(1) = \{\{read, post\}, \{read, post, logout\}\}$$
$$Acc(2) = \{\{response\}, \{response, ban\}\}$$
$$Acc(3) = \{\emptyset\}$$

Fig. 1. A MAS *Server*

Fig. 2. Two models of the MAS *Server*

model. As a result, although the actions *logout* and *ban* are optional, at least one of the two must be present in any model of *Server*. This kind of constraint entails that MAS are more expressive than modal transition systems (MTS) [2]. In this case, marking the state 3 is used to express the termination of the service, as the marked state has no outgoing transition, but one may also mark some states with outgoing transitions to ensure the reachability of checkpoints or a liveness property.

Consequently, the MAS *Server* specifies the behavior of a forum-like site: after having logged in, one can read messages or post a new message and may eventually log out. The server may also eventually decide to ban users.

A specification theory must support a set of crucial operators to be regarded as complete [3]. This is the case for the one implemented in MAccS which supports satisfaction checking, consistency and refinement for substitutability. It also supports product for the composition of MAS, quotient for the decomposition of MAS and conjunction for the merge of viewpoints modeled as MAS. These operators preserve the reachability of marked states and thus guarantee by design some reachability properties.

2 The Tool MAccS

MAccS offers a Graphical User Interface (GUI) featuring an interactive view of transition systems and MAS allowing to edit them easily and a sidebar to select and apply different operations defined on MAS. MAccS is also available as a library for integration in other programs or automatic processing.

MAccS is written in standard C++; the graphs underlying the transition systems and MAS are handled by the Boost Graph Library [4]. The GUI is

```
init {{login}}
wait {{read,post},{read,post,logout}}
...
init -login-> wait
wait -read-> reply
reply -response-> wait
...
```

Fig. 3. Excerpt of the textual form of the MAS given in Fig. 1

made with the framework Qt and Dot [5] is used to generate the layout of the transition systems and MAS. MAccS does not make use of platform-specific libraries and should thus compile and run on most desktop operating systems.

In addition to being created and modified through the GUI, the transition systems and MAS may be written in a simple textual format. An excerpt of this format is shown in Fig. 3 which corresponds to the MAS *Server* in Fig. 1. It is also possible to import and export them from and to the Dot format [5].

After creating (or importing) some transition systems or some MAS, several operations are available that we now introduce briefly.

Satisfaction checking. As mentioned in the introduction, a MAS characterizes a set of transition systems. One may first test in MAccS if a transition system M is a model of a given MAS S.

For example, it can be verified that the left-hand side transition system in Fig. 2 is a model of the MAS *Server* in Fig. 1. It corresponds to the implementation of *Server* in which users are never banned: after the *login* transition, the set $\{read, post, logout\}$ was selected from the Acc(1) and the set $\{response\}$ was chosen from Acc(2).

Refinement of MAS. Refinement allows one to replace, in any context, a specification by a more detailed version of it. Substitutability of a MAS S_2 by a MAS S_1 is allowed when every model satisfying the refinement S_1 also satisfies the larger specification S_2. Inclusion of the sets of models, also referred as thorough refinement in the literature, can be tested for two MAS in MAccS thus enabling to decide refinement.

Product of MAS. Two MAS S_1 and S_2 may be composed using the *product* operation (denoted $\otimes$), which synchronizes their actions. However, reachability is not compositional in general meaning that there may exist some models M_1 of S_1 and M_2 of S_2 such that from some states of $M_1 \times M_2$ no pair of marked states can be reached.

In order to enable the concurrent implementation of MAS while guaranteeing some reachability constraints, we have proposed in [1] a *compatible reachability* criterion which is a precondition for the computation of $S_1 \otimes S_2$ and allows to check if a pair of marked states is always reachable in the product of any two models of the MAS.

$$Acc(0') = \{\{login\}\}$$
$$Acc(1') = \{\{read, post, logout\}\}$$
$$Acc(2') = \{\{response, ban\}\}$$
$$Acc(3') = \{\emptyset\}$$

Fig. 4. MAS *Client*

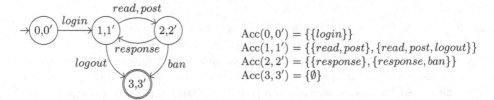

$$Acc(0, 0') = \{\{login\}\}$$
$$Acc(1, 1') = \{\{read, post\}, \{read, post, logout\}\}$$
$$Acc(2, 2') = \{\{response\}, \{response, ban\}\}$$
$$Acc(3, 3') = \{\emptyset\}$$

Fig. 5. Result of *Server* ⊗ *Client*

For example, the MAS *Server* given in Fig. 1 and *Client* given in Fig. 4 have a compatible reachability and their product is shown in Fig. 5.

When some MAS S_1 and S_2 do not have a compatible reachability, MAccS proposes to compute the largest refinement S_2' of S_2 such that S_1 and S_2' have a compatible reachability.

Quotient of MAS. Conversely, we may decompose specifications with the *quotient* operation. Intuitively, it is the opposite of the product: given two MAS S and S_1, the MAS S/S_1 is such that any of its models composed with any model of S_1 is a model of S. It also allows component reuse as S_1 may be typically the specification associated to a grey box component available off-the-shelf.

For example, consider the MAS *ROServer* in Fig. 6. This specification corresponds to a read-only forum: logged users may read messages and log out, but if they try to post a message, the server will ban them.

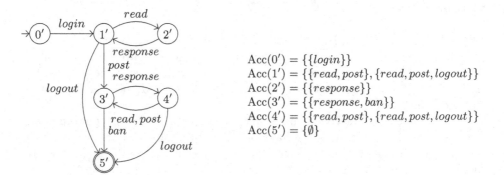

$$Acc(0') = \{\{login\}\}$$
$$Acc(1') = \{\{read, post\}, \{read, post, logout\}\}$$
$$Acc(2') = \{\{response\}\}$$
$$Acc(3') = \{\{response, ban\}\}$$
$$Acc(4') = \{\{read, post\}, \{read, post, logout\}\}$$
$$Acc(5') = \{\emptyset\}$$

Fig. 6. Specification *ROServer*

Now the Fig. 7 shows the quotient of *Server* and *ROServer*. Note that a priority P is generated to enforce the eventual choice of the transition labeled *ban* in any model $M_/$ and thus guarantee that, regardless of the implementation choices that are made when building a model M of *ROserver*, $M \times M_/$ will satisfy the reachability constraint included in *Server*. A screenshot of MAccS with the result of this quotient is shown in Fig. 8.

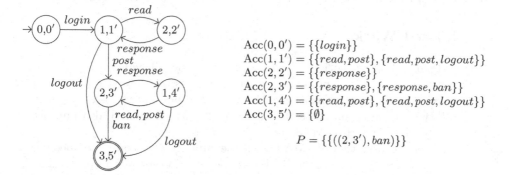

$$\mathrm{Acc}(0, 0') = \{\{login\}\}$$
$$\mathrm{Acc}(1, 1') = \{\{read, post\}, \{read, post, logout\}\}$$
$$\mathrm{Acc}(2, 2') = \{\{response\}\}$$
$$\mathrm{Acc}(2, 3') = \{\{response\}, \{response, ban\}\}$$
$$\mathrm{Acc}(1, 4') = \{\{read, post\}, \{read, post, logout\}\}$$
$$\mathrm{Acc}(3, 5') = \{\emptyset\}$$

$$P = \{\{((2, 3'), ban)\}\}$$

Fig. 7. Result of *Server/ROServer*

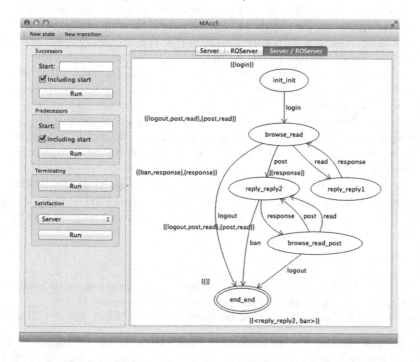

Fig. 8. Screenshot of MAccS with the result of *Server/ROServer*

Conjunction and consistency of MAS. It is a current practice to attach to a given (sub)system several specifications, each of them describing a different aspect or viewpoint of the (sub)system. These specifications have to be interpreted in a conjunctive way.

The tool MAccS addresses viewpoint-design by implementing a conjunction operator for MAS: given two MAS S_1 and S_2, the MAS $S_1 \wedge S_2$, whose set of models is exactly the intersection of the set of models of S_1 and S_2, can be computed. If this intersection is empty, the two MAS are declared inconsistent.

3   Related Work

MAS extend modal transition systems (MTS) [2] by allowing to specify any combination of actions and not only the sets of actions which belong to an interval defined by may/must transitions. Moreover, the possibility to require some reachability constraints on states is only available for MAS and also improves expressivity with respect to MTS.

MAccS is the first tool for MAS with the support of a complete specification theory. MTS have been identified as a specification formalism particularly suitable for interface-based design [3,6], contract-based design [7], software product lines description [8] and model merging [9] but only a few tools support them. The tool MTSA [10] supports refinement, product and conjunction of MTS but no quotient. The tools MIO workbench [11] and MICA [12] are dedicated to MTS enriched with input and output actions. They both support a complete specification theory but restricted to the modal case and their operators do not guarantee concurrent reachability. The tool MoTRAS [13] also proposes a complete specification theory for MTS, which are less expressive than MAS. MoTRAS allows for LTL model-checking of specifications but this is not enough to go along with reachability constraints as advocated in [1]. Several non-deterministic MTS variants, namely Disjunctive MTS [14], Boolean MTS and Parametric MTS [15], which have a similar expressive power as acceptance specifications (without marked states), are also under the scope of MoTRAS, but only for a reduced set of operations: there is no quotient for DMTS and only refinement and the deterministic hull for BMTS and PMTS. Last, the tools ECDAR [16] and PyECDAR [17] support a complete timed specification theory.

References

1. Verdier, G., Raclet, J.-B.: Quotient of acceptance specifications under reachability constraints. In: LATA 2015. LNCS, vol. 8977 (2015, to appear)
2. Larsen, K.G., Thomsen, B.: A modal process logic. In: LICS, pp. 203–210, IEEE (1988)
3. Raclet, J.B., Badouel, E., Benveniste, A., Caillaud, B., Legay, A., Passerone, R.: A modal interface theory for component-based design. Fundam. In. **108**(1–2), 119–149 (2011)
4. Siek, J., Lee, L.Q., Lumsdaine, A.: The Boost Graph Library. Addison-Wesley, Boston (2002)

5. Gansner, E.R., North, S.C.: An open graph visualization system and its applications to software engineering. Softw. Pract. Exp. **30**(11), 1203–1233 (2000)
6. Larsen, K.G., Nyman, U., Wąsowski, A.: Modal I/O automata for interface and product line theories. In: De Nicola, R. (ed.) ESOP 2007. LNCS, vol. 4421, pp. 64–79. Springer, Heidelberg (2007)
7. Benveniste, A., Caillaud, B., Nickovic, D., Passerone, R., Raclet, J.-B., Reinkemeier, P., Sangiovanni-Vincentelli, A., Damm, W., Henzinger, T., Larsen, K.G.: Contracts for system design. Research report, RR-8147, 65 pp., Nov 2012. https://hal.inria.fr/hal-00757488
8. Asirelli, P., ter Beek, M.H., Fantechi, A., Gnesi, S.: A logical framework to deal with variability. In: Méry, D., Merz, S. (eds.) IFM 2010. LNCS, vol. 6396, pp. 43–58. Springer, Heidelberg (2010)
9. Uchitel, S., Chechik, M.: Merging partial behavioural models. In: SIGSOFT FSE, pp. 43–52, ACM (2004)
10. D'Ippolito, N., Fischbein, D., Chechik, M., Uchitel, S.: MTSA: The modal transition system analyser. In: ASE, pp.475–476, IEEE (2008)
11. Bauer, S.S., Mayer, P., Legay, A.: MIO workbench: a tool for compositional design with modal input/output interfaces. In: Bultan, T., Hsiung, P.-A. (eds.) ATVA 2011. LNCS, vol. 6996, pp. 418–421. Springer, Heidelberg (2011)
12. Caillaud, B.: Mica: a modal interface compositional analysis library (Oct 2011). http://www.irisa.fr/s4/tools/mica
13. Křetínský, J., Sickert, S.: MoTraS: a tool for modal transition systems and their extensions. In: Van Hung, D., Ogawa, M. (eds.) ATVA 2013. LNCS, vol. 8172, pp. 487–491. Springer, Heidelberg (2013)
14. Larsen, K.G., Xinxin, L.: Equation solving using modal transition systems. In: Proceedings of the Fifth Annual IEEE Symposium on Logic in Computer Science, pp. 108–117, Philadelphia, Pennsylvania, USA, 4–7 June 1990
15. Beneš, N., Křetínský, J., Larsen, K.G., Møller, M.H., Srba, J.: Parametric modal transition systems. In: Bultan, T., Hsiung, P.-A. (eds.) ATVA 2011. LNCS, vol. 6996, pp. 275–289. Springer, Heidelberg (2011)
16. David, A., Larsen, K.G., Legay, A., Nyman, U., Wąsowski, A.: ECDAR: an environment for compositional design and analysis of real time systems. In: Bouajjani, A., Chin, W.-N. (eds.) ATVA 2010. LNCS, vol. 6252, pp. 365–370. Springer, Heidelberg (2010)
17. Legay, Axel, Traonouez, Louis-Marie: PYECDAR: towards open source implementation for timed systems. In: Van Hung, Dang, Ogawa, Mizuhito (eds.) ATVA 2013. LNCS, vol. 8172, pp. 460–463. Springer, Heidelberg (2013)

MPass: An Efficient Tool for the Analysis of Message-Passing Programs

Parosh Aziz Abdulla[1], Mohamed Faouzi Atig[1], Jonathan Cederberg[1],
Subham Modi[3], Othmane Rezine[1(✉)], and Gaurav Saini[2]

[1] Uppsala University, Uppsala, Sweden
othmane.rezine@it.uu.se
[2] Indian Institute of Technology, Ropar, India
[3] Indian Institute of Technology, Kanpur, India

Abstract. MPass is a freely available open source tool for the verification of message passing programs communicating in an asynchronous manner over unbounded channels. The verification task is non-trivial as it involves exploring state spaces of arbitrary or even infinite sizes. Even for programs that only manipulate finite range variables, the size of the channels could grow unboundedly, and hence the state space that need to be explored could be of infinite size. MPass addresses the bounded-phase reachability problem, where each process is allowed to perform a bounded number of phases during any run of the system. In each phase, a process can perform either send transitions or receive transitions (but not both). However, this does not bound the number of context switches between processes or the size of the channels but just the number of alternations between receive and send transitions of each process. Currently, MPass can decide bounded-phase reachability problem for three types of channel semantics, namely lossy, stuttering and unordered channels. Messages inside these channels can be lost, duplicated and re-arranged, respectively. MPass efficiently and uniformly reduces the bounded-phase reachability problem into the satisfiability of quantifier-free Presburger formula for each of the above mentioned semantics.

1 Introduction

MPass is a tool dedicated to the verification of state reachability for message-passing programs communicating in an asynchronous manner via unbounded channels. The reachability problem is undecidable in the case where the channels are *perfect*, i.e. channels that behave as non-lossy queues [6]. Because of the unbounded size of the channels, this message passing programs can be in fact considered as infinite state systems, even if the number of the states of the program itself is finite. Nevertheless, the problem becomes decidable if we consider other than perfect channel kind of semantics for the communication

This research was in part funded by the Uppsala Programming for Multicore Architectures Research Center (UPMARC) and by the Programming Platform for Future Wireless Sensor Networks project (ProFun).

I. Lanese and E. Madelaine (Eds.): FACS 2014, LNCS 8997, pp. 198–206, 2015.
DOI: 10.1007/978-3-319-15317-9_13

medium, namely *lossy, stuttering* or *unordered* channel semantics [1,9,12,14]. *Lossy* semantic allows loss of messages from any channel at any possible transition of the program. *Stuttering* on the other hand allows any message in any channel to be replicated any number of times. Finally, no order of arrival is kept in the *unordered* semantic, i.e. the channel is a multiset of messages where only the number of copies of each message is kept. It turns out that the state reachability of message passing programs for these semantics still comes with a high complexity. Therefor, different approaches have been suggested in order to reduce the complexity of the reachability problem. Most of these approaches consists in some sort of under approximation analysis of the system, allowing the system to evolve up to a certain fixed bound, thus limiting the state space that has to be explored in order to check the reachability of a given program state. One of these approaches consists in bounding the number of *context switches* between processes [11]. Since many bugs get exposed after a small number of context switches, it appears that these kind of approaches are very helpful when it comes to find bugs. On the other hand, they can tell about the program safety only up to a certain bound, the one under which the analysis has been carried. More specific to message passing communicating programs, La Torre et al. considered in [8] a bounded context switch analysis for perfect channel communicating processes, where processes are allowed to receive from only one channel in each context.

Parosh et al. considered in [3] a different approach, called *bounded phase* analysis. A *phase* of the program is a run in which each process is either performing send operations or receive operations, but not both. For instance, consider a program composed of two processes p_1 and p_2. A run of this program consists of only one phase if the following conditions are met: (i) p_1 is either receiving or sending messages, but not both, and (ii) p_2 is either receiving or sending messages, but not both. If p_1 is only receiving (resp. sending) messages, we say that p_1 is in a *receiving* (resp. *sending*) phase. Say one process (e.g. p_1) switches from receiving to sending or from sending to receiving during a run of the system, then two phases are needed in order to describe the run of the process. In that sense, a phase is *local* to each process. The run of the system as a whole is composed of only one phase if the run of each one of its processes is composed of only one local phase. Note that the number of send and receive operations within a phase is not bounded, and the number of channels to which processes are sending to (resp. receiving from) is only bounded by the number of channels composing the system. Also, this approach does not put any restriction on the length of the run or on the size of the buffers. Finally, it allows multiple processes to be running at the same time and allows an arbitrary number of context switches.

A variant of this approach has been demonstrated in a prototype, ALTERNA-TOR [2]. The phase in this variant is *global*, i.e. phases are defined not for each process, but for the whole system. This variant is more coarse-grained than the local (per-process) phase bounding approach. The tool ALTERNATOR proceeds in two steps in order to analyse the program within the phase bound. First, it translates the bounded phase reachability problem of the program to the satisfiability problem of a quantifier-free Presburger formula. Second, it feeds the generated formula to an SMT-solver. This allows leveraging the full power of state-of-the-art SMT-solvers for obtaining a very efficient solution to the bounded-phase reachability problem for all above mentioned semantics. The promising results of this prototype motivated its reimplementation into a more efficient tool, MPASS, that we present here in this paper.

MPASS turns the bounded phase state reachability verification task into a push-button exercise. Moreover, it comes with the following features:

- Users of MPASS can feed the tool with: (i) The protocol specification in XML, (ii) the target state for which the reachability analysis should be conducted, (iii) the semantic of the channel and (iv) the phase bound. Details of the input format are provided in Sect. 2.
- MPASS can handle three different kinds of channel semantics: *lossy* (LCS), *stuttering* (SLCS) and *multiset-unordered* (UCS) semantics which allow the messages inside the channels to be, respectively, lost, duplicated or re-ordered.
- MPASS allows a local (per process) bounded phase analysis. This fine grained analysis explores more behaviours than the global (per program) bounded phase analysis implemented in ALTERNATOR.
- Several optimisations have been implemented in MPASS, in particular in the SMT-formula generation phase (see Sect. 3).
- MPASS uses the Z3 SMT-solver http://z3.codeplex.com.
- If MPASS finds a bug then it is a real bug of the input program (under the considered channel semantic).
- If the bound on the number of phases increases then the set of explored program behaviours increases. In the limit, every run of the programs can then be explored.
- Users are provided with the computational time needed both by the constraint generation engine and by the SMT-solver in order to analyse the reachability of the provided protocol and state.
- MPASS output is generated in a user friendly manner, by generating a tex file. More information regarding this feature can be found in the manual of the tool [4].
- Finally, MPASS is an open source tool which can be interfaced with other SMT-solvers.

Targeted Users MPASS can be used by the following group of users:

1. **Researchers** and **computer scientists** can use the freely available and open source code of MPASS to:
   (a) Compare the bounded phase approach with other approaches for the verification of message-passing programs,
   (b) Improve and optimize the implemented techniques, either by generating a different SMT-formula or by using a different SMT-solver.
   (c) Target new platforms and programs (e.g. by adding shared variables or considering other channel semantics).

2. **Teachers** of distributed systems and concurrent programming classes can use (and augment) MPASS to get their students accustomed with message-passing programs and protocols. In particular, the precision of MPASS can concretely illustrates the difficulty of writing a correct distributed protocol or algorithm.
3. **Software designers** that are working on message-passing programs can use MPASS to evaluate the safety of their tentative solutions. It can also be used to check faultiness of an already used protocol by verifying the reachability of some error state.

2   Input Format

Examples on which we run our protocols are mostly taken from [7] which are further described in [10] and [13]. Bounded Retransmission Protocol (BRP) is also adapted from [5]. All protocols used for our experiments can be found in the `Includes/Protocols` folder. In [7] and in ALTERNATOR, the authors used a tabular format to specify a protocol (`.csv` file) from which an XML description could be extracted. Our tool works directly on the XML description. More specifically, MPASS takes as input a `settings` file where users can feed the tool with a structured input containing the following informations:

XML file: Path to the XML file where the protocol is specified.
Channel semantic: Either `lossy` (LCS), `stuttering` (SLCS) or `unordered` (UCS) channel semantic.
Phase bound: How many phases are allowed per process.
Bad state: It takes pairs of values. First is the name of the process, second is the (bad) state (of that process) for which state reachability is to be checked. Note that several bad states can be entered.

For instance, in order to ask MPASS to check the 3-phase-bounded reachability of the state `Invalid` of the process `RECEIVER` of the BRP protocol using the `lossy` semantic, the user can feed the tool with the file depicted in Fig. 1a, which you can also find in the `src` directory of MPASS.

Protocol Specification. The XML specification of all protocols used for our experiments can be found in the `Includes/Protocols` folder. Variants of these protocols can be specified by modifying their corresponding XML specification. Also, new protocols can be specified by writing a new XML specification. An XML protocol description contains: 1. The name of the protocol (Example: `Altenating Bit Protocol`), 2. the set of messages exchanged between processes, 3. the set of channels, and 4. a list of process specifications. The specification of each process contains: 1. The name of the process, 2. the set of states of the process, and 3. the set of transitions of the process. Each process transition is specified as an XML *rule*. An example of such a rule is depicted in Fig. 1b. The set of transition rules, together with the set of states defines a process. The set of processes, together with channel and message definitions, defines a protocol.

```
<rule id="Q0_ack1_INBOUND">
  <pre>
    <current_state>Q0</current_state>
    <received_message>ack1</received_message>
    <channel>c1</channel>
  </pre>
  <post>
    <next_state>Q1</next_state>
    <send_message>mesg0</send_message>
    <channel>c0</channel>
  </post>
</rule>
```

```
file ../Includes/Protocols/
BRP.xml
semantics lossy
bound 3
bad RECEIVER Invalid
channel_type process
```

(a) Example of a settings file.

(b) XML representation of process transition (of the ABP protocol) The above rule specifies two transitions from state Q0 to state Q1. The first transition consists in receiving message ack1 from channel c1. The second transition consists in sending message mesg0 to the channel c0.

Fig. 1. Input format

3   Implementation

The tool is available on GitHub [4]. It includes sources files, protocol specifications in XML and the user manual. MPASS tool is implemented in C++ with the help of lemon and pugixml libraries. In order to use MPASS, the SMT-solver Z3 is also required.

From the XML Protocol Specification to Automata Representation. Protocols are specified in XML files in the Includes sub-folder of the tool repository. They can be modified in a simple manner by adding, modifying or removing the XML rules and new protocols can be specified by writing their specification into an XML file. The first task of MPASS is to translate the protocol specification into a set of Non-Deterministic Finite Automaton (NFA). It does so by parsing the XML file which path is given as input in the settings file (using the plugixml library). Then, it makes use of the lemon library to translate the protocol into a set of NFA, each NFA defining one process from the protocol. For each such generated NFA, MPASS proceeds by extracting two automata, one containing all except the receive transitions (*send copy* of that process), the other one containing all except the send transitions (*receive copy* of that process). In total, MPASS would have extracted $2 * N$ automata from the input protocol (N being the number of processes composing the protocol).

From Automata to Quantifier-Free Presburger Formulas. The reachability problem of a given protocol state is analyzed by generating a *quantifier-free*

Presburger formula from the set of extracted send an receive automata. If the SMT-solver proves the quantifier free Presburger formula to be satisfiable, then the state is reachable and we have an unsafe condition. Otherwise, the formula is unsatisfiable, the state is unreachable and the program is safe. Note that the result of the reachability analysis should be interpreted with regard to the phase bound and to the channel semantic under which the analysis has been carried.

More information regarding the translation of the bounded phase state reachability to the satisfiability of *quantifier-free Presburger formula* can be found in [3], but here are some details concerning this translation. In order to generate the quantifier-free Presburger formula, a certain number of variables need to be defined in order to encode states and transitions of every NFA. This includes the `index`, the `occurrence` and the `match` variables. Variables `index` are integer variables used in order to index all states of all automata, while `occurrence` are boolean variables that apply to transitions and tell if the transition has been taken or not with respect to a given run. Variables `match` apply to receive transitions and check whether the receive transition matches a *previous* send operation. By enforcing that for every two consecutive receiving transitions, the order through which the matching sending transitions happens is the same as the order through which the receiving transitions happens, we encode the first-in-first-out lossy semantic of the channels. On the other hand, the unordered channel semantic is encoded by enforcing that every two distinct received message are matched by two distinct receive operations. The respective receiving operations and sending operations order does not matter for this semantic. Finally, the order of visited states and fired transitions along a run is encoded by ordering the indices (`index` variables) of the states.

Optimisations. Various optimizations were implemented in order to increase the efficiency of the approach described in [3] and implemented in ALTERNATOR [2]:

Reduction of the number of copies per process: Since the reachability analysis is carried under a certain phase bound k, the original approach consisted in making k copies of each process from the protocol specification. Instead of that, we make only two copies per process (send and receive copies). MPASS then generates variables for both send and receive copies of each process and duplicates them k times which are then further used to generate the Presburger formula. Thus, by duplicating variables instead of processes, we have saved space and time during the Presburger formula generation phase.

Removal of strongly connected components: We evaluate all the strongly connected components (SCC) of the send copy of each process. Then, we replace each SCC by two new states, s_{Scc}^{in} and s_{Scc}^{out}. For every send operation occurring between two states in the SCC, we add the same transition between s_{Scc}^{in} and s_{Scc}^{out}. s_{Scc}^{in} will be the entering point for any transition inbounding this SCC, while s_{Scc}^{out} will be the source state for all transitions leaving the SCC. Thus, the number of states and transitions per process is

Table 1. Verification Results for examples from [10] and [7]

P	Bad	Sem	Const. gen.	SMT check	Total time	Assert. Nb.	Ph	Res
ABP	RECEIVER, Invalid	UCS	0.07	74	74.07	4025	4	Unsafe
ABP	RECEIVER, Invalid	LCS	0.04	1	1.04	2519	3	Safe
ABP	RECEIVER, Invalid	SLCS	0.03	2	2.03	2519	3	Safe
BRP	RECEIVER, Invalid	UCS	0.3	2	2.3	23461	3	Safe
BRP	RECEIVER, Invalid	LCS	0.28	2	2.28	23461	3	Safe
BRP	RECEIVER, Invalid	SLCS	0.28	1	1.28	23461	3	Safe
STP	A, Invalid	UCS	0.03	4	4.03	2354	6	Unsafe
STP	A, Invalid	LCS	0.02	0	0.02	1348	4	Safe
STP	A, Invalid	SLCS	0.02	0	0.02	1348	4	Safe

reduced, which, in consequence, reduces the number of generated variables and assertions in the SMT-formula.

Reduction of the number of assertions: The z3 single command `create_distinct_statement` was used in order make all state indices distinct, thus replacing all assertions of the form `index(state₁) != index(state₂)`. This considerably reduced the number of assertions fed to the SMT solver.

4   Experimental Results

Table 1 displays the results of running MPASS tool on some examples; whereas Table 2 shows the results of running MPASS on some protocols which were intentionally modified in order to introduce some errors. The displayed examples are taken from [7] which are further described in [10] and [13]. Bounded Retransmission Protocol (BRP) is also adapted from [5].

Columns of both tables should be interpreted as follows: 1. **P** lists the name of the protocol under analysis. 2. **Bad** indicates both the process and the state of

Table 2. Verification Results for buggy (faulty) examples

P	Bad	Sem	Const. gen.	SMT check	Total time	Assert. Nb.	Ph	Res
ABP_F	RECEIVER, Invalid	SLCS	0.04	1	1.04	1275	2	Unsafe
ABP_F	RECEIVER, Invalid	UCS	0.04	1	1.04	1275	2	Unsafe
SLIDINGWINDOW_F	RECEIVER, Invalid	SLCS	0.02	0	0.02	913	1	Unsafe
SLIDINGWINDOW_F	RECEIVER, Invalid	UCS	0.03	0	0.03	913	1	Unsafe
SYNCHRONOUS_F	B, Invalid	SLCS	0.02	0	0.02	713	3	Unsafe
SYNCHRONOUS_F	B, Invalid	UCS	0.02	0	0.02	713	3	Unsafe

the process for which the state reachability analysis is conducted. 3. **Sem** indicated the channel semantic used for the analysis: *lossy* (LCS), *stuttering* (SLCS) or *unordered* (UCS). 4. Constraint generation (**Const. gen.**), 5. **Smt check** and 6. **Total time** lists, respectively, the time taken by MPASS to generate the SMT-formula, the time taken by the SMT solver z3 to check the satisfiability of that formula and the total time of the analysis (time is given in seconds). 7. **Assert. Nb.** lists the number of assertions fed to the SMT solver. 8. **Ph.** indicates the bound on the number of phases. Finally, 9. **Res** gives the result of the analysis. The result is either **Unsafe** if the bad state is reachable (i.e. the SMT formula is satisfiable), or **Safe** if the bad state is not reachable under the bounded-phase assumption and for the considered channel semantic (i.e. the SMT formula is unsatisfiable).

Results displayed here are for few protocols only. Rest of the results are available online at [4] in the `docs` folder.

Table 1 shows that seven out of nine examples have been proved by MPASS to be safe in less than three seconds. Also, MPASS found two safe examples to be faulty when we raised the phase bound from 3 to 4 for ABP and from 4 to 6 for STP. In both cases, the `unordered` channel semantic has been considered. It seems that this particular channel semantic (UCS) exposes more false negatives than the stuttering and the lossy one (SLCS and LCS). Also, it seems that rising the phase bound makes the reachability analysis explore more behaviours of the system in general. On the other hand, regarding the (faulty) examples listed in Table 2, all of them have been proved to be unsafe in less than two seconds and within less than three phases. Finally, we would like to mention that comparing ALTERNATOR with MPASS would be hazardous since a phase does not have the same semantic in both of the tools.

References

1. Abdulla, P., Jonsson, B.: Verifying programs with unreliable channels. In: LICS (1993)
2. Abdulla, P.A., Atig, M.F., Cederberg, J.: https://github.com/it-apv/alternator
3. Abdulla, P.A., Atig, M.F., Cederberg, J.: Analysis of message passing programs using SMT-solvers. In: Van Hung, D., Ogawa, M. (eds.) ATVA 2013. LNCS, vol. 8172, pp. 272–286. Springer, Heidelberg (2013)
4. Abdulla, P.A., Atig, M.F., Modi, S., Saini, G.: https://github.com/vigenere92/MPass
5. Abdulla, P.A., Collomb-Annichini, A., Bouajjani, A., Jonsson, B.: Using forward reachability analysis for verification of lossy channel systems. FMSD **25**(1), 39–65 (2004)
6. Brand, D., Zafiropulo, P.: On communicating finite-state machines. J. ACM **30**(2), 323–342 (1983)
7. Marques Jr., A.P., Ravn, A., Srba, J., Vighio, S.: https://github.com/csv2uppaal
8. La Torre, S., Madhusudan, P., Parlato, G.: Context-bounded analysis of concurrent queue systems. In: Ramakrishnan, C.R., Rehof, J. (eds.) TACAS 2008. LNCS, vol. 4963, pp. 299–314. Springer, Heidelberg (2008)

9. Lipton, R.: The reachability problem requires exponential time. Technical report TR 66 (1976)
10. Marques, A.P., Ravn, A.P., Srba, J., Vighio, S.: Tool supported analysis of web services protocols. In: TTCS, pp. 50–64. University of Oslo (2011)
11. Qadeer, S., Rehof, J.: Context-bounded model checking of concurrent software. In: Halbwachs, N., Zuck, L.D. (eds.) TACAS 2005. LNCS, vol. 3440, pp. 93–107. Springer, Heidelberg (2005)
12. Rackoff, C.: The covering and boundedness problems for vector addition systems. Theor. Comput. Sci. **6**, 223–231 (1978)
13. Ravn, A.P., Srba, J., Vighio, S.: Modelling and verification of web services business activity protocol. In: Abdulla, P.A., Leino, K.R.M. (eds.) TACAS 2011. LNCS, vol. 6605, pp. 357–371. Springer, Heidelberg (2011)
14. Schnoebelen, P.: Verifying lossy channel systems has nonprimitive recursive complexity. Inf. Process. Lett. **83**(5), 251–261 (2002)

Scheduling, Time, and Hybrid Systems

Widening the Schedulability of Hierarchical Scheduling Systems

Abdeldjalil Boudjadar[✉], Alexandre David, Jin Hyun Kim,
Kim Guldstrand Larsen, Marius Mikučionis, Ulrik Nyman, and Arne Skou

Computer Science, Aalborg University, Aalborg, Denmark
jalil@cs.aau.dk

Abstract. This paper presents a compositional approach for schedulability analysis of hierarchical systems, which enables to prove more systems schedulable by having richer and more detailed scheduling models. We use a lightweight method (statistical model checking) for design exploration, easily assuring high confidence in the correctness of the model. A satisfactory design can be proved schedulable using the computation costly method (symbolic model checking). In order to analyze a hierarchical scheduling system compositionally, we introduce the notion of a stochastic supplier modeling the supply of resources in each component. We specifically investigate two different techniques to widen the set of provably schedulable systems: (1) a new supplier model; (2) restricting the potential task offsets. We also provide a way to estimate the minimum resource supply (budget) that a component is required to provide.

1 Introduction

The use of hierarchical scheduling systems is a new trend in software architecture that integrates a number of individual components into a single system running on one execution platform. Hierarchical scheduling systems have reached a maturity where they are used in real automotive and space systems [10,15]. A class of analytical methods has been developed for hierarchical scheduling systems [19,20]. Due to their rigorous nature, analytical methods are easy to apply once proven correct, but very hard to prove correct. They also suffer from the abstractness of the models; they do not deal with any detail of the system behavior and thus grossly overestimate the amount of needed resources. Model-based methodologies for schedulability analysis [6,8,10] allow modeling more detailed and complicated behavior of individual tasks, relative to analytical methods while powerful analysis tools can be applied. Profiting from the technological advances in model checking, we provide a model based methodology for the schedulability analysis of hierarchical scheduling systems. We model tasks, resources, schedulers and suppliers as Parameterized Stopwatch Automata (PSA) [9]. The models can be quickly analyzed using statistical methods (UPPAAL SMC), which provide

The research presented in this paper has been partially supported by EU Artemis Projects CRAFTERS and MBAT.

© Springer International Publishing Switzerland 2015
I. Lanese and E. Madelaine (Eds.): FACS 2014, LNCS 8997, pp. 209–227, 2015.
DOI: 10.1007/978-3-319-15317-9_14

guarantees with a selected statistical margin. Once a satisfying model design has been found, the model can be analyzed using symbolic model checking (UPPAAL). Our approach aims at increasing resource utilization by (1) adjusting task offsets relative to the component period; (2) providing a new supplier model where the supply of resources is delayed as much as possible according to task requests. Our methodology also has the advantage that it is possible for system engineers to update the models in order to have a more realistic analysis of the system. In this way, they can utilize detailed knowledge of the system that they are working with; something that cannot be achieved with a classical analytical approach.

An example of a hierarchical scheduling system is depicted in Fig. 1. It includes two top level components Controls and Display and Nav. Ctrl scheduled according to the Earliest Deadline First (EDF) policy. Each component is characterized by timing requirements consisting of period and execution time (e.g. (10, 6) for Nav. Ctrl). The attributes of tasks are similar to the ones of components. Task deadlines are the same as the task periods.

According to the CARTS tool [19], the hierarchical scheduling system of Fig. 1 is not schedulable. However using the specific approach shown in this paper, this system can be shown to be schedulable using different offset parameters and/or a new supplier model.

Symbolic model checking offers absolute certainty that the verified properties are correct. However, it suffers from state space explosion

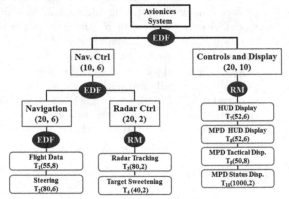

Fig. 1. A hierarchical scheduling systems.

and undecidability, thus some models might not be feasible to check and others will take a long time to verify. Statistical model checking provides high confidence in the results that one obtains in contrast to symbolic model checking.

This paper presents a methodology for performing compositional schedulability analysis of hierarchical scheduling systems. The general methodology consists of using a light weight statistical method and a costly but absolute certain symbolic method that operates on identical models. Design space exploration can be carried out at low cost using the statistical model checking in order to determine optimal system parameters that could be impossible to find using classical analytical methods. The use of automata and statistical model checking enables a larger class of tasks and resource supply models to be analyzed compared to the conventional real-time analytical method while still being efficient. Allowing designing systems based on a confidence level can be highly beneficial for soft real-time systems. In order to verify the schedulability of the system found using statistical methods we use the symbolic method on the final system design. The end goal of the methodology is to widen the set of concrete systems that can be proved schedulable. We instantiate our methodology using PSA models,

UPPAAL SMC and UPPAAL. Using the general methodology and our specific tools, we investigate two concrete techniques that affect the resource utilization. The first technique decreasing the needed resources relies on an update of the stochastic supplier model, such that it defers resource consumption until a task is ready. Secondly, we describe a way of giving a potential decrease in the needed resources of a component by ensuring more synchronicity between the initial off-set of tasks and the starting point of the parent component's period. In order to enable compositional verification, we introduce the concept of a stochastic supplier model. We evaluate our methodology by comparing our results to the ones obtained using the state of the art tool CARTS [19]. Our verification results are consistent with the results obtained from CARTS. In one particular case, we have uncovered a significant difference between CARTS and our methodology. After further investigation, this turned out to be an error in the implementation of CARTS and not the underlying theory. This has been confirmed by the developers of CARTS. When checking the schedulability of a system, our tools can prove the non-schedulability by means of a counterexample. Our methodology, which builds on previous work in [6], is very scalable because both design and analysis are compositional.

The rest of this paper is organized as follows: Sect. 2 describes our methodology. Section 3 presents our compositional modeling and analysis of hierarchical scheduling systems using UPPAAL and UPPAAL SMC. Section 4 describes two techniques to improve resource utilization. Section 5 compares our results with a state of the art tool. Section 6 describes related work. Section 7 is a conclusion.

2   Methodology and Preliminaries

This paper presents a general methodology, a specific approach and investigates two concrete techniques. The methodology could be instantiated using any modeling formalism supporting both a lightweight statistical analysis and a more costly formal verification. In this paper the methodology is instantiated as a specific approach using Parameterized Stopwatch Automata (PSA) together with the verification suite UPPAAL SMC and UPPAAL.

The two concrete techniques for enhancing the resource utilization are described in Sect. 4. Figure 2 shows a graphical conceptual representation of different sets of systems that different methods can show to be schedulable. Systems that are easily proven schedulable using classical analytical approaches can also be proven correct using symbolic model checking. Systems that can be shown, with a high degree of certainty, to be correct using statistical model checking (SMC) cannot always be proven to be correct using symbolic model checking due to

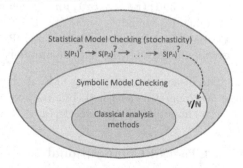

- Statistical M.C: Light weight and very expressive.
- Symbolic M.C: Very expressive and costly.
- Classical analysis: Light weight and weak expressive.

Fig. 2. Classes of systems that different methods can prove schedulable.

state space explosion. In the same way some complex systems that are analyzable using model checking cannot be proved correct using analytical approaches [8]. Our methodology consists of exploring system models with different sets of parameters $(S(P_i))$ searching for a realistic configuration that optimally satisfies the requirements. These experiments are performed using SMC with a high confidence level. Using SMC one can easily and interactively obtain either a high degree of confidence that the model is correct or a counterexample showing an error trace. When a satisfying final configuration has been found the system can be proven to be schedulable using symbolic model checking. In very rare cases an error could be found at this stage, but this is highly unlikely due to the confidence levels obtained using SMC.

2.1 Statistical Model Checking

We use both SMC and classical symbolic model checking techniques to analyze the schedulability of hierarchical scheduling systems. The UPPAAL verification suite provides both symbolic and SMC. The models which in practice can be analyzed statistically, using the UPPAAL SMC verification engine, are larger and can contain more features.

Meanwhile, SMC provides much faster responses. The speed of such responses depends entirely on the degree of certainty that one wants to obtain. The reason is that SMC consists in running a sufficiently high number of simulations of the system under analysis. The advantage of SMC resides in: (1) SMC provides a quick response in terms of less than a minute. This is also true in the case of non-schedulability were SMC produces counter-example witnesses; (2) SMC enables quantitative performance measurements instead of the Boolean (true, false) evaluation that symbolic model checking techniques provide. We can summarize the features of UPPAAL SMC that we use in the following:

- Stopwatches [9] are clocks that can be stopped and resumed without a reset. They are very practical to measure the execution time of preemptable tasks.
- Simulation and estimation of the value of expressions, `E[bound](min:expr)` and `E[bound](max:expr)`, for a given simulation time and/or number of runs specified by `bound`.
- Probability evaluation (`Pr[bound] P`) for a property `P` to be satisfied for a given simulation time and/or number of runs specified by `bound`.

The disadvantage of using SMC is that it will not provide complete certainty that a property is satisfied, but only verify it up to a specific confidence level, given as an analysis parameter [7].

2.2 Classical Compositional Framework

In this section, we provide the formal basis of our model-based compositional analysis approach. In fact, our theory conforms with the formal basis given in the compositional framework [21] for hierarchical scheduling systems.

A scheduling unit C is defined as a tuple (W, A) where W is a workload, consisting of a set of tasks $T_i = (p_i, e_i)$, and a scheduling policy A. Each task $T_i = (p_i, e_i)$ has timing attributes in the form of a period p_i and an execution time e_i. Task deadlines are the same as periods. The scheduling unit C (Fig. 3) is given a collective timing requirement $\Gamma = (\Pi, \Theta)$

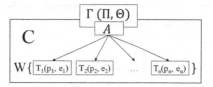

Fig. 3. Component and sub-tasks in a compositional framework

called interface, where Π is a period and Θ is a budget for the component. The collective timing requirement Γ is a representative of all timing requirements of tasks constituting the workload W. In the compositional framework [21], the schedulability of the system is checked by the following relation:

$$\mathbf{dbf}(W, A, t) \leq \mathbf{sbf}_\Gamma(R, t) \tag{1}$$

where t is a time interval. In this relation, the demand bound function $\mathbf{dbf}(W, A, t)$ computes the maximum amount of resource required by W under scheduling algorithm A during t time units. The supply bound function $\mathbf{sbf}_\Gamma(R, t)$ returns the minimum amount of resource that the resource model R allocates during a time interval t according to the resource requirement Γ. The system is said to be schedulable under the EDF policy if and only if it satisfies relation (1) for any value t.

2.3   Conceptual Models of Our Approach

In our model-based approach, we realize the compositional framework in the form of PSA models. We implemented the **dbf** as a set of tasks together with a scheduling algorithm, while the **sbf** is implemented by the supplier model. Such a supplier model (R_{PSA}) represents the classical resource model R in accordance with the contract Γ. The time when the workload can use resources follows from the scheduling algorithm, and is also constrained by the resource model R_{PSA}.

PSA supports stopwatches, which are clocks that can be stopped and resumed without a reset. The modeling formalism allows for having different rates of progression for stopwatches, but we only utilize the values 1 (running) and 0 (stopped). In our PSA models, the stopwatch is used to express the preemption of a task's execution. The execution of a task is preempted, i.e.

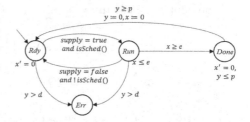

Fig. 4. Task model in PSA

the associated clock stops, in two cases: when it is preempted by a higher priority task or when any of the needed resources is not provided by the supplier.

Figure 4 is a conceptual model of a task, which we will realize using PSA in Sect. 3. The clock x stops progressing in the locations where its derivative x' is set to 0. The clock x keeps progressing at other locations. The task starts at the initial location Rdy and moves to Run when the two following conditions hold: the task is scheduled to use a resource pid, $(isSched(pid))$ and there is a supply of necessary resources $(supply = true)$. The clock x measures the execution time of the task while it is in the location Run. If either of the two conditions is false at the location Run, the task moves back to the location Rdy. The task stays at location Run until the stopwatch x reaches the execution time e, and then jumps to location $Done$ delaying until the next period. A task joins the error location Err when its deadline d is missed $(y > d)$. Throughout this paper we keep the assumption that $e \leq d \leq p$.

In the following, we relate the analytical view of the supply bound function and the resource model with the way they are implemented as a supplier model in our approach. We use the Periodic Resource Model (PRM) [21] as an example.

Figure 5 shows an example of the resource allocations of the PRM which guarantees the resource requirement $\Gamma = (\Pi, \Theta)$ where Π is 5 and Θ is 2. Σ represents a delay until the

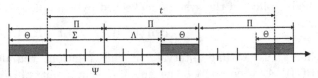

Fig. 5. Resource allocations of periodic resource model

next period and Λ is the delay located between the beginning of a period and the start of supply (slack time). The resource allocation in PRM does not need to be synchronized with the execution of tasks, thus Λ is deviated between 0 and $\Pi - \Theta$. The consecutive delay of Σ and Λ is denoted by Ψ, where no resource is allocated at all.

Property 1. The interval Ψ varies between 0 and the maximum consecutive delays of Σ and Λ, i.e. $0 \leq \Psi \leq 2(\Pi - \Theta)$.

The delay Λ varies between 0 and $\Pi - \Theta$ by the definition of the PRM. After a supply of Θ time units, the delay Σ is deviated between 0 and $\Pi - \Theta$. Consequently, $0 \leq \Lambda + \Sigma \leq 2(\Pi - \Theta)$.

The supply bound function $\mathbf{sbf}_\Gamma(R, t)$ based on the PRM is formulated as:

$$\mathbf{sbf}_\Gamma(PRM, t) = \left\lfloor \frac{t - (\Pi - \Theta)}{\Pi} \right\rfloor \cdot \Theta + \epsilon_s \tag{2}$$

$$\epsilon_s = \max\left(t - 2(\Pi - \Theta) - \Pi \left\lfloor \frac{t - (\Pi - \Theta)}{\Pi} \right\rfloor, 0 \right) \tag{3}$$

Our PSA model for the PRM (R_{PSA}) is designed to generate all possible allocations of resources in compliance with $\Gamma = (\Pi, \Theta)$.

One can remark that our resource model supplies the whole budget non-preemptively in one chunk, however according to [21] if one considers only worst cases, both preemptive and non-preemptive resource models provide the same analysis results. Thus we will use a non-preemptive supplier model (Fig. 6) both in this conceptual description as well in the computation models. Figure 6 shows the conceptual model of PSA resource model. In this model, the variable *supply* represents the resource allocation, which is a shared variable with the task model. Thus the supply is only enabled for Θ time units within the period Π. The location Rdy of R_{PSA} corresponds to the delay Λ in PRM of Fig. 5. This represents a situation where a new period started but the resource allocation has not been started. The location Sup corresponds to Θ where the resource is allocated, and $Done$ corresponds to Σ where the resource model waits for the next period.

In order to realize a compositional approach, our resource model R_{PSA} does not synchronize with the execution of tasks similarly to the resource allocation of PRM. Thus the resource model can stay at the location Rdy up to $\Pi - \Theta$ or immediately

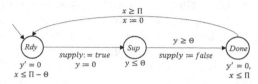

Fig. 6. Conceptual PRM model in PSA notation

move to the location Sup. This resource model is designed to generate all possible resource allocations including the maximum duration of no resource allocation Ψ.

3   Compositional Analysis Approach

In this section we present concrete PSA models based on the conceptual models presented in the previous section. The implementation contains a resource model (supplier template) and a task template. The scheduling policy is modeled as a separate PSA template, which is represented as a parameter when instantiating the concrete system. This increases the reconfigurability of our approach. We have modeled three different scheduling policies EDF, RM and FIFO but we only use EDF and RM in the experiments. Moreover, all tasks in the system are instances of the same Task template but with different parameters.

3.1   Stochastic Periodic Resource Model

In [22] the resource allocation by the supplier does not necessarily synchronize with tasks periods. That is, if the workloads of tasks start at time t_w and the resource allocation begins at time t_r then [22] assumes that t_w is not necessarily equal to t_r. This assumption leads to a stochastic periodic supplier model, where the supply of resources follows a uniform probability distribution within the supplier period. Thus,

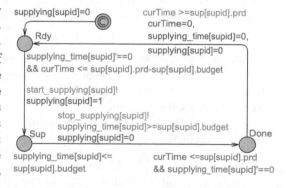

Fig. 7. Stochastic periodic resource model

we impose no obligation on the scheduler at the parent level of providing resources at a certain point in time. We only consider that the whole budget should be provided before the end of the supplier period. Figure 7 shows the supplier template, which communicates with the other templates through two output broadcast channels (start_supplying and stop_supplying) and a shared variable (supplying). These channels are used in the template Task to keep track of the resource supply. The initial location of the Supplier template is marked with double circles. Such a location is also marked with a "c" which indicates that it is a committed location, this leads the supplier to move instantaneously to the next location Rdy. Slack time is the maximum amount of time that can elapse before the supplier starts to supply resources. It is used in several places of Supplier and written as $sup[supid].prd - sup[supid].budget$. The location Rdy has an invariant consisting of a conjunction of two parts. The first part $supplying\_time[supid]' == 0$ means that the clock representing the supplied amount of resources does not progress while the template resides in the location Rdy. The second part $curTime <= sup[supid].prd - sup[supid].budget$ ensures that once $curTime$ has reached the end of the slack time the template leaves the location Rdy.

At some point in time between time zero and the slack time, the supplier moves to the location Sup. In this location, the progress rate of the clock supplying_time[supid] is set to 1, signifying that the supplier keeps supplying resources. While the likelihood of delays happening at location Rdy would be the same, we treat such a non-deterministic wait via a uniform probability distribution when performing statistical analysis. One can notice that non-determinism motivates the use of statistical model checking. The supplier can not provide more resources than budgeted and will move to the location Done when it has provided the needed resources. At the start of the next period, the supplier moves to the location Rdy.

3.2 Task Model

The task model in this paper has various execution attributes, such as the worst case execution time, deadline, initial offset and regular offset. Thus, our framework can easily be used to describe complicated hierarchical scheduling systems. Formally, a task within the workload $W = \{T_1, T_2, ..., T_n\}$ is defined by

- pri: Task priority.
- initial_offset: The offset of the initial period of the task.
- offset: The offset from the beginning of each period until task release.
- bcet: Best-case execution time.
- wcet: Worst-case execution time.
- preemptable: Whether a task is preemptable.
- tid: Task identifier.

Figure 8 shows the PSA task template. It begins its execution by waiting, non-deterministically, for an amount of time up to the initial offset (initial_offset). Using this parameter, we can adjust the synchronicity of the task execution with the supplier. This will be further explained in Sect. 4. The stopwatch twcrt is used to measure the worst-case response time of the task. The behavior of the

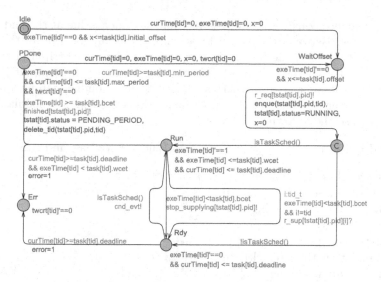

Fig. 8. Task model

task model consists mainly in checking whether a resource is available or not, by checking the supplier status $supplying[tstat[tid].pid]$, which is done inside the function isTaskSched().

The execution of a task can always be suspended whenever the supplier stops providing the task's requested resource. A task may travel several times between location Ready and location Run due to preemption by other tasks in the same component. This preemption is implemented at the level of the scheduling policy. Once the execution of a task is achieved within its deadline, the task moves to the location PDone, before starting the next period. If a task misses its deadline it moves to the location Err where it assigns 1 to the global variable error. This variable is used when analyzing the schedulability. The models used are available at http://people.cs.aau.dk/~ulrik/submissions/721641/models.zip. The top level system is formed by a parallel composition of component suppliers together with a scheduling policy. The schedulability of the top level system is performed according to [6]. The PSA models of scheduling algorithms are not included in the paper because their behavior is trivial, but they are provided in the above link.

3.3 Automated Computation of the Supplier Budget

We have automated a technique for directly estimating the supplier budget. Such an automation is realized by adding a helper template to the system and exploiting the expressiveness of the UPPAAL SMC query language. Figure 9 shows the modified initial states of the Supplier template. We do not show the helper because of

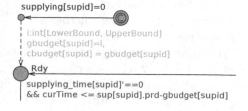

Fig. 9. Modified resource model

its simple behavior consisting of one transition, storing a value at the end of the simulation time. Between the initial location and the Rdy location of the modified supplier template, the budget is assigned a uniformly distributed random value between 0 and the period of the supplier, given in the template as the two constants LowerBound and UpperBound. The minimal budget can be found by searching for every budget value which makes the system non schedulable. To this end, we use the following query:

$$\text{Pr[cbudget[1]} <= \text{rbudget]} \quad (<> \text{globalTime} >= \text{simTime and error)} \qquad (4)$$

where cbudget[1] is the budget candidate for the supplier in a given run, rbudget is a constant value that is larger than any of the potential budgets, and globalTime is the current simulation time (clock). In the helper template, cbudget[1] is assigned a value larger than rbudget when the simulation has executed for simTime time units. Thus, this query finds every number between 0 and the supplier's budget for which

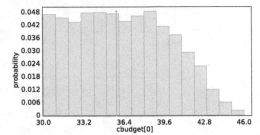

Fig. 10. Probability distribution of supplier's budgets that make component S_2 of Table 2 non schedulable under EDF

UPPAAL SMC finds a run where a task misses its deadline before the expiry of simTime, i.e. globalTime>=simTime.

Figures 10 and 11 show the probability distributions of budgets that UPPAAL SMC produces after checking the system using query (4). Figure 10 shows that for every potential budget between 0 and 45 a run where a deadline has been missed was found. In other words, a budget greater than 45 *can* make the system schedulable.

Given a budget, the schedulability of a component and its workload can be checked using the following query:

$$\text{Pr[}<= \text{simTime]}(<> \text{error)} \qquad (5)$$

Such a query computes the probability of a component to finally (<>) reach an error, where simTime is a simulation time and error is a global variable indicating whether a task has missed its deadline or not.

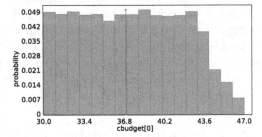

Fig. 11. Probability distribution of supplier's budgets that make component S_2 of Table 2 non schedulable under RM

By using the budget found via query (4) as a parameter value for component S_2 of Table 2 when checking query (5), we can see that this indeed makes component S_2 schedulable under EDF. Figure 11 is the estimation results of the same component under RM, showing that a supplier budget greater than 47 can make component S_2 schedulable. By using query (4), we can obtain a very good estimate for the minimal budget. In practice one might still need to check two or three values using query (5) after having applied query (4). Once a candidate budget is strongly determined, we apply symbolic model checking to be absolutely certain.

4 Enhancement of Resource Utilization

This section presents two techniques for enhancing the utilization of a resource: (1) introducing a new supplier model; (2) making tasks more synchronous with their suppliers by adjusting tasks initial offset.

4.1 Synchronous Periodic Resource Model

In order to increase the resource utilization by trying to avoid supplying resource when it is not needed, i.e. no waiting task, we introduce a new supplier model. The new supplier relies on delaying the resource supply, while no task is requesting resource, until a task request is received. Such a delay is up to the component slack time (period-budget).

Figure 12 depicts the PSA template that implements our new supplier model. Once started, the supplier joins location Rdy and keeps waiting while the slack time is not expired. Such a constraint is implemented by the location invariant curTime$\leq$ sup[supid].prd-sup[supid].budget, where prd and budget are respectively the period and budget of the supplier. One can remark that, at location Rdy, the stopwatch measuring the resource supply is not progressing (supplying_time[supid]'==0). Non deterministically, the supplier moves from location Rdy to the location Sup by either receiving a task request (guard isReq() over the crooked edge), or once the slack time is expired (guard curTime$\geq$sup[supid].prd-sup[supid].budget over the vertical edge).

At location Sup, the supplier keeps supplying resource before moving to the location Done. Such a location can be reached once the whole budget is supplied. From location Done and once the period is expired, the supplier joins location Rdy to start new period and resets its clocks.

Table 1 shows the gain in resource utilization obtained when applying the new supplier model. At the first stage, using the periodic resource model

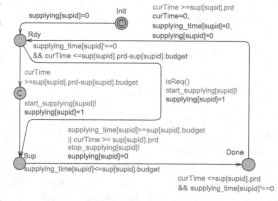

Fig. 12. Synchronous periodic resource model in PSA

PRM, we compute the component budgets of the avionics system we mentioned earlier. The component budgets obtained via CARTS (2nd column) and UPPAAL

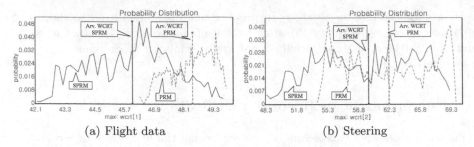

(a) Flight data   (b) Steering

Fig. 13. Probability distributions of WCRT of flight data and steering tasks. The queries $E[<= 100000; 1000](max : wcrt[1])$ and $E[<= 100000; 1000](max : wcrt[2])$ are used to generate the probability distributions using UPPAAL SMC.

SMC (3rd column) are identical; (10,6) (20,6) (20,2) (20,10). By replacing PRM with our new supplier model, we recompute the minimum budgets making the avionics components schedulable using UPPAAL SMC (4th column). For components Nav.Radar Ctrl and Navigation, the budgets are decreased to 5 in each case, with a gain of 17 % thanks to our new supplier model. We have checked and confirmed such new budgets using the UPPAAL symbolic model checking (MC).

In order to evaluate the effects of introducing a new supplier model, we have made a statistical experiment using the two tasks in the component Navigation. Figure 13 shows the probability distributions of

Table 1. Resource utilization comparison

Analysis Tool	CARTS	SMC	SMC & MC
Resource Model	PRM	PRM	Synchronous PRM
Nav. Radar Ctrl	(10, 6)	(10, 6)	**(10, 5)**
Navigation	(20, 6)	(20, 6)	**(20, 5)**
Radar Ctrl	(20, 2)	(20, 2)	(20, 2)
Control & Display	(20, 10)	(20, 10)	(20, 10)

WCRT using two different resource models. This shows that the average WCRT is enhanced using the new supplier model SPRM. There is no significant difference in the actual WCRT. By using these plots we can see how much a hierarchical system can be improved by using different system settings. The fact that we can easily generate such plots also shows the versatility of a model and simulation based approach.

4.2   Offset Manipulation

Our second technique consists in limiting the initial offset for the arrival of all tasks. Explicitly including offsets in the schedulability analysis was initiated in [23]. By limiting this initial offset to a certain percentage of the supplier period, the given component can be schedulable with a lower budget. This is an assumption that we are making about the system. It is the responsibility of the system engineers to confirm that the offset that they chose actually conforms with the real system. Thus we are not computing optimal offsets making the system schedulable, but investigating the impact of different offsets on the individual component resource requirements. As shown in Table 3, the smallest supplier budget can be obtained if all tasks arrive exactly synchronously with the start of the supplier period. This could be hard to achieve in practice. On the other hand, we think that it is indeed very possible to make the tasks synchronized with the supplier period such that all tasks arrive within either the first 20 % or 50 % of the supplier period. For these realistic values, we still obtain significant savings in the budget that a given component needs in order to be schedulable (See column 6 to 9 of Table 3). The percentage value is a parameter that can be easily changed in our setting when checking the schedulability. Similarly to Table 2, all statistical results in Table 3 are found using a confidence level of 0.95.

Another observation that we have made is that, the length of the period of the supplier can have a great impact on the budget that a component needs in order to be schedulable. This can be seen in Table 3 for component S_5. We have analyzed the same component with two different supplier periods. The first period is not a common divisor of the task periods (50000), while the second supplier period (10000) is a common divisor of the task periods. For the first experiment, the component can be schedulable with 30 % of the complete system resources, while in the second case it can be schedulable using only 18.8 % of the system resources (see column 4). In fact, this observation is an experimental result that can be found using both our approach and the CARTS tool (see Table 2 for component S_4).

4.3   Confirming Uppaal SMC Results with Model Checking

In order to give absolute responses about the schedulability analysis performed using UPPAAL SMC, we have verified some of the UPPAAL SMC results by means of symbolic model checking. These are marked in Table 3 by a gray background color in the cells. The reason for only verifying some of our results, but not all, is that for some of the models the verification time is as much as a couple of days.

According to our experience, statistical model checking is a good way to deal with the undecidability challenge of symbolic model checking in schedulability analysis, but does not represent an alternative.

5   Evaluation and Comparison

In order to evaluate the correctness of our model-based approach, we compare the component budgets from our estimation to the budgets obtained by the CARTS tool [19] for the same hierarchical system configurations. All the results presented in Table 2 are obtained with a confidence 0.95. When UPPAAL SMC returns a result where the estimated probability of missing a deadline is an interval from zero to some low value ϵ (e.g. [0,0.0973938]), this means that UPPAAL SMC did not find any trace in which a deadline was missed, i.e. with 95 % confidence a deadline will not be missed with the given budget and probability distribution. If a higher confidence is needed, the confidence value can be increased and the query can be rerun.

Table 2 shows the comparison we have done with the CARTS tool. Column 1 (Comp) contains 4 different components on which we have performed the

Table 2. Comparison of the estimated budgets of CARTS and Uppaal SMC

Comp	Tasks	P, WCET	CARTS		SMC	
			EDF	RM	EDF	RM
S_1	T_1	500, 30	100, 32.5	100, 32.5	100, 33	100, 33
	T_2	500, 100				
S_2	T_1	170, 30	100, 46.67	100, 47.5	100, 47	100, 48
	T_2	500, 100				
S_3	T_1	250, 40	**150, 42.5**	**150, 42.5**	**150, 45**	**150, 45**
	T_2	750, 50				
S_4	T_1	80000, 6890	50000, 15082	50000, 15082	50000, 15082	50000, 15082
	T_2	100000, 8192				
	T_3	200000, 2644	10000, 1880	10000, 2155.6	10000, 1875	10000, 2155
	T_4	1000000, 5874				

experiment. The workload of each component is stated on the second column (Tasks). In fact, each of component S_1, S_2 and S_3 is a parallel composition of 2 tasks (T_1, T_2), while S_4 contains 4 tasks $(T_1, \ldots, T_4)$. The third column specifies the period and the worst case execution time for each task. In order to perform a more thorough comparison, we have considered two different scheduling policies; EDF and RM. According to the CARTS tool, the minimum budget that the resource supplier should provide each 100 time units, for which the component S_1 is schedulable under EDF and RM, is **32.5**. For the same parameters, the minimum budget we have computed in our framework using Uppaal SMC is **33**, which is very close to that obtained by CARTS. The two tools produce almost identical results. CARTS has the advantage of being an extremely fast method, while our approach is extremely flexible and configurable.

5.1   Uppaal SMC Counterexample for One CARTS Result

During the schedulability analysis of a specific component configuration, we obtained a result from CARTS that was in conflict with our own results.

This was for the specific case (bold gray numbers) of component S_3 in Table 2. According to CARTS's computations, the minimal necessary budget for S_3 to be schedulable under EDF and RM is **42.5**. With the use of Uppaal SMC, we first estimated the minimal budget to be 45, which has a considerable difference with the results from CARTS.

Our estimation using Uppaal SMC immediately produced a counterexample trace which shows that

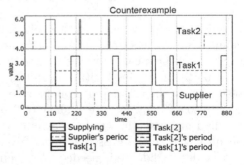

Fig. 14. Counterexample for the deadline missing of T_1 in S_3 with the budget 43 under RM in Table 2

Table 3. Enhancement of resource usability using the maximal offset of task's initial period. The cases marked with a grey background are symbolic model checking

S_i	T_i	P, WCET	Δ_{init} of supplier's period							
			$\Delta_{init} = 100\%$		$\Delta_{init} = 50\%$		$\Delta_{init} = 20\%$		$\Delta_{init} = 0\%$	
			EDF	RM	EDF	RM	EDF	RM	EDF	RM
1	T_1	500, 30	100, 33 (33%)	100, 33 (33%)	100, 33 (33%)	100, 33 (33%)	100, 29 (29%)	100, 29 (29%)	100, 26 (26%)	100, 26 (26%)
	T_2	500, 100								
2	T_1	170, 30	100, 47 (46 %)	100, 48 (48 %)	100, 47 (46 %)	100, 48 (47 %)	100, 42 (42 %)	100, 44 (44 %)	100, 38 (38 %)	100, 44 (44 %)
	T_2	500, 100								
3	T_1	250, 40	150, 45 (30 %)	150, 45 (30 %)	150, 45 (30 %)	150, 45 (30 %)	150, 44 (30 %)	150, 45 (30 %)	150, 40 (27 %)	150, 40 (27 %)
	T_2	750, 50								
4	T_1	10000, 1406	5000, 1406 (28 %)	5000, 1406 (28 %)	5000, 1406 (28 %)	5000, 1406 (28 %)	5000, 1325 (26 %)	5000, 1406 (28 %)	5000, 1057 (21 %)	5000, 1057 (21 %)
	T_2	40000, 2826								
5	T_1	80000, 6890	50000, 15082 (30 %)	50000, 15082 (30 %)	50000, 15082 (30 %)	50000, 15082 (30 %)	50000, 12531 (25 %)	50000, 14948 (30 %)	50000, 12400 (29 %)	50000, 13261 (27 %)
	T_2	100000, 8192								
	T_3	200000, 2644	10000, 1875 (18.8 %)	10000, 2155 (21.6 %)	10000, 1875 (18.8 %)	10000, 2155 (21.6 %)	10000, 1875 (18.8 %)	10000, 2060 (20.6 %)	10000, 1872 (18.7 %)	10000, 1985 (19.9 %)
	T_4	1000000, 5874								

Task1 (T_1) can miss its deadline with a supplier budget of 43. The counterexample is depicted in Fig. 14 in terms of a plot that was also produced by UPPAAL SMC. The bottom of the plot shows the supplier; the dashed spikes represent the length of the supplier period and the solid line illustrates when the supplier is supplying. Each of the other two groups illustrates the behavior of a task. The solid line shows when the task is executing, and the dashed line goes up when the task is released and down when the task has finished its computation. Approximately at time 880, Task1 is executing on its third period but fails to complete before its deadline. In order to confirm our findings, we also calculated the minimum supplier budget according to the theory underlying the CARTS tool. We calculated this both using the equations from [22] and equations from [21]. The results of such calculations confirmed our findings in that we calculated the minimal budget to be 45. This leads us to conclude that there must be an error in the implementation of CARTS while the underlying theory is correct. We reported this anomaly and it has been confirmed by the developers of the CARTS tool that CARTS has an implementation error.

6 Related Work

In an engineering setting, providing effective parameters that make a system realizable is very practical in terms of time and cost. In this paper, while we explore the schedulability analysis of hierarchical scheduling systems by profiting from the technological advances made in the area of model checking, we propose a compositional analysis approach to determine and increase the potential configurations making much more hierarchical scheduling systems schedulable.

The concept of hierarchical scheduling systems was first introduced as 2 levels systems in [11], and then generalized as a real-time multi-level system by [16]. An example of the increasing use of hierarchical scheduling systems is the standard ARINC 653 [2] for avionics real-time operating systems.

Several compositional analysis techniques [1,8,12,13,21,22] have been proposed. An analytical compositional framework was presented in [22] as a basis for the schedulability analysis of hierarchical scheduling systems. Such a framework relies on the abstraction and composition of system components, which are given by periodic interfaces. The interfaces state the components timing requirement without any specification of the tasks concrete behavior. In [20], the authors extend their previous work [22] to a hierarchical scheduling framework for multiprocessors based on cluster-based scheduling. They used analytical methods to perform the analysis. However, in both [20,22], the proposed framework is limited to a set of formulas describing an abstraction of the system entities, given in terms of periodic interfaces, without any specification of the tasks behavior and interaction. CARTS (Compositional Analysis of Real-Time Systems) [19] is tool that implements the theory given in [20,22]. Compared to our approach CARTS is a mature tool that is easy to use. On the other hand, we provide a more detailed modeling and analysis.

As common traits, analytical approaches assume computations with deterministic Execution Time usually coincident with the Worst Case Execution

Time (WCET), and they provide pessimistic results [8]. Recent research within schedulability analysis gives tremendous attention to model-based approaches, because of their expressiveness that allows for modeling more complicated behavior of systems, and also due to the technological advances made in the area of model-based simulation and analysis tools. In [4], the authors analyzed the schedulability of hierarchical scheduling systems using the TIMES tool [1,3], and implemented their model-based framework in VxWorks [4]. They constructed an abstract task model as well as scheduling algorithms focusing on the component under analysis. However, the authors not only consider the timing attributes of the component under analysis but also the timing attributes of the other components that can preempt the execution of the current component. Thus, the proposed approach is not fully compositional. The authors of [8] provided a compositional framework modeled as preemptive Time Petri Nets for the verification of hierarchical scheduling systems using the ORIS tool [17]. They only analyze systems using two specific scheduling algorithms severely restricting the class of systems they can handle. In [10], the authors introduced a model-based framework using UPPAAL for the schedulability analysis of single layered scheduling systems, modeling the concrete task behavior as a sequence of timed actions.

We have been inspired by the work in [10] but generalizing and lifting it to a compositional approach for hierarchical scheduling systems. Resource efficiency constitutes one of the most important factors in the performance evaluation of hierarchical scheduling systems. Such resources are often represented by either periodic [21] or explicit deadline periodic [12] resource models. The resource models represent an interface between a component and the rest of the system. In [14], the authors introduced the Dual Periodic Resource Model (DPRM) and presented an algorithm for computing the optimal resource interface, reducing the overhead suffered by the classical periodic resource models. In [18], the authors introduced a technique for improving the schedulability of real-time scheduling systems by reducing the resource interferences between tasks.

In contrast, we propose a model-based framework for the modeling of hierarchical scheduling systems with a generic resource model, while we use UPPAAL and UPPAAL SMC to analyze the schedulability of components in a compositional manner. We also introduce two novel techniques for improving resource efficiency, and computing the minimum resource supply of system components.

7   Conclusion

In this paper we have presented a compositional methodology for schedulability analysis using a combination of statistical and symbolic model checking. The methodology could be instantiated with any modeling formalism supporting both a lightweight statistical analysis and a more costly formal verification.

The methodology we propose is instantiated in a concrete approach using Parameterized Stopwatch Automata (PSA), UPPAAL SMC and UPPAAL. Our approach is model based, compositional and highly configurable. We have compared the results we obtained on different system configurations with results obtained from the CARTS tool. The results from the two tools are almost identical. We discovered one case with a large difference, which has been confirmed as an implementation error by the developers of CARTS. Our configurable approach can be instantiated and updated for many different applications and system configurations including scheduling policies. We have investigated two specific techniques for enhancing the resource utilization: a new resource model and offset manipulation. Both techniques are investigated using statistical model checking. We also provided a faster method for estimating the minimal budget of a supplier, instead of performing a binary search of potential budgets. The main contribution of the paper is that systems, which cannot be proven schedulable using classical analytic approaches, can potentially be proven schedulable using our approach.

A perspective of this work could be a study of the impact of the two techniques, we proposed for the enhancement of resource utilization, on the systems energy efficiency [5].

References

1. Amnell, T., Fersman, E., Mokrushin, L., Pettersson, P., Yi, W.: Times: A tool for schedulability analysis and code generation of real-time systems. In: Larsen, K.G., Niebert, P. (eds.) FORMATS 2003. LNCS, vol. 2791, pp. 60–72. Springer, Heidelberg (2004)
2. ARINC 653. Website. https://www.arinc.com/cf/store/documentlist.cfm
3. Åsberg, M., Nolte, T., Pettersson, P.: Prototyping and code synthesis of hierarchically scheduled systems using TIMES. J. Conver. (Consum. Electron.) 1(1), 77–86 (2010)
4. Behnam, M., Nolte, T., Shin, I., Åsberg, M., Bril, R.: Towards hierarchical scheduling in VxWorks. In: OSPERT 2008, pp. 63–72 (2008)
5. Boudjadar, A., David, A., Kim, J., Larsen, K., Nyman, U., Skou, A.: Schedulability and energy efficiency for multi-core hierarchical scheduling systems. In: Proceedings of the International Congres on Embedded Real Time Software and Systems ERTS^2 (2014)
6. Boudjadar, A., David, A., Kim, J.H., Larsen, K.G., Mikučionis, M., Nyman, U., Skou, A.: Hierarchical scheduling framework based on compositional analysis using uppaal. In: Fiadeiro, J.L., Liu, Z., Xue, J. (eds.) FACS 2013. LNCS, vol. 8348, pp. 61–78. Springer, Heidelberg (2014)
7. Bulychev, P.E., David, A., Larsen, K.G., Mikucionis, M., Poulsen, D.B., Legay, A., Wang, Z.: UPPAAL-SMC: statistical model checking for priced timed automata. In: Wiklicky, H., Massink, M. (eds.) QAPL, vol. 85, pp. 1–16. Electronic Proceedings in Theoretical Computer Science (2012). doi:10.4204/EPTCS.85.1
8. Carnevali, L., Pinzuti, A., Vicario, E.: Compositional verification for hierarchical scheduling of real-time systems. IEEE Trans. Softw. Eng. 39(5), 638–657 (2013)
9. Cassez, F., Larsen, K.G.: The impressive power of stopwatches. In: Palamidessi, C. (ed.) CONCUR 2000. LNCS, vol. 1877, p. 138. Springer, Heidelberg (2000)
10. David, A., Larsen, K.G., Legay, A., Mikučionis, M.: Schedulability of Herschel-Planck revisited using statistical model checking. In: Margaria, T., Steffen, B. (eds.) ISoLA 2012, Part II. LNCS, vol. 7610, pp. 293–307. Springer, Heidelberg (2012)

11. Deng, Z., Liu, J.W.S.: Scheduling real-time applications in an open environment. In: Proceedings of the 18th RTSS, pp. 308–319. Society Press (1997)
12. Easwaran, A., Anand, M., Lee, I.: Compositional analysis framework using EDP resource models. In: Proceedings of the 28th IEEE International Real-Time Systems Symposium, pp. 129–138 (2007)
13. Easwaran, A., Anand, M., Lee, I., Phan, L.T.X., Sokolsky, O.: Simulation relations, interface complexity, and resource optimality for real-time hierachical systems (2009)
14. Lee, J., Phan, L.T.X., Chen, S., Sokolsky, O., Lee, I.: Improving resource utilization for compositional scheduling using DPRM interfaces. SIGBED Rev. 8(1), 38–45 (2011)
15. Bril, R.J., Holenderski, M., Lukkien, J.J.: An efficient hierarchical scheduling framework for the automotive domain. In: Babamir, S.M. (ed.) Real-Time Systems, Architecture, Scheduling, and Application, pp. 67–94. InTech (2012)
16. Mok, A.K., Feng, X.A., Chen, D.: Resource partition for real-time systems. In: Proceedings of RTAS 2001, pp. 75–84. IEEE Computer Society (2001)
17. ORIS. Website. http://www.oris-tool.org/
18. Phan, L.T.X., Lee, I.: Improving schedulability of fixed-priority real-time systems using shapers. In: Proceedings of RTAS 2013, Washington, DC, USA, pp. 217–226. IEEE Computer Society (2013)
19. Phan, L.T.X., Lee, J., Easwaran, A., Ramaswamy, V., Chen, S., Lee, I., Sokolsky, O.: CARTS: a tool for compositional analysis of real-time systems. SIGBED Rev. 8(1), 62–63 (2011)
20. Shin, I., Easwaran, A., Lee, I.: Hierarchical scheduling framework for virtual clustering of multiprocessors. In: ECRTS, pp. 181–190. IEEE Computer Society (2008)
21. Shin, I., Lee, I.: Periodic resource model for compositional real-time guarantees. In: RTSS, pp. 2–13. IEEE Computer Society (2003)
22. Shin, I., Lee, I.: Compositional real-time scheduling framework with periodic model. ACM Trans. Embedded Comput. Syst. 7(3), 1–39 (2008)
23. Tindell, K.: Adding time-offsets to schedulability analysis. University of York, Department of Computer Science (1994)

Adding Formal Meanings to AADL with Hybrid Annex

Ehsan Ahmad[1,2], Yunwei Dong[1], Shuling Wang[2], Naijun Zhan[2(✉)], and Liang Zou[2]

[1] School of Computer Science, Northwestern Polytechnical University, Xi'an 710072, People's Republic of China
[2] State Key Laboratory of Computer Science, Institute of Software, Chinese Academy of Sciences, No. 4, South Fourth Street, Zhong Guan Cun, Beijing 100190, People's Republic of China
znj@ios.ac.cn

Abstract. AADL is a Model-Based Engineering language for architectural analysis and specification of real-time embedded systems with stringent performance requirements (e.g. fault-tolerance, security, safety-critical etc.). However, core AADL lacks of a mechanism for modeling continuous evolution of physical processes which are controlled by digital controllers. In our previous work, we have introduced Hybrid Annex—an AADL extension for continuous behavior and cyber-physical interaction modeling based on Hybrid Communicating Sequential Processes (HCSP). In this paper, we present formal semantics of the synchronous subset of AADL models annotated with Hybrid Annex specifications using HCSP. The semantics are then used to verify correctness of AADL models (with Hybrid Annex specifications) using an in-house developed theorem prover — Hybrid Hoare Logic (HHL) prover.

Keywords: AADL · Formal semantics · HCSP · Hybrid Annex · Hybrid systems

1 Introduction

Embedded Systems (ESs) make use of computer units to control physical processes so that the behavior of the controlled processes meets expected requirements. They have become ubiquitous in our daily life, e.g. automotive, aerospace, consumer electronics, communications, medical, manufacturing and so on. ESs are used to carry out highly complex and often critical functions such as to monitor and control industrial plants, complex transportation equipment, communication infrastructure, etc. The development process of ESs is widely recognized as a highly complex and challenging task. A thorough validation and verification activity is necessary to enhance the quality of ESs and, in particular, to fulfill the quality criteria mandated by the relevant standards engineers. How to design correct embedded systems is a grand challenge for computer science and control theory. Model-Based Engineering (MBE) is considered as an effective way of

© Springer International Publishing Switzerland 2015
I. Lanese and E. Madelaine (Eds.): FACS 2014, LNCS 8997, pp. 228–247, 2015.
DOI: 10.1007/978-3-319-15317-9_15

developing correct complex ESs, and has been successfully applied in industry [7,9]. In the framework of MBE, a model of the system to be developed is defined at the beginning; then extensive analysis and verification are conducted based on the model so that errors can be detected and corrected at early stages of design of the system. Afterwards, model transformation techniques are applied to transform abstract formal models into more concrete models, even into source code. Hybrid Systems (HSs) are mathematical models with precise mathematical semantics for ESs, wherein continuous physical dynamics are combined with discrete transitions. Based on HSs, rigorous analysis and verification of ESs become feasible.

Architectural Analysis & Design Language (AADL) is an SAE International standard and is an architecture description language for ESs [13]. It is based on architectural-centric MBE approach. It has been introduced to cope with embedded system design challenges by minimizing model inconsistency, decreasing mismatched assumptions of different stakeholders and supporting dependability predictions through analyzable architecture development. However, core AADL only provides support for structural modeling of embedded computing units and nothing related to detailed behavior of the software and physical processes which are controlled by the software can be modeled. So, as a result not only the reliability prediction, performance analysis and verification of AADL models are not precise enough, but also the cost is very high. To address these issues, Behavior Annex (BA) and BLESS annex are introduced for more precise behavior modeling using state transition systems with guards and actions [12,14]. Both BA and BLESS annex are intended to model discrete behavior of a control system. However, in practice, it is quite common that a control system contains continuous behavior, in particular, the behavior of controlled physical processes. In [17], we have introduced a lightweight language extension to AADL called the Hybrid Annex (HA) for continuous behavior and cyber-physical interaction modeling.

In addition, formal semantics are especially important for safety-critical systems and are the basis for formal analysis and verification of these systems. Although considerable amount of literature is available on formalization of AADL for performance and dependability analysis but the majority of the literature is focused on discrete behavior (behavior of the computing units) only and formalization of the continuous part of hybrid systems and the cyber-physical interaction (communication between the computing unit and the physical processes) is not addressed at all.

Hence, in order to use AADL for modeling and verification of hybrid system, it is required not only to define the formal semantics of the core language but also define the formal semantics of the dedicated annex (HA) used for continuous behavior modeling, in such a language which is designed to model and formally verify the HSs.

1.1   A Running Example

Throughout this paper, we use the Water Level Control System (WLCS) [8] as a running example to explain the motivation, to illustrate how to apply the HA extension to model HSs, as well as the use of proposed formal semantics for

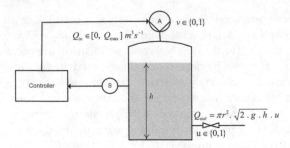

Fig. 1. WLCS diagram - a classical hybrid system

verification. As depicted in Fig. 1, WLCS consists of two main parts, the *water tank* and the *controller*. Continuous change of water level h in the water tank is described by

$$\begin{cases} \dot{h} = v \cdot Q_{max} - \pi \cdot r^2 \cdot \sqrt{2 \cdot g \cdot h} \\ \dot{v} = 0 \qquad v \in \{0, 1\} \end{cases}$$

where $Q_{max} = 0.007\,\mathrm{m^3s^{-1}}$, $\pi = 3.14$, $r = 0.0254\,\mathrm{m}$, and $g = 9.8\,\mathrm{ms^{-2}}$. $v \cdot Q_{max}$ is the water inflow Q_{in} into the tank, which takes the value 0 or Q_{max} depending on if the valve v is close or open. $\pi \cdot r^2 \cdot \sqrt{2 \cdot g \cdot h}$ stands for water outflow Q_{out}, which follows Torricelli's law.[1] S, v, and A represent the sensor, inflow valve and the actuator used to control inflow valve (v) respectively. The main goal of WLCS is to maintain water level h between a specified limit which is 0.30 m to 0.60 m, by controlling the inflow valve v to be close or open. The control command is computed by the controller based on the water level observed by sensor S and the predefined control strategy. The command is then sent to actuator A to control the inflow valve v appropriately.

Core AADL with HA can be used to model the structural architecture of the controller, continuous behavior of the water tank and the cyber-physical interaction between them. Assurance of the correct system behavior and the certification of real-time and dependability related properties demand a system level formal verification approach which is not addressed at all in the existing literature on formalization of AADL. In this paper, formal semantics for AADL models with HA specifications are proposed to fill this gap.

Contributions: In this paper, we propose formal semantics of AADL execution model with synchronous communication and HA using HCSP. The contribution of the paper is twofold. Firstly, we illustrate the use of HA to model the continuous behavior and the communication between the controller and the physical process. Continuous system behavior specified using HA can easily be attached to predefined AADL components. Secondly, formal semantics of AADL execution model and synchronous communication mechanism based on a language (HCSP) suitable for hybrid systems modeling and analysis is presented. Formal

---

[1] Normally, $Q_{out} = \pi \cdot r^2 \cdot \sqrt{2 \cdot g \cdot h} \cdot u$. But for simplicity, we take $u = 1$ here.

semantics are then used to verify correctness of AADL model annotated with HA specifications using an in-house developed theorem prover known as HHL prover [16,19].

Outline: Section 2 introduces HCSP, HHL and AADL with its execution model and synchronous communication semantics. Section 3 presents the continuous behavior and cyber-physical interaction modeling using HA and Sect. 4 discusses the formal semantics of AADL execution model along with synchronous communication. Section 5 illustrates verification of the case study using HHL prover. Section 6 presents a summary of the related work. Section 7 concludes this paper and discusses the future work.

2   Preliminaries

This section presents an overview of HCSP by highlighting primitive language constructs. The specification logic HHL for reasoning about HCSP behavior is then introduced briefly. Basic AADL notions and notations are also presented with emphases on execution model and synchronous data communication semantics.

2.1   Overview of HCSP

HCSP is an extension of Hoare's Communicating Sequential Processes (CSP) for modeling HSs [5,8]. In HCSP, differential equations are introduced to model continuous evolution of the physical processes along with interrupts, so both discrete and continuous behaviors are still modeled as *processes*. A hybrid system in HCSP is a parallel composition of networked sequential processes interacting through dedicated channels, or a repetition of a sub-system. Note that processes in parallel can only interact through communication and no shared variables are allowed. The set of variables is denoted by $\mathcal{V} = \{x, y, z, ...\}$ and the set of channels is denoted by $\Sigma = \{ch_1, ch_2, ch_3, ...\}$. The processes of HCSP are constructed as follows:

$$P ::= \textbf{skip} \mid x := e \mid wait\ d \mid ch?x \mid ch!e \mid P; Q \mid B \to P \mid P \sqcup Q \mid \|_{i \in I}(ch_i* \to Q_i) \mid P^*$$
$$\mid \langle \mathcal{F}(\dot{s}, s) = 0 \& B \rangle \mid \langle \mathcal{F}(\dot{s}, s) = 0 \& B \rangle \trianglerighteq_d Q \mid \langle \mathcal{F}(\dot{s}, s) = 0 \& B \rangle \trianglerighteq \|_{i \in I}(ch_i* \to Q_i)$$
$$S ::= P \mid S^* \mid S \| S$$

Here P, Q, and Q_i represent sequential processes, whereas S stands for a (sub)system; $ch, ch_i \in \Sigma$ are communication channels, while ch_i* is a communication event which can be either an input event $ch?x$ or an output event $ch!e$; B and e are boolean and arithmetic expressions respectively, and d is a non-negative real constant.

Process **skip** terminates immediately without updating variables, and process $x := e$ assigns the value of expression e to x and then terminates. Process $wait\ d$ keeps idle for d time units without any change to respective variables. Interaction between processes is based on two types of communication events: $ch!e$ sends the value of e along channel ch and $ch?x$ assigns the value received along channel ch to variable x. Communication takes place when both the source process and the destination process are ready.

HCSP supports both sequential and concurrent composition. A sequentially composed process $P; Q$ behaves as P first, and if it terminates, as Q afterwards. The alternative process $B \to P$ behaves as P only if B is true and terminates otherwise. Internal choice between processes P and Q, denoted as $P \sqcup Q$ is resolved by the process itself. Communication controlled external choice $[\![_{i \in I}(ch_i* \to Q_i)$ specifies that as soon as one of the communications ch_i* takes place, the process starts behaving as respective process Q_i. The repetition P^* executes P for an arbitrary finite number of times, and the choice of the number of times is nondeterministic.

Continuous evolution is specified as $\langle \mathcal{F}(\dot{s}, s) = 0 \& B \rangle$. Real variables s evolve continuously according to differential equations $\mathcal{F}$ as long as the boolean expression B is true. B defines the domain of s. Interruption of continuous evolution due to B (as soon as it becomes false) is known as *Boundary Interrupt*. Continuous evolution can also be preempted due to the following interrupts:

- *Timeout Interrupt*: $\langle \mathcal{F}(\dot{s}, s) = 0 \& B \rangle \trianglerighteq_d Q$ behaves like $\langle \mathcal{F}(\dot{s}, s) = 0 \& B \rangle$, if the continuous evolution terminates before d time units. Otherwise, after d time units of evolution according to $\mathcal{F}$, it moves on to execute Q.
- *Communication Interrupt*: $\langle \mathcal{F}(\dot{s}, s) = 0 \& B \rangle \trianglerighteq [\![_{i \in I}(ch_i* \to Q_i)$ behaves like $\langle \mathcal{F}(\dot{s}, s) = 0 \& B \rangle$, except that the continuous evolution is preempted whenever one of the communications ch_i* takes place, which is followed by respective Q_i.

Finally, S defines a HCSP system on the top level. A parallel composition $S_1 \| S_2$ behaves as if S_1 and S_2 run independently except that they need to synchronize along the common communication channels.

2.2 Overview of Hybrid Hoare Logic (HHL)

In [10], we have extended Hoare Logic to hybrid systems, by adding history formulas to describe continuous properties that hold throughout the whole execution of HCSP processes. The history formulas are defined by Duration Calculus (DC), which is a real arithmetic extension of Interval Temporal Logic (ITL) for specifying and reasoning about real-time systems. The mainly used assertion $\lceil S \rceil$, where S is a state formula, means that S holds everywhere inside the considered interval.

In HHL, the specification for a sequential process P is of the form $\{Pre\}\, P$ $\{Post; HF\}$, where $Pre, Post$ represent pre-/post-conditions, expressed by first-order logic, to specify properties of variables held at starting and termination of the execution of P, and HF is a history formula, expressed by DC, to record the execution history of P, including real-time and continuous properties. The specification for a parallel process is then defined by assigning to each sequential component the respective pre-/post-conditions and history formula, that is

$$\{Pre_1, Pre_2\}\, P_1 \| P_2\, \{Post_1, Post_2; HF_1, HF_2\}$$

In HHL, each HCSP construct is axiomatized by a set of axioms and inference rules. Based on the inference system, we have implemented an interactive theorem prover for HHL in proof assistant Isabelle/HOL. The tool can be downloaded from lcs.ios.ac.cn/~znj/HHLProver. For further details on HCSP, HHL and HHL prover, we refer to [16].

The WLCS can be modeled, using HCSP, as a parallel composition of the water tank and the controller, whose specification is given as follows:

$$\{Pre_1, Pre_2\} \; Watertank \| Controller \{0.30 \leq h \leq 0.60, \; True; \; \lceil 0.30 \leq h \leq 0.60 \rceil, \; True\}.$$

As shown by the postcondition and history formula corresponding to *Watertank*, the water level h will always be kept in the range $[0.30, 0.60]$. The details for the modeling and verification of the WLCS system are described in the rest of the paper.

2.3   Overview of AADL

AADL contains components for both the application software, and the execution hardware of an embedded system, and supports textual, graphical and XML Metadata Interchange (XMI) specification formats. Components with *type* and *implementation* classifiers are instantiated and connected together to structure the system architecture. AADL core language constructs are categorized into application software, execution platform and composite components. The *system* component represents a composite entity containing software, execution platform or system components.

Components and Connections. Execution platform category represents computation and communication resources including *processor, memory, bus* and *device* components. A processor component represents the hardware and software responsible for thread scheduling and execution. Properties can be assigned to a processor component to specify scheduling policies, high-level operating system services and communication protocols. A memory component is used to represent storage entities for data and code. A device component can model a physical entity in the external environment: a plant or the software simulation of the plant. It can also be used as an interactive component like sensor or actuator. A bus component represents the physical connections among execution platform components.

Application software category consists of *process, data, subprogram, thread*, and *thread group* components. A process component represents the protected address space, which is bound to a memory component. A data component can be used to abstract data type, local data or parameter of a subprogram. A subprogram models the executable code which is called, with parameters, by thread and other subprograms. Thread is the only schedulable component with execution semantics to model system execution behavior. A thread represents sequential flow of the execution and the associated semantic automation describes life cycle of the thread.

A component type declaration defines interface elements and may contain *Features*. Features contain communication ports. AADL supports *data, event*

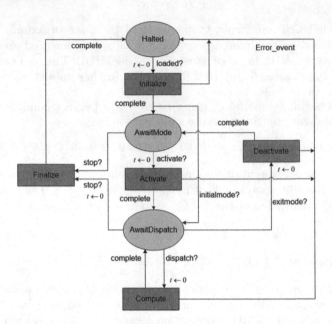

Fig. 2. Thread execution state machine

and *event data* ports to transmit and receive data, control, and control and data respectively. Port communication is typed and directional. An *in* port receives data/control and an *out* port sends data/control while an *in out* port can send and receive data/control. Communication is realized through *connections* between ports, parameters and access to shared data.

This paper is focused on formalizing execution model semantics of AADL with synchronous communication in which threads are communicating through data ports. Due to the page limitation, these two aspects are briefly discussed in the rest of this section. We refer to AADL standard document AS5506-B [13] for further details.

Execution Model. AADL structure model (hierarchical composition of the components) does not contain explicit information about the execution model, instead it is specified by the execution control automaton and properties at model and project level. AADL execution model deals with execution control automaton, thread dispatch strategy, scheduling and execution and fault handling. Our focus in this paper is on the execution model and (synchronous) communication formalism and the formalization of thread fault handling and modal semantics will be subject of a later paper.

Thread execution life cycle, as depicted in Fig. 2 is same for every thread. Thread execution life cycle consists of two types of states: *action states* and *rest states*. Threads in action states are forced to execute associated program code while in rest states threads do not perform any execution. *Initialize*, *Activate*, *Deactivate*, *Compute*, and *Finalize* are the action states while *Halted*,

AwaitMode, and *AwaitDispatch* are the rest states. Active states can have properties specifying the source code entry points, computation time and deadlines.

Thread in *AwaitDispatch* state is active in current operational mode (AADL supports more than one operational modes) and is waiting for dispatch. Thread dispatch condition is type dependant. A Periodic thread is dispatched after a fixed time interval specified in its *Period* property. An aperiodic thread, if its predefined dispatch port is not connected, is dispatched each time it receives an event, otherwise it is dispatched each time it receives an event on dispatch port.

A thread is initialized after the respective process is loaded into memory and is directly moved to *AwaitDispatch* state if it is active in current process mode otherwise it is moved to *AwaitMode* state. Thread dispatch is controlled by *Enabled(t)* function and *Wait_For_Dispatch* invariant in *AwaitDispatch* state. The clock variable t is reset each time an active state is entered, and the timing assertion *assert* $t \leq (state\_Deadline + Recover\_Deadline)$ is placed in the active state to specify deadline violation. If assertion in any active state is violated, thread is moved to the *Halted* state.

Synchronous Communication. Inter-thread communication in synchronous data flow communication pattern can either be *immediate* or *delayed* depending on data port connections. For an immediate connection, data is transmitted whenever the source thread completes its execution and meanwhile destination thread is suspended. The value received at destination is the value produced at the latest completion of source thread. For immediate connection, threads must share a common dispatch. For a delayed connection the output is transmitted at the deadline of the source thread so it is available to the destination thread at the next dispatch. The value received at destination is the value produced at the latest deadline of the source thread. For delayed connection, threads do not need to share a common dispatch.

2.4   WLCS Discrete Behavior Modeling

Depicted using the AADL graphical notations, Fig. 3 shows the architecture of the controller of the running example (WLCS), while the detailed behavior of the water tank is presented in Listing 1 and is discussed in the next section. The continuous state of the water tank, i.e. the water level h, is measured by a *sensor* and the output is sent to the controller process *Wlcs.impl* through connection $C1$, which contains two periodic threads *get_data* and *com_cmd*. Threads are connected through an immediate connection *Conn*. Thread *get_data* samples sensor data through its in data port s along connection $C2$ on every dispatch and sends computed data to *com_cmd* thread through out data port w along connection *Conn*. Control command according to control laws, is computed by *com_cmd* thread and is sent to *actuator* through out data port c using connections $C3$ and $C4$.

In relation to execution model and synchronous communication mechanisms discussed earlier, threads *get_data* and *com_cmd* share same execution life cycle presented in Fig. 2 and the immediate connection *Conn* between them is as discussed in Sect. 2.3. Formal semantics of this discrete behavior of the controller

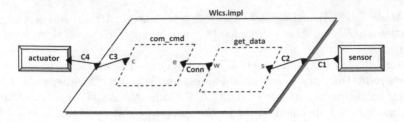

Fig. 3. AADL model of WLCS using graphical notations

component (consisting of threads and communication between them) are presented in Sect. 4 in detail.

3   Hybrid Annex

Hybrid Annex (HA) has been proposed to equip AADL for hybrid system modeling and analysis [17]. An HA specification can be attached to either the implementation classifier of an AADL device component or to an abstract component to model the continuous behavior of the interactive components (i.e. sensors and actuators) or to model the behavior of a physical process respectively. An HA specification may contain six sections: `assert`, `invariant`, `variables`, `constants`, `channels`, and `behavior` to specify predicates, predicates that must hold throughout continuous behavior model, local variables, constants, communication channels and continuous behavior respectively.

Listing 1 presents the complete textual AADL model with HA specifications of the water tank of WLCS–the running example. The type classifier declares the interface of the `WaterTank` component with two data ports. The out data port `wl` is used to send the current water level, while the in data port `cc` is used to receive the control command. The `WaterTank` is connected to the sensor and actuator using ports `wl` and `cc` with appropriate connections. The `WaterLevel` and `ValveStatus` refer to AADL Data Model Annex components in package `WLCS` that specifies the details of the range and measuring units of the data types used in this model.

The implementation of the `WaterTank` component in Listing 1 is specified using three HA sections: `variables`, `constants`, and `behavior`. Below we explain each of these sections in the context of the running example. The formal syntax, grammar and details on each section of HA are presented in [17].

3.1   Variables Section

Local variables in the scope of current HA subclause are declared in `variables` section. A variable may either be discrete or continuous depending on the component to which HA specification is attached and must have a data type specified by AADL component classifier reference. In Listing 1, the `variables` section contains `t`, `v`, and `h` to specify the current time, status of the inflow valve and the

Listing 1. AADL WaterTank Component Specification using Hybrid Annex

```
abstract WaterTank
  features
    cc: in data port WLCS::ValveStatus;
    wl: out data port WLCS::WaterLevel;
  end WaterTank;
abstract implementation WaterTank.impl
annex hybrid {**
  variables
    t :   WLCS::Time   -- value of current time
    v :   WLCS::ValveStatus  -- inflow valve status
    h :   WLCS::WaterLevel  -- current water level
  constants
    Qmax = 0.007 cmps  -- maximum water inflow
    g    = 9.8 mpss  -- gravitational force
    pi   = 3.14
    r    = 0.0254 m  -- radius of outflow valve
    u    = 1  -- outflow valve status, permanently open
    period = 0.01 sec  -- sampling period
  behavior
    Plant ::= t := 0 &
            'DT 1 h =(v*Qmax)-(pi*(r^2)*1.414*(g^0.5)*(h^0.5)*u)' &
            'DT 1 v = 0' <(t<period)> [[> wl!(h)]]> GetCmd
    GetCmd ::= cc?(v)
    WaterTank ::= repeat (Plant)
**};
end WaterTank.impl;
```

current water level. Variable v can take value either 0 or 1 to represent the *close* and *open* status of the inflow valve.

3.2 Constants Section

In the standard way, **constants** section is used to define constants that are used in modeling continuous behavior of the physical process. Constants are only initialized once at declaration by either integer or real value, along with appropriate measuring unit specification.

The **constants** section in Listing 1 contains six constants. Constant **Qmax** with value 0.007 specifies the maximum water inflow through valve v. Measuring unit of the water inflow $m^3 s^{-1}$ is specified as **cmps**. Constant **g** is the gravitational force with 9.8 and measuring unit ms^{-2} specified as **mpss**. Constants **pi** and **u** represent the value of π and status of the outflow valve without any measuring unit specification. The constant **period** with value 0.01 and measuring unit seconds specified as **sec** represents the sampling period of the controller. Radius of the outflow valve **r** takes value 0.0254 and is measured in meters specified as **m**.

3.3   Behavior Section

The `behavior` section in HA contains parallel composition of networked sequential processes to specify the continuous behavior and cyber-physical interaction between AADL components and the physical processes. Each behavior specification is represented as a HCSP process explained in Sect. 2.1. Specification of a continuous evolution consists of differential expression along with boolean conditions followed by one or more communication events denoting interrupts. Differential expression contains differential equations specified using the keyword `DE` followed by the order of the differential equation and the dependant and independent variables. Keeping in view the extensive use of time derivation in real-time modeling, separate notation is defined for time derivation specification consisting of the keyword `DT` followed by the order and the dependant variable.

The `behavior` section in Listing 1 shows HA specification for the water tank of the running example. Continuous evolution of water level h is modeled using time derivation 'DT 1 h = (v*Qmax)-(pi*(r^2)*1.414*(g^0.5)*(h^0.5)*u)' with boundary condition `t < period` as process `Plant`. Here, `(v*Qmax)` is the total water inflow if the value of v is 1 and `(pi*(r^2)*1.414*(g^0.5)*(h^0.5)*u)`' is the total water outflow at a particular time `t`. 'DT 1 v = 0' represents the rate of change of variable v with respect to time, which is 0 in this case. The continuous evolution of the water level `h` is preempted by the communication event on out data port `wl`. This communication interrupt is modeled using `[[> wl!(h) ]]>` followed by the process `GetCmd`. Process `GetCmd` contains the communication event `cc?(v)` used to get the control command from the controller on port `cc`. The repeating continuous behavior of the water tank is modeled by the `WaterTank` process where every iteration starts by resetting the time clock `t:=0`.

HA is expressive enough to model physical processes with complex continuous dynamics attached to AADL ports and mapped with AADL connections.[2]

4   Formal Semantics

4.1   Formalization of Synchronous Subset of AADL

Algorithm 1 lists the main steps followed for defining formal semantics of the AADL execution model with synchronous communications. Here, Tr is a set of threads in an AADL model, and for every $tr \in Tr$, processes ACT_{tr}, DIS_{tr}, and COM_{tr} are generated to specify activation, dispatch and computation behavior of the thread. Based on specific properties, associated connections and timing constraints, each active thread corresponding to state machine shown in Fig. 2 is translated into one HCSP process.

---

[2] The details of the AADL textual model for the Controller component and all proof files (discussed in Sect. 5) related to the running example are available at https://github.com/ehah/FACS2014.

Algorithm 1. Translation of an AADL model into HCSP processes

---

Require: AADL instance model
Ensure: Generate HCSP processes for periodic threads and connections
 1: **for all** $tr \in Tr$ **do**
 2:     generate an activation process ACT_{tr} (Sect. 4.1)
 3:     generate a dispatch process DIS_{tr} (Sect. 4.2)
 4:     generate a compute process COM_{tr} (Sect. 4.3)
 5: **end for**
 6: **for all** $c_{tr} \in CON_{tr}$ **do**
 7:     **if** tr is source in c_{tr} **then**
 8:         update COM_{tr} for c_{tr} (Sect. 4.4)
 9:     **else**
10:         update DIS_{tr} for c_{tr} (Sect. 4.5)
11:     **end if**
12: **end for**

Separate activation and dispatch processes are defined for each thread to specify the activation and dispatch behavior of the thread. AADL modal semantics is not considered here, so every thread has only one operational mode. Following parallel composition of ACT, DIS and COM processes represents the HCSP process corresponding to an AADL periodic thread.

$$ThrdName(period, deadline, bcet, wcet) \triangleq ACT^* \| DIS^* \| COM^*$$

Here, *period*, *deadline*, *bcet*, and *wcet* are process parameters to represent *Period*, *Deadline*, minimum and maximum *Compute_Execution_Time* properties respectively. Processes ACT, DIS and COM have repeating behavior and can only communicate through common channels.

Process ACT is used to specify the behavior of a thread which had already been initialized, activated and is ready for dispatch. Behavior of ACT process, as shown below, is quite simple. It only signalizes process DIS via output communication event *complete_act!*, which shows the execution completion of source code contained in a file associated with *Activate_Entrypoint_Source_Text* property of a thread.

$$ACT \triangleq complete\_act!$$

Below we explain dispatch (DIS) and compute (COM) processes in detail.

4.2   Dispatch Process

A periodic thread is dispatched after every fixed time interval specified in its *Period* property. The dispatch process for a periodic thread is specified as:

$DIS \triangleq complete\_act?; wait\ period; dispatch!dis; GetData(data); trans!data;$
$\qquad complete\_comp?$

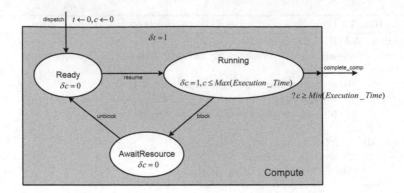

Fig. 4. Thread execution and actions in compute state

At the start, process *DIS* is ready to receive activation completion event from process *ACT*. Then it keeps idle for the period of the thread, after which it is ready to send dispatch event (*dis*) over channel *dispatch*. Thread execution completion event is received across channel *complete_comp* and after which the process is repeated again. Periodic thread inputs value from *in* data ports at dispatch time and outputs values to out data ports at completion time. Process *GetData* shows getting *data* from all *in* data ports at dispatch time. The data is then sent along channel *trans* to compute process (*COM*) which is explained below.

4.3   Compute Process

Compute process itself is a parallel composition of *Ready*, *Running*, and *AwaitResource* processes with clock variables c and t to be initialized at the start, as depicted in Fig. 4. Continuous evolution of variable t represents the total amount of time since the dispatch event received from the dispatch process while the continuous evolution of variable c specifies execution time in the current dispatch. Therefore, the clock t is always progressing in all the sub-states (represented by $\delta t = 1$), while c is only progressing in *Running* sub-state (represented by $\delta c = 1$).

Process *COM* below specifies behavior of a compute process. After the dispatch event, it first receives data x_2 along channel *trans*, then communications along tri_k for $k = 1, 2, 3$ are performed, not only to coordinate the execution order between the four parallel sub-processes, but also to transmit x_2 to processes *Ready*, *Running*, and *AwaitResource*. The boolean variable *isReady* indicates whether the ready state is enabled.

$$
\begin{aligned}
COM \triangleq\ & (dispatch?\mathrm{x};\ trans?x_2;\ tri_1!x_2;\ tri_2!x_2;\ tri_3!x_2) \\
& \|(tri_1?y_1;\ t := 0;\ isReady := 1;\ (isReady \rightarrow Ready)^*) \\
& \|(tri_2?y_2;\ c := 0;\ Running^*)\|(tri_3?y_3;\ AwaitResource^*)
\end{aligned}
$$

Thread execution in *Compute* state (see Fig. 4) is controlled by the scheduler modeled using AADL *processor* component. Detailed specification of the scheduling policies and protocols is beyond the scope of this paper as we are not aiming for schedulability analysis. Although, in this paper, we use a simplified static scheduler with predefined unique thread priorities assigned at design level, proposed semantics can be enhanced to model dynamic scheduling by adding a separate process to specify the respective behavior. Whenever the executing thread completes its execution or is blocked due to required resources, the processor is allocated to the highest priority thread in the *Ready* state (modeled as *Ready* process). Execution of the thread can only be interrupted due to required resources blocked by any other thread. This waiting for resource behavior is specified by *AwaitResource* process.

Process *Ready* maintains a continuous variable t to model the deadline of the thread. Continuous evolution of time t starts once a dispatch event is received from *DIS* process on *dispatch* channel by the parent process *COM*. After process *Ready* receives an event from the scheduler via *run* channel, indicating that current thread is ready to run, it then sends current value of time t via *resume* channel to process *Running*. After this communication, it is ready to accept the new value of t via *unblock* channel sent by *AwaitResouce* process. If the new value of t is equal to the *deadline*, the ready state is disabled, as a result the thread will need re-initialization and re-activation. The *Ready* process is specified as below:

$$Ready \triangleq \langle t = 1 \& t < deadline \rangle \unrhd (run? \rightarrow (resume!t; unblock?t));$$
$$t = deadline \rightarrow isReady := 0$$

Process *Running* maintains variable ct to record current time t sent by process *Ready* via *resume* channel, and variable c (defined in *COM* process) to record execution time. The boundary condition for continuous evolution is to check if c is less than or equal to WCET and ct is less than or equal to the deadline. Continuous evolution can be interrupted by an event from the scheduler along *res_busy* channel, indicating that the shared resource is blocked, then the *Running* process will send the current value of ct along *block* channel to *AwaitResource*. Continuous evolution can also be interrupted by an event to the scheduler along *complete_exec* channel, indicating the execution completion of the source code specified in a file associated with *Compute_Entrypoint_Source_Text* property of the thread in the dispatch. The *Running* process will then signal the successful execution completion along *complete_comp*! to process *DIS*. To ensure determinism, it is checked that the thread must execute at least till BCET otherwise it has to wait for $(bcet - c)$ time units. Process $SetData(x_r)$ represents the computation of new values x_r based on the received data y_2 (as shown in the parent *COM* process) and then sending new values to the out data ports. As an illustration, it is instantiated and explained in [18] in detail for our running example. The *Running* process is specified as below:

$$Running \triangleq resume?\,ct;\,\langle \dot{c} = 1, \dot{ct} = 1\&c \leq wcet \wedge ct \leq deadline\rangle \trianglerighteq$$
$$((res\_busy? \rightarrow block!ct)[(complete\_exec! \rightarrow (SetData(x_r);$$
$$complete\_comp! \rightarrow c < bcet \rightarrow wait\,(bcet - c))))$$

When an executing thread accesses a shared data component locked by any other thread, it is blocked. Such waiting behavior is specified by *AwaitResource* process. It receives current time via *block* channel from process *Running* and stores it in variable *act*. After it receives an event via *res_free* channel from the scheduler, indicating that the required resource is available, the current value of *act* is sent via *unblock* channel to *Ready* process. Below is the specification of *AwaitResource* process.

$$AwaitResource \triangleq block?\,act;\,\langle \dot{act} = 1\&act \leq deadline\,\rangle \trianglerighteq (res\_free? \rightarrow unblock!act);$$

The lock/un-clock mechanism of shared resources depends on the implementation strategies and does not affect analysis at architecture level so it is not discussed here.

4.4 Connection Process

The connection between two threads or between a thread and a device has an ultimate *source* and an ultimate *destination*. Synchronous communication in AADL is realized through periodic thread with data ports. Based on communication semantics explained in Sect. 2.3, the behavior of a connection is specified by

$$Conn_{tr} \triangleq StC?\,x_c;\,CtD!\,x_c.$$

StC is a communication channel between the source and the connection process (*Conn_{tr}* in this case). $StC?\,x_c$ shows input communication event ready to occur when the respective source thread completes its execution and is ready to send dispatch event, and moreover, receives the data x_c from the source state. The dispatch event together with the data x_c is sent across channel *CtD* to destination thread to start its execution.

For every connection $c_{tr} \in CON_{tr}$ in which thread *tr* is a source thread, the *Running* process is updated based on connection type: *immediate* or *delayed*. In case of immediate connection it sends the complete event on execution completion together with data x_r to connection process *Conn_{tr}* via *StC* as defined below.

$$Running_i \triangleq resume?\,ct;\,\langle \dot{c} = 1, \dot{ct} = 1\&c \leq wcet \wedge ct \leq deadline\rangle \trianglerighteq$$
$$... (SetData(x_r); complete\_comp! \rightarrow$$
$$c < bcet \rightarrow wait(bcet - c); StC!x_r) ...$$

The behavior of the *Running* process, in case of a source thread with delayed connection, is specified below, in which the completion event *complete_comp!*

together with data x_r is sent after the deadline.

$$Running_d \triangleq resume?ct; \langle \dot{c} = 1, \dot{ct} = 1 \& c \leq wcet \wedge ct \leq deadline \rangle \trianglerighteq \dots$$
$$(ct = deadline \rightarrow StC! \; x_r; complete\_comp!) \dots$$

For every connection $c_{tr} \in CON_{tr}$ in which tr is a destination thread, the respective *DIS* process is updated to wait for complete event with the data from the connection process $Conn_{tr}$ via *CtD* channel. As a result, process *DIS* does not need to specify the period of the thread. Instead, after the complete event with data z is received from channel *CtD*, the dispatch *dis* event is sent across channel *dispatch* which is received by respective *COM* process. The behavior of modified *DIS* process of a destination thread is specified as follows:

$$DIS \triangleq complete\_act?; CtD?z; dispatch!dis; GetData(data); trans!data; complete\_comp?$$

4.5   WLCS Hybrid System Modeling

The structure of the running example (WLCS) has been simplified to focus tightly on the elements needed to present a description of hybrid behavior of the system using plant and the controller while the internal behavior of the sensor and actuator is not discussed. So, connections $C1$ and $C2$ in Fig. 3 are specified as channel *wl* and connections $C3$ and $C4$ are mapped to channel *cc* resulted in a cyber-physical interaction supported by HA. HA uses ports to communicate with other AADL component and channels for internal process communication. Both of these communication mechanisms are mapped as channel communications for verification in terms of HCSP. The hybrid system of the running example (WLCS as whole), as specified below, is modeled as parallel composition of the *WaterTank* and the *Controller*.

$$\begin{aligned}
WLCS & \triangleq Watertank \| Controller \\
Watertank & \triangleq (t := 0; Plant)^* \\
Plant & \triangleq \langle \dot{h} = v \cdot Q_{max} - \pi \cdot r^2 \cdot \sqrt{2 \cdot g \cdot h}, v = 0 \& t < 0.01 \rangle \\
& \trianglerighteq wl! \; h \rightarrow cc?v; \\
Controller & \triangleq get\_data \| Conn \| com\_cmd
\end{aligned}$$

Behavior of the *WaterTank* is specified in Listing 1 and the behavior of *Controller* is obtained by applying the translation approach explained in Algorithm 1 to the AADL model of Fig. 3. The process Controller is composed of three subprocesses: *get_data*, *Conn*, and *com_cmd* executing in parallel. These processes specify behavior of thread *get_data*, immediate connection *Conn* and thread *com_cmd* respectively.

The complete HCSP model of the running example, along with parameters (obtained from respective AADL properties) and details of the subprocesses *get_data*, *Conn*, and *com_cmd*, are presented in [18]. As HA is based on HCSP so each notation of HA automatically corresponds to a respective HCSP notation.

5   Verification Using HHL Prover

In this section, we show how to use HHL prover to formally verify an AADL model with HA specification through the running example WLCS.

The main goal of WLCS is to maintain water level h between a specified limit which is 0.30 m to 0.60 m, by controlling the inflow valve v to be close or open. The control algorithm of the system is designed as follows: every 0.01 s, the controller samples the value of h, and when h is greater than 0.59 m, it assigns value 0 to v, while when h is less than 0.31 m, v assigned value 1. We can investigate the safety of the WLCS system from two aspects:

– it is deadlock-free, under the assumption that the scheduler is well-behaved
– the property $0.30 \le h \le 0.60$ always holds for the WLCS system

The deadlock-freedom can be checked by some existing CSP checkers, like the known CSP tool FDR. Here we focus on the verification of the second property, which is mostly related to the hybrid behavior of the system. Thus, we abstract away various communications for synchronizing AADL components, and obtain a simplified controller for the WLCS system with the same control behavior as the *Controller* in the translated HCSP model:

$$Controller = (\text{wait } period; \ wl?x; x \ \le \ 0.31 \ \rightarrow \ y := 1; x \ge 0.59 \rightarrow \ y := 0; cc!y)^*$$

where *period* is 0.01 s as mentioned above. The resulting model for the WLCS system covers the continuous plant, the controller containing the corresponding control algorithm, and the interactions between them.

By applying the HHL prover, we have proved the following specification for the WLCS system:

$$\{t = 0 \wedge h = 0.31 \wedge v = 1, y = 0 \vee y = 1\} \ WLCS$$
$$\{0.30 \le h \le 0.60, True; \lceil 0.30 \le h \le 0.60 \rceil, True\}$$

indicating that from the initial state when t is 0 s, h is 0.31 m and v is *open*, throughout the execution of *WLCS*, the safety requirement $0.30 \le h \le 0.60$ always holds for the water tank.

6   Related Work

Formalization of AADL has been explored a lot. Here we summerize some of the important work. Yang et al [15] have formalized BA by translating it into Time Abstract State Machine (TASM). Process algebra interpretation of AADL models is presented in [11]. They have translated AADL models to process algebra ACSR and Real-Time Calculus (RTC) for performance evaluation using VERSA and RTC Toolbox respectively. COMPASS toolset used a variant of AADL called SLIM and SuSMv model checker for safety, dependability and performance evaluation [4]. In [6], a tool called AADL2BIP based on BIP (Behavior Interaction Priority) for safety property verification has been introduced.

Considerable amount of efforts are made to formalize AADL, but most of them are focused on control systems with discrete behavior. To our best knowledge, formalization of the continuous time modeling based on a dedicated annex has not been explored before. The proposed formal semantics based on language purely designed for hybrid system is novel and the first step to enhance AADL modeling and formal analysis capabilities for systems with both discrete and continuous dynamics.

There have been a number of modeling languages proposed for formalizing hybrid systems. The most popular is hybrid automata [1,2], with real-time temporal logics interpreted on their behaviors as specification languages. However, analogous to state machines, hybrid automata provides little support for structured description and composition. As an alternative approach, Platzer [3] proposed hybrid programs and the related differential dynamic logic for the compositional modeling and deductive verification of hybrid systems. However, in his work, parallelism and communication were not well handled, that occur ubiquitously in AADL models.

Based on HA for continuous behavior modeling and AADL core for discrete modeling, our approach of defining formal semantics for verification is scalable and can be used to verify complex HSs.

7   Conclusion and Future Work

The AADL with Hybrid Annex can model continuous behavior of the physical process to be monitored and controlled by the control system. Formal semantics, based on HCSP, of synchronous subset of AADL annotated with Hybrid Annex are presented to furnish AADL for modeling and verification of hybrid systems. The application of the Hybrid Annex for modeling and formal semantics for verification is illustrated through a benchmark of hybrid system, i.e., the example of water level control system. AADL model is verified using an in-house developed theorem prover called HHL prover. Being the first step towards formalization of continuous behavior and cyber-physical interaction modeling and verification using AADL, this study has opened new horizon for research in AADL.

Our future work includes enhancement of the current approach to cover asynchronous subset of AADL which is based on aperiodic thread with event-driven communication models and the development of a plug-in to Open-Source AADL Tool Environment (OSATE), the development environment for AADL modeling, for automatic translation of AADL models (with Hybrid Annex specifications) to HCSP processes and verification using HHL prover.

Acknowledgements. The work has been partly supported by the National Basic Research Program of China under Grant No. 2014CB340700, by Natural Science Foundation of China under Grant No. NSFC-91118007 and NSFC-6110006, by the CAS/SAF-EA International Partnership Program for Creative Research Teams, and by the National Infrastructure Software Plan under Grant No. 2012ZX01041-002-003.

References

1. Alur, R., Courcoubetis, C., Henzinger, T., Ho, P.: Hybrid automata: an algorithmic approach to the specification and verification of hybrid systems. In: Grossman, R.L., Ravn, A.P., Rischel, H., Nerode, A. (eds.) HS 1991 and HS 1992. LNCS, vol. 736, pp. 209–229. Springer, Heidelberg (1993)
2. Manna, Z., Pnueli, A.: Verifying hybrid systems. In: Grossman, R.L., Ravn, A.P., Rischel, H., Nerode, A. (eds.) HS 1991 and HS 1992. LNCS, vol. 736, pp. 4–35. Springer, Heidelberg (1993)
3. Platzer, A.: Differential dynamic logic for hybrid systems. J. Autom. Reason. 41(2), 143–189 (2008)
4. Bozzano, M., Cimatti, A., Katoen, J.-P., Nguyen, V.Y., Noll, T., Roveri, M., Wimmer, R.: A model checker for AADL. In: Touili, T., Cook, B., Jackson, P. (eds.) CAV 2010. LNCS, vol. 6174, pp. 562–565. Springer, Heidelberg (2010)
5. Zhou, C., Wang, J., Ravn, A.: A formal description of hybrid systems. In: Alur, R., Sontag, E.D., Henzinger, T.A. (eds.) HS 1995. LNCS, vol. 1066, pp. 511–530. Springer, Heidelberg (1996)
6. Chkouri, M.Y., Robert, A., Bozga, M., Sifakis, J.: Translating AADL into BIP - application to the verification of real-time systems. In: Chaudron, M.R.V. (ed.) MODELS 2008. LNCS, vol. 5421, pp. 5–19. Springer, Heidelberg (2009)
7. Henzinger, T.A., Sifakis, J.: The embedded systems design challenge. In: Misra, J., Nipkow, T., Sekerinski, E. (eds.) FM 2006. LNCS, vol. 4085, pp. 1–15. Springer, Heidelberg (2006)
8. He, J.: From CSP to hybrid systems. In: Roscoe, A.W. (ed.) A Classical Mind, pp. 171–189. Prentice Hall, Hertfordshire (1994)
9. Lee, E.: What's ahead for embedded software? IEEE Comput. 33(9), 18–26 (2000)
10. Liu, J., Lv, J., Quan, Z., Zhan, N., Zhao, H., Zhou, C., Zou, L.: A calculus for hybrid CSP. In: Ueda, K. (ed.) APLAS 2010. LNCS, vol. 6461, pp. 1–15. Springer, Heidelberg (2010)
11. Sokolsky, O., Lee, I., Clarke, D.: Process-algebraic interpretation of AADL models. In: Kordon, F., Kermarrec, Y. (eds.) Ada-Europe 2009. LNCS, vol. 5570, pp. 222–236. Springer, Heidelberg (2009)
12. SAE Internatinal, Architecture Analysis & Design Language (AADL) Annex Volume 2: Annex D: Behavior Annex, SAE International Standards (2011)
13. SAE International, Aarchitecture Analysis & Design Language (AADL), revision: B, SAE International Standards (2012)
14. Larson, R.B., Chalin, P., Hatcliff, J.: BLESS: formal specification and verification of behaviors for embedded systems with software. In: Brat, G., Rungta, N., Venet, A. (eds.) NFM 2013. LNCS, vol. 7871, pp. 276–290. Springer, Heidelberg (2013)
15. Yang, Z., Kai, H., Ma, D., Lei, P.: Towards a formal semantics for the AADL behavior annex. In: Proceedings of DATE 2009, pp. 1166–1171 (2009)
16. Zhan, N., Wang, S., Zhao, H.: Formal modelling, analysis and verification of hybrid systems. In: Liu, Z., Woodcock, J., Zhu, H. (eds.) Unifying Theories of Programming and Formal Engineering Methods. LNCS, vol. 8050, pp. 207–281. Springer, Heidelberg (2013)
17. Ahmad, E., Larson, R.B., Barrett, C.S., Zhan, N., Dong, Y.: Hybrid annex: An AADL extension for continuous behavior and cyber-physical interaction modeling. In: Proceedings of HILT 2014, pp. 29–38 (2014)

18. Ahmad, E., Dong, Y., Wang, S., Zhan, N., Zou, L.: Adding formal meanings to AADL with hybrid annex, Technical report ISCAS-SKLCS-14-09, State key Lab. of Computer Science, Institute of Software, Chinese Academy of Sciences, Beijing 100190. China (2014)
19. Zou, L., Lv, J., Wang, S., Zhan, N., Tang, T., Yuan, L., Liu, Y.: Verifying chinese train control system under a combined scenario by theorem proving. In: Cohen, E., Rybalchenko, A. (eds.) VSTTE 2013. LNCS, vol. 8164, pp. 262–280. Springer, Heidelberg (2014)

Component-Based Modeling and Observer-Based Verification for Railway Safety-Critical Applications

Marc Sango[1,2](✉), Laurence Duchien[2], and Christophe Gransart[1]

[1] IFSTTAR, COSYS/LEOST, 59650 Villeneuve-d'Ascq, France
{marc.sango,christophe.gransart}@ifsttar.fr
[2] INRIA Lille-Nord Europe, LIFL CNRS UMR 8022, University of Lille 1,
59650 Villeneuve-d'Ascq, France
laurence.duchien@inria.fr

Abstract. One of the challenges that engineers face, during the development process of safety-critical systems, is the verification of safety application models before implementation. Formalization is important in order to verify that the design meets the specified safety requirements. In this paper, we formally describe the set of transformation rules, which are defined for the automatic transformation of safety application source models to timed automata target models. The source models are based on our domain-specific component model, named SARA, dedicated to SAfety-critical RAilway control applications. The target models are then used for the observer-based verification of safety requirements. This method provides an intuitive way of expressing system properties without requiring a significant knowledge of higher order logic and theorem proving, as required in most of existing approaches. An experimentation over a chosen benchmark at rail-road crossing protection application is shown to highlight the proposed approach.

Keywords: Software component · Timed automata · Transformation · Verification · Safety-critical applications

1 Introduction

Safety-critical systems must conform to safety standards defined by domain standardizations, such as the European standard of software for railway control and protection systems, EN 50128 [8]. This is why one of the challenges that engineers face, during the development process of safety-critical systems, is the verification of safety application models before implementation. Over the last few years, the complexity of safety applications has increased. Then the modeling and formalization of safety applications is becoming a very difficult task.

Component-Based Software Engineering (CBSE) is a possible software modeling solution. It is an established approach for modeling a complex software and for facilitating integration by a third party [20]. There are several research works that facilitate component-based development in general or in domain-specific

© Springer International Publishing Switzerland 2015
I. Lanese and E. Madelaine (Eds.): FACS 2014, LNCS 8997, pp. 248–266, 2015.
DOI: 10.1007/978-3-319-15317-9_16

purposes [2,5,10,21]. In this paper, we use our domain-specific component model, named SARA, dedicated to the development of SAfety-critical RAilway control applications [17]. The objective of our approach consists in modeling and enforcing dependability requirements during the development process of safety-critical applications in order to facilitate their certification process.

On the other hand, design models have to be mapped to formal models for automatic verification. In this work, we focus on verification approaches that take advantage of the flexibility of reliable component models and analysis facilities offered by formal models in order to satisfy timing requirements. There are several research works that propose the transformation of informal or semi-formal models into formal models, which are supported by available verification tools [1,4,15]. For example, for the safety of rail-road protection systems, Mekki et al. use the model-driven architecture approach to systematically transform the UML state machine into the Timed Automata (TA) in order to validate some temporal requirements [15]. In this approach, the three-tier approach for the composition of pre-verified components is not explicitly considered. Based on pre-defined formal models of source and target models, Soliman et al. transform the function block diagram to the Uppaal timed automata [19]. In the same way, Bhatti et al. suggest an approach for the verification of IEC 61499 function block applications by using the observer-based verification [4].

In this paper, we focus on the transformation phase from our SARA model to the TA model, which is one of the most popular models adapted for the verification of timing properties [3]. The transformation algorithm consists of transformation rules. Both the source and the target domain models have been formally defined. Then, these formal definitions are used for the definition of transformation rules. The target models and the timing requirement observers are next used for the observer-based verification of safety applications. This method provides an intuitive way of expressing system properties without requiring a significant knowledge of higher order logic and theorem proving, as required in most of the existing approaches [4]. Indeed, users can use predefined observer patterns or can enhance them for their verification tasks.

The remainder of this paper is organized as follows. In Sect. 2, we motivate our approach by an example of rail-road crossing protection system. In Sect. 3, we give an overview of the suggested process of modeling and verification. In Sect. 4, we introduce the formal definitions of the SARA component model and the formal definitions in terms of the TA formalism. Then, based on these definitions, the transformation rules are defined. In Sect. 5, based on a use case of our motivating example, the observer patterns of some safety requirements are presented. These observer models are synchronized with the use case model to do the verification. Finally, we discuss related works in Sect. 6 before concluding and pointing out future directions of our research in Sect. 7.

2   Motivating Example

Our approach is motivated by using a rail-road intersection protection system. Figure 1 presents an implementation of a rail-road level crossing control application by using software components. Note that, in this section, we focus on its global description. The elements, component types and component connections types will be detailed in Sect. 4.1. The component *Sensor* embedded in the train reads information from track sensors to detect an approaching and an exiting of trains in the monitored intersection. This information is translated into a sequence of events *appr* and *exit* depending on the distance *dist* of trains from the intersection. The intersection gate is operated through the *Gate* component which closes or opens the gate. The *Gate* component responds to events by moving barriers *up* or *down*. The component *Controller* acts as a mediator between the other two components. It receives events from the sensor component and decides to open or not the gate to road traffic.

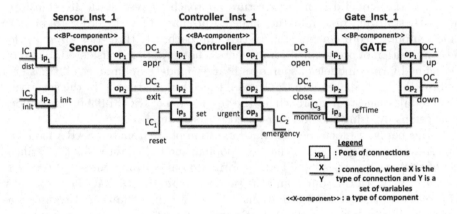

Fig. 1. The example of SARA components

For example, when the approach signal *appr* is received (respectively *exit*), the component instance *Controller_Inst_1* sends immediately a *close* signal (respectively *open*) to the gate instance *Gate_Inst_1*. In general, the behavior of controller instance depends on operation rules, i.e., in some operation scenarios. In fact, railway level crossing behavior depends generally on the national operation rules [22]. But in most European countries, the automatic protection system gives absolute or relative priority to railway traffic, while preventing road users from crossing whenever a train is approaching [15]. In this work, we use an adapted use case, which is presented in detail in Sect. 5.

It is possible that the interaction of components in Fig. 1 results in the violation of system safety requirements specification, such as:

Requirement 1: "the gate must be down whenever a train is inside the rail-road crossing section" (adapted from [4]);

Requirement 2: "when the gate is opened to road traffic, it must stay open at least T_{min} time units, where T_{min} represents the minimum desired period of time separating two successive closing cycles of gate" (adapted from [15]);

Requirement 3: "once closed and when there is no train approaching meanwhile, the gate must be kept closed at least (T_{begin}) and at most (T_{end}), where T_{begin} and T_{end} are the time limits prescribed" (adapted from [15]).

The above application architecture and these safety requirements under verification are used throughout the rest of the paper.

3   Overview

Figure 2 shows the schematic structure of our component-based modeling and observer-based verification approach. It is composed of two development paths and one verification tool.

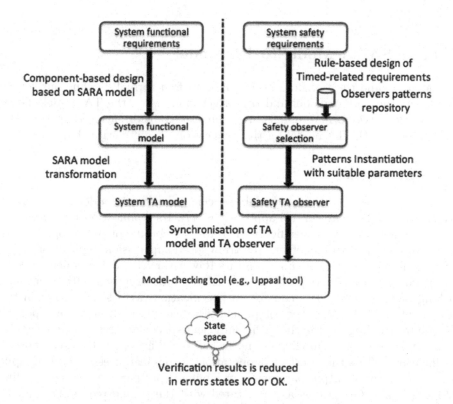

Fig. 2. Our methodology

The path on the left of Fig. 2 represents the system functional development path. It is responsible for performing the functional requirements. Functional requirements are modeled according to a component-based paradigm. In this paper, we use our SARA component model. Then, this model is translated into the TA formal model. One of the main parts of our method is the transformation of the SARA model to the TA model, as detailed in Sect. 4. The result of this path is a system TA model.

The path on the right of Fig. 2 represents the system safety development path. It is responsible for monitoring safety requirements. Generally, safety requirements depend on operation rules developed with a rule-based paradigm. For each safety requirement, the appropriate observation pattern is selected from the generic patterns and then instantiated to produce a corresponding safety requirement observer, as detailed in Sect. 5. The result of this development path is a safety TA observer.

In the end, the safety TA observers instantiated are synchronized with the system TA model obtained to generate a system global TA model. Then, by using a verification tool (e.g., Uppaal model checkers), the verification task is reduced to a reachability search of an error or no-error states (KO or OK states) on the global TA model.

4   From SARA Model to TA Model

In order to define the transformation rules, we first formally define our source model, i.e., the SARA model and the target model, i.e., the TA model. Then, based on these two formal models, we define the transformation rules from the SARA model to the TA model for the verification of safety-critical applications.

4.1   SARA Model

SARA component model is a domain-specific component model dedicated to SAfety-critical RAilway control applications [17]. Its Application Programming Interface (API), which is specified with Ravenscar profile of Ada programming language, is defined to implement the train speed supervision application [16].

According to the SARA model and its Ravenscar API, a component specification is defined as an entity which encapsulates data structures with operations working on these data. The component specification (a) is separated from the component body (b), from the component instance (c) and from the component runtime (d) (see Fig. 3). Firstly, each component specification is distinguished by a unique name (e.g., CompTypeName in line 1 of Fig. 3.(a)). Each component specification defines the interface of operations for its instances by a set of input parameters, a set of output parameters or input/output parameters (e.g., see line 10 in Fig. 3.(a)). Operations are annotated with the timing requirement annotations (e.g., see lines 12–15 in Fig. 3.(a)). These annotations can be checked, as illustrated in Fig. 3.(d) with the Ada language annotations checking tool [9]. However, tasks and synchronization are not currently permitted in this tool.

Secondly, in the body of components, the behavior of component instances is defined by users (e.g., see lines 5–6 Fig. 3.(b)). Thirdly, SARA application, i.e., a top-level component named SARAProg, built from others connected components, can only be instantiated when the required resources are present (e.g., see lines 17–18 in Fig. 3.(c)), while components can only be instantiated within

(a)
```
1 package CompTypeName is
2   — Component type:
3   type CompType is new Sara.Comps↩
        with record
4     Time_Var : Integer ;
5     Train_Pos: Float ;
6   end record ;
7   — other data:
8   Tmax : constant Integer := 15;
9   — operations:
10  Procedure Op (C : in out ↩
        CompType)
11  — operation annotations:
12  with
13  pre => (C.Time_Var = 0),
14  Post => (C.Time_Var <= Tmax
15      and then C.Train_Pos=10.0);
16 end CompTypeName;
```

(b)
```
1 package body ↩
      CompTypeName is
2   Procedure Op (C : in↩
        out CompType) ↩
      is
3   begin
4     — user defined ↩
          behavior: e.g.,
5     C.Time_Var := 10;
6     C.Train_Pos := 12.0;
7   end Op;
8 end CompTypeName;
```

(c)
```
1  with CompTypeName;
2  Procedure SARAProg — Top-level component
3    — prog input parameters:
4    Train_Init : Integer := 0;
5    Train_X_Coord : Float := 0.0;
6    — prog component instances:
7    CompInst : Sara.Prog.CompType :=
8    (Time_Var => Train_Init ,
9     Train_Pos => Train_X_Coord);
10   — program component execution:
11   package Defined_Task is new Sara.↩
          Periodic_Task
12        (Comp_Type => Sara.Prog.CompType,
13         Comp_Inst => Sara.Prog.CompInst ,
14         Priority => 1, Period => 0.010,
15         Provided_Op => CompTypeName.Op);
16   — program resources:
17   use Defined_Task;
18   use Ada.Calendar; — or Ada.Real_Time
19   Start , Finish : Time;
20 begin
21   Start := Clock; — get system start time
22   ...
23 end SARAProg;
```

(d)

```
macbook-pro-de-christophe-gransart:test marcsango$ gnatprove -P SARAProg.gpr --report=all
Phase 1 of 3: frame condition computation ...
Phase 2 of 3: translation to intermediate language ...
Statistics logged in /Users/marcsango/Documents/papers/FACS-2014/test/gnatprove/gnatprove.out
(detailed info can be found in /Users/marcsango/Documents/papers/FACS-2014/test/gnatprove/*.alfa)
Phase 3 of 3: generation and proof of VCs ...
analyzing SARAProg, 1 checks
saraprog.adb:13:16: info: precondition proved
analyzing CompTypeName.Op, 1 checks
comptypename.ads:15:15: postcondition not proved
analyzing precondition for CompTypeName.Op, 0 checks
```

Fig. 3. (a) Specification (b) Body (c) Instance (d) run-time checks

an application or other components (e.g.; see lines 7–15 in Fig. 3.(c)). Finally, Fig. 3.(d) shows the screen shot of the runtime execution and runtime annotation checking of our application implementation based on SARA component model.

More formally, the SARA component model is defined as follows.

Definition 1 (SARAProg). A SARA program is defined as a tuple SARA-Prog = (ProgName, IP, OP, LV, CV, IO, ProgBody), where:

- ProgName is the name of the program, which is defined by its developer;
- IP is a set of input parameters, which enter the input ports of program components, e.g., IP = $\{dist, init, reset, monitorT\}$ in Fig. 1;
- OP is a set of output parameters, which exit the output ports of program components, e.g., OP = $\{up, down, emergency\}$ in Fig. 1;
- LV is a set of local variables of this program. For technical reasons, we assume that all the local variables of program components occur somewhere in the program structure. e.g., LV = $\{init, set, urgent, refTime\}$ in Fig. 1;
- CV is a set of clock variables that monitor the time, e.g., CV = $\{monitorT\}$.
- IO is a set of input/ouput variables of the program body, e.g., IO = $\{approach, exit, close, open\}$ $\cup$ IP $\cup$ OP $\cup$ LV $\cup$ CV in Fig. 1;
- ProgBody is a SARA program body. It is defined as a set of component instances which are interconnected using variables. The connections of component instances are defined as a program configurations, ProgConfigs (Definition 2).

Definition 2 (ProgConfig). A program component configuration is defined as a tuple ProgConfig = (CompInsts, CompConnects), where

- CompInsts is a set of component instances (see Definition 3),
- CompConnects is a set of component connections (see Definition 5).

Definition 3 (CompInst). A component Instance is defined as a tuple (Inst-Name, CompTypeName, Priority), where:

- InstName is a user defined name of specific instance of a component type;
- CompTypeName is the name of the corresponding component type, Comp-Type (see Definition 4);
- Priority is an integer that defines the execution order of component instances in the context of the component configuration. For instance, the execution order of Fig. 1 is: Gate_Inst_1 < Controller_Inst_1 < Sensor_Inst_1. This means that Sensor_Inst_1 has a highest priority than Controller_Inst_1 and Controller_Inst_1 has a highest priority than Gate_Inst_1.

Definition 4 (CompType). A component type is defined as a tuple Comp-Type = (CompTypeName, IP, OP, LV, Annotation, CompBody), where:

- CompTypeName is the name of the component type, which is defined by its developer. We distinguish two kinds of component type: active and passive components. An active component has its own dedicated thread of execution.

While a passive component is directly processed in the context of the calling thread of an active component. Note that a component is either a basic component or a hierarchical component. A hierarchical component contains other components that can be themselves hierarchical or basic (e.g. SARAprog of Fig. 3 (c) that contains basic component instances of Fig. 1). Whereas, a basic component directly encapsulates behavior (e.g., in Fig. 1, BP-component is a basic passive component, and BA-component is a basic active component);

- IP $= \{ip_1, ip_2, ..., ip_n\}$ is a set of input ports;
- OP $= \{op_1, op_2, ..., op_n\}$ is a set of output ports;
- LV is a set of local variables of this component type;
- Annotation is a time annotation of component body operations, e.g., see lines 12-15 of Fig. 3 (a);
- CompBody defines the behavior of instances of component type. The body can be written in any programming language. For example, we use the Ada programming language, e.g., see Fig. 3 (b).

Definition 5 (CompConnect). A component connection is defined as a set of four types of connection, CompConnect = {DC, IC, LC, OC}, where:

- DC is a set of direct connections between IP of component instances and OP of component instances. It is defined as:
  - $DC_n : InstName_i.op_j \rightarrow InstName_k.ip_l$,
  - e.g., $DC_1 : Sensor\_Inst\_1.op_1 \rightarrow Controller\_Inst\_1.ip_1$ in Fig. 1;
- IC is a set of connections that connect input parameters $ip_j \in IP$ of SARA-Prog to an input port $ip_l \in IP$ of kth component instance or to a program local variable $lv_k \in LV$. It is defined as:
  - $IC_n: ProgName.ip_j \rightarrow InstName_k.ip_l$, or
  - $IC_n: ProgName.ip_j \rightarrow ProgName.vl_k$,
  - e.g., $IC_1 : dist \rightarrow Sensor\_Inst\_1.ip_1$ in Fig. 1 or
  - e.g.,: $IC_2 : init \rightarrow Sensor\_Inst\_1.init$ in Fig. 1;
- LC is a set of connections that involves local variables of a program that do not occur in IC. A local variable $lv_i \in LV$ of SARAProg may be connected to an input port $ip_j \in IP$ of the kth component instance, an output port $op_l \in OP$ of the kth component instance or an output parameters $op_m \in OP$ of SARAProg. It is defined as:
  - $LC_n: ProgName.lv_i \rightarrow InstName_k.ip_j$, or
  - $LC_n: InstName_k.op_l \rightarrow ProgName.lv_i$, or
  - $LC_n: ProgName.lv_i \rightarrow ProgName.op_m$
  - e.g., $LC_1 : reset \rightarrow Controller\_Inst\_1.set$, or
  - e.g., $LC_2: Controller\_Inst\_1.op_3 \rightarrow emergency$ in Fig. 1;
- OC is a set of output connections between $op_i \in OP$ of the kth component instance and output variables $op_j \in OP$ of SARAProg. It is defined as: $OC_n : InstName_k.op_i \rightarrow ProgName.op_j$, e.g.: $OC_1 : Gate\_Inst\_1.op_1 \rightarrow up$ in Fig. 1.

4.2   Time Annotations

In this section, we provide predefined time annotations, which are used to anno-
tate our component operations (e.g., lines 12–15 in Fig. 3.(a)). This predefi-
nition facilitates the expression of timing constraints commonly used. While
analysing various types of common temporal requirement classifications [7,12],
we found out that most of requirements can be expressed either as a set of
obligation rules or as a set of interdiction rules. Table 1 shows some examples of
timing response obligation annotations and their descriptions. Generally, in common temporal requirements, an event e, named here *monitored event e* should
occur permanently or temporarily in response to a stimulus event, named here
referenced event e′.

Table 1. Time annotations

Time annotations	Descriptions
$between(e, T_{begin}, T_{end}, i, e')$	Ensures that a monitored event e must occur within a temporal interval $[T_{begin}, T_{end}]$ after the ith occurrence of referenced event e'
$mindelay(e, T_{min}, i, e')$	Ensures that a monitored event e must occur after a minimum delay T_{min} time unit after the ith occurrence of referenced event e'
$maxdelay(e, T_{max}, i, e')$	Ensures that a monitored event e must occur before a maximum delay T_{max} time unit after the ith occurrence of event e'
$exactdelay(e, T, i, e')$	Ensures that a monitored event e must occur exactly at a delay T time unit after the ith occurrence of event e'

In this paper, we also give to users the possibility to express requirements
that refer not only to the timed interval relatively to a given event, but also to
the occurrence i^{th} of this event appearance. For example, stating only the timed
obligation pattern (e.g., *event e* **must occur after** *event e′*) is ambiguous since
the assertion does not specify the response time limit within which e may occur
after e'. In addition, it does not specify if e may occur after the first or the
last occurrence of e'. However, affirming that *event e* **must occur before a**
maximum delay of 3 time units after the first occurrence *of event e′*
avoid confusion. In this example, the assertion obtained is identified in Table 1
as the $maxdelay(e, T_{max}, 1, e')$ annotation, where $T_{max} = 3$ time units (e.g.,
seconds) and $i = 1^{th}$, i.e., the first occurrence of e'.

The goal of these timed annotations is to guide users during the modeling
in order to produce a clear and accurate description, while manipulating simple
and precise concepts.

4.3   TA Model

Timed Automata (TA) is one of the most popular models adapted to real-time system [3]. First, TA models are well adapted for the verification of time properties for real-time components because temporal requirements are explicitly modeled by using state invariants, transition guards and setting or resetting clock variables. Second, a number of methods based on variants of the TA model (or other similar models such as timed Petri nets) have been proposed [11,13,14]. In this paper, we use timed automata over input or output actions, called the Timed Automata with Inputs and Outputs (TAIO) [13]. Finally, a number of automatic model checker tools for TA have been efficiently developed, e.g., Uppaal [14] and Kronos [24]. In this work, we use Uppaal as one of these tools for the verification process. It offers a convenient graphical user interface for simulation. In the following the TA system, based on Uppaal TA system, is defined to facilitate the transformation process of the SARA model. This means that all parts which are not used by the transformation process are not included in the definitions.

Definition 6 (TASys). A TA verification system can be defined as a tuple TA = (TAModels, TADeclarations), where:

- TAModels is a set of all TA models used in a system global model. In this work, every TA model is defined according to TAIO (see Definition 7);
- TADeclarations is the declaration part that contains all input/output variables of all component instances and all input/output/local variables of the program (see Definition 10).

Definition 7 (TAModel). A TA model is defined as a tuple TAModel = (TAName, TASyntax, TASemantic), where:

- TAName is the name of the TA model which appears in the system declarations part to arrange priorities on TAModels;
- TASyntax is the syntax of the state-transition description of TAIO extended with boolean and integer variables (see Definition 8);
- TASemantic is the semantic (see Definition 9).

Definition 8 (TASyntax). TAIO is represented by the tuple A = (L, l_0, V, Act, Clock, Inv, T), where:

- L is a finite set of locations;
- $l_0 \in L$ is the initial location;
- V = $V_{bool} \cup V_{int} \cup V_{act} \cup V_{const} \cup V_{clock}$ is a finite set of variables (boolean, bounded integer, channel, constant or clock) declared in the TADeclarations part (see Definition 10);
- Act = $V_{act} \times \{!, ?\}$ is a set of synchronization actions over channel variables V_{act}. It is the partitioned set of input and output actions, $Act = Act_{in} \cup Act_{out}$. Input actions are denoted a?, b?, etc., and output actions are denoted a!, b!, etc.;
- Clock is a finite set of real-valued clocks, $\{x_1, x_2, ..., x_n\}$;

- Inv is a function, that assigns an invariant to each location. $Inv(V_{clock}, V_{int})$ is the set of invariants over clocks $x_j \in Clock$ and integer variables $c \in V_{int}$;
- T is a finite set of edges for transitions.

  Each edge T is a tuple (l, g, r, a, l'), where:

- $l, l' \in L$ are respectively the source and destination locations;
- g is a set of time constraints of the form $x \bullet c$, where $x \in Clock$ is a clock variable, $c \in V_{const}$ is an integer constant and $\bullet \in \{<, \leq, =, \geq, >\}$;
- $r \in Clock$ is a set of clocks to reset to zero, $(r := 0$, where 0 is the initial valuation of the clock);
- $a \in Act$ is a set of actions to update $(a := b$, where b is another action).

Definition 9 (TASemantic). The semantic of A = (L, l_0, V, Act, Clock, Inv, T) is defined by the Timed Labeled Transition System (TLTS) [13]. TLTS is a tuple (S, s_0, Act, T_d, T_t), where:

- $S = L \times \mathbb{R}_+^X$ is a set of timed states associated to locations of A;
- $s_0 = (q_0, \mathbf{0})$ is the initial state. $\mathbf{0}$ is the valuation assigning 0 to every clock $x \in Clock$ of A;
- T_d is a set of discrete transitions of the form $(s, a, s') = (s', v) \xrightarrow{a} (s', v')$, where $a \in Act$ and there is an edge $E = (l, g, r, a, l',)$, such that v satisfies g and v' is obtained by resetting to zero all clocks in r and leaving the others unchanged; where $t \in \mathbb{R}_+$. T_t must be deterministic.

Definition 10 (TADeclarations). In order to facilitate the transformation process of SARA model to TA model, TADeclarations are partitioned to a TA model declaration part (TAModelDecl) and to a system model declaration part (TASysDecl). TAModelDecl = (dataType, variableName, value), where: - *dataType* is a set of project-specific data types. In this work, we use the Uppaal declaration types: constant, boolean, bounded integer, channels, array or clock; - *variableName* represents the name of the variable and - *value* is considered either the initial value or the constant according to the data type.

TASysDecl defines the execution order by assigning priority to TA models. For example in the example of Fig. 1, input connections (e.g., IC_1) have the highest priority, followed by component instances (e.g., Controller_Inst_1), followed by other connection types according to the execution order defined (e.g., DC_1) and finally followed by output connections (e.g., OC_1).

4.4   Transformation Rules

This sub-section presents the transformation rules developed to translate SARA application models to TA models. They are based on the above SARA and TA formal models.

Rule 1 (mapping of declarations). The objective of this rule is to transform the input and output variables of each component instance (CompInst) and all the variables declared in the SARA program (SARAProg) into TA declaration parts (TADeclarations). It is composed of two parts:

- **Rule 1.1.** For each CompInst = ($InstName_i$, CompTypeName, Priority), where CompType = (CompTypeName, IP, OP, LV, Annotation, CompBody), insert $ip_j \in IP_i$ and $op_j \in OP_i$ in TADeclarations, where $i = 1, 2, ..., n$ and n is the number of CompType instances, as shown in the left hand of Fig. 4;
- **Rule 1.2.** For each *ProgName* of SARAProg, where $ip_m \in IP$, $op_n \in OP$ and $lv_p \in LV$ insert corresponding variables in TADeclarations, as shown in the right hand of Fig. 4.

//Sensor_Inst_1 of Fif. 1 TA declaration	*//Fig1. program TA declaration*
Const int N = 2; // number of trains	*int dist;*
typedef int[0,N-1] id; // bounded integer,	*bool init;*
clock x1, x2, x3; // sensor clock variables	*bool reset;*
int ip_1_list_for_dist[N];	*...*
bool ip_2_list_for_init[N];	*...*
chan op_1_channel_for_approach[N];	*bool up;*
chan op_2_channel_for_exit[N];	*bool down;*

Fig. 4. Example of Fig. 1 TAdeclarations

Rule 2 (mapping of CompInsts). The objective of this rule is to transform CompInsts to TAModels. For each CompInst = (InstName, CompTypeName, Priority), where CompType = (CompTypeName, IP, OP, LV, Annotation, CompBody), insert the corresponding TAModel to TASys with TAName = InstName by using a user predefined TAModel library and by taking into account the annotations in order to add the suitable state invariants and transition guards according to rule 4. For example, see Fig. 7, which corresponds to our use case TAModel corresponding to the three component instances of Fig. 1.

Rule 3 (Mapping of annotations). This rule is invoked from rule 3 when a component type contains time annotations as shown in Table 1, and illustrated in lines 12–15 of Fig. 3 (a). These annotations are translated into boolean conditions in TASyst by respecting the TASemantic shown in Definition 8.

Rule 4 (mapping of connections). The objective of this rule is to transform connections. For each connection in CompConnect = (DC, IC, LC, OC), a TAModel in TASys is inserted by respecting the following rule parts:

- **Rule 4.1.** For each DC_n : $InstName_i.op_j \rightarrow InstName_k.ip_l$, insert a TAModel $(L, l_0, V, Act, Clock, Inv, T)$ with name DC_n, where $L = \{l_0\} = \{DC_n\}$, $V = \{op_j, ip_l\}$, $Inv = \{\}$, and $T = \{(q, g, r, a, q')\}$, with $g = \{op_j \oplus ip_l\}$, where $\oplus$ or XOR represents the inequality function between the output op_j and the input ip_l, $r \in Clock \wedge r = \{\}$ and $a \in Act \wedge a = \{ip_l := op_j\}$ (e.g., DC_3 in Fig. 5);
- **Rule 4.2.** For each IC_n : $ProgName.ip_j \rightarrow InstName_k.ip_l$ or $ProgName.ip_j \rightarrow ProgName.vl_k$, insert a TAModel with name IC_n (e.g., IC_1 in Fig. 5);
- **Rule 4.3.** For each LC_n : $ProgName.vl_i \rightarrow InstName_k.ip_j$, $InstName_k.op_l \rightarrow ProgName.lv_i$ or $ProgName.lv_i \rightarrow ProgName.op_m$, insert a TAModel, with name LC_n (e.g., LC_1 in Fig. 5);

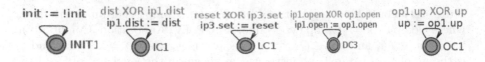

Fig. 5. Example of Fig. 1 TA connections

- **Rule 4.4.** For each $OC_n : InstName_k.op_i \rightarrow Program.op_j$, insert a TAModel with name OC_n, (e.g., OC_1 in Fig. 5);

Rule 5 (Initial input mapping). The objective of this rule is to allow manual validation by using TASys like Uppaal simulator. For this, input variables IP of the SARA program are allowed to be changed by the user. For each $ProgName.ip_j$ in IP, insert TAModel with name $INIT_n$, where $L = \{INIT_n\}$, $V = \{ip_j\}$ and $T = \{(q, g, r, a, q')\}$, with $a \in Act \wedge a = \{ip_j := !ip_j\}$, $r \in Clock \wedge r = \{\} \wedge g = \{\}$, (e.g., $INIT1$ in Fig. 5).

Rule 6 (mapping of execution flow). The objective of this rule is to define the execution flow of the TASys by using priorities on TA models. Based on priority defined in CompInst = (InstName, CompTypeName, Priority) shown in Definition 3, assign priority to each TAName in TASysDecl (see Definition 10).

The validation of these transformation rules are realized through their application in some use case scenarios of SARA model. The preservation of syntax and semantic information across the transformations was checked whenever the TA output models are successful processed by the Uppaal simulation tool.

5   Proof of Concept

In this section, a simulation scenario of a use case is translated into the TA model for the verification of system-level requirements presented in Sect. 2.

5.1   Use Case

The safety of rail-road Level Crossing (LC) has long been a major concern for railway and road stakeholders since LC accidents often generate serious material damage, traffic disruption and human losses. As a consequence, the LC system has already been used as a benchmark in several previous verification approaches [4, 15]. Figure 6 shows the LC topography considered in this paper. It is composed of the following features: (1) double-track railway lines ($UpLine$ and $DownLine$); (2) roads with traffic in both directions; (3) traffic lights to manage the road traffic in the LC zone; (4) sound alarms to signal train arrival; (5) two half-barriers used to prevent road users from crossing while trains are passing; (6) three train sensors An_i, Ap_i and Ex_i in both track lines. For example, in $DownLine$, the An_2 is the anticipation sensor, which allows the detection of the approaching train speed, necessary to alert road users with sound alarm and road lights. The sensor Ap_2 is used to detect the arrival of trains in the

LC zone and the exit sensor Ex_2 is used to announce the departure of trains after exiting the LC zone. Since several trains with different speeds (passenger or freight trains) can circulate on railway lines, the required durations between sensors are expressed with intervals in Fig. 6. For example, $d_1 = [10, 15]$ second (s) is a required interval of durations between An_i and Ap_i. This interval and the others must be respected by trains circulating in the railway track lines.

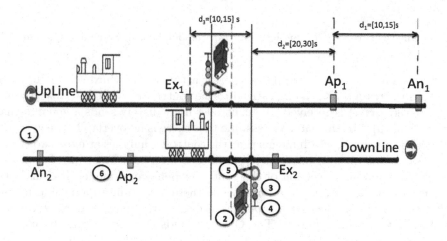

Fig. 6. Level crossing topography

5.2   Transformation of Simulation Scenario to TA Model

In this step, the SARA model of a simulation scenario is translated into the TA model. Figures 1 and 3 present an architecture and an implementation of a simulation example of our use case by using software components (Sensor, Controller, Gate). These components are executed in parallel and are synchronized through various events, e.g., *appr*, *close*, etc., in order to provide the automatic LC control system. This LC model is manually transformed to the Uppaal TA model in oder to use its simulation tool for the verification of our requirements. Figure 7 shows the Uppaal TA model of a LC system scenario, presented as follows.

When a train arrives in the monitored area, it activates the first sensor instance An_i, (i.e., An_1 for the *UpLine* direction and An_2 for the *DownLine* direction) and it sends the *appr* event with its *id* (*appr*[*id*]! in Fig. 6) to the controller. In the same way, when it approaches the crossing section, it activates the second sensor Ap_i and sends the *close*[*id*]! event to the controller. The train spends at least 10 s and at most 15 s in this first section (between An_i and Ap_i, i.e., between *appr* sending and *close* sending). This timing requirement is presented as an invariant of state *Near*1 (i.e., $x1 >= 10$ in Fig. 6) and the guard of a transition to state *Near*1 to *Near*2 (i.e., $x1 <= 15$). The train leaves the crossing section at least 30 s and at most 45 s after sending the *close* event.

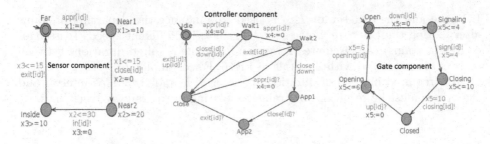

Fig. 7. The level crossing TA model: Controller model, Sensor model and Gate model

When a train leaves the crossing section, it activates the third sensor instance Ex_i, and the train sends an *exit*! signal to the controller. When the *close*? signal (respectively *exit*?) is received, the controller immediately sends a *down*! signal (respectively *up*!) to the gate. We assume that there is no overlap between trains in the same direction, which means that the controller handles at most two trains at the same time, i.e., at most one train in each direction. The controller model of Fig. 7 is a simplified version of the controller behavioral model. It deals with the case when the gate is closed and when there is a train approaching meanwhile, the controller decides to open immediately the gate or to wait certain duration before open the gate. The Gate responds to *down*? signal by moving down and takes 10 s to be completely closed. Indeed, it takes 4 s to activate the light warning the vehicles approaching the LC and 6 s to close the gate. Conversely, it responds to *up* signal by moving up and it takes 6 s to be completely open.

5.3   Requirement Validation Using Observer Patterns

The verification consists in checking that the parallel composition of the application model under test and its safety requirements observers never enters an erroneous state. The system-level safety requirements stated in Sect. 2 are checked based on the predefined observer patterns.

Requirement 1 validation. This requirement is a critical condition aiming to avoid train-car collisions in the crossing zone. It states that "The gate is *never open* when the train is *inside*". This requirement will be expressed as an *exclusion pattern* between *open* state and *inside* state. Firstly, this textual description of the requirement, which is presented as an annotation in the SARA component model (see Fig. 3 (a)), is intuitively presented as an exclusion observer pattern in the TA model. Figure 8 (a) presents the graphical representation of this exclusion pattern, which is used to check that a given situation (state $S1$ and $S2$ are activated at the same time with event $b1$? and $a1$?) is never reached.

Secondly, once identified, the patterns are instantiated with the appropriate parameters. In our case, the exclusion pattern is instantiated with $in[id]$, $exit[id]$, $opening[id]$ and $down[id]$ events, instead of $a1$, $a0$, $b1$ and $b0$, respectively. Thirdly, once generated, the TA patterns are synchronized with the

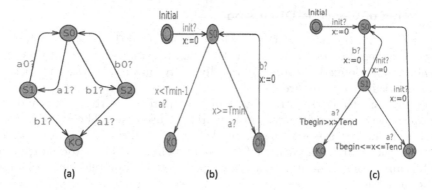

Fig. 8. (a) Exclusion observer pattern, (b) Forbidden before observer pattern, (c) Obligation between observer pattern

system model to generate a global system. Finally, the verification of our use case is carried out on the Uppaal model checker. The "KO" node in the TA observers is never reached, which means that this requirement "the gate must be down when the train is inside the crossing" is always evaluated to true.

Requirement 2 validation. In our scenario model shown in Sect. 5.2, we firstly supposed that the Gate should stay in the *open* state at least 15 s before becoming closed again. According to the Gate model in Fig. 7, the Gate takes 4 s to signal when vehicles can traverse, and 6 s to be closed. So, the time that separates the *up* and *down* detection is $Tmin = 15$ s $- 4$. This means that the *down* detection should be done at least 11 s after the *up* detection. With the Uppaal model checker, the "KO" node of Fig. 3 (b) observer pattern instantiation ($down[id]$ instead of a and $up[id]$ instead of b) is reached. Indeed, the path that violates the requirement can be expressed as follows: (1) the first train leaves the critical section and sends $exit[id1]$ signal. Exit detection triggers the $up[id1]$ sending. Consequently, the gate is open; (2) suppose that a second train is simultaneously entering the LC section, an $appr[id2]$ signal is detected; (3) the second train takes 10 s to trigger the close signal, which triggers the $down[id2]$ sending; (4) As a result, 10 s is computed between $up[id1]$ and $down[id2]$, which violates this requirement: "when the gate is opened to road traffic, it must stay open at least T_{min} time units, where $T_{min} = 11$ s". This verification result helps the designer to search the accepted time parameter between open cycles.

Requirement 3 validation. "once closed and when there is no train approaching meanwhile, the gate must be kept closed at least T_{begin} and at most T_{end}." For the validation of this requirement, we determine the different speed intervals allowed in the track lines. In the beginning, the train speed interval considered in our double-track railway lines of Fig. 6 is [14,45] m/s. The counter examples given by Uppaal model checker, allow to identify new speed intervals that validate the requirement, and so on. The obtained speed intervals that validate this requirement an above requirements are: {[14, 15[, [15, 16[, [16, 18[, [18, 20[, [20, 22[, [22, 30[, [30, 45]}.

5.4   Proof of Concept Discussion

The first results obtained in the previous "proof in use" are encouraging and show the correctness of the defined rules. However, the more formal validation still need to be defined in order to formally verify that the syntax and specially the semantic information are indeed preserved across the transformation.

Having said that, the strong goal of our approach is to express and verify requirements relative to certain scenarios of use cases. The scenario-based description, rather the entire system description, allows a limitation of the explored space search, and hence a first reduction in the combinatorial explosion, which is an important limitation for the application of model checking techniques in complex software projects [23]. For this reason, the strong assumptions we made about the SARA model is that the designer is able to identify all possible interactions between components of the system and between the system and its environment. We justify this strong hypothesis, particularly in the field of embedded systems, by the fact that the designer of a component needs to know precisely and completely the context, i.e., constraints, conditions, of its system for properly developing it. It would be necessary to study formally the validity of this working assumption for scalability in the targeted applications. In this paper, we do not address this aspect, which is planned for our future work.

6   Related Work

Automating the verification process of applications increases development productivity and quality [1]. There are several research works in this direction. These works are mainly based on the transformation of the source models to the target formal models, which are next used for verification purposes by exploiting verification tools [18]. For example, Solimaan et al. transform function block diagram to timed automata for the automated formal verification by using the Uppaal model checker [19]. Textual safety requirements are converted to CTL properties and are checked on the Uppaal TA system using the verifier tool. This verification process requires significant knowledge of higher order logic and theorem proving. This process has two main limitations. The first one is that users must be familiar with the higher order logic in CTL. The second is the lack of patterns for high-level system properties. In contrast, in our verification methodology, we use observer-based verification by providing the timed annotation patterns which promote reusability. As demonstrated in [4], the verification of safety properties by using observer-based verification does not require learning another language for the purpose of property specification. The verification task can be reduced to a simple reachability analysis. Our method suggests using generic predefined observation patterns [6] to check the temporal requirements of a given system.

In this work, we focus on the verification approach that takes advantage of the flexibility of the source model and the analysis facilities offered by a target formal model. In the same way, Mekki et al., based on the flexibility an the expressiveness of UML State Machine (UML SM), transform this semi-formal model to the TA model [15]. This method allows the automated verification of temporal requirements, initially expressed in a semi-formal formalism, through the model transformation. This work is focused on the validation of new functional requirements that prevent several accidents at LCs with model-checking techniques [15]. We use the suggested new LC topography as our use case. In contrast, our work focuses on the integrated development approach. Indeed, given a software requirement specification of safety-critical software, the proposed development process is to guide developers at the first design stage for the identification of requirement types, for the modeling of requirements and for the verification of requirement models before implementation.

7   Conclusion

The main challenge we face in this paper is how to transform a source model of safety-critical applications to a target model suitable for automatic formal verification. In order to face this challenge, we formalize our SARA component model and the TA model. Based on these formal models, transformation rules were then defined. A component model of a simulation scenario is manually transformed to the Uppaal TA model to validate some safety requirements. The counter examples discovered during the verification process can help the developer to identify the software components that should be modified before the implementation and the integration. After the verification phase, the scenario model is implemented with the Ravenscar profile of Ada language, which is one of the recommended languages in the development of railway safety-critical applications. The complete process to validate the safety requirements shows the understanding of the transformation process and the applicability of the proposed approach.

This is very encouraging to automate the transformation of our SARA model to the TA model. We are currently working on the development of this automation. As a consequence, our future work targets the automation process for the automatic verification of timing requirement annotations, which are not supported by the annotation checking tool [9], used in this paper. In addition, the application of our approach to several use case scenarios is another direction to demonstrate the efficiency and the scalability of our approach.

Aknowledgements. This work is supported by IFSTTAR Institute and ANR VEGAS Project.

References

1. Adler, R., Schaefer, I., Trapp, M., Poetzsch-Heffter, A.: Component-based modeling and verification of dynamic adaptation in safety-critical embedded systems. ACM Trans. Embed. Comput. Syst. **10**(2), 20:1–20:39 (2011)
2. Akerholm, M., Moller, A., Hansson, H., Nolin, M.: Towards a dependable component technology for embedded system applications. In: 10th International Workshop on Object-Oriented Real-Time Dependable Systems, pp. 320–328, February 2005

3. Alur, R., Dill, D.L.: A theory of timed automata. Theor. Comput. Sci. **126**(2), 183–235 (1994)
4. Bhatti, Z., Sinha, R., Roop, P.: Observer based verification of iec 61499 function blocks. In: Industrial Informatics (INDIN), pp. 609–614, July 2011
5. Crnkovic, I., Sentilles, S., Vulgarakis, A., Chaudron, M.R.V.: A classification framework for software component models. IEEE Trans. Softw. Eng. **37**(5), 593–615 (2011)
6. Dong, J.S., Hao, P., Qin, S., Sun, J., Yi, W.: Timed automata patterns. IEEE Trans. Softw. Eng. **34**(6), 844–859 (2008)
7. Dwyer, M.B., Avrunin, G.S., Corbett, J.C.: Patterns in property specifications for finite-state verification. In: Proceedings of ICSE'99, pp. 411–420 (1999)
8. EN-50128. Railway applications—communication, signalling and processing systems—software for railway control and protection systems, January 2011
9. Hi-lite. Simplifying the use of formal methods: verification by contract. http://www.open-do.org/projects/hi-lite/
10. IEC-61499. IEC 61499 function blocks for industrial-process measurement and control systems. Geneva, Switzerland (2005)
11. Kaynar, D.K., Lynch, N., Segala, R., Vaandrager, F.: The Theory of Timed I/O Automata. Morgan & Claypool Publishers, Cambridge (2006)
12. Konrad, S., Cheng, B.H.C.: Real-time specification patterns. In: Proceedings of the 27th ICSE, pp. 372–381 (2005)
13. Krichen, M., Tripakis, S.: Conformance testing for real-time systems. Form. Methods Syst. Des. **34**(3), 238–304 (2009)
14. Larsen, K.G., Pettersson, P., Yi, W.: Uppaal in a nutshell. Int. J. Softw. Tools Technol. Transf. **1**(1–2), 134–152 (1997)
15. Mekki, A., Ghazel, M., Toguyeni, A.: Validation of a new functional design of automatic protection systems at level crossings with model-checking techniques. IEEE Trans. Intell. Transp. Syst. **13**(2), 714–723 (2012)
16. Sango, M.: Application of sara approach to ertms/etcs on-board train control system. Technical report, IFSTTAR, April 2013. http://urls.fr/sara
17. Sango, M., Gransart, C., Duchien, L.: Safety component-based approach and its application to ERTMS/ETCS on-board train control system. In: TRA2014 Transport Research Arena 2014, Paris, France, April 2014
18. Sendall, S., Kozaczynski, W.: Model transformation: The heart and soul of model-driven software development. IEEE Softw. **20**(5), 42–45 (2003)
19. Soliman, D., Thramboulidis, K., Frey, G.: Transformation of function block diagrams to uppaal timed automata for the verification of safety applications. Ann. Rev. Control **36**(2), 338–345 (2012)
20. Szyperski, C.: Component Software: Beyond Object-Oriented Programming. Addison-Wesley Longman Publishing Co. Inc., Boston (1998)
21. Tamura, G., Casallas, R., Cleve, A., Duchien, L.: Qos contract-aware reconfiguration of component architectures using e-graphs. In: FACS'10, pp. 34–52 (2010)
22. Taylor, K.: Addressing road user behavioural changes at railway level crossings. In: ACRS-Travelsafe National Conference, pp. 368–375, Brisbane, Australia (2008)
23. Whittle, J.: Specifying precise use cases with use case charts. In: Bruel, J.-M. (ed.) MoDELS 2005. LNCS, vol. 3844, pp. 290–301. Springer, Heidelberg (2006)
24. Yovine, S.: A verification tool for real-time systems. Int. J. Softw. Tools Technol. Transf. **1**(1–2), 123–133 (1997). Springer

Other Verification Approaches

Intransitive Non-Interference by Unfolding

Paolo Baldan[1]([✉]), Francesco Burato[1], and Alberto Carraro[2]

[1] Dipartimento di Matematica,
Università di Padova, Padua, Italy
baldan@math.unipd.it, francesco.burato@gmail.com
[2] DAIS, ANR Projet Récré,
Università Ca' Foscari, Venice, Italy
acarraro@dsi.unive.it

Abstract. Non-interference characterises the absence of undesired information flows in a computing system, by asking that actions with higher level of confidentiality do not cause any observable effect at the lower levels. In many concrete applications, this requirement is too strict and the abstract model is enriched with some form of downgrading, namely with the possibility of declassifying information, thus allowing for a controlled form of leakage. This paper focuses on BINI (Bisimilarity-based Intransitive non-interference), a formalisation of non-interference with downgrading in the setting of Petri nets. Generalising some previous works, we provide a causal characterisation of BINI in terms of the unfolding semantics, a true concurrent semantics of Petri nets. Building on this, we design an algorithm for checking BINI on safe Petri nets which relies on the construction of suitable complete prefixes of the unfolding. The algorithm is implemented in a prototype tool and some preliminary tests are quite encouraging as they suggest that the management of downgrading does not cause any significant performance decay.

1 Introduction

The theory of *information flow control*, and more specifically of *non-interference*, identifies different *levels* (or *domains*) to which components of a computing system (function, variable, process, resource, etc.) are mapped. The levels are organised in a partial order (sometimes in a lattice [1]) and information may flow from lower levels to higher levels but not vice versa: the higher is the level, the more classified are the data or entities belonging to it.

The concept of non-interference was introduced in [2] in order to provide a formal foundation for the specification and analysis of information flow security policies and the mechanisms that enforce them. The common intuition is that information *flows* from a level A to a level B if the behaviour of some component of level B is affected by some component of level A in some run of the system.

The classical theory of non-interference [2] dealt with *transitive multilevel security policies*. According to this view $A \leq B$ implies that information is

---

Work supported by the project Récré (ANR) and the MIUR PRIN project CINA.

I. Lanese and E. Madelaine (Eds.): FACS 2014, LNCS 8997, pp. 269–287, 2015.
DOI: 10.1007/978-3-319-15317-9_17

allowed to flow from level A to level B; of course if, additionally, $B \leq C$, then information is also allowed to flow from A to C. Some multilevel security policies do not allow all transitive flows: admitted flows are expressed by a reflexive, possibly not transitive, relation $\rightsquigarrow \subseteq \leq$, the meaning of $A \rightsquigarrow B$ being that "information is allowed to flow from level A to level B". For practical security problems a requirement like $A \not\rightsquigarrow B$ (complete absence of flows from A to B) is in general too strong and suitable weakenings can be appropriate which allow one to *declassify* information (e.g., a certain secret becomes obsolete or a password has to be checked against the one provided by the user). An early approach is [3], where declassification is rendered in the form of *downgrading* (or *channel control*). One adds an intermediate level D with $A \rightsquigarrow D \rightsquigarrow B$: the level D is acting as a *downgrader* so that any flow from A to B is required to happen *only through* the intermediary D and not directly from A to B. A general treatment of intransitive policies is provided in [4,5] where computing systems are abstracted away as automata or labelled transition systems. The first work adapting intransitive non-interference to a programming language setting is [6], that provides a type-based approach to the enforcement of intransitive multilevel security policies for imperative languages. Intransitive non-interference has been widely studied also in the context of process calculi (see, e.g., [7]) and Petri nets [8,9].

In the simplest view, the system has a high (secret) part H and a low (public) part L. The high part H should not *interfere* with the low part L, meaning that whatever is done in H produces no "visible" effect on L, where the idea of visibility is based on some observational semantics which can be trace or bisimulation equivalence (see, e.g., [10–12]).

In those concurrent formalisms which include forms of composition and synchronisation, such as process calculi and Petri nets, a popular formulation of non-interference is the so-called NDC (Non-Deducibility on Composition), which looks at the system under analysis as a component possibly interacting with the surrounding environment. It states that a process (or net) S is free of interferences whenever S running in isolation, seen from the low level, is behaviourally equivalent to S interacting with any parallel high level process (or net) that may synchronise on high actions (or transitions) [8,10,13–16].

The fact that the behaviour of S is not altered by composition is often described by referring to some informal notion of causality – the activity at high level should not cause visible effects on the behaviour at low level – but formalised in terms of interleaving semantics. Some steps towards a causal characterisation of non-interference can be found in [15], where several notions of non-interference, in particular BNDC (Bisimilarity-based NDC), are studied over contact-free elementary nets (or equivalently pure safe nets) and trace nets. A purely causal characterisation of BNDC on safe Petri nets is provided in [16], in terms of a classical true concurrent semantics of Petri nets, the unfolding semantics [17]. The interest for a causal characterisation is not only of theoretical nature. On the pragmatic side the use of a true concurrent semantics, which represents interleavings only implicitly, is helpful for facing the state explosion problem which affects the verification of concurrent systems. Indeed, the efficiency of this approach is supported by evidences provided by a prototype tool UBIC which checks BNDC on safe Petri nets by implementing the algorithm proposed in [16], outperforming other tools based on interleaving semantics.

In this paper we show that the unfolding-based approach to non-interference proposed in [16] for Petri nets can be generalised to deal with a form of declassification. We work with the formalisation in [8,9], where the two-level approach based on the distinction between high H (confidential) and low L (public) actions, is enriched with the addition of so-called *downgrading* actions D. The occurrence of a downgrading action declassifies all the high actions that have occurred before, which are no longer considered confidential. These high actions can thus be observed at the low level without any concern about information leakage. The notion of observation is formalised by taking bisimilarity as a reference equivalence, so that the resulting property is called *Bisimilarity-based Intransitive Non-Interference* (BINI) [8].

We provide a structural characterisation of BINI: a safe net is BINI if and only if its unfolding reveals neither a direct causality (given by a *weak causal* place), with a token flowing from a high to a low level transition without passing through a downgrading transition, nor a direct conflict (represented by a *weak conflict* place) between a low level and a non-downgraded high level transition.

The structural characterisation, in turn, enables the checking of the BINI property on a suitably defined complete prefix of the unfolding: we present an algorithm that actually performs this verification. A potential advantage of our approach, compared to other techniques that construct (or explore) the reachability graph of the net, is a great gain of efficiency for highly concurrent systems, since the unfolding prefix is, in these cases, much smaller than the complete state space (see e.g. [18] and references therein). The unfolding-based algorithm for checking BINI has been implemented in a prototype tool UBIC2 [19]. Dealing with downgrading requires a refined notion of completeness for prefixes and, consequently, UBIC2 has to manage additional data structures with respect to the tool UBIC in [16]. In practice the overhead, both in terms of time and memory consumption, turns out to be reasonably light and the performances of UBIC2 are in line with those of UBIC, which in [16] are argued to outperform those of interleaving-based tools like ANICA [20] and PNSC [9]. We discuss some preliminary test runs which show promising results.

The rest of the paper is structured as follows. In Sect. 2 we define the basics of Petri nets and their unfoldings semantics, and we present the BINI property. In Sect. 3 we give a characterisation of BINI based on weak causal and conflict places. In Sect. 4 we provide an unfolding-based characterisation of BINI which is then exploited in Sect. 5 for devising a corresponding algorithm. Implementation and experimental results are discussed in Sect. 6. Finally, in Sect. 7 we draw some conclusions.

2   Preliminaries

In this section we review the basics of Petri nets and their unfolding semantics, and we define BINI, the reference non-interference property for the paper.

2.1   Petri Nets

A *Petri net* is a tuple $N = (P, T, F)$ where P, T are disjoint sets of *places* and *transitions*, respectively and $F : (P \times T) \cup (T \times P) \to \{0, 1\}$ is the *flow relation*. Graphically, places and transitions are drawn, respectively, as circles and rectangles, while the flow relation is rendered by means of directed arcs connecting places and transitions. For example if $F(p, t) = 1$ then there is an arc from p to t. For $x \in P \cup T$ we define its *pre-set* ${}^{\bullet}x = \{y \in P \cup T : F(y, x) = 1\}$ and its *post-set* $x^{\bullet} = \{y \in P \cup T : F(x, y) = 1\}$. We will only consider nets where ${}^{\bullet}t \neq \emptyset$ for all $t \in T$.

A *marking* of N is a function $m : P \to \mathbb{N}$. A transition $t \in T$ is *enabled* at a marking m, denoted $m[t\rangle$, iff $m(p) \geq F(p, t)$ for all $p \in P$. If $m[t\rangle$ then t can be *fired* leading to a new marking m', written $m[t\rangle m'$, defined by $m'(p) = m(p) + F(t, p) - F(p, t)$ for all places $p \in P$. The enabling and firing relations are extended to $\sigma \in T^*$ (finite sequences of elements of T) by defining $m[\varepsilon\rangle m$ (where ε is the empty sequence) and $m[\sigma t\rangle m''$ when $m[\sigma\rangle m'$ and $m'[t\rangle m''$.

A *marked Petri net* is a pair $\mathbf{N} = (N, m_0)$ where N is a Petri net and m_0 is a marking of N. A marking m' is *reachable* if there exists $\sigma \in T^*$ such that $m_0[\sigma\rangle m'$. The set of reachable markings of $\mathbf{N}$ is denoted by $[m_0\rangle$. When $m[t\rangle m'$, the marking m', uniquely determined by m and t, is denoted by $\langle m[t\rangle$. Analogously, for $\sigma \in T^*$, if $m[\sigma\rangle$ we can define the marking $\langle m[\sigma\rangle$. In pictures markings are represented as black dots, called *tokens*, inside places (the presence of n dots inside place p means that $m(p) = n$).

The net $\mathbf{N}$ is *safe* if for every $p \in P$ and $m \in [m_0\rangle$ we have $m(p) \leq 1$. In a safe net every marking m can be seen as a subset of places and we write $p \in m$ instead of $m(p) = 1$.

2.2   Bisimulation-Based Intransitive Non-Interference

A *net system* is a Petri net N where T is partitioned into three disjoint sets H, L and D. We sometimes write $N = (P, H, L, D, F)$ making the three sets of transitions explicit. The idea is to model a system with two distinguished classes of "users": high level users and low level users. Transitions in H, called *high transitions*, are thought of as visible only to the high level users, while the *low transitions* in L are globally visible. Transitions in D are called *downgrading transitions*. Their firing "declassify" prior occurrences of high transitions.

The idea of secure net system in the presence of downgrading is made precise by the definition of *Bisimulation-based Intransitive Non-Interference* (BINI).

As a first step we need to recall *Bisimilarity-based Non-Deducibility on Composition* (BNDC, for short) [8,15], the security notion which has been formulated for *two-level net systems*, where $D = \emptyset$ (no downgrading transitions). A net system N is called *high* when $L = \emptyset$ and $D = \emptyset$.

A two-level net system $\mathbf{N}$ is deemed free of interferences when, seen from the low level, the system $\mathbf{N}$ interacting with any parallel high system is indistinguishable from $\mathbf{N}$ restricted to the low transitions. The formalisation of this intuition requires (parallel) composition and restriction operators on net systems, as in [8].

Definition 1 (parallel composition). *Let N and N' be two-level net systems such that $P \cap P' = \emptyset$, $(H' \cap L) \cup (H \cap L') = \emptyset$, and $(P \cap T') \cup (P' \cap T) = \emptyset$. The parallel composition of N and N' is the net system $N \,|\, N' = (P \cup P', H \cup H', L \cup L', F \cup F')$. The composition of marked two-level net systems $\mathbf{N} = (N, m_0)$ and $\mathbf{N}' = (N', m_0')$ is the two-level marked net system $\mathbf{N} \,|\, \mathbf{N}' = (N \,|\, N', m_0 \cup m_0')$.*

Intuitively, $N \,|\, N'$ is the superposition of N and N', synchronised on the common transitions.

Definition 2 (restriction). *Given a net system N and a subset $T_1 \subseteq T$, the restriction of N by T_1 is the net system $N \backslash T_1 = (P, H - T_1, L - T_1, D - T_1, F \backslash T_1)$ where $F \backslash T_1$ is the restriction of F to $(P \times (T - T_1)) \cup ((T - T_1) \times P)$. For a marked net system $\mathbf{N}$, the restriction $\mathbf{N} \backslash T_1$ is $(N \backslash T_1, m_0)$.*

As a last ingredient, we need to define the *low view* (see [15, Definition 3.1]) of a sequence $\sigma \in T^*$, which represents the view of a low level user on σ in a two-level net system $\mathbf{N}$. It is defined inductively by $\nu_N(\varepsilon) = \varepsilon$ and $\nu_N(t\,\sigma) = t\,\nu_N(\sigma)$ if $t \in L$ and $\nu_N(t\,\sigma) = \nu_N(\sigma)$ if $t \in H$.

Definition 3 (low view bisimulation). *A low view simulation between two marked net systems $\mathbf{N}$ and $\mathbf{N}'$ is a binary relation $R \subseteq [m_0\rangle \times [m_0'\rangle$ such that (i) $(m_0, m_0') \in R$ and (ii) for all $(m, m') \in R$, if $m[\sigma\rangle$ there exists σ' such that $m'[\sigma'\rangle$, $(\langle m[\sigma\rangle, \langle m'[\sigma'\rangle) \in R$ and $\nu_N(\sigma) = \nu_{N'}(\sigma')$. The relation R is a low view bisimulation if both R and R^{-1} are low view simulations. In this case, we say that $\mathbf{N}$ and $\mathbf{N}'$ are low view bisimilar and write $\mathbf{N} \approx \mathbf{N}'$.*

Intuitively, the low transitions are supposed to be observed by the low level users, while the high transitions cannot be observed and should hopefully be kept secret, i.e. they should not be revealed to the low level users by the observation of the firing sequences in which they occur. This is formalised by saying that a two-level net system $\mathbf{N}$ is BNDC when no behavioural difference can be detected, by a low level observer, between $\mathbf{N} \backslash H$ (i.e. $\mathbf{N}$ running in isolation and without firing high transitions) and $(\mathbf{N} \,|\, \mathbf{N}') \backslash (H - H')$ (i.e., $\mathbf{N}$ running in parallel with an arbitrary high net $\mathbf{N}'$, thus possibly synchronising on high transitions).

Definition 4 (BNDC). *A two-level marked net system $\mathbf{N}$ is BNDC if for every high marked net system $\mathbf{N}'$ we have that $\mathbf{N} \backslash H \approx (\mathbf{N} \,|\, \mathbf{N}') \backslash (H - H')$.*

Figure 1(a) represents a two-level net system $\mathbf{C}$ (without downgrading transitions): high transitions are double edged rectangles. It models a batch service S that checks digital signatures of digital documents. The files to be checked are enqueued in a buffer. For each file an algorithm generates a pair of keys (pK, sK): the secret key sK is used by the signer to sign the file (transition *set key*) and then the public key pK is received by S (transition *get key*). In the meantime the file is sent to S (transition *send file*) and immediately after pK is used by S to verify the signature (transition *check key*) once the file has been received. According to the outcome of the verification operation the sender receives a message (either *ok* or *fail*). The net system $\mathbf{C}$ is not BNDC, since

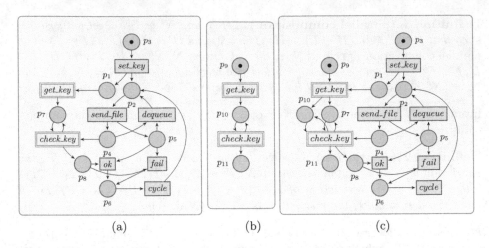

Fig. 1. (a) A net system $\mathbf{C}$; (b) A high net system $\mathbf{D}$; (c) $(\mathbf{C}\,|\,\mathbf{D}) \setminus (H_C - H_D)$.

the fact that the low level receives the outcome of the signature check results in a leak of information from the high level. More formally, the net system $\mathbf{D}$ of Fig. 1(b) is such that $\mathbf{C} \setminus H_C$ is not bisimilar to $(\mathbf{C}\,|\,\mathbf{D}) \setminus (H_C - H_D)$ (Fig. 1(c)). In this case $(\mathbf{C}\,|\,\mathbf{D}) \setminus (H_C - H_D)$ coincides with $\mathbf{C}\,|\,\mathbf{D}$, since $H_C - H_D = \emptyset$.

This example illustrates the strictness of BNDC: the system $\mathbf{C}$ is rejected by this security policy, even if the fact that "public level" will know the outcome of the signature check seems unavoidable.

Bisimulation-based Intransitive Non-Interference (BINI) is a more relaxed security policy obtained with the insertion of downgrading transitions. Downgrading transitions may be observed by the low level user, but when such transitions occur, they declassify the prior occurrences of high transitions which does not need to be kept secret any longer.

As usual we let $T^*D = \{\sigma d : \sigma \in T^*,\ d \in D\}$. A d-*marking* of a marked net system $\mathbf{N}$ is any marking $m = \langle m_0[\sigma\rangle$, for some $\sigma \in \{\varepsilon\} \cup T^*D$.

Definition 5 (BINI [8]). *A marked net system $\mathbf{N}$ is BINI when for every d-marking m the two-level net system $(N \setminus D, m)$ is BNDC.*

The intuition behind Definition 5 is as follows: BINI is a clocked version of BNDC, where the ticks of the clock are the downgrading transitions. In fact every time a downgrading transition d is fired the system reaches a d-marking: all the high transitions that can be fired afterwards (without firing another downgrading transition) are required to be non-observable w.r.t. low view bisimulation. Instead there is no requirement on the high transitions that might have occurred *before* d: they may be revealed by the downgrading transition itself or by subsequent low transitions without breaking the security policy.

The net system $\mathbf{P}$ of Fig. 2(a) is a slight modification of the net system $\mathbf{C}$ of Fig. 1(a): it includes downgrading transitions, identifiable as rounded edge

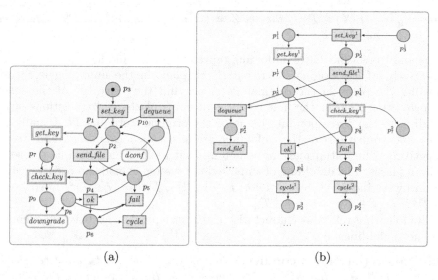

(a)   (b)

Fig. 2. (a) A net system **P** modelling signature checking with declassification and (b) partial unfolding of the net system in Fig. 1(a).

rectangles. In particular **P** "extends" **C** with downgrading transitions which declassify the signature check, thus making the system BINI.

2.3   Unfolding Semantics and Related Notions

Given a Petri net **N**, the unfolding construction [17] produces a Petri net $\mathcal{U}(\mathbf{N})$ whose places are a reification of the tokens that circulate in **N** and whose transitions are copies of the transitions of **N**, representing their possible firings. The unfolding provides an implicit representation of the marking graph of **N**, a directed graph whose nodes are the reachable markings of **N**. The unfolding can be infinite, but when **N** is safe along the lines of the seminal work in [21,22], finite fragments can be constructed containing a representation of all the reachable markings and, for highly concurrent systems, possibly exponentially smaller than the marking graph.

The unfolding is constructed inductively starting from the initial marking of **N** and then adding, at each step, an occurrence of each transition of **N** which is enabled by (the image of) a coverable subset of the places already generated. Below we indicate by π_1 the projection over the first component of tuples.

Definition 6 (unfolding). *Let* **N** *be a safe marked Petri net and let* $\perp$ *be an element not in* P, T, F. *Define the Petri net* $U^{(0)} = (T^{(0)}, P^{(0)}, F^{(0)})$ *as* $T^{(0)} = \emptyset$, $P^{(0)} = \{(p, \perp) : p \in m_0\}$ *and* $F^{(0)} = \emptyset$. *Then the unfolding is the least Petri net* $\mathcal{U}(\mathbf{N}) = (P^{(\omega)}, T^{(\omega)}, F^{(\omega)})$ *containing* $U^{(0)}$ *and such that*

– if $t \in T$ *and* $X \subseteq P^{(\omega)}$ *with* X *reachable and* $\pi_1(X) = {}^{\bullet}t$, *then* $(t, X) \in T^{(\omega)}$;

– *for any* $e = (t, X) \in T^{(\omega)}$, *the set* $Z = \{(p, e) : p \in \pi_1(e)^\bullet\} \subseteq P^{(\omega)}$; *moreover* ${}^\bullet e = X$, *and* $e^\bullet = Z$.

Places and transitions in the unfolding represent tokens and firing of transitions, respectively, of the original Petri net. Each place in the unfolding is a tuple recording the place in the original Petri net and the "history" of the token. The projection π_1 over the first component maps places and transitions of the unfolding to the corresponding items of the original Petri net $\mathbf{N}$. Usually the places and transitions of the unfolding are also called *conditions* and *events*, respectively. The initial marking is left implicit as it is identified as the set of minimal places. The unfolding of a marked net system is made an occurrence net system by setting $H^{(\omega)} = \{e \in T^{(\omega)} : \pi_1(e) \in H\}$, $L^{(\omega)} = \{e \in T^{(\omega)} : \pi_1(e) \in L\}$ and $D^{(\omega)} = \{e \in T^{(\omega)} : \pi_1(e) \in D\}$.

The following relations characterise the interdependencies between events in Petri net unfoldings.

Definition 7 (causality, conflict). *Causality* $<$ *is the least transitive relation on* $P^{(\omega)} \cup T^{(\omega)}$ *such that if* $x \in {}^\bullet y$ *then* $x < y$. *By* $\leq$ *we denote the reflexive closure of* $<$. *Conflict* $\sharp$ *is the least symmetric relation on* $P \cup T$ *such that if* $t, t' \in T$, $t \neq t'$ *and* ${}^\bullet t \cap {}^\bullet t' \neq \emptyset$ *then* $t \sharp t'$ *and if* $x < x'$ *and* $x \sharp y$ *then* $x' \sharp y$.

Two events are in conflict when they can never occur in the same computation: for example $ok^1 \sharp fail^1$ in the net system $\mathbf{C}$ of Fig. 1.(c).

The *causes* of an event $e \in T^{(\omega)}$ are $[e] = \{e' \in T^{(\omega)} : e' \leq e\}$ and we write $[e)$ for the *strict causes*, i.e., $[e) = [e] - \{e\}$. The computations of $\mathbf{N}$ are represented by configurations in $\mathcal{U}(\mathbf{N})$, i.e., causally closed and conflict-free subsets of $T^{(\omega)}$.

Definition 8 (configuration). *A configuration of* $\mathcal{U}(\mathbf{N})$ *is a finite subset* $C \subseteq T^{(\omega)}$ *such that* $\sharp \cap (C \times C) = \emptyset$ *and* $[e] \subseteq C$ *for all* $e \in C$. *The set of all configurations of* $\mathcal{U}(\mathbf{N})$ *is denoted by* $\mathcal{C}(\mathcal{U}(\mathbf{N}))$.

A configuration of $\mathcal{U}(\mathbf{N})$ can be associated with a reachable marking of $\mathbf{N}$, obtained by firing all its transitions in any order compatible with causality. The *frontier* of a configuration C is the set $C^\circ = (P^{(0)} \cup \bigcup_{e \in C} e^\bullet) - (\bigcup_{e \in C} {}^\bullet e)$; it induces a marking $\mathsf{M}(C)$ on $\mathbf{N}$ defined by $\mathsf{M}(C) = \{\pi_1(b) : b \in C^\circ\}$. The unfolding has been shown to be marking complete in the sense that $m \in [m_0\rangle$ iff there exists $C \in \mathcal{C}(\mathcal{U}(\mathbf{N}))$ such that $\mathsf{M}(C) = m$ (see [17,21]).

3   BINI Through Causal and Conflict Places

The paper [15] characterises BNDC for contact-free elementary Petri nets (safe nets without self-loops) in terms of the absence of suitably defined *causal* and *conflict* places. Later [9] adapted this approach to the BINI property, still for contact-free elementary Petri nets. Here we provide a different structural characterisation of the BINI property for safe net systems in terms of what we call weak causal and conflict places. The qualification weak is motivated by the fact that our requirements are weaker than those in [9], a fact which plays a pivotal role for the development of the unfolding-based algorithm.

Notation. Given a net system $\mathbf{N}$, a place $p \in P$ and a transition $t \in T$, we set $t^- = \{p \in P : F(t,p) < F(p,t)\}$ and $t^+ = \{p \in P : F(t,p) > F(p,t)\}$.

Definition 9 (weak causal place). *A place p of a net system $\mathbf{N}$ is* weak causal *if there are transitions $l \in L$, $h \in H$ and a sequence $\tau \in (L \cup H)^*$ satisfying (1) $p \in \,^{\bullet}l \cap h^+$ and (2) there is a reachable marking m such that $m[h\tau l\rangle$.*

In words, a token in place p is needed by l (i.e. p is in the pre-set of l) and h contributes positively to such place. Furthermore, there exists a firing sequence $m[h\tau l\rangle$ in which h puts a token in p, that may afterwards travel through the net moved by transitions (the sequence τ, which does not include downgradings), and eventually goes back to p where it is essential for the firing of l. Intuitively, this witnesses a causal information flow from the high to the low level since the firing of l depends on the firing of a non-downgraded occurrence of h. An example of weak causal place is p_8 in Fig. 1(a). Clearly $p_8 \in check\_key^+ \cap \,^{\bullet}ok$. Moreover if $m_0[set\_key \; get\_key \; send\_file\rangle m$ and $m[check\_key \; ok\rangle$ (with $\tau = \varepsilon$, in the notation of Definition 9).

A notion of weak conflict place can be defined along the same lines.

Definition 10 (weak conflict place). *A place p of a net system $\mathbf{N}$ is* weak conflict *if there are transitions $l \in L$, $h \in H$ and a sequence $\tau \in (L \cup H)^*$ satisfying (1) $p \in \,^{\bullet}l \cap h^-$ and (2) there is a reachable marking m such that $m[h\rangle$ and $m[\tau l\rangle$.*

Notice that a token in place p is needed by l (since $p \in \,^{\bullet}l$) and consumed by h. Moreover there is a marking in which there is a choice: either high transition h fires, "stealing" a token from p, or a sequence τ (not containing downgrading transitions) is executed which leads to the firing of l. Intuitively, the firing of l is possible only in absence of the firing of a non-downgraded occurrence of h. An example of weak conflict place is p_4 in Fig. 1(a). Clearly $p_4 \in check\_key^- \cap \,^{\bullet}dequeue$. Moreover $m_0[set\_key \; get\_key \; send\_file\rangle m$ and $m[check\_key\rangle$, $m[dequeue\rangle$ (again $\tau = \varepsilon$ with the notation of Definition 10).

Theorem 1 (BINI in safe net systems). *A safe marked net system $\mathbf{N}$ is not BINI iff it contains either a weak causal place or a weak conflict place.*

4   Intransitive Non-Interference in the Unfolding

In this section we show how the presence of weak causal and conflict places in a safe net $\mathbf{N}$ can be characterised in the unfolding $\mathcal{U}(\mathbf{N})$. In view of Theorem 1 this will provide also a characterisation of the BINI property. This is the basis for devising unfolding-based algorithms for checking BINI (see Sect. 5).

4.1   Weak Causal and Conflict Places Through the Unfolding

Notation. For a condition b and an event e in $\mathcal{U}(\mathbf{N})$ we set $e^+ = \{b \in P^{(\omega)} : \pi_1(b) \in \pi_1(e)^+\}$ and $e^- = \{b \in P^{(\omega)} : \pi_1(b) \in \pi_1(e)^-\}$. Moreover transitions denoted by d, h and l, possibly with subscripts, will be implicitly assumed to be downgrading, high and low transitions, respectively.

Lemma 1. *Let* **N** *be a net system.*

(i) If p is a weak causal place in **N**, *then there are events* h', l' *and a condition* b *in* $\mathcal{U}(\mathbf{N})$ *such that* $b \in {}^\bullet l' \cap h'^+$, $\pi_1(b) = p$ *and* $\{d' \in D^{(\omega)} : h' < d' < l'\} = \emptyset$;

(ii) if p is a weak conflict place in **N**, *then there are events* h', l' *and a condition* b *in* $\mathcal{U}(\mathbf{N})$ *such that* $b \in {}^\bullet l' \cap h'^-$, $[h'] \cup [l'] \in \mathcal{C}(\mathcal{U}(\mathbf{N}))$, $\pi_1(b) = p$ *and for all* $d' \in D^{(\omega)}$ *if* $d' \# h'$, *then* $d' \not< l'$.

Lemma 1 gives structural conditions that the unfolding $\mathcal{U}(\mathbf{N})$ necessarily satisfies if **N** contains either a weak causal or a weak conflict place. Specifically, a weak causal place in **N** is witnessed by the presence of a condition $b \in {}^\bullet l' \cap h'^+$ in the unfolding, such that h' is not downgraded by an event causally following h' and preceding l'. A weak conflict place is witnessed by the presence of a condition $b \in {}^\bullet l' \cap h'^-$ such that h' is not ruled out by any downgrading event necessary for the occurrence of l'.

One can prove that also the converse holds and thus we get a characterisation of BINI for safe net systems in terms of the absence, in the unfolding, of conditions satisfying the structural properties indicated in the following theorem.

Theorem 2 (BINI in the unfolding of safe net systems). *A safe net system* **N** *is not BINI iff there are events* h', l' *and a condition* b *in* $\mathcal{U}(\mathbf{N})$ *such that either (1)* $b \in {}^\bullet l' \cap h'^+$ *and* $\{d' \in D^{(\omega)} : h' < d' < l'\} = \emptyset$ *or (2)* $b \in {}^\bullet l' \cap h'^-$, $[h'] \cup [l'] \in \mathcal{C}(\mathcal{U}(\mathbf{N}))$ *and for all* $d' \in D^{(\omega)}$ *if* $d' \# h'$, *then* $d' \not< l'$.

4.2   Complete Prefixes for Interferences

The characterisation of BINI in Theorem 2 paves the way to an unfolding-based checking algorithm for such property. The general idea of unfolding-based verification techniques, originating from the seminal work [21], consists in constructing a causally closed subnet of the unfolding, referred to as an unfolding prefix, which is complete for the property of interest. In [21] the focus is on reachability and a prefix U of the unfolding is deemed *complete* when any marking reachable in **N** is in the image of the marking produced by some configuration of U. This has been later extended to more general properties [22].

In [16] it was observed that a prefix which is complete for reachability (and also for executability of transitions), could lack relevant information for interferences. The solution adopted in [16] consists in considering *extended markings*, which also record the security level of transitions producing tokens on the frontier. This is not enough in presence of downgradings. Consider for instance the net in Fig. 3 (a), its unfolding (b) and a prefix of the unfolding (c). The unfolding prefix (c) is marking complete even if we take into account the security level of the transition producing the tokens (i.e., it is extended marking complete in the sense of [16]). The event l_1^2 can be omitted in (c) since $[l_3^2]$ produces the same marking as $[l_1^2]$, namely $\{p_2, p_3\}$, and in both cases only p_3 is filled with a token generated by a high transition (h_1). However, the prefix (c) does not contain an occurrence of place p_3 satisfying the conditions of Theorem 2(1), witnessing that p_3 is a weak causal place. In fact, the only occurrence is $p_3^1 \in {}^\bullet l_2^2 \cap h_1^{1+}$,

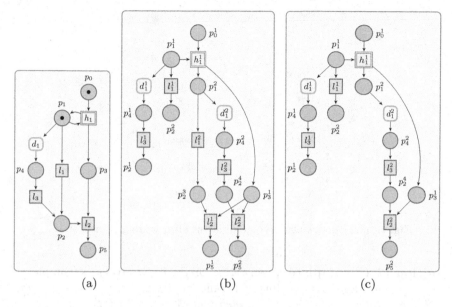

Fig. 3. (a) A not BINI net system, (b) its unfolding and (c) a prefix not including an interference.

but $\{d' \in D^{(\omega)} : h_1^1 < d' < l_2^2\} = \{d_1^2\} \neq \emptyset$. Thus the prefix does not witness the fact that the net system is not BINI.

In order to produce a complete prefix which captures all interferences, we need to further enrich the marking associated with a configuration.

Definition 11 (downgrading marking). *Let* **N** *be a safe net system,* $\mathcal{U}(\mathbf{N})$ *its unfolding and let* $C \in \mathcal{C}(\mathcal{U}(\mathbf{N}))$. *The* downgrading marking *of* C *is* $\mathsf{M}^d(C) = \langle \mathsf{M}(C), \delta_C \rangle$ *where* $\delta_C \subseteq \mathsf{M}(C) \times \mathsf{M}(C)$ *is the relation*

$$\delta_C = \{(\pi_1(b), \pi_1(b')) : (\exists h' \in H^{(\omega)}.\ b' \in h'^+) \Rightarrow (\exists d' \in D^{(\omega)}.\ h' < d' < b)\}.$$

Roughly, when a token has been produced using a downgrading transition, its presence in a marking can downgrade the confidentiality level of some tokens produced by high transitions. The relation δ_C is intended to capture exactly this information: given $b, b' \in C^\circ$, we have that $\pi_1(b)\delta_C\pi_1(b')$ if b' is produced by a high-level transition h' and b "declassifies" b', in the sense that the presence of a token in b witnesses the previous firing of a downgrading transition d' caused by h'. If, instead, b' is not produced by a high transition then $\pi_1(b')$ is already public, and indeed $\pi_1(b)\delta_C\pi_1(b')$ trivially holds, i.e., b' is declassified by any condition (in particular by b' itself).

For instance, consider again the unfolding (b) of Fig. 3. Note that $\mathsf{M}^d([l_1^2]) \neq \mathsf{M}^d([l_3^2])$ because $p_2\delta_{[l_3^2]}p_3$ but $\neg(p_2\delta_{[l_1^2]}p_3)$. Therefore in a prefix of the unfolding of (a), complete with respect to downgrading markings, none of the events l_1^2 and l_2^1 can be safely omitted. Hence the prefix will contain a witness of the weak causal place p_3 satisfying condition (1) of Theorem 2.

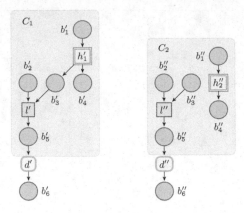

Fig. 4. The d-markings become different after adding transition d'.

Definition 12 (d-complete prefix). *A prefix U of $\mathcal{U}(\mathbf{N})$ is* complete for downgrading marking reachability *(d-complete), when for any configuration $C \in \mathcal{C}(\mathcal{U}(\mathbf{N}))$ there exists $C' \in \mathcal{C}(U)$ such that $\mathsf{M}^d(C) = \mathsf{M}^d(C')$.*

Given a safe net system $\mathbf{N}$, a d-complete prefix U of $\mathcal{U}(\mathbf{N})$ contains sufficient information for deciding whether or not $\mathbf{N}$ contains a weak causal place.

Theorem 3 (d-completeness for weak causal places). *Let $\mathbf{N}$ be a safe net system and let U be an d-complete prefix of $\mathcal{U}(\mathbf{N})$. Then p is a weak causal place in $\mathbf{N}$ iff there exist high and low events h', l' and a condition b in U such that $b \in {}^{\bullet}l' \cap h'^{+}$, $\{d' \in D^{(\omega)} : h' < d' < l'\} = \emptyset$ and $\pi_1(b) = p$.*

5   Unfolding-Based Algorithms

Even if d-complete prefixes of $\mathcal{U}(\mathbf{N})$ determine whether $\mathbf{N}$ is BINI or not, there are some technical difficulties concerning the actual construction of a d-complete unfolding prefix. The problem lies in the fact that two configurations with the same d-marking, once extended with an occurrence of the same transition, might not have the same d-marking. For instance, consider configurations C_1 and C_2 - marked by a grey background - in Fig. 4, where we assume that items denoted by x' and x'' are occurrences of x. Then $\mathsf{M}^d(C_1) = \mathsf{M}^d(C_2) = \langle\{b_5, b_4\}, \delta\rangle$ but the equality of the d-markings no longer holds after adding the occurrences of d. As a consequence Lemma 2 (cut-off elimination) would fail, thus invalidating the construction of a complete prefix. Speaking in terms of the theory of *canonical prefixes* [22], d-markings do not provide a valid *cutting context*. In order to cope with this problem we further enrich the information recorded in the marking.

Definition 13 (ad-marking). *Let $\mathbf{N}$ a safe net system, $\mathcal{U}(\mathbf{N})$ its unfolding and $C \in \mathcal{C}(\mathcal{U}(\mathbf{N}))$. The* algorithmic downgrading marking *(ad-marking) of C is $\mathsf{M}^{ad}(C) = \langle \mathsf{M}(C), \delta_C, \zeta_C \rangle$, where ζ_C is the function given, for each $h \in H$, by $\zeta_C(h) = \{\pi_1(b) : b \in C^{\circ} \wedge \exists h'. \ \pi_1(h') = h \wedge h'^{+} \cap C^{\circ} \neq \emptyset \wedge h' < b\}$.*

Ad-markings contain an additional component $\zeta_C(h)$, which provides an indication of those tokens which have non-downgraded instances of the high transition h in their history. A downgrading transition using this token will determine the downgrading of all tokens produced by h in the current marking.

Consider again configurations C_1 and C_2 in Fig. 4. Note that $b_5 \in \zeta_{C_1}(h) - \zeta_{C_2}(h)$, so that $\mathsf{M}^{ad}(C_1) \neq \mathsf{M}^{ad}(C_2)$.

A key notion for constructing ad-complete prefixes is that of cut-off, which is roughly a transition in the unfolding that produces an ad-marking already produced by other transitions with smaller history. The idea of cut-off events goes back to [21]. The word "smaller" is formalised by fixing an order $\prec$ on configurations. We can take $C \prec C'$ is $|C| < |C'|$, as in [21], but finer adequate orders (see [22]) can be considered for reducing the size of complete prefixes and improving the efficiency (this actually is done in the tool UBIC2).

Definition 14 (cut-off). *Let $\mathbf{N}$ be a safe net system, $\mathcal{U}(\mathbf{N})$ its unfolding and U a prefix of the unfolding. An event $t \in T_U$ is a cut-off when either (1) $\mathsf{M}^{ad}([t]) = \mathsf{M}^{ad}(\emptyset)$, i.e. it as the same ad-marking as the initial marking, (2) or there exists event $t' \in T_U$ such that $\mathsf{M}^{ad}([t]) = \mathsf{M}^{ad}([t'])$ and $[t'] \prec [t]$.*

A procedure that unfolds a net system by adding events with $\prec$-minimal history and stopping at cut-offs produces an ad-complete prefix of the unfolding. This requires Lemma 2 to be proved and follows from the general theory in [22].

Lemma 2 (cut-off elimination). *Let $\mathbf{N}$ be a finite safe net system, $\mathcal{U}(\mathbf{N})$ its unfolding and $C \in \mathcal{C}(\mathcal{U}(\mathbf{N}))$ a configuration. There exists a configuration $C' \in \mathcal{C}(\mathcal{U}(\mathbf{N}))$ without cut-offs such that $\mathsf{M}^{ad}(C) = \mathsf{M}^{ad}(C')$.*

Relying on the results developed so far we are finally close to provide an algorithm for checking the BINI property for safe net systems. Note that ad-complete and d-complete prefixes are only ensured to witnesses causal interferences. However along the lines of [16], we can show that given a safe net system a constructive procedure allows us to obtain a net which is BINI if and only if the original net is, and where all interferences have been reduced to causal ones.

Lemma 3 (causal reduction). *Let $\mathbf{N}$ be a safe net system. It is possible to build a safe net called causal reduct of $\mathbf{N}$, denoted by $\gamma(\mathbf{N})$, such that $\mathbf{N}$ is BINI iff $\gamma(\mathbf{N})$ has a weak causal place.*

The details of the construction of $\gamma(\mathbf{N})$ are omitted here since such construction for the BINI property is very similar to the one for BNDC in [16]. It causes at most the doubling of the size of the net.

On these bases we developed Algorithm 1. It first computes the causal reduct $\mathbf{N}' = \gamma(\mathbf{N})$ of $\mathbf{N}$. Then it builds an ad-complete prefix of the unfolding $\mathcal{U}(\mathbf{N}')$, looking, at each step, for the presence of causal dependencies between high and low transitions satisfying the conditions in Theorem 3. The starting unfolding prefix U is the initial marking of $\mathbf{N}'$. At each step, a *possible extension* of U, namely an event e' of $\mathcal{U}(\mathbf{N}')$ such that $\bullet e' \subseteq C^\circ$ for some configuration C of U, is added. The set of possible extensions is updated by the procedure PE.

Data: A safe c-net system **N**
Result: 'yes' iff **N** is *BINI*
compute $\gamma(\mathbf{N})$;
$U := \gamma(m_0)$;
PE(U, pe);
while $pe \neq \emptyset$ **do**
    | take $t \in pe$ s.t. $[t]$ is $<$-minimal;
    | **if** $\pi_1(t) \in L$ **then**
    | **if** $\exists h \in H_U, p' \in P_U : p' \in {}^{\bullet}t \cap h^+ \wedge \{d \in D_U | h < d < t\} = \emptyset$ **then**
    | | **return** *'no'*
    | **end**
    | **end**
    | **if** t *is not a cut-off* **then**
    | add t to U;
    | **end**
    | PE(U,pe);
end
return *'yes'*

Algorithm 1. Algorithm to decide BINI on safe net systems.

Theorem 4 (correctness of the algorithm for safe net systems). *Let* **N** *be a safe net system. Then Algorithm 1 always terminates and provides the answer 'yes' iff* **N** *is BINI.*

6 Implementation and Experimental Results

A tool UBIC2 (*Unfolding-Based Interference Checker 2*) [19], which checks the property BINI on safe net systems by resorting to Algorithm 1, has been implemented as an extension of the tool UBIC for BNDC [16]. Both UBIC and UBIC2 are based on CUNF [23], a toolset for the computation of the unfolding of contextual Petri nets.

The tool UBIC2 takes as input a safe net **N** in the PEP ll_net format, documented in [23]. The security level of transitions is determined by the first character of their name: "h" stands for high, "d" for downgrading any other character for low. Depending on the selected option, the tool can either stop when the first interference witness is found (if any) or compute a complete unfolding prefix.

The benefits arising from resorting to a true-concurrent semantics rather than to an interleaving one have been already discussed in [16], where UBIC is shown to outperform in several cases tools based on interleaving approaches like ANICA [20] (which in turn has better performances than PNSC [9]).

The discussions and tests which follows are thus mainly aimed at assessing to what extent the increased complexity and the additional data structures needed for managing the downgrading influence the performances. As such, they focus on the tools UBIC and UBIC2. We also keep an eye on the comparison with the tool ANICA, based on the interleaving semantics, in order to get a confirmation

Table 1. Test results on **C** nets.

| Size | Places | Trans | UBIC | | UBIC2 | | ANICA |
			Time (sec)	Mem (MB)	Time (sec)	Mem (MB)	Time (sec)
25	200	200	0.032	8.277	0.037	8.367	1.167
50	400	400	0.145	25.922	0.166	25.918	4.616
100	800	800	1.010	84.738	1.074	84.469	25.730
200	1600	1600	7.947	293.113	8.022	291.605	210.695
300	2400	2400	31.634	615.156	32.900	615.898	779.620

of the gain of efficiency provided by a true concurrent approach in the case of highly concurrent systems.

The tests have been run on a laptop mounting Intel®Core™i3-3227U CPU @ 1.90GHz, 4GB of RAM @ 1.90GHz and XUbuntu GNU/Linux version 13.04. For each test the following data are reported:

- *Size:* size of the net w.r.t. parameters that depend on the kind of net,
- *Places:* number of places in the net before any kind of processing,
- *Trans:* number of transitions in the net before any kind of processing,
- *X Time (sec):* time needed by tool X to analyse the net (in seconds),
- *X Mem (MB):* memory consumed by tool X to analyse the net (in MB).

The tests presented below have been conducted on two families of systems.

1. Generalisations $\mathbf{C}(m)$ of the file signature checker Fig. 1, with m multiple parallel components. The results are reported in Table 1. All the instances are not BNDC (whence not BINI). The tools have been invoked by requiring to find all possible interferences. We did not report the memory usage for ANICA because it invokes subprocesses, a fact that makes it very difficult to get an accurate measure. Hence very few can be said about the comparison of UBIC2 and ANICA in terms of memory usage. We also compared UBIC2 and ANICA on the checking of property BINI using variations of net system **C** with downgrading transitions, namely on systems consisting of parallel copies of the net system **P** in Fig. 2 (UBIC was not included in the comparison as it does not deal with downgradings). The results are almost identical to those in the last two columns of Table 1, hence not reported.
2. Nets $\mathbf{R}(m)$ implementing a simple mutual exclusion algorithm described in [16], parametric with respect to the number m of processes competing for the resource. The results are reported in Table 2. All the instances are not BNDC and hence they are not BINI.

The experimental results in Tables 1 and 2 are quite reassuring. They show that, when verifying BNDC, UBIC2 has almost the same performances as UBIC in terms of execution time and memory consumption. In turn, UBIC was shown in [16] to often outperform interleaving based tools and this is confirmed here.

Table 2. Test results on **R** nets.

Size	Places	Trans	UBIC Time (sec)	UBIC Mem (MB)	UBIC2 Time (sec)	UBIC2 Mem (MB)
10	64	62	0.010	2.562	0.015	2.777
20	124	122	0.044	7.234	0.065	7.965
30	184	182	0.169	15.840	0.219	17.352
50	304	302	1.369	51.152	1.499	55.059
100	604	602	22.548	300.465	24.348	316.121

An overhead in memory usage is expected due to the additional data recorded in ad-markings with respect to what happens for the algorithm verifying BNDC in [16]. If ad-markings for histories are explicitly stored, the memory consumption for markings increases of a factor $O(2|H| \cdot |P|)$. The factor $|P|$ is due to the maximal size of a marking (at most all places are marked in the net), while the factor $2|H|$ is due to the number of components in the ad-marking. Roughly, we can expect that the increase in memory consumption for UBIC2 w.r.t. UBIC will be proportional to the number of high transitions in the net. Indeed this effect is visible in the tests reported in Table 2 where nets with a significant number of high transitions are considered.

Concerning the execution time, there are two kinds of overhead: the computation of the ad-marking and the exploration of histories in search of downgrading transitions. They do not seem to have a relevant impact, possibly due to the fact that the data structures used by CUNF are optimised for these operations.

7   Conclusions and Future Work

We provided a "causal" characterisation of non-interference by focusing on Petri nets and on Bisimilarity-based Intransitive Non-Interference (BINI). For the class of safe net systems, we characterised BINI on the unfolding, in terms of causalities and conflicts between high and low level transitions. Our work led to an algorithm for checking BINI based on the generation of a suitable finite prefix of the unfolding. We also developed a prototype tool UBIC2 (Unfolding-Based Interference Checker 2) [19] that implements the algorithm proposed in this paper. The algorithm, despite being in a prototypical form, exhibits promising performances compared to other tools based on interleaving semantics.

The paper mostly deals with safe Petri nets, which are widely used in system modelling and verification. This is quite convenient when resorting to unfolding techniques. A generalisation to non-safe (but still finite-state) Petri nets is possible at the price of technical complications and a reduced efficiency.

As future lines of research, we intend to explore causal characterisations of non-interference for other formalisms including process calculi and imperative languages. This would allow to establish a formal and possibly fruitful link with the huge literature on non-interference in these settings. The connection could rely on Petri net encodings of these formalisms. For process calculi many proposals can be found in the literature (see, e.g., [24–26]). For imperative languages a suitable encoding, properly capturing dependencies between computational steps, could require more sophisticated Petri net models. In particular Petri nets extended with read arcs, capable of representing the concurrent read access to shared resources, could be helpful. The use of read arcs can lead to a gain of efficiency for unfolding-based verification techniques (see, e.g., [27]). Preliminary investigations suggest that the extension of the framework in the present paper to Petri nets with read arcs is algorithmically feasible and yet non-trivial.

Our paper develops in a two-level setting, where we only consider a private and a public level. We believe that this choice is more suited for presenting the fundamental ideas and difficulties, which could be obfuscated in a more realistic and fine-grained context. The extension to an arbitrary number of security levels does not seem to oppose serious conceptual complications (the security check in a multi-level setting can be reduced to a number of checks in a two-level setting), although it could impact on performances. Another interesting refinement is the use of *selective declassification* [28], where each downgrading action d can declassify only a subset $\mathcal{H}(d) \subseteq H$ of high actions. Again, we believe that our approach can be easily adapted by slightly changing the notion of ad-marking.

Opacity has been studied in the setting of Petri nets [29] as a general notion, capable of capturing various confidentiality properties, including non-interference notions with downgrading. Exploring the possibility of exploiting causal semantics in this setting appears as an interesting venue of future research. We would also like to investigate the relation with other approaches which exploit Petri nets and causal semantics in the presence of partial information. In particular, *diagnosability* properties [30] (roughly, the possibility of deducing hidden action occurrences from the observation of visible ones) seem similar in spirit to non-interference properties.

Acknowledgements. We are grateful to the the anonymous referees for their insightful comments and suggestions on the submitted version of this paper.

References

1. Denning, D.E.: A lattice model of secure information flow. Commun. ACM **19**(5), 236–243 (1976)
2. Goguen, J.A., Meseguer, J.: Security policies and security models. In: IEEE Symposium on Security and Privacy, pp. 11–20 (1982)
3. Rushby, J.M.: Design and verification of secure systems. In: SOSP 1981, pp. 12–21. ACM (1981)
4. Haigh, J.T., Young, W.D.: Extending the noninterference version of mls for sat. IEEE Trans. Softw. Eng. **13**(2), 141–150 (1987)
5. Rushby, J.: Noninterference, transitivity and channel-control security policies. Technical report. Technical report CSL-92-02, SRI International (1992)

6. Mantel, H., Sands, D.: Controlled declassification based on intransitive noninterference. In: Chin, W.-N. (ed.) APLAS 2004. LNCS, vol. 3302, pp. 129–145. Springer, Heidelberg (2004)
7. Bossi, A., Piazza, C., Rossi, S.: Modelling downgrading in information flow security. In: CSFW2004, pp. 187–201. IEEE (2004)
8. Best, E., Darondeau, P., Gorrieri, R.: On the decidability of non interference over unbounded Petri nets. In: SecCo 2010. EPTCS, vol. 51, pp. 16–33 (2010)
9. Gorrieri, R., Vernali, M.: On intransitive non-interference in some models of concurrency. In: Aldini, A., Gorrieri, R. (eds.) FOSAD 2011. LNCS, vol. 6858, pp. 125–151. Springer, Heidelberg (2011)
10. Focardi, R., Gorrieri, R., Martinelli, F.: Classification of security properties. In: Focardi, R., Gorrieri, R. (eds.) FOSAD 2001. LNCS, vol. 2946, pp. 139–185. Springer, Heidelberg (2004)
11. McCullough, D.: Noninterference and the composability of security properties. In: IEEE Symposium on Security and Privacy, pp. 178–186. IEEE (1988)
12. Wittbold, J., Johnson, D.: Information flow in nondeterministic systems. In: IEEE Symposium on Security and Privacy, pp. 148–161. IEEE (1990)
13. Ryan, P., Schneider, Y.: Process algebra and non-interference. J. Comput. Secur. 9(1/2), 75–103 (2001)
14. Mantel, H.: Possibilistic definitions of security - an assembly kit. In: CSFW 2000, pp. 185–199. IEEE (2000)
15. Busi, N., Gorrieri, R.: Structural non-interference in elementary and trace nets. Math. Struct. Comput. Sci. 19(6), 1065–1090 (2009)
16. Baldan, P., Carraro, A.: Non-interference by unfolding. In: Ciardo, G., Kindler, E. (eds.) PETRI NETS 2014. LNCS, vol. 8489, pp. 190–209. Springer, Heidelberg (2014)
17. Nielsen, M., Plotkin, G., Winskel, G.: Petri nets, event structures and domains, part 1. Theor. Comput. Sci. 13, 85–108 (1981)
18. Esparza, J., Heljanko, K.: Unfoldings - A Partial order Approach to Model Checking. EACTS Monographs in Theoretical Computer Science. Springer, Heidelberg (2008)
19. Baldan, P., Burato, F., Carraro, A.: UBIC2: unfolding-based interference checker 2 (2014). https://bitbucket.org/fburato/ubic2/
20. Technology, S.: ANICA: automated non-interference check assistant (2011). http://service-technology.org/anica
21. McMillan, K.L.: A technique of state space search based on unfolding. Formal Meth. Syst. Des. 6(1), 45–65 (1995)
22. Khomenko, V., Koutny, M., Vogler, W.: Canonical prefixes of Petri net unfoldings. Acta Informatica 40, 95–118 (2003)
23. Rodríguez, C., Schwoon, S.: Cunf: a tool for unfolding and verifying Petri nets with read arcs. In: Van Hung, D., Ogawa, M. (eds.) ATVA 2013. LNCS, vol. 8172, pp. 492–495. Springer, Heidelberg (2013)
24. Gorrieri, R., Montanari, U.: SCONE: a simple calculus of nets. CONCUR 1990. LNCS, vol. 458, pp. 2–31. Springer, Heidelberg (1990)
25. Devillers, R., Klaudel, H., Koutny, M.: A compositional Petri net translation of general pi-calculus terms. Formal Aspects Comput. 20(4–5), 429–450 (2008)
26. Meyer, R., Khomenko, V., Hüchting, R.: A polynomial translation of π-calculus (FCP) to safe Petri nets. In: Koutny, M., Ulidowski, I. (eds.) CONCUR 2012. LNCS, vol. 7454, pp. 440–455. Springer, Heidelberg (2012)
27. Baldan, P., Corradini, A., König, B., Schwoon, S., Rodríguez, C.: Efficient unfolding of contextual Petri nets. Theor. Comput. Sci. 449(1), 2–22 (2012)

28. Best, E., Darondeau, P.: Deciding selective declassification of Petri nets. In: Degano, P., Guttman, J.D. (eds.) Principles of Security and Trust. LNCS, vol. 7215, pp. 290–308. Springer, Heidelberg (2012)
29. Bryans, J., Koutny, M., Ryan, P.: Modelling dynamic opacity using Petri nets with silent actions. In: Dimitrakos, T., Martinelli, F. (eds.) FAST. IIFIP, vol. 173, pp. 159–172. Springer, Heidelberg (2005)
30. Haar, S.: Types of asynchronous diagnosability and the reveals-relation in occurrence nets. IEEE Trans. Autom. Control **55**(10), 2310–2320 (2010)

Reduction and Abstraction Techniques for BIP

Mohamad Noureddine[2]($\boxtimes$), Mohamad Jaber[2],
Simon Bliudze[1], and Fadi A. Zaraket[2]

[1] Ecole Polytechnique Fédérale de Lausanne, Station 14, 1015 Lausanne, Switzerland
simon.bliudze@epfl.ch
[2] American University of Beirut, Beirut, Lebanon
{man17,mj54,fz11}@aub.edu.lb

Abstract. Reduction and abstraction techniques have been proposed to address the state space explosion problem in verification. In this paper, we present reduction and abstraction techniques for component-based systems modeled in BIP (Behavior, Interaction and Priority). Given a BIP system consisting of several atomic components, we select two atomic components amenable for reduction and compute their product. The resulting product component typically contains constants and branching bisimilar states. We use constant propagation to reduce the resulting component. Then we use a branching bisimulation abstraction to compute an abstraction of the product component. The presented method is fully implemented and scales to large designs not possible to verify with existing techniques.

1 Introduction

As systems become more complex, verifying their correctness becomes harder, especially in the presence of state explosion. Researchers have proposed reduction and abstraction techniques to address this problem [11,14,17]. We discuss and compare to them in Sect. 6.

We target component-based systems (CBS) expressed in the BIP (Behavior, Interaction and Priority) framework [2]. BIP uses a dedicated language and toolset supporting a rigorous design flow. The BIP language allows to build complex systems by coordinating the behavior of a set of atomic components. Behavior is described with Labeled Transition Systems (LTS) where transitions are annotated with data and functions written in C. Coordination between components is layered. The first layer describes the interactions between components that allow synchronization and data transfer. The second layer describes dynamic priorities between the interactions to express scheduling policies. The combination of interactions and priorities characterizes the overall architecture of a system. Moreover, BIP has rigorous operational semantics: the behavior of a composite component is formally described as the composition of the behaviors

---

Mohamad Noureddine – The presented work was partially realised while this author was at EPFL for a summer internship. The authors are listed alphabetically.

I. Lanese and E. Madelaine (Eds.): FACS 2014, LNCS 8997, pp. 288–305, 2015.
DOI: 10.1007/978-3-319-15317-9_18

of its atomic components. This allows a direct relation between the underlying semantic model and its (automatically synthesized) implementation.

The BIP framework uses: (1) DFinder [3], a compositional and incremental verification tool-set, and (2) NuSMV [8] model checker, to verify BIP system invariants.

In this paper, we present reduction and abstraction techniques for component-based systems modeled in BIP. Given a BIP system consisting of several atomic components, our method automatically selects a pair of candidate components that have a high reduction potential based on their data dependencies and their synchronization. Our method uses component selection heuristics similar to [9,10,19] and provides a user-defined selection API. Then, our method computes the product of the selected pair of atomic components which renders the interaction data transfer operations into transition data transfer operations. This often uncovers opportunities for constant propagation in the product component that were hidden before. Moreover, the product operation results in product transitions of two types: (1) *non-observable* transitions involved only in a singleton interaction (i.e., a singleton interaction involves only one component) and with no actions; (2) *observable* transitions involved in either multiparty interactions or in a singleton interaction but with actions. Non-observable transitions form a branching bisimilar equivalence relation that partitions the state space. Our method detects and merges equivalence classes into representative states resulting in an abstraction of the product component.

The presented techniques are fully implemented. We evaluate our method using (1) traffic light controller case study and (2) medium to large configurations of an Automatic Teller Machine (ATM). The results show that our method drastically reduces the state space and enables verifying invariants more efficiently. In this paper, we make the following contributions:

- We abstract a BIP system with a branching bisimulation equivalence that we formalize and that leverages observable and non-observable transitions in the BIP context.
- We provide structural heuristics for selecting candidate pairs of components amenable for reduction and abstraction.
- We also provide an API for user-defined component selection criteria.
- We formalize the product operation between two BIP components and embed constant propagation in it.

The rest of the paper is structured as follows. Section 2 discusses needed background information about BIP. We present the merging and constant propagation techniques in Sect. 3, and the branching bisimulation reduction in Sect. 4. Section 5 illustrates the results obtained from verifying models reduced using our method. We summarize related work in Sect. 6 and conclude in Sect. 7.

2   BIP - Behavior, Interaction, Priority

We recall the necessary concepts of the BIP framework [2]. BIP allows to construct systems by superposing three layers of modeling: Behavior, Interaction, and Priority. The *behavior* layer consists of a set of atomic components represented by transition systems. Atomic components are Labeled Transition Systems (LTS) extended with C functions and data. Transitions are labeled with sets of communication ports. The *interaction* layer models the collaboration between components. Interactions are described using sets of ports. The *priority* layer is used to specify scheduling policies applied to the interaction layer, given by a strict partial order on interactions.

Atomic Components. An atomic component is endowed with a finite set of local variables X taking values in a domain Data. Atomic components synchronize and exchange data with each others through *ports*. Below, we will denote by $\mathbb{B}[X]$ the set of boolean predicates over X and by $Exp[X]$ the set of assignment statements of the form $X := f(X)$.

Definition 1 (Port). *A port $p[X_p]$, where $X_p \subseteq X$, is defined by a port identifier p and some data variables in a set X_p (referred to as the support set). We will also denote this set of variables by $p.X$.*

Definition 2 (Atomic component). *An atomic component B is defined as a tuple (P, L, X, T), where P is a set of ports,[1] L is a set of control locations, X is a set of variables and $T \subset L \times P \times \mathbb{B}[X] \times Exp[X] \times L$ is a transition relation, such that, for each transition $\tau = (l, p[X_p], g_\tau, f_\tau, l') \in T$, $g_\tau \in \mathbb{B}[X]$ is a Boolean guard over X and $f_\tau \in Exp[X]$ is a partial mapping associating to some $x \in X$ the corresponding statement $f_\tau^x(X)$.*

For $\tau = (l, p[X_p], g_\tau, f_\tau, l') \in T$ a transition of the LTS, l (resp. l') is referred to as the source (resp. destination) location and p is a port through which an interaction with another component can take place. Transition τ can be executed only if the guard g_τ evaluates to true, and f_τ is a computation step: a set of assignments to local variables in X.

In the sequel we use the dot notation. Given a transition $\tau = (l, p[X_p], g_\tau, f_\tau, l')$, $\tau.src$, $\tau.port$, $\tau.guard$, $\tau.func$, and $\tau.dest$ denote l, p, g_τ, f_τ, and l', respectively. Also, the set of variables used in a transition is defined as $var(f_\tau) = \{x \in X \mid x := f^x(X) \in f_\tau\}$. Given an atomic component B, $B.P$ denotes the set of ports of the atomic component B, $B.L$ denotes its set of locations, etc. We denote by $\mathbf{X}$ the set of valuations of the variables X.

Semantics of Atomic Components. The semantics of an atomic component is an LTS over configurations and ports, formally defined as follows:

Definition 3 (Semantics of Atomic Components). *The semantics of the atomic component $B = (P, L, X, T)$ is defined as the LTS $S_B = (Q_B, P_B, \rightarrow)$,[2] where $Q_B = L \times \mathbf{X}$, $P_B = P \times \mathbf{X}$ denotes the set of labels, that is, ports augmented with valuations of variables and $\rightarrow = \{((l, v), p(v_p), (l', v')) \mid$*

---

[1] All sets are finite.

[2] Here and below, we omit the index on $\rightarrow$, since it is always clear from the context.

$\exists \tau = (l, p[X_p], g_\tau, f_\tau, l') \in T : g_\tau(v) \wedge v'$ *is equal to the value of* $f_\tau(v_p/v)\}$, *where* v_p *is a valuation of the variables* X_p.

Transition $(l, v) \xrightarrow{p(v_p)} (l', v')$ is possible iff there exists a transition $(l', p[X_p], g_\tau, f_\tau, l)$, such that $g_\tau(v') = \mathtt{true}$. As a result, the valuation of variables X is updated to $v' = f_\tau(v_p/v)$, i.e. the values of variables X_p are updated to v_p before the application of f.

Creating Composite Components. Atomic components interact by synchronizing transitions. Upon synchronization, data values can be transferred between components.

Definition 4 (Interaction). *An interaction* a *is a tuple* (P_a, G_a, F_a), *where* $P_a \subseteq \bigcup_{i=1}^{n} B_i.P$ *is a nonempty set of ports that contains at most one port of every component, that is,* $\forall i : 1 \leq i \leq n : |B_i.P \cap P_a| \leq 1$. *Denoting by* $X_a = \bigcup_{p \in P_a} X_p$ *the set of variables available to* a, $G_a \in \mathbb{B}[X_a]$ *is a boolean guard and* $F_a : \mathbf{X_a} \rightarrow \mathbf{X_a}$ *is an update function.* P_a *is the set of connected ports called the support set of* a.

Definition 5 (Semantics of Composite Components). *Let* $\mathcal{B} = \{B_1, \ldots, B_n\}$ *be a set of atomic components with their respective semantic LTS* $S_{B_i} = (Q_{B_i}, P_{B_i}, \rightarrow)$ *(recall, Definition. 3, that the states* Q_{B_i} *and labels* P_{B_i} *comprise valuations of data variables); let* γ *be a set of interactions. The composition of* $\mathcal{B}$ *with* γ *is the LTS* $\gamma(\mathcal{B}) = (Q, \gamma, \rightarrow)$, *where* $Q = Q_{B_1} \times \ldots \times Q_{B_n}$ *and* $\rightarrow$ *is the least set of transitions satisfying the following rule*

$$\frac{a = (\{p_i\}_{i \in I}, G_a, F_a) \in \gamma \qquad G_a(\{v_{p_i}\}_{i \in I})}{\forall i \in I, \; q_i \xrightarrow{p_i(v_i)}_i q_i' \wedge v_i = F_a^i(\{v_{p_i}\}_{i \in I}) \qquad \forall i \notin I, \; q_i = q_i'}{(q_1, \ldots, q_n) \xrightarrow{a} (q_1', \ldots, q_n')}$$

where v_{p_i} *denotes the valuation of the variables attached to port* p_i *and* F_a^i *is the partial function derived from* F_a *restricted to the variables associated with* p_i.

The meaning of the above rule is the following: if there exists an interaction a such that all its ports are enabled in the current state and its guard evaluates to $\mathtt{true}$, then the interaction can be fired. When a is fired, all involved components evolve according to the interaction and not involved components remain in the same state.

Finally, we consider systems defined as a parallel composition of components together with an initial state.

Definition 6 (System). *A BIP system* $\mathcal{S}$ *is a tuple* $(B, Init, v)$ *where* B *is a composite component,* $Init \in B_1.L \times \ldots \times B_n.L$ *is the initial state of* B, *and* $v \in \mathbf{X^{Init}}$ *where* $X^{Init} \subseteq \bigcup_{i=1}^{n} B_i.X$.

3   Merging and Constant Propagation

In this section we present two techniques *merging* and *constant propagation* in order to reduce the state space of the system. First, we select candidate components for merging based on a set of heuristics. Then, we apply a constant propagation technique [16] that will reduce the state space by removing some data variables.

3.1   Merging Components

Throughout this paper, we assume that the input BIP systems have no priority rules and that all the automata in the BIP atomic components are complete. An automaton is complete iff in any location, the disjunction of guards of the outgoing transitions evaluates to true.

Let $\mathcal{B}$ be a set of atomic components and γ be an interaction model. Consider two atomic components $B_1, B_2 \in \mathcal{B}$ and denote $I(B_1, B_2) = \{a \in \gamma \mid P_a \subseteq B_1.P \cup B_2.P\}$ the set of interactions involving only B_1 and B_2; $P_{12} = \bigcup_{a \in I(B_1, B_2)} P_a$ the set of all ports that are part of some interaction $a \in I(B_1, B_2)$ and p_a a new port corresponding to an interaction $a \in I(B_1, B_2)$. Assume further that all ports involved in interactions between B_1 and B_2 are not involved in interactions with any other atomic components, i.e., for any $a \in \gamma$, either $a \in I(B_1, B_2)$, or $P_a \cap P_{12} = \emptyset$.

Definition 7 (Product Component). *Let B_1 and B_2 be two atomic components as above. Their product is an atomic component $prod(B_1, B_2) = (P, L, X, \rightarrow)$, where:*

- $P = B_1.P \cup B_2.P \cup \{p_a \mid a \in I(B_1, B_2)\} \setminus P_{12}$,
- $X = B_1.X \cup B_2.X$,
- $\rightarrow$ *is the minimal transition relation induced by the following rules,*

$$\frac{a \in I(B_1, B_2) \quad P_a = \{p_1, p_2\} \quad l_1 \xrightarrow{(p_1, g_1, f_1)} l_1' \quad l_2 \xrightarrow{(p_2, g_2, f_2)} l_2'}{(l_1, l_2) \xrightarrow{\left(p_a,\ g_1 \wedge g_2 \wedge G_a,\ (f_1 \cup f_2) \circ F_a\right)} (l_1', l_2')},$$

$$\frac{\{i, j\} = \{1, 2\} \quad p \in B_i.P \setminus P_{12} \quad l_i \xrightarrow{(p, g, f)} l_i' \quad l_j' = l_j}{(l_1, l_2) \xrightarrow{(p, g, f)} (l_1', l_2')},$$

- $L = \{(l_1, l_2) \in B_1.L \times B_2.L \mid \exists (l_1', l_2') \in B_1.L \times B_2.L : (l_1, l_2) \rightarrow (l_1', l_2')\}$.

Informally, the product component operation is a syntactic analogue of the semantic *parallel composition* operation of two atomic components as defined in Definition 5.

Definition 8 (Component Merging). *Let $\gamma(\mathcal{B})$ be a composite component and B_1, B_2 be atomic components as above. We define the component merging operation $merge(\gamma(\mathcal{B})) = \gamma'(\mathcal{B}')$ where*

- $\mathcal{B}' = \mathcal{B} \cup \{prod(B_1, B_2)\} \setminus \{B_1, B_2\}$, *and*
- $\gamma' = \big(\gamma \setminus I(B_1, B_2)\big) \cup \big\{(\{p_a\}, \texttt{true}, \texttt{id}) \mid a \in I(B_1, B_2)\big\}$

By Definition 5 system $\gamma'(\mathcal{B}')$ is semantically equivalent to $\gamma(\mathcal{B})$ since the product component $prod(B_1, B_2) \in \mathcal{B}'$ from Definition 7, where B_1 and B_2 are atomic components in $\mathcal{B}$, is semantically equivalent to a *parallel composition*.

Several heuristics for selecting candidate components have been presented for LTS systems with no data transfer [9,10,19]. These heuristics consider merging pairs of components and favor the ones that result in smaller components. Our method *iteratively* selects and merges candidate components for merging based on a set of heuristics that take data transfer and component synchronization into consideration.

The first heuristic favors the pairs of components with the largest amount of data transfer. Intuitively, larger data transfer operations offer more room for stuck at constant variables that we detect and eliminate using constant propagation. The width of the data transfer considers the type of data variables (integers are wider than Boolean variable). The second heuristic favors the components that are highly synchronized since they produce more compact products. Intuitively, the product of highly synchronized components results in a large unreachable state space that is easily detected. Both are structural analysis heuristics and take polynomial running time with respect to the size of the system.

Our method also supports a merge selection API that users can implement to rank candidate component pairs. The API passes a pair of components to the user implementation and the implementation evaluates the pair and returns a merging rank value. The pair with highest rank is considered for merging.

Product components can be very large which is a problem to compositional model checking techniques in DFinder and NuSMV. Our method considers the product of components B_1 and B_2 if the maximum number of possible transitions of $B_1 \times B_2$ is smaller than a threshold value $n_1 \times n_2 \le n_t$ where n_1 and n_2 are the number of transitions in B_1 and B_2, respectively.

3.2 Constant Propagation

We remove stuck-at-constant data variables by following the basic definition of constant propagation from [16,20]. A variable is stuck-at-constant if it is constant on all possible control locations of an atomic component. Applying constant propagation as an intermediate step in compositional verification tools is not novel and is a well established technique [12,15]. To the best of our knowledge, we are the first to apply it in the context of BIP systems.

Given a composite component $\gamma(\{B_i\}_{i \in I})$ and an atomic component B_k such that $k \in I$, we construct the composite component $\gamma(\{B_j\}_{j \in J}, B'_k)$ where $J = I \setminus \{k\}$ and B'_k is an atomic component such that $B'_k.L = B_k.L$, $B'_k.X = B_k.X \setminus X_c$ where $X_c \subseteq B_k.X$ is the set of stuck-at-constant variables in B_k, and $B'_k.T = T'$ where T' is T with each constant variable $x \in X_c$ is replaced by its constant value appropriately.

Algorithm 1. Algorithm for building CFG of an atomic component

$l_0 \leftarrow$ initial location of B
Create vertex v_{init} s.t. $v_{init}.l = l_0$ and $v_{init}.f =$ initial valuation of $B.X$
Create vertex v_{l_0} s.t. $v_{l_0}.l = l_0$ and $v_{l_0}.f = \phi$
Create vertex (v_{init}, v_{l_0})
$Vertices[l_0] \leftarrow v_{l_0}$
$stack.push(l_0)$
while $\neg stack.isEmpty()$ **do**
   $l \leftarrow stack.pop()$
   Set l as visited
   $v_l \leftarrow Vertices[l]$
   for all τ s.t. $\tau.src = l$ **do**
      Create vertex v s.t. $v.l = l$ and $v.f = \tau.f$
      Create edge (v_l, v)
      if $\tau.dest$ visited **then**
         Create edge $(v, Vertices[\tau.dest])$
      else
         Create vertex v_{dest} s.t. $v.dest.l = \tau.dest$ and $v_{dest}.f = \phi$
         Create edge (v, v_{dest})
         $Vertices[\tau.dest] \leftarrow v_{dest}$
         $stack.push(\tau.dest)$
      end if
   end for
end while

Definition 9 (Control Flow Graph). *The control flow graph (CFG) of an atomic component B is a directed graph (V, E) where:*

- *V is a set of vertices, each representing a control location $l \in B.L$ and a set of computational steps in B. We denote by $v.l$ and $v.f$ the control location and the set of computational steps in $v \in V$, respectively.*
- *E is a set of edges, such that $(v_1, v_2) \in E$ iff $\exists (\tau \in B.T). (v_1.l = \tau.src \wedge v_2.l = \tau.dest) \wedge (v_1.f = \tau.f \vee v_2.f = \tau.f).$*

Listing 1 shows the algorithm used for constructing the CFG of an atomic component B. We create an empty vertex for each control location in B. We denote by v_l the empty vertex corresponding to control location $l \in B.L$. Then we perform a depth first traversal of the LTS of B. For each control location l, for every outgoing transition τ, we create a vertex v_τ such that $v_\tau.l = l$ and $v_\tau.f = \tau.f$, and create edges (v_l, v_τ) and $(v_\tau, v_{\tau.dest})$. The empty vertices can be easily discarded, but we keep them to simplify the constant propagation step. Intuitively, this step is conservative as it abstracts away guards and may not consider some potential stuck-at-constant variables. Alternatively, symbolic computation can be used to take advantage of that.

Definition 10 (Lattice element). *A lattice element is a representation of static knowledge of the value of a variable x during the execution of a constant propagation algorithm [20]. A lattice element can have one of three types:*

– $\top$: x is likely to have a yet to be determined constant value.
– $\bot$: x's value cannot be determined statically.
– c_i: x has the value i.

Definition 11 (Lattice element meet). *The meet ($\sqcup$) operation of two lattice elements is an operation such that: (1) $\top \sqcup any = any$; (2) $\bot \sqcup any = \bot$; (3) $c_i \sqcup c_j = c_i$ if $i = j$; and (4) $c_i \sqcup c_j = \bot$ if $i \neq j$.*

Listing 2 shows the constant propagation algorithm. Given an atomic component B, we start by constructing the CFG $G(B) = (V, E)$. At each vertex $v \in V$, a variable is associated with two lattice elements, an entry element and an exit element. We initialize all variables to have the $\top$ lattice element. Variables that take part in any interaction are directly assigned the $\bot$ element since their values cannot be predicted from the component itself. Visiting a vertex v consists of computing the entry lattice elements for each variable $x \in var(v.f)$, where $var(v.f)$ is the set of variables referenced in $v.f$. This is done by performing a meet operation on the exit lattice elements of all vertices v' such $(v', v) \in E$. We then evaluate $v.f$ based on the new entry elements. The rules for the evaluation of the addition operator on lattice elements are: (1) $\top + (\top \text{ or } c_i) = \top$; (2) $\bot + any = \bot$; and (3) $c_i + c_j = c_{i+j}$. The rules for the rest of operators follow similarly.

If the evaluation of $v.f$ causes a change in the exit lattice element of any variable $x \in B.X$, all vertices v'' such that $(v, v'') \in E$ are marked for visiting. A fixed point is reached once no further exit elements are changes and no vertices are still marked for visiting. After reaching the fixed point, we form the set of stuck at constant variables $X_c = \{x : x \in B.X \text{ and } \forall v \in V. \, Entry[v][x] \text{ is constant}\}$ that have constant lattice elements at the entry of every vertex. Finally, we construct $T' = \{(l, p, g'_\tau, f'_\tau, l') \mid (l, p, g_\tau, f_\tau, l') \in T\}$ where g'_τ and f'_τ are the new guards and actions. We substitute the X_c variables with their corresponding constant values in the guards $g'_\tau = g_\tau[x \in X_c / Entry[v][x]]$ where $v.f = f_\tau$. We do the same for the actions $f'_\tau = (f_\tau \setminus \{x := f^x(X) \mid x \in X_c\})[x \in X_c / Entry[v][x]]$ but after removing the assignment statements corresponding to X_c variables.

4   Branching Bisimulation Abstraction

To cope with the increase in the number of control locations introduced by the component merging process, we apply a *branching bisimulation* based abstraction [13]. A branching bisimulation equivalence relation partitions the control locations into disjoint sets of locations that are branching bisimilar [21]. We recall the definition of branching bisimulation for LTS systems from [5,13] and apply it in the BIP context.

Definition 12 (Partition of control locations). *Given an atomic component B, $\pi \subseteq 2^{B.L}$ is partition of the set of control locations $B.L$ iff (1) $\bigcup_{L \in \pi} L = B.L$; and (2) $\forall L', L'' \in \pi, \, L' \neq L'' \Rightarrow L' \cap L'' = \emptyset$.*

We denote by $\pi(l)$ the block $L \in \pi$ containing the control location l.

Algorithm 2. Constant propagation algorithm

$G \leftarrow CFG(B)$
for all $v \in G.V$ **do**
    for all $x \in var(v.f)$ **do**
        $Entry[v][x] \leftarrow Exit[v][x] \leftarrow \top$
    end for
end for
$v_0 \leftarrow G.v_{init}$
$stack.push(v_0)$
while $\neg stack.isEmpty()$ **do**
    $v \leftarrow stack.pop()$
    for all $x \in var(v.f)$ **do**
        $Entry[v][x] \leftarrow meet(Exit[v'][x]$ $\forall v' \in G.V$ s.t. $(v', v) \in G.E)$
    end for
    for all $x \in var(v.f)$ **do**
        $Exit[v][x] = evaluate(v.f)$
        if $Exit[v][x]$ *changed* **then**
            for all v'' s.t. $(v, v'') \in E$ **do**
                $stack.push(v'')$
            end for
        end if
    end for
end while

Definition 13 (Non-observable transition). *Given a composite component* $\gamma(\{B_i\}_{i \in I})$, *an atomic component* B_k *for* $k \in I$, *a transition* $\tau = (l, p, g_\tau, f_\tau, l') \in B_k.T$ *is a non-observable transition iff (1)* $f_\tau = \emptyset$; *and (2)* $\forall a = (P_a, G_a, F_a) \in \gamma$, $p \in P_a \Rightarrow (P_a = \{p\} \wedge F_a = \emptyset)$.

Informally, non-observable transitions involved only in a singleton interaction and with no actions. Non-observable transitions form a branching bisimilar equivalence relation that partition the state space.

    Let $\varepsilon = \{(l, l') \mid \exists \tau = (l, p, g_\tau, f_\tau, l') \in B_k.T$ *and* τ is non-observable$\}$. The set ε^* denotes the reflexive transitive closure of ε. We use the notation $l \xrightarrow{p} l'$ for $\tau = (l, p, g_\tau, f_\tau, l') \in B.T$.

Definition 14 (Branching bisimilarity relation). *Given a composite component* $\gamma(\{B_i\}_{i \in I})$, *an atomic component* B_k *for* $k \in I$, *a relation* $\mathfrak{B} = B_k.L \times B_k.L$ *is a branching bisimilarity relation on* B_k *iff:*

– $\mathfrak{B}$ *is symmetric*
– *Given* $l, \ell \in B_k.L$, $(l, \ell) \in \mathfrak{B}$ *iff* $\forall l, l_1$, $l \xrightarrow{p} l_1$,

$$\begin{cases} (l, l_1) \in \varepsilon \wedge (l_1, \ell) \in \mathfrak{B} \\ \vee \\ \exists (l_2, \ell_1 \in B_k.L), \ (\ell_1 \xrightarrow{p} l_2) \wedge (\ell, \ell_1) \in \varepsilon^* \wedge (l, \ell_1) \in \mathfrak{B} \wedge (l_1, l_2) \in \mathfrak{B} \end{cases}$$

We write $l_1 \sim l_2$ when $(l_1, l_2) \in \mathfrak{B}$. We denote by π^b the partition under the branching bisimilarity equivalence.

Definition 15 (Quotient branching bisimilar component). *Given a composite component* $\gamma(\{B_i\}_{i \in I})$, *and an atomic component* B_k *for* $k \in I$, *let* $\mathfrak{B}$ *be the largest branching bisimulation relation over* B_k, *an atomic component* B *is the quotient branching bisimilar component of* B_k *iff* B *is the atomic component with the smallest number of states such that*

1. $B.L = \pi^b$
2. $B.T = \{(\pi^b(l), p, g, f, \pi^b(l')) \mid (l, p, g, f, l') \in B_k.T \wedge ((l \sim l') \Rightarrow ((l, l') \notin \varepsilon))\}$
3. $B.P = \{p \mid \exists \tau = (l, p, g, f, l') \in B.T\}$.

Definition 16 (Branching bisimulation abstraction). *Given a composite component* $\gamma(\{B_i\}_{i \in I})$ *and an atomic component* B_k *for* $k \in I$, *we define the branching bisimulation abstraction operation*

$$abstract(k, \gamma(\{B_i\}_{i \in I})) = \gamma(\{B_i\}_{i \in I})|_{B_k = B}$$

where B_k *is replaced by its quotient branching bisimilar component* B.

Construction. We follow the signature refinement approach for branching bisimulation abstraction as presented in [5,21]. It is based on computing a *signature* for each control location $l \in B.L$. At the end of the algorithm, control locations with the same signature $sig(l)$ are bisimilar with respect to the branching bisimilarity relation $\mathfrak{B}$. Given an atomic component B, we start from an initial partition $\pi^0 = \{B.L\}$. We then keep refining the partition π w.r.t. $\mathfrak{B}$ until a fixed point is reached and we are left with a minimal partition π^b of $B.L$.

Definition 17 (Branching bisimulation signature function). *Given an atomic component* B *and a partition* π *of* $B.L$, *the branching bisimulation signature function of a control location* $l \in B.L$ *is defined as:* $sig(l) = \{(p, \pi(l_1)) \mid \exists l_2 \in B.L \text{ s.t. } (l, l_2) \in \varepsilon^* \wedge l_2 \xrightarrow{p} l_1 \wedge ((l_2, l_1) \notin \varepsilon \vee \pi(l_1) \neq \pi(l)))\}$.

Listing 3 shows the algorithm we used for computing the minimal partition π^b of the control locations $B.L$; it is a direct adaptation of the single threaded algorithm presented in [5]. Constructing the quotient atomic component from the computed partition is a direct translation of Definition 15.

Correctness. As noticed in [4], a straightforward consequence of Bloom's results [6] is that composition with sets of interactions (Definition 5), called "BIP glue operators" in [4], preserves bisimilarity. Since the only transitions that we consider non-observable in this paper do not modify the data variables of atomic component and do not participate in any of the interactions, it follows that branching bisimilarity is preserved by composition with interactions.

Algorithm 3. Branching bisimulation abstraction algorithm

BranchingBisimilarityAbstraction(B)
$\pi' \leftarrow \pi \leftarrow B.L$
repeat
   $\pi \leftarrow \pi'$
   $\pi' \leftarrow refinePartition(B, \pi)$
until $\pi' \leftarrow \pi$

---

refinePartition(B, π)
for all $l \in B.L$ **do**
   $sig \leftarrow \emptyset$
   for all $l' \in B.L$ *s.t.* $(l, p, g, f, l') \in B.T$ **do**
     if $((l, p, l') \neq \varepsilon) \vee (\pi(l') \neq \pi(l))$ **then**
       $sig \leftarrow sig \cup (p, \pi(l'))$
     end if
   end for
   insertSignature(B, π, l, sig)
end for
return $\{\{l' \in B.L \mid sig(l') = sig(l)\} \mid l \in B.L\}$

---

insertSignature(B, π, l, sig)
$sig(l) \leftarrow sig(l) \cup sig$
for all $l' \in B.L$ *s.t.* $l' \xrightarrow{\varepsilon} l$ **do**
   if $\pi(l) = \pi(l')$ **then**
     insertSignature(B, π, l', sig)
   end if
end for

The branching bisimulation abstraction introduces new behaviors as follows. Observable transitions are allowed to introduce changes to the state of the component by changing the values of the internal variables. The branching bismilarity relation only considers ports as transition labels and ignores differences in actions. Thus grouping locations and building the quotient component may introduce new sequences of transitions, especially in the cases where guards on the transitions are not mutually exclusive. Nevertheless, the interactions between the different components in the system are preserved, i.e., synchronization between the components is not affected.

5 Results

We illustrate our method using a traffic light controller case study and evaluate it using several configurations of medium to large ATM systems. We use the NuSMV [8] model checker to verify deadlock freedom of the BIP systems before and after reduction. We report on the number of BDD nodes allocated, and on the execution time taken to perform the verification. Moreover, we also report on the execution time taken by DFinder [3] to prove the deadlock freedom of the ATM design. All experiments are run on a machine with an Intel Core i7 processor and 4 GB of physical memory. We set a time-out for verification of 5000 seconds, and do not set a limit on the memory usage other than the physical limit of the machine. We use the default configuration of NuSMV and do not add any further optimizations. We use the command `check_fsm` to verify deadlock freedom of the designs.

5.1 Traffic Light Controller

Figure 1 shows a traffic light controller system modeled in BIP. It is composed of two atomic components, `timer` and `light`. The timer counts the amount of time for which the light must stay in a specific state (i.e. a specific color of the light). The light component determines the color of the traffic light. Additionally, it informs the timer about the amount of time to spend in each location through a data transfer on the interaction a between the two components.

The interaction a between the components creates a data dependence between the two. This data dependence hides the fact that the variable n has a constant value at each location in the timer component. Figure 2a shows the product component of the light and timer components. Since the `done` ports of the two components are synchronized, we replace them by a single port `donedone`. Subsequently, the interaction a is replaced by an interaction a' based solely on the newly created port. Note that this synchronization between the two `done` ports renders some transitions in the product automaton obsolete, i.e. they can never be taken and are thus removed.

Performing constant propagation on the resulting product yields to detecting that both the variables n and m are constants at each control location. We replace these variables by their constant values at each control location, and remove them from the component as shown in Fig. 2b.

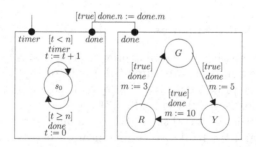

Fig. 1. Traffic light in BIP

Table 1 shows the results of running NuSMV on the translated BIP models before and after applying our reduction techniques. The *Locations* and *Transitions* columns show the total number of control locations and transitions in the

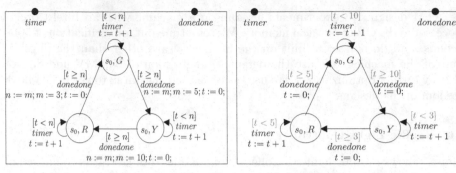

(a) Before constant propagation   (b) After constant propagation

Fig. 2. The product of the timer and light components

Table 1. Results for traffic light controller

Before reduction				After reduction			
Locations	Transitions	BDD nodes	Time(s)	Locations	Transitions	BDD nodes	Time(s)
4	5	8589	0.0088	1	6	1425	0.0016

BIP system, respectively. The *BDD Nodes* and *Time* columns show the number of allocated BDD nodes and the time taken for verification, respectively. Using branching bisimulation reduction, we are able to reduce the number of control locations from 4 to a single location. Although the component merging operation introduced an increase in the number of transitions, this addition did not affect neither the number of allocated BDD nodes nor the verification time. Our method reduced the verification time by a factor of 5 and the number of allocated BDD nodes by a factor of 6.

5.2   Automatic Teller Machine

An ATM is a computerized system that provides financial services for users in a public space. Figure 3 shows a structured BIP model of an ATM system adapted from the description provided in [7]. The system is composed of four atomic components: (1) the User, (2) the ATM, (3) the Bank Validation and (4) the Bank Transaction. It is the job of the ATM component to handle all interactions between the users and the bank. No communication between the users and the bank is allowed.

The ATM starts from an idle location and waits for the user to insert his card and enter the confidential code. The user has 5 time units to enter the code before the counter expires and the card is ejected by the ATM. Once the code is entered, the ATM checks with the bank validation unit for the correctness of the code. If the code is invalid, the card is ejected and no transaction occurs. If the code is valid, the ATM waits for the user to enter the desired amount of

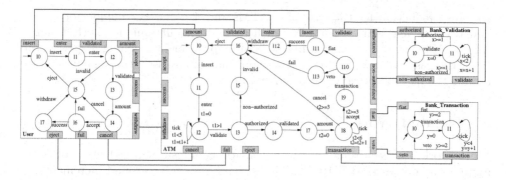

Fig. 3. Modeling of ATM system in BIP

money for the transaction. The time-out for entering the amount of money is of 6 time units.

Once the user enters the desired transaction amount, the ATM checks with the bank whether the transaction is allowed or not by communicating with the bank transaction unit. If the transaction is approved, the money is transferred to the user and the card is ejected. If the transaction is rejected, the user is notified and the card is ejected. In all cases, the ATM goes back to the idle location waiting for any additional users. In our model, we assume the presence of a single bank and multiple ATMs and users.

Table 2 shows the improvement obtained by applying our reduction method on the ATM design for a number of ATMs ranging from 2 to 50. We show the number of control locations and transitions before and after applying our reduction method. We also present the number of allocated BDD nodes and the verification time in seconds in each case for NuSMV, and the verification time taken by DFinder to prove deadlock freedom. Note that in all cases, the results were conclusive and no spurious counter-examples were generated. Our method reduced by 3 times the number of control locations in the design and by 2 times the number of transitions. Under NuSMV, it introduced large improvements in both the number of allocated BDD nodes and the verification time, achieving

Table 2. Results for ATM system

| | | | | | | NuSMV | | | | DFinder | |
| | Locations | | Transitions | | Reduction | BDD nodes | | Time (s) | | Time (s) | |
ATMs	Orig.	Red.	Orig.	Red.	Time (s)	Orig.	Red.	Orig.	Red.	Orig.	Red.
2	50	18	68	32	0.066	977,712	542,901	1.4	0.2	3	2
3	73	25	98	44	0.073	6,183,118	921,076	142.6	10.3	4	3
4	96	32	128	56	0.079	18,630,028	1,893,192	3,360.9	281.3	6	4
5	119	39	158	68	0.086	N/A	N/A	N/A	N/A	7	5
10	234	74	308	128	0.133	N/A	N/A	N/A	N/A	24	8
50	1,154	354	1,508	608	0.472	N/A	N/A	N/A	N/A	267	37

10 times reduction for the case of 4 ATMs and 4 users. For number of ATMs and users higher than 4, NuSMV reached the time-out limit for both designs. As for DFinder, our method achieved high improvement reaching a speedup of 10 in the case of 50 ATMs and users. Note that in all cases, the time needed to reduce the designs is negligible as shown in Table 2.

6   Related Work

Much work has been done on the automatic compositional reduction of communicating processes [1,9,10,19]. The techniques revolve around incrementally composing and minimizing individual components of an input system modulo an equivalence relation. Most of the techniques focus on finding heuristics for selecting components to be composed in a way that minimizes the size of the largest intermediate composed component.

The work in [9] presents a comparative study of three component selection heuristics. The first is proposed in [19] and aims at finding components such that the number of transitions that can be removed (hidden) after their parallel composition is as high as possible. The authors in [9] improve on the heuristics defined in [19] by introducing metrics to estimate the number of the transitions that can be removed after parallel composition. Our transformations can make use of the aforementioned heuristics to select candidate components for merging. In fact, our supporting tool provides an easy to use programming interface for adding and testing selection heuristics.

The work in [10] uses the concept of networks of LTSs introduced in [18] to support compositional reduction using different compositional operators. The authors use a heuristic similar to the ones presented in [9] to estimate the number of internal transitions that can be removed after applying the composition operators, and compare the obtained metric for possible compositions. Our technique differs from the work in [10] in that our transformations are solely targeted towards BIP systems, and need not be as general as the techniques presented in [10].

Additionally, the idea of computing the product of communicating finite state machines and then reducing them using a notion of state equivalence is presented in [1]. The authors propose a method to iteratively multiply the components of a given design and reduce the product at each iteration using a notion of input-output equivalence. This leads to the construction of a minimal product finite state machine representing the entire input system, on which verification is to be performed. We follow a similar approach to that presented in [1], but we do not compute the product of the entire system, component merging is based on a set of user defined heuristics and is done while considering the state explosion introduced by the product operation.

In [11], the authors address the problem of using program analysis in order to assist reduction techniques, mainly *symmetry reduction*, in limiting state-space explosion in systems composed of multiple communicating processes. Such a system is symmetric if its transition relation is invariant under some given permutations of the communicating processes. States in the system that are identical up to these permutations are considered equivalent, and lead to generating a reduced system that is bisimilar to the original system. The authors argue that symmetry reduction is affected by local state explosion in the each of the processes, and propose the usage of static analysis techniques such as *static local reachability analysis* in order to benefit the efficiency of symmetry reduction. In our work, we also make use of constant propagation, a static program analysis technique, in the benefit of reducing the number of internal variables and thus help the model checker in deciding the problem.

Graf and Steffen [14] focus on presenting a compositional minimization technique for finite state concurrent systems. This technique makes use of *interface specifications* to remove unreachable transitions of the system. Interface specifications are provided by the user and are used to define sets of observable sequences at the interfaces between communicating processes. The authors present a method that takes interface specifications into consideration when performing iterative composition and minimization, thus avoiding the state-space explosion at the intermediate composition levels. We resemble the aforementioned approach in that we consider port synchronization between components when performing merging, thus leading to removing unreachable transitions from the product component.

Compositional minimization via static analysis (CMSA) [22] selects candidate components for minimization using a mincut based algorithm such that the number of component outputs is significantly smaller that the number of inputs. CMSA then partitions the state space into equivalence classes relevant to the outputs, selects representative states of the equivalence classes, and computes a reduced circuit using a bisimulation based transformation that targets state space reduction. CMSA is applicable to circuit designs only. Our method differs in that it works on BIP systems, and resembles CMSA in that it considers merged components as candidate components, and applies a branching bisimulation abstraction with respects to the ports of the resulting product component.

7   Conclusion

Our work makes contributions to efficiently verify component-based systems modeled in BIP. First, we select pairs of components amenable for reduction and abstraction using structural heuristics. Then we merge the selected components using a product operation and we reduce the resulting component using constant propagation. Finally, we use abstraction techniques based on merging branching bisimilar states in order to reduce the size of the system and its complexity. Spurious counterexamples are detected by translating the counterexample to the original system and simulating it. Our contributions are complementary to tools that are used to verify BIP systems such as DFinder and BIP-to-NuSMV. Our reduction and abstraction techniques are completely implemented in a supporting tool that provides an API to specify user defined merging heuristics.

In the future, we plan to extend our work to handle priorities in the BIP context. We also plan to define feedback guidance to refine the abstraction in case a spurious counterexample is generated. We also plan to use the component selection heuristics defined in the literature in our tool, compare them on different designs and propose new heuristics that are targeted towards the efficient compositional reduction of BIP systems.

References

1. Aziz, A., Singhal, V., Swamy, G., Brayton, R.K.: Minimizing interacting finite state machines: a compositional approach to language to containment. In: ICCD, pp. 255–261 (1994)
2. Basu, A., Bensalem, S., Bozga, M., Combaz, J., Jaber, M., Nguyen, T.H., Sifakis, J.: Rigorous component-based system design using the bip framework. IEEE Softw. **28**(3), 41–48 (2011)
3. Bensalem, S., Bozga, M., Nguyen, T.-H., Sifakis, J.: D-Finder: a tool for compositional deadlock detection and verification. In: Bouajjani, A., Maler, O. (eds.) CAV 2009. LNCS, vol. 5643, pp. 614–619. Springer, Heidelberg (2009)
4. Bliudze, S., Sifakis, J.: A notion of glue expressiveness for component-based systems. In: van Breugel, F., Chechik, M. (eds.) CONCUR 2008. LNCS, vol. 5201, pp. 508–522. Springer, Heidelberg (2008)
5. Blom, S., Orzan, S.: Distributed branching bisimulation reduction of state spaces. Electron. Notes Theor. Comput. Sci. **89**(1), 99–113 (2003). PDMC 2003, Parallel and Distributed Model Checking (Satellite Workshop of CAV 2003)
6. Bloom, B.: Ready simulation, bisimulation, and the semantics of CCS-like languages. Ph.D. thesis, Massachusetts Institute of Technology (1989)
7. Chaudron, M., Eskenazi, E., Fioukov, A., Hammer, D.: A framework for formal component-based software architecting. In: OOPSLA, pp. 73–80 (2001)
8. Cimatti, A., Clarke, E., Giunchiglia, E., Giunchiglia, F., Pistore, M., Roveri, M., Sebastiani, R., Tacchella, A.: NuSMV 2: an opensource tool for symbolic model checking. In: Brinksma, E., Larsen, K.G. (eds.) CAV 2002. LNCS, vol. 2404, pp. 359–364. Springer, Heidelberg (2002)
9. Crouzen, P., Hermanns, H.: Aggregation ordering for massively compositional models. In: 2010 10th International Conference on Application of Concurrency to System Design (ACSD), pp. 171–180. IEEE (2010)
10. Crouzen, P., Lang, F.: Smart reduction. In: Giannakopoulou, D., Orejas, F. (eds.) FASE 2011. LNCS, vol. 6603, pp. 111–126. Springer, Heidelberg (2011)
11. Emerson, E.A., Wahl, T.: Efficient reduction techniques for systems with many components. Electr. Notes Theor. Comput. Sci. **130**, 379–399 (2005)
12. Garavel, H., Sifakis, J.: Compilation and verification of lotos specifications. PSTV **10**, 359–376 (1990)
13. van Glabbeek, R.J., Weijland, W.P.: Branching time and abstraction in bisimulation semantics. J. ACM **43**(3), 555–600 (1996)
14. Graf, S., Steffen, B.: Compositional minimization of finite state systems. In: CAV, pp. 186–196 (1990)
15. Groote, J.F., Ponse, A.: The syntax and semantics of μCRL. In: Ponse, A., Verhoef, C., van Vlijmen, S.F.M. (eds.) Algebra of Communicating Processes, pp. 26–62. Springer, London (1995)

16. Kildall, G.A.: A unified approach to global program optimization. In: POPL 1973, pp. 194–206. ACM, New York (1973)
17. Komuravelli, A., Gurfinkel, A., Chaki, S., Clarke, E.M.: Automatic abstraction in SMT-based unbounded software model checking. In: Sharygina, N., Veith, H. (eds.) CAV 2013. LNCS, vol. 8044, pp. 846–862. Springer, Heidelberg (2013)
18. Lang, F.: Exp.Open 2.0: a flexible tool integrating partial order, compositional, and on-the-fly verification methods. In: Romijn, J.M.T., Smith, G.P., van de Pol, J. (eds.) IFM 2005. LNCS, vol. 3771, pp. 70–88. Springer, Heidelberg (2005)
19. Tai, K.C., Koppol, P.V.: Hierarchy-based incremental analysis of communication protocols. In: Proceedings of the 1993 International Conference on Network Protocols, 1993, pp. 318–325. IEEE (1993)
20. Wegman, M.N., Zadeck, F.K.: Constant propagation with conditional branches. ACM Trans. Program. Lang. Syst. **13**(2), 181–210 (1991)
21. Wimmer, R., Herbstritt, M., Hermanns, H., Strampp, K., Becker, B.: SIGREF – a symbolic bisimulation tool box. In: Graf, S., Zhang, W. (eds.) ATVA 2006. LNCS, vol. 4218, pp. 477–492. Springer, Heidelberg (2006)
22. Zaraket, F.A., Baumgartner, J., Aziz, A.: Scalable compositional minimization via static analysis. In: ICCAD, pp. 1060–1067 (2005)

Compositionality for Quantitative Specifications

Uli Fahrenberg[1], Jan Křetínský[2]([⊠]), Axel Legay[1],
and Louis-Marie Traonouez[1]

[1] IRISA/Inria Rennes, Rennes, France
[2] IST Austria, Klosterneuburg, Austria
jan.kretinsky@ist.ac.at

Abstract. We provide a framework for compositional and iterative design and verification of systems with quantitative information, such as rewards, time or energy. It is based on disjunctive modal transition systems where we allow actions to bear various types of quantitative information. Throughout the design process the actions can be further refined and the information made more precise. We show how to compute the results of standard operations on the systems, including the quotient (residual), which has not been previously considered for quantitative non-deterministic systems. Our quantitative framework has close connections to the modal nu-calculus and is compositional with respect to general notions of distances between systems and the standard operations.

1 Introduction

Specifications of systems come in two main flavors. *Logical* specifications are formalized as formulae of modal or temporal logics, such as the modal μ-calculus or LTL. A common way to verify them on a system is to translate them to automata and then analyze the composition of the system and the automaton. In contrast, in the *behavioral* approach, specifications are given, from the very beginning, in an automata-like formalism. Such properties can be verified using various equivalences and preorders, such as bisimilarity or refinement. Here we focus on the latter approach, but also show connections between the two.

Behavioral formalisms are particularly apt for component-based design. Indeed, specifications can be easily composed as well as separately refined into more concrete ones. The behavioral formalisms we work here with are *modal transition systems* (MTS) [30] and their extensions. MTS are like automata, but with two types of transitions: *must*-transitions represent behavior that has to be present in every implementation; *may*-transition represent behavior that is allowed, but not required to be implemented.

J. Křetínský—This research was funded in part by the European Research Council (ERC) under grant agreement 267989 (QUAREM), by the Austrian Science Fund (FWF) project S11402-N23 (RiSE), and by the Czech Science Foundation, grant No. P202/12/G061.

I. Lanese and E. Madelaine (Eds.): FACS 2014, LNCS 8997, pp. 306–324, 2015.
DOI: 10.1007/978-3-319-15317-9_19

A simple example of a vending machine specification, in Fig. 1 on the left, describes that any correct implementation must be ready to accept money, then may offer the customer to choose extras and must issue a beverage. While the must-transitions are preserved in the refinement process, the may-transitions can be either implemented and turned into must-transitions, or dropped.

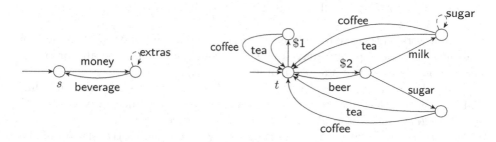

Fig. 1. Two specifications of a vending machine

This low-level refinement process is, however, insufficient when the designer wants to get more specific about the implemented actions, such as going from the coarse specification just described to the more fine-grained specification on the right of Fig. 1. In order to relate such specifications, MTS with *structured labels* were introduced [5]. Given a preorder on labels, relating for instance coffee $\preccurlyeq$ beverage, we can refine a transition label into one which is below, for example implement "beverage" with its refinement "coffee". Then t will be a refinement of s.

This framework can be applied to various pre-orders. For example, one can use labels with a discrete component carrying the action information and an interval component to model time durations or energy consumption. As an example, consider the simple real-time property to the right: "after a

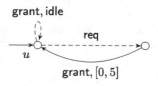

req(uest), grant has to be executed within 5 time units without the process being idle meanwhile". The transition (grant, $[0, 5]$) could be safely refined to (grant, $[l, r]$) for any $0 \leq l \leq r \leq 5$.

However, here we identify several shortcomings of the current approaches:

Expressive power. The current theory of structured labels is available only for the basic MTS. Very often one needs to use richer structures such as *disjunctive* MTS (DMTS) [8, 31] or acceptance automata [23, 35]. While MTS generally cannot express disjunction of properties, DMTS can express any Boolean combinations of properties. This allows, for instance, to prohibit deadlocks as in the example to the left in Fig. 2. The disjunctive must, depicted as a branching arrow, requires at least one of the transitions to be present. Thus we allow the deadline for grant to be reset as long as additional work is generated. Note that specifying

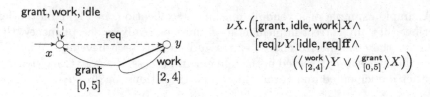

Fig. 2. A DMTS and its ν-calculus translation

grant and work as two separate must-transitions would not allow postponing the deadline; and two separate may-transitions would not guarantee any progress, as none of them has to be implemented.

The additional expressive power of DMTS is also justified by the fact that DMTS are equivalent to the modal ν-calculus [7]. We hence propose *DMTS with structured labels* and also extend the equivalence between DMTS and the ν-calculus to our setting. Figure 2 (right) shows a ν-calculus translation of the DMTS on its left.

Robustness. Consider again the request-grant example x in Fig. 2, together with the two labeled transition systems in Fig. 3 (left). While i_1, issuing grant after precisely 5 time units, is a valid implementation of x, if there is but a small positive drift in the timing, like in i_2, it is not an implementation anymore. However, this drift might be easily mended or just might be due to measuring errors. Therefore, when models and specifications contain such quantitative information, the standard Boolean notions of satisfaction and refinement are of limited utility [25] and should be replaced by notions more robust to perturbations. For another example, the DMTS to the right of Fig. 3 is *not* a refinement of the second one in Fig. 2, but for all practical purposes, it is very close.

One approach to robustness is to employ metric *distances* instead of Boolean relations; this has been done for example in [12,14,15,17,24,36,38] and many other papers. An advantage of behavioral specification formalisms is that models and specifications are closely related, hence distances between models can easily be extended to distances between specifications. We have developed a distance-based approach for MTS in [3,4] and shown in [4,20] that a good general setting

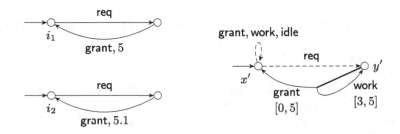

Fig. 3. Two implementations (left) and another DMTS specification (right)

is given by recursively specified trace distances on an abstract quantale. Here we extend this to DMTS.

Compositionality. The framework should be compositional. In the quantitative setting, this in essence means that the operations we define on the systems should behave well with respect not only to satisfaction, but also to the distances. For instance, if s_1 is close to t_1 and s_2 close to t_2, then also the structural composition $s_1\|s_2$ should be close to $t_1\|t_2$. We prove this for the usual operations; in particular, we give a construction for such a well-behaved *quotient*.

The quotient of s by t is the most general system that, when composed with t, refines s. This operation is thus useful for computing missing parts of a system to be implemented, when we already have several components at our disposal. The construction is complex already in the non-quantitative setting [7] and the extension of the algorithm to structured labels is non-trivial.

Our contribution. To sum up, we extend the framework of structured labels to DMTS and the modal ν-calculus. We equip this framework with distances and give constructions for the structured analogues of the standard operations, so that they behave compositionally with respect to the distances. The full proofs can be found in [19].

Further related work. Refinement of components is a frequently used design approach in various areas, ranging from subtyping [32] over the Java modeling language JML [27] or correct-by-design class diagrams operations [18] to interface theories close to MTS such as interface automata [16] based on alternating simulation. A variant of alternating simulation called covariant-contravariant simulation has been compared to MTS modal refinement in [1]. The graphical representability of these variants was studied in [7,9]. Quantities have been introduced also to the modal mu-calculus. At first, the focus lied on probabilities [26,33,34], but later predicates with values in arbitrary metric spaces were also introduced [15]. However, no refinement has been considered.

2   Structured Labels

Let Σ be a poset with partial order $\preccurlyeq$. We think of $\preccurlyeq$ as *label refinement*, so that if $a \preccurlyeq b$, then a is less permissive (more restricted) than b.

We say that a label $a \in \Sigma$ is an *implementation label* if $b \preccurlyeq a$ implies $b = a$ for all $b \in \Sigma$, *i.e.*, if a cannot be further refined. The set of implementation labels is denoted Γ, and for $a \in \Sigma$, we let $[\![a]\!] = \{b \in \Gamma \mid b \preccurlyeq a\}$ denote the set of its implementations. Note that $a \preccurlyeq b$ implies $[\![a]\!] \subseteq [\![b]\!]$ for all $a, b \in \Sigma$.

Example 1. A trivial but important example of our label structure is the *discrete* one in which label refinement $\preccurlyeq$ is equality (and $\Gamma = \Sigma$). This is equivalent to the "standard" case of *unstructured* labels.

A typical label set in quantitative applications consists of a discrete component and real-valued weights. For specifications, weights are replaced by (closed) weight *intervals*, so that $\Sigma = U \times \{[l, r] \mid l \in \mathbb{R} \cup \{-\infty\}, r \in \mathbb{R} \cup \{\infty\}, l \le r\}$ for a finite set U, *cf.* [4,5]. Label refinement is given by $(u_1, [l_1, r_1]) \preccurlyeq (u_2, [l_2, r_2])$ iff $u_1 = u_2$ and $[l_1, r_1] \subseteq [l_2, r_2]$, so that labels are more refined if they specify smaller intervals; thus, $\Gamma = U \times \{[x, x] \mid x \in \mathbb{R}\} \approx U \times \mathbb{R}$.

For a quite general setting, we can instead start with an arbitrary set Γ of implementation labels, let $\Sigma = 2^\Gamma$, the powerset, and $\preccurlyeq \, = \, \subseteq$ be subset inclusion. Then $\llbracket a \rrbracket = a$ for all $a \in \Sigma$. (Hence we identify implementation labels with one-element subsets of Σ.) □

2.1   Label Operations

Specification theories come equipped with several standard operations that make compositional software design possible [2]: conjunction for merging viewpoints covering different system's aspects [6,37], structural composition for running components in parallel, and quotient to synthesize missing parts of systems [31]. In order to provide them for DMTS, we first need the respective atomic operations on their action labels.

We hence assume that Σ comes equipped with a partial conjunction, *i.e.*, an operator $\oslash : \Sigma \times \Sigma \rightharpoonup \Sigma$ for which it holds that

(1) if $a_1 \oslash a_2$ is defined, then $a_1 \oslash a_2 \preccurlyeq a_1$ and $a_1 \oslash a_2 \preccurlyeq a_2$, and
(2) if $a_3 \preccurlyeq a_1$ and $a_3 \preccurlyeq a_2$, then $a_1 \oslash a_2$ is defined and $a_3 \preccurlyeq a_1 \oslash a_2$.

Note that by these properties, any two partial conjunctions on Σ have to agree on elements for which they are both defined.

Example 2. For discrete labels, the unique conjunction operator is given by

$$a_1 \oslash a_2 = \begin{cases} a_1 & \text{if } a_1 = a_2, \\ \text{undef.} & \text{otherwise}. \end{cases}$$

For labels in $U \times \{[l, r] \mid l, r \in \mathbb{R}, l \le r\}$, the unique conjunction is

$$(u_1, [l_1, r_1]) \oslash (u_2, [l_2, r_2]) = \begin{cases} \text{undef.} & \text{if } u_1 \ne u_2 \text{ or } [l_1, r_1] \cap [l_2, r_2] = \emptyset, \\ (u_1, [l_1, r_1] \cap [l_2, r_2]) & \text{otherwise}. \end{cases}$$

Finally, for the case of specification labels as sets of implementation labels, the unique conjunction is $a_1 \oslash a_2 = a_1 \cap a_2$. □

For structural composition and quotient of specifications, we assume a partial *label synchronization* operator $\odot : \Sigma \times \Sigma \rightharpoonup \Sigma$ which specifies how to compose labels. We assume $\odot$ to be associative and commutative, with the following technical property which we shall need later: For all $a_1, a_2, b_1, b_2 \in \Sigma$ with $a_1 \preccurlyeq a_2$ and $b_1 \preccurlyeq b_2$, $a_1 \odot b_1$ is defined iff $a_2 \odot b_2$ is, and if both are defined, then $a_1 \odot b_1 \preccurlyeq a_2 \odot b_2$.

Example 3. For discrete labels, the conjunction of Example 2 is the same as CSP-style composition, but other compositions may be defined.

For labels in $U \times \{[l, r] \mid l, r \in \mathbb{R}, l \leq r\}$, several useful label synchronization operators may be defined for different applications. One is given by *addition* of intervals, *i.e.*,

$$
(u_1, [l_1, r_1]) \stackrel{+}{\oplus} (u_2, [l_2, r_2]) = \begin{cases} \text{undef.} & \text{if } u_1 \neq u_2, \\ (u_1, [l_1 + l_2, r_1 + r_2]) & \text{otherwise}, \end{cases}
$$

for example modeling computation time of actions on a single processor. Another operator uses *maximum* instead of addition:

$$
(u_1, [l_1, r_1]) \stackrel{\mathrm{max}}{\oplus} (u_2, [l_2, r_2]) = \begin{cases} \text{undef.} & \text{if } u_1 \neq u_2, \\ (u_1, [\max(l_1, l_2), \max(r_1, r_2)]) & \text{otherwise}. \end{cases}
$$

Here we wait for the slower action. This models a blocking synchronization where both synchronized actions have to be performed before we can continue. Yet another operator uses interval *intersection* instead, *i.e.*, $\stackrel{\cap}{\oplus} = \oslash$; this is useful if the intervals model deadlines.

For set-valued specification labels, we may take any synchronization operator $\oplus$ given on implementation labels Γ and lift it to one on Σ by $a_1 \oplus a_2 = \{b_1 \oplus b_2 \mid b_1 \in [\![a_1]\!], b_2 \in [\![a_2]\!]\}$. $\qquad \square$

3   Specification Formalisms

In this section we introduce the specification formalisms which we use in the rest of the paper. The universe of models for our specifications is the one of standard *labeled transition systems*. For simplicity of exposition, we work only with *finite* specifications and implementations, but most of our results extend to the infinite (but finitely branching) case.

A *labeled transition system* (LTS) is a structure $\mathcal{I} = (S, s^0, \longrightarrow)$ consisting of a finite set S of states, an initial state $s^0 \in S$, and a transition relation $\longrightarrow \subseteq S \times \Gamma \times S$. We usually write $s \stackrel{a}{\longrightarrow} t$ instead of $(s, a, t) \in \longrightarrow$. Note that transitions are labeled with *implementation* labels.

3.1   Disjunctive Modal Transition Systems

A *disjunctive modal transition system* (DMTS) is a structure $\mathcal{D} = (S, S^0, \dashrightarrow, \longrightarrow)$ consisting of finite sets $S \supseteq S^0$ of states and initial states, respectively, may-transitions $\dashrightarrow \subseteq S \times \Sigma \times S$, and disjunctive must-transitions $\longrightarrow \subseteq S \times 2^{\Sigma \times S}$. It is assumed that for all $(s, N) \in \longrightarrow$ and $(a, t) \in N$ there is $(s, b, t) \in \dashrightarrow$ with $a \preccurlyeq b$.

Note that we allow multiple (or zero) initial states. We write $s \stackrel{a}{\dashrightarrow} t$ instead of $(s, a, t) \in \dashrightarrow$ and $s \longrightarrow N$ instead of $(s, N) \in \longrightarrow$. A DMTS $(S, S^0, \dashrightarrow, \longrightarrow)$ is an *implementation* if $\dashrightarrow \subseteq S \times \Gamma \times S$, $\longrightarrow = \{(s, \{(a, t)\}) \mid s \stackrel{a}{\dashrightarrow} t\}$, and $S^0 = \{s^0\}$ is a singleton; DMTS implementations are hence isomorphic to LTS.

DMTS were introduced in [31] in the context of equation solving, or *quotient* of specifications by processes. They are a natural extension of *modal* transition systems [30], which are DMTS in which all disjunctive must-transitions $s \longrightarrow N$ lead to singletons $N = \{(a,t)\}$; in fact, DMTS are the closure of MTS under quotient [31].

We introduce a notion of modal refinement of DMTS with structured labels. For discrete labels, it coincides with the classical definition [31].

Definition 4. *Let* $\mathcal{D}_1 = (S_1, S_1^0, \dashrightarrow_1, \longrightarrow_1)$, $\mathcal{D}_2 = (S_2, S_2^0, \dashrightarrow_2, \longrightarrow_2)$ *be DMTS. A relation* $R \subseteq S_1 \times S_2$ *is a* modal refinement *if it holds for all* $(s_1, s_2) \in R$ *that*

- *for all* $s_1 \overset{a_1}{\dashrightarrow}_1 t_1$ *there is* $s_2 \overset{a_2}{\dashrightarrow}_2 t_2$ *such that* $a_1 \preccurlyeq a_2$ *and* $(t_1, t_2) \in R$, *and*
- *for all* $s_2 \longrightarrow_2 N_2$ *there is* $s_1 \longrightarrow_1 N_1$ *such that for all* $(a_1, t_1) \in N_1$ *there is* $(a_2, t_2) \in N_2$ *with* $a_1 \preccurlyeq a_2$ *and* $(t_1, t_2) \in R$.

$\mathcal{D}_1$ refines $\mathcal{D}_2$, denoted $\mathcal{D}_1 \leq_m \mathcal{D}_2$, if there exists a modal refinement R for which it holds that for every $s_1^0 \in S_1^0$ there is $s_2^0 \in S_2^0$ for which $(s_1^0, s_2^0) \in R$.

We write $\mathcal{D}_1 \equiv_m \mathcal{D}_2$ if $\mathcal{D}_1 \leq_m \mathcal{D}_2$ and $\mathcal{D}_2 \leq_m \mathcal{D}_1$. The *implementation seman-tics* of a DMTS $\mathcal{D}$ is $[\![\mathcal{D}]\!] = \{\mathcal{I} \leq_m \mathcal{D} \mid \mathcal{I} \text{ implementation}\}$. We say that $\mathcal{D}_1$ *thoroughly refines* $\mathcal{D}_2$, and write $\mathcal{D}_1 \leq_{th} \mathcal{D}_2$, if $[\![\mathcal{D}_1]\!] \subseteq [\![\mathcal{D}_2]\!]$. The below propo-sition, which follows directly from transitivity of modal refinement, shows that modal refinement is *sound* with respect to thorough refinement; in the context of specification theories, this is what one would expect.

Proposition 5. *For all DMTS* $\mathcal{D}_1$, $\mathcal{D}_2$, $\mathcal{D}_1 \leq_m \mathcal{D}_2$ *implies* $\mathcal{D}_1 \leq_{th} \mathcal{D}_2$.   □

3.2   Acceptance Automata

A (non-deterministic) *acceptance automaton* (AA) is a structure $\mathcal{A} = (S, S^0, \text{Tran})$, with $S \supseteq S^0$ finite sets of states and initial states and $\text{Tran} : S \to 2^{2^{\Sigma \times S}}$ an assignment of *transition constraints*. The intuition is that a transition constraint $\text{Tran}(s) = \{M_1, \ldots, M_n\}$ specifies a disjunction of n choices $M_1, \ldots, M_n$ as to which transitions from s have to be implemented.

An AA is an *implementation* if $S^0 = \{s^0\}$ is a singleton and it holds for all $s \in S$ that $\text{Tran}(s) = \{M\} \subseteq 2^{\Gamma \times S}$ is a singleton; hence AA implementations are isomorphic to LTS. Acceptance automata were first introduced in [35], based on the notion of acceptance trees in [23]; however, there they are restricted to be *deterministic*. We employ no such restriction here.

Let $\mathcal{A}_1 = (S_1, S_1^0, \text{Tran}_1)$ and $\mathcal{A}_2 = (S_2, S_2^0, \text{Tran}_2)$ be AA. A relation $R \subseteq S_1 \times S_2$ is a *modal refinement* if it holds for all $(s_1, s_2) \in R$ and all $M_1 \in \text{Tran}_1(s_1)$ that there exists $M_2 \in \text{Tran}_2(s_2)$ such that

$$
\begin{aligned}
&\text{for all } (a_1, t_1) \in M_1 \text{ there is } (a_2, t_2) \in M_2 \text{ with } a_1 \preccurlyeq a_2 \text{ and } (t_1, t_2) \in R, \\
&\text{for all } (a_2, t_2) \in M_2 \text{ there is } (a_1, t_1) \in M_1 \text{ with } a_1 \preccurlyeq a_2 \text{ and } (t_1, t_2) \in R.
\end{aligned} \tag{1}
$$

The definition reduces to the one of [35] in case labels are discrete. We will write $M_1 \preccurlyeq_R M_2$ if M_1, M_2, R satisfy (1).

In [7], the following translations were discovered between DMTS and AA: For a DMTS $\mathcal{D} = (S, S^0, \dashrightarrow, \longrightarrow)$ and $s \in S$, let $\mathrm{Tran}(s) = \{M \subseteq \Sigma \times S \mid \forall (a, t) \in M : s \overset{a}{\dashrightarrow} t, \forall s \longrightarrow N : N \cap M \neq \emptyset\}$ and define the AA $da(\mathcal{D}) = (S, S^0, \mathrm{Tran})$. For an AA $\mathcal{A} = (S, S^0, \mathrm{Tran})$, define the DMTS $ad(\mathcal{A}) = (D, D^0, \dashrightarrow, \longrightarrow)$ by

$$D = \{M \in \mathrm{Tran}(s) \mid s \in S\}, \qquad D^0 = \{M^0 \in \mathrm{Tran}(s^0) \mid s^0 \in S^0\},$$
$$\longrightarrow = \{(M, \{(a, M') \mid M' \in \mathrm{Tran}(t)\}) \mid (a, t) \in M\},$$
$$\dashrightarrow = \{(M, a, M') \mid \exists M \longrightarrow N : (a, M') \in N\}.$$

Similarly to a theorem of [7,21], we can now show the following:

Theorem 6. *For DMTS $\mathcal{D}_1$, $\mathcal{D}_2$ and AA $\mathcal{A}_1$, $\mathcal{A}_2$, $\mathcal{D}_1 \leq_m \mathcal{D}_2$ iff $da(\mathcal{D}_1) \leq_m da(\mathcal{D}_2)$ and $\mathcal{A}_1 \leq_m \mathcal{A}_2$ iff $ad(\mathcal{A}_1) \leq_m ad(\mathcal{A}_2)$.* $\qquad\square$

This structural equivalence will allow us to freely translate forth and back between DMTS and AA in the rest of the paper. Note, however, that the state spaces of $\mathcal{A}$ and $ad(\mathcal{A})$ are not the same; the one of $ad(\mathcal{A})$ may be exponentially larger. [21] shows that this blow-up is unavoidable.

From a practical point of view, DMTS are a somewhat more useful specification formalism than AA. This is because they are usually more compact and easily drawn and due to their close relation to the modal ν-calculus, see below.

3.3 The Modal ν-Calculus

In [7], translations were discovered between DMTS and the modal ν-calculus, and refining the translations in [21], we could show that for discrete labels, these formalisms are *structurally equivalent*. We use the representation of the modal ν-calculus by equation systems in Hennessy-Milner logic developed in [29]. For a finite set X of variables, let $\mathcal{H}(X)$ be the set of *Hennessy-Milner formulae*, generated by the abstract syntax $\mathcal{H}(X) \ni \phi ::= \mathbf{tt} \mid \mathbf{ff} \mid x \mid \langle a \rangle \phi \mid [a]\phi \mid \phi \wedge \phi \mid \phi \vee \phi$, for $a \in \Sigma$ and $x \in X$. A *ν-calculus expression* is a structure $\mathcal{N} = (X, X^0, \Delta)$, with $X^0 \subseteq X$ sets of variables and $\Delta : X \to \mathcal{H}(X)$ a *declaration*.

We recall the greatest fixed point semantics of ν-calculus expressions from [29], but extend it to structured labels. Let $(S, S^0, \longrightarrow)$ be an LTS, then an *assignment* is a mapping $\sigma : X \to 2^S$. The set of assignments forms a complete lattice with order $\sigma_1 \sqsubseteq \sigma_2$ iff $\sigma_1(x) \subseteq \sigma_2(x)$ for all $x \in X$ and lowest upper bound $\left(\bigsqcup_{i \in I} \sigma_i\right)(x) = \bigcup_{i \in I} \sigma_i(x)$.

The semantics of a formula in $\mathcal{H}(X)$ is a function from assignments to subsets of S defined as follows: $(\!|\mathbf{tt}|\!)\sigma = S$, $(\!|\mathbf{ff}|\!)\sigma = \emptyset$, $(\!|x|\!)\sigma = \sigma(x)$, $(\!|\phi \wedge \psi|\!)\sigma = (\!|\phi|\!)\sigma \cap (\!|\psi|\!)\sigma$, $(\!|\phi \vee \psi|\!)\sigma = (\!|\phi|\!)\sigma \cup (\!|\psi|\!)\sigma$, and

$$(\!|\langle a \rangle \phi|\!)\sigma = \{s \in S \mid \exists s \overset{b}{\longrightarrow} t : b \in [\![a]\!], t \in (\!|\phi|\!)\sigma\},$$
$$(\!|[a]\phi|\!)\sigma = \{s \in S \mid \forall s \overset{b}{\longrightarrow} t : b \in [\![a]\!] \implies t \in (\!|\phi|\!)\sigma\}.$$

The semantics of a declaration Δ is then the assignment defined by $(\!|\Delta|\!) = \bigsqcup\{\sigma : X \to 2^S \mid \forall x \in X : \sigma(x) \subseteq (\!|\Delta(x)|\!)\sigma\}$; the greatest (pre)fixed point of Δ.

An LTS $\mathcal{I} = (S, s^0, \longrightarrow)$ *implements* (or models) the expression $\mathcal{N}$, denoted $\mathcal{I} \models \mathcal{N}$, if there is $x^0 \in X^0$ such that $s^0 \in (\!|\Delta|\!)(x^0)$.

In [21] we have introduced another semantics for ν-calculus expressions, which is given by a notion of refinement, like for DMTS and AA. For this we need a normal form for ν-calculus expressions:

Lemma 7 ([21]). *For any ν-calculus expression $\mathcal{N}_1 = (X_1, X_1^0, \Delta_1)$, there exists another expression $\mathcal{N}_2 = (X_2, X_2^0, \Delta_2)$ with $[\![\mathcal{N}_1]\!] = [\![\mathcal{N}_2]\!]$ and such that for any $x \in X$, $\Delta_2(x)$ is of the form $\Delta_2(x) = \bigwedge_{i \in I} \left(\bigvee_{j \in J_i} \langle a_{ij}\rangle x_{ij} \right) \wedge \bigwedge_{a \in \Sigma} [a]\left(\bigvee_{j \in J_a} y_{a,j} \right)$ for finite (possibly empty) index sets I, J_i, J_a and all $x_{ij}, y_{a,j} \in X_2$.* □

As this is a type of *conjunctive normal form*, it is clear that translating a ν-calculus expression into normal form may incur an exponential blow-up. We introduce some notation for ν-calculus expressions in normal form. Let $\mathcal{N} = (X, X^0, \Delta)$ be such an expression and $x \in X$, with $\Delta(x) = \bigwedge_{i \in I} \left(\bigvee_{j \in J_i} \langle a_{ij}\rangle x_{ij} \right) \wedge \bigwedge_{a \in \Sigma} [a]\left(\bigvee_{j \in J_a} y_{a,j} \right)$ as in the lemma. Define $\Diamond(x) = \{\{(a_{ij}, x_{ij}) \mid j \in J_i\} \mid i \in I\}$ and, for each $a \in \Sigma$, $\Box^a(x) = \{y_{a,j} \mid j \in J_a\}$. Intuitively, $\Diamond(x)$ collects all $\langle a\rangle$-requirements from x, whereas $\Box^a(x)$ specifies the disjunction of $[a]$-properties which must hold from x. Note that now,

$$\Delta(x) = \bigwedge_{N \in \Diamond(x)} \left(\bigvee_{(a,y) \in N} \langle a\rangle y \right) \wedge \bigwedge_{a \in \Sigma} [a]\left(\bigvee_{y \in \Box^a(x)} y \right). \tag{2}$$

Let $\mathcal{N}_1 = (X_1, X_1^0, \Delta_1)$, $\mathcal{N}_2 = (X_2, X_2^0, \Delta_2)$ be ν-calculus expressions in normal form and $R \subseteq X_1 \times X_2$. The relation R is a *modal refinement* if it holds for all $(x_1, x_2) \in R$ that

- for all $a_1 \in \Sigma$ and $y_1 \in \Box_1^{a_1}(x_1)$ there is $a_2 \in \Sigma$ and $y_2 \in \Box_2^{a_2}(x_2)$ with $a_1 \preccurlyeq a_2$ and $(y_1, y_2) \in R$, and
- for all $N_2 \in \Diamond_2(x_2)$ there is $N_1 \in \Diamond_1(x_1)$ such that for all $(a_1, y_1) \in N_1$ there exists $(a_2, y_2) \in N_2$ with $a_1 \preccurlyeq a_2$ and $(y_1, y_2) \in R$.

We say that a ν-calculus expression (X, X^0, Δ) in normal form is an *implementation* if $X^0 = \{x^0\}$ is a singleton, $\Diamond(x) = \{\{(a,y)\} \mid y \in \Box^a(x), a \in \Sigma\}$ and $\Box^a(x) = \emptyset$ for all $a \notin \Gamma$, for all $x \in X$. We can translate a LTS $(S, S^0, \longrightarrow)$ to a ν-calculus expression (S, S^0, Δ) in normal form by setting $\Diamond(s) = \{\{(a,t)\} \mid s \xrightarrow{a} t\}$ and $\Box^a(s) = \{t \mid s \xrightarrow{a} t\}$ for all $s \in S$, $a \in \Sigma$. This defines a bijection between LTS and ν-calculus implementations, hence, like for DMTS and AA, an embedding of LTS into ν-calculus. One of the main results of [21] is that for discrete labels, the refinement semantics and the fixed point semantics of the modal ν-calculus agree; the proof can easily be extended to our case of structured labels:

Theorem 8. *For any LTS $\mathcal{I}$ and any ν-calculus expression $\mathcal{N}$ in normal form, $\mathcal{I} \models \mathcal{N}$ iff $\mathcal{I} \leq_m \mathcal{N}$.* □

For a DMTS $\mathcal{D} = (S, S^0, \dashrightarrow, \longrightarrow)$ and all $s \in S$, let $\Diamond(s) = \{N \mid s \longrightarrow N\}$ and, for each $a \in \Sigma$, $\Box^a(s) = \{t \mid s \overset{a}{\dashrightarrow} t\}$. Define the (normal-form) ν-calculus expression $dn(\mathcal{D}) = (S, S^0, \Delta)$, with Δ given as in (2). For a ν-calculus expression $\mathcal{N} = (X, X^0, \Delta)$ in normal form, let $\dashrightarrow = \{(x, a, y) \in X \times \Sigma \times X \mid y \in \Box^a(x)\}$, $\longrightarrow = \{(x, N) \mid x \in X, N \in \Diamond(x)\}$ and define the DMTS $nd(\mathcal{N}) = (X, X^0, \dashrightarrow, \longrightarrow)$. Given that these translations are entirely syntactic, the following theorem is not a surprise:

Theorem 9. *For DMTS $\mathcal{D}_1$, $\mathcal{D}_2$ and ν-calculus expressions $\mathcal{N}_1$, $\mathcal{N}_2$, $\mathcal{D}_1 \leq_m \mathcal{D}_2$ iff $dn(\mathcal{D}_1) \leq_m dn(\mathcal{D}_2)$ and $\mathcal{N}_1 \leq_m \mathcal{N}_2$ iff $nd(\mathcal{N}_1) \leq_m nd(\mathcal{N}_2)$.* $\qquad\square$

4 Specification Theory

Structural specifications typically come equipped with operations which allow for *compositional reasoning*, *viz.* conjunction, structural composition, and quotient, *cf.* [2]. On deterministic MTS, these operations can be given easily using simple structural operational rules (for such semantics of weighted systems, see *e.g.*, [28]). For non-deterministic systems this is significantly harder; in [7] it is shown that DMTS and AA permit these operations and, additionally but trivially, disjunction. Here we show how to extend these operations on non-deterministic systems to our quantitative setting with structured labels.

We remark that structural composition and quotient operators are well-known from some logics, such as, *e.g.*, linear [22] or spatial logic [10], and were extended to quite general contexts [11]. However, whereas these operators are part of the formal syntax in those logics, for us they are simply operations on logical expressions (or DMTS, or AA). Consequently [21], structural composition is generally only a sound over-approximation of the semantic composition.

Given the equivalence of DMTS, AA and the modal ν-calculus exposed in the previous section, we will often state properties for all three types of specifications at the same time, letting $\mathcal{S}$ stand for any of the three types.

4.1 Disjunction and Conjunction

Disjunction of specifications is easily defined as we allow multiple initial states. For DMTS $\mathcal{D}_1 = (S_1, S_1^0, \dashrightarrow_1, \longrightarrow_1)$, $\mathcal{D}_2 = (S_2, S_2^0, \dashrightarrow_2, \longrightarrow_2)$, we can hence define $\mathcal{D}_1 \vee \mathcal{D}_2 = (S_1 \cup S_2, S_1^0 \cup S_2^0, \dashrightarrow_1 \cup \dashrightarrow_2, \longrightarrow_1 \cup \longrightarrow_2)$ (with all unions disjoint). For conjunction, we let $\mathcal{D}_1 \wedge \mathcal{D}_2 = (S_1 \times S_2, S_1^0 \times S_2^0, \dashrightarrow, \longrightarrow)$, with

- $(s_1, s_2) \overset{a_1 \oslash a_2}{\dashrightarrow} (t_1, t_2)$ whenever $s_1 \overset{a_1}{\dashrightarrow}_1 t_1$, $s_2 \overset{a_2}{\dashrightarrow}_2 t_2$ and $a_1 \oslash a_2$ is defined,
- for all $s_1 \longrightarrow N_1$, $(s_1, s_2) \longrightarrow \{(a_1 \oslash a_2, (t_1, t_2)) \mid (a_1, t_1) \in N_1, s_2 \overset{a_2}{\dashrightarrow}_2 t_2, a_1 \oslash a_2$ defined$\}$,
- for all $s_2 \longrightarrow N_2$, $(s_1, s_2) \longrightarrow \{(a_1 \oslash a_2, (t_1, t_2)) \mid (a_2, t_2) \in N_2, s_1 \overset{a_1}{\dashrightarrow}_1 t_1, a_1 \oslash a_2$ defined$\}$.

Theorem 10. *For all specifications $\mathcal{S}_1$, $\mathcal{S}_2$, $\mathcal{S}_3$,*

- $\mathcal{S}_1 \vee \mathcal{S}_2 \leq_m \mathcal{S}_3$ *iff* $\mathcal{S}_1 \leq_m \mathcal{S}_3$ *and* $\mathcal{S}_2 \leq_m \mathcal{S}_3$,
- $\mathcal{S}_1 \leq_m \mathcal{S}_2 \wedge \mathcal{S}_3$ *iff* $\mathcal{S}_1 \leq_m \mathcal{S}_2$ *and* $\mathcal{S}_1 \leq_m \mathcal{S}_3$,
- $[\![\mathcal{S}_1 \vee \mathcal{S}_2]\!] = [\![\mathcal{S}_1]\!] \cup [\![\mathcal{S}_2]\!]$, *and* $[\![\mathcal{S}_1 \wedge \mathcal{S}_2]\!] = [\![\mathcal{S}_1]\!] \cap [\![\mathcal{S}_2]\!]$.

With bottom and top elements given by $\bot = (\emptyset, \emptyset, \emptyset)$ and $\top = (\{s\}, \{s\}, \text{Tran}_\top)$ with $\text{Tran}_\top(s) = 2^{2^{\Sigma \times \{s\}}}$, our classes of specifications form *bounded distributive lattices* up to $\equiv_m$.

4.2 Structural Composition

For AA $\mathcal{A}_1 = (S_1, S_1^0, \text{Tran}_1)$, $\mathcal{A}_2 = (S_2, S_2^0, \text{Tran}_2)$, their *structural composition* is $\mathcal{A}_1 \| \mathcal{A}_2 = (S_1 \times S_2, S_1^0 \times S_2^0, \text{Tran})$, with $\text{Tran}((s_1, s_2)) = \{M_1 \odot M_2 \mid M_1 \in \text{Tran}_1(s_1), M_2 \in \text{Tran}_2(s_2)\}$ for all $s_1 \in S_1$, $s_2 \in S_2$, where $M_1 \odot M_2 = \{(a_1 \odot a_2, (t_1, t_2)) \mid (a_1, t_1) \in M_1, (a_2, t_2) \in M_2, a_1 \odot a_2 \text{ defined}\}$.

Remark a subtle difference between conjunction and structural composition, which we expose for discrete labels and CSP-style composition: for the DMTS $\mathcal{D}_1$, $\mathcal{D}_2$ shown to the right, both $\mathcal{D}_1 \wedge \mathcal{D}_2$ and $\mathcal{D}_1 \| \mathcal{D}_2$ have only one state, but $\text{Tran}(s_1 \wedge t_1) = \emptyset$ and $\text{Tran}(s_1 \| t_1) = \{\emptyset\}$, so that $\mathcal{D}_1 \wedge \mathcal{D}_2$ is inconsistent, whereas $\mathcal{D}_1 \| \mathcal{D}_2$ is not.

This definition extends the structural composition defined for modal transition systems, with structured labels, in [4]. For DMTS specifications (and hence also for ν-calculus expressions), the back translation from AA to DMTS entails an exponential explosion.

Theorem 11. *Up to* $\equiv_m$*, the operator* $\|$ *is associative, commutative and monotone.*

Corollary 12 (Independent implementability). *For all specifications* $\mathcal{S}_1$, $\mathcal{S}_2$, $\mathcal{S}_3$, $\mathcal{S}_4$, $\mathcal{S}_1 \leq_m \mathcal{S}_3$ *and* $\mathcal{S}_2 \leq_m \mathcal{S}_4$ *imply* $\mathcal{S}_1 \| \mathcal{S}_2 \leq_m \mathcal{S}_3 \| \mathcal{S}_4$. $\qquad\qquad\square$

4.3 Quotient

Because of non-determinism, we have to use a power set construction for the quotient, as opposed to conjunction and structural composition where product is sufficient. For AA $\mathcal{A}_3 = (S_3, S_3^0, \text{Tran}_3)$, $\mathcal{A}_1 = (S_1, S_1^0, \text{Tran}_1)$, the quotient is $\mathcal{A}_3 / \mathcal{A}_1 = (S, \{s^0\}, \text{Tran})$, with $S = 2^{S_3 \times S_1}$ and $s^0 = \{(s_3^0, s_1^0) \mid s_3^0 \in S_3^0, s_1^0 \in S_1^0\}$. States in S will be written $\{s_3^1/s_1^1, \ldots, s_3^n/s_1^n)\}$ instead of $\{(s_3^1, s_1^1), \ldots, (s_3^n, s_1^n))\}$. Intuitively, this denotes that such state when composed with s_1^i conforms to s_3^i for each i; we call this *consistency* here.

We now define Tran. First, $\text{Tran}(\emptyset) = 2^{\Sigma \times \{\emptyset\}}$, so $\emptyset$ is universal. For any other state $s = \{s_3^1/s_1^1, \ldots, s_3^n/s_1^n\} \in S$, its set of *permissible labels* is defined by

$$pl(s) = \{a_2 \in \Sigma \mid \forall i = 1, \ldots, n : \forall (a_1, t_1) \in\in \text{Tran}_1(s_1^i) :$$

$$\exists (a_3, t_3) \in\in \text{Tran}_3(s_3^i) : a_1 \odot a_2 \preccurlyeq a_3\},$$

that is, a label is permissible iff it cannot violate consistency. Here we use the notation $x \in\in z$ as a shortcut for $\exists y : x \in y \in z$.

Now for each $a \in pl(s)$ and each $i \in \{1, \ldots, n\}$, let $\{t_1 \in S_1 \mid (a, t_1) \in\in \text{Tran}_1(t_1^i)\} = \{t_1^{i,1}, \ldots, t_1^{i, m_i}\}$ be an enumeration of all the possible states in S_1

after an a-transition. Then we define the set of all sets of possible assignments of next-a states from s_3^i to next-a states from s_1^i:

$$pt_a(s) = \{\{(t_3^{i,j}, t_1^{i,j}) \mid i = 1, \ldots, n, j = 1, \ldots, m_i\} \mid \forall i : \forall j : (a, t_3^{i,j}) \in\in \mathrm{Tran}_3(s_3^i)\}$$

These are all possible next-state assignments which preserve consistency. Now let $pt(s) = \bigcup_{a \in pl(s)} pt_a(s)$ and define

$$\mathrm{Tran}(s) = \{M \subseteq pt(s) \mid \forall i = 1, \ldots, n : \forall M_1 \in \mathrm{Tran}_1(s_1^i) :$$

$$\exists M_3 \in \mathrm{Tran}_3(s_3^i) : M \triangleright M_1 \preccurlyeq_R M_3\},$$

where $M \triangleright M_1 = \{(a_1 \oplus a, t_3^i) \mid (a, \{t_3^1/t_1^1, \ldots, t_3^k/t_1^k)\}) \in M, (a_1, t_1^i) \in M_1\}$, to guarantee consistency no matter which element of $\mathrm{Tran}_1(s_1^i)$, s is composed with.

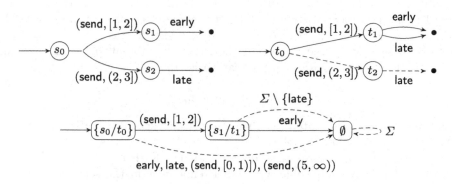

Fig. 4. Two DMTS and their quotient.

Example 13. Consider the two simple systems in Fig. 4 and their quotient under $\overset{\circ}{\oplus}$, *i.e.*, where label synchronization is intersection. During the construction and the translation back to DMTS, many states were eliminated as they were inconsistent (their Tran-set was empty). For instance, there is no may transition to state $\{s_2/t_2\}$, because when it is composed with t_2 there is no guarantee of late-transition, hence no guarantee to refine s_2.

Theorem 14. *For all specifications $\mathcal{S}_1$, $\mathcal{S}_2$, $\mathcal{S}_3$, $\mathcal{S}_1 \| \mathcal{S}_2 \leq_m \mathcal{S}_3$ iff $\mathcal{S}_2 \leq_m \mathcal{S}_3/\mathcal{S}_1$.*

5   Robust Specification Theories

We proceed to lift the results of the previous sections to a *quantitative* setting, where the Boolean notions of modal and thorough refinement are replaced by refinement *distances*. We have shown in [4,20] that a good setting for quantitative analysis is given by the one of *recursively specified trace distances* on an abstract commutative quantale as defined below; we refer to the above-cited papers for a detailed exposition of how this framework covers all common approaches to quantitative analysis.

Denote by $\Sigma^\infty = \Sigma^* \cup \Sigma^\omega$ the set of finite and infinite traces over Σ.

5.1   Recursively Specified Trace Distances

Recall that a *(commutative) quantale* consists of a complete lattice $(\mathbb{L}, \sqsubseteq_{\mathbb{L}})$ and a commutative, associative addition operation $\oplus_{\mathbb{L}}$ which distributes over arbitrary suprema; we denote by $\bot_{\mathbb{L}}, \top_{\mathbb{L}}$ the bottom and top elements of $\mathbb{L}$. We call a function $d : X \times X \to \mathbb{L}$, for a set X and a quantale $\mathbb{L}$, an $\mathbb{L}$-*hemimetric* if it satisfies $d(x, x) = \bot_{\mathbb{L}}$ for all $x \in X$ and $d(x, z) \sqsubseteq_{\mathbb{L}} d(x, y) \oplus_{\mathbb{L}} d(y, z)$ for all $x, y, z \in X$. $\mathbb{L}$-hemimetrics are generalizations of distances: for $\mathbb{L} = \mathbb{R}_{\geq 0} \cup \{\infty\}$ the extended real line, an $(\mathbb{R}_{\geq 0} \cup \{\infty\})$-hemimetric is simply an extended hemimetric.

A *recursive trace distance specification* $\mathcal{F} = (\mathbb{L}, \mathsf{eval}, d_{\mathsf{tr}}^{\mathbb{L}}, F)$ consists of a quantale $\mathbb{L}$, a quantale morphism $\mathsf{eval} : \mathbb{L} \to \mathbb{R}_{\geq 0} \cup \{\infty\}$, an $\mathbb{L}$-hemimetric $d_{\mathsf{tr}}^{\mathbb{L}} : \Sigma^{\infty} \times \Sigma^{\infty} \to \mathbb{L}$ (called *lifted trace distance*), and a *distance iterator* function $F : \Sigma \times \Sigma \times \mathbb{L} \to \mathbb{L}$. F must be monotone in the third and anti-monotone in the second coordinate and satisfy an extended triangle inequality: for all $a, b, c \in \Sigma$ and $\alpha, \beta \in \mathbb{L}$, $F(a, b, \alpha) \oplus_{\mathbb{L}} F(b, c, \beta) \sqsupseteq_{\mathbb{L}} F(a, c, \alpha \oplus_{\mathbb{L}} \beta)$.

F is to specify $d_{\mathsf{tr}}^{\mathbb{L}}$ recursively in the sense that for all $a, b \in \Sigma$ and all $\sigma, \tau \in \Sigma^{\infty}$ (and with "." denoting concatenation),

$$d_{\mathsf{tr}}^{\mathbb{L}}(a.\sigma, b.\tau) = F(a, b, d_{\mathsf{tr}}^{\mathbb{L}}(\sigma, \tau)). \tag{3}$$

The *trace distance* associated with such a distance specification is $d_{\mathsf{tr}} : \Sigma^{\infty} \times \Sigma^{\infty} \to \mathbb{R}_{\geq 0}$ given by $d_{\mathsf{tr}} = \mathsf{eval} \circ d_{\mathsf{tr}}^{\mathbb{L}}$.

Note that $d_{\mathsf{tr}}^{\mathbb{L}}$ specializes to a distance on labels (because $\Sigma \subseteq \Sigma^{\infty}$); we require that this is compatible with label refinement in the sense that $a \preccurlyeq b$ implies $d_{\mathsf{tr}}^{\mathbb{L}}(a, b) = \bot_{\mathbb{L}}$. Then (3) implies that whenever $a \preccurlyeq b$, then $F(a, b, \bot_{\mathbb{L}}) = d_{\mathsf{tr}}^{\mathbb{L}}(a, b) = \bot_{\mathbb{L}}$. As an inverse property, we say that F is *recursively separating* if $F(a, b, \alpha) = \bot_{\mathbb{L}}$ implies that $a \preccurlyeq b$ and $\alpha = \bot_{\mathbb{L}}$.

Example 15. It is shown in [4,20] that all commonly used trace distances obey recursive characterizations as above. We give a few examples, all of which are recursively separating:

- The *point-wise* distance from [14], for example, has $\mathbb{L} = \mathbb{R}_{\geq 0} \cup \{\infty\}$, $\mathsf{eval} = \mathsf{id}$ and
$$d_{\mathsf{tr}}^{\mathbb{L}}(a.\sigma, b.\tau) = \max(d(a, b), d_{\mathsf{tr}}^{\mathbb{L}}(\sigma, \tau)),$$
  where $d : \Sigma \times \Sigma \to \mathbb{R}_{\geq 0} \cup \{\infty\}$ is a hemimetric on labels. For the label set $\Sigma = U \times \{[l, r] \mid l \in \mathbb{R} \cup \{-\infty\}, r \in \mathbb{R} \cup \{\infty\}, l \leq r\}$ from Example 1, one useful example of such a hemimetric is $d((u_1, [l_1, r_1]), (u_2, [l_2, r_2])) = \sup_{x_1 \in [l_1, r_1]} \inf_{x_2 \in [l_2, r_2]} |x_1 - x_2| = \max(l_2 - l_1, r_1 - r_2, 0)$ if $u_1 = u_2$ and ∞ otherwise, *cf.* [3].
- The *discounting* distance, also used in [14], again uses $\mathbb{L} = \mathbb{R}_{\geq 0} \cup \{\infty\}$ and $\mathsf{eval} = \mathsf{id}$, but
$$d_{\mathsf{tr}}^{\mathbb{L}}(a.\sigma, b.\tau) = d(a, b) + \lambda d_{\mathsf{tr}}^{\mathbb{L}}(\sigma, \tau)$$
  for a constant $\lambda \in [0, 1)$.

– For the limit-average distance used in [12] and others, $\mathbb{L} = (\mathbb{R}_{\geq 0} \cup \{\infty\})^{\mathbb{N}}$, $\mathrm{eval}(\alpha) = \liminf_{j \in \mathbb{N}} \alpha(j)$, and

$$d_{\mathrm{tr}}^{\mathbb{L}}(a.\sigma, b.\tau)(j) = \frac{1}{j+1} d(a,b) + \frac{j}{j+1} d_{\mathrm{tr}}^{\mathbb{L}}(\sigma,\tau)(j-1).$$

– The *discrete* trace distance is given by $d_{\mathrm{tr}}(\sigma, \tau) = 0$ if $\sigma \preccurlyeq \tau$ and ∞ otherwise (here we have extended $\preccurlyeq$ to traces in the obvious way). It has a recursive characterization with $\mathbb{L} = \mathbb{R}_{\geq 0} \cup \{\infty\}$, $\mathrm{eval} = \mathrm{id}$, and $d_{\mathrm{tr}}(a.\sigma, b.\tau) = d_{\mathrm{tr}}(\sigma, \tau)$ if $a \preccurlyeq b$ and ∞ otherwise.

For the rest of this paper, we fix a recursively specified trace distance.

5.2   Refinement Distances

We lift the notions of modal refinement, for all our formalisms, to distances. Conceptually, this is done by replacing "∀" quantifiers by "sup" and "∃" by "inf" in the definitions, and then using the distance iterator to introduce a recursive functional whose least fixed point is the distance.

Definition 16. *The* lifted refinement distance *on the states of DMTS $\mathcal{D}_1 = (S_1, S_1^0, \dashrightarrow_1, \longrightarrow_1)$, $\mathcal{D}_2 = (S_2, S_2^0, \dashrightarrow_2, \longrightarrow_2)$ is the least fixed point to the equations*

$$d_{\mathsf{m}}^{\mathbb{L}}(s_1, s_2) = \max \begin{cases} \displaystyle\sup_{s_1 \overset{a_1}{\dashrightarrow} t_1} \inf_{s_2 \overset{a_2}{\dashrightarrow} t_2} F(a_1, a_2, d_{\mathsf{m}}^{\mathbb{L}}(t_1, t_2)), \\[2ex] \displaystyle\sup_{s_2 \longrightarrow N_2} \inf_{s_1 \longrightarrow N_1} \sup_{(a_1, t_1) \in N_1} \inf_{(a_2, t_2) \in N_2} F(a_1, a_2, d_{\mathsf{m}}^{\mathbb{L}}(t_1, t_2)). \end{cases}$$

For AA $\mathcal{A}_1 = (S_1, S_1^0, \mathrm{Tran}_1)$, $\mathcal{A}_2 = (S_2, S_2^0, \mathrm{Tran}_2)$, the equations are instead

$$d_{\mathsf{m}}^{\mathbb{L}}(s_1, s_2) = \\ \sup_{M_1 \in \mathrm{Tran}_1(s_1)} \inf_{M_2 \in \mathrm{Tran}_2(s_2)} \max \begin{cases} \displaystyle\sup_{(a_1, t_1) \in M_1} \inf_{(a_2, t_2) \in M_2} F(a_1, a_2, d_{\mathsf{m}}^{\mathbb{L}}(t_1, t_2)), \\[2ex] \displaystyle\sup_{(a_2, t_2) \in M_2} \inf_{(a_1, t_1) \in M_1} F(a_1, a_2, d_{\mathsf{m}}^{\mathbb{L}}(t_1, t_2)), \end{cases}$$

and for ν-calculus expressions $\mathcal{N}_1 = (X_1, X_1^0, \Delta_1)$, $\mathcal{N}_2 = (X_2, X_2^0, \Delta_2)$,

$$d_{\mathsf{m}}^{\mathbb{L}}(x_1, x_2) = \max \begin{cases} \displaystyle\sup_{a_1 \in \Sigma, y_1 \in \Box_1^{a_1}(x_1)} \inf_{a_2 \in \Sigma, y_2 \in \Box_2^{a_2}(x_2)} F(a_1, a_2, d_{\mathsf{m}}^{\mathbb{L}}(y_1, y_2)), \\[2ex] \displaystyle\sup_{N_2 \in \Diamond_2(x_2)} \inf_{N_1 \in \Diamond_1(x_1)} \sup_{(a_1, y_1) \in N_1} \inf_{(a_2, y_2) \in N_2} F(a_1, a_2, d_{\mathsf{m}}^{\mathbb{L}}(y_1, y_2)). \end{cases}$$

Using Tarski's fixed point theorem, one easily sees that the lifted refinement distances are indeed well-defined. (Here one needs monotonicity of F in the third coordinate, together with the fact that sup and inf are monotonic.)

Note that we define the distances using *least* fixed points, as opposed to the *greatest* fixed point definition of standard refinement. Informally, this is because our order is reversed: we are not interested in maximizing refinement relations, but in *minimizing* refinement distance.

The lifted refinement distance between specifications is defined by

$$d_m^{\mathbb{L}}(\mathcal{S}_1, \mathcal{S}_2) = \sup_{s_1^0 \in S_1^0} \inf_{s_2^0 \in S_2^0} d_m^{\mathbb{L}}(s_1^0, s_2^0).$$

Analogously to thorough refinement, there is also a *lifted thorough refinement distance*, given by $d_{th}^{\mathbb{L}}(\mathcal{S}_1, \mathcal{S}_2) = \sup_{\mathcal{I}_1 \in \llbracket \mathcal{S}_1 \rrbracket} \inf_{\mathcal{I}_2 \in \llbracket \mathcal{S}_2 \rrbracket} d_m^{\mathbb{L}}(\mathcal{I}_1, \mathcal{I}_2)$. Using the eval function, one gets distances $d_m = \text{eval} \circ d_m^{\mathbb{L}}$ and $d_{th} = \text{eval} \circ d_{th}^{\mathbb{L}}$, with values in $\mathbb{R}_{\geq 0} \cup \{\infty\}$, which will be the ones one is interested in for concrete applications.

Example 17. We compute the *discounting* refinement distance between the DMTS x and x' in Figs. 2 and 3, assuming sup-inf distance on quantitative labels. We have

$$d_m(x, x') = \max(0 + \lambda d_m(x, x'), 0 + \lambda d_m(y, y')),$$
$$d_m(y, y') = \max(0 + \lambda d_m(x, x'), 1 + \lambda d_m(y, y'),$$

the least fixed point of which is $d_m(x, x') = \frac{\lambda}{1-\lambda}$. Similarly, $d_m(x', x) = \frac{\lambda}{1-\lambda}$. Note that $x \not\leq_m x'$ and $x' \not\leq_m x$.

The following quantitative extension of Theorems 6 and 9 shows that our translations preserve and reflect refinement distances.

Theorem 18. *For all DMTS $\mathcal{D}_1, \mathcal{D}_2$, all AA $\mathcal{A}_1, \mathcal{A}_2$ and all ν-calculus expressions $\mathcal{N}_1, \mathcal{N}_2$:*

$$d_m^{\mathbb{L}}(\mathcal{D}_1, \mathcal{D}_2) = d_m^{\mathbb{L}}(da(\mathcal{D}_1), da(\mathcal{D}_2)) \qquad d_m^{\mathbb{L}}(\mathcal{A}_1, \mathcal{A}_2) = d_m^{\mathbb{L}}(ad(\mathcal{A}_1), ad(\mathcal{A}_2))$$
$$d_m^{\mathbb{L}}(\mathcal{D}_1, \mathcal{D}_2) = d_m^{\mathbb{L}}(dn(\mathcal{D}_1), dn(\mathcal{D}_2)) \qquad d_m^{\mathbb{L}}(\mathcal{N}_1, \mathcal{N}_2) = d_m^{\mathbb{L}}(nd(\mathcal{N}_1), nd(\mathcal{N}_2))$$

We sum up important properties of our distances:

Proposition 19. *The functions $d_m^{\mathbb{L}}$, $d_{th}^{\mathbb{L}}$ are $\mathbb{L}$-hemimetrics, and d_m, d_{th} are hemimetrics. For specifications $\mathcal{S}_1, \mathcal{S}_2$, $\mathcal{S}_1 \leq_m \mathcal{S}_2$ implies $d_m^{\mathbb{L}}(\mathcal{S}_1, \mathcal{S}_2) = \perp_{\mathbb{L}}$, and $\mathcal{S}_1 \leq_{th} \mathcal{S}_2$ implies $d_{th}^{\mathbb{L}}(\mathcal{S}_1, \mathcal{S}_2) = \perp_{\mathbb{L}}$. If F is recursively separating, then also the reverse implications hold.*

For the discrete distances, $d_m(\mathcal{S}_1, \mathcal{S}_2) = 0$ if $\mathcal{S}_1 \leq_m \mathcal{S}_2$ and ∞ otherwise. Similarly, $d_{th}(\mathcal{S}_1, \mathcal{S}_2) = 0$ if $\mathcal{S}_1 \leq_{th} \mathcal{S}_2$ and ∞ otherwise.

As a quantitative analogy to the implication from (Boolean) modal refinement to thorough refinement (Proposition 5), the next theorem shows that thorough refinement distance is bounded above by modal refinement distance. Note that for the discrete trace distance (and using Proposition 19), this is equivalent to the Boolean statement.

Theorem 20. *For all specifications $\mathcal{S}_1, \mathcal{S}_2$, $d_{th}^{\mathbb{L}}(\mathcal{S}_1, \mathcal{S}_2) \sqsubseteq_{\mathbb{L}} d_m^{\mathbb{L}}(\mathcal{S}_1, \mathcal{S}_2)$.*

5.3 Disjunction and Conjunction

In order to generalize the properties of Theorem 10 to our quantitative setting, we introduce a notion of relaxed implementation semantics:

Definition 21. *The α-relaxed implementation semantics of $\mathcal{S}$, for a specification $\mathcal{S}$ and $\alpha \in \mathbb{L}$, is $[\![\mathcal{S}]\!]^\alpha = \{\mathcal{I} \text{ implementation} \mid d_m^{\mathbb{L}}(\mathcal{I}, \mathcal{S}) \sqsubseteq \alpha\}$.*

Hence, $[\![\mathcal{S}]\!]^\alpha$ comprises all labeled transition systems which are implementations of $\mathcal{S}$ up to α. Note that by Proposition 19 and for F recursively separating, $[\![\mathcal{S}]\!]^{\perp_{\mathbb{L}}} = [\![\mathcal{S}]\!]$.

Theorem 22. *For all specifications $\mathcal{S}_1$, $\mathcal{S}_2$, $\mathcal{S}_3$ and $\alpha \in \mathbb{L}$,*

- $d_m^{\mathbb{L}}(\mathcal{S}_1 \vee \mathcal{S}_2, \mathcal{S}_3) = \max(d_m^{\mathbb{L}}(\mathcal{S}_1, \mathcal{S}_3), d_m^{\mathbb{L}}(\mathcal{S}_2, \mathcal{S}_3))$,
- $d_m^{\mathbb{L}}(\mathcal{S}_1, \mathcal{S}_2 \wedge \mathcal{S}_3) \sqsupseteq_{\mathbb{L}} \max(d_m^{\mathbb{L}}(\mathcal{S}_1, \mathcal{S}_2), d_m^{\mathbb{L}}(\mathcal{S}_1, \mathcal{S}_3))$,
- $[\![\mathcal{S}_1 \vee \mathcal{S}_2]\!]^\alpha = [\![\mathcal{S}_1]\!]^\alpha \cup [\![\mathcal{S}_2]\!]^\alpha$, and $[\![\mathcal{S}_1 \wedge \mathcal{S}_2]\!]^\alpha \subseteq [\![\mathcal{S}_1]\!]^\alpha \cap [\![\mathcal{S}_2]\!]^\alpha$.

The below example shows why the inclusions above cannot be replaced by equalities. To sum up, disjunction is quantitatively sound and complete, whereas conjunction is only quantitatively sound.

Fig. 5. LTS $\mathcal{I}$ together with DMTS $\mathcal{D}_1$, $\mathcal{D}_2$ and their conjunction. For the point-wise or discounting distances, $d_m(\mathcal{I}, \mathcal{D}_1) = d_m(\mathcal{I}, \mathcal{D}_2) = 1$, but $d_m(\mathcal{I}, \mathcal{D}_1 \wedge \mathcal{D}_2) = \infty$.

Example 23. For the point-wise or discounting distances, the DMTS in Fig. 5 are such that $d_m(\mathcal{I}, \mathcal{D}_1) = d_m(\mathcal{I}, \mathcal{D}_2) = 1$, but $d_m(\mathcal{I}, \mathcal{D}_1 \wedge \mathcal{D}_2) = \infty$. Hence $d_m(\mathcal{I}, \mathcal{S}_1 \wedge \mathcal{S}_2) \neq \max(d_m(\mathcal{I}, \mathcal{S}_1), d_m(\mathcal{I}, \mathcal{S}_2))$, and $\mathcal{I} \in [\![\mathcal{D}_1]\!]^1 \cap [\![\mathcal{D}_2]\!]^1$, but $\mathcal{I} \notin [\![\mathcal{D}_1 \wedge \mathcal{D}_2]\!]^1$.

5.4 Structural Composition and Quotient

We proceed to devise a quantitative generalization of the properties of structural composition and quotient exposed in Sect. 4. To this end, we need to use a *uniform composition bound* on labels:

Let $P : \mathbb{L} \times \mathbb{L} \to \mathbb{L}$ be a function which is monotone in both coordinates, has $P(\alpha, \perp_{\mathbb{L}}) = P(\perp_{\mathbb{L}}, \alpha) = \alpha$ and $P(\alpha, \top_{\mathbb{L}}) = P(\top_{\mathbb{L}}, \alpha) = \top_{\mathbb{L}}$ for all $\alpha \in \mathbb{L}$. We require that for all $a_1, b_1, a_2, b_2 \in \Sigma$ and $\alpha, \beta \in \mathbb{L}$ with $F(a_1, a_2, \alpha) \neq \top$ and $F(b_1, b_2, \beta) \neq \top$, $a_1 \oplus b_1$ is defined iff $a_2 \oplus b_2$ is, and if both are defined, then

$$F(a_1 \oplus b_1, a_2 \oplus b_2, P(\alpha, \beta)) \sqsubseteq_{\mathbb{L}} P(F(a_1, a_2, \alpha), F(b_1, b_2, \beta)). \quad (4)$$

Note that (4) implies that $d_{\mathsf{tr}}(a_1 \oplus a_2, b_1 \oplus b_2) \sqsubseteq_\mathbb{L} P(d_{\mathsf{tr}}(a_1, b_1), d_{\mathsf{tr}}(a_2, b_2))$. Hence P provides a *uniform bound*[1] on distances between synchronized labels, and (4) extends this property so that it holds recursively. Also, this is a generalization of the condition that we imposed on $\oplus$ in Sect. 2; it is shown in [4] that it holds for all common label synchronizations.

The following theorems show that composition is uniformly continuous (*i.e.*, a quantitative generalization of independent implementability; Corollary 12) and that quotient preserves and reflects refinement distance (a quantitative generalization of Theorem 14).

Theorem 24. *For all specifications* S_1, S_2, S_3, S_4, $d_{\mathsf{m}}^\mathbb{L}(S_1 \| S_2, S_3 \| S_4) \sqsubseteq_\mathbb{L} P(d_{\mathsf{m}}^\mathbb{L}(S_1, S_3), d_{\mathsf{m}}^\mathbb{L}(S_2, S_4))$.

Theorem 25. *For all specifications* S_1, S_2, S_3, $d_{\mathsf{m}}^\mathbb{L}(S_1 \| S_2, S_3) = d_{\mathsf{m}}^\mathbb{L}(S_2, S_3 / S_1)$.

6   Conclusion

We have presented a framework for compositional and iterative design and verification of systems which supports quantities and system and action refinement. Moreover, it is robust, in that it uses distances to measure quantitative refinement and the operations preserve distances.

The framework is very general. It can be applied to a large variety of quantities (energy, time, resource consumption etc.) and implement the robustness notions associated with them. It is also agnostic with respect to the type of specifications used, as it applies equally to behavioral and logical specifications. This means that logical and behavioral quantitative specifications can be freely combined in quantitative system development.

References

1. Aceto, L., Fábregas, I., de Frutos-Escrig, D., Ingólfsdóttir, A., Palomino, M.: On the specification of modal systems: a comparison of three frameworks. Sci. Comput. Program. **78**(12), 2468–2487 (2013)
2. Bauer, S.S., David, A., Hennicker, R., Guldstrand Larsen, K., Legay, A., Nyman, U., Wąsowski, A.: Moving from specifications to contracts in component-based design. In: de Lara, J., Zisman, A. (eds.) Fundamental Approaches to Software Engineering. LNCS, vol. 7212, pp. 43–58. Springer, Heidelberg (2012)
3. Bauer, S.S., Fahrenberg, U., Juhl, L., Larsen, K.G., Legay, A., Thrane, C.: Weighted modal transition systems. Form. Meth. Syst. Des. **42**(2), 193–220 (2013)
4. Bauer, S.S., Fahrenberg, U., Legay, A., Thrane, C.: General quantitative specification theories with modalities. In: Hirsch, E.A., Karhumäki, J., Lepistö, A., Prilutskii, M. (eds.) CSR 2012. LNCS, vol. 7353, pp. 18–30. Springer, Heidelberg (2012)

---

[1] Indeed, P bears some similarity to the concept of *modulus of continuity* used in analysis.

5. Bauer, S.S., Juhl, L., Larsen, K.G., Legay, A., Srba, J.: Extending modal transition systems with structured labels. Math. Struct. Comput. Sci. **22**(4), 581–617 (2012)
6. Ben-David, S., Chechik, M., Uchitel, S.: Merging partial behaviour models with different vocabularies. In: [12]
7. Beneš, N., Delahaye, B., Fahrenberg, U., Křetínský, J., Legay, A.: Hennessy-Milner logic with greatest fixed points. In: [12]
8. Beneš, N., Černá, I., Křetínský, J.: Modal transition systems: composition and LTL model checking. In: Bultan, T., Hsiung, P.-A. (eds.) ATVA 2011. LNCS, vol. 6996, pp. 228–242. Springer, Heidelberg (2011)
9. Boudol, G., Larsen, K.G.: Graphical versus logical specifications. Th. Comp. Sci. **106**(1), 3–20 (1992)
10. Caires, L., Cardelli, L.: A spatial logic for concurrency. Inf. Comp. **186**(2), 194–235 (2003)
11. Cardelli, L., Larsen, K.G., Mardare, R.: Modular Markovian logic. In: Aceto, L., Henzinger, M., Sgall, J. (eds.) ICALP 2011, Part II. LNCS, vol. 6756, pp. 380–391. Springer, Heidelberg (2011)
12. Černý, P., Henzinger, T.A., Radhakrishna, A.: Simulation distances. Th. Comp. Sci. **413**(1), 21–35 (2012)
13. D'Argenio, P.R., Melgratti, H. (eds.): CONCUR 2013 – Concurrency Theory. LNCS, vol. 8052. Springer, Heidelberg (2013)
14. de Alfaro, L., Faella, M., Henzinger, T.A., Majumdar, R., Stoelinga, M.: Model checking discounted temporal properties. Th. Comp. Sci. **345**(1), 139–170 (2005)
15. de Alfaro, L., Faella, M., Stoelinga, M.: Linear and branching system metrics. IEEE Trans. Softw. Eng. **35**(2), 258–273 (2009)
16. de Alfaro, L., Henzinger, T.A.: Interface automata. In: ESEC/SIGSOFT FSE. ACM (2001)
17. Desharnais, J., Gupta, V., Jagadeesan, R., Panangaden, P.: Metrics for labelled Markov processes. Th. Comp. Sci. **318**(3), 323–354 (2004)
18. Fahrenberg, U., Acher, M., Legay, A., Wąsowski, A.: Sound merging and differencing for class diagrams. In: Gnesi, S., Rensink, A. (eds.) FASE 2014 (ETAPS). LNCS, vol. 8411, pp. 63–78. Springer, Heidelberg (2014)
19. Fahrenberg, U., Křetínský, J., Legay, A., Traonouez, L.-M.: Compositionality for quantitative specifications. Technical Report abs/1408.1256, arXiv.org (2014)
20. Fahrenberg, U., Legay, A.: The quantitative linear-time-branching-time spectrum. Th. Comp. Sci. (2014). http://dx.doi.org/10.1016/j.tcs.2013.07.030
21. Fahrenberg, U., Legay, A., Traonouez, L.-M.: Structural refinement for the modal nu-calculus. In: Ciobanu, G., Méry, D. (eds.) ICTAC 2014. LNCS, vol. 8687, pp. 169–187. Springer, Heidelberg (2014)
22. Girard, J.-Y.: Linear logic. Th. Comp. Sci. **50**, 1–102 (1987)
23. Hennessy, M.: Acceptance trees. J. ACM **32**(4), 896–928 (1985)
24. Henzinger, T.A., Majumdar, R., Prabhu, V.S.: Quantifying similarities between timed systems. In: Pettersson, P., Yi, W. (eds.) FORMATS 2005. LNCS, vol. 3829, pp. 226–241. Springer, Heidelberg (2005)
25. Henzinger, T.A., Sifakis, J.: The embedded systems design challenge. In: Misra, J., Nipkow, T., Sekerinski, E. (eds.) FM 2006. LNCS, vol. 4085, pp. 1–15. Springer, Heidelberg (2006)
26. Huth, M., Kwiatkowska, M.Z.: Quantitative analysis and model checking. In: LICS. IEEE Computer Society (1997)
27. Jacobs, B., Poll, E.: A logic for the java modeling language JML. In: Hussmann, H. (ed.) FASE 2001. LNCS, vol. 2029, p. 284. Springer, Heidelberg (2001)

28. Klin, B., Sassone, V.: Structural operational semantics for stochastic and weighted transition systems. Inf. Comput. **227**, 58–83 (2013)
29. Larsen, K.G.: Proof systems for satisfiability in Hennessy-Milner logic with recursion. Th. Comp. Sci. **72**(2&3), 265–288 (1990)
30. Larsen, K.G., Thomsen, B.: A modal process logic. In: LICS. IEEE Computer Society (1988)
31. Larsen, K.G., Xinxin, L.: Equation solving using modal transition systems. In: LICS. IEEE Computer Society (1990)
32. Liskov, B., Wing, J.M.: A behavioral notion of subtyping. ACM Trans. Program. Lang. Syst. **16**(6), 1811–1841 (1994)
33. Mio, M.: Probabilistic modal μ-calculus with independent product. In: Hofmann, M. (ed.) FOSSACS 2011. LNCS, vol. 6604, pp. 290–304. Springer, Heidelberg (2011)
34. Morgan, C., McIver, A.: A probabilistic temporal calculus based on expectations. In: Groves, L., Reeves, S. (eds.) Formal Methods. Springer, Singapore (1997)
35. Raclet, J.-B.: Residual for component specifications. Publication interne 1843, IRISA, Rennes (2007)
36. Romero Hernández, D., de Frutos Escrig, D.: Defining distances for all process semantics. In: Giese, H., Rosu, G. (eds.) FORTE 2012 and FMOODS 2012. LNCS, vol. 7273, pp. 169–185. Springer, Heidelberg (2012)
37. Uchitel, S., Chechik, M.: Merging partial behavioural models. In: SIGSOFT FSE. ACM (2004)
38. van Breugel, F., Worrell, J.: A behavioural pseudometric for probabilistic transition systems. Th. Comp. Sci. **331**(1), 115–142 (2005)

Safety and Liveness of Composition

Algorithmic Verification of Procedural Programs in the Presence of Code Variability

Siavash Soleimanifard[(✉)] and Dilian Gurov

KTH Royal Institute of Technology, Stockholm, Sweden
{siavashs,dilian}@csc.kth.se

Abstract. We present a generic framework for verifying temporal safety properties of procedural programs that are dynamically or statically configured by replacing, adapting, or adding new components. To deal with such a variability of a program, we require programmers to provide local specifications for its variable components, and verify the global properties by replacing these specifications with maximal models. Our framework is a generalization of a previously developed framework that abstracts from all program data. In this work, we capture program data and thus significantly increase the range of properties that can be verified. Our framework is generic by being parametric on the set of observed program events and their semantics. We separate program structure from the behavior it induces to facilitate independent component specification and verification. We provide tool support for an instantiation of our framework to programs written in a procedural language with pointers as the only datatype.

1 Introduction

In modern computing systems code changes frequently. Components evolve rapidly or exist in multiple versions customized for different users, and in open and mobile contexts a system may even automatically reconfigure itself. As a result, systems are no longer developed as monolithic applications; instead they are composed of ready-made off-the-shelf components, and each component may be dynamically replaced by a new one that provides improved or additional functionality. The design and implementation of systems with such static and dynamic *variability* has been attracting considerable attention over the past years. However, there has been less attention to their formal verification. In this paper, we develop a generic framework for the verification of temporal safety properties of such systems.

The verification of *variable systems* is challenging because the code of the variable components is either not available at verification time or changes frequently. Therefore, an ideal verification technique for such systems should (i) *localize* the verification of variable components, and (ii) *relativize* the *global* properties of the system on the correctness of its variable components. This can be achieved through a compositional verification scheme where system components are specified *locally* and verified independently, while the correctness of

© Springer International Publishing Switzerland 2015
I. Lanese and E. Madelaine (Eds.): FACS 2014, LNCS 8997, pp. 327–345, 2015.
DOI: 10.1007/978-3-319-15317-9_20

its global properties is inferred from these local specifications. As a result, this allows an independent evolution of the implementations of individual components, only requiring the re-establishment of their local correctness. An algorithmic technique for realization of this verification scheme is to replace the local specifications by so-called *maximal models* [12]. These are most general models satisfying the specifications. Thus, if such models exist, they can replace the specifications of variable components in the verification of the global properties.

The work presented in this paper is the second, final, and conceptually more complicated phase of developing a compositional verification framework for temporal properties of procedural programs with variability exploiting maximal models. In the first phase, we developed a compositional verification technique that separates program structure from its operational semantics (behavior) to allow independent evolution of components [13,15]. The technique abstracts away all program data to achieve algorithmic and practical verification. Such a drastic abstraction, while allowing the verification of certain control flow safety properties [25], significantly reduces the range of properties that can be handled. For instance, properties of sequences of method invocations such as "method m_1 is not called after method m_2 is called" can be verified, but not properties that involve program data, such as "method m_1 is called only if variable V is not pointing to `null`". In this work, we generalize this technique to capture program data, and thus bring the usability of our work to a whole new level.

The two main limitations of any verification technique that is based on maximal models are (i) the computationally complex maximal model construction and (ii) the difficulty of producing component specifications. In our previous works, these limitations were softened by full data abstraction. As we show in Sect. 2, including program data (if done in the straightforward fashion) makes the maximal model construction and property specification impractical: the program models and properties become too detailed and large, maximal model construction becomes unmanageably complex, and the program models become overly specific to one programming language. Our present proposal captures program data without adding extra complexity to the maximal model construction, and keeps the complexity of property specification within practical limits.

We define a novel notion of program structure that is parametric on a set of *actions* that model single instructions of a selected type, and a set of Hoare-style state *assertions* that capture abstractly the effect of a series of statements between consecutive actions. We combine the abstraction provided by assertions with the precision provided by actions to define a uniform control flow graph representation of programs that can be tuned for the verification of the class of properties of interest. The abstraction provided by assertions prevents the local specifications from becoming overly verbose, and allows us to capture program data without adding extra complexity to the maximal model construction. From a wider perspective, by providing Hoare-style assertions and precise ordering of actions these models allow to combine Hoare-style with temporal logic reasoning.

To the extent of our knowledge, our previous framework and consequently the one presented in this paper are the only ones for algorithmic verification of

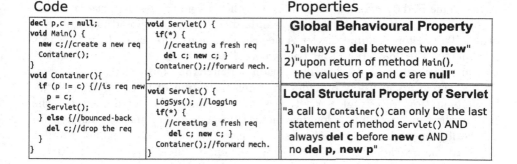

Code

Properties

Fig. 1. Web Server Application

temporal properties of procedural languages that allow the proofs to be relativized on component specifications. From a technical point of view, the main
contributions of this paper compared to our previous works are: (i) a novel structural model that combines the precise ordering of selected instructions with
abstract representation of the remaining ones, and its operational semantics
(a behavioral model), (ii) a proof that the original maximal model construction
can be adapted for the case with data (possibly from infinite domains) with
minimal additional cost, (iii) a proof of the correctness of the technique by (non-
trivial) re-establishment of our previous results, and (iv) tool support for an
instantiation of the framework to programs with pointers as the only datatype.
The extended version of this paper including additional examples and proofs can
be found in the accompanying report [24].

2   Overview of the Approach

This section provides an overview of our framework by demonstrating its use on
an example that mimics the method invocation style of real-life web applications.
Although the technique we propose applies to procedural languages in general,
we illustrate it here on *Pointer Programs* (PoP), a language with *pointers* as
the only datatype [23]. The language supports pointer creation and deletion,
assignments and conditional statements, loops, and method-calls with call-by-
reference parameter passing. The statement **new** x allocates a fresh chunk of
memory and assigns its pointer to variable x, while del x deletes the memory
that x is pointing to and assigns null to x (and all its aliases). The guards for
the conditional statements and loops are equality (alias) and inequality checks
on variables, and non-deterministic choice, denoted by ∗. Being able to deal with
this language is of interest, since it can give rise to infinite state spaces, for two
reasons: unbounded stacks of procedure calls, and unbounded pointer creation.
Due to space constraints, the formal instantiation of our generic verification
framework to the PoP language is delegated to the accompanying report [24].

We use this language to implement a program that mimics the method invocation style of Java enterprise web applications. The execution of such applications

starts in method `Container` where based on the current request a *Servlet* is called to prepare the output. As a coding standard [17], servlets should not call each other. Thus if for example servlet A needs to make use of servlet B, it forwards a request to the `Container` that triggers a call to B. We model this so-called forwarding mechanism by explicit invocation of `Container` in servlets.

The program in Fig. 1 provides an implementation of a container and two implementations of a single servlet, in which the one at the bottom extends the one at the top by adding a logging facility through calling method `LogSys`. In the code, the variables are pointers to requests. The global variables `p` and `c` point to the previous (last-received) and current requests, respectively. At the beginning of the execution, the request `c` is initialized by `Main` and `Container` is called. In `Container` if the current request is different with the previous one, the current request is stored in `p` and method `Servlet` is called, which non-deterministically generates a fresh request and calls back `Container`. By this, we mimic the call-backs to `Container` (forwarding mechanism) in a real web-application when servlets call each other via the container. `Container` drops (i.e., deletes) the requests that are bounced back to it (when `p` = `c`) to avoid cycles in the computation. The code of method `LogSys` is not shown here, but we assume that it does not modify the global variables. Here, we consider each method as a component, but in general a component can consist of several methods.

In this example, we assume that the method `Servlet` is the variable part of the program. The structural local specification of method `Servlet` and two behavioral global properties are given in the figure. In the remainder of this section, we explain how to apply to this program the verification technique developed in the later sections, in different variability scenarios.

Verification Technique. In our framework, we divide the verification of variable programs into two independent sub-tasks:

(i) a check that the implementation of each variable component satisfies its local specification, and
(ii) a check that the composition of the local specifications together with the implementations of the non-variable components entails the global property.

By this division we localize the verification of variable components (with sub-task (i)), and relativize the correctness of global properties of the program on the local specifications of its variable components (with sub-task (ii)). Thus, adding or changing the implementation of a variable component does not require the global property to be re-verified, just its local specification (with sub-task (i)). Also notice that, if the local specifications are specified as completely as possible (*i.e.*, are not tailored toward particular global properties), once the local checks of sub-task (i) are performed, the verification of new global properties will not require the re-specification and verification of variable components. In fact, variable components are often implemented and specified as general-purpose libraries that can be used in arbitrary contexts and should thus not be specified toward specific global properties.

In most variability scenarios, variable systems would be verified once (with sub-tasks (i) and (ii)) before delivering the software to customers, and would be re-verified every time a variable component is modified by performing sub-task (i) on the customer's side. Ideally, sub-task (i) should be performable quickly and thus in isolation from the non-variable part of the system, which is (usually) significantly larger than the modified component. This is difficult to achieve for local specifications that express properties of the execution of programs, *i.e. behavioral* specifications, but is natural for those that express properties of the code (program text) itself, *i.e. structural* specifications. The reason is that the latter can be checked against the component's code rather than the execution of the whole program. For example, a behavioral specification of method `Servlet` would be "c points to `null` at any return point of method `Servlet`", which cannot be checked for method `Servlet` in isolation from `Container` and `LogSys`, while the structural specification given in Fig. 1 can be checked against `Servlet`'s code, independent from the rest of the program. In practice, these local specifications should be provided by the developers. This requires the knowledge of the safety requirements of the system.

Let us now mimic some dynamic variability scenarios. First assume that no implementation of `Servlet` is available, for example because it is not implemented yet or should be imported from a third-party library. Still, the incomplete program can be verified from the given structural local property of method `Servlet` and the implementation of methods `Main` and `Container` by performing sub-task (ii). Later, when the implementation of method `Servlet` at the top becomes available, it is only checked against its specification, as in sub-task (i). Now assume that, after a while, the implementation of `Servlet` is updated to the one at the bottom. Again, only the local check of sub-task (i) needs to be performed, this time for the new implementation.

For static variability scenarios, assume that the two implementations of `Servlet` are available and each of them together with `Container` make an application that is delivered to customers based on their needs and budget (as in product families). To verify the global property, the local specification of method `Servlet` is checked for each of the implementations separately (sub-task (i)). Independently, the composition of this local specification with the implementation of `Container` is checked against the global property (sub-task (ii)).

To verify programs in such variability scenarios, we model the structure of non-variable components with *flow graphs*, and convert local specifications of the variable components to *maximal flow graphs*. Here, we present these notions informally and describe how they are used in our verification framework.

Flow Graphs. A flow graph is a finite collection of *method graphs*, each of which represents the control flow structure of a method. Our flow graphs are parametric on the class of program instructions that need to be explicitly represented for the verification of the properties of interest, while using an abstract representation of all other instructions. The rationale is that in temporal reasoning one is usually interested in the ordering of certain events of interest, here called *actions*. The exact ordering of the other events can be abstracted away; only their cumulative

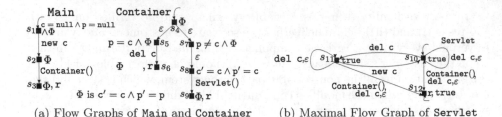

(a) Flow Graphs of Main and Container   (b) Maximal Flow Graph of Servlet

Fig. 2. (a) Flow Graphs of Main and Container (b) Maximal Flow Graph of Servlet

effect needs to be captured. We represent the effect of a series of consecutive events between two actions in a Hoare style, through logical *assertions*. The combination of the precise ordering of actions and abstract representation of data provided by assertions yields a flexible program model that potentially allows to combine Hoare-style with temporal logic reasoning. Here, however, we use these models only for the verification of control flow properties.

In our flow graphs, the actions have parameters and are represented by transition labels, while the assertions are assigned to control nodes[1]. Besides assertions, return nodes are tagged by the atomic proposition r. Entry nodes of method graphs represent the beginning of methods.

As an example, Fig. 2a shows a flow graph of the code of methods Main and Container. We want to verify properties talking about order of new and del statements, e.g., global properties in the figure, thus in this example, actions are new and del. We add a neutral action ε to simplify the presentation of the flow graphs. Assertions are equality and inequality checks on the variables at the beginning and the end of a block of code between two actions. They express the cumulative effect of condition evaluation and assignments. We use variable names (such as p and c) and their primed version (p' and c') to refer to the values at the beginning and the end of blocks, respectively. For example, state s_8 in the figure represents the assignment statement $p := c$ in the code of Container.

Maximal Flow Graphs. A maximal flow graph for a specification is a flow graph that represents the structure of *any* code satisfying it. To verify global properties, in our framework the variable components are replaced with maximal flow graphs constructed from their specifications (in sub-task (ii)). By this, we decouple the concrete implementations of variable components from the global correctness reasoning, thus allowing independent evolution of their code. In Sect. 5, we define formally maximal flow graphs, prove their existence and uniqueness for our specification logic, and provide an algorithm to construct them. Here, we only give an intuitive explanation of their specifics in the present setup.

Local specifications often specify constraints on a small subset of the program variables only, namely the variables whose values should be captured for

---

[1] This (maybe non-standard) design choice allows a clear distinction between actions and assertions, which is crucial for our framework.

the verification of the class of properties of interest. For example, the specification of method `Servlet` does not specify any constraint on the variables p and c since their values don't have any effect on the global properties. In such situations, there are (possibly infinitely) many implementations for a component that respect its specification. A maximal flow graph should capture the structure of all these implementations. It is therefore of size exponential in the number of unspecified variables and their values, and is thus infeasible to construct in practice with standard algorithms, e.g., [12,13,20], where data is represented concretely.

In our structural models, however, data is represented symbolically through logical assertions. We use a *semantic entailment* relation on assertions to reduce the size and complexity of the construction of the maximal flow graphs. The idea is that a control node with assertion ϕ can represent any set of nodes that are tagged with assertions entailing ϕ. For example, consider the maximal flow graph constructed from the local specification of `Servlet` shown in Fig. 2b. In the graph the assertions (`true`) do not specify any constraints on the variables, so any similar flow graph that for example has $c' = c$ or $p' = p$ as assertions at its control nodes will be represented by the given maximal flow graph.

Verification. In our framework we support verification of structural and behavioral global properties by performing the sub-tasks (i) and (ii) as follows. (i) The flow graph extracted from the available implementation of `Servlet` is model checked against its local specification. (ii) The maximal flow graph of `Servlet` and the flow graph of `Container` are composed by means of set-theoretic union. This composition can be directly model checked against structural global properties. However, the verification of behavioral global properties requires that a behavioral model is induced from the composition. Intuitively this model (called *flow graph behavior*) should capture all possible runs (executions) of the flow graph. Therefore, it should model the call stack and represent the values of variables at each point of the execution, in which the latter requires the semantics of the transition labels and state assertions. Also, to allow model checking of such models, values should be from finite domains. Then the model can be represented by means of pushdown automata. These models are defined in Sect. 3.

3   Program Model

We first define an abstract notion of *model* on which our representations of program structure and behavior are based. A model is a *Kripke* structure extended with transition labels and a set of state assertions.

Definition 1 (Model). *A* model *is a tuple* $\mathcal{M} = (S, L, \rightarrow, A, P, \lambda_A, \lambda_P)$ *where S is a set of states, L a set of labels, $\rightarrow \subseteq S \times L \times S$ a labeled transition relation, A a finite set of atomic propositions (or atoms), P a finite set of state assertions, $\lambda_A : S \rightarrow 2^A$ and $\lambda_P : S \rightarrow P$ valuations assigning to each state a set of atoms and a state assertion, respectively. An* initialized model S *is a pair* $(\mathcal{M}, E)$ *with $\mathcal{M}$ a model and $E \subseteq S$ a set of initial states.*

Models are composed through disjoint union $\uplus$. We assume the set of state assertions P to be equipped with a semantic entailment relation, denoted by $\sqsubseteq$. This relation is used to define simulation preorder, logical satisfaction, and maximal model construction.

In contrast to models without data, the states of models with data are additionally tagged with state assertions. As we shall see, these assertions together with the atomic propositions provide the basis for the symbolic and concrete representation of data, respectively. State assertions are used in structural models to capture how data may change at the states (nodes) of the model, while atomic propositions are used in behavioral models to represent the values of variables at each point of the program execution.

We mentioned that a maximal model is the most general model satisfying a property. The generality relation on models is technically defined w.r.t. a preorder relation called *simulation*. The definition of simulation preorder is parametric on the semantic entailment $\sqsubseteq$.

Definition 2 (Simulation). *A simulation on S is a binary relation R on S such that whenever $(s,t) \in R$ then $\lambda_A(s) = \lambda_A(t)$, $\lambda_P(s) \sqsubseteq \lambda_P(t)$, and whenever $s \xrightarrow{a} s'$ then there is some $t' \in S$ such that $t \xrightarrow{a} t'$ and $(s',t') \in R$. We say that t simulates s, written $s \leqslant t$, if there is a simulation R such that $(s,t) \in R$.*

Simulation on two disjoint models $\mathcal{M}_1$ and $\mathcal{M}_2$ is defined, as usual, as simulation on their union. Simulation is extended to initialized models $(\mathcal{M}_1, E_1)$ by defining $(\mathcal{M}_1, E_1) \leqslant (\mathcal{M}_2, E_2)$ if there is a simulation R such that for each $s \in E_1$ there is some $t \in E_2$ with $(s,t) \in R$.

As mentioned earlier, we compose models to verify global properties. The following theorem establishes that simulation is preserved by model composition.

Theorem 1 (Monotonicity). *If $\mathcal{S}_1 \leqslant \mathcal{S}_1'$ and $\mathcal{S}_2 \leqslant \mathcal{S}_2'$ then $\mathcal{S}_1 \uplus \mathcal{S}_2 \leqslant \mathcal{S}_1' \uplus \mathcal{S}_2'$.*

3.1 Flow Graphs

Intuitively, a *flow graph* is a collection of *method graphs*, one for each method of the program, as illustrated in Fig. 2a. W.l.o.g., we assume that method names are distinct and taken from a countably infinite set of method names *Meth*. The notion of method graph is an instance of the generic notion of initialized model defined above, with particular sets of assertions P and labels L. Let $\mathcal{A}$ be a set of *actions* with data parameters. The set of flow graph labels is $L = L_{\mathcal{A}} \cup L_{call}$, where $L_{\mathcal{A}} = \{\alpha(a_1, ..., a_n) \mid \alpha \in \mathcal{A}\}$ are action-induced labels and $L_{call} = \{m(a_1, ..., a_w) \mid m \in Meth\}$ are labels representing method invocations.

Definition 3 (Method Graph). *A method graph for method name $m \in Meth$ over a set $M \subseteq Meth$ of method names is an initialized model $(\mathcal{M}_m, E_m)$ where $\mathcal{M}_m = (S_m, L_m, \rightarrow_m, A_m, P_m, \lambda_{A_m}, \lambda_{P_m})$ is a finite model and $E_m \subseteq S_m$ is a non-empty set of entry points of m. S_m is the set of control nodes of m, $L_m \subseteq L$, $A_m = \{m, r\}$, $P_m \subseteq P$, $\lambda_{P_m} : S_m \rightarrow P_m$ is a valuation for transition propositions, and $\lambda_{A_m} : S_m \rightarrow \{\{m\}, \{m, r\}\}$ is a valuation for atoms so that* *each node is tagged with its method name, and* return nodes *are additionally tagged with r.*

We sometimes write $s \models m$ to denote $m \in \lambda_A(s)$. Notice that with the above definition, control nodes of flow graphs do not in general correspond to single program points in the actual program's code, but rather to sets of them.

Example 1. The definition of method graphs for PoP programs is an instantiation of the definition above where $\mathcal{A}_{pop}$ is formed from PoP actions and P_m are the PoP assertions. Recall that the set of PoP actions is $\mathcal{A}_{pop} = \{\mathtt{del}, \mathtt{new}, \varepsilon\}$ where the arities of $\mathtt{new}$ and $\mathtt{del}$ are one and of ε is zero. The set of PoP assertions P_{pop} is formed by equality and inequality constraints on the values of variables at the beginning (non-primed variables) and end (primed variables) of the code block that has collapsed into a state. Figure 2a shows a flow graph for the non-variable components (methods `Main` and `Container`) of the PoP program in Fig. 1.

Given the definition of PoP assertions above, semantic entailment $\sqsubseteq$ on P_{pop} is defined as logical implication. $\qquad\qquad\qquad\qquad\qquad\qquad\qquad\qquad\qquad\qquad$ $\square$

In contrast to the flow graphs defined here, the ones without data do not have state assertions, because all variables and their values are abstracted away.

Every flow graph $\mathcal{G}$ is equipped with an *interface* I, denoted by $\mathcal{G} : I$. A *flow graph interface* consists of a triple $I = (M^+, M^-, Modify)$, where $M^+, M^- \subseteq Meth$ are finite sets of *provided* and *required* methods, respectively, and $Modify$ is the set of the global variables of the program that are modified in the code of the provided methods. As we shall see, interfaces are needed when constructing maximal flow graphs, which in turn are used for compositional verification.

The definition of *flow graph simulation*, denoted by $\leqslant_s$, is an instantiation of the general notion of simulation on models (see Definition 2) to flow graphs.

3.2   Flow Graph Behavior

Program states $\sigma \in \Sigma$ are defined as usual as mappings from the set of program variables V to their values taken from $\mathcal{D}$. Behavioral transitions conceptually capture the occurrence of actions together with data transformations as specified by assertions. An assertion ϕ is interpreted over pairs of program states, written $(\sigma, \sigma') \models \phi$, and is defined to hold when the closed formula $\phi[\sigma, \sigma']$ is logically valid (here σ, σ' are used as syntactic substitutions for the non-primed and primed variables, respectively). We define *behavioral states* $\langle s, \sigma, \sigma' \rangle$ as consisting of a control node and a pair of program states that satisfies the assertion of the node.

Example 2. PoP programs can create infinitely many pointers. However, at any point of the execution (behavior), only finitely many of them are referenced by program variables. Following [23] we exploit this fact and abstractly represent the infinite pointers of PoP programs by finitely many *equivalence classes*. Two variables are deemed to be equivalent whenever they are pointing to the same memory. Thus, PoP program states are essentially *partitionings* of variables into such equivalence classes. In Example 3 we show how these program states are used to form an execution of the PoP program in Fig. 1.   □

Next we define flow graph behavior. Behavioral transitions are labeled with "m_1 call $m_2(a_1, \ldots, a_w)$" for an invocation of method m_2 by method m_1 with parameters $a_1, \ldots, a_w$, "m_2 ret m_1" for the corresponding return from the call, or $\alpha(a_1, ..., a_n) \in L_A$ for the (method-local) transfer of control by action α with parameters $a_1, ..., a_n$. The definition of flow graph behavior is parametric on externally provided (denotational) semantic mappings $[\![\cdot]\!]$ over states and state pairs that specify the (local) effect of actions, calls and returns.

Definition 4 (Flow Graph Behavior). *Let* $\mathcal{S} = (\mathcal{M}, E) : (M^+, M^-, \text{Modify})$ *be a flow graph s.t.* $\mathcal{M} = (S, L, \rightarrow, A, P, \lambda_A, \lambda_P)$. *The behavior of* $\mathcal{S}$ *is defined as the initialized model* $b(\mathcal{S}) = (\mathcal{M}_b, E_b)$ *where* $\mathcal{M}_b = (S_b, L_b, \rightarrow_b, A_b, P_b, \lambda_{A_b}, \lambda_{P_b})$, *with* $S_b \subseteq (S \times \Sigma \times \Sigma) \times (S \times \Sigma)^*$, *i.e., states (or configurations) are pairs of behavioral states* $\langle s, \sigma, \sigma' \rangle$ *and stacks* γ *over pairs of control nodes and program states,* $L_b = L_A \cup \{m_1 \text{ call } l_{m_2} \mid m_1 \in M^+ \wedge l_{m_2} \in L_{call}\} \cup \{m_1 \text{ ret } m_2 \mid m_1, m_2 \in M^+\}$, $A_b = A \cup (\Sigma \times \Sigma)$, $P_b = \{tt\}$, $\lambda_{A_b}(\langle s, \sigma, \sigma' \rangle, \gamma) = \lambda_A(s) \cup \{(\sigma, \sigma')\}$, *and* $\rightarrow_b \subseteq S_b \times L_b \times S_b$ *is defined by the following transition rules:*

$[\alpha]$ $(\langle s_1, \sigma_1, \sigma_1' \rangle, \gamma) \xrightarrow{\alpha(\sigma'(a_1), \ldots, \sigma'(a_n))} (\langle s_2, \sigma_2, \sigma_2' \rangle, \gamma)$ *if* $s_1 \xrightarrow{\alpha(a_1, \ldots, a_n)} s_2 \wedge$
$(\sigma_1, \sigma_1') \models \lambda_P(s_1) \wedge$
$(\sigma_2, \sigma_2') \models \lambda_P(s_2) \wedge$
$\sigma_2 = [\![\alpha]\!]\sigma_1'$

$[call]$ $(\langle s_1, \sigma_1, \sigma_1' \rangle, \gamma)$ *if* $s_1 \xrightarrow{m'(a_1, \ldots, a_w)} s_2 \wedge s \models m' \wedge$
$\qquad\qquad \xrightarrow{m \text{ call } m'(\sigma'(a_1), \ldots, \sigma'(a_w))} (\langle s, \sigma, \sigma' \rangle, \langle s_2, \sigma_1' \rangle \cdot \gamma)$ $s_1, s_2 \models m \wedge m, m' \in M^+ \wedge$
$(\sigma_1, \sigma_1') \models \lambda_P(s_1) \wedge$
$(\sigma, \sigma') \models \lambda_P(s) \wedge$
$\sigma_2 = [\![call]\!]\sigma_1'$

$[ret]$ $(\langle s_1, \sigma_1, \sigma_1' \rangle, \langle s_2, \sigma_2 \rangle \cdot \gamma) \xrightarrow{m \text{ ret } m'} (\langle s_2, \sigma_3, \sigma_3' \rangle, \gamma)$ *if* $s_1 \models r \wedge m, m' \in M^+ \wedge$
$s_2 \models m' \wedge (\sigma_1, \sigma_1') \models \lambda_P(s_1) \wedge$
$s_1 \models m \wedge (\sigma_3, \sigma_3') \models \lambda_P(s_2) \wedge$
$\sigma_3 = [\![ret]\!](\sigma_1', \sigma_2)$

The initial configurations are $E_b = \{(\langle s, \sigma_0, \sigma_0' \rangle, \epsilon) \mid s \in E \wedge (\sigma_0, \sigma_0') \models \lambda_P(s)\}$, *where* σ_0 *and* ϵ *denote the initial program state and the empty stack, respectively.*

In the behavioral models variables are explicitly assigned to values and therefore the set of assertions P_b should be empty. However, to be faithful to Definition 1, we use the (dummy) value tt which we assign to all behavioral states. It should further be noted that if $\mathcal{D}$ is finite, flow graph behavior can also be defined by means of *pushdown automata*, as in [13].

Example 3. The above definition is instantiated to PoP programs through the denotational semantics of PoP transition labels: PoP actions, call and ret. Due to space limitation, here we only provide an intuitive explanation of the semantics and delegate the formal definitions to the accompanying technical report [24]. Intuitively, the semantics of ε is the identity function, $\text{del}(v)$ moves v and all of its aliases to the equivalence class of null, $\text{new}(v)$ maps v to a fresh equivalence class, call initializes a program state for the called method, and ret recomputes the equivalence classes of variables upon a return from a call. Consider the composition of flow graphs shown in Fig. 2a and b. An example run through this flow graph is shown below[2]. In the run, the boxes represent the equivalence classes of variables, where the left box always represents the class of null, e.g., $\boxed{\text{p}\,|\,\text{c}}$ shows that variables p is in the equivalence class of null and c is in a different one.

$$(\langle s_1, \boxed{\text{p, c}\,|}, \boxed{\text{p, c}\,|}\rangle, \epsilon) \xrightarrow{\text{new c}} (\langle s_2, \boxed{\text{p}\,|\,\text{c}}, \boxed{\text{p}\,|\,\text{c}}\rangle, \epsilon) \xrightarrow{\text{Main call Container()}} (\langle s_4, \boxed{\text{p}\,|\,\text{c}}, \boxed{\text{p}\,|\,\text{c}}\rangle, \langle s_3, \boxed{\text{p}\,|\,\text{c}}\rangle)$$

$$\xrightarrow{\varepsilon} (\langle s_7, \boxed{\text{p}\,|\,\text{c}}, \boxed{\text{p}\,|\,\text{c}}\rangle, \langle s_3, \boxed{\text{p}\,|\,\text{c}}\rangle) \xrightarrow{\varepsilon} (\langle s_8, \boxed{\text{p}\,|\,\text{c}}, \boxed{|\,\text{p, c}}\rangle, \langle s_3, \boxed{\text{p}\,|\,\text{c}}\rangle)$$

$$\xrightarrow{\text{Container call Servlet()}} (\langle s_{10}, \boxed{|\,\text{p, c}}, \boxed{\text{p, c}\,|}\rangle, \langle s_9, \boxed{|\,\text{p, c}}\rangle, \langle s_3, \boxed{\text{p}\,|\,\text{c}}\rangle)$$

$$\xrightarrow{\varepsilon} (\langle s_{12}, \boxed{\text{p, c}\,|}, \boxed{\text{p, c}\,|}\rangle, \langle s_9, \boxed{|\,\text{p, c}}\rangle, \langle s_3, \boxed{\text{p}\,|\,\text{c}}\rangle) \xrightarrow{\text{Servlet ret Container}} (\langle s_9, \boxed{\text{p, c}\,|}, \boxed{\text{p, c}\,|}\rangle, \langle s_3, \boxed{\text{p}\,|\,\text{c}}\rangle)$$

$$\xrightarrow{\text{Container ret Main}} (\langle s_3, \boxed{\text{p, c}\,|}, \boxed{\text{p, c}\,|}\rangle, \epsilon)$$

Observe how assertions and transitions change the equivalence classes of variables, and states are pushed to and popped from the stack. E.g., the first transitions, new c, changes the equivalence class of c from null to a fresh one; the assertion of state s_8 moves p to the equivalence class of c; and the second transition pushes $\langle s_3, \boxed{\text{p}\,|\,\text{c}}\rangle$ to the stack, that is popped by the last transition. $\square$

In contrast to the above definition of behavior, the one without data does not have program states Σ, and the only action is ε. Thus, at calls control nodes are simply pushed to the stack and these are popped at returns. Also the set of atomic propositions A_b is equal to A, only consisting of method names and r.

Again, we instantiate the general definition of simulation (Definition 2) to flow graph behavior, and denote it by $\leqslant_b$. A result that we later exploit for compositional verification is that if two flow graphs are related by structural simulation, then their behaviors are related by behavioral simulation.

Theorem 2 (Simulation Correspondence). *For flow graphs A and B, if $A \leqslant_s B$ then $b(A) \leqslant_b b(B)$.*

4   Logic

As a property specification language we use the safety fragment of Modal Equation Systems [21], that is without diamond modalities. This logic is equal in expressive power to the safety fragment of the modal μ-calculus [19]. Here, we employ the former logic for technical reasons that will become clear later, but a user is free to use either. The translation of μ-calculus to simulation logic defined

---

[2] This example is simplified for the presentation in this paper. For complete examples please see [24].

in Definition 6 below is based on Bekič's principle described in [6, 8]. The translation in the other direction is straightforward and done simply by replacing each fixed point by an equation.

Following Larsen [21], we define the syntax and semantics of the specification language in two steps: first we define a basic modal logic that is parametrized on a set of labels L, state assertions P, and atoms A, and then we add recursion by means of equation systems in Definition 6. *Basic simulation logic* is a variant of Hennessy-Milner logic [14] without diamond modalities.

Definition 5 (Basic Simulation Logic: Syntax). *The formulas of* basic simulation logic *are inductively defined by:*

$$\phi ::= a \mid \neg a \mid p \mid \neg p \mid X \mid \phi_1 \wedge \phi_2 \mid \phi_1 \vee \phi_2 \mid [l]\phi$$

where $a \in A$, $p \in P$, $l \in L$, *and* X *ranges over a set of propositional variables* $\mathcal{V}$. *Formulas of the shape* a, $\neg a$, p, *and* $\neg p$ *are called* atomic formulas.

The semantics of a formula ϕ of basic simulation logic over L, P, and A is defined relative to a model M and an environment $\rho : \mathcal{V} \to 2^S$ as an extension of the standard definition (see [26]) with the following additional clauses.

$$\|p\|\rho \stackrel{\text{def}}{=} \{s \in S \mid \lambda_P(s) \sqsubseteq p\} \qquad \text{and} \qquad \|\neg p\|\rho \stackrel{\text{def}}{=} S \setminus \|p\|\rho$$

Definition 6 (Modal Equation System). *A* modal equation system $\Pi = \{X_i = \Phi_i \mid i \in J\}$ *over* L *and* A *for a set of indexes* J *is a finite set of* defining equations *such that the variables* X_i *are pairwise distinct and each* Φ_i *is a formula of basic simulation logic over* L, P, *and* A. *The set of variables occurring in* Π *is partitioned into the set of* bound *variables, defined by* $\text{bv}(\Pi) = \{X_i \mid i \in J\}$, *and the set of* free *variables* $\text{fv}(\Pi)$.

The semantics of a closed modal equation system $\|[\Pi]\|\rho$ is defined as its greatest fixed point. We use n-ary versions of conjunction and disjunction, setting $\bigwedge \emptyset = \text{tt}$ (*true*) and $\bigvee \emptyset = \text{ff}$ (*false*). We use $Labels(X)$ and $Atoms(X)$ to refer to the set of labels and atoms of the defining equation for X, respectively.

Finally, using the definitions of basic simulation logic and modal equation systems, the formulas of *simulation logic* are defined by $\Phi[\Pi]$ over L, P, and A, where Φ is a formula of basic simulation logic and Π is a modal equation system. The semantics of $\Phi[\Pi]$ w.r.t. model M and environment ρ is defined by $\|\Phi[\Pi]\|\rho \stackrel{\text{def}}{=} \|\Phi\|\rho[\|\Pi\|\rho]$. We say that a state s of a model M satisfies $\Phi[\Pi]$, written $(M, s) \models \Phi[\Pi]$, if $s \in \|\Phi[\Pi]\|\rho$ for all ρ. For initialized model (M, E) we define $(M, E) \models \Phi[\Pi]$ if $(M, s) \models \Phi[\Pi]$ for all $s \in E$.

Simulation logic is capable of expressing safety properties of sequences of observed actions, calls and returns. We use two instantiations of this logic to represent structural and behavioral properties. Structural logic expresses properties of flow graphs (Definition 3), therefore it is instantiated by $a \in A$, $p \in P$, and $l \in L$. Behavioral logic, however, expresses properties of flow graph behaviors (Definition 4), therefore it is instantiated by $a \in A_b$, $p \in P_b$, and $l \in L_b$.

Example 4. The structural local property "Container can only be called as the last statement of the method Servlet" in Fig. 1 is specified by the structural formula $X[\Pi]$, where Π is

$$X = [\text{Container}()]r \wedge \bigwedge_{l \in L_{\text{Servlet}} \setminus \text{Container}()} [l]X$$

The second behavioral global property in Fig. 1 is specified by the behavioral formula $X[\Pi]$, where Π is $X = ((\text{Main} \wedge r) \Rightarrow (p = \text{null} \wedge c = \text{null})) \wedge \bigwedge_{l \in L_b} [l]X$.

5   Maximal Models and Flow Graphs

To construct maximal models, we generalize our previous algorithm for models without program data [13], following closely the treatment there. We therefore only sketch our construction here, and refer the reader to [13] for the details. Our construction algorithm is defined on the general notion of model (Definition 1).

5.1   Maximal Model Construction

We define two auxiliary functions θ and χ which form a *Galois connection* between finite models and formulas in simulation logic. Function χ translates a *finite* model into a formula, while θ translates a formula into a (finite) model. Both functions are defined on formulas in a so-called *simulation normal form* (SNF). In this section, we define SNF and show that every formula of simulation logic has an SNF representation and provide an algorithm to convert a formula to its SNF. The construction of maximal models basically consists of translating a given formula into SNF and applying function θ on the result.

Definition 7 (χ). *Function χ maps a finite initialized model $(\mathcal{M}, E)$ into its characteristic formula $\chi(\mathcal{M}, E) = \phi_E[\Pi_\mathcal{M}]$, where $\phi_E = \bigvee_{s \in E} X_s$, and $\Pi_\mathcal{M}$ is defined by the equations:*

$$X_s = \bigwedge_{l \in L} [l] \bigvee_{s \xrightarrow{l} t} X_t \wedge \bigwedge_{a \in \lambda_A(s)} a \wedge \bigwedge_{b \notin \lambda_A(s)} \neg b \wedge \lambda_P(s)$$

Example 5. Function χ maps the flow graph of method Main to its characteristic formula $(X_1)[\Pi_{\text{Main}}]$, where Π_{Main} is the modal equation system

$$X_1 = \bigwedge_{l \in L \setminus \{\text{new } c\}} [l]\text{ff} \wedge [\text{new } c]X_2 \wedge \neg r \wedge \text{Main} \wedge \Phi$$
$$X_2 = \bigwedge_{l \in L \setminus \{\text{Container}()\}} [l]\text{ff} \wedge [\text{Container}()]X_3 \wedge \neg r \wedge \text{Main} \wedge \Phi$$
$$X_3 = \bigwedge_{l \in L} [l]\text{ff} \wedge r \wedge \text{Main} \wedge \Phi$$

and where L is the set of structural labels. Recall that $\text{ff} = \bigvee \emptyset$.   □

The next result shows that function χ precisely translates an initialized model to a formula. This is a variation of an earlier result by Larsen [21].

Theorem 3. *Let S_1 and S_2 be two initialized models and let S_2 be finite. Then $S_1 \leqslant S_2$ if and only if $S_1 \models \mathcal{X}(S_2)$.*

Definition 8 (Simulation Normal Form). *A formula $\phi[\Pi]$ of simulation logic over L, A, and P is in* simulation normal form (SNF) *if ϕ has the form $\bigvee \mathcal{Z}$ for some finite set $\mathcal{Z} \subseteq bv(\Pi)$ and all equations of Π have the following state normal form*

$$X = \bigwedge_{l \in L} [l] \bigvee \mathcal{Y}_{X,l} \wedge \bigwedge_{a \in B_X} a \wedge \bigwedge_{b \notin A \setminus B_X} \neg b \wedge p \qquad (1)$$

where each $\mathcal{Y}_{X,l} \subseteq bv(\Pi)$ is a finite set of variables, $B_X \subseteq A$ is a set of atomic propositions, and $p \in P$ is a state assertion.

Example 6. The property shown in Example 5 is in simulation normal form. $\square$

To translate simulation logic formulas into SNF we generalize the algorithm of [13] that works as follows. For a given set of atoms A, labels L, and a formula $\phi[\Pi]$, it saturates each equation of Π by conjoining its missing labels as $\bigwedge_{l \in L \wedge l \notin Labels(X)} [l] \; tt$, and atoms as $\bigwedge_{a \in A \wedge a \notin Atoms(X)}(a \vee \neg a)$, and then transforms the resulting formula to SNF by introducing new equations for disjunctions of formulas not guarded by any box. Our adaptation of this algorithm to formulas $\phi[\Pi]$ of Definition 6 proceeds in two steps. First, we apply the above algorithm to $\phi[\Pi]$, simply carrying over the assertions of the equations. In the second step, we conjoin the top element of the lattice of P to the resulting equations that do not have any assertions. In this way we simplify the saturation of assertions, that would otherwise be very inefficient or even impossible when the set of variables and their values is large or infinite.

Theorem 4. *Every formula of simulation logic has an equivalent one in SNF.*

Definition 9 (θ). *Function θ translates a formula $(\bigvee \mathcal{X})[\Pi]$ over L, A, and P, that is in SNF as in (1), to the (finite) initialized model $\theta((\bigvee \mathcal{X})[\Pi]) = ((S, L, \rightarrow, A, P, \lambda_A, \lambda_P), E)$ where $S = bv(\Pi)$, $E = \mathcal{X}$ and for every $X \in \mathcal{X}$ the equation for X induces transitions $\{X \xrightarrow{l} Y \mid Y \in \mathcal{Y}_{X,l}\}$, $\lambda_A(X) = B_X$, and $\lambda_P(X) = p$.*

Theorem 5 (Maximal Model Theorem). *For any ϕ in SNF, we have $S \leqslant \theta(\phi)$ if and only if $S \models \phi$.*

Thus, the model $\theta(\phi)$ is a maximal model for ϕ, in the sense that $\theta(\phi)$ is a model that satisfies ϕ and simulates all models satisfying it.

5.2   Maximal Flow Graph Construction

Maximal models constructed from structural properties by the above algorithm are in general not legal flow graphs. To restrict these to legal flow graphs, we conjoin the property with a so-called *characteristic formula* C_I constructed from the interface $I = (M^+, M^-, Modify)$. C_I describes precisely the models that constitute flow graphs with interface I:

$$C_I = \Phi_I[\Pi_I], \quad \Phi_I = \bigvee_{m \in M^+} X_m$$
$$\Pi_I = \{X_m = \bigwedge_{l \in L}[l]X_m \wedge a_m \wedge p_m \mid m \in M^+\}$$
$$a_m = m \wedge \bigwedge\{\neg m' \mid m' \in M^+, m' \neq m\}$$
$$p_m = \bigwedge\{v = v' \mid v \notin Modify \wedge v \in V\}$$

With the help of C_I we obtain a variant of Theorem 5 for flow graphs.

Theorem 6. *Let $I = (M^+, M^-, Modify)$ be an interface. For any initialized model $S = (\mathcal{M}, E)$ over L and $A = M^+ \cup \{r\}$ we have:*

1. $S \models C_I$ *if and only if* $\mathcal{R}(S) : I$
2. $S \leqslant_s \theta(\phi \wedge C_I)$ *if and only if* $S \models \phi$ *and* $\mathcal{R}(S) : I$

where $\mathcal{R}(S)$ denotes the reachable part of S.

6 Compositional Verification and Tool Support

As mentioned in Sect. 5, for models and formulas as defined in Definitions 1 and 6, maximal models exist and are unique up to isomorphism. Therefore, for this choice of model and logic we can provide the following principle for compositional verification that is sound and complete for finite models: "To show $\mathcal{M}_1 \uplus \mathcal{M}_2 \models \psi$, it suffices to show $\mathcal{M}_1 \models \phi$, i.e., that component $\mathcal{M}_1$ satisfies a suitably chosen *local specification* ϕ, and $\theta(\phi) \uplus \mathcal{M}_2 \models \psi$, i.e., that $\mathcal{M}_2$, when composed with the maximal model $\theta(\phi)$, satisfies the *global property* ψ."

We exploit Theorem 6 to adapt this principle to flow graphs (as models) and structural logic and use the maximal flow graph construction from Sect. 5.2 to obtain the rule below.

$$\frac{\mathcal{G}_1 \models \phi \qquad \theta(\phi \wedge C_I) \uplus \mathcal{G}_2 \models \psi}{\mathcal{G}_1 \uplus \mathcal{G}_2 \models \psi} \tag{2}$$

The rule states that the composition of flow graphs $\mathcal{G}_1$ and $\mathcal{G}_2$ satisfies the structural property ψ if flow graph $\mathcal{G}_1$ satisfies a local structural property ϕ, and the composition of flow graph $\mathcal{G}_2$ with the maximal flow graph for ϕ and interface I satisfies ψ.

Theorem 7. *Rule (2) is sound and complete.*

We restrict local specifications to structural properties, and by exploiting the fact that structural simulation implies behavioral simulation (Theorem 2), we obtain a complete compositional verification rule for global behavioral properties, thus avoiding the possibility of false negatives. However, adapting the compositional verification principle to local behavioral specifications is more problematic, as behavioral properties in general do not give rise to unique maximal flow graphs. We can represent the set of flow graphs satisfying the local specification by a (pushdown) model that simulates the behavior of these flow graphs, but this necessarily leads to approximate (i.e., sound but incomplete) solutions, since such a model cannot be guaranteed to be a legal flow graph behavior.

Tool Support and Evaluation. We have extended our compositional verification toolset [16] for the verification of PoP programs in the presence of variability. Besides the necessary data structures, the toolset includes a maximal flow graph constructor, a tool to induce behaviors from flow graphs, and external model checkers CWB [9] and Moped [18]. We used this toolset to verify a Java J2EE application consisting of 1087 lines of code, of which 297 lines are variable.

We focused on properties of *database connections*, such as "at the end of the execution, all database connections should have been closed". We therefore abstracted away all program data except variables of this type, constructed and destructed by invoking methods `getConnection` and `close`, respectively. To extract flow graphs with this abstraction, we first extracted a data-less flow graph from the Java code with our flow graph extractor tool CoNFLEx [11]. Then we manually inserted all 4 database connection variables of the program into the extracted flow graphs and replaced any call to `getConnection` and `close` methods with `new` and `del` actions, respectively. This was necessary because currently we do not have a tool to extract PoP flow graphs from code. We also specified each method of the program with a structural local specification, expressing its safe sequences of invocation of methods `getConnection` and `close` (here renamed to `new` and `del`). We then (i) model checked the flow graphs of variable components against their corresponding local specifications with CWB (took 0.5 sec.), and (ii) constructed maximal flow graphs from the local specifications of the variable components (took 4.1 sec.), composed them with the flow graphs of the other components and model checked the result against a property of database connection with Moped (took 2.1 sec.). Recall that to re-verify the program after a change in the variable components only sub-task (i) needs to be repeated.

7   Related Work

In the context of compositional verification of temporal properties, the maximal model technique was first proposed by Grumberg and Long for ACTL, the universal fragment of CTL [12], and later generalized by Kupferman and Vardi for ACTL* [20]. These works do not address the verification of infinite state systems. In our previous work, we used maximal models constructed from safety μ-calculus formulas to verify infinite state context-free behaviors, where the program data is disregarded [13]. In this work we extend our previous work to a generic framework that captures program data.

For a different class of properties, Hoare logic provides a popular framework for compositional verification of programs, (see e.g. [22]) that is technically capable of verifying programs with variability. Also, of particular interest to our technique is the work by Alur and Chaudhuri [3], which proposes a unification of Hoare logic and Manna-Pnueli-style temporal reasoning by defining a set of proof rules for the verification of some particular classes of (non-regular) temporal properties. Our technique is partially inspired by this work.

Related to our approach of relativizating global properties on local specifications, Andersen introduces partial model checking in which global properties of concurrent systems are reduced to local properties of their components (processes) [5]. The work only considers finite-state systems; however, the approach suggests the possibility of extending our technique to generate local properties for variable components of programs when the global properties are fixed.

Several successful tools and techniques exist for (non-compositional) verification of behavioral properties of procedural programs. However, as mentioned, compositionality is essential for the verification of variable programs. Still, related to our two-step verification procedure, tools such as SLAM [7] and ESP [10] divide the verification into (local) intra- and (global) inter-procedural analysis to achieve scalability. It is interesting to explore if the ideas presented here can be used to adapt these tools for the verification of systems with variability.

Closely related to our flow graph model are *recursive state machines* [2], defined by Alur and others as a formalism to model procedural programs with recursive calls. The authors propose efficient LTL and CTL* model checking algorithms. However, they do not address compositional verification.

As for specification languages, the temporal logic of nested calls and returns [4] and its generalization to nested words [1] are of particular interest to this work. These logics are capable of abstracting internal computations by moving from a call to its corresponding return point in one step. However, they do not make a clear separation of structure and behavior, and may therefore require more involved maximal model constructions.

8   Conclusion

This paper presents a generic framework for compositional verification of temporal safety properties of sequential procedural programs in the presence of variability. The framework is a generalization of a previously developed framework which disregards program data. Our technique relies on local specifications of the variable components, in that the correctness of global properties of the program is relativized on the composition of the maximal flow graphs constructed from these local specifications and the flow graphs of the stable components.

The framework is parametric on a set of selected "visible" program instructions that are explicitly represented as transition labels, while the effect of all other instructions is captured abstractly by means of Hoare-style state assertions. This distinction allows to keep the level of detail of specifications within practical limits. It also allows a (symbolic) formulation of the maximal model construction for program models with data that does not add to the complexity of the construction for models without data. To evaluate our technique in practice, we provide tool support for the verification of evolving PoP programs.

In the current setting, our (symbolic) flow graphs induce behaviors with concrete data from finite domains. We conjecture that program data can be represented symbolically in the behaviors as well, using the state assertions of the structural program model (Definition 1). We plan to investigate the expressiveness of symbolic behaviors. We are currently working on a parametric flow graph extractor to extract flow graphs of Java programs for the given sets of actions and assertions. We also plan to provide tool support for the verification of programs with other datatypes, such as integers and Booleans.

References

1. Alur, R., Arenas, M., Barcelo, P., Etessami, K., Immerman, N., Libkin, L.: First-order and temporal logics for nested words. In: LICS, pp. 151–160 (2007)
2. Alur, R., Benedikt, M., Etessami, K., Godefroid, P., Reps, T., Yannakakis, M.: Analysis of recursive state machines. TOPLAS **27**, 786–818 (2005)
3. Alur, R., Chaudhuri, S.: Temporal reasoning for procedural programs. In: Barthe, G., Hermenegildo, M. (eds.) VMCAI 2010. LNCS, vol. 5944, pp. 45–60. Springer, Heidelberg (2010)
4. Alur, R., Etessami, K., Madhusudan, P.: A temporal logic of nested calls and returns. In: Jensen, K., Podelski, A. (eds.) TACAS 2004. LNCS, vol. 2988, pp. 467–481. Springer, Heidelberg (2004)
5. Andersen, H.: Partial model checking. In: LICS, pp. 398–407 (1995)
6. Arnold, A., Niwiński, D.: Rudiments of μ-Calculus. Studies in Logic and the Foundations of Mathematics, vol. 146. Elsevier, Amsterdam (2001)
7. Ball, T., Rajamani, S.K.: The SLAM project: debugging system software via static analysis. In: POPL, pp. 1–3 (2002)
8. Bekič, H.: Definable operators in general algebras, and the theory of automata and flowcharts. Technical report, IBM Laboratory (1967)
9. Cleaveland, R., Parrow, J., Steffen, B.: A semantics based verification tool for finite state systems. In: IFIP WG6.1, pp. 287–302 (1990)
10. Das, M., Lerner, S., Seigle, M.: ESP: path-sensitive program verification in polynomial time. In: PLDI, pp. 57–68. ACM (2002)
11. de Carvalho Gomes, P., Picoco, A., Gurov, D.: Sound control flow graph extraction from incomplete Java bytecode programs. In: Gnesi, S., Rensink, A. (eds.) FASE 2014 (ETAPS). LNCS, vol. 8411, pp. 215–229. Springer, Heidelberg (2014)
12. Grumberg, O., Long, D.: Model checking and modular verification. TOPLAS **16**(3), 843–871 (1994)
13. Gurov, D., Huisman, M., Sprenger, C.: Compositional verification of sequential programs with procedures. Inf. Comput. **206**(7), 840–868 (2008)
14. Hennessy, M., Milner, R.: Algebraic laws for nondeterminism and concurrency. J. ACM **32**, 137–161 (1985)
15. Huisman, M., Aktug, I., Gurov, D.: Program models for compositional verification. In: Liu, S., Araki, K. (eds.) ICFEM 2008. LNCS, vol. 5256, pp. 147–166. Springer, Heidelberg (2008)
16. Huisman, M., Gurov, D.: CVPP: a tool set for compositional verification of control-flow safety properties. In: Beckert, B., Marché, C. (eds.) FoVeOOS 2010. LNCS, vol. 6528, pp. 107–121. Springer, Heidelberg (2011)
17. Servlet Development. Release 2 (9.0.3). http://docs.oracle.com/cd/A97688_16/generic.903/a97680/develop.htm#1007089
18. Kiefer, S., Schwoon, S., Suwimonteerabuth, D.: Moped–a model-checker for pushdown systems. http://www.informatik.uni-stuttgart.de/fmi/szs/tools/moped/
19. Kozen, D.: Results on the propositional μ-calculus. TCS **27**, 333–354 (1983)
20. Kupferman, O., Vardi, M.: An automata-theoretic approach to modular model checking. TOPLAS **22**(1), 87–128 (2000)

21. Larsen, K.G.: Modal specifications. In: Sifakis, J. (ed.) Automatic Verification Methods for Finite State Systems. LNCS, vol. 407, pp. 232–246. Springer, Heidelberg (1989)

22. Müller, P. (ed.): Modular Specification and Verification of Object-Oriented Programs. LNCS, vol. 2262. Springer, Heidelberg (2002)

23. Rot, J., de Boer, F., Bonsangue, M.: Unbounded allocation in bounded heaps. In: Arbab, F., Sirjani, M. (eds.) FSEN 2013. LNCS, vol. 8161, pp. 1–16. Springer, Heidelberg (2013)

24. Soleimanifard, S., Gurov, D.: Algorithmic verification of procedural programs in the presence of code variability. Technical report, KTH (2013). http://urn.kb.se/resolve?urn=urn:nbn:se:kth:diva-128950

25. Soleimanifard, S., Gurov, D., Huisman, M.: Procedure-modular specification and verification of temporal safety properties. Softw. Syst. Model. (2013). doi:10.1007/s10270-013-0321-0

26. Stirling, C.: Modal and Temporal Logics of Processes. Springer, New York (2001)

Place-Liveness of ComSA Applications

Abderrahim Ait Wakrime[✉], Sébastien Limet, and Sophie Robert

University of Orléans, INSA Centre Val de Loire, LIFO, EA 4022,
45067 Orléans, France
{abderrahim.ait-wakrime,sebastien.limet,sophie.robert}@univ-orleans.fr

Abstract. Interactive scientific visualization applications are based on heterogeneous codes to implement simulation, visualization and interaction parts. These different parts need to be precisely assembled to construct high performance applications allowing efficient interactions. Thanks to their programming paradigm, component-based approaches are suitable to construct this kind of applications. However, building a correct application using this paradigm is a difficult task. Even starting up such an application may be a difficult problem since the composition may lead to deadlocks. This paper defines a sufficient condition that ensures place-liveness of a subclass of FIFO nets. This result is used to provide tools that help a user to analyze his application. Especially, this analysis aims at avoiding deadlocks and starting the application up in a way that ensures its liveness i.e. all its components are active.

Keywords: FIFO nets · Component-based approaches · Analysis tools

1   Introduction

Component-based approaches are widely used in many different domains. The main advantages of such approaches are their great ability to integrate heterogeneous codes in a single application and the separation of concerns and the code reusability that they favor. Scientific computing, including scientific visualization, is a domain which can benefit from component-based approaches since it requires applications that integrate very specific and sophisticated codes from different fields. In this sense, scientific workflows (e.g. [8]) are often component-based approaches.

The work presented in this paper takes place in the domain of interactive scientific visualization, *i.e.* scientific applications that include a simulation coupled with a real-time visualization as well as interaction means allowing the user to interact with the simulation or the visualization. Such applications are made from different kinds of modules. They can be parallel codes for shared or distributed memory systems or they can be sequential codes. Thus, the modules can have very different behaviors: some can be very slow, others can be very fast. Finally, the interactivity introduces performance constraints since the result of

This work was supported by the French Agency for Research (Grant "ExaViz", ANR-11-MONU-003).

I. Lanese and E. Madelaine (Eds.): FACS 2014, LNCS 8997, pp. 346–363, 2015.
DOI: 10.1007/978-3-319-15317-9_21

an interaction should be quickly visible to the user to understand what he does. A component-based approach can help to resolve these constraints thanks to exogenous coordination. In this case, some connectors, which express very specific communication policies, are used to coordinate the components when assembling them in an application [11]. For example, coupling a parallel simulation with a visualization can generate buffer overflows on the visualization. But it may be unnecessary to render all the simulation results thus a connector based on a greedy policy can solve the problem. Our connectors are similar to Reo [2] connectors. However, they are not based on a *request-response* protocol unlike the channel-based coordination model of Reo. The connectors deliver data when the receiver is ready to consume them. Therefore the sender is able to run at its own rate. That is why the exogenous coordination need to be precisely defined with connectors able to specify synchronization policies taking into account the application specificities.

The ComSA component model, subject of our paper, meets the needs of interactive scientific visualization applications. It can be implemented in frameworks like FlowVR [1] which is specifically designed to provide exogenous coordination that fits the constraints of interactive applications [6].

Building a ComSA application can be a difficult task especially for users who are not computer experts. Particularly, the composition needs to be well defined in order to ensure that the application can start and also to prevent run time issues. Solving these problems is often based on the analysis of the application deadlocks. For component-based approaches, the deadlocks are widely studied as illustrated by the recent work [3]. In this context, our goal is to provide a set of tools that helps to build the application and to analyze it. In particular, the analysis tools aim to correct the application by detecting deadlocks. They also target to start properly the application which may be non-trivial.

Petri nets are extensively used as formal models for concurrent systems. For the component-based approaches they are also frequently utilized because of their analysis and verification ability as in [4,16] where the application behavior analysis and refinement are based on colored Petri nets. Moreover, they offer a simple graphical representation that can be used for simulation purposes.

This paper proposes to complete ComSA with a toolkit based on a special class of FIFO nets called strict colored FIFO nets (sCFN). The formal semantics offered by sCFN models finely the behavior of high performance interactive visualization applications. This can be used for simulation purposes to test the global behavior of an application for example. But such a modeling is also helpful to specify some properties on the structure of the application to ensure that it can be started and that it can run without blocking because of deadlocks. This kind of analysis usually relies on liveness properties of Petri nets. Sufficient conditions to insure liveness of some classes of Petri nets most often use the well known Commoner property that relies on the notions of siphons and traps [5,10]. Such conditions also provide a way to build a proper initial marking that makes the Petri net live. The deadlock freedom of the applications presented in this paper relies on a place-liveness property of the sCFNs that model them. The place-liveness is demonstrated using a reduction of the problem to a class of ordinary Petri nets and are based on liveness results of the asymmetric choice Petri nets.

The remainder of this paper is structured as follows: the ComSA component model is presented in Sect. 2 with an example to present the problem. Section 3 defines the class of sCFN and presents the semantics of ComSA applications using sCFNs. Section 4 presents a sufficient condition for place-liveness of sCFNs and shows how it is used to help the user to build and start his application. Finally Sect. 5 concludes and gives some perspectives.

2   The ComSA Model

The component-based approach for Scientific Applications (ComSA) aims to design and develop interactive applications including visualization components. It can model applications developed with the FlowVR middleware. The model is first described and some examples are given. The examples are used to illustrate how our model fits with the targeted application constraints and to show the need of analysis tools to check application properties as the existence of a start configuration which guarantees all the components will actually run.

2.1   The Component Model

A *component* is an existing piece of software composed of *input ports* and *output ports* which are the interfaces between a component and the outside.

Definition 1. *A component is a quadruple* $C = (Id, pIn \cup \{s\}, pOut \cup \{e\}, IR)$, *where Id is its unique identifier, pIn a set of input data ports, s an input triggering port, pOut a set of output data ports, e an output signal port and IR a subset of* $\mathcal{P}(pIn) \times \mathcal{P}(pOut)$ *called* incidence relations.

For a component C, Id_C, pIn_C, $pOut_C$ and IR_C denote respectively its identifier, input ports, output ports and its incidence relations.

The component *behavior* is described by the incidence relations. Each of them represents an operational mode of the component and can be linked to a specific service provided by the component. Data exchanges between component are performed through messages and during an iteration a component can read at most one message on each of its input port and produce at most one message on each of its output port.

Definition 2. *Given a component C, an incidence relation is a pair* $r = \langle I, O \rangle$ *s.t.* $I \subseteq pIn_C$ *is the set of* input ports *of r and* $O \subseteq pOut_C$ *its set of* output *ports.* I *and* O *are denoted* $IR^{in}(r)$ *and* $IR^{out}(r)$ *respectively. r is said* satisfied *if each port* $p \in IR^{in}(r)$ *contains data.*

The behavior of a component C named *wait-get-put* is the following: *wait* until *at least one* of its incidence relation is satisfied, *get* one message from the input ports of *all* satisfied incidence relations of C, *put* one new message to the output ports of all satisfied incidence relations of C and emit a signal on port e.

It is important to remark that at each iteration, all the satisfied incidence relations are triggered and all the corresponding results are produced. The incidence relations describe different computations the component can make according to the inputs and only one result is computed for each output port. For a component C, let $\mathcal{P}(IR_C)$ be the set of all the non-empty subsets of IR_C, each set $S \in \mathcal{P}(IR_C)$ is a behavior of C s.t. $\forall r \in S$, r is fired.

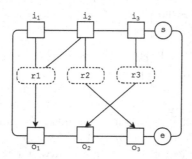

Fig. 1. Example of incidence relations.

For example, the component illustrated Fig. 1 has three incidence relations. However, if i_2 and i_3 are fed then both r_2 and r_3 are executed and if all the input ports are fed, all the incidence relations are fired. So, the component has two behaviors in addition to those corresponding to r_1, r_2 and r_3. It is also important to remark that if the input port s of a component C is connected in an application, it becomes an implicit input port of *all* incidence relations of C. This way, it is possible to control the component iterations from the outside.

Assembling components to realize an application, consists in defining a communication schema allowing the exchanges of data between the components. This schema is based on communication connectors in charge of the communication policy and on links.

Definition 3. *A connector is a quadruple* $c = (Id, \{i, s\}, \{o\}, t)$ *where Id is the identifier of c, i is an input port, s a triggering input port, o an output port and t the type of the connector.*

For a connector c, the notations $Id_c, pIn_c, pOut_c$ and t_c stand respectively for the identifier, the set of input ports, the set of output ports and the type of c. The *behavior of a connector* depends on its type. Three types of connectors are available:

- The **sFIFO** connector is a plain FIFO connection. To prevent overflows, the sender waits for a triggering signal on its s port usually sent by the receiver.
- **bBuffer** and **nbBuffer** connectors keep their incoming messages and dispatch the oldest one when they receive a triggering signal on their s port. **nbBuffer** is the non-blocking variant of **bBuffer** *i.e.* it generates an empty message to the receiver when triggered while it has no message waiting.

– **bGreedy** and **nbGreedy** connectors keep only the last message provided by
the sender and send it when they receive a triggering signal on their s port.
nbGreedy is the non-blocking variant of the **bGreedy** connector.

The links are used to connect components and connectors via their ports.

Definition 4. *A link is a pair $\langle x^p, y^q \rangle$ where x, y are components or connectors,
$p \in pOut_x$ and $q \in pIn_y$. When, $p \neq e$, $q \neq s$ and either x or y is a connector
the link $\langle x^p, y^q \rangle$ is called a* data link*. When, $p = e$, $q = s$ and x is a component,
the link $\langle x^p, y^q \rangle$ is called a* trigger link.

Two data links $\langle x_1^{p_1}, y_1^{q_1} \rangle$ and $\langle x_2^{p_2}, y_2^{q_2} \rangle$ are *compatible* if $y_1^{q_1} \neq y_2^{q_2}$. Each input
port cannot belong to more than one link.

An application is described by a graph that connects the output ports to
the input ports of components and connectors. Thus, its vertices are the components and the connectors. Its edges are the links. Formally, an application App
is defined by a graph $(Comp \bigcup Conn, Dl \bigcup Tl)$ where $Comp$ is a set of components, $Conn$ a set of connectors, Dl a set of pairwise compatible data links and
Tl a set of trigger links.

It is important to remark that data links must be compatible to prevent that
an input port is fed concurrently by two different producers. On the other hand,
a s port can be the end of several trigger links and it will be fed with a signal
at the end of the iteration of all the emitter components.

Definition 5. *Let $App = (Comp \bigcup Conn, Dl \bigcup Tl)$ and $C \in Comp$, each $r \in$
IR_C is said* active *if $\forall p \in IR^{in}(r) \exists l \in Dl$ and $c \in Conn$ s.t. $l = \langle c^i, C^p \rangle$.*

If for each $C' \in Comp \exists r \in IR_{C'}$ s.t. r is active then the application App is
said *well-formed.*

Figure 2 illustrates an application graph for the scientific visualization of a molecular dynamics simulation. Thus, Components I1 and I2 represent *interaction*
components, S1, S2 and S3 *computation* components and V is the *visualization* component. Therefore, I1 and I2 provide some events as mouse clicks,
3D or analog positions. For example they can be respectively associated to a
Omni®Phantom (an haptic device with force feedback and a 3D position sens-
ing) and a SpaceBall (a 3D motion controller). Component S1 transforms these
events into actions and interprets raw the 3D positions it receives. Component
S2 is the simulation component. It provides the atom positions and their energy
according to the molecular dynamics it implements. The molecular dynamics can
be influenced by a force applied on some atoms that S2 can receive. Component
S3 computes this force when it receives the right event and sends it to both
Component S2 and I1 that is able to produce a feedback to the user. Finally,
Component V renders the atoms and the forces when applied on atoms. Component V also receives the actions and the 3D position which is used to represent
an avatar. This avatar allows atom selections from which forces are computed
using the distance between this avatar and the nearest atom at the time of the
selection.

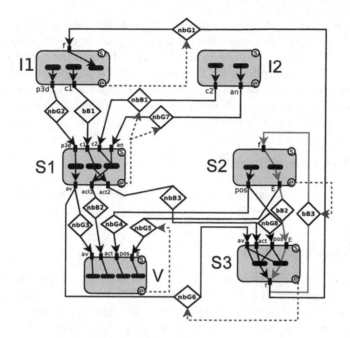

Fig. 2. Application of a molecular dynamics simulation

The incidence relations of each component describe its behaviors. For example, the component S2 has two behaviors. It produces atom positions at each iteration and an energy only at the reception of a force on its input port. Its incidence relations are $\{\langle \emptyset, \{pos\}\rangle, \langle\{f\}, \{E\}\rangle\}$. The component S3 computes a force from the avatar and the atom positions according to the action message it receives on its *act* port. As soon as it receives an energy it also updates the force to modulate its norm for example. Therefore its incidence relations are $\{\langle\{pos, av, act\}, \{f\}\rangle, \langle\{pos, av, E\}, \{f\}\rangle\}$.

To ensure the application runs as fast as possible, communications are based on *nbGreedy* connectors in order to not saturate the slowest components thanks to message loss and to not delay the fastest ones. However, events as mouse clicks cannot be lost. Indeed they trigger specific computations. For example the mouse click from $c1$ of I1 is interpreted by S1 into an action that triggers a force computation of the S3 component. That is why, a *Buffer* connector was chosen to connect $c1$ of I1 (resp. $c2$ of I2) to $c1$ (resp. $c2$) of S1. We choose a blocking or non blocking mode for these connectors according to the component capacity to interpret empty messages. The energy must not be lost for the force computation and the component S2 must interpret all the forces from S3. To ensure that no information is lost *bBuffer* connectors were chosen between the E and the f ports of S2 and S3.

It is simple to check that an application *App* is well-formed which ensures that all the components may be operational. However, it does neither guarantee that the application starts nor all its components are live, in the sense they can actually receive data. Therefore, it may be very difficult for a user to start and verify the liveness of such application because of cycles in the application graph. That is why, it is essential to define analysis tools to help the user to check the good properties of his application. These tools rely on an operational semantics of the ComSA model in terms of strict Colored Fifo Nets (sCFN), a subclass of FIFO nets. In the following, we describe how the formal semantics offered by sCFN models the ComSA applications.

3   The ComSA Semantics

Some definitions and notations of Petri nets are first recalled, then the sFIFO nets are defined and finally the ComSA semantics is presented.

3.1   Ordinary Petri Nets

The place-liveness property of strict color FIFO nets uses a place-liveness sufficient condition on ordinary Petri nets. Hence, definitions, notations and results on Petri nets used in the remainder are presented. For more details see e.g. [5].

An *ordinary Petri net* (OPN) is a tuple $\langle P, T, A, M \rangle$ where P is a finite set of places, T is a finite set of transitions (with $P \cap T = \emptyset$), A a set of arcs either of the form $\langle p, t \rangle$ or of the form $\langle t, p \rangle$ where $p \in P$, $t \in P$. Finally M is a function which assigns a positive number of tokens to each place. The notation $\langle P, T, A \rangle$ refers to the structure of the net $\langle P, T, A, M \rangle$.

The following definitions are used to express the dynamics of an OPN. In an OPN $\langle P, T, A, M \rangle$, $\bullet x$ where $x \in P \cup T$ denotes the set $\{y | \exists \langle y, x \rangle \in A\}$ and symmetrically $x \bullet$ denotes the set $\{y | \exists \langle x, y \rangle \in A\}$. Note that if $x \in P$ $\bullet x$ and $x \bullet$ are subsets of T and vice versa. Let E be a subset of P or of T, $\bullet E$ denotes the set $\bigcup_{x \in E} \bullet x$ and $E \bullet$ denotes the set $\bigcup_{x \in E} x \bullet$. A set of places E is said to be *marked* if $\exists p \in E$ such that $M(p) > 0$. A place p such that $\bullet p = \emptyset$ is called a *source* place. A place p such that $|p \bullet| > 1$ is called a *conflict* and in this case, the elements of $p \bullet$ are called conflicting transitions.

In an OPN $\langle P, T, A, M \rangle$, a transition $t \in T$ is *enabled* if $\forall p \in \bullet t$ $M(p) > 0$. Firing an enabled transition consists in consuming one token in each of its input places and putting one token to each of its output places. The OPN $\langle P, T, A, M \rangle$ can evolve to $\langle P, T, A, M' \rangle$ when firing transition t (denoted $\langle P, T, A, M \rangle \rightarrow_t \langle P, T, A, M' \rangle$), if t is an enabled transition of $\langle P, T, A, M \rangle$ and M' is the marking defined as follows

$$M_R(p) = \begin{vmatrix} M(p) - 1 & \text{if } p \in \bullet t \\ M(p) & \text{otherwise} \end{vmatrix} \qquad M'(p) = \begin{vmatrix} M_R(p) + 1 & \text{if } p \in t \bullet \\ M_R(p) & \text{otherwise} \end{vmatrix}$$

Note that M_R is just an auxiliary marking that helps to define M' especially for the places of $t \bullet \cap \bullet t$. For an OPN $\langle P, T, A \rangle$, a marking M' is said *reachable in one step* from a marking M if $\langle P, T, A, M \rangle \rightarrow_t \langle P, T, A, M' \rangle$ for some $t \in T$, it is denoted $M \rightarrow_{\langle P, T, A \rangle} M'$ or $M \rightarrow M'$ if $\langle P, T, A \rangle$ is clear from context.

The reflexive transitive closure of $\to$ is denoted $\to^*$. A marking M' is *reachable* from the marking M if $M \to^* M'$.

An OPN $\langle P, T, A, M \rangle$ is said to be *live* if for any marking M' reachable from M and any transition $t \in T$ there exists a marking M'' reachable from M' such that t is enabled in $\langle P, T, A, M'' \rangle$. Moreover, it is said *place-live* if for every marking M' reachable from M and for every place $p \in P$, there exists a marking M'' which marks p.

In the following all the OPNs are considered to contain at least one place and one transition and to be connected in order to not consider several sub-nets in demonstrations *i.e.* they do not contain an isolated place.

Lemma 1. *If an OPN is live then it is place-live.*

Now, let us give some definitions and properties related to the structure of an OPN. First of all, an OPN $\langle P, T, A \rangle$ is an *asymmetric choice net* (ACN) iff $\forall p_1, p_2 \in P$ $p_1 \bullet \cap p_2 \bullet \neq \emptyset \implies p_1 \bullet \subseteq p_2 \bullet$ or $p_2 \bullet \subseteq p_1 \bullet$.

Let $\langle P, T, A \rangle$ be an OPN. A set of places $E \subseteq P$ is called a *siphon* if $\bullet E \subseteq E \bullet$ and it is called a *trap* if $E \bullet \subseteq \bullet E$. It is well-known that if a siphon is unmarked for a marking M then it remains unmarked for every marking M' reachable from M. Symmetrically if a trap is marked for a marking M then it remains marked for every marking M' reachable from M. Those properties are very important to prove the liveness of an ACN [13].

Theorem 1. *If every siphon of an ACN contains a marked trap, then it is live.*

3.2   sCFN Definition

OPNs are too weak to express the semantics of ComSA applications since their tokens are all alike this is why sCFNs are introduced. sCFN is a subclass of FIFO nets [7] that are colored Petri nets [9] where places are FIFO queues to ensure that tokens leave a place in the order they entered this place. These two features fit our needs to model the behavior of the components. sCFN imposes that each transition consumes exactly one token in each of its input places and produces exactly one token on its output places. Moreover, some transitions have priorities, represented by a weight, which is the number of input places of each transition to resolve the conflict between these transitions.

Definition 6. *A strict colored FIFO net is a tuple $\langle P, T, A, M \rangle$ where P is a finite set of places which are FIFO queues of tokens, T is a finite set of transitions (with $P \cap T = \emptyset$), A a set of arcs either of the form $\langle p, t, e \rangle$ or of the form $\langle t, p, e \rangle$ where $p \in P$, $t \in T$ and e is an expression that may contain variables. Finally M is a function which associates a FIFO queue to each place. Note that transitions have a weight that is a positive integer denoted by W_t.*

In order to illustrate the sCFN, let us denote a FIFO queue as a list of elements $(a_1, \ldots, a_n)$ where a_1 is the oldest element of the queue and a_n the most recent one. The empty FIFO is denoted $\emptyset$. Moreover we use the following notations.

Let f a FIFO queue, $f+e$ denotes the addition of an element in the FIFO, $f \uparrow$ denotes the oldest element of the FIFO and $f--$ the removing of the oldest element (only defined if $f \neq \emptyset$).

Most of the notations used for OPNs apply to sCFNs. However the dynamics of the net is quite different. In a sCFN $\langle P, T, A, M \rangle$ a place is said *marked* if $M(p) \neq \emptyset$. A transition $t \in T$ is *enabled with the binding* σ if $\forall p \in \bullet t \ M(p) \neq \emptyset$ and $\forall \langle p, t, e \rangle \in A$, $\sigma(e) = M(p) \uparrow$ where σ simply maps variables of e to values. Note that unlike OPN, it is not sufficient that the input places of a sCFN are marked to make it enabled. However, when a transition is fired only one token is consumed from the input places and only one token is put to the output places.

Firing an enabled transition consists in consuming the oldest token in each of its input places and putting one token to each of its output places. If several conflicting transitions are enabled, only those of the greater weight can be fired. The sCFN $\langle P, T, A, M \rangle$ can evolve to $\langle P, T, A, M' \rangle$ when firing transition t (denoted $\langle P, T, A, M \rangle \rightarrow_t \langle P, T, A, M' \rangle$), if t is an enabled transition of $\langle P, T, A, M \rangle$ such that there is no other enabled transition in conflict with t and having a strictly greater weight. In this case, M' is the marking defined as follows

$$M_R(p) = \begin{vmatrix} M(p)-- & if \ p \in \bullet t \\ M(p) & otherwise \end{vmatrix} \quad M'(p) = \begin{vmatrix} M_R(p) + \sigma_t^M(e) & if \ \langle t, p, e \rangle \in A \\ M_R(p) & otherwise \end{vmatrix}$$

Note that if two conflicting transitions are enabled, the one with the greater weight is applied, if they have the same weight, only one is applied in a don't know way.

Figure 3 illustrates the dynamics of a sCFN. In the sCFN of Fig. 3(a), P_m contains a token $[]$ that represents the empty list and therefore P_m is not empty. In this sCFN, both t_{in} and t_{out} have no empty input places but only t_{in} is enabled (with $\sigma_1 = \{e \mapsto 1, L \mapsto []\}$). Indeed the arc from P_m to t_{out} is labeled with a list containing one element $([e])$ which cannot match the empty list. Firing t_{in} with σ_1 removes 1 from P_i and $[]$ from P_m and puts $\sigma_1([e])$ (i.e. [1]) to P_m. The resulting sCFN is displayed in Fig. 3(b). In this sCFN, both t_{in} and t_{out} are enabled, t_{in} is fired (but t_{out} could have been also) with $\sigma_2 = \{e \mapsto 2, L \mapsto [1]\}$ which gives the sCFN of Fig. 3(c). Note that this step discards token 1. Figure 3(d) illustrates the result after firing of t_{out} with $\sigma_3 = \{e \mapsto 2\}$. P_s becomes empty and P_m gets again a token that is the empty list. Finally, transition t_{back} is fired with $\sigma_4 = \{e \mapsto 2\}$ which empties P_o and puts 1 in P_s and 2 in P_i (since places are FIFOs, 2 enters at the end of this FIFO). This kind of sCFN is used to express greedy connection since t_{in} let tokens coming from P_i, enter into P_m but instead of adding it to the place, it replaces the old token by the new one. The place P_s represents the signal port that indicates when the token stored in P_m must be sent to the recipient.

3.3   Semantics Based on sCFNs

The semantics of our component model is given by a function Ψ that defines the sCFN describing the behavior of an application. This function is decomposed in

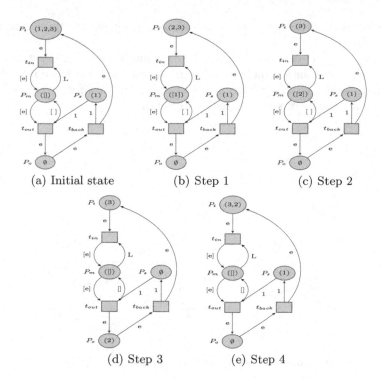

(a) Initial state   (b) Step 1   (c) Step 2

(d) Step 3   (e) Step 4

Fig. 3. An example of sCFN and its dynamics

several parts to define the sCFN of each $C \in Comp$, the sCFN of each $c \in Conn$ and finally the sCFN of the application graph in linking the sCFN representing components and connectors. For lack of space, Ψ is detailed only for components and connectors.

The general idea to define the semantics of a component C consists in representing each port of the component by a place and each behavior by a transition. In the following, to ensure the uniqueness of the places and transitions names, they are denoted using the component or the connector Id they represent. For example the P_s place of a component C_1 will be denoted $P_s^{C_1}$. However, if there is no ambiguity the Id will be omitted.

As explained in Sect. 2, the incidence relations IR_C of a component C describe all its behaviors from $\mathcal{P}(IR_C)$. If $B_C^{in} = \{\bigcup_{r \in E} IR^{in}(r) | E \in \mathcal{P}(IR_C)\}$ then $IP \in B_C^{in}$ is a set of input ports which trigger a behavior of C.

For a component $C = (Id, I, O, IR)$, $\Psi_C(C) = \langle P_C^{port} \cup P_C^{Sig}, T_C^{IR} \cup T_C^{Sig}, A_C \rangle$ where $P_C^{port} = \{P_p | p \in I \cup O\}$ is the set of places representing the ports, $P_C^{Sig} = \{P_{it}, P_{es}\}$ are places that control the passage from one iteration to the other, $T_C^{IR} = \{t_i | i \in B_C^{in}\}$ is the set of transitions that model the different behaviors of the component and $T_C^{Sig} = \{t_e, t_s\}$ are the transitions to send to the outside the signal of the iteration end and to receive activation signals from outside. A_C is detailed later.

A component iterates only when all the input ports of at least one of its incidence relations contain messages. Then, all satisfied incidence relations are triggered. To translate this behavior to a sCFN, a transition t_i is created for all possible combinations of satisfied incidence relations.

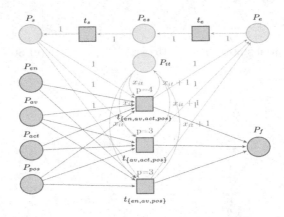

Fig. 4. Ψ_C applied on the component S3 (Fig. 2).

These transitions have a weight that is the number of input places. This weight guarantees that all the satisfied incidence relations are activated. On the example in Fig. 4, the transitions $t_{\{av,act,pos\}}$ and $t_{\{en,av,pos\}}$ model the two incidence relations of $S3$ with a priority of 3. Messages in the application are represented by tokens composed of the iteration of the component whose produced the message and the message itself.

The set A_C is the union of five sets. The two first ones A_C^P and A_C^T encode consumption and production of messages for each behavior.

$A_C^P = \{\langle P_p, t_i, \langle x_p, m_p \rangle\rangle | P_p \in P_C^{IR}, p \in i\}$ tells that for a behavior i the component consumes one message in each input port of this behavior.

$A_C^T = \bigcup_{E \in \mathcal{P}(\mathcal{IR}_C)} \{\langle t_i, P_p, \langle x_{it}, m_p \rangle\rangle | i = IR^{in}(E), p \in IR^{out}(E)\}$ expresses that one message stamped with the iteration number of the component, is produced in each output port of the behavior.

In an application, component synchronizations are managed thanks to the ports s and e of each component. To model these controls, the place P_s must be marked to trigger any transition $t \in T_C^{IR}$ which must then send an ending signal to the place P_e. The transition t_i, if triggered, must also update the iteration number in sending the current iteration number to the P_{it} place and receiving the incremented number. Hence, the additional arcs are defined by

$A_C^{P_e} = \{\langle t_i, P_e, 1\rangle | t_i \in T_C^{IR}\}$, $A_C^{P_s} = \{\langle P_s, t_i, 1\rangle | t_i \in T_C^{IR}\}$,

$A_C^{Sig} = \{\langle P_e, t_e, 1\rangle, \langle t_e, P_{es}, 1\rangle, \langle P_{es}, t_s, 1\rangle, \langle t_s, P_s, 1\rangle\}$ and

$A_C^{it} = \{\langle P_{it}, t_i, x_{it}\rangle, \langle t_i, P_{it}, x_{it}+1\rangle | t_i \in T_C^{IR}\}$.

The sCFN model of a connector c is defined by the function $\Psi_c(c)$ according to the type of c. The sFIFO connector sCFN consists of two places P_i and P_o to represent respectively the input and the output port and a transition to transmit messages from P_i to P_o. For other connectors given in Fig. 5, in addition to the P_i and P_o places they also have a place P_s to represent the triggering port and a place P_m that represents the memory of the connector (the list of messages it stores). In the bBuffer sCFN, the buffering is done thanks to the transition t_{in} that stores new incoming messages in the place P_m. The transition t_{out} delivers the messages stored in P_m when a signal arrives in P_s. The sCFN of the bGreedy connector models the message loss using a list in P_m that is either empty or contains a single element. This list is initialized to the empty list. Each time a new message arrives in P_i the list contained in P_m is replaced by the list that contains only the new message. This way only the last message is stored in P_m. When a signal arrives in P_s, if the list of P_m is empty the transition t_{out} is not enabled, otherwise the message contained in the list of P_m is delivered to P_o and the empty list is put in P_m. The non blocking versions of those two connectors just add a transition t_s that is enabled once a signal is in the place P_s and is able to deliver an empty message $m_\emptyset$ to P_o. However the weight of t_s is smaller than the weight of t_{out} so that when a real message is available in P_m, this message is delivered to P_o.

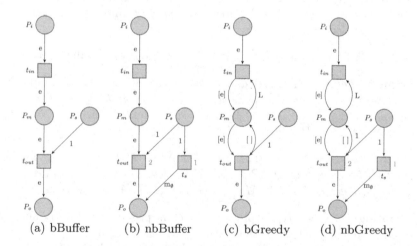

(a) bBuffer   (b) nbBuffer   (c) bGreedy   (d) nbGreedy

Fig. 5. sCFNs of the different connectors

The additional transitions and arcs used to represent the links in the application are not presented here for lack of space. However they do not cause any structural problems in the resulting net since they mainly duplicate tokens or synchronize some signals.

An initial marking M_{init} is necessary to define the application sCFN. M_{init} consists in initializing with a (1) the P_s places of the components when $\bullet P_s = \{t_s\}$.

M_{init} also initializes the P_{it} places with a (0) for each component. This initial marking will be completed in Sect. 4 which deals with the construction of the start configuration which guarantees that all the components of the application are live.

4   Deadlock Analysis of ComSA Applications

This section first proves a sufficient condition for place-liveness of a subclass of sCFNs, then it shows how this result can be used to help the user to build a deadlock-free application.

4.1   Place-Liveness of sCFNs

The deadlock freedom of our applications is based on a place-liveness property of sCFNs. This property expresses that all the component ports in the application graph eventually receive data during the application running. This section presents a sufficient condition to insure the place-liveness of sCFNs. This result relies on Theorem 1 that gives a sufficient condition for liveness of ACNs. The general idea consists in simulating sCFNs by OPNs in such way places containing tokens in the sCFNs are the same as the corresponding ones in the OPN.

Definition 7. *Let $N = \langle P, T, A \rangle$ be an OPN, and M and M' are two markings of N such that $M(p) > 0 \Leftrightarrow M'(p) > 0$, then M and M' are said mark-equivalent. It is denoted $M \leftrightarrow M'$.*

If $M \leftrightarrow M'$, $\langle P, T, A, M \rangle$ and $\langle P, T, A, M' \rangle$ have the same enabled transitions.

Definition 8. *Let $N = \langle P, T, A \rangle$ and $N' = \langle P', T', A' \rangle$ be two OPNs and N, N' do not contain isolated place. N' is a sub-net of N if $P' \subseteq P$, $T' \subseteq T$ and $A' \subseteq A$ with $\forall \langle x, y \rangle \in A'$ $x, y \in P' \cup T'$. N' is said underlying N if it is a sub-net of N s.t. $P' = P$ and $A' = \{\langle x, y \rangle \in A | x \in T' \text{ or } y \in T'\}$.*

Lemma 2. *Let $N = \langle P, T, A \rangle$ be an OPN and $N' = \langle P, T', A' \rangle$ an OPN underlying N. Let M_1 be a marking s.t. $\langle P, T', A', M_1 \rangle$ is live. If $\forall M_2$ s.t. $\langle P, T, A, M_1 \rangle \rightarrow_t \langle P, T, A, M_2 \rangle$ we have $\langle P, T', A', M_2 \rangle$ is live then $\langle P, T, A, M_1 \rangle$ is place-live.*

Proof. Proving $\langle P, T, A, M_1 \rangle$ is place-live means proving that $\forall M_2$ such that $M_1 \rightarrow_N^* M_2$, $\forall p \in P$, $\exists M_3$ such that $M_2 \rightarrow_N^* M_3$ and $M_3(p) > 0$.

First let us remark that if $\langle P, T, A, M_1 \rangle$ where M_1 is such that $\langle P, T', A', M_1 \rangle$ is live then $\forall p \in P$ $\exists M_2$ such that $M_2(p) > 0$ and $M_1 \rightarrow_N M_2$. Indeed, since $\langle P, T', A', M_1 \rangle$ is live, it is place-live, i.e. $\forall p \in P$ $\exists M_2$ such that $M_1 \rightarrow_{N'} M_2$ and $M_2(p) > 0$. Since N' is underlying N all transitions used in $M_1 \rightarrow_{N'} M_2$ are transitions of N therefore $M_1 \rightarrow_N M_2$.

Now, by hypothesis N is s.t. if $\langle P, T', A', M_1 \rangle$ is live then $\forall M_2$ such that $\langle P, T, A, M_1 \rangle \rightarrow_t \langle P, T, A, M_2 \rangle$, M_2 verifies $\langle P, T', A', M_2 \rangle$ is live. Thus, by an easy induction, it is obvious that any marking M_3 reachable from a marking M_1 making N' live, is s.t. $\langle P, T', A', M_3 \rangle$ is live. So, from the remark above, $\forall p \in P$ $\exists M_4$ reachable from M_3 that marks p therefore $\langle P, T, A, M_1 \rangle$ is place-live.

Now let us define a class of OPN that preserves the liveness of an underlying ACN. For that some additional definitions have to be introduced.

Definition 9. *Let $\langle P, T, A \rangle$ an OPN. $t \in T$ is said covering if $\exists T' \subset T$ such that $t \notin T'$, $\bullet t = \bullet T'$ and $t \bullet = T' \bullet$.*

Lemma 3. *Let $\langle P, T, A, M \rangle$ an OPN where t is covering $T' \subset T$ and M' s.t. $\langle P, T, A, M \rangle \rightarrow_t \langle P, T, A, M' \rangle$ then $\exists \overline{M} \leftrightarrow M$ and $\overline{M'} \leftrightarrow M'$ s.t. $\langle P, T, A, \overline{M} \rangle \rightarrow^* \langle P, T, A, \overline{M'} \rangle$ where each transition of T' is fired once in the derivation.*

Proof. Since $\langle P, T, A, M \rangle \rightarrow_t \langle P, T, A, M' \rangle$, M' is such that $M'(p) > 0 \; \forall p \in t \bullet$ and $M'(p) = M(p) - 1 \; \forall p \in \bullet t \setminus t \bullet$.

Let M_t be the marking such that $M_t(p) = \begin{vmatrix} M(p) - 1 + |p \bullet \cap T'| & if \; p \in \bullet t \\ M(p) & otherwise \end{vmatrix}$ since M enables t ($\forall p \in \bullet t, M(p) > 0$) and M_t only adds tokens in $\bullet t$, $M \leftrightarrow M_t$. Moreover, for each place $p \in \bullet t$, $M_t(p)$ is greater than the number of transitions of T' whose p is an input place. As a consequence, it is possible to fire each transition of T' once from M_t. The resulting marking M'_t is such that $M'_t(p) > 0$ for any $p \in T' \bullet$ (recall $T' \bullet = t \bullet$) and $M'_t(p) = M_t(p) - |p \bullet \cap T'| = M(p) - 1$ for any $p \in \bullet T' \setminus T' \bullet$. Thus $M'_t(p) \leftrightarrow M'$.

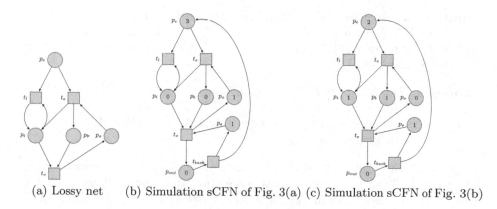

(a) Lossy net   (b) Simulation sCFN of Fig. 3(a) (c) Simulation sCFN of Fig. 3(b)

Fig. 6. Lossy nets and simulation

Definition 10. *A lossy net is an OPN such that $Lossy = \langle P_L, T_L, A_L \rangle$ as shown Fig. 6(a). The transition t_l is called lossy transition.*

A lossy OPN is used to simulate a lossy connection. p_b is a buffer that accepts only one token. This is controlled by places p_o that indicates the buffer is empty and p_i that indicates the buffer is full. The transition t_l is used to discard tokens that arrive in p_e while p_b contains a token. More precisely, starting from a marking such that p_o contains one token and all other places are empty, when a token arrives at place p_e the transition t_e is enabled. Once t_e is fired, a token is placed in p_i and p_b and p_e is emptied. As a consequence t_e is not enabled but as soon as a token arrives to p_e, t_l is. While the transition t_o is not fired, tokens arriving in p_e can be discarded using t_l. When t_o is fired, places p_i and p_b become empty and place p_o contains one token which indicates that the next token arriving at p_e will be put in the buffer.

A lossy OPN is not an ACN one since both $p_e \bullet$ and $p_i \bullet$ contain t_l but none of these sets includes the other. However, lossy OPN preserves the liveness of the underlying ACN.

Definition 11. *Let $N = \langle P, T, A \rangle$ an OPN, N contains a lossy net $N' = \langle P_L, T_L, A_L \rangle$ that is connected by $\{p_e, t_o\}$ if the only arcs between N' and $N \setminus N'$ are the following $\{\langle t, p_e \rangle | t \in T \setminus T_L\}$, $\{\langle t_o, p \rangle | p \in P \setminus P_L\}$ and $\{\langle p, t_o \rangle | p \in P \setminus P_L\}$.*

Lemma 4. *Let N be an OPN s.t. it contains a sub-net N' that is a lossy net connected by $\{p_e, t_o\}$. Let M a marking s.t. $M(p_o) = 1$ and $M(p_i) = M(p_b) = 0$. Then every marking M' reachable from M is s.t. if t_l is enabled then $M'(p_b) = 1$.*

Proof. Since $p_i \in \bullet t_l$, t_l is enabled means that p_i is not empty. Since $\bullet p_i = \{t_e\}$, p_i is marked when t_e is fired, p_b is also marked since $p_b \in t_e \bullet$. t_e cannot be enabled until p_o is empty. Thus both p_i and p_b cannot contain more than one token. When t_o is fired, p_i and p_b are emptied and p_o receives a token.

Definition 12. *An extended asymmetric choice net (EACN for short) is an OPN $N = \langle P, T, A \rangle$ such that the underlying net $\langle P, T', A' \rangle$ is ACN where $T' = T \setminus (\{t \in T | t \text{ is covering}\} \bigcup \cup_{L \in \mathcal{L}(N)} \{t_l\})$ with $\mathcal{L}(N)$ the set of all the lossy nets connected by some $\{p_e, t_o\}$ in N.*

Theorem 2. *Let $N = \langle P, T, A \rangle$ an EACN whose underlying ACN is $N' = \langle P, T', A' \rangle$ and M_1 a marking such that $\langle P, T', A', M_1 \rangle$ marks one trap in every siphon of N'. Any marking M_2 such that $\langle P, T, A, M_1 \rangle \to_t \langle P, T, A, M_2 \rangle$, marks one trap in every siphon of N'.*

Proof. First, note that if N' is an ACN and M marks a trap in every siphon of N, from the liveness property of ACN we know that any marking reachable from M also marks a trap in any siphon of N'. Now, let us prove Theorem 2. Three cases must be distinguished according to the kind of transitions t.

- If $t \in T'$, the property is verified since N' is an ACN.
- If t is covering, then from Lemma 3 we know that $\langle P, T, A, M_1 \rangle \to_t \langle P, T, A, M_2 \rangle$ corresponds to a derivation $\langle P, T, A, \overline{M_1} \rangle \to_{N'}^* \langle P, T, A, \overline{M_2} \rangle$ such that $M_1 \leftrightarrow \overline{M_1}$ and $M_2 \leftrightarrow \overline{M_2}$. Thus $\overline{M_2}$ is such that every siphon of N' contains a marked trap, so M_2 also verifies this property.
- If t is a lossy transition, the only place that may be empty after firing t is the place p_e associated to t. It can be remarked that every trap of N' containing this place p_e contains either the p_i or the p_b place associated to t. Since t is enabled in M_1, from Lemma 4 both p_i and p_b are marked in M so they are in M_2. So every trap of N' marked in M_1 remains marked in M_2.

Definition 13. *Let $N = \langle P, T, A \rangle$ be a sCFN, $\overline{N} = \langle \overline{P}, \overline{T}, \overline{A} \rangle$ be an OPN and three onto functions $\Phi_P : \overline{P} \to P$, $\Phi_T : \overline{T} \to T$ and $\Phi_M : FIFO \to \mathbb{N}$ where the last two are applications. N' simulates N through Φ_P, Φ_T and Φ_M if for every marking M_1 and M_2 $\langle P, T, A, M_1 \rangle \to_t \langle P, T, A, M_2 \rangle$ iff $\langle \overline{P}, \overline{T}, \overline{A}, \Phi_M(M_1) \rangle \to_{\Phi_T(t)} \langle \overline{P}, \overline{T}, \overline{A}, \Phi_M(M_2) \rangle$.*

The OPN of Fig. 6(b) simulates the bGreedy sCFN of Fig. 3(a) with $\Phi_P = \{p_e \mapsto p_i, p_b \mapsto p_m, p_s \mapsto p_s, p_{out} \mapsto p_o\}$, $\Phi_T = \{t_l \mapsto t_{in}, t_e \mapsto t_{in}, t_o \mapsto t_{out}, t_{back} \mapsto t_{back}\}$ and $\Phi_M(x)$ is the number of elements of x for any FIFO x except ([]) where $\Phi_M(([])) = 0$. Fig. 6(c) displays the result of firing transition t_l which corresponds to the net simulating the sCFN of Fig. 3(b).

Theorem 3. *Let S be a sCFN and N be an OPN that simulates S through Φ_P, Φ_T and Φ_M, if N is place-live then S is place-live too.*

It is obvious from Definition 13 and Theorem 2. Of course, it is not always possible to find an OPN that simulates a sCFN. Fortunately, the sCFNs describing the semantics of our component model can be simulated by OPNs using generalization of functions Φ_T, Φ_P and Φ_M described above. The obtained OPN is in the class of EACN when the active elementary incidence relations respect asymmetric choice condition (i.e. $IR^{in}(r_1) \cap IR^{in}(r_2) \neq \emptyset \Rightarrow IR^{out}(r_1) \subseteq IR^{out}(r_2) \vee IR^{out}(r_2) \subseteq IR^{out}(r_1)$). Indeed in this case, there are two kinds of places which do not verify the ACN conditions; namely the places encoding input ports and the p_e places of lossy sub-nets. In both cases the transitions that are in the post set of the place are either covering or respect ACN condition.

Note that a sCFN that is place live may not be live but, in this case, the only transitions that are not live are those representing compositions of elementary behaviors of the components. This is not a problem since each elementary behavior is live. On the other hand, weights on transitions may prevent the firing of some transitions. Once again, this is not a real problem since in the sCFN built from an application, if a transition t conflicts with another t' and $W(t) > W(t')$ then t is covering. This means t is a behavior that includes the behavior t'.

The analysis of the EACN that simulates the sCFN of an application makes possible to detect whether the application can be launched and be live.

4.2   Start Configuration and Experiments

The process to start ComSA application consists of three main steps.

ACN condition. The first step consists in verifying that the set of active incidence relations of the application respect the ACN condition. If it is not the case, it is proposed to the user to lock several behaviors of involved components which is equivalent to replace two relations $\langle I_1, O_1 \rangle$ and $\langle I_2, O_2 \rangle$ by the relation $\langle I_1 \cup I_2, O_1 \cup O_2 \rangle$. This way non asymmetric incidence relations are eliminated. The consequence is that the application would not exploit all the asynchrony allowed by the component but it is the price to pay to avoid deadlocks.

Siphon-trap condition. The second stage consists in verifying that all the siphons of the application sCFN contain a trap. Indeed, if it is not the case the application cannot be live. If some siphons do not contain a trap, the cycles they form in the application are highlighted so that the user can modify the application to make it deadlock free.

Start configuration. Finally, when all the siphons contain a trap, the initial marking M_{init} (Sect. 3.3) is used to find out the traps still unmarked. In each of these traps, a blocking connector is randomly chosen to deliver a first empty message. The random choice may be replaced by user's choice.

The first and the last steps are straightforward and do not require much computations but the second one is known to be NP-hard. This step has been implemented using the method described in [14]. This method consists in transforming the original problem into a SAT problem. The open-source SAT solver [15] has been used to solve the problem.

The application illustrated Fig. 2 contains 18 incidence relations such that all components verified the ACN condition. Its sCFN has 76 transitions and 71 places excluding the P_{it} places. For this case, the second phase lasts 95s on a standard laptop. The result is the determination of 9 siphons all containing a trap. For example, one of this siphon allowed to highlight the cycle illustrated by the red path on the Fig. 2. The initial marking M_{init} is completed by marking of a randomly chosen connector P_s place in unmarked traps. In the application, this marking is interpreted as a set of connectors, blocking or not, which need to send a first empty message. Thus, the sCFN analysis offers the automatic construction of a proper start configuration.

5   Conclusion

In this paper, the ComSA component model has been presented. This approach is dedicated to design interactive scientific visualization applications. The ComSA semantics has been defined by means of sCFN whose place-liveness has been proved under specific conditions. These results are used to help users to build correct applications without deadlocks and to start those applications.

The results presented in this paper are the basis of a set of tools dedicated to the design and the analysis of ComSA applications. Those tools include simulation of the application, analysis of its structure to control its starting and its liveness. sCFN semantics should also help to design algorithms to reconfigure on the fly a running application without stopping it completely. This involves to stop some components, verify that the new configuration is deadlock-free and start the new composition. The tools are still under construction. Some preliminary experiments on real applications show their practical usefulness in particular in automating the construction of a start configuration. However, they need to be optimized for larger applications and the use of a hierarchical construction of the application should be of great interest. Further analysis on the global behavior of ComSA applications should be possible thanks to the sCFN modeling. For example, it should be possible to express data coherence problems which is an important issue for applications that allow lossy communications. This analysis could rely on previous work [12] that defines some ways to control data loss.

References

1. Allard, J., Gouranton, V., Lecointre, L., Limet, S., Melin, E., Raffin, B., Robert, S.: FlowVR: a middleware for large scale virtual reality applications. In: Danelutto, M., Vanneschi, M., Laforenza, D. (eds.) Euro-Par 2004. LNCS, vol. 3149, pp. 497–505. Springer, Heidelberg (2004)
2. Arbab, F.: Reo: a channel-based coordination model for component composition. Math. Struct. Comput. Sci. **14**(3), 329–366 (2004)
3. Attie, P.C., Bensalem, S., Bozga, M., Jaber, M., Sifakis, J., Zaraket, F.A.: An abstract framework for deadlock prevention in BIP. In: Beyer, D., Boreale, M. (eds.) FORTE/FMOODS 2013. LNCS, vol. 7892, pp. 161–177. Springer, Heidelberg (2013)
4. Bastide, R., Barboni, E.: Software components: a formal semantics based on coloured Petri nets. ENTCS **160**(0), 57–73 (2006)
5. Desel, J., Esparza, J.: Free Choice Petri Nets. Cambridge University Press, New York (1995)
6. Dreher, M., Piuzzi, M., Turki, A., Chavent, M., Baaden, M., Férey, N., Limet, S., Raffin, B., Robert, S.: Interactive molecular dynamics: scaling up to large systems. In: ICCS. Procedia Computer Science, vol. 18, pp. 20–29. Elsevier (2013)
7. Finkel, A., Memmi, G.: FIFO nets: a new model of parallel computation. In: Cremers, A.B., Kriegel, H.-P. (eds.) Theoretical Computer Science. LNCS, vol. 145, pp. 111–121. Springer, Heidelberg (1982)
8. Goodale, T., Allen, G., Lanfermann, G., Massó, J., Radke, T., Seidel, E., Shalf, J.: The cactus framework and toolkit: design and applications. In: Palma, J.M.L.M., Sousa, A.A., Dongarra, J., Hernández, V. (eds.) VECPAR 2002. LNCS, vol. 2565, pp. 197–227. Springer, Heidelberg (2003)
9. Jensen, K., Kristensen, L.M.: Coloured Petri Nets - Modelling and Validation of Concurrent Systems. Springer, Berlin (2009)
10. Jiao, L., Cheung, T.Y., Lu, W.: On liveness and boundedness of asymmetric choice nets. Theor. Comput. Sci. **311**(1–3), 165–197 (2004)
11. Lau, K.K., Safie, L., Stepan, P., Tran, C. M.: A component model that is both control-driven and data-driven. In: CBSE, pp. 41–50 (2011)
12. Limet, S., Robert, S., Turki, A.: Controlling an iteration-wise coherence in dataflow. In: Arbab, F., Ölveczky, P.C. (eds.) FACS 2011. LNCS, vol. 7253, pp. 241–258. Springer, Heidelberg (2012)
13. Murata, T.: Petri nets: properties, analysis and applications. Proc. IEEE **77**(4), 541–580 (1989)
14. Oanea, O., Wimmel, H., Wolf, K.: New algorithms for deciding the siphon-trap property. In: Lilius, J., Penczek, W. (eds.) PETRI NETS 2010. LNCS, vol. 6128, pp. 267–286. Springer, Heidelberg (2010)
15. Sörensson, N., Een, N.: Open-source SAT solver (2008). http://minisat.se/
16. Yu, Y., Li, T., Liu, Q., Dai, F.: Approach to modeling components in software architecture. JSW **6**(11), 2196–2200 (2011)

Admit Your Weakness: Verifying Correctness on TSO Architectures

Graeme Smith[1], John Derrick[2], and Brijesh Dongol[2](✉)

[1] School of Information Technology and Electrical Engineering,
The University of Queensland, Brisbane, Australia
[2] Department of Computing, University of Sheffield, Sheffield, UK
B.Dongol@sheffield.ac.uk

Abstract. Linearizability has become the standard correctness criterion for fine-grained non-atomic concurrent algorithms, however, most approaches assume a sequentially consistent memory model, which is not always realised in practice. In this paper we study the correctness of concurrent algorithms on a *weak* memory model: the TSO (Total Store Order) memory model, which is commonly implemented by multicore architectures. Here, linearizability is often too strict, and hence, we prove a weaker criterion, *quiescent consistency* instead. Like linearizability, quiescent consistency is compositional making it an ideal correctness criterion in a component-based context. We demonstrate how to model a typical concurrent algorithm, *seqlock*, and prove it quiescent consistent using a simulation-based approach. Previous approaches to proving correctness on TSO architectures have been based on linearizabilty which makes it necessary to modify the algorithm's high-level requirements. Our approach is the first, to our knowledge, for proving correctness without the need for such a modification.

1 Introduction

This paper is concerned with correctness of concurrent algorithms that typically arise in the multicore processor context, in which shared variables or data structures such as queues, stacks or hashtables are accessed concurrently by several processes. These are becoming prevalent in libraries such as `java.util.concurrent` and operating system kernels. To increase efficiency, these algorithms dispense with locking, or only lock small parts of a data structure. Thus the shared variables or data structure might be concurrently accessed by different processors executing different operations — correctness of such algorithms is therefore a key issue.

To date, the subject of correctness has focussed on a condition called *linearizability* [11]. This requires that fine-grained implementations of access operations (e.g., reading or writing of a shared variable) appear as though they take effect instantaneously at some point in time within the operation's interval of execution — thereby achieving the same effect as an atomic operation. There has been an enormous amount of interest in deriving techniques for verifying linearizability. These range from using shape analysis [1,4] and separation

© Springer International Publishing Switzerland 2015
I. Lanese and E. Madelaine (Eds.): FACS 2014, LNCS 8997, pp. 364–383, 2015.
DOI: 10.1007/978-3-319-15317-9_22

logic [4] to rely-guarantee reasoning [21] and refinement-based simulation methods [6,8].

The vast majority of this work has assumed a *sequentially consistent* memory model, whereby program instructions are executed by the hardware in the order specified by the program [14]. However, processor cores within modern multicore systems often communicate via shared memory and use (local) store buffers to improve performance. Whilst these *weak* memory models give greater scope for optimisation, sequential consistency is lost (as the effect of a *write* to the shared memory is delayed by the local buffer). One such memory model is the TSO (Total Store Order) model which is implemented in the x86 multicore processor architecture [19].

The purpose of this paper is to investigate correctness of concurrent algorithms in the TSO memory model. There has been limited work in this area so far, with current approaches [3,9] based on linearizabilty, which makes it necessary to modify the algorithm's high-level requirements. Instead, we focus here on the weaker notion of *quiescent consistency* as a correctness criterion. Like linearizability, quiescent consistency is compositional making it an ideal correctness criterion in a component-based context. Quiescent consistency was introduced in [2,18] and has been advocated recently by Shavit as the correctness condition to be used in the multicore age [17]. Although these papers provide neither a formal definition nor a proof method for quiescent consistency, both these shortcomings were addressed in [5], for sequentially consistent architectures.

Like linearizability [11], the definition in [5] is formalised in terms of histories of invocations and responses of the operations of the concurrent algorithm, while the proof method is based on coupled simulations [7] of history-enhanced data types [6]. However, the methods in [5] only address concurrent data structures that are designed to be quiescent consistent and execute under sequentially consistent memory. The aim of this paper is to investigate the use of quiescent consistency as the correctness requirement under TSO memory, then adapt the proof method in [5] to verify such algorithms. We are not proposing that quiescent consistency is the definitive correctness criterion for TSO, but rather that it is an alternative to linearizability that may be useful in some circumstances. We illustrate this with our running example in the paper.

We make three contributions. First, we show how we can adapt the definition of quiescent consistency to a TSO memory model (Sect. 2). Second, we show in Sect. 3 how we can use Z to model algorithms on a TSO architecture, then in Sect. 4 using this model we show how we can adapt the simulation-based proof method to verify quiescent consistency. We conclude in Sect. 5.

2   Background

2.1   The TSO Memory Model

In the TSO (Total Store Order) architecture (see [19] for a good introduction), each processor core uses a write buffer, which is a FIFO queue that stores pending writes to memory. A processor core performing a *write* to a memory location enqueues the write to the buffer and continues computation without waiting for the write to be committed to memory. Pending writes do not become visible to other cores until the buffer is *flushed*, which commits (some or all) pending writes to memory.

The value of a memory location read by a process is the most recent value for that location in the processor's local buffer. If there is no such value (e.g., initially or when all writes corresponding to the location have been flushed), the value of the location is fetched from memory. The use of local buffers allows a read by one process, occurring after a write by another, to return an older value as if it occurred before the write.

In general, flushes are controlled by the CPU. However, a programmer may explicitly include a *fence*, or *memory barrier*, instruction in a program's code to force a flush to occur. Therefore, although TSO allows some non-sequentially consistent executions, it is used in many modern architectures on the basis that these can be prevented, where necessary, by programmers using fence instructions. To model concurrent algorithms on TSO we assume the following behaviour, which is reflected our Z models [20]:[1]

- A *write* operation to a memory location adds the entry to the tail of its store buffer.
- The head of the store buffer is *flushed* into the memory. This flush is under the control of the CPU and thus happens non-deterministically.
- A *read* of a memory location takes as its value the most recent value in the store buffer if available, and the value from memory otherwise.

Example 1. Consider the following example, with two global variables x and y which are both initially 0, and operations to write to and read from the variables.

```
word x=0, y=0;

set_x(in word d) {x=d;}          set_y(in word d) {y=d;}
read_x(out word d) {d=x;}        read_y(out word d) {d=y;}
```

A possible execution in TSO is the following sequence of operation calls and flushes:

$$s_1 = \langle (p, \mathsf{set\_x}(1)), (p, \mathsf{read\_y}(0)), (q, \mathsf{set\_y}(1)), (q, \mathsf{read\_x}(0)),$$
$$\mathtt{flush}(p), \mathtt{flush}(q) \rangle$$

where $(p, \mathsf{read\_y}(0))$, for example, means that process p performs a read_y operation that returns 0, and $\mathtt{flush}(p)$ corresponds to a CPU flush of a single value from p's buffer. Note that both reads return 0, which is not possible on a sequentially consistent architecture. This is because the corresponding *set* operations write to the process's *local* buffer, and these writes are not globally visible until that process's buffer is flushed. Here that happens at the end of the execution. □

---

[1] We do not need a full formal semantics of TSO, but interested readers are referred to [15,16] for formal definitions.

2.2   Concurrent Consistency Models

In what sense is a concurrent algorithm correct? Not only do we have executions as in the example above, but the fine-grained nature of operations means that processes do not perform the whole operation at once — an operation's steps might be interleaved with steps of another operation executed by another process. To formally capture the fact that operations can overlap in this way, we introduce the notion of *histories* as sequences of *events*. *Events* in the sequential world are invocations or returns of operations. In TSO, they will be an invocation, response or a flush. The sets of events are denoted $Event$ and $Event_{TSO}$ respectively. Flushes are performed by the CPU and operate on a particular process's buffer.

A method is *pending* if it has been invoked but has not yet returned. A history is *sequential* if all invoke events are immediately followed by their matching returns. Where this is not the case, methods overlap. A *quiescent* state is one in which there are no pending methods, and all buffers have been flushed.

Invocations and returns of operations from a set I are performed by a particular process from a set P with an input or output value V. We let $\perp$ denote empty inputs/outputs and assume that $\perp \in V$. Thus we define:

$$Event ::= inv\langle\!\langle P \times I \times V \rangle\!\rangle \mid ret\langle\!\langle P \times I \times V \rangle\!\rangle$$
$$Event_{TSO} ::= inv\langle\!\langle P \times I \times V \rangle\!\rangle \mid ret\langle\!\langle P \times I \times V \rangle\!\rangle \mid flush\langle\!\langle P \rangle\!\rangle$$

Example 2. A TSO history corresponding to the sequence s_1 above is:[2]

$$h_1 = \langle inv(p, \mathsf{set\_x}, 1), ret(p, \mathsf{set\_x},), inv(p, \mathsf{read\_y},), ret(p, \mathsf{read\_y}, 0),$$
$$inv(q, \mathsf{set\_y}, 1), ret(q, \mathsf{set\_y},), inv(q, \mathsf{read\_x},), ret(q, \mathsf{read\_x}, 0),$$
$$flush(p), flush(q)\rangle$$

It is in a quiescent state initially and at its end but not anywhere in between. □

Correctness means that the histories of an implementation should correspond 'in some sense' to those of its abstract specification (in which overlapping operations are not possible). Varying the meaning of 'in some sense' results in different correctness conditions [10]. Of these, *linearizability* has been widely used as the correctness criterion in sequentially consistent architectures. However, issues arise in the context of TSO since the direct application of linearizability to TSO requires the natural abstract specification to be weakened (see the approaches of both [3,9]). Thus it seems that linearizability might impose too many constraints to be a useful criterion for a weak memory model such as TSO since it requires sequential consistency amongst the system processes [10]. Instead, here we use an alternative (weaker) correctness criterion, *quiescent consistency* [17]. Informally it states that operations separated by quiescent states should appear to take effect in their (real-time) order.

---

[2] We elide empty inputs or outputs in the events, e.g., write $ret(p, \mathsf{set\_x},)$ for $ret(p, \mathsf{set\_x}, \perp)$.

Quiescent consistency has been recently formalised in [5] for sequentially consistent architectures and a proof method developed for it. Our first task therefore is to adapt the definition for a TSO model. First of all some preliminaries. For a history h, $\#h$ is the *length* of the sequence, and $h(n)$ its nth element (for $n : 1..\#h$). Predicates $inv?(e)$, $ret?(e)$, and $flush?(e)$ are used to check whether an event $e \in Event \cup Event_{TSO}$ is an invoke, return or flush, respectively. We let $e.p \in P$, $e.i \in I$ and $e.v \in V$ be the process executing the event e, the operation to which the event belongs, and the input/output value of v, respectively. Furthermore, for a TSO event e that is a return or flush, we assume $e.bv$ is the boolean corresponding to the event, which holds iff all local buffers are empty immediately after e occurs. Finally, we let $Ret!$ be the set of all TSO return events.

We now need a preliminary definition saying what it means to be a matching pair of invocation and return, a pending invocation, a legal history (where each process calls at most one operation at a time), and a quiescent history (a history which is in a quiescent state at its end). Unlike, earlier work, we record concrete flush events in the concrete histories to handle TSO memory, and hence, the definition below differs from [5,6], which were defined for SC architectures.

Definition 1. *Suppose* $h \in seqEvent \cup seqEvent_{TSO}$. *Two positions* $m, n : 1..\#h$ *form a* matching pair *iff* $mp(m, n, h)$ *holds*; n *in* h *is a* pending invocation *iff* $pi(n, h)$ *holds*; h *is* legal *iff* $legal(h)$ *holds*; *and* h *is* quiescent *iff* $qu?(h)$ *holds, where:*

$$mp(m, n, h) \triangleq h(m).p = h(n).p \wedge h(m).i = h(n).i \wedge inv?(h(m)) \wedge ret?(h(n)) \wedge$$
$$\forall k \bullet m < k < n \wedge h(k).p = h(m).p \Rightarrow flush?(h(k))$$
$$pi(n, h) \triangleq inv?(h(n)) \wedge \forall m \bullet n < m \leq \#h \wedge h(m).p = h(n).p \Rightarrow flush?(h(n))$$
$$legal(h) \triangleq h \in seqEvent_{TSO} \wedge h \neq \langle\rangle \wedge inv?(h(1)) \wedge$$
$$\forall n : 1..\#h \bullet \text{if } inv?(h(n)) \text{ then } pi(n, h) \vee \exists m \bullet mp(n, m, h)$$
$$\text{elseif } ret?(h(n)) \text{ then } \exists m \bullet mp(m, n, h)$$
$$qu?(h) \triangleq legal(h) \wedge h(\#h).bv \wedge \forall n : 1..\#h \bullet \neg pi(n, h) \qquad \square$$

Both linearizability and quiescent consistency are defined by comparing the histories generated by concurrent implementations with the sequential histories of some given abstract atomic specification. Here we will adapt the standard definitions to TSO.

Our formal definitions of linearizability and quiescent consistency for TSO are given below. Both are defined using a function $smap$ that maps the indices of the concurrent history to a sequential history, and linearizability uses an additional function $complete$ that removes all pending invokes. Bijections from X to Y are denoted $X \rightarrowtail\!\!\!\rightarrow Y$. We assume a function $remflush(h, z)$ which transforms h to z by removing all flushes from h, but keeps the order of all other events in h the same. Function $remflush$ can be defined recursively, but its formal definition is elided here for space reasons.

$$eveq(e, e') \triangleq e \in Event \wedge e' \in Event_{TSO} \wedge e.p = e'.p \wedge e.i = e'.i \wedge e.v = e'.v$$
$$smap(h, f, hs) \triangleq \exists z : seqEvent_{TSO} \bullet remflush(h, z) \wedge f \in 1..\#z \rightarrowtail\!\!\!\rightarrow 1..\#hs \wedge$$
$$\forall m, n : 1..\#z \bullet eveq(hs(f(n)), z(n)) \wedge$$
$$(mp(m, n, z) \Rightarrow f(m) + 1 = f(n))$$

Definition 2 (Linearizability and Quiescent consistency on TSO). *Let h be a TSO history, hs a sequential history. The history h is said to be* quiescent consistent *with hs iff* $qcons(h, hs)$ *holds and* linearizable *with respect to hs iff* $lin(h, hs)$ *holds, where:*

$$qcons(h, hs) \cong \exists f \bullet smap(h, f, hs) \wedge$$
$$\forall m, n, k : 1..\#h \bullet m < n \wedge m \leq k \leq n \wedge$$
$$qu?(h[1..k]) \wedge ret?(h(m)) \wedge inv?(h(n)) \Rightarrow f(m) < f(n)$$
$$lrel(h, hs) \cong \exists f \bullet smap(h, f, hs) \wedge$$
$$\forall m, n, m', n' : 1..\#h \bullet$$
$$n < m' \wedge mp(m, n, h) \wedge mp(m', n', h) \Rightarrow f(n) < f(m')$$
$$lin(h, hs) \cong \exists h_0 : seqRet! \bullet legal(h \frown h_0) \wedge lrel(complete(h \frown h_0), hs) \qquad \square$$

The key point to note is that quiescent consistency allows the operations of processes *between* quiescent states to be reordered, whereas linearizablity does not. As in [5], we have the following property.

Proposition 1 (Linearizability implies quiescent consistency). *For any* $h \in seqEvent_{TSO}$ *and* $hs \in seqEvent$, $lin(h, hs) \Rightarrow qcons(h, hs)$. $\qquad \square$

Example 3. Let us return to Example 1 above. In what sense is this correct with respect to an abstract specification which has one operation for each concrete one? Consider h_1 again. Because of the effect of the local buffers, both read operations return 0. This is only possible at the abstract level if the reads occur before the writes. For example, h_1 could be mapped to sequential history:

$$h_2 = \langle inv(p, \mathsf{read\_y},), ret(p, \mathsf{read\_y}, 0), inv(q, \mathsf{read\_x},), ret(q, \mathsf{read\_x}, 0),$$
$$inv(p, \mathsf{set\_x}, 1), ret(p, \mathsf{set\_x},), inv(q, \mathsf{set\_y}, 1), ret(q, \mathsf{set\_y},)\rangle$$

Such a reordering is possible under quiescent consistency, but not line-arizability. $\qquad \square$

This example highlights a typical consequence of using a TSO architecture. We should allow for programmers to exploit such consequences in order to improve the efficiency of their algorithms. Therefore, in some circumstances it makes sense to adopt quiescent consistency as the correctness criterion for TSO. The only existing work on correctness on TSO [3,9] has looked at linearizability, and to do so has needed to modify the high-level requirements of the algorithms by either adding implementation-level details such as buffers and flushes, or nondeterminism reflecting operation reorderings to the abstract specifications. There has been no work, as far as we are aware, on quiescent consistency as the correctness criterion for TSO.

3   Modelling an Algorithm on the TSO Architecture

As a more complex motivating example, we examine the Linux locking mechanism *seqlock* [13], which allows reading of shared variables without locking the global memory, thus supporting fast write access. We begin by showing that while *seqlock* is linearizable on a standard architecture, it is neither linearizable nor quiescent consistent on TSO without the use of memory barriers. We then turn our attention to a one-writer variant of *seqlock* (based on the non-blocking write protocol of [12]) which we show is quiescent consistent in Sect. 4.

Example 4. In the usual *seqlock* algorithm all processes can read and write. A process wishing to *write* to the shared variables x1 and x2 *acquires* a lock and increments a counter c. It then proceeds to write to the variables, and finally increments c again before *releasing* the lock. The lock ensures synchronisation between writers, and the counter c ensures the consistency of values read by other processes. The two increments of c ensure that it is odd when a process is writing to the variables, and even otherwise. Hence, when a process wishes to *read* the shared variables, it waits in a loop until c is even before reading them. Also, before returning it checks that the value of c has not changed (i.e., another write has not begun). If it has changed, the process starts over. A typical implementation of *seqlock* (based on that in [3]) is given in Fig. 1. A local variable c0 is used by the **read** operation to record the (even) value of c before the operation begins updating the shared variables. In general, the **release** operation does not include a fence instruction and so does not flush the buffer.   □

```
word x1 = 0, x2 = 0;
word c = 0;                          read(out word d1,d2) {
                                       word c0;
write(in word d1,d2) {                 do {
    acquire;                             do {
    c++;                                   c0 = c;
    x1 = d1;                             } while (c0 % 2 != 0);
    x2 = d2;                             d1 = x1;
    c++;                                 d2 = x2;
    release; }                         } while (c != c0); }
```

Fig. 1. Seqlock implementation

Abstract specification - AS. The algorithm is captured abstractly in Z [20], a state-based specification formalism that allows specification of data types by defining their state (variables), initial state and operations. All these are given as *schemas*, consisting of variable declarations plus predicates further constraining the variables. Input and output variables are decorated by '?' and '!', respectively, and notation v' denotes the value of a variable v in the post state of an operation. Unprimed variables of a schema S are introduced into another schema by including S in the declaration, and both unprimed and primed variables are introduced using ΞS or ΔS, the former constraining variables to remain unchanged. For the program in Fig. 1, the abstract specification is:

$$\boxed{\begin{array}{l} \underline{\;AS\;} \\ x_1, x_2 : \mathbb{N} \end{array}}$$

$$\boxed{\begin{array}{l} \underline{\;ASInit\;} \\ AS \\ \hline x_1 = x_2 = 0 \end{array}}$$

$$\boxed{\begin{array}{l} \underline{\;Write_q\;} \\ \Delta AS \\ d_1?, d_2? : \mathbb{N} \\ \hline x_1' = d_1? \wedge x_2' = d_2? \end{array}}$$

$$\boxed{\begin{array}{l} \underline{\;Read_q\;} \\ \Xi AS \\ d_1!, d_2! : \mathbb{N} \\ \hline d_1! = x_1 \wedge d_2! = x_2 \end{array}}$$

The abstract state (as defined by schema AS) consists of two variables x_1 and x_2 of type $\mathbb{N}$, representing x1 and x2 in Fig. 1, respectively. The initial state is given by $ASInit$, which ensures that execution begins in a state in which the value of both x_1 and x_2 is 0. Parameterised schemas $Write_q$ and $Read_q$, where q denotes the process performing the step, represent abstractions of the fine-grained operations write and read in Fig. 1, respectively. $Write_q$ (atomically) sets the values of x_1 and x_2 by ensuring the values of x_1' and x_2' equal to $d_1?$ and $d_2?$, respectively. $Read_q$ sets the outputs $d_1!$ and $d_2!$ to x_1 and x_2, respectively.

Histories of the abstract specification are generated by initialising the state as specified by $ASInit$, then repeatedly choosing a process q and schema $Write_q$ or $Read_q$ non-deterministically, and transitioning to the next state as specified by the chosen schema.

Proposition 2. *Seqlock is linearizable with respect to the abstract specification AS on a sequentially consistent architecture.*

Choosing the final statement of each concrete operation as its *linearization point* (i.e., the point where the operation appears to take effect), the proposition can be proved using the existing approach of Derrick et al. [6].   □

Proposition 3. *Seqlock is not linearizable with respect to the abstract specification AS on the TSO architecture, nor is it quiescent consistent.*

Proof. By Proposition 1 linearizability does not hold if quiescent consistency does not hold. To show quiescent consistency does not hold, we provide a counter example, which follows from the fact that flushes from successive writes can interleave resulting in inconsistent reads. For example, in the following concrete history process r reads the values 3 and 2 for x1 and x2, respectively, which cannot occur according to the abstract specification:

$$\langle inv(p, \texttt{write}, (1,2)), ret(p, \texttt{write},), inv(q, \texttt{write}, (3,4)), ret(q, \texttt{write},),$$
$$flush(p), flush_F(p), flush(q), flush(q), flush(q), flush(q), flush(p), flush(p),$$
$$inv(r, \texttt{read},), ret(r, \texttt{read}, (3,2))\rangle$$

The four flushes for each of p and q correspond to the flushing of the first write to c, the write to x1, the write to x2, and the second write to c, respectively. Note that this counter-example is only possible since the write operations may not include a fence.   □

To avoid such inconsistent behaviour in practice, a memory barrier is required at the end of the write operation. Since reads cannot complete while a write operation is pending, with this memory barrier there are no behaviours possible on TSO other than those possible on a sequentially consistent architecture. Hence, the algorithm can be proved linearizable by Proposition 2.

To illustrate correctness proofs on a TSO architecture further, we examine a variant of *seqlock* in which all processes can read, but only one can write. In this case, no writer lock is required and the write operation can be simplified by removing the acquire and release commands. To verify quiescent consistency (or indeed linearizability) we need a formal specification of this system, which we give now.

Concrete specification - CS. Let P be a set of processes and PC denote program counter values.

$$PC ::= 1 \mid w_1 \mid w_2 \mid w_3 \mid r_1 \mid r_2 \mid r_3 \mid r_4$$

The state CS comprises both the global variables, and program counters, local variables and buffers for each process.

CS	$CSInit$
$x_1, x_2, c : \mathbb{N}$	CS
$pc : P \to PC$	
$d_1, d_2, c_0 : P \to \mathbb{N}$	$x_1 = x_2 = c = 0$
$b : P \to seq(\{x_1, x_2, c\} \times \mathbb{N})$	$\forall q : P \bullet pc(q) = 1 \wedge b(q) = \langle \rangle$

The elements of the processes' buffers (denoted by variable b) are ordered pairs, the first element of which identifies a global variable (using a label, e.g., x_1, written in sans serif), and the second the value written to it by the process. To simplify the presentation of the operation specifications, we adopt the following two conventions:

1. Any values (of variables or in the range of functions) that are not explicitly defined in an operation are unchanged.
2. $\overline{x_1}(q)$ denotes the value of x_1 read by a process q. This value is either the most recent in its buffer or, when no such value exists, the value of the global variable x_1. Similarly, for $\overline{x_2}(q)$ and $\overline{c}(q)$.

Let $p : P$ denote the writer process. The write operation is captured by four operations in Z: one for each of its lines (given that the acquire and release commands have been removed). The subscript p acts as a parameter to the operations.

$$\begin{array}{|l} \hline W1_p \\ \hline \Delta CS \\ d_1?, d_2? : \mathbb{N} \\ \hline pc(p) = 1 \land pc'(p) = w_1 \\ d_1'(p) = d_1? \land d_2'(p) = d_2? \\ b'(p) = b(p) \,^\frown\, \langle (\mathsf{c}, \overline{c}(p) + 1) \rangle \\ \hline \end{array}$$

$$\begin{array}{|l} \hline W2_p \\ \hline \Delta LS \\ \hline pc(p) = w_1 \land pc'(p) = w_2 \\ b'(p) = b(p) \,^\frown\, \langle (\mathsf{x}_1, d_1) \rangle \\ \hline \end{array}$$

$$\begin{array}{|l} \hline W3_p \\ \hline \Delta CS \\ \hline pc(p) = w_2 \land pc'(p) = w_3 \\ b'(p) = b(p) \,^\frown\, \langle (\mathsf{x}_2, d_2) \rangle \\ \hline \end{array}$$

$$\begin{array}{|l} \hline W4_p \\ \hline \Delta CS \\ \hline pc(p) = w_3 \land pc'(p) = 1 \\ b'(p) = b(p) \,^\frown\, \langle (\mathsf{c}, \overline{c}(p) + 1) \rangle \\ \hline \end{array}$$

The **read** operation is captured by 5 operations in Z: $R1_q$ for one iteration of the inner do-loop[3], $R2_q$ for the assignment to local variable d1, $R3_q$ for the assignment to local variable d2, $R4_q$ for starting a new iteration of the outer do-loop (when $c \neq c_0$), and $R5_q$ for returning the read values (when $c = c_0$). In each case, the subscript $q : P$ is a parameter identifying the process performing the operation. There is also an operation $Flush_p$ corresponding to a CPU flush of the writer process's buffer.

$$\begin{array}{|l} \hline R1_q \\ \hline \Delta CS \\ \hline pc(q) = 1 \lor pc(q) = r1 \\ c_0'(p) = c \land \textbf{if } c_0'(q) \bmod 2 \neq 0 \\ \qquad \textbf{then } pc'(q) = r1 \\ \qquad \textbf{else } pc'(q) = r2 \\ \hline \end{array}$$

$$\begin{array}{|l} \hline R2_q \\ \hline \Delta CS \\ \hline pc(q) = r_2 \land pc'(q) = r_3 \\ d_1'(q) = \overline{x_1}(q) \\ \hline \end{array}$$

$$\begin{array}{|l} \hline R3_q \\ \hline \Delta CS \\ \hline pc(q) = r_3 \land pc'(q) = r_4 \\ d_2'(q) = \overline{x_2}(q) \\ \hline \end{array}$$

$$\begin{array}{|l} \hline R4_q \\ \hline \Delta CS \\ \hline pc(q) = r4 \land c_0(q) \neq \overline{c}(q) \\ pc'(q) = r1 \\ \hline \end{array}$$

---

[3] Any command, and in particular a write to c, occurring between the assignment to c0 and the check of the loop condition will have the same effect as if it occurred after the check. Hence, no potential behaviour is prohibited by modelling the two commands by a single operation.

$\underline{\ \ R5_q\ }$
ΔCS
$d_1!, d_2! : \mathbb{N}$
$pc(q) = r4 \wedge c_0(q) = \overline{c}(q)$
$d_1! = d_1(p) \wedge d_2! = d_2(q)$
$pc'(q) = 1$

$\underline{\ \ Flush_p\ }$
ΔCS
$b(p) \neq \langle \rangle$
$(b(p)(1)).1 = x_1 \Rightarrow x_1' = (b(p)(1)).2$
$(b(p)(1)).1 = x_2 \Rightarrow x_2' = (b(p)(1)).2$
$(b(p)(1)).1 = c \Rightarrow c' = (b(p)(1)).2$
$b'(p) = tail\, b(p)$

4   Showing Quiescent Consistency on the TSO Architecture

With this model in place we now consider how we can verify that it is indeed quiescent consistent. First of all we consider why linearizability is not appropriate.

Proposition 4. *Seqlock with one writer process is not linearizable with respect to the abstract specification AS on a TSO architecture.*

This follows from Example 5 below, which gives a history in which reads from the writer process p and another process q occur in an order that is not possible at the abstract level.   □

Example 5. The following concrete history is possible.

$$\langle inv(p, \mathtt{write}, (1,2)), ret(p, \mathtt{write},), inv(p, \mathtt{read},), ret(p, \mathtt{read}, (1,2)),$$
$$inv(q, \mathtt{read},), ret(q, \mathtt{read}, (0,0)), \mathit{flush}(p), \mathit{flush}(p), \mathit{flush}(p), \mathit{flush}(p)\rangle$$

The first flush occurs after q's read so c will be even, which allows the read to proceed. The first read in the history (by p) reads the values of x1 and x2 from p's buffer. The second (by q) reads from the global memory. The overall effect is that the second read returns older values than the first; hence, there is no corresponding abstract history.   □

Burckhardt et al. [3] prove this variant of *seqlock* is linearizable on TSO. However, in order to do this, they are forced to use an abstract specification that, like the concrete algorithm, has local buffers and CPU flushes. Hence, reading of older values after newer values have been read (as in the history above) is allowed by the abstract specification. It is our goal, however, to show correctness with respect to the stronger, and more intuitive, abstract specification AS — since an abstract description of *seqlock* should not mention buffers and flushes.

Under quiescent consistency, the above history could be reordered as the following abstract sequential history:

$$hs = \langle inv(q, \mathtt{read},), ret(q, \mathtt{read}, (0,0)), inv(p, \mathtt{write}, (1,2)), ret(p, \mathtt{write},),$$
$$inv(p, \mathtt{read},), ret(p, \mathtt{read}, (1,2))\rangle$$

Proposition 5. *Seqlock with one writer process is quiescent consistent with respect to abstract specification AS on a TSO architecture.*   □

We describe a proof methodology in Sect. 4.1 and then give an outline proof of this proposition using the schemas from AS and CS in Sect. 4.2.

4.1   Simulation Rules for Quiescent Consistency

We adapt a refinement-based proof method for verifying quiescent consistency on sequentially consistent memory models defined in [5]. Let our abstract specification be given as $A = (AState, AInit, (AOp_{p,i})_{p \in P, i \in I})$ and concrete specification be given as $C = (CState, CInit, (COp_{p,j})_{p \in P, j \in J})$ where the sets I and J are used to index the abstract and concrete operations and P is the set of all process identifiers. The function $abs : J \rightarrow I$ maps each concrete operation to the abstract operation it implements. In the definitions below, we treat operations as functions in the following two ways: $AOp_{p,i}(in_i, out_i)$ denotes an operation with its input and output parameters, and in $COp_{p,j}(in, cs, cs')$ we have made the before and after states explicit.

The simulation rules for quiescent consistency use a non-atomic, or coupled, simulation [7] which matches the concrete return events that result in a quiescent state with a sequence of abstract operations, and (abstractly) views all other concrete events as *skips*. For this to work, we need to keep track of the progress of the concrete operations in non-quiescent states. Thus we extend the retrieve relation R (between abstract and concrete states) with a history H, giving a family of retrieve relations R^H. For transitions to a quiescent state, we need to match up with a sequence of *all* abstract operations corresponding to the invoke and return events occurring in H. Quiescent consistency allows us to potentially reorder H to achieve this.

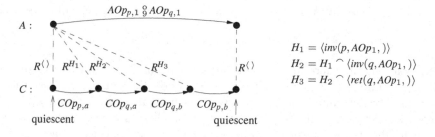

Fig. 2. Coupled simulation for some example run

Figure 2, taken from [5], illustrates an example where the abstract operation $AOp_{p,1}$ is implemented as $COp_{p,a} \mathbin{\text{§}} COp_{p,b}$ (so abs maps both a and b to 1). Processes p and q execute concrete steps. In the initial and final quiescent states, the systems are related by $R^{\langle \rangle}$. In non-quiescent states the systems are related by a retrieve relation that has recorded (via invocation and return events) the concrete operations that have completed. These will ultimately have to be matched when transitioning to a quiescent state. As with all simulations, to apply the proof method one needs to define the simulation rules, and prove that all the squares (and triangles) in diagrams such as Fig. 2 commute.

Notation: The definition of coupled simulation uses predicates $inv?(Op)$, $ret?(Op)$, $int?(Op)$, and $flush?(Op)$ that hold iff the concrete operation Op is an invocation, return, internal (i.e., neither invoke, return or flush), and flush event respectively.

To allow the concrete reordering we write $hs \simeq H$ for two histories hs : $seq Event$ and $H : seq Event_{TSO}$ iff $hs \sim H \setminus \{| \; flush \; |\}$ where $\sim$ is permutation equivalence and $H \setminus \{| \; flush \; |\}$ removes all flushes from the history H.

Furthermore, we let AOP denote the set of all abstract operations and define a function $hist$ which constructs the sequential history corresponding to a sequence of abstract operations:

$$hist(\langle AOp_{p_1,1}(in_1, out_1), \ldots, AOp_{p_n,n}(in_n, out_n) \rangle) \cong$$
$$\langle inv(p_1, AOp_1, in_1), ret(p_1, AOp_1, out_1), \ldots, inv(p_n, AOp_n, in_n), ret(p_n, AOp_n, out_n) \rangle$$

For a sequential history hs and abstract states as and as' we define

$$seqhist(hs, as, as') \cong \exists aops : AOP^* \bullet aops(as, as') \wedge hist(aops) = hs,$$

which holds iff (a) there is some abstract sequence of operations $aops$ whose composition (in order) is a relation between as and as', and (b) the sequential history generated from $aops$ is hs.

Example 6. The abstract history hs of Example 5 maps the state $as = \{x_1 \mapsto 0, x_2 \mapsto 0\}$ to $as' = \{x_1 \mapsto 1, x_2 \mapsto 2\}$. Hence, we have $seqhist(hs, as, as')$. □

A coupled simulation for proving quiescent consistency is given below. It uses the following definition where h is an abstract history and cs is a concrete state:

$$qu(h, cs) \cong \forall n : 1..\#h \bullet \neg pi(n, h) \wedge \forall p : P \bullet cs(b(p)) = \langle \rangle$$

which holds iff (a) there are no pending invocations in h, and (b) all process buffers are empty in cs, where we assume b models the buffer for each process. This is used to determine when an execution is in a quiescent state. For example, in seqlock `reads` are completed by their returns, whereas `writes` require at least one flush after their return to complete. Therefore, we reach a quiescent state in one of the following two ways. Either all buffers are empty and the lasting pending `read` returns, or all processes are idle and a flush empties the last non-empty buffer.

Note that unlike Definition 2, which uses concrete histories to determine quiescence, Definition 3 below uses both the histories H and the concrete state built up in R^H.

Definition 3 (QC Coupled simulation for TSO). *Let A and C be abstract and concrete specifications. Let $H : seqEvent_{TSO}$. A family of relations $R^H \subseteq AState \times CState$ is a* QC *(quiescent consistent) coupled simulation from A to C iff $\forall\, as : AState,\, cs, cs' : CState,\, in, out : V,\, p : P,\, i : I,\, j : J$ such that $R^H(as, cs)$, each of the following holds:*

1. $COp_{p,j}(in, cs, cs') \wedge inv?(COp_{p,j}) \Rightarrow R^{H^\frown \langle inv(p, AOp_{abs(j)}, in) \rangle}(as, cs')$
2. $COp_{p,j}(cs, cs') \wedge int?(COp_{p,j}) \Rightarrow R^H(as, cs')$
3. $COp_{p,j}(cs, cs', out) \wedge ret?(COp_{p,j}) \Rightarrow$

   if $\neg qu(H^\frown \langle ret(p, AOp_{abs(j)}, out) \rangle, cs')$ **then** $R^{H^\frown \langle ret(p, AOp_{abs(j)}, out) \rangle}(as, cs')$
   else $\exists\, as' : AState \bullet R^{\langle \rangle}(as', cs') \wedge$
   $\qquad \exists\, hs \bullet hs \simeq H^\frown \langle ret(p, AOp_{abs(j)}, out) \rangle \wedge seqhist(hs, as, as')$
4. $COp_{p,j}(cs, cs') \wedge flush?(COp_{p,j}) \Rightarrow$

   if $\neg qu(H^\frown \langle flush(p) \rangle, cs')$ **then** $R^{H^\frown \langle flush(p) \rangle}(as, cs')$
   else $\exists\, as' : AState \bullet R^{\langle \rangle}(as', cs') \wedge$
   $\qquad \exists\, hs \bullet hs \simeq H^\frown \langle flush(p) \rangle \wedge seqhist(hs, as, as')$

together with the **initialisation** *condition: $\forall\, ci : CInit \bullet \exists\, ai : AInit \bullet R^{\langle \rangle}(ai, ci)$.* $\qquad\square$

We now describe these proof obligations. Rule 1 is for a step that starts (invokes) an operation, e.g., $W1_p$, where the event corresponding to the step is added to the history H collected thus far. The proof obligation requires that if R^H holds before the invocation then $R^{H^\frown \langle inv(p, AOp_{abs(j)}, in) \rangle}$ holds after, and the abstract system does not take a step. Rule 2 applies to steps that are neither invocations nor returns, e.g., $W2_p$, and requires that R^H is maintained. Again, the abstract system does not take a step.

Rule 3 applies to a return step, e.g., $W4_p$, and has two cases. The case is determined by appending the corresponding return event to H and testing whether or not qu holds. For a return to non-quiescent step, the abstract state does not change, but $R^{H^\frown \langle ret(p, AOp_{abs(j)}, out) \rangle}$ must hold in the poststate provided R^H holds in the prestate. Return to quiescence is more complicated, and requires that there exists a sequential history hs that is a permutation of $H^\frown \langle ret(p, AOp_{abs(j)}, out) \rangle$ such that overall effect of the steps corresponding to hs is equivalent to a transition from the abstracting start state as to as'. Furthermore, as' is related to the concrete poststate cs' via $R^{\langle \rangle}$, where the history collected thus far is empty because the system has returned to quiescence.

These rules are in essence same as those for sequentially consistent architectures in [5]. For TSO, we need an additional rule for flushes, Rule 4. This rule is similar to Rule 3. For a return to non-quiescent step, the abstract state does not change, and $R^{H^\frown \langle flush(p) \rangle}$ must hold in the poststate provided R^H holds in the prestate. Return to quiescence requires that there exists a sequential history hs that is a permutation of $H^\frown \langle flush(p) \rangle$ such that overall effect of the steps corresponding to hs is equivalent to a transition from the abstracting start state as to as'. Again, as' is related to the concrete poststate cs' via $R^{\langle \rangle}$.

Quiescent consistency, as with linearizability, is a *safety property* and no liveness is guaranteed. Therefore, Definition 3 does not mention any applicability conditions.

Following the proof strategy in [5], it can be shown that coupled simulation is a sound proof technique for quiescent consistency (the proof of this follows from the definition).

Theorem 1. *Let A and C be abstract and concrete specifications, respectively. If there is a coupled simulation R^H from A to C, then C is quiescent consistent wrt. A.*   □

4.2   Proof Outline for Seqlock

To apply Definition 3 one needs to define R^H and also give the explicit reordering of the concrete history on returning to quiescence (conditions 3 and 4). R^H is a conjunction of a number of individual cases corresponding to possible values of the buffer in any state. The proof consists of a number of small proof steps which individually are not complicated but we do not have space to give them all here. Rather we just aim to give a flavour of what is involved.

First we need to determine which condition(s) of Definition 3 needs to be proved for each of the concrete Z operations. Condition 1 needs to be proved for $W1_p$ and $R1_q$ which are the invocation events of the **write** and **read** operations respectively. Condition 3 needs to be proved for $W4_p$ and $R5_q$ which are the return events of the **write** and **read** operation respectively, and condition 4 for the occurrence of $Flush_p$. Condition 2 needs to be proved for all other operations.

1. Defining $R^{\langle\rangle}$: $R^{\langle\rangle}$ relates abstract states and quiescent concrete states. The latter are those in which $pc(q) = 1$ for all processes q, and the buffer of the writer process p is empty. In these states, the abstract and concrete values of x_1 and x_2 are equal, and c is even. That is, letting $A.x_1$ and $A.x_2$ denote the abstract variables x_1 and x_2, $R^{\langle\rangle}$ is true when

$$A.x_1 = x_1 \land A.x_2 = x_2 \land c \bmod 2 = 0 \land (\forall q : P \bullet pc(q) = 1) \land b(p) = \langle\rangle$$

2. Defining R^H: For $H \neq \langle\rangle$, R^H includes a number of conjuncts depending on the values of pc and b for the individual processes. For example, when H's last event is an invocation of the **write** operation with input values $d1?$ and $d2?$, R^H includes the following conjuncts.

– If $pc(p) = w_1$ the inputs from the pending **write** operation are in $d_1(p)$ and $d_2(p)$.

$$pc(p) = w_1 \Rightarrow d_1(p) = d_1? \land d_2(p) = d_2? \tag{1}$$

– If $pc(p) = w_2$ the inputs from the pending **write** operation are either in the last entry of $b(p)$ and $d_2(p)$, or x_1 and $d_2(p)$ when the writer process's buffer has been completely flushed.

$$pc(p) = w_2 \wedge b(p) \neq \langle\,\rangle \Rightarrow last\ b(p) = (x_1, d_1?) \wedge d_2(p) = d_2? \qquad (2)$$

$$pc(p) = w_2 \wedge b(p) = \langle\,\rangle \Rightarrow x_1 = d_1? \wedge d_2(p) = d_2? \qquad (3)$$

3. Proof obligations for initialisation and non-quiescent states.
Given the complete definition of R^H it is possible to prove the initialisation condition and the coupled simulation conditions for each concrete Z operation that does not result in a quiescent state. For example, consider just the conjuncts (1) to (3) above.

The invocation event for the write operation is $W1_p$. This operation sets $d1(p)$ to $d_1?$, and $d2(p)$ to $d_2?$, and so establishes the consequent of (1). Since $pc(p) = w1$ in its poststate, (1) to (3) hold.

Operation $W2_p$ is an internal event. It adds $(x_1, d1(p))$ to the end of $b(p)$. Since (1) holds in the prestate of the operation, $last\ b(p) = (x_1, d_1?)$ in the poststate. Also since (1) holds in the prestate and the operation does not change $d_2(p)$, $d_2(p) = d_2?$ in the poststate. Hence, the consequent of (2) is established. Since $W2_p$ also establishes $pc(p) = w2$ and $b(p) \neq \langle\,\rangle$ in its poststate, (1) to (3) hold.

When $pc(p) = w1$ or $pc(p) = w_2$, a $Flush_p$ operation can also result in a non-quiescent state. It does not change $pc(p)$. When $pc(p) = w1$, since the consequent of (1) holds in the prestate of the operation, it will also hold in the poststate since $Flush_p$ does not change $d_1(p)$ or $d_2(p)$. Hence, (1) to (3) hold.

When $pc(p) = w_2$, since $b(p) \neq \langle\,\rangle$ in the prestate of $Flush_p$ the consequent of (2) holds. If in the poststate $b(p) \neq \langle\,\rangle$ then, since $Flush_p$ does not change $last\ b(p)$ or $d_2(p)$, the consequent of (2) continues to hold as required. If in the poststate $b(p) = \langle\,\rangle$ then in the prestate there was only one entry in the buffer which we know from the consequent of (2) is $(x_1, d_1?)$. Hence, in the operation's poststate we have $x_1 = d_1?$ and, since $Flush_p$ does not change $d_2(p)$, $d_2(p) = d_2?$. Hence, the consequent of (3) holds as required. Therefore in both cases, (1) to (3) hold.

Finally, when $pc(p) = w_1$ or $pc(p) = w_2$, a process other than p can do any of the concrete Z operations capturing the read operation, as an invocation or internal event. In each case, since no local variables of p nor any global variables are changed, (1) to (3) will continue to hold.

In the full proof, the above reasoning would be extended to all conjuncts which comprise R^H for each concrete history H beginning from a quiescent state.

4. Proof obligations for quiescent states.
The remaining steps of the proof require showing that each concrete Z operation that results in a quiescent state simulates an abstract history which is a reordering of the concrete history since the last quiescent state. As discussed earlier there are two ways of a reaching a quiescent state. The first is when all buffers are empty and the lasting pending read returns. In this case, the else condition of Rule 3 applies. The other case is when all processes are idle and a flush empties the last non-empty buffer. In this case the else condition of Rule 4 applies.

To prove the rules we are required to find a reordering of the sequence of the concrete history, which can be determined for both Rule 3 and 4 as follows.

Case 1: $ret(p, \mathtt{read}, (\_, \_))$ occurs between $ret(p, \mathtt{write}, (\_, \_))$ and the final $flush(p)$ of that $\mathtt{write}$.
In this case, there is no to reorder the operations (since the $\mathtt{read}$ is from p's buffer and so is consistent with the $\mathtt{write}$) and the abstract history corresponds to the order of returns.

Case 2: $ret(q, \mathtt{read}, (\_, \_))$ occurs between $ret(p, \mathtt{write}, (\_, \_))$ and the final $flush(p)$ of that $\mathtt{write}$.
In this case, the clue for finding a valid reordering is found in Example 5 where a process reads an older value after a newer value has been read. To avoid this situation, we can reorder the concrete history as follows. In the reordered abstract history, we want the $\mathtt{read}$ by q to occur before the $\mathtt{write}$ by p. Therefore, we move the return (and if necessary, invocation) of the $\mathtt{read}$ to be immediately before the return of the $\mathtt{write}$. As in Case 1, the order of the abstract history is then the order of the returns. If there is more than one such $\mathtt{read}$ operation, the order they appear in before the $\mathtt{write}$ operation is arbitrary.

Case 3: $ret(p, \mathtt{read}, (\_, \_))$ occurs after both $ret(p, \mathtt{write}, (\_, \_))$ and the final $flush(p)$ of that $\mathtt{write}$.
In this case, there is no to reorder the operations and the abstract history corresponds to the order of returns.

Case 4: $ret(q, \mathtt{read}, (\_, \_))$ occurs after both $ret(p, \mathtt{write}, (\_, \_))$ and the final $flush(p)$ of that $\mathtt{write}$.
In this case, there is no to reorder the operations and the abstract history corresponds to the order of returns.

The reordered concrete history will have no $\mathtt{read}$ operations on q while a $\mathtt{write}$ operation on p is pending or has not yet been completely flushed to the global memory. Hence, there will be no effects from writes being delayed: all reads by processes other than the writer process will occur either before the write begins, or after it has been completely flushed to memory. Therefore, there will be an abstract history corresponding to the reordered concrete one. As an example, consider the following concrete history with a single $\mathtt{write}$ and three reads.

$\langle inv(p, \mathtt{write}, (1, 2)), inv(r, \mathtt{read},), ret(p, \mathtt{write},), inv(p, \mathtt{read},), \ inv(q, \mathtt{read},),$
$ret(q, \mathtt{read}, (0, 0)), flush(p), flush(p), ret(p, \mathtt{read}, (1, 2)), flush(p), flush(p),$
$ret(r, \mathtt{read}, (1, 2)) \rangle$

At the end of this history, we are in a quiescent state. All buffers are empty and the lasting pending $\mathtt{read}$ returns, hence Rule 3 applies. To reorder this, we note that Case 1 applies to the $\mathtt{read}$ by p and Case 4 to the $\mathtt{read}$ by r. Therefore, no reordering is required. For the $\mathtt{read}$ by q Case 2 applies. Therefore, the return of this $\mathtt{read}$ is moved to immediately before the return of the $\mathtt{write}$. In this case, we also need to move the invocation of the $\mathtt{read}$ (since it occurs after the return of the $\mathtt{write}$.

The reordered concrete history is therefore as follows.

$\langle inv(p, \mathtt{write}, (1, 2)), inv(r, \mathtt{read},), inv(q, \mathtt{read},), ret(q, \mathtt{read}, (0, 0)),$
$ret(p, \mathtt{write},), inv(p, \mathtt{read},), flush(p), flush(p), ret(p, \mathtt{read}, (1, 2)), flush(p),$
$flush(p), ret(r, \mathtt{read}, (1,2)) \rangle$

The order of the operations in the corresponding sequential abstract history hs is given by the order of returns above:

$\langle inv(q, \mathtt{read},), ret(q, \mathtt{read}, (0, 0)), inv(p, \mathtt{write}, (1, 2)), ret(p, \mathtt{write},),$
$inv(p, \mathtt{read},), ret(p, \mathtt{read}, (1, 2)), inv(r, \mathtt{read},), ret(r, \mathtt{read}, (1,2)) \rangle .$

5   Conclusions

This paper has investigated methods for proving correctness of concurrent algorithms on TSO architectures. Due to the apparent reorderings of reads and writes in a TSO memory model, we have focussed on quiescent consistency as a correctness criterion. We have shown how to model an algorithm and prove quiescent consistency using a simulation-based approach. This was illustrated with a running example based on seqlock, but is applicable to other algorithms running on TSO.

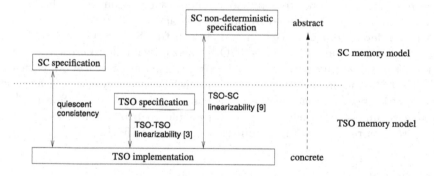

Fig. 3. Comparison of different approaches

Other work on correctness of algorithms on TSO have altered the definition of linearizability. For example, TSO-TSO linearizability [3] and TSO-SC linearizability [9] have been defined. These approaches, however, prove correctness with respect to abstract specifications which have been altered to include either low-level details of local buffers and CPU flushes (TSO-TSO linearizability), or nondeterminism to account for possible operation reorderings (TSO-SC linearizability). Gotsman et al. [9] provide the following abstract specification of seqlock, where the abstract state is modelled as queue: writes are added to the head of the queue, and reads do not return the last value in the queue

but any previously written values. In their notation, this is written as follows
[9, pp. 20–21].

```
Queue q = {(0, 0)};              read(out word d1, d2) {
                                   while (*)
write(in word d1, d2) {            q.dequeue();
  q.enqueue(d1,d2); }            (d1,d2) = q.top(); }
```

This is in contrast to our more natural specification where reads return the most
recently written values.

Burckhardt *et al.* also use a more natural specification:

```
word x1 = 0, x2 = 0;

write(in word d1, d2) { lock; x1 = d1; x2 = d2; unlock; }

read(out word d1, d2) { lock; d1 = x1; d2 = x2; unlock; }
```

However, to cope with the effects of TSO memory, each `write` operation of
the abstract specification takes place in two atomic steps: a write to a store
buffer and a memory flush. Therefore, while the abstract specification is seem-
ingly natural, its underlying semantics is architecturally dependant and includes
local store buffers and CPU flushes. As acknowledged by Burckhardt *et al.*, their
notion of linearizability is "different from the classical definition of linearizability on a sequentially consistent memory model, which requires methods in the
specification to be implemented by one atomic action" [3, p. 100].

An overview of our approach in comparison to TSO-TSO and TSO-SC linearizability is given in Fig. 3. TSO-TSO linearizability fails to cross the boundary from the TSO implementation to a sequentially consistent (SC) abstraction,
while TSO-SC linearizability crosses this boundary at the cost of a weaker non-
deterministic specification. On the other hand, by weakening the linearizability
criterion to quiescent consistency, it is possible to prove a relationship with
respect to a more intuitive deterministic abstract specification.

References

1. Amit, D., Rinetzky, N., Reps, T., Sagiv, M., Yahav, E.: Comparison under abstraction for verifying linearizability. In: Damm, W., Hermanns, H. (eds.) CAV 2007.
   LNCS, vol. 4590, pp. 477–490. Springer, Heidelberg (2007)
2. Aspnes, J., Herlihy, M., Shavit, N.: Counting networks. J. ACM **41**(5), 1020–1048
   (1994)
3. Burckhardt, S., Gotsman, A., Musuvathi, M., Yang, H.: Concurrent library correctness on the TSO memory model. In: Seidl, H. (ed.) ESOP 2012. LNCS, vol. 7211,
   pp. 87–107. Springer, Heidelberg (2012)
4. Calcagno, C., Parkinson, M., Vafeiadis, V.: Modular safety checking for fine-grained
   concurrency. In: Riis Nielson, H., Filé, G. (eds.) SAS 2007. LNCS, vol. 4634,
   pp. 233–248. Springer, Heidelberg (2007)

5. Derrick, J., Dongol, B., Schellhorn, G., Tofan, B., Travkin, O., Wehrheim, H.: Quiescent consistency: defining and verifying relaxed linearizability. In: Jones, C., Pihlajasaari, P., Sun, J. (eds.) FM 2014. LNCS, vol. 8442, pp. 200–214. Springer, Heidelberg (2014)
6. Derrick, J., Schellhorn, G., Wehrheim, H.: Mechanically verified proof obligations for linearizability. ACM Trans. Program. Lang. Syst. **33**(1), 4 (2011)
7. Derrick, J., Wehrheim, H.: Using coupled simulations in non-atomic refinement. In: Bert, D., Bowen, J.P., King, S., Waldén, M. (eds.) ZB 2003. LNCS, vol. 2651, pp. 127–147. Springer, Heidelberg (2003)
8. Doherty, S., Groves, L., Luchangco, V., Moir, M.: Formal verification of a practical lock-free queue algorithm. In: de Frutos-Escrig, D., Núñez, M. (eds.) FORTE 2004. LNCS, vol. 3235, pp. 97–114. Springer, Heidelberg (2004)
9. Gotsman, A., Musuvathi, M., Yang, H.: Show no weakness: sequentially consistent specifications of TSO libraries. In: Aguilera, M.K. (ed.) DISC 2012. LNCS, vol. 7611, pp. 31–45. Springer, Heidelberg (2012). Extended edition http://software.imdea.org/~gotsman
10. Herlihy, M., Shavit, N.: The Art of Multiprocessor Programming. Morgan Kaufmann, San Mateo (2008)
11. Herlihy, M., Wing, J.M.: Linearizability: a correctness condition for concurrent objects. ACM Trans. Program. Lang. Syst. **12**(3), 463–492 (1990)
12. Kopetz, H., Reisinger, J.: The non-blocking write protocol NBW: a solution to a real-time synchronization problem. In: Real-Time Systems Symposium, pp. 131–137 (1993)
13. Lameter, C.: Effective synchronisation on Linux/NUMA systems. In: Gelato Conference. Silicon Graphics, Inc. (2005)
14. Lamport, L.: How to make a multiprocessor computer that correctly executes multiprocess programs. IEEE Trans. Comput. **28**(9), 690–691 (1979)
15. Owens, S.: Reasoning about the Implementation of concurrency abstractions on x86-TSO. In: D'Hondt, T. (ed.) ECOOP 2010. LNCS, vol. 6183, pp. 478–503. Springer, Heidelberg (2010)
16. Sewell, P., Sarkar, S., Owens, S., Nardelli, F.Z., Myreen, M.O.: x86-TSO: a rigorous and usable programmer's model for x86 multiprocessors. Commun. ACM **53**(7), 89–97 (2010)
17. Shavit, N.: Data structures in the multicore age. Commun. ACM **54**(3), 76–84 (2011)
18. Shavit, N., Zemach, A.: Diffracting trees. ACM Trans. Comput. Syst. **14**(4), 385–428 (1996)
19. Sorin, D.J., Hill, M.D., Wood, D.A.: A Primer on Memory Consistency and Cache Coherence. Synthesis Lectures on Computer Architecture. Morgan & Claypool Publishers, San Rafael (2011)
20. Spivey, J.M.: The Z Notation: A Reference Manual. Prentice Hall, Upper Saddle River (1992)
21. Vafeiadis, V.: Modular fine-grained concurrency verification. Ph.D. thesis, University of Cambridge (2007)

Author Index

Printed in the United States
By Bookmasters